THE EUROPEAN UNION AND CONFLICT PREVENTION

POLICY AND LEGAL ASPECTS

THE EUROPEAN UNION AND CONFLICT PREVENTION

POLICY AND LEGAL ASPECTS

Edited by

Vincent Kronenberger

and

Jan Wouters

T·M·C·Asser Press

The Hague

Published by T.M.C.ASSER PRESS
P.O.Box 16163, 2500 BD The Hague, The Netherlands
www.asserpress.nl

T.M.C.ASSER PRESS' English language books are distributed exclusively by:

Cambridge University Press, The Edinburgh Building, Shaftesbury Road,
Cambridge CB2 2RU, UK,
or
for customers in the USA, Canada and Mexico:
Cambridge University Press, 40 West 20th Street, New York, NY 10011-4211, USA
www.cambridge.org

ISBN 90-6704-171-8

SUMMARY OF CONTENTS

PART TWO C
Selected geographical case studies

PART THREE
Experience of other actors

PART THREE A
International organisations

PART THREE B
Other actors

LIST OF ABBREVIATIONS

ABD	Asian Development Bank
ACC	Administrative Committee on Coordination
ACP	Africa, Caribbean and Pacific states
AfDB	African Development Bank
AFSJ	Area of freedom, security and justice
AFSOUTH	Allied Forces Southern Europe
AII	Adriatic-Ionian Initiative
AIV	Advisory Council on International Affairs
ALA	Asia/Latin America
ASEAN	Association of South-East Asian Nations
ASEM	Asia-Europe Meeting
AU	African Union
BiH	Bosnia and Herzegovina
BSEC	Black Sea Economic Cooperation
BTF	Bosnia/Balkans Task Force
BTWC	Biological and Toxin Weapons Convention
Bull.	Bulletin of the European Communities
Bull. EU	Bulletin of the European Union
CAF	Conflict Analysis Framework
CAFAO	Customs and Fiscal Assistance Office
CAP	Common agricultural policy
CARDS	Community Assistance for Reconstruction, Development and Stabilisation
CAS	Country Assistance Strategy
CBD	Convention on Biological Diversity
CBM	Confidence-Building Measures Programme
CBSS	Council of the Baltic Sea States
CCD	Convention to Combat Desertification
CDA	Conflict-related Development Analysis
CDD	Community-driven development
CDF	Comprehensive Development Framework
CEEC	Central and Eastern European Country
CEFTA	Central European Free Trade Association
CEI	Central European Initiative
CEMAC	Economic and Monetary Community of Central Africa
CEP	Civil Emergency Planning
CFI	Court of First Instance of the European Communities
CFSP	Common Foreign and Security Policy
CIAS	Conflict Impact Assessment System
CIDSE	Coopération Internationale pour le Développement et la Solidarité

CIME	Committee on International Investment and Multinational Enterprises
C i O	Chairman-in-Office
CIS	Commonwealth of Independent States
CITES	Convention on International Trade in Endangered Species
CIVCOM	Committee for the Civilian Aspects of Crisis Management
CJTF	Combined Joint Task Force
CLRAE	Congress of Local and Regional Authorities of Europe
CM	Crisis management
CMC	Crisis Management Cell
CML Rev.	Common Market Law Review
CMTF	Crisis Management Task Force
COCPO	Oil, Gas and Chemicals Department of the World Bank
CoEDM	Council of Europe Decentralisation Mission in Kosovo
COMESA	Common Market for Eastern and Southern Africa
COPOL	Comité politique/Political Committee
COPS	Comité politique et de sécurité
COREPER	Committee of Permanent Representatives in the Council of the European Union
COSCE	Council of the OSCE
CPA	Cooperation and Partnership Agreement
CPC	Conflict Prevention Centre
CPDC	Conflict, Peace and Development Cooperation
CPIA	Country Policy and Institutional Analysis
CP	Conflict prevention
CPA	Conflict Prevention Associates
CPN	Conflict Prevention Network
CPN Yearbook	Conflict Prevention Network Yearbook
CPOM	Conflict Prevention Officials Meeting
CPR Unit	Conflict Prevention and Reconstruction Unit (World Bank)
CPRN	Post-Conflict Reconstruction Network
CPT	Committee for the Prevention of Torture
CPU	Conflict Prevention Unit (European Commission)
CSBMs	Confidence and Security-Building Measures
CSCE	Conference on Security and Co-operation in Europe
CSP	Country Strategy Papers
CSR	Corporate Social Responsibility
CTBT	Comprehensive Nuclear Test-Ban Treaty
CU	Customs Union
DABLAS Task Force	Danube-Black Sea Region Task Force
DAC	Development Assistance Committee
DCI	Defense Capabilities Initiative
DDA	Doha Development Agenda
DECRG	Development Economics Research Group (World Bank)
DFID	Department for International Development (UK)
DG	Directorate-General
DGF	Development Grant Facility

DG RELEX	External Relations DG
DLP	Democratic Leadership Programme
DPA	Department of Political Affairs
DPC	Defence Planning Committee
DRC	Defence Review Committee
DRC	Democratic Republic of Congo
DSACEUR	Deputy Supreme Allied Commander Europe
DTC	Diamond Trading Company
EAC	East African Community
EAP	Environmental Action Programme
EAPC	Euro-Atlantic Partnership Council
EAs	Europe Agreements
EBA	Everything-but-arms
EBRD	European Bank for Reconstruction and Development
EC	European Community
ECCAS	Economic Community of Central African States
ECDPM	European Center for Development Policy Management
ECHO	European Commission Humanitarian Aid Office
ECHR	European Convention on Human Rights
ECJ	Court of Justice of the European Communities
ECMM	European Community Monitoring Mission
ECOWAS	Economic Community of West African States
ECR	European Court Reports
ECRI	European Commission against Racism and Intolerance
ECSA Rev.	European Community Studies Association Review
EDF	European Development Fund
EDSP	European Security and Defence Policy
EEA	European Economic Area
EEIG	European Economic Interest Grouping
EFA	Education for All
EFA Rev.	European Foreign Affairs Review
EFTA	European Free Trade Area
EIB	European Investment Bank
EIDHR	European Initiative for Democracy and Human Rights
EITI	Extractive Industries Transparency Initiative
EMP	European Monitoring Platform
EP	European Parliament
EPA	Economic Partnership Agreement
EPC	European Political Cooperation
EPC Working Papers	European Policy Centre Working Papers
EPLO	European Peacebuilding Liaison Office
ESDI	European Security and Defence Identity
ESDP	European Security and Defence Policy
ESF Working Papers	European Security Forum Working Papers
ESSD	Environmentally and Socially Sustainable Development
EU	European Union
EUMC	EU Military Committee

EUMM	EU Monitoring Mission
EUMS	EU Military Staff
EUPM	European Union Police Mission
EUSR	EU Special Representative
FAO	Food and Agricultural Organisation
FCCC	Framework Convention on Climate Change
FDI	Foreign direct investment
FINCR	Finance and Credit Risk Department of the World Bank
FLEGT	Forest Law Enforcement, Governance and Trade
FPA	Framework Partnership Agreement
FRM	Resource Mobilisation Department of the World Bank
FRY	Federal Republic of Yugoslavia
FYROM	Former Yugoslav Republic of Macedonia
FSC	Forest Stewardship Council
GAC	General Affairs Council
GAERC	General Affairs and External Relations Council
GATS	General Agreement on Trade in Services
GCC	Gulf Co-operation Council
GDP	Gross Domestic Product
GLP	Good laboratory practices
GMES	Global Monitoring for Environment and Security
GSP	Generalized System of Preferences
GTZ	Deutsche Gesellschaft für Technische Zusammenarbeit
HCNM	High Commissioner on National Minorities
HIPC	Heavily Indebted Poor Countries
HIPS	High-Indebted Poor Countries
HR	High Representative
IBRD	International Bank for Reconstruction and Development
ICC	International Criminal Court
ICJ	International Court of Justice
ICLQ	International Comparative Law Quarterly
ICONS	Impeding Crisis Online New Systems
ICPBS	International Commission for the Protection of the Black Sea
ICPDR	International Commission for the Protection of the Danube River
ICRC	International Committee of the Red Cross
ICTY	International Criminal Tribunal for the former Yugoslavia
IDA	International Development Association (World Bank)
IDP	Internally displaced people
IFF	Intergovernmental Forum on Forests
IFOR	Implementation Force (NATO led)
IGC	Intergovernmental Conference
IGAD	Intergovernmental Authority on Development
IGO	Intergovernmental organisation
IFOR	International Fellowship of Reconciliation

ILM	International Legal Materials
ILO	International Labour Organisation
IMF	International Monetary Fund
IMS	International Military Staff
IO	International organisations
IOC	Indian Ocean Commission
IPF	Intergovernmental Panel on Forests
IPM	Inventory of Preventive Measures
IPR	Intellectual property rights
IRIN	Integrated Regional Information Networks
IS	International Staff
ISPA	Instrument for Structural Policies for Pre-assession
IPTF	International Police Task Force
JHA	Justice and Home Affairs
JIU	UN Joint Inspection Unit
KEDO	Korean Peninsula Energy Development Organisation
KFOR	Kosovo Force (NATO led)
LDA	Local Democracy Agencies
LDC	Least developed countries
LICUS	Low-Income Countries Under Stress
LRRD	Link between relief, rehabilitation and development
MAP	Mediterranean Action Plan
MAPE	Multinational Advisory Police Element
MC	Military Committee
MCPFE	Ministerial Conference for the Protection of Forests in Europe
MCSD	Mediterranean Commission for Sustainable Development
MEAs	Multilateral Environmental Agreements
MEDA	Mediterranean Development Programme
MEPs	Members of the European Parliament
METAP	Mediterranean Technical Assistance Programme
MIP	Multi-annual Indicative Programme
MOC	Media Operations Center
MONUC	UN Mission in the Democratic Republic of Congo
MPLA	Movement for the Liberation of Angola
MRO	Military Response Options
NAC	North Atlantic Council
NAFTA	North American Free Trade Agreement
NATO	North-Atlantic Treaty Organisation
NCRS	NATO Crisis Response System
NEPAD	New Partnership for Africa's Development
NGOs	Non-governmental Organisation
NIP	National Indicative Programmes
NIS	Newly Independent States

NIWS	NATO Intelligence and Warning System
NLA	National Liberation Army
NPS	NATO Precautionary System
NRC	NATO Russia Council
NRF	NATO Response Force
NSA	Non-State Actors
NUC	NATO/Ukraine Commission
OAU	Organisation of African Unity
OCHA	Office for Coordination of Humanitarian Affairs
ODA	Official Development Assistance
ODIHR	OSCE Office for Democratic Institutions and Human Rights
OECD	Organisation for Economic Co-operation and Development
OED	Operations Evaluation Department
OHCHR	Office of the High Commissioner for Human Rights
OHR	Office of the High Representative in Bosnia and Herzegovina
OJEC/EU	Official Journal of the European Communities/European Union
OPCS	Operational Policy and Bank Procedures Statements (World Bank)
OSCE	Organisation for Security and Co-operation in Europe
PC	Political Committee
PCA	Partnership and Cooperation Agreements
PCF	Post-Conflict Fund
PCG	Policy Coordination Group
PCPI	Post-Conflict Progress Indicators
PfP	Partnership for Peace
PJCC	Police and Judicial Cooperation in Criminal Matters
PMF	Political Military Framework
PREM	Poverty Reduction and Economic Management Network (World Bank)
PRSP	Poverty Reduction Strategy Paper
PSC	Political and Security Committee
PU	Policy Unit
REACT	Rapid Expert Assistance and Co-operation Teams
RERP	Regional Environmental Reconstruction Programme
RICR	Revue internationale de la Croix-Rouge
RRM	Rapid Reaction Mechanism
RSP	Regional Strategy Papers
RTA	Regional trade agreements
RUF	Revolutionary United Front
SAA	Stability and Association Agreement
SADC	Southern Africa Development Community
SADCC	Southern African Development Coordination Conference
SAIS Review	The Paul H. Nitze School of Advanced International Studies Review

SALW	Small arms and light weapons
SAMs	Sanctions Assistance Missions
SAP	Stabilisation and Association Process
SCEPC	Senior Civil Emergency Planning Committee
SECI	Southeast European Cooperation Initiative
SEE	South Eastern Europe
SEECP	South East Cooperation Process
SFOR	Stabilisation Force in Bosnia and Herzegovina
SG	Secretary General
SHAPE	Supreme Headquarters Allied Powers Europe
SIPO	Strategic Indicative Development Plan for the Organ
SIPRI Yearbook	Stockholm International Peace Research Institute Yearbook
SITCEN	Situation Center
SMAP	Medium-Term Priority Environmental Action Programme
SMEs	Small and medium-sized enterprises
SWP	Stiftung Wissenschaft und Politik
SWP Comments	Stiftung Wissenschaft und Politik Comments
TACIS	Technical Assistance for the Commonwealth of Independent States
TBT	Technical Barriers to Trade
TEC	Treaty establishing the European Community
TEU	Treaty on European Union
TFT	Tropical Forest Trust
TRIPs	Trade-Related Aspects of Intellectual Property Rights
TSS	Transitional Support Strategy
UN	United Nations
UNCED	UN Conference on Environment and Development
UNCTAD	UN Conference on Trade and Development
UN OCHA	UN Organisation for the Coordination of Humanitarian Assistance
UNDP	UN Development Programme
UNDHA	UN Department of Humanitarian Affairs
UNECE	UN Economic Commission for Europe
UNEP	UN Environment Programme
UNHCR	UN High Commissioner for Refugees
UNIDO	UN Industrial Development Organisation
UNITA	National Union for Total Independence of Angola
UNMIK	UN Interim Administration Mission in Kosovo
UNPREDEP	UN Preventive Deployment Force
UNPROFOR	UN Protection Force
UNRWA	UN Relief and Works Agency
UNSC	UN Security Council
UNSG	UN Secretary General
USAID	United States Agency for International Development

WAEMU	West African Economic and Monetary Union
WB	Western Balkans
WBI	World Bank Institute
WDC	World Diamond Council
WEU	Western European Union
WMDs	Weapons of Mass Destruction
WSSCC	Water Supply and Sanitation Collaborative Council
WSSD	World Summit on Sustainable Development
WTO	World Trade Organisation
ZEI Discussion Papers	Zentrum für Europäische Integrationsforschung Discussion Papers

INTRODUCTION

The European integration process is first and foremost a peace project. In 1951, the six High Contracting Parties to the Treaty establishing the European Coal and Steel Community (ECSC) solemnly declared 'that world peace can be safeguarded only by creative efforts commensurate with the dangers that threaten it' and emphasised 'that the contribution which an organised and vital Europe can make to civilization is indispensable to the maintenance of peaceful relations' in order 'to substitute for age old rivalries the merging of their essential interests' and 'to create (...) the basis for a broader and deeper community among peoples long divided by bloody conflicts'.[1] Such an overall peace-building aim between the Member States has constantly been recalled in the subsequent treaties that have deepened the integration of the European Community (EC),[2] culminating in 1992 with the creation of a European Union (EU),[3] that should most probably soon enjoy its own Constitution.[4]

The success that the EU has encountered by preventing violent conflicts from reoccurring within its borders rapidly leads one to the idea that the EU can also contribute to the prevention of conflicts outside its territory. However, the emphasis on conflict prevention as an integral and explicit part of the EU's external policies has emerged only recently, dating back to the very beginning of

---

[1] Preamble to the Treaty establishing a European Coal and Steel Community, signed at Paris on 18 April 1951, available at <http://europa.eu.int/abc/obj/treaties/en/entoc29.htm>. This treaty was concluded for a period of 50 years from the date of its entry into force (cf., Article 97). It consequently expired on 23 July 2002.

[2] See the Preamble to the Treaty establishing the European Economic Community, signed at Rome on 25 March 1957.

[3] The European Union was created by the Treaty of Maastricht, signed on 7 February 1992 (published in *OJEC* [1992] C 191/1). This treaty was amended in 1997 (Treaty of Amsterdam) and in 2001 (Treaty of Nice). A consolidated version of the Treaty on European Union (TEU) has been published in *OJEC* [2002] C 325/1. Broadly speaking, the European Union is based on the so-called 'three pillars', namely the European Communities (now, since the expiry of the ECSC, the European Community and the European Atomic Energy Community (signed in Rome on 25 March 1957)) and two intergovernmental policies, i.e., a Common Foreign and Security Policy (CFSP) and Police and Judicial Cooperation in Criminal Matters (PJCC) (cf., Article 1 TEU).

[4] See the Draft Treaty establishing a Constitution for Europe, *OJEC* [2003] C 169/1 and the provisional consolidated version of the Treaty which was agreed upon in Brussels in June 2004 (IGC Doc. No. 86/04), 25 June 2004, available at <http://ue.eu.int/cms3_applications/Applications/igc/doc_register.asp?lang=EN&cmsid=576>.

V. Kronenberger and J. Wouters, eds., The European Union and Conflict Prevention
© *2004, T·M·C·Asser Press, The Hague, The Netherlands*

the 21st century.[5] This book precisely aims at providing a comprehensive analysis of the EU's strategy for preventing the eruption and the reignition of violent conflicts in third States. While this question has received attention among political scientists and policy think-tanks both prior to the launch of the EU's strategy[6] and, to a certain extent, since then,[7] the ambition of this book is also to analyse aspects of the EU's involvement in conflict prevention from a legal perspective. The book's structure is described in more detail at the end of this introduction.

BRIEF HISTORICAL BACKGROUND

Even before endorsing an explicit strategy for the prevention of violent conflicts, the EC/EU has exported the 'virtuous circle' of political and economic stability to its closest neighbours. Probably the most remarkable aspect generating tangible results relates to the agreements which the EC has concluded with neighbouring countries, aiming ultimately at offering them membership in the organisation. Although the EC/EU has never formally included the prior solving of conflicts in its accession criteria,[8] it has,

---

[5] It was at the June 2001 Göteburg European Council that the Heads of State and Government of the then 15 Member States of the European Union indicated that 'conflict prevention is one of the main objectives of the Union's external relations and should be integrated in all its relevant aspects (...)'. For a historical overview, see Chapter 3 in this volume.

[6] See the work carried out between 1997 and 2001 under the auspices of the Conflict Prevention Network (CPN), a network of academic institutions, NGOs and experts financed by the European Community, which contributed, *inter alia*, to the development of the Commission's indicators to identify potential conflicts (cf., Chapter 1 in this volume). These contributions appear in the following CPN Yearbooks: P. Cross (ed.), *Contributing to Preventive Action* (Baden-Baden, SWP-CPN Yearbook 1997/1998, Nomos Verlagsgesellschaft 1998); P. Cross and G. Rasamoelina (eds.), *Conflict Prevention Policy of the European Union* (Baden-Baden, SWP-CPN, Yearbook 1998/1999, Nomos Verlagsgesellschaft 1999); M. Lund and G. Rasamoelina (eds.), *The Impact of Conflict Prevention Policy* (Baden-Baden, SWP-CPN Yearbook 1999/2000, Nomos Verlagsgesellschaft 2000); and L. van de Goor and Martina Huber (eds.), *Mainstreaming Conflict Prevention* (Baden-Baden, SWP-CPN Yearbook 2000/2001, Nomos Verlagsgesellschaft 2002).

[7] See, e.g., T. Debiel and M. Fischer, 'Crisis Prevention and Conflict Management by the EU: concepts, capacity and problems of coherence' (2000), available at <www.berghof-center.org/publication/>; C. Hill, 'The EU's Capacity for Conflict Prevention', 6 *EFA Rev.* (2001), p. 315; F. Nkundabagenzi, C. Pailhe and V. Peclow, *L'Union européenne et la prévention des conflits: concepts et instruments d'un nouvel acteur* (Brussels, Les Rapports du GRIP 2002).

[8] Hence, the Community did not require Greece to solve its conflict with Turkey prior to accession; see, F. Hoffmeister, 'Changing requirements for membership' in A. Ott and K. Inglis (eds.), *Handbook on European Enlargement. A Commentary on the Enlargement Process* (The Hague, T.M.C. Asser Press 2002), p. 96. Note that, in respect of the accession negotiations of the CEECs (Czech Republic, Hungary, Slovakia, Estonia, Lithuania, Latvia, Slovenia, Poland), Cyprus and Malta, the EU's position included, *inter alia*, the undertaking by each candidate state that it would resolve any border dispute (see L. Mauer, 'Negotiations in Progress', in A. Ott and K. Inglis (eds.),

however, used its 'power of attraction'[9] on several occasions in order to anchor peace and freedom in the candidate States, such as in the cases of Greece (1982), Spain and Portugal (1986),[10] and, more recently, to defuse tensions or crises by linking the solving thereof to the negotiations on association agreements with the EC, including the future prospect of membership. As far as the Central and Eastern European Countries (CEECs) are concerned, the EC particularly used this 'carrot and stick approach' as a powerful tool to decrease inter-state tensions in the dispute which pitted Hungary and Slovakia against each other over the construction of the Gabcikovo-Nagymáros hydroelectric project on the Danube.[11] In Estonia, the EC also put a great deal of pressure on the Estonian government to resolve the status of the Russian minority,[12] in line with the respect for minority rights, as part of the accession criteria laid down by the 1993 Copenhagen European Council,[13] while linking an amicable solution with Russia to the

---

op. cit. p. 116), which was undoubtedly meant to address the situation in Cyprus; however, such a condition was subsequently set aside. On 1 May 2004, and despite UN/EU efforts to bring the parties to an agreement, only the internationally recognised Republic of Cyprus joined the EU. In addition to the political issues that this situation may cause, the legal problems should not be underestimated either. Examples are already given by the three Anastasiou judgements delivered by the Court of Justice of the European Communities (Cases C-432/92 [1994] ECR I-3087, C-219/98 [2000] ECR I-5241 and C-140/02 [2003] not yet reported) which concerned the interpretation of the 1977 Protocol to the 1972 EC-Cyprus Association Agreement and a Community directive as far as certificates of origin delivered by the authorities in the self-proclaimed 'Turkish Republic of Northern Cyprus' were concerned. Such issues are likely to arise in the future. On the two first cases, see P. Koutrakos, 'Legal issues of EC-Cyprus trade relations', 50 *ICLQ* (2003), p. 489.

[9] This expression has been borrowed from G. Munuera, *Preventing Armed Conflict in Europe: Lessons from Recent Experience* (Paris, 15-16 Chaillot Papers, WEU Institute for Security Studies 1994), p. 91, available at <http://aei.pitt.edu/archive/00000467/01/chai156e.html>.

[10] See, e.g., the (favourable) opinion of the Commission on the accession of Spain and Portugal, delivered on 31 May 1985 (*OJEC* [1985] L 302/3) which stresses that 'the enlargement of the Communities through the accession of the Kingdom of Spain and the Portuguese Republic will help to strengthen safeguards for peace and freedom in Europe'.

[11] See G. Munuera, op. cit. n. 9. The author highlights that the pressure by the European Community was crucial in defusing the crisis. In particular, whereas the two States agreed to peacefully settle the dispute by submitting the case to the International Court of Justice, European Commissioner Van den Broek, in a statement delivered on 4 March 1993, clearly emphasised the link between that decision and the renegotiation of the Europe Agreement between the Slovak Republic and the EC (which entailed a reference to the future accession of the country to the EC).

[12] The 1991 Estonian Law on Foreigners restricted citizenship to the descendants of those who had been citizens before 1940. This measure threatened to render non-Estonian speakers stateless, among whom are the important Russian-speaking minority. As a consequence, Russian-speaking inhabitants in Narva and Sillamä voted in July 1993 to secede from Estonia, a referendum declared illegal by the Estonian government. The Russian President B. Yeltsin then threatened to intervene by sending troops stationed in Estonia.

[13] The 1993 Copenhagen European Council's conditions required each candidate state to achieve a) the stability of institutions guaranteeing democracy, the rule of law, human rights and respect for and protection of minorities (political criterion); b) the existence of a functioning market economy as well as the capacity to cope with competitive pressure and market forces within the EU (economic

negotiations of the Europe Agreement (namely the opening of markets and the future prospect for membership), which effectively started in 1994.[14] This 'light prevention' through effective diplomatic mediation by the EC, together with the Organisation for Security and Cooperation in Europe (OSCE), proved sufficient to defuse the crisis and eventually avoid its escalation.[15] Overall, one may say that the accession to the EU of ten new Member States on 1 May 2004, despite the political, socio-economic and legal difficulties it may cause, enlarges the 'community of peace'[16] and prosperity to a wider circle of European States.

When it comes to third States having no prospect of membership, either for political or geographic reasons, the EC made very little contribution to the prevention of conflicts. For example, its development cooperation policy, in particular with the African, Caribbean and Pacific States (ACP)[17] among which an important number of States have been undermined by severe crises and devastating inter- and intrastate wars,[18] solely focused on trade and development aid until the early 1990s, with no emphasis on conflict prevention.[19]

The situation changed dramatically in the 1990s due to the combination of ground-breaking interlinked events, which in turn led the EU to embrace the cause of conflict prevention. The powerful destabilisation effect of the collapse of the Soviet Union, in particular in the Western Balkans and in African States, the lack of appropriate mechanisms at regional and international level aimed at resolving rapidly, coherently and adequately the outbreak of conflicts which devastated Bosnia-Herzegovina (1992-1995) and the Horn of Africa, convinced the international community to endorse the United Nations Secretary General's

---

criterion); and c) the ability to take on the obligations of membership including adherence to the aims of political, economic and monetary union (legal criterion, linked to capacity to adopt the *acquis communautaire*).

[14] G. Munuera, op. cit. n. 9.

[15] See H. Miall, 'Preventing Potential Conflicts: Assessing the Impact of "Light" and "Deep" Conflict Prevention in Central and Eastern Europe and the Balkans', in M. Lund and G. Rasamoelina (eds.), *The Impact of Conflict Prevention Policy* (Baden-Baden, SWP Conflict Prevention Network, Yearbook 1999/2000, Nomos 2000), p. 23 at 33.

[16] EU Programme for the Prevention of Violent Conflicts, endorsed at the Göteborg European Council, June 2001, available at <www.eu2001.se/static/eng/pdf/violent.PDF>.

[17] The ACP group of States encompasses 79 members, all of which, save Cuba, are signatories to the partnership agreement with the EC (also called the Cotonou Agreement (which replaced the Lomé Conventions in June 2000)). A total of 48 States are from Sub-Saharan Africa, 16 from the Caribbean region and 15 from the Pacific.

[18] In 2000, 31 of the 51 African States composing this continent were either subject to inter-state or intrastate war, or afflicted by violent internal crises: cf., the speech delivered by Commissioner P. Nielson, 'From declaration to deeds, from resolutions to results. The EU and Africa after the Cairo Summit', Brussels, 22 May 2000.

[19] See, e.g., F. Nkundabagenzi, *L'Union européenne et la prévention des conflits africains* (Brussels, Les Rapports du GRIP 2000), p. 13.

idea of 'preventive diplomacy'[20] and to promote the 'culture of prevention'. Faced with new responsibilities within a new European architecture and with the outbreak of the most disastrous conflict and human rights violations in Europe since the Second World War, the Heads of State and Government of the EC had little choice but to embark upon a deeper coordination of their foreign and security policies, a project that had long been postponed. A Common Foreign and Security Policy (CFSP) emerged from the Treaty on European Union signed in Maastricht in February 1992, which entered into force in November 1993. Without dwelling too long on the historical background, which is further scrutinised in Chapter 3 of this book, the creation of the CFSP and its reinforcement in the amendments brought by the Treaty of Amsterdam that entered into force in May 1999, paved the way for the progressive transfer from the Western European Union (WEU)[21] of the so-called 'Petersberg tasks' to the EU, i.e., humanitarian and rescue tasks, peacekeeping tasks, tasks of combat forces in crisis management, including peacemaking,[22] a transfer which is now legally enshrined in the TEU since the entry into force of the Treaty of Nice in February 2003.[23] However, so far the list of 'Petersberg tasks' does not mention conflict prevention. In fact, the EU's conflict prevention policy has emerged and developed without any precise legal basis in the TEU.[24] This is not to say that

---

[20] Cf., the Report by UN Secretary General Boutros Boutros Ghali *Agenda for Peace, Preventive Diplomacy, peacemaking and peacekeeping*, A/47/277, S/24111, 17 June 1992, available at <http://www.un.org/Docs/SG/agpeace.html>. The Report (point 20) defined preventive diplomacy as 'action to prevent disputes from arising between parties, to prevent existing disputes from escalating into conflicts and to limit the spread of the latter when they occur'.

[21] The WEU was established by the 1948 Brussels Treaty as a collective self-defence organisation between Belgium, France, the Netherlands, Luxembourg and the United Kingdom. The Treaty was modified in 1954 to include Germany and Italy. Currently, the WEU is composed of 10 Members (Greece, Portugal and Spain, in addition to the seven above), six Associate Members (Czech Republic, Hungary, Iceland, Norway, Poland and Turkey), five observers (Austria, Denmark, Ireland, Finland, Sweden) and seven Associate Partners (Bulgaria, Estonia, Latvia, Lithuania, Romania, Slovakia and Slovenia). Article V of the modified Brussels Treaty deals with collective self-defence (currently WEU's residual competence). The WEU's two main bodies are the Council (meeting at 21 or 28 (with associate partners)) and the Assembly. The link between the WEU and the EU is further symbolised by a common Secretary General Mr. J. Solana, Secretary General of the Council of the EU and High Representative for CFSP.

[22] In the 1992 Petersberg Declaration, the WEU redefined its own tasks beyond its original defence functions, by indicating that the military units of the WEU Member States 'apart from contributing to the common defence in accordance with Article V of the Washington Treaty and Article V of the modified Brussels Treaty respectively (...) could be employed for: humanitarian and rescue tasks; peacekeeping tasks; tasks of combat forces in crisis management, including peacemaking'. See further on the relationship between the WEU and the EU, R.A. Wessel, 'The EU as a black widow: devouring the WEU to give birth to the European Security and Defence Policy', in V. Kronenberger (ed.), *The European Union and the International Legal Order: Discord or Harmony?* (The Hague, T.M.C. Asser Press 2001), pp. 405-434.

[23] See Article 17(2) TEU.

[24] As further developed in this book, this situation will certainly change when the Treaty establishing a Constitution for Europe will enter into force. Indeed, the Draft Treaty specifically refers to

when the EU actions are aimed at the prevention of violent conflicts, the organisation acts *ultra vires*. On the contrary, the EU relies on instruments and acts that are based on the TEU, whether they concern its first (EC), second (CFSP) or third pillar (PJCC). In reality, the EU has extended its external policy instruments to serve the overall aim of preventing violent conflicts. It has actually decided to mainstream conflict prevention into its policies, as further illustrated in this book (cf., especially Chapters 7-13).

DEFINITION OF CONFLICT PREVENTION

At this juncture, we feel that it is important and necessary to focus on the notion of conflict prevention. Conflict prevention may often be considered as a catch-all concept. In an extremely broad sense, it could be depicted as any action that promotes peace. However, such an approach would deny the very nature of the concept which relates to actions that take place when, at least, a potential risk of conflict exists within a given State or region. For the purpose of this book, conflict prevention should first be understood as the prevention of *violent* conflicts. Indeed not all individual and collective conflicts take violent forms and need to be prevented. It is when conflicts might develop into violence that a preventive mechanism should be activated. This is one of the reasons why appropriate analytical tools are crucial for identifying potential conflicts. At the EU level, the institutions (Commission and Council) have developed their own set of indicators of sources of violent conflicts (cf., especially Chapters 1 and 2). Second, the concept should be understood as the prevention of violent conflicts *within or between States*. Since the early 1990s, it has been rightly noted that conflicts have increasingly shifted from inter-state to intrastate.[25] This shift has given rise to delicate problems which might explain the reticence of the international community in deciding to act on past occasions. First, the trend has rendered more complex the analysis of the origins of conflicts (ethnic, religious, linguistic, cultural, socio-economic) and consequently the establishment of rapid and appropriate mechanisms to solve them. Second, the engagement of international actors in preventing intrastate conflicts was also stigmatised as a possible intrusion in internal affairs, risking hampering States' sovereign rights.[26]

---

conflict prevention in several of its provisions (cf., Articles I-40(1) and III-210(1) of the Draft Constitution).

[25] A. Wenger and D. Möckli, *Conflict Prevention. The untapped potential of the business sector* (Boulder, Lynne Rienner Publishers 2003), at pp. 21-25, indicate that, between 1989 and 2000, there were more than 100 intrastate violent conflicts but only seven interstate armed conflicts around the world.

[26] At the September 1992 Jakarta Conference of Non-Aligned States, Malaysia circulated a draft resolution on the UN Secretary General's *Agenda for Peace* which expressed worries concerning the recent tendency in intervening in internal affairs with the pretext of safeguarding human rights or

While this may be a risk if preventive engagement takes the form of a military operation without the appropriate mandate from the UN Security Council (cf., below), it may be excluded when the conflict prevention instruments used amount to diplomatic or economic instruments, such as trade and development policy measures (even including trade sanctions or conditional foreign aid).

This having been said, negatively defined, conflict prevention should be distinguished both from conflict management and conflict resolution. Whereas conflict prevention is essentially meant to avoid a conflict from taking place, conflict management presupposes that a conflict has broken out, rendering certain action necessary which is essentially aimed at halting hostilities at the request and/or with the consent of the warring parties. In this sense, conflict management is a concept closer to peacemaking and peace enforcement,[27] both being enshrined in the EU's Petersberg tasks-list mentioned above. Conflict prevention is also a wider concept than conflict resolution. The latter has been defined as 'efforts to increase cooperation among the parties to a conflict and deepen their relationship by addressing the conditions that led to the dispute, fostering positive attitudes and allaying distrust through reconciliation initiatives, and building or strengthening the institutions and processes through which the parties interact. Conflict resolution can be used to reduce the chances of violence or to consolidate the cessation of a violent conflict in order to prevent re-escalation'.[28] While conflict resolution also presupposes the eruption of a conflict, unlike conflict prevention, it has, however, a close relationship with the latter in its form of post-conflict reconstruction. Indeed, post-conflict reconstruction can serve as a powerful tool to avoid the reignition of a violent conflict.

Several authors have attempted positively to define the concept of conflict prevention. For P. Douma, L. van de Goor and K. van Walraven, there are two definitions of conflict prevention. 'In the first, more narrowly defined approach, conflict prevention denotes any kind of (political, economic, military) activity with the aim to prevent the eruption of violence as such. In other words, in the first definition conflict prevention can only exist if a conflict has not yet reached a violent stage. In the second, more broadly defined approach, conflict prevention denotes any kind of (political, economic, military) activity with the aim to prevent either the eruption of violence or the escalation of a violent conflict. In

---

preventing conflicts. However, after guarantees were given by the UN Secretary General that the UN would never intervene in conflicts without the consent of all parties involved and diplomatic efforts by Indonesia, the final resolution noted the useful contribution that the *Agenda for Peace* brought to the discussion on the UN's role: see B. Boutros-Ghali, *Mes années à la maison de verre* (Paris, Fayard 1999), pp. 51-52.

[27] See A. Wenger and D. Möckli, *Conflict Prevention. The untapped potential of the business sector* (Boulder, Lynne Rienner Publishers 2003), pp. 33-34.

[28] See the abridged version of the thesaurus and glossary of early warning and conflict prevention terms by Alex P. Schmid Pioom (Erasmus University 1998), available at <http://www.fewer. org/pubs/index.htm>.

this second approach conflict prevention is related to concepts as reduction, conflict containment or management, and even conflict mediation'.[29] For M.S. Lund, 'conflict prevention refers to actions, policies or institutions to keep emerging internal or inter-state disputes in specific vulnerable places and periods from escalating into significant, ongoing violence ("vertical escalation"), while simultaneously promoting opportunities and movement wherever possible towards non-violent reconciliation of basic clashing interests. By implication, this includes avoiding re-eruption of violence where conflict has abated as well as keeping active conflicts from igniting conflict in a new, hitherto peaceful peace ("horizontal escalation"). Prevention thus focuses on changes that are needed and possible in the medium term, rather than, on the one hand, attempting wholesale structural socio-economic and political transformations to improve human condition, which are achievable only in the long run, or on the other hand, diplomatic and military efforts to merely manage a crisis or end a raging conflict in the short-term.'[30] This definition can be qualified as 'semi-narrow'. It encompasses conflict resolution elements which, strictly speaking, go beyond conflict prevention, but narrows down the concept by referring solely to medium-term measures. This definition does not exactly correspond to the EU's strategy, at least as it is formulated by the European Commission's Communication of 11 April 2001.[31] Indeed, although the Commission has not dwelt on the difficulties of advancing a definition of its own, it distinguishes between long-term and short-term prevention. Long-term prevention chiefly refers to what the Carnegie Commission for Preventing Deadly Conflicts has described, in 1997, as 'structural prevention',[32] namely actions that are meant to address the root causes of conflicts. Short-term prevention essentially refers to 'operational pre-vention',[33] i.e., measures which are aimed at reacting rapidly to nascent conflicts and avoiding imminent violence. Without imposing a specific definition of conflict prevention on the authors of this book, we have nevertheless chosen to draw heavily on the dichotomy highlighted above in the structure of this volume.

---

[29] P. Douma, L. van de Goor, K. van Walraven, 'Research Methodologies and Practice: A Comparative Perspective on Methods for Assessing the Outbreak of Conflict and the Implementation in Practice by International Organisations', in P. Cross and G. Rasamoelina (eds.), *Conflict Prevention Policy of the European Union*, op. cit. n. 6, p. 80.

[30] M.S. Lund, 'Preventing Violent Conflicts: Progress and Shortfall' in P. Cross (ed.), *Contributing to Preventive Action*, op. cit. n. 6, p. 27. This definition is a refined version of a proposal made in his earlier groundbreaking essay *Preventing Violent Conflicts: Strategy for Preventive Diplomacy* (Washington DC, United States Institute of Peace Press 1996), p. 37.

[31] European Commission Communication on Conflict Prevention, COM (2001) 211 final, 11 April 2001.

[32] See Chapter 4 of the Final Report of the Carnegie Commission on Preventing Deadly Conflicts, available at <http://www.wilsoncenter.org/subsites/ccpdc/pubs/rept97/finfr.htm>. This concept is equivalent to H. Miall's expression 'deep prevention' referred to above (cf., n. 15).

[33] See Chapter 3 of the Final Report of the Carnegie Commission, op. cit. n. 32. H. Miall, op. cit. n. 15, refers to 'light prevention'.

However, we have opted to focus more precisely on the concept and the application of 'structural prevention' given the wide range of instruments which the EU may use to achieve such a goal (cf., Chapters 7-13).

THE EUROPEAN UNION AND CONFLICT PREVENTION IN CONTEXT

That a regional organisation such as the EU decides to embark upon the prevention of conflicts beyond the territory of its Member States or of its closest neighbours, may raise some questions as to its motives, its setting of priorities and to respect for international law.

If the moral responsibility of the EU to avoid human suffering is often referred to as one of the altruistic reasons for engaging in conflict prevention,[34] the EU's action is also increasingly linked to the belief that prevention ensures security, both outside and inside its territory.[35] It also relies on the pragmatic idea that, in any event, preventive engagement, even though its benefits may never be seen, serves to avoid being called at a later stage to take more costly and painful actions, such as military intervention.[36] From an economic perspective, it is also clear that, in the long run, the EU obtains more benefits to deal with stable and peaceful trade partners than with countries afflicted by violent conflicts. If these motives may sufficiently explain the EU's engagement in conflict prevention, they do not shed any light on why that engagement should extend to all parts of the world. The explanation may well be summarised by the European Security Strategy proposed by J. Solana, the High Representative for the CFSP at the Thessaloniki European Council of June 2003 and endorsed at the Brussels European Council in December 2003, according to which the EU is a global actor and should be ready to share in the responsibility for global security.[37] This ambitious and courageous objective should, however, be balanced against the necessity to prioritise some regions or actions over others, in order to avoid wasting resources or the duplication of work with other international organisations or States.[38] In this respect, the EU's security strategy mainly focuses on the necessity to build security in the EU's neighbourhood, essentially at the Eastern borders of the EU-25 and around the Mediterranean region. Without excluding actions beyond this area, in particular in regions having close historical links with EU Member States, such as illustrated by the EU-led military

---

[34] See EU Programme for the Prevention of Violent Conflicts, op. cit. n. 16.

[35] J. Solana, 'A secure Europe in a better World', Brussels European Council, 12 December 2003, p. 1.

[36] Cf., M. Rocard, 'Prévention des conflits: une synergie d'efforts internationaux', in P. Cross/G. Rasamoelina (eds.), op. cit. n. 6, p. 13.

[37] J. Solana, 'A secure Europe in a better world', op. cit. n. 35, p. 1.

[38] See the call for 'discrimination' in the EU's action expressed by C. Hill, op. cit. n. 7, p. 331.

mission in Congo, operation *Artemis*,[39] it is indeed most probably within the above-mentioned geographic zones that the EU may add value. In any event, the EU's engagement in the prevention of conflicts should be carried out with full respect for international law, in particular the United Nations Charter. The adherence to the principles of the UN Charter for the maintenance of peace and the reinforcement of international security is specifically mentioned in Article 11 TEU, which is even considered as an objective of the EU's CFSP. But the engagement in conflict prevention raises questions as to the EU's status according to the UN Charter. In the UN constitutional framework, 'regional arrangements and agencies' are governed by Chapter VIII of the UN Charter. According to Article 52 of the UN Charter '[n]othing in the present Charter precludes the existence of regional arrangements or agencies for dealing with such matters relating to the maintenance of international peace and security as are appropriate for regional action, provided that such arrangements or agencies and their activities are consistent with the Purposes and Principles of the United Nations'. In essence, Article 52(2) and (3) limits the actions of such arrangements or agencies to the pacific settlement of local disputes. Article 53 states that '[t]he Security Council shall, where appropriate, utilize such regional arrangements or agencies for enforcement action under its authority. But no enforcement action shall be taken under regional arrangements or by regional agencies without the authorization of the Security Council'. Despite the absence of a definition of a 'regional arrangement or agency' within the meaning of the Charter[40] and the legal debate these provisions have raised,[41] it is generally agreed that the criteria

---

[39] See Council Joint Action 2003/423/CFSP of 5 June 2003 on the European Union military operation in the Democratic Republic of Congo, *OJEC* [2003] L 143/50 and Council Decision 2003/432/CFSP of 12 June on the European Union military operation in the Democratic Republic of Congo, *OJEC* [2003] L 147/42. The operation was established in implementation of the mandate provided in the UN Security Council Resolution 1484 of 30 May 2003 asking for the creation of an Interim Emergency Multinational Force in the Ituri region, in particular in the town of Bunia, in co-operation with the UN mission in the Democratic Republic of the Congo (MONUC). The operation was indisputably of a preventive nature in order to limit the escalation and the spread of violence to the whole country. However, the operation also had a conflict management dimension on the basis of the mandate of the UN Security Council Resolution which, in particular, referred, on several instances, to the existence of a conflict in Ituri and to breaches of international humanitarian law.

[40] International practice seems to admit self-proclamation of regional organisations as regional arrangements, as was done by the Organisation of American States in 1948 and the Arab League in 1948. In the 1992 UN Agenda for Peace op. cit. n. 20, the UN Secretary General emphasised that the 'Charter deliberately provides no precise definition of regional arrangements and agencies, thus allowing useful flexibility for undertakings by a group of States to deal with a matter appropriate for regional action which also could contribute to the maintenance of international peace and security. Such associations or entities could include treaty-based organisations, whether created before or after the founding of the United Nations, regional organisations for mutual security and defence, organisations for general regional development or for cooperation on a particular economic topic or function, and groups created to deal with a specific political, economic or social issue of concern'.

[41] See for a discussion on this debate, E. Kodjo, 'Article 52' in J.P. Cot and A. Pellet (eds.), *La Charte des Nations Unies, commentaire article par article* (Paris, Economica 1985), pp. 800-803 as

which have to be fulfilled are threefold: the regional arrangement or agency shall a) be consistent with the purposes and principles of the United Nations; b) aim at pacifically solving matters of regional dimension (local disputes) by an action having regional characteristics; and c) deal with matters relating to the maintenance of international peace and security. Since whether or not the arrangement has legal personality is irrelevant,[42] and even though the EU has not officially claimed to be a regional arrangement or agency,[43] given the explicit reference to the UN Charter in the TEU and the EU's aim of maintaining peace and security and in the light of the flexible criteria of Article 52 of the UN Charter, it may be argued that the EU can be considered as a regional arrangement or agency. However, the crucial issue is whether such an arrangement is competent, on its own initiative, to act outside the territory of its Member States. Since local disputes are commonly understood as disputes exclusively involving States which are parties to the regional arrangement or agency concerned, it is generally argued that the reply to this question is in the negative.[44] This may naturally cause a dilemma for the EU since the objective of enabling it to prevent and manage conflicts beyond its borders lies at the core of its new responsibilities. If international practice and organs of the UN have accepted that the North Atlantic Treaty Organisation (NATO) engages in peace maintenance operations (i.e., outside its traditional collective security/defence mission) outside the territory of the Atlantic Alliance,[45] this situation cannot *stricto sensu* be extended to the EU, since, so far, it is not a collective self-defence organisation, within the meaning of Article 51 of the UN Charter, this task being still carried out in Europe by the WEU and NATO.[46] Such a

---

well as the judgment of the ICJ delivered on 26 November 1984, *Military and Paramilitary activities in Nicaragua*, ICJ Reports 392.

[42] In Europe, the CSCE was considered to constitute a regional arrangement, even though it lacked legal personality: cf., UN General Assembly Resolutions 47/10 (28 October 1992) and 48/19 (16 November 1993). Its successor, the OSCE, is likewise considered as fulfilling all the tasks of a regional arrangement (cf. Resolution 52/22 of the UN General Assembly (16 January 1998)).

[43] Note, however, that, in a resolution adopted on 14 May 1998 (*OJEC* [1998] C 167/190), the European Parliament referred explicitly to Article 52 of the UN Charter to designate the European Union. See on this, V. Kronenberger, 'La dimension institutionnelle de la Politique européenne de commune de sécurité et de défense (PECSD) de l'Union européenne', 10 *Europe* (2000), p. 3, at 7. J. Wouters and F. Naert have recently argued that it is perhaps time for the EU to claim this status, which could contribute to a more structured and organised relationship with the UN: see, 'Linking Global and Regional Organisations: the case of the United Nations and the European Union', April 2004, p. 5, available at <http://www.law.kuleuven.ac.be/iir/nl/opinies/index.html>.

[44] See E. Kodjo, op. cit. n. 41, p. 814.

[45] Cf., N Figà-Talamanca, 'The role of NATO in the Peace Agreement for Bosnia-Herzegovina, 7 *European Journal of International Law* (1996), p. 165 and S. Duke, 'From Amsterdam to Kosovo: Lessons for the Future of CFSP', 2 *EIPASCOPE* (1999), p. 12, the two authors asking respectively whether NATO could be considered as a regional arrangement and whether its missions had been properly authorised by the UN Security Council.

[46] See in general on the triangular relationship between the EU, WEU and NATO, R.A. Wessel, op. cit. n. 22, at 423-431.

possibility might, however, be used on the basis of the Draft Treaty establishing a Constitution for Europe.[47] In any event, as far as EU conflict prevention missions outside its territory are concerned, respecting Chapter VIII of the UN Charter would imply that missions having a non-coercive character (such as civilian conflict prevention missions) could be legally carried out either with the consent of the parties (States/regions) concerned, with the authorisation of the UN Security Council or within the ambit of other regional arrangements, such as the OSCE or the Arab League, having mandated the EU to act on the territory of one or several of its participatory States. For preventive actions having a coercive character, those should be authorised by the UN Security Council, in compliance with Article 53 of the UN Charter.

This point leads also one to strongly emphasise that the EU efforts run largely together and in parallel with the initiatives of other international organisations, having global or regional mandates, within the sphere of conflict prevention (cf., Chapters 16-22).

STRUCTURE OF THE BOOK

This book is divided into three Parts and 25 Chapters. The Chapters are up to date so as to reflect the factual and legal situation at the first trimester of 2004.

Part One (Chapters 1 and 2) is dedicated to the practice of EU institutions which relates to the identification of conflict indicators. Sources of conflicts are often numerous and complex, intrinsically dependent on the historical, ethnic, political and socio-economic context in which they occur. It is consequently very difficult to identify a set of theoretical tools or indicators which would signal in every single case the eminent occurrence of a conflict. Nonetheless, the EU institutions have developed a set of indicators that may help to identify the causes of potential conflict situations which, consequently, could enable them to initiate appropriate preventive mechanisms before it is too late. Part One describes the efforts made by the EU institutions to develop these indicators and, to a certain extent, whether these indicators are reliable and how they have been used.

Part Two (Chapters 3-15) describes and assesses the state reached by the EU in its conflict prevention strategy and practice. It discusses the institutional dimension and the financial dimension of conflict prevention within the EU architecture. It also analyses extensively the EU's instruments for the prevention

---

[47] Cf., Article I-40 (7) of the Draft Constitution, according to which if a Member State is the victim of armed aggression on its territory, the other Member States shall have an obligation towards it to render aid and assistance by all the means in their power, in accordance with Article 51 of the UN Charter. Article I-40 (7) however adds that this shall not prejudice the specific character of the security and defence policy of certain Member States and that commitments and cooperation in this area shall be consistent with commitments under NATO, 'which, for those States which are members of it, remains the foundation of their collective defence and the forum for its implementation'.

of conflicts, in particular, in terms of structural conflict prevention. More precisely, Part Two raises the question whether the whole range of EU instruments and policies, from 'soft' to 'hard' law measures, which may contribute to prevent the occurrence or reignition of violent conflicts, have been appropriately used. It finally focuses on concrete EU actions in two regions of the world, namely the Western Balkans and Sub-Saharan Africa.

Part Three (Chapters 16-25) discusses the experience and initiatives of other actors in preventing conflicts, as well as their cooperation with the EU in this field. Firstly, it focuses on other international organisations, whether their mandate or reach is global, such as the UN, the G8 or the World Bank, or regional, such as the OSCE, NATO and the Council of Europe. In terms of cooperation with the EU, while concrete and positive coordinated actions shall be noted, the discussion reveals that cooperation in the field of conflict prevention remains essentially *ad hoc* and lacks a more structural and institutionalised basis. Secondly, Part Three provides an overview of the relations that the EU enjoys with the International Committee of the Red Cross, NGOs and the business sector. Finally, the book draws the main conclusions of the three parts and provides some concrete proposals for improvements or changes, in the light of the Draft Treaty establishing a Constitution for Europe.

ACKNOWLEDGMENTS

We are naturally indebted to the twenty-three other authors who have agreed to contribute to this project and have provided valuable suggestions throughout the publication process of this book. This book would never have seen the light without the commitment and precious language revision of Peter Morris, University of Utrecht, and the encouragement, support and advice of Marjolijn H. Bastiaans and Philip van Tongeren, from T.M.C. Asser Press. We are also thankful to Mieke Eijdenberg and Serena Crespi for their very helpful contribution to the sub-editing and the indexing of the book.

Luxembourg/Leuven, July 2004   Vincent KRONENBERGER
                                                                 Jan WOUTERS

PART ONE

INDICATORS TO PREVENT CONFLICTS: THE PRACTICE OF EU INSTITUTIONS

Chapter 1
CONFLICT INDICATORS DEVELOPED BY THE COMMISSION – THE CHECK-LIST FOR ROOT CAUSES OF CONFLICT/EARLY WARNING INDICATORS

by Javier Niño Pérez[1]

1. INTRODUCTION: THE EU AND CONFLICT PREVENTION

According to the new Draft Treaty establishing a Constitution for Europe, the European Union (EU) shall work towards preserving peace, *preventing conflicts* and strengthening international security, in conformity with the principles of the United Nations Charter.[2] The Draft Treaty also states that, when pursuing its foreign policy objectives, the EU may use civilian and military means, including joint disarmament operations, humanitarian and rescue tasks, military advice and assistance tasks, *conflict prevention* and peace-keeping tasks, tasks of combat forces in crisis management, including peacemaking and post-conflict stabilization.[3]

The explicit reference to conflict prevention as one of the objectives of the Union's external action constitutes a novelty in the legal framework of the EU. Indeed, although a number of foreign policy objectives are laid down in the Treaty on European Union and in the Treaty establishing the European Community such as the promotion of respect for human rights, democracy and the rule of law, to foster sustainable economic and social development, to campaign against poverty, to contribute to international peace and security and to foster the integration of developing countries into the world economy, etc., there had been no mention so far of conflict prevention policies and activities.

However, even if the issue, as such, had not been explicitly included among the objectives of the EU's external action, the EU has, since its origins, engaged

---

[1] Administrator, European Commission, DG External Relations, Conflict prevention, crisis management and ACP political issues. All views expressed are those of the author only.

[2] Articles I-40 (1) and III-193(2)(c) of the Draft Treaty establishing a Constitution for Europe of 18 July 2003 (CONV 850/03), available via <http://www.europa.eu.int/futurum/index_en.htm> and published at *OJEC* [2003] C 169/1.

[3] Article III-210(1) of the Draft Treaty.

V. Kronenberger and J. Wouters, eds., The European Union and Conflict Prevention
© 2004, T·M·C·ASSER PRESS, *The Hague, The Netherlands*

in conflict prevention through a number of instruments directly or indirectly relevant to this particular area of foreign policy.[4]

The very nature of the EU helps to explain the rationale behind this commitment to conflict prevention: the EU is in itself a peace project, and a supremely successful one. It has underpinned the reconciliation and peaceful development of Western Europe over the last half century, helping to consolidate democracy and to assure prosperity. Given the importance of the EU on the international scene, its interests and ambitions and the considerable resources it has committed to assistance and cooperation, there is no doubt that the EU should seek to project stability also beyond its own borders. This is above all a moral and political imperative, but it also makes economic sense. It is a lot cheaper to channel conflict into dialogue and constructive action than to deal with the consequences once it has degenerated into violent confrontation.

During the mid-1990s, in the context of the changing international environment after the end of the Cold War and of the change of the European integration process that resulted, *inter alia*, in the establishment of the CFSP as its second pillar, the EU issued a number of policy statements on conflict prevention that led to the definition of a conceptual and policy framework for addressing violent conflict. This framework combines sophisticated analyses of conflicts with a realistic acknowledgement of the concrete possibilities and limits of EU action.

The above cited framework contains three main elements regarding the objective, the approach as well as the definition itself of conflict prevention:[5]

Objective: When dealing with the issue of violent conflict, this policy framework defines structural stability as the overarching strategic objective which informs all levels of the EU's actions in relation to conflict-prone areas. Structural stability can be described as a situation characterized by sustainable economic development, democracy and respect for human rights, viable political structures and healthy social and environment conditions, with the capacity to manage change without resorting to violent conflict.

Approach: Although the means available to the European Union are limited compared to the magnitude of the task of effectively preventing, managing and resolving conflicts, the Union should aspire to maximize its leverage through an optimal use of its instruments and resources. Thus its approach should be (i) pro-

---

[4] Among these are the following: development cooperation and external assistance, economic cooperation and trade policy instruments, humanitarian aid, social and environmental policies, diplomatic instruments such as political dialogue and mediation, as well as economic or other sanctions, and ultimately the new instruments of ESDP (including information gathering for anticipating potential conflict situations and monitoring international agreements). For a short historical overview, see the chapter by J. Wouters and F. Naert in this volume.

[5] These elements are clearly defined in the Communication from the Commission on the European Union and the issue of Conflicts in Africa: peace-building, Conflict Prevention and Beyond, 6 March 1996, SEC (96) 332. It is worth noting that they have also been endorsed by the DAC guidelines (OECD) on the prevention of violent conflicts (1997 and 2001).

active because the European Union, without prejudging the basic principle that ultimately those directly concerned by violent conflict are primarily responsible for handling the issue of violent conflicts, has not only an important interest but also an important potential for actively addressing this issue and (ii) comprehensive in so far as the European Union, within its competencies, should address the entire cycle of conflict and peace.

Definition: In contrast to widespread international confusion on conflict-related terminology, the EU has constructed a set of working definitions for conflict prevention both in a narrow and in a wider sense:

In a narrow sense, conflict prevention relates to the activities undertaken over the short-term to reduce manifest tensions and/or to prevent the outbreak or recurrence of violent conflict. These activities will therefore apply mainly in a situation of tension, that is where conflict in society becomes apparent (e.g., when open fighting between organized or disorganized forces begins or extreme social unrest emerges) and whose gravity depends on certain events as well as existing political power.

In a wider sense, it can be defined as the activities undertaken over the medium and long-term to address root causes of violent conflict in a targeted manner. Thus, in this sense conflict prevention also applies to situations where a country is seemingly stable and largely quiet but where (structural) causes of potential conflict may be discerned. Thus, activities of conflict prevention in a wider sense could be summarized under the term peace-building.[6]

2.   THE ROLE OF THE EUROPEAN COMMISSION

This wide definition of conflict prevention implies that conflict prevention can occur at two points in a typical conflict's life history: 1) when there has not been a violent conflict in recent years, and before significant violence signals possible escalation. In this case, conflict prevention aims to keep a conflict from escalating; and 2) when there has been a recent violent conflict but peace is being restored. Here conflict prevention aims to avoid 'a relapse or reigniting of violence'.[7]

This will have an impact in terms of both clarifying core issues and identifying instruments which could increase the EU's capacity to prevent and resolve violent conflicts. As regard the identification of instruments, conflict prevention offers a practical rationale for integrating all external functions of the EU which fall

---

[6] See the Annex for a complete set of activities to be included under the term conflict prevention.

[7] See Alex P. Schmid Pioom's abridged version of his *Thesaurus and Glossary of Early Warning and Conflict Prevention Terms* (Erasmus University 1998), available at <http://www.fewer.org/pubs/index.htm>. who quotes Michael S. Lund.

under both the first and second pillar of the institutional framework of the EU where the European Commission has a very significant role to play.

The First Pillar of the European Union contains institutions, procedures and instruments assigned to the European Community (EC) by the Treaties. It covers the EC's original areas of competence, such as agriculture, industrial policy, and the common market. Also included in the EC portfolio are external policy areas connected to the common market, such as international trade and development where the EU can engage in conflict prevention through a wide range of external assistance policy frameworks (for ACP – Africa, Caribbean and Pacific, ALA – Asia/Latin America, MED – Mediterranean countries, PHARE and TACIS – Central and Eastern European countries and CARDS – Balkan countries), through targeted economic measures (regional integration, relief, rehabilitation and development), and through special programmes for human rights, gender and democratization.

The scope of the European Commission for engaging in conflict prevention through the EC Pillar is extensive as, in this context, it stands as a centralized, relatively autonomous body with the exclusive right of initiative and is primarily responsible for the definition and implementation of actions related to these pre-viously cited instruments.

The EU's Second Pillar, the Common Foreign and Security Policy (CFSP), was established in 1992 (Maastricht Treaty on European Union) in order to give expression to the EU's emerging international political identity and increased op-tions for *de facto* engagement in international relations. It lays out the rules, means and mechanisms by which EU foreign policy is made and implemented. The link between the CFSP and conflict prevention policy and actions is self-evi-dent.

The CFSP is not implemented in the same way as Community policies (e.g., the agricultural, environmental, transport and research policies). In view of the sensitive nature of questions affecting international relations, the Treaty naturally attaches great importance to the Member States and the bodies of the European Union in which they directly participate, i.e., the Council and its competent in-stances (committees, working parties). Nevertheless, the Commission also plays a treaty-specific role in CFSP. The Commission is fully associated with the work carried out in the field of CFSP. The Commission may, as may any Member State, refer to the Council any question relating to CFSP and may submit propos-als to the Council – although it does not have the sole right to do so as in Com-munity matters. The Commission may also, as well as the Member States, request the Presidency to convene an extraordinary Council meeting and implement the CFSP budget (under the EC budget) including through appropriate financial pro-posals.

Both within the framework of the first and the second pillars, the Commission already possesses a wide range of instruments to address various phases of the conflict cycle. The setting up in 2001 of a unit dealing with conflict prevention and crisis management issues within the Directorate General for External Relations is a reflection of its determination to play a more proactive role and to enhance the impact and consistency of the different Commission's and in a larger context EU's initiatives in this area. The objective of the unit is to act as the main focal point and driving force within the Commission for conflict prevention activities.

3. CONFLICT PREVENTION / EARLY WARNING INDICATORS

One of the aims of policy-makers and decision-makers concerned with conflict resolution and prevention is to acquire the ability to anticipate the outbreak of violent conflicts before they occur. This early warning would help them to determine the best course of action and to prioritize resource allocation. Moreover, conflict management and humanitarian relief organizations can more effectively plan and target their activities.

Early warning can be defined as: 'the systematic collection and analysis of information coming from areas of crises for the purpose of: (a) anticipating the escalation of violent conflict; (b) development of strategic responses to these crises; and (c) the presentation of options to key decision makers'.[8]

The analysis of the information is not an end in itself but is rather intended for the development of early response such as the design of policies and/or interventions, including humanitarian, aimed at preventing violence and to help build sustainable peace and security.

Conflicts are rarely mono-causal and the most frequent underlying causes of post-1945 conflicts have been a combination of factors related to: ethnicity (disputes arising out of ethnic, religious or linguistic differences); governance (e.g., efforts to change the form of government or the party in power); independence (either in the form of decolonization or separatist state formation); control of natural resources (oil, water); strategic (to gain an economic or geopolitical advantage) and/or territorial. Studies carried out by the Clingendael Institute in the Netherlands show that, whereas military/political conditions serve as triggers for the outbreak of violent conflict, economic and social indicators are important for the structural background conditions within societies that provide a potential breeding ground for discontent.[9] Thus, there is no clear-cut international understanding on what are the causes of violent conflict that should inform an analysis of potentially conflict-prone areas. The logical corollary to this is that there is no

---

[8] See the definition given by Alex P. Schmid Pioom, op. cit. n. 7.

[9] K. van Walraven and J. van der Vlugt, *Conflict Prevention and Early Warning in the Political Practice of International Organizations* (The Hague, Clingendael Institute Research Essays 1996) and L. van de Goor and S. Verstegen, *Conflict Prognosis: Bridging the Gap from Early Warning to Early Response* (The Hague, Clingendael Institute 1999).

consensus as to what type of indicators most accurately predict the emergence of a conflict. Generally, early warning techniques are classified as either data-based (quantitative) or judgment-based (qualitative[10]) where the former includes the collection and analysis of large data sets and the latter is based on the subjective assessment of experts. There is an old-age battle over the merits of quantitative, qualitative or mixed-method approaches to conflict prevention and early warning mechanisms.

Notwithstanding the ongoing debate on the definition and nature of the most reliable early warning indictors, and since the mid-to-late 1990s, early warning research has progressed significantly both in terms of its ability to be accurate (as many disasters had already been preceded by warnings) and its potential to impose principles of cost-effectiveness in the resource allocation of external affairs departments. Thus, it could be argued that a consensus has been reached on:

a) the acknowledgement that effective early warning requires the use of a range of data sources and analytical methods:

- Local, e.g., events and perceptions not covered by the media;
- dynamic newswire reports (e.g., Reuters);
- structural data (e.g., World Bank) – these usually change very slowly and include political factors (regime type, democracy, military), economic factors (stability, inequality, security and environmental stress/resources), socio-cultural factors (media propaganda, institutional, religious). Early warning techniques are used to identify and analyze relevant early warning data from these sources;

b) the necessity for conflict/early warning indicators to cover four main areas:[11]

- **Governance**: level of democracy, human rights violations (arbitrary arrests, failure of the rule of law, in particular, lack of judiciary and the police; weakness of state situations and repression of civil society organizations), corruption;

- **Economics/economic performance**: economic growth, per capita income, secondary education, dependency on primary commodities and natural re-

---

[10] D.K. Gupta, 'An Early Warning About Forecasts: Oracle to Academics' in S. Schmeidl and H. Adelman (eds.), *Synergy in Early Warning. Conference Proceedings* (York University, York Center for International and Security Studies, 1997), pp. 375-397.

[11] See, e.g., M.P Sirseloudi, Conflict and Peace Indicators – Great Lakes, November 2000 (FEWER 2000) available at <http://www.reliefweb.int/w/rwb.nsf/0/c764c0220d1ae788c12569ba003a5601?OpenDocument>.

sources, employment and social insecurity, prevalence of poverty, income disparities and land distribution, environmental degradation;

- **Socio-cultural/social cohesion**: levels of trust and association, ethnic dominance, ethno-linguistic fractionalization index, geographic concentration, lack of access to mass media; discrimination on racial or ethnic grounds; and

- **Security**: length of peacetime since last war, size of ethnic diasporas, political killings, disappearances; availability of arms; crime rates, inter-personal violence, geopolitical aspects.

4. THE COMMISSION'S CHECK-LIST FOR ROOT CAUSES OF CONFLICT

The EU has also acknowledged that a key to an effective policy in this area is the definition of a long-term approach to peace and security whose objective rests upon identifying and addressing the causes of violent conflicts in a targeted manner.

The corollary to this principle is the need to use early warning indicators signalling potential conflict as a way of assessing the need for early action, taking account of coherence and coordination. In order to achieve effective early action, there is a need to enhance capacity for political monitoring and analysis, early warning, the elaboration of scenarios and policy options and the careful scrutiny of the relevant EU policy-making mechanisms. The gap between analysis, early warning and action must be reduced, in particular by enhancing capacities for political analysis, through the elaboration of scenarios and policy options and the careful scrutiny of the relevant EU policy-making mechanisms.

The need to 'move the timescale for EU action forward, becoming progressively more pro-active and less reactive'[12] is reflected in the Communication from the Commission on conflict prevention[13] which highlights the 'evident need for enhanced common analysis of root causes of conflict and of signs of emerging conflict' and suggests that 'an early identification of risk factors increases the chances of timely and effective action to address the underlying causes of conflict'. Equally, the EU programme for the prevention of violent conflicts[14] highlights the need for the EU to improve its early warning capacities.

---

[12] Joint report presented by the High representative/Commission on improving the Coherence and Effectiveness of EU action in the field of conflict prevention, December 2000 <http://register.consilium.eu.int/pdf/en/00/st14/14088en0.pdf>.

[13] COM (2001) 211 final, 11 April 2001, available at <europa.eu.int/comm/external_relations/cfsp/news/com2001_211_en.pdf>.

[14] Göteborg, European Council, June 2001 available at <http://ue.eu.int/en/Info/eurocouncil/index.htm>.

It is in this context that the European Commission, in cooperation with the Conflict Prevention Network,[15] and cognizant of the key role that it ought to play in this area, developed the check-list for root causes of conflict/early warning indicators in 2001.

Root causes of violent conflict refer to the characteristics of a country's historically dominant economic, political and social institutions, practices, and capacities (e.g., cultural norms and rules, government structure and processes, leadership make-up, public policies, etc.), which may create the preconditions for social conflict. In this sense, they may redispose, in a latent fashion, a particular area to conflict. Root causes are thus pervasive factors, which have become more or less built into the policies, structures and culture of a society. They can nonetheless be relatively influenced by human action, including social and political actors and government policies.

The list is only one of the tools that the Commission has at its disposal for monitoring and early warning. Others include regular reporting from Delegations and desk officers on issues related to the economic and political developments in concerned countries, open source information via the Commission's crisis room and the ECHO's disaster monitoring system ICONS (Impeding Crisis Online New System).

The Commission Crisis Room, in addition to tasks relating to information gathering, also serves as an Operation centre in crisis situations and provides Crisis management support, reacting to events such as acts of terrorism, non-military incidents, acts of war or emergencies (including the evacuation of staff in third countries). It is organized in two main sections, a conference room for audio/video conferences and multimedia briefings and a communications room which is designed to serve as the hub for all telecommunications and information resources for crisis managers.

4.1 Objectives of the check-list

The check-list should serve as a tool for generating political attention and facilitating pro-active agenda setting. Hence, its objective is twofold:

a) Awareness raising/early warning: to increase awareness within the EU decision-making forums of the problems of those countries/regions with the highest assessed risk of an outbreak, continuation or re-emergence of conflict.

As a framework for analysis, the list should help those concerned to structure their own thinking, encourage them to take a more comprehensive look at poten-

---

[15] The Conflict Prevention Network (CPN) was a network of academic institutions, NGOs and independent experts, and was a project managed by the German Institute for International and Security Affairs. In 2000, it was mandated by the European Commission to prepare a document which could be used as a basis to prepare the check-list. The final list, elaborated by the Conflict Prevention Unit of the European Commission, benefited significantly from the work of the CPN.

tial conflict cases as well as sensitizing them to the interrelatedness of different areas of concern as well as areas of preventive action. Indicators do not lead directly to preventive measures and recommendations. Yet, an indicator-based analysis may sensitize different policy sectors which are affecting a certain area. The framework should additionally enhance in-house understanding of the need for conflict-sensitive policies in various sectors which may seem irrelevant for the conflict potential at first sight. Also, a number of areas that are of concern to different policy sectors will be linked by the different actors on the connections between indicator categories and problem areas. The analysis is to remain focused (cluster areas); yet it is to be placed in a context that makes it explicitly imperative to gear different policy areas more clearly towards conflict prevention.

b) Agenda setting/mainstreaming: to heighten the effort to ensure that EU policies (and in particular those managed by the European Commission) contribute to conflict prevention/resolution. This objective reflects the need to establish an in-house 'culture of prevention' and to provide appropriate means and procedures to effectively follow a policy of 'mainstreaming' conflict prevention. In other words, conflict prevention should thus systematically be incorporated in, and become an integral and equal part of, all essential areas of engagement, within the framework of the EU's external relations. Regarding this objective, the list is a practical instrument which has been drawn up to help better identify the root causes of conflict and their manifestation, so as to reflect them in the Country or regional Strategy Papers. These documents constitute the guiding framework for political and economic cooperation between the European Commission and third countries. They normally have a five-year duration and undergo mid-term reviews. They are drafted by the geographical services of the Commission (both at headquarters and in the field) with the help of thematic units and other Directorates General concerned (trade, environment, ECHO). They define the Commission's cooperation strategy and are co-signed by the recipient country target. Thus, in the context of the Strategy Papers, the list should assist in drawing attention to those areas where Community instruments might/should intervene, thus being a useful first step in preparing for programming activities.

These two objectives complement each other: conflict causes are often well known, yet a specific case frequently fails to receive adequate attention. This will not only raise awareness of the need to cooperate and further improve inner and interinstitutional coordination but will also facilitate an integrated approach to conflict prevention within and among these actors.

4.2   The indicators

Conflict indicators can be used for very different purposes. As indicated above, the indicators of the check-list were selected with a view to constituting an instrument for early warning and agenda setting as opposed, for instance, to conflict impact assessment.

Taking into account the goals to be achieved, other existing instruments, internal working structures and decision-making processes, it was agreed that the indicators should: a) combine the quantitative and qualitative approaches, b) be short and precise yet broad and comprehensive enough to point to all potential risks, c) be sorted according the volatile nature of the situation with the help of, e.g., the phases, definitions and terminology developed in the practical guide, d) indicate the current trend for each situation (degrading, improving, unchanged), e) in a very brief and digestible format point to key problems in each country concerned and f) be presented to the Commission at regular intervals.

The list of indicators agreed refers to the following eight areas:

1. Legitimacy of the State;
2. The rule of law;
3. Respect for fundamental rights;
4. Civil society and the media;
5. Relations between communities and dispute-solving mechanisms;
6. Sound economic management;
7. Social and regional inequalities, and
8. The geopolitical situation.

These areas reflect the set of four root causes of violent conflict that the EU has developed and which merit particular attention for the purpose of conflict prevention. It is worth examining in a more detailed manner what these four root causes entail so as to better understand the rationale behind the check-list.

4.2.1 *Imbalance of political, social, economic and cultural opportunities among different identity groups*

Societies vulnerable to violent conflict may be characterized by a serious imbalance of opportunities among the main identity groups, in such areas as employment, education and basic physical safety.

Some of these settings may even be called 'exclusionary societies', while 'ethnic cleansing' and forced displacement may become extreme manifestations of this exclusion process. On a more common level, certain groups are routinely kept outside the formal economy, social services and the political process. Others are at least marginalized by not enjoying the same rights as ordinary citizens and being condemned not to voice their grievances publicly, although they may have indirect ways of expressing their needs. This discrimination may apply particularly to indigenous peoples, ethnic and religious groups (whether numerically majorities or minorities), castes, social classes, and the young. Such practices may be the result of an ancient heritage and are sometimes accepted by those who are neglected – at least to a certain extent. Most systems of exclusion are meant to maintain the uneven distribution of power, income and wealth. Lack of access to government services may be a deliberate policy to perpetuate this imbalance. In the absence of guarantees for minority rights, the imbalance of opportunities can be preserved or even accentuated after the introduction of formally democratic procedures. Faced with such an opportunity, marginalized groups and regions may vote for opposition parties, if these are allowed to exist, or show other signs of disloyalty, but may then be 'punished', for example, by the withholding of necessary investments in roads and other infrastructure.

4.2.2   Lack of democratic legitimacy and effectiveness of governance

Most violent conflicts are characterized by 'bad governance', which may partly be related to deficits in legitimacy. Public authority may indeed not be accepted by the population or there is no popular participation in the political process. The rule of law is not guaranteed either. Some regimes may seek to maintain legitimacy by using the state for patronage, extending employment in state enterprises or by manipulating the army or other security sector forces. The problem of inadequate governance may also partly arise from the increasing inefficiency of the state when it is based on such clientele practices. In extreme cases, the state is unable to perform its basic functions and reaches the brink of collapse. Laws are not enacted, order is not preserved, citizens are not protected and they therefore feel physically threatened, and basic public socio-economic functions are not performed. Where governments fail to maintain legitimacy and support, repression often becomes an alternative. Governments may even consider waging an interstate war to shift attention away from their internal legitimacy deficit. Regimes may also engage in massive human rights violations against regions, identity groups or political opponents (with potential spill-over effects to neighbouring states). Sometimes, they lose control over parts of the armed forces or provoke violent rebellion.

4.2.3   Absence of opportunities for the peaceful conciliation of group interests and for bridging dividing lines among different identity groups

When societies succeed in dealing with the root causes of violent conflicts, they have usually found traditional and modern ways to channel the inevitable competition that occurs among differing social interests, and to contain the scope of emerging societal problems and related tensions. Democratic institutions, including an independent and efficient judicial system, may provide the most effective mechanisms to peacefully regulate that competition. Usually, the lack of a broad and diverse public debate reduces the opportunity for a system to know about growing dissatisfaction, as it lacks information and cannot react. Alternative ways to transmit grievances may be lacking after the erosion of traditional authority, while, at the same time, those concerned may feel excluded from the decision-making process. Most societies have developed some mutually accepted dispute resolution mechanisms within or outside the formal institutional set-up. However, they sometimes only work locally or are no longer accepted by all the major players, and thus require outside actors to play a role in mediating in inter as well as intrastate conflicts. Regional organizations may therefore have an important potential to contribute to the peaceful (or violent) settlement of conflicts. Where they are inoperative, a crucial opportunity for preventing or managing emerging political disputes is lost.

4.2.4   *Lack of a vibrant civil society*

A civil society which operates largely independently of the state and the dominant political forces can provide the arena for negotiated solutions, when political conflict and policy debate become deadlocked. Where it is non-existent, suppressed or politicized, however, it cannot provide this alternative. Civil society organizations and civilian institutions thus have the potential to play a vital role in monitoring government policies as well as state adherence to constitutional frameworks, holding public institutions accountable and ensuring the legitimate and transparent conduct of the security sector. The interests of private businessmen in stability may also prevent the outbreak of hostilities. However, where economic activity is tightly controlled or hampered by the state, a growing proportion of the business community may have an interest in the breakdown of public authority. When values shared by many identity groups within society lose importance, parts of the population look for guidance from charismatic leaders and religious extremists on the one hand, and economic opportunities beyond legal frameworks on the other, thus developing 'uncivil' patterns of behaviour. An independent media can be a major guarantee of diversified debate and the comprehension of opposing interests. Unprofessional and extremist media, on the other hand, may become a major factor in exacerbating violent conflict.

4.3   **The questionnaire**

Building on the check-list, the Commission developed a more comprehensive questionnaire in order to assess on a more in-depth basis the situation of a given country with regard to the four root causes of conflicts developed beforehand. Thus, the list is divided into self-explanatory lead questions linked to each of the indicators indicating conflict potential as well as imminent trouble spots.

These questions are meant to: (i) be self-explanatory in order to be used easily, (ii) address general issues that do not too easily preclude one form of conflict (like genocide), (iii) be precise in their formulation as questions as opposed to mere indictors that could still be interpreted in different ways, (iv) record different intensities and stages (long-term potential and short-term events) and (v) leave space for interpretation and for qualitative/relative weight to be given within the comments/answers.

5. Two Years On and the Way Ahead

All policy actors concerned (in the Commission context, primarily desk officers and delegations) have so far expressed satisfaction with the usefulness of the check-list. Based on this list, conflict assessments are carried out annually for more than 120 countries by the Commission's services. They are used to prepare discussions between the Commission and the EU Council's Policy Unit in order to prepare a confidential 'watch list' of countries which is, at the start of each EU Presidency (i.e., six-monthly), made known to the General Affairs and External Relations Council for a broad consideration of potential conflict issues.

In addition, when drafting the political analysis section of the CSP/RSP,[16] risk factors contained in the list are now systematically checked by the Commission's geographical services and on the basis of this conflict analysis, attention is then given to conflict prevention focused activities that external aid should target. Thus, at the level of programming the assistance, the Commission is already placing more emphasis on strengthening the rule of law, supporting democratic institutions (e.g., election monitoring), developing the civil society, reforming the security sector or specific post-conflict measures. Those sectors of intervention had been identified in the Communication as a key to supplanting conflict or preventing its re-emergence.

These are just two very tangible outcomes of the work carried out thus far confirming that, two years after its adoption, it can be safely argued that the check-list for root causes of conflict has made a very significant contribution to the overall objective of further rooting the culture of conflict prevention in the day to day work of the Commission services as well as constituting an effective means for raising awareness in the EU of the conflict prevention approach and to making more systematic and more coordinated use of EU instruments to get to the root causes of conflict.

Nevertheless, it should be borne in mind that the process is still at an initial stage and that a number of questions are still open as to how the list could develop its full potential and produce even more notable results in the future. Among these questions one could cite the appropriateness of revising the indicators so as, for instance, to adapt it to the different geographical areas, the need to enhance its potential in the Commission's interactions with partners within (Member States) or outside (the countries concerned, other international organizations, NGOs) the EU as well as devising more sophisticated training methods for delegations and geographical services.

---

[16] The Country (or Regional) Strategy Papers (CSP or RSP) were identified in the previously cited Communication on conflict prevention as key tools to integrate conflict prevention in the programming of development cooperation.

ANNEX

European Commission check-list for root causes of conflict

1.   **Legitimacy of the State**

Are there proper checks and balances in the political system?
Respect for the Constitution, ability of Parliament and the judiciary to check on the executive, devolution of powers and the ability of regional authorities (if any) to counterbalance central power.

How inclusive is the political/administrative power?
Ethnic and religious representativeness of the government, equality of access to political activity, participative decision-making, fair recruitment in the administration and other public institutions.

What is the overall level of respect for national authorities?
Historical resentment against State authority, existence of independentist movements, parties advocating extreme solutions (revolutionary or reactionary) to perceived shortcomings, perceived ability of the State to answer people's needs.

Is corruption widespread?
Overall level of corruption, existence of anti-corruption programmes, widespread bribery in bureaucracies, collusion between the private sector and civil servants.

2.   **Rule of law**

How strong is the judicial system?
Independence and effectiveness of the judiciary, equality of all citizens before the law, effective possibility to undertake legal action against state decisions, enforcement of legal decisions.

Does unlawful state violence exist?
Participation of security forces in illegal activities (road blocks, extortion, others), effective prosecution of human rights abuses by security forces, existence of a minimal human rights framework for their operation, prison conditions.

Does civilian power control security forces?
Influence of security forces on political decision-making, role of the Parliament in debating/checking their use, existence of open debate and media/academic scrutiny of the security sector.

Does organized crime undermine the country's stability?
Control of a significant part of the country/economy by criminal networks (drugs, natural resources, human trafficking), existence of private armies or armed para-

military groups acting with impunity, proper reintegration of former combatants into social life.

3. Respect for fundamental rights

Are civil and political freedoms respected?
Respect of right to vote/eligibility, protection of civil liberties including freedom of speech and of assembly, free and fair elections respecting the rights of the opposition.

Are religious and cultural rights respected?
Punishment by law of religious, ethnic or cultural discrimination, recognition of minority languages, e.g., in education, definition of the state with no reference to a dominant religious/cultural identity.

Are other basic human rights respected?
Prosecution of human rights violations (torture, illegal detention), gender equality, freedom of private practices (dress codes, private life, etc.), adherence to and implementation of commitments under international human rights treaties and conventions, effective operation of human rights monitoring by NGOs and/or international organizations

4. Civil society and the media

Can civil society operate freely and efficiently?
Protection of NGOs and the right of association by the state, liveliness of civil society, access to staff, training, resources and others, ability to influence policy processes and solve tensions between communities.

How independent and professional are the media?
Censorship by the government, independence of the media from partisan agendas and political or private interests, ability to reflect the views of all social groups, access of journalists to professional training.

5. Relations between communities and dispute-solving mechanisms

How good are relations between identity groups?
Ability of major identity groups to mix together, frequency of outbursts of racial/religious violence, perpetuation of negative stereotypes or mutual suspicions by collective memory and culture, existence and effectiveness of reconciliation mechanisms (e.g., justice commissions).

Does the state arbitrate over tensions and disputes between communities?
Existence and effectiveness of mechanisms arbitrating between conflicting parties

(wisemen, elders, ombudsmen), political manipulation of ethnic/identity differences, existence of regional forums for conflict prevention/resolution.

Are there uncontrolled flows of migrants/refugees?
Social friction between migrant and host communities (e.g., adverse pressure on food, water, etc.), respect for basic rights of migrants/refugees, impact of migration flows on ethnic/identity balance of host regions.

6.   Sound economic management

How robust is the economy?
Income dependency on a limited number of sectors (e.g., one single agricultural product or industry or remittance), capacity to react to natural disasters or international conditions (for instance massive swings in commodity prices).

Is policy framework conducive to macro-economic stability?
Stability of main macro-economic fundamentals (inflation, public deficit, current accounts), ability to attract investment (both domestic and FDI), implementation of policies negotiated with IFIs.

How sustainable is the state's environmental policy?
Fairness of management of natural resources (e.g., water), anticipation of possible internal or external conflicts over natural resources, risk of serious environmental degradation (for instance desertification) forcing people into exile or threatening traditional ways of life.

7.   Social and regional inequalities

How are social welfare policies addressed?
Overall level of literacy, health, sanitation, development of safety nets and income policies (or, by default, the existence of alternative social mechanisms ensuring local or family solidarity), correct anticipation of massive demographic changes by public policies (especially urbanisation and youth unemployment).

How are social inequalities tackled?
Trend for poverty and marginalisation (especially in absolute terms), vulnerability of least-favoured segments of society, fairness of access to education, health care, jobs, economic opportunities (including women and minorities), existence of public policies addressing inequalities among communities through land reform, quota systems, social programmes or others.

How are regional disparities tackled?
Urban/rural gaps, existence of regions lagging behind in terms of economic development or particularly affected by lack of vital resources, redistributive policies between regions.

8.   Geopolitical situation

How stable is the region's geopolitical situation?
Relations with the country's neighbours, pending border issues, dependency of the country on unstable neighbours for vital assets (e.g., access to sea or water), effectiveness of regional conflict-resolution mechanisms.

Is the state affected by external threats?
Destabilising policies of outside forces, existence of proactive ethnic communities/diasporas abroad, ability to control arms trafficking.

Is the state affecting regional stability?
Support to militias or rebel groups operating on neighbouring territories, protection of war criminals or rebel groups from neighbouring states, exploitation of the country's natural resources for foreign policy purposes, presence of illicit international activities on the country's territory.

Chapter 2
THE COUNCIL'S EARLY WARNING PROCESS

by Niall Burgess[1]

1. INTRODUCTION

The importance of early warning as a basis for more active external action has been stressed repeatedly in the European Council conclusions. The conceptual basis for conflict prevention was set out in a series of texts considered by the European Council in 2000/2001. In December 2000, the Nice European Council considered a report from the High Representative for Common Foreign and Security Policy (CFSP), Javier Solana, and Commissioner Chris Patten on conflict prevention which stressed the importance of early warning in conflict prevention.[2] The principles set out in this report were given more concrete shape in the Göteborg Programme for the Prevention of Violent Conflicts adopted by the European Council in June 2001.[3]

Since then, work has been set in motion to structure an early warning process which can enable the European Union (EU) to be more active, more coherent and more capable in preventing crises, both in its neighbourhood and further afield. What follows is a snapshot of a work in progress. This brief account looks first at the **context** in which early warning is being developed. It outlines the new **resources** for information, analysis and decision-making which are now available, particularly through the development of the European Security and Defence Policy (ESDP). It links these to the **processes** which have been put in place as we develop an early warning **capability** and considers the link between these resources and the development of an early warning capability. It looks at early warning **in practice**, and, finally, considers **future** perspectives on early warning. Much of what is now integral to the early warning process is new. In three years time, there will be more and the process will undoubtedly have developed.

---

[1] Head of the Task Force dealing with Security Issues at the European Union Policy Unit, Council of the European Union, Brussels. All views expressed are those of the author alone.

[2] *Improving the Coherence and Effectiveness of European Union Action in the Field of Conflict Prevention*, Doc. 14088/00, 30 November 2000, available at <register.consilium.eu.int/pdf/en/00/st14/14088en0.pdf>.

[3] Doc. 9537/1/01 REV 1, 7 June 2001, available at <register.consilium.eu.int/pdf/ en/01/st09/09537-r1en1.pdf>.

V. Kronenberger and J. Wouters, eds., The European Union and Conflict Prevention
© 2004, T·M·C·ASSER PRESS, *The Hague, The Netherlands*

2. THE POLICY CONTEXT: A MORE ACTIVE FOREIGN AND SECURITY
    POLICY

The EU's CFSP is undergoing a profound transformation. New units have been
established to do new things. Field operations have been launched in the Western
Balkans and in Africa – three of them in under six months. More will follow.
New EU Special Representatives have been appointed in the Western Balkans,
Southern Caucasus and Afghanistan. Enlargement is bringing new resources –
and new priorities – to the fore. And, of course, the world has moved on. The
threats posed by international terrorism, the proliferation of weapons of mass destruction and organised crime combine with a better awareness of the more familiar problems of violent conflict to create a new orientation in security thinking.

If Europe's CFSP had a physical shape at present, it would be the shape of the
Western Balkans. Failure to prevent the spread of conflict through the region in
the 1990s highlighted serious deficits in the fledgling political Union. Foremost
among these was the political consensus on how to handle the evolving crisis.
Beyond this, the capacity of the EU to influence the situation on the ground was
limited to economic, trade and humanitarian assistance and delivery was slow.
The EU had no crisis management capabilities. For these it was wholly reliant on
other organisations – NATO, the UN and OSCE – with other decision-making
structures.

This has changed with the development of the ESDP and with the allocation of
new resources in support of external policy. Through the 1990s the Union was
largely reactive to developments – and often its reaction was more declamatory
than real. The emergence of a new political will to engage in crisis resolution,
combined with the development of military and civilian crisis management capabilities has enabled the EU to become more proactive in addressing concerns.
During its first year of operations, the EU has launched two police missions and
one military mission in the Western Balkans as well as a military mission in the
Democratic Republic of Congo. It has signalled its willingness to assume responsibility from NATO for peacekeeping in Bosnia and is preparing for its first police mission in Africa. Although these operations have a limited timeframe, they
signal a different level of engagement and commitment by the European Union to
long-standing crises in its neighbourhood and further afield.

Increased concerns over terrorism, organized crime and proliferation have
prompted a re-evaluation of security priorities leading to agreement on the EU's
first security strategy in 2003.[4] In short, the EU has progressed in a few short
years from a largely reactive stance to events, to a more active approach leading
to a strategic approach. The role and development of the early warning function
should be seen against this background.

---

[4] See section 7 below.

3. RESOURCES FOR EARLY WARNING

Early warning operates at several levels within the EU. Some **Member States** have considerable resources for information acquisition, assessment, evaluation and policy elaboration within their diplomatic, military and security structures. Their early warning processes use and combine in different ways the resources of their foreign, defence and interior ministries. The **Commission** employs conflict indicators, using the resources in its Delegations, to better target programming within its country strategies.

The Council Secretariat has few early warning sources of its own. The challenge facing it has not been to create new resources, but to retrieve existing resources through diplomatic, military or civilian channels, to integrate them and put them at the disposal of EU policy makers. The Council's ability to leverage these resources for early warning and integrate them in support of policy objectives has grown with the development of ESDP and CFSP. The Council Secretariat currently has a staff of around 2,500 of whom some 10% work on foreign and security policy issues. An increasing flow of information is now routed through the **new structures** established to support CFSP and ESDP. These include:

– The **Political and Security Committee** (PSC) which was set up primarily to exercise the strategic direction and coordination of crisis management operations.[5] All Member States and the Commission are represented at senior official level. The PSC is supported by a Military Committee (EUMC) which gives military advice and brings together the representatives of the Chiefs of Defence of all Member States. Unlike its predecessor, the Political Committee (COPOL), which met generally once a month, the PSC is Brussels-based and meets twice weekly, more often if necessary. This has enabled it to act as a focal point for the early warning and policy formulation bodies – most of them also new. These include the Policy Unit, the EU Military Staff and the EU Joint Situation Centre.

– The **Policy Unit** (PU) was set up under the Amsterdam Treaty[6] to provide support to the High Representative. This is a small unit of 15 seconded diplomats,[7] one from each Member State, and officials from the Commission, Council Secretariat and WEU. One of its tasks is to monitor and analyse developments and provide timely assessments and early warning of events or situations which may have significant repercussions, including potential political crises. Its composition makes it an important entry point to the Council

---

[5] Council Decision 2001/78/CFSP of 22 January 2001, *OJEC* [2001] L 27/1.

[6] Declaration 6 annexed to the Amsterdam Treaty, *OJEC* [1997] C 340.

[7] This will increase to 25 with the enlargement taking place on 1 May 2004.

structures for national diplomatic information. It is organised around task forces, one of which coordinates the receipt and evaluation of information for early warning purposes.

– The **Joint Situation Centre** (SITCEN) operates round-the-clock with both civil and military staff and is linked both to the Member States and to other Situation Centres, as well as to the EU Satellite Centre. It provides assessments and early warning.

– The **EU Military Staff**[8] provides early warning, situation assessment and strategic planning for crisis management operations. Its intelligence division draws on national intelligence capabilities and includes representatives of Member States' defence forces. It reports to the EU Military Committee.

In addition to these newer bodies, the Council maintains a field presence through its network of **EU Special Representatives**, appointed under the Treaty with a mandate in relation to particular policy issues. Recent years have seen the creation of new mandates in the Former Yugoslav Republic of Macedonia (FYROM)[9] in 2001, Bosnia and Herzegovina[10] and Afghanistan[11] in 2002, and the South Caucasus[12] in 2003 in addition to long-standing mandates in the Middle East[13] and the African Great Lakes Region.[14] They are an indispensable resource for information assessment and early warning – most are based in the field and supported by small teams of seconded experts.

The **EU Monitoring Mission**[15] in the Western Balkans comprises around 120 international monitors covering political and security developments as well as border monitoring, interethnic issues and refugee returns in the region under the direction of the High Representative. Work is underway on the further development of an EU monitoring capability.

---

[8] Council Decision 2001/79/CFSP of 22 January 2001, *OJEC* [2001] L 27/4.

[9] Council Joint Action 2001/760/CFSP of 29 October 2001 concerning the appointment of a Special Representative of the EU in the former Yugoslav Republic of Macedonia, *OJEC* [2001] L 287/1.

[10] Council Joint Action 2002/211/CFSP of 11 March 2002 on the appointment of the EU Special Representative in Bosnia and Herzegovina, *OJEC* [2002] L 70/7.

[11] Council Joint Action 2003/448/CFSP of 16 June 2003 extending the mandate of the Special Representative of the European Union in Afghanistan, *OJEC* [2003] L 150/73.

[12] Council Joint Action 2003/496/CFSP of 7 July 2003 concerning the appointment of an EU Special Representative for the South Caucasus, *OJEC* [2003] L 169/74.

[13] Council Joint Action 2002/965/CFSP of 10 December 2002 amending and extending the mandate of the European Union Special Representative for the Middle East peace process, *OJEC* [2002] L 334/11.

[14] Council Joint Action 2003/447/CFSP of 16 June 2003 extending the mandate of the European Union Special Representative for the African Great Lakes Region, *OJEC* [2003] L 150/72.

[15] Council Joint Action 2000/811/CFSP of 22 December 2000 on the European Union Monitoring Mission, *OJEC* [2000] L 328/53.

These new bodies bring together formidable resources for collecting and integrating early warning and analysis. In addition to these bodies, many of them relatively new, there are others which can play a crucial role in early warning. The **European Commission** has a network of delegation offices and a range of field activities and personnel with enormous potential for the early warning process.[16] These resources provide the essential linkage between the EU's political and security action and its trade, humanitarian and development activities. EU **Heads of Mission** are another resource, whose potential has yet to be fully tapped. Recent field operations in the Balkans and Africa have led to intensified contact with the United Nations and with other regional organisations, most notably NATO and the OSCE. Information exchange with these organisations is being deepened.

4. EARLY WARNING IN PRACTICE

The EU is as much the product of events as of design. While resources for early warning and for integration were being developed, crises in the Western Balkans, Africa and elsewhere have tested the ability of the EU to monitor and evaluate unfolding events and to respond to them effectively. They have also helped to mould the early warning process.

Faced with successive security and political crises in the **Presevo Valley** in Southern Serbia and in Northern **FYROM** in 2001, the Council, through its High Representative Javier Solana stepped up diplomatic engagement with the authorities in Belgrade and Skopje and with other actors in the region, particularly the United States and NATO. The Commission took steps to speed up the delivery of assistance. EUMM monitoring teams were deployed to the Presevo Valley and the number of monitoring teams in FYROM was increased. The Council appointed an EU Special Representative, resident in Skopje, working under the direction of J. Solana and supported, among others, by staff seconded from the Policy Unit in Brussels. The experience underlined a number of factors for effective functioning in a crisis:

–   the need for focus at the highest political level, willing to engage in continuous political dialogue, to be present frequently in the region and empowered to act on behalf of the EU;
–   the need for continuous engagement of Member States – in this case through the PSC;
–   the value of a resident representative (EUSR) in support of the High Representative, acting where possible as a focus for coordination between the numerous EU bodies present on the ground;

---

[16] See Chapter 1 above.

- the importance of monitoring teams deployed to trouble spots;
- the importance of close articulation with other actors (in this case the United States, NATO and OSCE).

Each of these elements played a role in ensuring an adequate information flow and a linkage with the policy-making process.

These lessons have been applied since to other emerging concerns. EU Special Representatives have since been appointed in Afghanistan and the Southern Caucasus. Each works under the operational direction of the High Representative and is supported by staff who are also close to the policy-making process. Each reports regularly from the field and directly to the PSC.

The crises in the Balkans fit clearly into the familiar pattern of crisis in the region. The chain of events set in motion by the **terrorist attacks** of 11 September 2001 and most recently of 11 March 2004 have signalled a very different type of threat. Within two weeks of the attacks, an Extraordinary European Council has met to reaffirm Europe's determination to address the threats posed by terrorism and to adopt a comprehensive plan of action which included intensified cooperation and exchange of information between intelligence services. This and subsequent actions against terrorism and organized crime have underlined the need for global engagement and for intelligence sharing in response to new threats.

A brief overview of these developments raises the question as to what precisely should be the focus of the Council early activities - early warning of what? The answer is complex. EU concerns range from conflict (internal and inter-state) to complex emergencies, humanitarian and human rights violations, state failure and new security threats such as terrorism and proliferation. Although these issues can be closely linked, each engages a distinct range of actors who must be linked to the early warning process. It implies that early warning operates across a range of timeframes: early warning of the imminent crisis of underlying developments which could lead to crisis (and conflict) in the longer term. The context for early warning is also complex. It plays a crucial role in conflict prevention but also in other policy objectives such as the prevention of threats, of complex humanitarian emergencies, genocide and human rights and humanitarian violations.

5.   BUILDING RESOURCES INTO A CAPABILITY FOR EARLY WARNING

The European Union has been speaking of capabilities for crisis management since 1999 when the European Council at Helsinki established the first Headline Goal for military capabilities, followed by goals in the areas of the police and the administration of justice six months later at Feira. The ability to undertake conflict prevention and crisis management tasks requires a range of capabilities, not all of them quantified or explicitly set down in Council conclusions. Early warning is one such capability. The existence of resources for early warning – however rich – does not in itself constitute an early warning capability for EU policy makers. They are transformed into a capability when they are integrated and developed into an evaluation which becomes a collective basis for action by the EU as a whole. Early warning cannot stand in isolation from the policy-making process. Unless it is a foundation for action, it has no value. Early warning is part of a policy-making continuum, which anticipates problems, evaluates their impact, sets out policy options and strategic considerations for policy makers.[17] Put simply, it sets out to answer three related questions:

– **What is going on?** The EU can only respond to emerging situations if it has a clear picture of what is happening on the ground. The issue is rarely one of a lack of information. On the contrary, an overload of information – from both public and internal sources – can also impede the policy-making process. The emphasis for the Council has been on securing a steady flow of relevant and reliable information from known sources whether from within the Council Secretariat structures, from Member States or from partner organisations. The confidential nature of much of this information has necessitated the creation of a secure IT infrastructure and the development of a security-conscious culture among staff involved in handling confidential information. This has had to be reconciled with the need to maintain close contact also with the humanitarian and non-governmental organisations which are also invaluable sources of field information.

– **What does it all mean?** A common analysis can be a powerful basis for collective action. Conversely, when Member States have different perceptions of what is going on they will respond in different ways – as we have seen in Iraq. Good analysis is every bit as important as good information.

– **What are we going to do about it?** It is one thing to identify an emerging crisis; another thing to identify realistic and feasible answers. Those involved in the policy elaboration need to understand not only the issue itself but also the European Union if their proposals are to meet with a positive response. There are many NGOs and think-tanks whose excellent analysis is often marred by policy recommendations to the EU which are vague, poorly thought-through or simply unrealistic. This is often the result of a poor under-

---

[17] This is reflected in much of the conceptual work on early warning, e.g., in the 1997 FEWER definition of early warning as the 'systematic collection and analysis of information coming from areas of crisis for the purpose of: a) anticipating the escalation of violent conflict; b) the development of strategic responses to these crises; and c) the presentation of options to critical actors for the purposes of decision-making': quoted in Alex P. Schid Pioom's *Thesaurus and glossary of early warning and conflict prevention terms* (Erasmus University 1998) available at <http://www.fewer. org/pubs/index.htm>.

standing of the EU's complex decision-making procedures and of the resources and capabilities at its disposal.

6.   THE PROCESS: A WORK IN PROGRESS

Significant progress has already been made in integrating existing national resources into a common early warning capability. This work has its roots in the
EU Programme for the Prevention of Violent Conflicts endorsed by the European
Council at Göteborg in June 2001. This set out the broad guidelines for early
warning at Council level:

–   the need for the Council Secretariat early warning bodies (currently the
    Policy Unit, Military Staff and Joint Situation Centre) and the Commission to
    provide regular information on developments of potential conflict situations
    and to develop standard formats and methods for early warning reports;
–   the importance of exchanges of information with the UN, OSCE, other inter-
    national organisations and civil society;
–   the role of the PSC in monitoring concerns and drawing on information from
    early warning bodies, and in bringing issues to the attention of the Council;
–   and the commitment by the Council to schedule a broad consideration of con-
    flict prevention at the outset of each Presidency.

Because much of the information flowing into the Council is confidential, the
early warning reports using this material as well as details of the process are
themselves confidential. An essential prerequisite for this work has been the establishment of a secure IT infrastructure, as mentioned above. However,
organisational routines have been put in place which bring all early warning bodies together around the tasks of monitoring and evaluation. These routines are important in ensuring that information is exchanged and differing assessments are
explored and discussed. Regular formats for reporting have been developed and
key risk factors identified. Each of the early warning bodies uses its own methodology as a basis for contributing to this joint work. The time frame for early
warning is a six to twelve month perspective.
     Each of the early warning bodies brings distinct and complementary resources
to the table. The Policy Unit has access to diplomatic reporting from Member
States and is an important actor in the follow-up and policy formulation. Through
its programming it can play a vital role in addressing emerging issues. The EU
Military Staff and Joint SITCEN bring a security expertise and close links to the
new crisis management capabilities. The Commission, which has begun making
systematic use of conflict indicators for early warning, has close links to the humanitarian and development communities and an extensive network of delegations. In short, the Council early warning bodies have access to resources which

are particularly valuable for short-term early warning and crisis prevention, whereas the Commission resources are well adapted to longer term preventive measures. Harnessing both of these sets of resources is important in ensuring a coherent and integrated approach to prevention. The process has been jointly designed and reports are jointly authored by Council and Commission staff. Contact between the Council and the Commission is through contact points in the Policy Unit and in DG RELEX (External Relations DG) respectively and functions extremely smoothly.

The Council early warning process is focussed on the EU's own decision-making structures, primarily the PSC, which has assumed a central role in setting the broad parameters for monitoring and in considering early warning reports and assessments.[18] More systematic follow-up on early warning issues, through the involvement of Council working groups in the preparation of policy options for the PSC is also being developed. Involvement of the Council is important in ensuring that peripheral issues can find space on agendas and the Council has periodically taken stock of this work.

The process is, as stated at the outset, a work in progress. In the short-term, work is likely to focus on further developing exchanges, particularly between second and third pillars and between the EU and its partners, in increasing and systematising the flow of information from Member States and on improving follow through at policy level. Nonetheless, the process has come far in a short space of time.

7. FUTURE PERSPECTIVES: EARLY WARNING AND PLANNING IN A
    STRATEGIC FRAMEWORK

Two recent decisions by the European Council will influence the future development of the Council's early warning process.

The first is the adoption of Europe's first Security Strategy following a proposal by the EU High Representative, Javier Solana.[19] This provides a strategic framework – some would say long overdue – for work in the security and defence area. It grew from the realisation – following internal disagreements over war in Iraq – that Europe can only act effectively if it has a common perception of problems and how to deal with them. Prevention is a key theme of the strategy which sets out five key threats facing the European Union: terrorism, proliferation, organised crime, regional conflicts and failed states. It comments that these

---

[18] M. Winston (referred to by A.S. Pioom's thesaurus, op. cit. n. 17) speaks of recipients of early warning in the international sphere. For the EU, the primary recipients of early warning are EU decision-makers.

[19] *A Secure Europe in a Better World*, European Council of Thessaloniki, 20 June 2003, available at <ue.eu.int/pressdata/EN/reports/76255.pdf>.

threats are dynamic. Left alone, they will grow. If we wait for them to materialise, we may have waited too long. Europe must be 'able to act at the first signs of trouble'. The strategy sets out a series of objectives in response to these threats: a more secure neighbourhood and the development of more effective multilateralism. The strategy goes beyond identification of the threats and responses to draw conclusions for the development of the EU itself: foremost among these is the creation of a *'strategic culture that fosters early, rapid and when necessary, robust intervention'*. The emphasis not only on familiar or 'old' threats such as regional conflict, but also on 'new' ones such as terrorism, proliferation and organised crime, will place a premium on closer linkages between the second (external) and third (justice and home affairs) pillars. This is an area where exchanges of information can be slow and partial, not only at EU but also at national level. It will also place a premium on better integration of a broad range of intelligence sources – civil as well as military and diplomatic. Intelligence will play a growing role in foreign policy decisions in a world where terrorism and proliferation are increasingly occupying centre stage.

Second is the decision to establish a **planning cell** with civil/military components charged, among other things, with 'linking work across the EU on anticipating crises including opportunities for conflict prevention and post-conflict stabilisation' and with enhancing 'the capacity of the EUMS to conduct early warning, situation assessment and strategic planning'.[20] In addition a small EU cell will be established at NATO to improve the preparation of EU operations using NATO assets. While the modalities for establishing these cells have yet to be worked out, these bodies will help to reinforce the linkage between early warning and crisis management planning.

In the immediate future, expected agreement on a new Treaty framework will also have implications for the early warning process. The creation of an EU Foreign Minister - if backed up by a new external service, closer integration between Council and Commission and increased use of national diplomatic resources - will act as a catalyst for further developments in the process.

---

[20] European Defence; NATO/EU consultation, planning and operations. Presidency document presented to the European Council, December 2003; see <http//www.ue.eu.int/pressData/en/misc/78414.pdf>.

PART TWO

EU CONFLICT PREVENTION STRATEGY AND PRACTICE SO FAR

PART TWO A

HISTORY, STRATEGY AND INSTITUTIONS

Chapter 3
THE EU AND CONFLICT PREVENTION: A BRIEF HISTORIC OVERVIEW

by Jan Wouters[1] and Frederik Naert[2]

1. INTRODUCTION

Although the European Union ('EU') addresses conflict prevention in general only since fairly recently in a more or less systematic manner, it is not as such a novel subject within the EU context. In fact, one could submit that the establishment of the European Communities in the course of the 1950s was itself at least in part a measure of conflict prevention in Europe and in the world at large: did not the preamble of the – now defunct – European Coal and Steel Community Treaty recall the famous phrase of the Schuman Declaration that 'world peace can be safeguarded only by creative efforts commensurate with the dangers that threaten it' and that 'the contribution which an organized and vital Europe can make to civilization is indispensable to the maintenance of peaceful relations'?[3] The present contribution will not go that far back in time, though. It only aims to provide an overview of the EU's actions in the field of conflict prevention since the 1990s. In a first part, we will illustrate that the EU has been active in this field for quite some time, but that it has long adopted a rather fragmented approach, focusing in particular on specific regions or issues. While we will try to address all major initiatives, we will not attempt to give an exhaustive overview. In a second part, we will provide a brief overview of the more recent development towards a more general and more comprehensive approach to conflict prevention.

---

[1] Professor of International Law and the Law of International Organisations, KU Leuven; *Of Counsel,* Linklaters De Bandt, Brussels.

[2] Research and teaching assistant, Institute for International Law, KU Leuven.

[3] Treaty Establishing the European Coal and Steel Community, Paris, 18 April 1951, expired on 23 July 2002 (in conformity with its Article 97). See also the EU Programme for the Prevention of Violent Conflicts (EU Council Doc. 9537/1/01 REV 1, 7 June 2001, available at <http://register. consilium.eu.int>, endorsed by the General Affairs Council on 11-12 June and by the Göteborg European Council on 15-16 June 2001, see para. 52 Presidency Conclusions), para. 1 ('The European Union is a successful example of conflict prevention'). All European Council Presidency Conclusions since June 1994 are available at <http://ue.eu.int/cms3_applications/applications/newsRoom/ loadBook.asp?BID=76&LANG=1&cmsid=347>. Unless indicated otherwise, all URLs in this contribution were active as of June 2004.

V. Kronenberger and J. Wouters, eds., The European Union and Conflict Prevention
© 2004, T·M·C·ASSER PRESS, *The Hague, The Netherlands*

In both parts, we will also illustrate that the EU's actions can often be placed in the framework of broader international efforts at conflict prevention (without, however, clarifying in each instance the precise relationship between the EU and international efforts, which we leave to the more specific contributions).[4] We will conclude with a short look ahead, namely at the EU's Draft Constitution.

2.   Earlier EU Attempts At Conflict Prevention

In the sphere of external relations, the competence of the European Communities ('EC') was for a long time limited to economic areas and, to some extent, development.[5] However, coordination between EC Member States in the field of broader external relations gradually developed beyond these limits. At first, this occurred outside the EC, in particular by the establishment of the European Political Cooperation ('EPC') in 1970,[6] which was later given a treaty basis by the Single European Act in 1986.[7] While the latter essentially restricted the EPC's competence regarding (European) security questions to 'political and economic aspects of security', conflict prevention other than by military means clearly fell within the EPC's scope. Nevertheless it appears that the EPC hardly dealt with conflict prevention. Neither did the EC consciously use its external economic relations powers for conflict prevention purposes in any significant manner.[8]

This picture began to change in 1992 when the Maastricht Treaty on European Union[9] ('EU Treaty') established the EU and in essence brought the EPC into the

---

[4] On cooperation between international organisations in the field of conflict prevention, see Chapter 16 in this volume.

[5] On the EC's competences in the field of development policy before the Maastricht Treaty on European Union, see, e.g., W. Devroe and J. Wouters, *De Europese Unie. Het Verdrag van Maastricht en zijn uitvoering: analyse en perspectieven* [The European Union. The Treaty of Maastricht and its implementation: analysis and perspectives] (Leuven, Peeters 1996) pp. 546-547 and S. Keukeleire, *Het buitenlands beleid van de Europese Unie* [The foreign policy of the European Union] (Deventer, Kluwer 1998) p. 115.

[6] By a decision adopted by the Foreign Affairs Ministers of the Member States on 27 October 1970, see *Bull. EC* 11-1970, pp. 9-14. See also K. Lenaerts and P. Van Nuffel, *Constitutional Law of the European Union* (London, Sweet & Maxwell 1999) pp. 36-37 and W. Devroe and J. Wouters, op. cit. n. 5, at pp. 608-609.

[7] 17 and 28 February 1986, *OJEC* [1987] L 169/1 (Title III. Treaty provisions on European cooperation in the sphere of foreign policy, Art. 30). The Single European Act entered into force on 1 July 1987.

[8] See, e.g., P. Tsakaloyannis, 'Political Constraints for an Effective Community Foreign Policy', in J.K. De Vree et al. (eds.), *Towards a European Foreign Policy* (Dordrecht, Martinus Nijhoff 1987) p. 150, who, writing in 1985, argued in favour of a policy encouraging stability and regional integration and promoting the peaceful settlement of disputes, all related to conflict prevention, 'by using Europe's economic assets' but submitted that is was uncertain whether the Community was willing or capable of undertaking such a role.

[9] Treaty on European Union, Maastricht, 7 February 1992, *OJEC* [1992] C 191/1 (when reference will be hereafter made to the EU Treaty in its original version of the Maastricht Treaty, the expression the 'original EU Treaty' is used).

institutional framework of the EU, renaming it the Common Foreign and Security Policy ('CFSP', also referred to as the 'second pillar' of the EU).[10] Unlike the EPC, the scope of the CFSP is comprehensive and covers 'all areas of foreign and security policy'.[11] The objectives of the CFSP included 'to preserve peace and strengthen international security, in accordance with the principles of the United Nations Charter as well as the principles of the Helsinki Final Act and the objectives of the Paris Charter'.[12] The potential of conflict prevention under the CFSP was noted quite soon at the highest level: in 1992, the Report to the European Council in Lisbon on the likely development of the common foreign and security policy (CFSP) with a view to identifying areas open to joint action *vis-à-vis* particular countries or groups of countries, stated that

'[...] the CFSP should contribute to ensuring that the Union's external action is *less reactive* to events in the outside world, and more active in [...] the creation of a more favourable international environment. This will enable the European Union to have an improved capacity *to tackle problems at their roots in order to anticipate the outbreak of crises.*'[13] [emphasis added]

The same document lists a number of possible 'specific' objectives for joint actions, including 'contributing to the prevention and settlement of conflicts'.[14] Nevertheless, the initial focus of the EU's CFSP was, according to this report, to be twofold. On the one hand, priority was to be attached to a number of regions, namely 'Central and Eastern Europe, in particular the Commonwealth of Independent States and the Balkans, the Mediterranean, in particular the Maghreb, and the Middle East'. In respect of Central and Eastern Europe, encouragement of 'the prevention and settlement of conflicts' was specifically mentioned as an objective, albeit in the context of the Conference on Security and Cooperation in Europe ('CSCE') commitments. On the other hand, a number of priority 'horizontal' issues, in particular 'domains within the security dimension', were identified. However, these included no direct or specific reference to conflict preven-

---

[10] Ibid., Art. B and Title V (Arts. J-J.11), now Art. 2 and Title V (Arts. 11-28) EU Treaty.

[11] Ibid., Art. J.1.1, now Art. 11(1) EU Treaty.

[12] Art. J.1.2, third indent original EU Treaty, now Art. 11(1), third indent EU Treaty.

[13] This Report was published as Annex I to the Conclusions of the Lisbon European Council, 26-27 June 1992, *Bull. EC* 6-1992, para. I.31 (also available at the European Foreign Policy Bulletin database, Doc. No. 92/257, available at <http://www.iue.it/EFPB/Welcome.html>).

[14] Ibid. Moreover, all of the other possible 'specific' objectives listed may arguably also serve conflict prevention purposes, especially '(i) strengthening democratic principles and institutions, and respect for human and minority rights; (ii) promoting regional political stability and contributing to the creation of political and/or economic frameworks that encourage regional cooperation or moves towards regional or sub-regional integration; (iv) contributing to a more effective international coordination in dealing with emergency situations; (v) strengthening existing cooperation in issues of international interest such as the fight against arms proliferation, terrorism and the traffic in illicit drugs; (vi) promoting and supporting good government.'

tion, although they were certainly relevant to conflict prevention, especially the CSCE process.[15]

Thus the EU explicitly set its efforts, at least in part, in the broader international context, including the CSCE process. That is hardly surprising, since the end of the Cold War had led to a wave of enthusiasm and hopes and proposals for a more effective role of the CSCE and the UN in maintaining and restoring international peace and security. In the CSCE this was reflected above all in the 1990 Charter of Paris for a New Europe,[16] to which the EU Treaty refers,[17] and in the 1992 Helsinki (II) *Challenges for Change* Document.[18] Both documents highlight the importance of conflict prevention.[19] One of the main achievements of the CSCE's 1992 Helsinki Summit was the establishment and appointment of a High Commissioner on National Minorities ('HCNM'), who was to be 'an instrument of conflict prevention at the earliest possible stage'.[20]

At the UN level the post Cold War enthusiasm was evidenced by the Security Council's actions in respect of the Iraqi invasion of Kuwait, which showed that the UN could work (more or less) as had been envisaged by the Charter, and by the special Security Council summit of 31 January 1992, which led the UN Secretary General to draw up a very useful 1992 report entitled *An Agenda for Peace*.[21] This document, true to its name, contains an ambitious agenda for a more peaceful world and offers 'a coherent contribution towards securing peace in the spirit of the Charter'.[22] It repeatedly attaches great importance to conflict prevention, including the eradication of the root causes of conflict, and discusses various conflict prevention instruments.[23]

---

[15] Ibid. The other issues identified (apart from the CSCE process) were '(ii) the policy of disarmament and arms control in Europe, including confidence-building measures; (iii) nuclear non-proliferation issues; (iv) the economic aspects of security [...].'

[16] CSCE Summit, Charter of Paris for a New Europe, Paris, 19-21 November 1990, available at <http://www.osce.org/docs/english/1990-1999/summits/paris90e.htm>. Two excerpts may illustrate the enthusiasm of that period: 'a time of profound change and historic expectations' and 'a new era of democracy, peace and unity in Europe'.

[17] See Art. 11(1), third indent EU Treaty, previously Art. J.1(1), third indent.

[18] CSCE Summit, CSCE Helsinki Document 1992, Challenges of Change, Helsinki, 9-10 July 1992, available at <http://www.osce.org/docs/english/1990-1999/summits/hels92e.htm>.

[19] For a discussion of the CSCE/OSCE's role in conflict prevention, see Chapter 18 in this volume.

[20] CSCE, 9-10 July 1992, Helsinki, Helsinki Decision II (CSCE High Commissioner on National Minorities), para. 2. See also Helsinki, Helsinki Decision I (Strengthening CSCE Institutions and Structures), para. 23.

[21] An Agenda for Peace. Preventive Diplomacy, Peacemaking and Peacekeeping, Report of the Secretary General pursuant to the statement adopted by the Summit Meeting of the Security Council on 31 January 1992, UN Doc. A/47/277 – S/24111, 17 June 1992, available at <http://www.un.org/Docs/SG/agpeace.html>. Again, a quote illustrates the spirit of that time: 'In these past months a conviction has grown [...] that an opportunity has been regained to achieve the great objectives of the Charter' (para. 3).

[22] Ibid., para. 22.

[23] See especially paras. 13, 15 and 23-33.

Before the development of the EU's (Common) European Security and Defence Policy ('EDSP'), initiated by the June 1999 Cologne European Council and facilitated by the changes introduced by the Treaty of Amsterdam,[24] the Western European Union ('WEU') was of particular importance for the EU's CFSP, as the EU 'request[ed] the Western European Union (WEU), which [was] an integral part of the development of the Union, to elaborate and implement decisions and actions of the Union which have defence implications'.[25] The WEU, in turn, in its 1992 Petersberg Declaration, declared its willingness to 'support, on a case-by-case basis [...], the effective implementation of conflict-prevention and crisis-management measures, including peacekeeping activities of the CSCE or the United Nations Security Council'.[26] Therefore the EU could request the WEU to support CSCE or UN conflict prevention and crisis management measures which had 'defence implications' and which it could, at that time, not undertake itself.[27] Nevertheless, in respect of conflict prevention, the EU arguably had considerable room for action itself, as only few conflict prevention measures would appear to have defence implications.[28] Indeed, this is supported by the EU's conflict prevention initiatives predating the launch of ESDP, which we will discuss below.

Thus we see, after the end of the Cold War, a wide acceptance within international organisations of the importance of conflict prevention. This is a logical consequence of the adoption by these organisations, including the UN,[29] CSCE/

---

[24] The Treaty of Amsterdam (2 October 1997, *OJEC* [1997] C 340/1, entered into force on 1 May 1999) inserted the Petersberg tasks, i.e., the crisis management tasks which the WEU had adopted in 1992 (see *infra* n. 26), into Art. J.7(2) EU Treaty (now Art. 17(2) EU Treaty) and provided the possibility for the European Council to integrate the WEU into the EU (see then Art. J.1 EU Treaty).

[25] Art. J.4(2) original EU Treaty. This was essentially maintained by the Treaty of Amsterdam (*supra* previous note), except for the possibility that the European Council could change it (see *supra* previous note *in fine*), which happened with the launching of ESDP in 1999 (see *supra*). This explains the deletion of the reference to WEU in the present EU Treaty as amended by the Treaty of Nice (Treaty of Nice amending the Treaty on European Union, the Treaties Establishing the European Communities and Certain Related Acts, Nice, 26 February 2001, *OJEC* [2001] C 80/1, entered into force on 1 February 2003). A consolidated version of the EU and EC Treaties including the amendments made by the Treaty of Nice is published in *OJEC* [2002] C 325/1-184.

[26] Petersberg Declaration, WEU Council of Ministers, Bonn, 19 June 1992, available at <http://www.bits.de/NRANEU/docs/petersberg92.pdf>, para. I.2. In para. II.4 the kind of military operations which the WEU envisaged were defined as 'humanitarian and rescue tasks; peacekeeping tasks; tasks of combat forces in crisis management, including peacemaking'. These tasks were later included in Art. 17(2) EU Treaty.

[27] On the relationship between EU, WEU and OSCE, see, e.g., W. Devroe and J. Wouters, op. cit. n. 5, at pp. 652-654.

[28] Obviously, this depends on the interpretation of 'defence implications' and in particular whether these words cover only measures which affect the use of military means or also measures concerning a situation in which the use of military force might be possible.

[29] See generally An Agenda for Peace, *supra* n. 21, especially paras. 5, 12, 13 and 15. See also the practice of the Security Council, in particular relating to the expansion of the notion 'threat to international peace and security', which has been held to (actually or potentially) cover, *inter alia*, terrorism (see, e.g., UN Doc. S/RES/1269 (19 October 1999) and UN Doc. S/RES/1373 (28 Septem-

OSCE,[30] NATO,[31] WEU[32] and EU,[33] of a broad, or even comprehensive, security concept.

Returning to the EU, it seems that conflict prevention was clearly covered by CFSP but did not initially become an autonomous priority. Instead, it rather became an aspect of the EU's policy *vis-à-vis* certain regions or an effect of specific but limited horizontal measures or of broader general measures which did not primarily envisage conflict prevention. We will now illustrate this, albeit only by way of a brief and selective overview, as most of these case-studies are examined in more detail in other contributions in this book.

2.1   **Regional**

2.1.1   *The countries of Central and Eastern Europe ('CEEC')*

In the light of the attempts to overcome the division of Europe, it is quite obvious that the CEEC became one of the main priorities for the EU's external relations. Admittedly, these countries were also a priority for other European organisations,[34] in particular the Council of Europe, NATO and WEU: each of them

---

ber 2001)), internal conflicts or unrest (e.g., in Somalia: UN Documents S/RES/733 (23 January 1992) and S/RES/751 (24 April 1992) and following), the overturn of a democratically elected regime (Haiti, see UN Documents S/RES/841 (16 June 1993), S/RES/875 (16 October 1993), S/RES/ 917 (6 May 1994) and S/RES/940 (31 July 1994)) and the repression of civilians and/or minorities (see especially UN Doc. S/RES/688 (5 April 1991, para. 1) and UN Doc. S/RES/1296 (19 April 2000, para. 5)). See further UN Documents S/RES/1308 (17 July 2000, concerning AIDS) and S/ RES/1325 (31 October 2000, on women and peace and security). See also *infra* on Resolution 1366 (2001) on conflict prevention. All Security Council resolutions are available at <http://www.un.org/ documents/scres.htm>. See furthermore the *Declaration and Programme of Action on a Culture of Peace*, 13 September 1999, UN Doc. A/RES/53/243 (6 October 1999). All UN General Assembly resolutions are available at <http://www.un.org/documents/resga.htm>.

    [30] See especially Helsinki Final Act (1 August 1975, available at <http://www.osce.org/docs/ english/1990-1999/summits/helfa75e.htm>), at several passages; Charter of Paris for a New Europe (*supra* n. 16), para. 21 and the Charter for European Security (Istanbul, 18-19 November 1999, available at <http://www.osce.org/docs/english/1990-1999/summits/istachart99e.htm>), paras. 4, 5, 9. See also the contribution by E. Bakker in this volume.

    [31] See especially The Alliance's Strategic Concept (Washington DC, 24 April 1999, available at <http://www.nato.int/docu/pr/1999/p99-065e.htm>), para. 25. See also Chapter 19 in this volume.

    [32] See European Security: a Common Concept of the 27 WEU Countries (WEU, Extraordinary Council of Ministers, Madrid, 14 November 1995), para. 1.

    [33] Such a broad security concept clearly underlies the *European Security Strategy* adopted at the December 2003 Brussels European Council (*A Secure Europe in a Better World*, available at <http:// ue.eu.int>). Moreover, the EU's adherence to a broad security concept is also illustrated through the reference in Art. 11(1) EU Treaty to the CSCE's Charter of Paris for a New Europe (which endorses a comprehensive security concept, see *supra* n. 16) and the EU's development of civilian crisis management instruments and its focus on conflict prevention.

    [34] A point which is also stressed by Keukeleire (op. cit. n. 5, at pp. 380-381) as one of the factors having contributed to the success of the EU's policy *vis-à-vis* the CEEC.

reached out to the CEEC.[35] The Council of Europe was the first to accept them as Members. NATO started cooperating with these countries, and others, in the North Atlantic Cooperation Council, which was later transformed into the present Euro Atlantic Partnership Council, as well as in the framework of the Partnership for Peace. In 1999 it accepted three of the CEEC as Members (the Czech Republic, Hungary and Poland) and seven others (Bulgaria, Estonia, Latvia, Lithuania, Romania, Slovakia and Slovenia) joined the Alliance in April 2004.[36] The WEU granted the CEEC a form of participation short of full membership, namely that of associated partners. We will treat the countries of South Eastern Europe ('SEE'), i.e., the Balkan countries of Croatia, FYROM, Albania, FRY (Serbia & Montenegro) and Bosnia,[37] separately, as most of them have, due to the conflict in the former Yugoslavia, been treated differently from the CEEC and because they have been the subject of distinct EU actions (see *infra*).

While the 1992 Report to the European Council in Lisbon[38] cited above stressed the priority to be attached to 'Central and Eastern Europe', it added 'in particular the Commonwealth of Independent States and the Balkans'. It thereby could have given the impression that the rest of CEE was somehow less important. However, that certainly does not appear to have been the case when one looks at the EU's actions. In particular, the EC had already entered into extensive bilateral contractual relations with a number of CEEC, in particular the 'Europe Agreements', and granted considerable support to a number of CEEC through the PHARE programme, the EBRD and the EIB.[39]

Moreover, at the European Council of Copenhagen in June 1993, the EC offered the CEEC the prospect of joining the EU.[40] For the purposes of this contribution, the European Council's December 1994 Essen Summit is very significant. At this summit, the European Council decided to establish 'a set of guidelines for short and medium-term measures' in four priority areas, one of which was 'ensuring the lasting peace and stability of the European continent [...] by preparing for the future accession of the associated countries of Central and

---

[35] These different and mutually reinforcing processes were rightly stressed by the Essen European Council (9-10 December 1994) Presidency Conclusions: 'The structured relationship covering [CFSP] [...] can reinforce efforts in the framework of the Western European Union, NATO and the partnership for peace, the [CSCE] and the stability pact, to increase security and stability throughout Europe' (Annex IV, Report from the Council to the Essen European Council on a strategy to prepare for the accession of the associated CEEC, VI).

[36] The status of ratification of the accession protocols is available at <http://www.nato.int/issues/enlargement/ratification-e.htm>.

[37] On the European Commission's external relations website SEE is treated as a region comprising these five countries, see <http://europa.eu.int/comm/external_relations/see/>.

[38] *Supra* n. 13.

[39] See S. Keukeleire, op. cit. n. 5, at pp. 375-376.

[40] Copenhagen European Council, 21-22 June 1993, Presidency Conclusions (relevant excerpts, especially para. 7.A.iii, are available at <http://www.europarl.eu.int/enlargement/ec/cop_en.htm>).

Eastern Europe'.[41] Thus eventual membership was seen as a means to assure lasting peace and stability, in other words, as a conflict prevention measure, much like the EC itself was conceived, at least in part, as such a conflict prevention measure (see *supra*). To achieve this, the EU embarked on a programme 'to prepare for the accession of all European countries with which it ha[d] concluded Europe Agreements'.[42] It regarded 'the narrowing of the gap between the countries of Central and Eastern Europe and the EU and WEU as a contribution to security and stability in Europe'.[43]

There is no need to discuss here the whole evolution of the enlargement process, which meanwhile has been successfully concluded by most CEEC.[44] Rather, attention should be given to one major initiative that took place in the context of this process and that clearly demonstrates the conflict prevention objective, namely the Conference/Pact on stability in Europe, an initiative by the then French Prime Minister Balladur which was taken up by the EU.[45] It was aimed at preventing further conflicts such as the one in the former Yugoslavia,[46] and was described by the European Council as 'the Union's first exercise in preventive diplomacy'.[47] It was said to have 'contributed to the strategy for preparing for accession'.[48] The Conference consisted of an inaugural conference (held

---

[41] Essen European Council (9-10 December 1994) Presidency Conclusions. See also the Copenhagen Presidency Conclusions (21-22 June 1993): 'Peace and security in Europe depend on the success of' the 'courageous efforts undertaken by the associated countries to modernize their economies [...] and to ensure a rapid transition to a market economy' (para. 7.A.ii).

[42] Essen European Council (9-10 December 1994) Presidency Conclusions.

[43] Ibid.

[44] See generally A. Ott and K. Inglis, *Handbook on European Enlargement. A commentary on the enlargement process* (The Hague, T.M.C. Asser Press 2002).

[45] See the Presidency Conclusions of the Brussels European Council of 10-11 December 1993; Council Decision of 20 December 1993 concerning the joint action adopted by the Council on the basis of Article J.3 of the Treaty on European Union on the inaugural conference on the Stability Pact (93/728/CFSP), *OJEC* [1993] L 339/1 and Council Decision of 14 June 1994 on the continuation of the joint action adopted by the Council on the basis of Article J.3 of the Treaty on European Union on the inaugural conference on the Stability Pact (94/367/CFSP), *OJEC* [1994] L 165/2. See also European Parliament, Recommendation on the joint action on the Pact on Stability in Europe, *OJEC* [1994] C 128/418.

[46] See Ministère des Affaires étrangères [France], 'Common Foreign and Security Policy', February 1996, <http://www.france.diplomatie.fr/frmonde/euro/eu25.gb.html>.

[47] Report from the European Council to the European Parliament on the Progress Achieved by the European Union in 1995 (pursuant to Article D of the Treaty on European Union), *Bull. EU* 7/8-1996, para. II.B.iv, at p. 70. See also Art. 2 Council Decision of 93/728/CFSP, *supra* n. 45 ('The inaugural conference will put into effect preventive diplomacy') and the Presidency Conclusions of the Brussels European Council of 10-11 December 1993 ('the draft Pact on Stability in Europe is intended to promote preventive diplomacy [...] The aim of the initiative is to contribute to stability by averting tension and potential conflicts in Europe'). See also W. Devroe and J. Wouters, op. cit. n. 5, at p. 643.

[48] Cannes European Council, 26-27 June 1995, Presidency Conclusions, para. B.IX. See also UK Foreign and Commonwealth Office, 'The Pact on Stability in Europe, Background Brief', April 1995, available at <http://web.archive.org/web/19990901114333/http://193.114.50.5/reference/

in Paris in May 1994), followed up by two regional round tables (one for the Baltic region and another for the other Central and Eastern European countries and chaired by the EU) which considered issues relating to borders, minorities and regional economic cooperation, and it was concluded by the Final Conference on the Pact on Stability in Europe (held in Paris in March 1995), where a Final Declaration of the Pact on Stability was adopted by 52 States.[49] The Stability Pact[50] consists of this final (political) declaration and a list of about one hundred (existing and new[51]) agreements and was submitted to the OSCE for monitoring, albeit with EU support.[52] In the event of difficulties, resort to OSCE dispute settlement mechanisms was provided[53] and both the EU and the Council of Europe were to assist in the implementation.[54]

2.1.2   South Eastern Europe

Because of the nature of our contribution, we will be rather brief concerning the EU's conflict prevention efforts relating to the first series of conflicts in the former Yugoslavia,[55] i.e., those that ended with the Dayton Agreement[56] in 1995.

---

briefs/pactstab.html> ('A principal aim of the Pact was to remove obstacles to the applications of the countries of Central Europe for membership of the EU').

[49] See generally the references cited *supra* in nn. 45-48; S. Keukeleire, op. cit. n. 5, at pp. 200 and 221; W. Devroe and J. Wouters, op. cit. n. 5, at p. 622 and European Commission for Democracy Through Law (Venice Commission), Report on the Preferential Treatment of National Minorities by Their Kin-State, CDL-INF (2001) 19, 22 October 2001, <http://www.hhrf.org/statusztorveny/report.htm>.

[50] Text in *Bull. EU* 3-1995, para. 2.2.

[51] In fact, very few new treaties were concluded under the auspices of the Pact. The Venice Commission Report (*supra* n. 49) lists only 2, including one concluded after the end of the Conference. See also the UK Foreign and Commonwealth Office paper, *supra* n. 48.

[52] See the 1995 European Council Report (*supra* n. 47) and the UK Foreign and Commonwealth Office paper (*supra* n. 48).

[53] See paras. 15-16 Final Declaration (*supra* nn. 49-50); the Venice Commission Report (*supra* n. 49) and the Foreign and Commonwealth Office paper (*supra* n. 48).

[54] For the EU, these measures were taken as part of the PHARE programme, see the Cannes European Council Presidency Conclusions (26-27 June 1995), para. B.IX and S. Keukeleire, op. cit. n. 5, at p. 226. They include a programme on minorities carried out jointly with the Council of Europe, see Council of Europe, Parliamentary Assembly, Report on the Protection of National Minorities, Doc. 7899, 8 September 1997, <http://assembly.coe.int/Documents/WorkingDocs/Doc97/EDOC 7899.htm>, para. 24.

[55] For a chronology of the conflict in the former Yugoslavia from 1989 to May 1994, see D. Bethlehem and M. Weller (eds.), *The 'Yugoslav' Crisis in International Law: General Issues* (Cambridge, Cambridge University Press, 1997) pp. xix-lvi. See also UN, *The Blue Helmets. A Review of United Nations Peace-keeping* (New York, UN Department of Public Information 1996) pp. 487-509.

[56] General Framework Agreement for Peace in Bosnia and Herzegovina with Annexes (hereafter, Dayton Agreement), Paris, 14 December 1995, 35 *ILM* (1996) pp. 75 et seq., also available at <http://www.ohr.int>.

It may suffice to point to two aspects of its actions.[57] First, the EU (initially the EPC) undertook numerous but mostly rather unsuccessful diplomatic efforts to prevent, contain and resolve this conflict.[58] Second, it sent a European Community Monitoring Mission ('ECMM') to the area, which had a monitoring mandate but was also meant to contribute to 'reducing the risk of outbreaks of violence and promoting stabilisation'.[59] The ECMM, later renamed EUMM,[60] was deployed in several former Yugoslav republics and in some neighbouring countries and may have helped to prevent a further spillover of the conflict.

However, we should discuss in some more detail the EU's conflict prevention efforts after this first series of conflicts.[61] First, the EU played, and still plays, a major role in the post-conflict situation in Bosnia itself, in cooperation with numerous other actors, focusing mainly on economic reconstruction, humanitarian aid and considerable financial support,[62] and, since 2003, a police operation.[63] The EU also administered the city of Mostar from 1994 to 1996,[64] with the assistance, at its request, of a WEU police operation.[65] By these post-conflict measures, the EU was, and still is, helping to prevent a recurrence of the conflict.

---

[57] For a more elaborate discussion of the EU's role in these conflicts, including the later conflict in Kosovo, see, e.g., J. Wouters and F. Naert, 'How Effective is the European security Architecture? Lessons from Bosnia and Kosovo', 50 *ICLQ* (2001) pp. 540-576.

[58] The most prominent of these were the following. First, the Brioni talks, which resulted in the Brioni Declaration (Joint Declaration of the Six Yugoslav Republics and the EC, 7 July 1991, available at <http://web.archive.org/web/19980101-20010101re_/http://www.dalmatia.net/croatia/politics/brioni_declaration.htm>) and in the ECMM (see *infra*). Second, the EC-sponsored Conference on Peace in Yugoslavia, which started on 7 September 1991 (D. Bethlehem and M. Weller (eds.), op. cit. n. 55, at p. xxix). In July 1992, this Conference was 'replaced' by the International Conference on the Former Yugoslavia ('ICFY'), led by an EC and a UN envoy (ibid., at pp. xxxvii-xxxviii). In May 1994 a Contact Group was established, which was to cooperate with the ICFY and consisted of the US, Russia, Germany, France and the UK and later also Italy (see P. Szasz, 'Introductory Note', 35 *ILM* (1996) pp. 75-77).

[59] ECMM, Role of the Mission, previously available at <http://ue.eu.int/pesc/ecmm/html/role.htm>.

[60] See Council Joint Action of 22 December 2000 on the European Union Monitoring Mission (2000/811/CFSP), *OJEC* [2000] L 328/53, later extended (presently until 31 December 2004). See generally the EUMM webpage, at <http://www.consilium.eu.int/cms3_fo/showPage.asp?id=622&lang=EN&mode=g>.

[61] For a more detailed discussion, see Chapter 14 in this volume.

[62] See J. Wouters and F. Naert, loc. cit. n. 57, at pp. 555-556.

[63] The EU has taken over, since 1 January 2003, the UN's International Police Task Force in Bosnia, see Council Joint Action of 11 March 2002 on the European Union Police Mission (2002/210/CFSP), *OJEC* [2002] L 70/1 (later amended). See for more details Chapter 14 in this volume and <http://ue.eu.int/cms3_fo/showPage.asp?id=585&lang=en&mode=g>. Furthermore, the EU has stated its willingness to take over the NATO-led military presence in Bosnia and is preparing itself for this operation.

[64] The EU Administration of Mostar was established by Council Decisions 94/308/CFSP, *OJEC* [1994] L 134/1 and 94/790/CFSP, *OJ* 1994 L 326/2, repeatedly extended and terminated by Decisions 96/442/CFSP, *OJEC* [1996] L 185/1, 96/476/CFSP, *OJEC* [1996] L 195/1, 96/508/CFSP, *OJEC* [1996] L 212/1 and 96/744/CFSP, *OJEC* [1996] L 340/1.

[65] See <http://www.weu.int/History.htm#4B>.

However, the EU also developed a more comprehensive regional approach after this conflict, initiated by the EU Council Conclusions of 26-27 February 1996.[66] This regional approach subsequently took shape through the 'Process of stability and good-neighbourly relations in South-Eastern Europe' (the 'Royaumont Process').[67]

The EU was also involved[68] in WEU's police operation in Albania, i.e., the Multinational Advisory Police Element ('MAPE'),[69] which, in cooperation with the Council of Europe[70] and the OSCE[71], aimed to stabilise the volatile situation in Albania in 1997.[72]

When the Kosovo crisis flared up, the EU's attempts to prevent an escalation and to contain it again essentially followed the dual track of diplomatic pressure and the use of the ECMM to prevent a spillover, with, in addition, humanitarian relief by the European Community's Humanitarian Office ('ECHO').[73] Furthermore, before and during the conflict, the EU, together with other international

---

[66] See especially Annex III thereto, see http://europa.eu.int/comm/external_relations/see/docs/reg_approach_96.htm.

[67] See the Common Position of 9 November 1998 defined by the Council on the basis of Article J.2 of the Treaty on European Union, concerning the process on stability and good-neighbourliness in South-East Europe (98/633/CFSP), *OJEC* [1998] L 302/1, implemented by Council Decision of 31 May 1999 implementing Common Position 98/633/CFSP defined by the Council on the basis of Article J.2 of the Treaty on European Union concerning the process on stability and good-neighbourliness in South-East Europe (1999/361/EC), *OJEC* [1999] L 141/1 and by Council Decision of 22 October 1999 implementing Common Position 98/633/CFSP concerning the process on stability and good-neighbourliness in South-East Europe (1999/694/CFSP), *OJEC* [1999] L 275/1. The main antecedents of the Common Position of 9 November 1998, which go back to the Paris Conference on Peace in Bosnia and Herzegovina where the Dayton Agreement was signed, are listed in its preamble.

[68] See, e.g., Council Decision of 22 September 1998 adopted on the basis of Article J.4(2) of the Treaty on European Union on the study of the feasibility of international police operations to assist the Albanian authorities (98/547/CFSP), *OJEC* [1998] L 263/1; Joint Action of 9 March 1999 adopted by the Council on the basis of Article J.3 of the Treaty on European Union concerning a contribution by the European Union to the re-establishment of a viable police force in Albania (99/189/CFSP), *OJEC* [1999] L 63/1; Council Decision of 9 March 1999 adopted on the basis of Article J.4(2) of the Treaty on European Union on the implementation of the Joint Action concerning a contribution by the European Union to the re-establishment of a viable police force in Albania (99/190/CFSP), *OJEC* [1999] L 63/3 and Council Joint Action of 16 June 2000 supplementing Joint Action 1999/189/CFSP concerning a contribution by the European Union to the re-establishment of a viable police force in Albania (2000/388/CFSP), *OJEC* [2000] L 145/1.

[69] On MAPE, see <http://www.weu.int/History.htm#5>.

[70] See, e.g., the joint EU-Council of Europe 'Albania programmes' mentioned in the Annex to the Council of Europe, '11th Quadripartite Meeting Council of Europe/European Union', press release, April 1998, <http://press.coe.int/cp/98/226a(98).htm>.

[71] On the OSCE's presence in Albania, see <http://www.osce.org/albania/overview/>.

[72] The situation was sufficiently grave for the Security Council to authorise an Italian-led military intervention, see UN Documents S/RES/1101 (28 March 1997) and S/RES/1114 (19 June 1997).

[73] See J. Wouters and F. Naert, loc. cit. n. 57, at pp. 557-560. On the diplomatic front, the EU efforts were largely coordinated with, and in support of, actions by the Contact Group, the Security Council and the G7/8.

organisations, especially the UN,[74] NATO[75] and the OSCE,[76] made considerable efforts to prevent the Kosovo conflict from spreading to Albania and FYROM.[77] After the conflict ended, the international community adopted a similar approach to that in Bosnia, consisting of a complex international presence in Kosovo to stabilise it and to prevent a recurrence of the conflict.[78] The EU again plays a major role in this multi-organisation effort, focusing once again mainly on economic reconstruction and humanitarian aid.[79] The EU also further developed its regional approach, in particular through the Stability Pact for South Eastern Europe,[80] which in effect succeeded the Royaumont process, and which 'is the first serious attempt by the international community to replace the previous, reactive crisis intervention policy in South Eastern Europe with a comprehensive, long-term conflict prevention strategy'.[81] The Stability Pact is not limited to the EU, but involves numerous international actors, both States and international organisations. Nevertheless, the EU was its main initiator[82] and plays a leading role in it.[83] In

---

[74] The UN had deployed a United Nations Preventive Deployment Force (UNPREDEP) to FYROM (see UN Doc. S/RES/983, 31 March 1995). Before that, the United Nations Protection force (UNPROFOR) had fulfilled a preventive role in FYROM (see UN Doc. S/RES/795, 11 December 1992).

[75] NATO undertook preventive and humanitarian action in Macedonia and Albania, see 'Historique des initiatives françaises', <http://www.diplomatie.fr/actual/dossiers/kossovo/kossovo14. html>; Clark, 'When force is necessary: NATO's military response to the Kosovo crisis', *NATO Review* (1999/2) pp. 17-18 (available at <http://www.nato.int/docu/review.htm>) and Balanzino, 'NATO's humanitarian support to the victims of the Kosovo crisis', ibid., pp. 9-13.

[76] The OSCE assigned additional tasks to its missions in Albania and FYROM (see OSCE Permanent Council Decision No. 218, 11 March 1998).

[77] For instance, the EU contributed, through ECHO, to the supply of humanitarian aid to Macedonia and Albania (see the ECHO annual reviews of 1998 and 1999, available at <http:// europa.eu.int/comm/echo/information/publications/annual_reviews_en.htm>) and the ECMM too was assigned tasks in Albania and Macedonia (J. Wouters and F. Naert, loc. cit. n. 62, at p. 560).

[78] See J. Wouters and F. Naert, loc. cit. n. 57, at pp. 561-566.

[79] Ibid., at pp. 563-564.

[80] See Council Common Position of 16 June 2000 repealing Common Position 98/633/CFSP on the Process on stability and good-neighbourliness in South-East Europe, *OJEC* [2000] L 144/35. The preamble of this decision clarifies that the repeal is due to the incorporation of the process' objectives and activities into the Stability Pact. The Stability Pact for South Eastern Europe was approved by the EU and the other participants on 10 June 1999. Its text is in 39 *ILM* (2000) pp. 962 et seq. and is also available at <http://www.stabilitypact.org>. For a more detailed discussion, see J. Wouters and F. Naert, loc. cit. n. 57, at pp. 566-568.

[81] See the page entitled 'About the Stability Pact', at <http://www.stabilitypact.org>.

[82] See also the Common Position of 17 May 1999 adopted by the Council on the basis of Article 15 of the Treaty on European Union, concerning a Stability Pact for South-Eastern Europe, *OJEC* [1999] L 133/1.

[83] E.g., the EU appoints its Special Coordinator. See para. 13 of the Stability Pact and, most recently, the Council Decision of 22 December 2003 on the appointment of the Special Coordinator of the Stability Pact for South-Eastern Europe (2003/910/EC), *OJEC* [2003] L 342/51. See also the Common Position of 17 May 1999 adopted by the Council on the basis of Article 15 of the Treaty on European Union, concerning a Stability Pact for South-Eastern Europe, *OJEC* [1999] L 133/1, Art. 1(1).

the meantime, the EU has moved beyond the Stability Pact and has offered the countries of SEE a perspective for EU membership, naturally based on the familiar conditionality, through its Stabilisation and Association process.[84]

A last EU conflict prevention effort in SEE which must be mentioned is that relating to FYROM. As has been noted above, before and during the conflict in Kosovo, the EU, together with other international organisations, undertook action in FYROM to prevent the Kosovo conflict from spreading to this country. While these joint efforts appear to have been fairly successful, tensions nevertheless escalated in FYROM, resulting in some, albeit fairly limited, armed confrontation in early 2001. The international community, especially the EU[85] and NATO acting in close cooperation,[86] exerted heavy pressure to de-escalate the conflict. This resulted in a peace agreement signed on 13 August 2001.[87] These European organisations also closely collaborated in assisting in the implementation of and in monitoring compliance with the peace agreement,[88] thus contributing to preventing a resurgence of the conflict. It was in this context that the EU, taking over from NATO on 31 March 2003, conducted its first military crisis management operation.[89] Apart from this, FYROM is included in the EU's regional approach to SEE set out above.

2.1.3 Africa

One of the EU's most explicit initiatives in conflict prevention was aimed at the African continent. It essentially started with the Essen European Council of December 1994, which advocated 'an intensive political dialogue between the European Union and the Organization for African Unity (OAU) in particular regarding conflict prevention in Africa'.[90] By this time, the EC had already set up rehabilitation programmes for countries that had been affected by conflict or

---

[84] See <http://europa.eu.int/comm/external_relations/see/actions/index.htm> and the detailed discussion Chapter 14 in this volume. See also the Commission's third annual report on the Stabilisation and Association process for South East Europe, COM(2004)202, 30 March 2004, available at <http://europa.eu.int/comm/external_relations/see/sap/rep3/strat_pap.pdf>.

[85] See Chapter 14 in this volume.

[86] See Chapter 19 in this volume.

[87] Ohrid Framework Agreement, 13 August 2001, available at <http://www.usip.org/library/pa/macedonia/pa_mac_08132001.html>.

[88] This was provided for in basic principle 2 of the Ohrid Agreement (*supra* n. 87) and in Annex C thereto.

[89] Operation Concordia, see generally <http://ue.eu.int/cms3_fo/showPage.asp?id=594&lang=en&mode=g> and Chapter 14 in this volume. See also Council Joint Action of 27 January 2003 on the European Union military operation in the Former Yugoslav Republic of Macedonia (2003/92/CFSP), *OJEC* [2003] L 34/26 and Council Decision 2003/202/CFSP of 18 March 2003 relating to the launch of the EU military operation in the Former Yugoslav Republic of Macedonia (2003/202/CFSP), *OJEC* [2003] L 76/43.

[90] Presidency Conclusions, 9-10 December 1994, title 'External relations', para. 8. On the background for this initiative, see M. Landgraf, 'Peace-building and conflict prevention in Africa', at <http://www.oneworld.org/thinktank/eucoop/edit4.htm>.

natural disasters as an intermediate phase between humanitarian aid and ordinary development assistance.[91] At least in respect of countries affected by conflicts, this can be qualified as a post-conflict (and conflict prevention) measure. In March 1995 the European Commission adopted a communication entitled 'The EU and the issue of conflicts in Africa: peace-building, conflict prevention and beyond'.[92] Subsequently, in December 1996 in Madrid, the European Council adopted specific conclusions on preventive diplomacy, conflict resolution and peace-keeping in Africa, which state, *inter alia*, that preventive diplomacy is a CFSP priority aim and which declare the EU's readiness to support African efforts in this field.[93]

This led, in turn, to the adoption and implementation of a common position concerning conflict prevention and resolution in Africa in 1997.[94] For the purposes of this contribution, two brief comments about this common position may suffice. First, in its Article 3, it states that

'[...] The Council notes that, in accordance with the relevant procedures, steps will be taken to ensure coordination of the efforts of the European Community and those of the Member States in this field, including with regard to development cooperation and the support for human rights, democracy, the rule of law and good governance'.

In part pursuant to this provision, the Council adopted a common position concerning human rights, democratic principles, the rule of law and good governance in Africa in 1998.[95] On the other hand, the role of development instruments in conflict prevention was, according to the Council's resolution of 5 June 1997 on the coherence of the EC's development cooperation with its other policies, to be studied more thoroughly.[96] Second, in its preamble the 1997 common position re-

---

[91] For more details, see the Court of Auditors' Special Report No. 4/2000 on rehabilitation actions for ACP countries as an instrument to prepare for normal development aid, accompanied by the Commission's replies, *OJEC* [2000] C 113/1.

[92] Communication from the Commission to the Council, The EU and the issue of conflicts in Africa: peace-building, conflict prevention and beyond, SEC(96)332, 6 March 1996, available at <http://web.archive.org/web/20030402085950/http://europa.eu.int/comm/development/prevention/communication-1996.htm>.

[93] Presidency Conclusions, 15-16 December 1995, Part A.III.B *juncto* Part B, Annex 13.

[94] Common position of 2 June 1997 defined by the Council on the basis of Article J.2 of the Treaty on European Union, concerning conflict prevention and resolution in Africa (97/356/CFSP), *OJEC* [1997] L 153/1, implemented by the Council decision of 20 October 1997 concerning the implementation of Common Position 97/356/CFSP defined by the Council on the basis of Article J.2 of the Treaty on European Union, concerning conflict prevention and resolution in Africa (97/690/CFSP), *OJEC* [1997] L 293/5.

[95] Common Position of 25 May 1998 defined by the Council on the basis of Article J.2 of the Treaty on European Union, concerning human rights, democratic principles, the rule of law and good governance in Africa (98/350/CFSP), *OJEC* [1998] L 158/1.

[96] EU Council Doc. 8631/97 Press 329, Part III.A1, available at <http://europa.eu.int/comm/development/body/theme/prevention/resolution-1997.htm>.

fers to initiatives taken at the level of the UN. Indeed, the UN too was starting to develop a conflict prevention strategy for Africa.[97] In 2001, the 1997 common position was repealed and replaced by the common position of 14 May 2001 concerning conflict prevention, management and resolution in Africa[98] (replaced again in early 2004[99]). Later that same year African leaders launched the New Partnership for Africa's Development ('NEPAD'),[100] which, *inter alia*, includes 'Strengthening mechanisms for conflict prevention, management and resolution at the subregional and continental levels, and to ensure that these mechanisms are used to restore and maintain peace'.[101] NEPAD was welcomed at the G8's 2002 Kananaskis Summit, in particular through the G8 Africa Action Plan, which also covers commitments in the field of conflict prevention.[102] Moreover, the Cotonou Agreement, which affects most African countries, also includes provisions on conflict prevention.[103]

Apart from this approach to the African continent as a whole, the EU has adopted several measures with a conflict prevention (often combined with a conflict resolution) dimension in respect of specific countries, conflicts, or regions

---

[97] A main starting point was the Report of the Secretary General on the Causes of Conflicts and the Promotion of Durable Peace and Sustainable Development in Africa (UN Doc. A/52/871-S/1998/318, 16 April 1998, available at <http://www.un.org/ecosocdev/geninfo/afrec/sgreport/index.html>). See furthermore several Security Council resolutions and Presidential statements, e.g., UN Documents S/RES1170 (28 May 1998), S/RES/1196 (16 September 1998), S/RES/1197 (18 September 1998), S/RES/1208 (19 November 1998), S/RES/1209 (19 November 1998), S/RES/1318 (7 September 2000), S/RES/1467 (18 March 2003), S/PRST/1997/46 (25 September 1997), S/PRST/1998/28 (16 September 1998), S/PRST/1998/29 (24 September 1998), S/PRST/1998/35 (30 November 1998), S/PRST/2002/2 (31 January 2002), S/PRST/2000/1 (13 January 2000), S/PRST/2001/10 (22 March 2001) and S/PRST/2002/31 (31 October 2002), the UN General Assembly's annual resolutions on Causes of conflict and the promotion of durable peace and sustainable development in Africa (starting with UN Doc. A/RES/53/92, 16 December 1998) and the Millennium Declaration (UN Doc. A/RES/55/2, 18 September 2000), Part VII. Furthermore, the Security Council established, in 2002, an Ad Hoc Working Group on Conflict Prevention and Resolution in Africa, see UN press release SC/7632, 14 January 2003 (and, for the terms of reference of this working group, UN Doc. S/2002/207, 1 March 2002) and discussed 'Africa's food crisis as a threat to peace and security' (see UN Doc. S/2002/1392, 20 December 2002).

[98] Council Common Position of 14 May 2001 concerning conflict prevention, management and resolution in Africa (2001/374/CFSP), *OJEC* [2001] L 132/3.

[99] Council Common Position 2004/85/CFSP of 26 January 2004 concerning conflict prevention, management and resolution in Africa and repealing Common Position 2001/374/CFSP (2004/86/CFSP), *OJEU* [2004] L 21/25.

[100] See generally <http://www.nepad.org>.

[101] The New Partnership for Africa's Development (NEPAD), October 2001, available at <http://www.nepad.org>, para. 49. See also ibid., paras. 71-78.

[102] G8 Africa Action Plan, adopted on 27 June 2002 in Kananaskis, Part I, see <http://www.g8.utoronto.ca/summit/2002kananaskis/africaplan.html>.

[103] Partnership Agreement between the Members of the African, Caribbean and Pacific Group of States of the One Part, and the European Community and Its Member States of the Other Part, Cotonou, 23 June 2000, *OJEC* [2000] L 317/3. See Chapter 15 in this volume.

within Africa. To give just a few examples:[104] the EU adopted a common position on the Great Lakes region[105] and sent a special envoy to that region[106] and it supported the peace process in the Democratic Republic of Congo,[107] including by sending *Operation Artemis*,[108] the EU's second military operation.

2.1.4 *The Mediterranean*

In December 1994 in Essen, the European Council established as one of its priorities not only peace and stability in Europe, but also in the neighbouring regions, in particular the Mediterranean. Its objective in this regard was 'ensuring the lasting peace and stability of [...] neighbouring regions by [...] developing in parallel the special relationship of the Union to its other neighbours, particularly the Mediterranean countries'.[109] To that effect, it was 'developing a programme to establish a Euro-Mediterranean partnership to promote peace, stability, prosperity and cooperation in the region' and stated its willingness to 'to support the Mediterranean countries in their efforts progressively to transform their region into a zone of peace, stability, prosperity and cooperation'.[110] The next European Council, at Cannes in June 1995, prepared the way for a Euro-Mediterranean Conference,[111] which was held in Barcelona on 27-28 November 1995 and at which the Barcelona Declaration was adopted.[112] One of the objectives of the comprehensive Euro-Mediterranean Partnership launched by this Declaration is the establishment of a common area of peace and stability: 'The participants ex-

---

[104] For other regional and country-specific examples, see Chapter 15 in this volume.

[105] Joint Action of 22 November 1996 adopted by the Council on the basis of Article J.3 of the Treaty on European Union on the Great Lakes Region (96/669/CFSP), *OJEC* [1996] L 312/1.

[106] See Joint Action of 25 March 1996 adopted by the Council on the basis of Article J.3 of the Treaty on European Union, in relation to the nomination of a Special Envoy for the African Great Lakes Region, *OJ* 1996 L 87/1, as repeatedly extended and replaced, most recently by Council Joint Action of 8 December 2003 amending and extending the mandate of the Special Representative of the European Union for the African Great Lakes Region (2003/869/CFSP), *OJEC* [2003] L 326/37.

[107] See Council Common Position of 8 November 1999 concerning EU support for the implementation of the Lusaka ceasefire agreement and the peace process in the Democratic Republic of Congo (1999/722/CFSP), *OJEC* [1999] L 286/1 and subsequent decisions amending or replacing this common position.

[108] See generally <http://ue.eu.int/cms3_fo/showPage.asp?id=605&lang=en&mode=g>. See also Council Joint Action of 5 June 2003 on the European Union military operation in the Democratic Republic of Congo (2003/423/CFSP), *OJEC* [2003] L 143/50 and Council Decision of 12 June 2003 on the launching of the European Union military operation in the Democratic Republic of Congo (2003/432/CFSP), *OJEC* [2003] L 147/42.

[109] Essen European Council (9-10 December 1994) Presidency Conclusions, 'Introduction'.

[110] Ibid., under the heading 'external relations'. See also the Council report for the European Council in Essen concerning the future Mediterranean Policy, attached to these Conclusions, especially para. 4.

[111] Cannes European Council, 26-27 June 1995, Presidency Conclusions, Part A.II.

[112] The text thereof is available at <http://europa.eu.int/comm/external_relations/euromed/bd.htm>.

press their conviction that the peace, stability and security of the Mediterranean region are a common asset which they pledge to promote and strengthen by all means at their disposal'.[113] On the EU side, this partnership is implemented, *inter alia*, through the MEDA programme,[114] reportedly 'the EC budget's second biggest external relations programme',[115] and through the conclusion of association agreements.[116] The objective 'to create an area of shared prosperity through an economic and financial partnership' is also retained in the Common Strategy of the European Union of 19 June 2000 on the Mediterranean region.[117] For the purposes of this contribution it may suffice to conclude that the EU's relations with the Mediterranean serve, at least in part, the purpose of assuring peace and stability and thus of preventing conflict.

2.2 Thematic

2.2.1 Arms control and non-proliferation[118]

Limitations on arms exports and proliferation of certain technologies and weapons, especially weapons of mass destruction, do not necessarily always help to prevent conflicts and in some cases a balance or minimal possession of certain arms and/or technology may even have a deterrent effect *vis-à-vis* aggressors. Nevertheless, it is clear that such limitations in many cases can help to prevent the outbreak, continuation or escalation of conflicts. Thus we will briefly mention the most important EU measures in this area.

One of the first of these measures was the regulation of the export of dual-use goods,[119] i.e., goods that can be used for both military and civilian use. The regime regulating these exports incorporates the commitments entered into in this

---

[113] Ibid.

[114] See <http://europa.eu.int/comm/external_relations/euromed/meda.htm>.

[115] See <http://europa.eu.int/comm/external_relations/med_mideast/intro/index.htm>.

[116] See <http://europa.eu.int/comm/external_relations/euromed/free_trade_area.htm> and <http://europa.eu.int/comm/external_relations/euromed/med_ass_agreemnts.htm> for more details.

[117] *OJEC* [2000] L 183/5, Part II, para. 7.

[118] For an overview of the EU's actions in this field, see, e.g., S. Keukeleire, op. cit. n. 5, at pp. 206-210.

[119] See initially the Council Decision of 19 December 1994 on the Joint Action adopted by the Council of the basis of Article J.3 of the Treaty on European Union concerning the control of exports of dual-use goods (94/942/CFSP), *OJEC* [1994] L 367/8 and Council Regulation (EC) No. 3381/94 of 19 December 1994 setting up a Community regime for the control of exports of dual-use goods, *OJEC* [1994] L 367/1, both repeatedly amended. The present regime is based solely on a Community act, see Council Decision of 22 June 2000 repealing Decision 94/942/CFSP on the joint action concerning the control of exports of dual-use goods, *OJEC* [2000] L 159/218. It is contained in Council Regulation (EC) No. 1334/2000 of 22 June 2000 setting up a Community regime for the control of exports of dual-use items and technology, *OJEC* [2000] L 159/1, as repeatedly amended. See also <http://europa.eu.int/comm/trade/goods/dualuse/legis.htm>.

field by the Member States in international export control mechanisms[120] such as the Wassenaar Arrangement, the Australia Group and the Missile Technology Control Regime.[121] Moreover, the EU as such takes part in these mechanisms: the Commission is a full member of the Australia Group, a permanent observer at the Nuclear Suppliers Group and the Zangger Committee and it participates in the EU Presidency Delegation in the Missile Technology Control Regime and in the EU Presidency Delegation in the Wassenaar Arrangement.[122]

Other EU measures regarding conventional arms include measures concerning the prevention and combating of illegal trafficking in conventional arms,[123] arms exports[124] and arms brokering[125] in general and the prevention of the spread of small arms and light weapons, both in general[126] and in relation to specific regions or countries.[127] Many of these actions have counterparts on a broader inter-

---

[120] Information on these mechanisms can be found at <http://www.fas.org/nuke/control/index. html>.

[121] See, e.g., the 4th consideration of Council Regulation (EC) No. 149/2003 of 27 January 2003 amending and updating Regulation (EC) No. 1334/2000 setting up a Community regime for the control of exports of dual-use items and technology, *OJEC* [2003] L 30/1. See also the Commission's answer to written question No. 3502/98, *OJEC* [1999] C 142/140 ('the entire Wassenaar dual-use list is integrated into the Union list of controlled dual-use products'), and the Council's answer to written question No. E-4065/98, *OJEC* [1999] C 297/127 ('The commitments of Member States under the Wassenaar arrangement, as well as under the other export control regimes, are transposed into an integrated EU system').

[122] See <http://europa.eu.int/comm/external_relations/cfsp/npd/index.htm>.

[123] EU Programme on illicit trafficking in conventional arms, 26 June 1997. See Chapter 12 in this volume.

[124] See especially the European Union code of conduct on arms exports, adopted by the Council on 8 June 1998, EU Council Doc. 8675/2/98 REV 2, 5 June 1998 (available at <http://register. consilium.eu.int> and at <http://ue.eu.int/uedocs/cmsUpload/8675_2_98_en.pdf>) and Council Declaration of 13 June 2000, issued on the occasion of the adoption of the common list of military equipment covered by the European Union code of conduct on arms export, *OJEC* [2000] C 191/1. See also generally <http://ue.eu.int/cms3_fo/showPage.asp?id=408&lang=en&mode=g>.

[125] See Council Common Position of 23 June 2003 on the control of arms brokering (2003/468/ CFSP), *OJEC* [2003] L 156/79.

[126] See Joint Action of 17 December 1998 adopted by the Council on the basis of Article J.3 of the Treaty on European Union on the European Union's contribution to combating the destabilising accumulation and spread of small arms and light weapons (1999/34/CFSP), *OJEC* [1999] L 9/1, later replaced by Council Joint Action of 12 July 2002 on the European Union's contribution to combating the destabilising accumulation and spread of small arms and light weapons and repealing Joint Action 1999/34/CFSP (2002/589/CFSP), *OJEC* [2000] L 191/1, and Council resolution of 21 may 1999 on conflict prevention, management and small arms and weapons, 21 May 1999, available at <http://www.webarchive.org/web/20030625170159>, <http://www.ib.be/grip/bdg/g1787.html> and cited in European Commission, *Small arms and light weapons. The response of the European Union* (Luxembourg, Office for Official Publications of the European Communities, 2001) pp. 17-18 (also available at <http://europa.eu.int/comm/external_relations/cfsp/doc/small_arms_en.pdf>). The latter publication also provides a good overview up to 2001.

[127] E.g., Council Decision of 11 November 2002 extending and amending Decision 1999/730/ CFSP concerning a European Union contribution to combating the destabilising accumulation and spread of small arms and light weapons in Cambodia (2002/904/CFSP), *OJEC* [2002] L 313/1 and

national level, e.g., in the UN,[128] the OSCE[129] and the G7/8,[130] and the EU attempts to 'build consensus in the relevant regional and international forums (for example, the UN and OSCE) and among affected States' on such measures 'as the basis for regional and incremental approaches to the problem and, where appropriate, global international instruments'.[131] Finally, one may also mention EU actions concerning anti-personnel landmines,[132] although these serve mostly humanitarian objectives and only limited conflict prevention purposes.[133]

In the field of weapons of mass destruction, the EU has also adopted a number of measures, although mostly only more recently. On the one hand, some of these

---

Council Decision of 21 July 2003 concerning the implementation of Joint Action 2002/589/CFSP with a view to a European Union contribution to combating the destabilising accumulation and spread of small arms and light weapons in Latin America and the Caribbean, *OJEC* [2003] L 185/59.

[128] For an overview of the UN's actions regarding disarmament, see <http://disarmament.un.org/>. In the field of conventional arms, the most important UN initiatives are the Protocol Against the Illicit Manufacturing of Trafficking in Firearms, Their Parts and Components and Ammunition, supplementing the United Nations Convention against Transnational Organised Crime (New York, 31 May 2000, available at <http://untreaty.un.org/English/TreatyEvent2003/Texts/treaty4E.pdf>), the Programme of Action to Prevent, Combat and Eradicate the Illicit Trade in Small Arms and Light Weapons in All Its Aspects (UN Doc. A/CONF.192/15, July 2001), the UN Register of Conventional Arms, and a number of Security Council decisions and statements, including UN Documents S/RES/1209 (19 November 1998), S/RES/1467 (18 March 2003), S/PRST/1999/28 (24 September 1999), S/PRST/2001/21 (31 August 2001) and S/PRST/2002/30 (31 October 2002) and numerous weapons embargoes relating to specific conflicts.

[129] See the OSCE Document on Small Arms and Light Weapons, Vienna, 24 November 2000, available at <http://www.osce.org/docs/english/fsc/2000/decisions/fscew231.htm>.

[130] See the G8 Miyazaki Initiatives for Conflict Prevention, adopted by the G8 Foreign Ministers' Meeting in Miyazaki (Japan) on 13 July 2000, covering, *inter alia*, small arms and light weapons, available at <http://www.g7.utoronto.ca/foreign/fm000713-in.htm>.

[131] See Art. 2 Council Joint Action 2002/589/CFSP of 12 July 2002, *supra* n. 126. For an example of joint efforts by the Member States in an international negotiation, see Council Common Position of 31 January 2000 on the proposed protocol against the illicit manufacturing of and trafficking in firearms, their parts and components and ammunition, supplementing the United Nations Convention against Transnational Organised Crime (2000/130/JHA), *OJEC* [2000] L 37/1.

[132] See, to name but a few, Joint Action of 28 November 1997 adopted by the Council on the basis of Article J.3 of the Treaty on European Union, on anti-personnel landmines (97/817/CFSP), *OJEC* [1997] L 338/1; Council Regulation (EC) No. 1725/2001 of 23 July 2001 concerning action against anti-personnel landmines in third countries other than developing countries, *OJEC* [2001] L 234/6; Regulation (EC) No. 1724/2001 of the European Parliament and of the Council of 23 July 2001 concerning action against anti-personnel landmines in developing countries, *OJEC* [2001] L 234/1 and Council Decision of 9 November 1998 adopted on the basis of Article J.3 of the Treaty on European Union concerning a specific action of the Union in the field of assistance for mine clearance (98/627/CFSP), *OJEC* [1998] L 300/1. See also generally <http://europa.eu.int/comm/external_relations/mine/intro/index.htm>.

[133] For instance, anti-personnel landmines were addressed within the framework of the Convention on Prohibitions or Restrictions on the Use of Certain Conventional Weapons which may Be Deemed to be Excessively Injurious or to Have Indiscriminate Effects (Geneva, 10 October 1980, available at <http://www.icrc.org/ihl>). Nevertheless, to the extent that mines hinder economic reconstruction and development, which may contribute to conflict prevention (see *infra*), they do have an impact on conflict prevention.

instruments focus on certain weapons or technologies. They include the control of technical assistance related to weapons of mass destruction,[134] *inter alia*, in furtherance of Member States' commitments under international export control regimes,[135] a Declaration on the prevention of proliferation of ballistic missiles,[136] and support for several international non-proliferation instruments and mechanisms, such as the International Code of Conduct Against Ballistic Missile Proliferation (elaborated by the Members of the Missile Technology Control Regime),[137] the Biological and Toxin Weapons Convention, especially in the framework of the review conferences,[138] the Nuclear Non-Proliferation Treaty, in particular in the framework of the review conferences of this treaty,[139] the Comprehensive Nuclear Test-Ban Treaty[140] and the Nuclear Suppliers

---

[134] Joint Action of 22 June 2000 concerning the control of technical assistance related to certain military end-uses (2000/401/CFSP), *OJEC* [2000] L 159/216.

[135] Ibid., especially the 2nd consideration of the preamble and Arts. 1(c) and 4(c).

[136] European Council of Göteborg, 15-16 June 2001, Presidency Conclusions, para. 54 and Annex I.

[137] See Council Common Position of 23 July 2001 on the fight against ballistic missile proliferation (2001/567/CFSP), *OJEC* [2001] L 202/1 and Council Joint Action of 27 May 2002 on financial support for the international negotiating process leading to the adoption of an international code of conduct against ballistic missile proliferation (2002/406/CFSP), *OJEC* [2002] L 140/1.

[138] See the Common position of 25 June 1996 defined by the Council on the basis of Article J.2 of the Treaty on European Union, relating to preparation for the Fourth Review Conference of the Convention on the prohibition of the development, production and stockpiling of bacteriological (biological) and toxin weapons and on their destruction (BTWC) (96/408/CFSP), *OJEC* [1996] L 168/3 and the Common Position of 4 March 1998 defined by the Council on the basis of Article J.2 of the Treaty on European Union, relating to progress towards a legally binding Protocol to strengthen compliance with the Biological and Toxin Weapons Convention (BTWC) and the intensification of work in the Ad Hoc Group to that end (98/197/CFSP), *OJEC* [1998] L 75/2, later replaced by the Common Position of 17 May 1999 adopted by the Council on the basis of Article 15 of the Treaty on European Union, relating to progress towards a legally binding Protocol to strengthen compliance with the Biological and Toxin Weapons Convention (BTWC), and with a view to the successful completion of substantive work in the Ad Hoc Group by the end of 1999 (1999/346/CFSP), *OJEC* [1999] L 133/3.

[139] See, e.g., the Council Decision of 25 July 1994 concerning the Joint Action regarding preparation for the 1995 Conference of the States Parties to the Treaty on the Non-proliferation of Nuclear Weapons (94/509/CFSP), *OJEC* [1994] L 205/1 and Council Common Position of 23 April 1998 relating to preparation for the second Preparatory Committee for the 2000 Review Conference of the Parties to the Treaty on the Non-proliferation of Nuclear Weapons (98/289/CFSP), *OJEC* [1998] L 129/1, replaced by Council Common Position of 13 April 2000 relating to the 2000 Review Conference of the Parties to the Treaty on the Non-proliferation of Nuclear Weapons (2000/297/CFSP), *OJEC* [2000] L 97/1.

[140] Council Common Position of 29 July 1999 relating to the European Union's contribution to the promotion of the early entry into force of the Comprehensive Nuclear Test-Ban Treaty (CTBT) (1999/533/CFSP), *OJEC* [1999] L 204/1; Council Decision of 9 April 2001 implementing Common Position 1999/533/CFSP relating to the European Union's contribution to the promotion of the early entry into force of the Comprehensive Nuclear Test-Ban Treaty (CTBT) (2001/286/CFSP), *OJEC* [2001] L 99/3 and Council Decision of 21 July 2003 implementing Common Position 1999/533/CFSP relating to the European Union's contribution to the promotion of the early entry into force of the Comprehensive Nuclear Test-Ban Treaty (CTBT) (2003/567/CFSP), *OJEC* [2003] L 192/53.

Group.[141] On the other hand, the EU has taken some actions targeted at specific countries, for instance, supporting non-proliferation and disarmament in Russia,[142] in parallel with US[143] and G8[144] efforts, and North Korea (by participating in the international Korean Peninsula Energy Development Organization ('KEDO')[145]). Moreover, the EU is developing a more comprehensive approach to the non-proliferation of weapons of mass destruction: on 16 June 2003, the External Relations Council gave its endorsement to 'basic principles for an EU strategy against proliferation of Weapons of Mass Destruction' and approved the Ac-

---

[141] See the Joint Action of 29 April 1997 adopted by the Council on the basis of Article J.3 of the Treaty on European Union on the European Union's contribution to the promotion of transparency in nuclear-related export controls (97/288/CFSP), *OJEC* [1997] L 120/1 and Council Decision of 25 January 1999 on the implementation of Joint Action 97/288/CFSP concerning the financing of a communication system to all members of the Nuclear Suppliers Group which are not Member States of the European Union (1999/74/CFSP), *OJEC* [1999] L 23/4, later repealed by Council Decision of 16 July 2001 repealing Council Decision 1999/74/CFSP on the implementation of Joint Action 97/288/CFSP concerning the financing of a communication system to all members of the Nuclear Suppliers Group which are not Member States of the European Union (2001/543/CFSP), *OJEC* [2001] L 194/56.

[142] See Council Joint Action of 17 December 1999 establishing a European Union Cooperation Programme for Non-proliferation and Disarmament in the Russian Federation (1999/878/CFSP), *OJEC* [1999] L 331/11; Council Decision of 25 June 2001 implementing Joint Action 1999/878/CFSP with a view to contributing to the European Union Cooperation Programme for Non-proliferation and Disarmament in the Russian Federation (2001/493/CFSP), *OJEC* [2001] L 180/2 and Council Joint Action of 24 June 2003 on the continuation of the European Union cooperation programme for non-proliferation and disarmament in the Russian Federation (2003/472/CFSP), *OJEC* [2003] L 157/69.

[143] In particular the Cooperative Threat Reduction programme, see <http://www.dtra.mil/ctr/ctr_index.html and http://www.fas.org/nuke/control/ctr/index.html>.

[144] See especially the G8 Global Partnership Against the Spread of Weapons and Materials of Mass Destruction, 27 June 2002, <http://www.g8.utoronto.ca/g7/summit/2002kananaskis/arms.html> (in which the G8 committed to raise up to $20 billion to support specific cooperation projects, initially in Russia, to address non-proliferation, disarmament, counter-terrorism and nuclear safety issues over ten years). At the June 2003 Evian Summit, the G8 adopted additional measures in the field of non-proliferation, see mainly the G8 Statement and Action Plan on Securing Radioactive Sources, the G8 Action Plan on a Global Partnership Against the Spread of Weapons and Materials of Mass Destruction and the G8 Declaration on the Non-proliferation of Weapons of Mass Destruction, all 2 June 2003 and all available at <http://www.g8.utoronto.ca/summit/2003evian/>. Considerations 3 and 4 of the preamble of Council Joint Action 2003/472/CFSP of 24 June 2003 (*supra* n. 142) explicitly refer to the 2002 G8 initiative and state that the EU supports its aim and principles.

[145] See the Joint Action of 5 March 1996 adopted by the Council on the basis of Article J.3 of the Treaty on European Union on participation of the European Union in the Korean Peninsula Energy Development Organization (KEDO) (96/195/CFSP), *OJEC* [1996] L 63/1 and the Common Position of 24 July 1997 defined by the Council on the basis of Article J.2 of the Treaty on European Union, on the Korean Peninsular Energy Development Organisation (KEDO) (97/484/CFSP), *OJEC* [1997] L 213/1, both repealed and replaced by Council Common Position of 6 December 2001 on participation by the European Union in the Korean Peninsular Energy Development Organisation (KEDO), *OJEC* [2001] L 325/1. The 1997 Agreement on the accession of the European Atomic Energy Community to KEDO was replaced by a Renewal Agreement in 2001 (both agreements are available at <http://www.kedo.org>. See also <http://europa.eu.int/comm/external_relations/cfsp/npd/index.htm>.

tion plan for the implementation of these basic principles,[146] and the December 2003 Brussels European Council adopted a full-fledged 'Strategy against Proliferation of Weapons of Mass Destruction'.[147]

This being said, it should be noted that several EU Member States are ranked among the 10 largest arms exporters in the world, including to developing countries.[148] This, together with debates in specific cases, such as, most recently, whether or not to lift the arms exports embargo to China, suggest that the implementation, often at the national level,[149] of agreed policies and guidelines, which are not always legally binding,[150] may be somewhat problematic.

2.2.2   Human rights, the rule of law and democracy[151]

As was noted above, most international organisations, including the EU, nowadays use a broad or even a comprehensive security concept. This concept also covers democracy, the rule of law and human and minorities' rights.[152] This was for instance expressly recognised by the 1991 Luxemburg European Council in its Declaration on Human Rights.[153]

Like disarmament and non-proliferation, this is an area in which the EU has been quite active in its external relations, especially since, in accordance with the 1991 Declaration on Human Rights, 'respecting, promoting and safeguarding hu-

---

[146] See the Conclusions of this Council meeting (EU Doc. 10369/03 Presse 166, p. 9, available at <http://ue.eu.int>). The documents approved are in EU Council Documents 10352/03, 10 June 2003 and 10354/1/03 REV 1, 13 June 2003.

[147] See para. 86 of the Presidency Conclusions of this European Council and EU Council Doc. 15708/03, 10 December 2003, available at <http://register.consilium.eu.int>.

[148] See (US) Congressional Research Service, Conventional Arms Transfers to Developing Nations, 1995-2002, 22 September 2003, <http://www.fas.org/man/crs/RL32084.pdf>. The main EU Member States exporting arms are France, the UK, Germany and Italy.

[149] E.g., the Council stated in respect of the Code of Conduct on arms exports (supra n. 124) that 'the day to day interpretation and application [...] is carried out by each Member State individually' and that 'It does not lie in the Council's purview to exercise a review of such decisions' (reply to written question No. E-2689/02, OJEC [2003] C 137/E/110). There is only an annual reporting duty which allows for a 'common assessment of the functioning of the Code' (Council reply to written question No. E-2899/02, OJEC [2003] C 137/E/137).

[150] E.g., the Code of Conduct on arms exports (supra n. 124) 'was not adopted in the form of a legally binding act, nor does it constitute an international agreement' (Council reply to written question No. E-2691/02, OJEC [2003] C 137/E/111).

[151] See generally <http://europa.eu.int/comm/external_relations/human_rights/intro/index.htm> and Chapter 11 in this volume.

[152] See supra nn. 29-33 and the accompanying text. Specific examples covering the rule of law, democracy and human rights include the UN Security Council practice relating to Haiti and the protection of minorities and civilians (supra n. 29) and the CSCE Helsinki Document 1992, Challenges of Change (supra n. 18), § 21 ('our comprehensive concept of security [...] relates the maintenance of peace to the respect for human rights and fundamental freedoms').

[153] Declaration on Human rights, Conclusion of the Luxembourg European Council , 28-29 June 1991, available at <http://europa.eu.int/comm/external_relations/human_rights/doc/hr_decl_91.htm>.

man rights is an essential part of international relations and one of the corner-stones of European cooperation as well as of relations between the Community and its member States and other countries'.[154] Rather than providing an overview of all EU external actions in support of democracy, human rights and the rule of law, we will focus on some initiatives which are specifically noteworthy from a conflict prevention angle.

It appears that the first major general EU initiative in this field, except the use of sanctions,[155] going beyond the numerous declarations and demarches and com-mitting considerable resources, was the European Initiative for Democracy and Human Rights ('EIDHR'), launched in 1994.[156] Essentially, this was the result of the European Parliament's bringing together of several separate budget headings dealing with the promotion of human rights together into one proper Chapter.[157] Funding under this initiative has gradually increased to a substantial amount.[158]

The current legal basis of most EU actions in support of developing and con-solidating democracy and the rule of law and of human rights in third countries are Council regulation Nos. 975[159] and 976[160] of 1999. Both regulations, in their preamble, explicitly cover conflict prevention measures. However, the aim of the regulations in respect of conflict prevention is 'support for measures to promote the respect for human rights and democratisation by preventing conflict and deal-ing with its consequences',[161] rather than the other way around.

It is submitted that the relationship between democracy, the rule of law and respect for human rights on the one hand, and conflict prevention on the other, is symbiotic: the former contribute to the latter, as the Declaration on Human Rights

---

[154] Ibid.

[155] Usually on the basis of a suspension of contractual advantages (see especially the 'human rights clause', *infra* n. 164) or on the basis of Security Council resolutions. See also Chapter 5 in this volume.

[156] See generally <http://europa.eu.int/comm/europeaid/projects/eidhr/index_en.htm>.

[157] See the Report from the Commission on the implementation of measures intended to promote observance of human rights and democratic principles in external relations for 1996-1999, COM(2000)726, 14 November 2000, available at <http://europa.eu.int/eur-lex/en/search/search_lip.html>. The budget Chapter concerned is B7-70 (ibid.).

[158] Ibid., noting a rise from 200,000 Euros in 1987 to 100 million Euros in 1999.

[159] Council Regulation (EC) No. 975/1999 of 29 April 1999 laying down the requirements for the implementation of development cooperation operations which contribute to the general objective of developing and consolidating democracy and the rule of law and to that of respecting human rights and fundamental freedoms, *OJ* 1999 L 120/1.

[160] Council Regulation (EC) No. 976/1999 of 29 April 1999 laying down the requirements for the implementation of Community operations, other than those of development cooperation, which, within the framework of Community cooperation policy, contribute to the general objective of devel-oping and consolidating democracy and the rule of law and to that of respecting human rights and fundamental freedoms in third countries, *OJEC* [1999] L 120/8.

[161] See the identical Art. 2 of Regulation 975/1999 (*supra* n. 159) and Art. 3 of Regulation 976/1999 (*supra* n. 160).

recognises,[162] but the latter also contributes to the former, as stated in the two 1999 regulations. For the purposes of this contribution, it is obviously mainly the impact of democracy, the rule of law and respect for human rights on conflict prevention that matters. In this respect, all the EU's actions regarding democracy, the rule of law and respect for human rights are relevant. They are far too numerous to list and it may suffice here to mention that they include, *inter alia*, an impressive number of statements and demarches, strong support for the International Criminal Court,[163] human rights clauses in contractual relations,[164] election assistance and observation missions[165] and initiatives aimed at specific countries or regions.[166] Moreover, in 2001, in response to a communication from the Commission,[167] the General Affairs Council committed itself to the 'mainstreaming' of human rights and democratisation into EU policies and actions.[168]

---

[162] See also the European Parliament Resolution of 25 April 2002 on the Communication from the Commission to the Council and the European Parliament on the European Union's role in promoting human rights and democratisation in third countries, *OJEC* [2003] C 131/E/147, consideration L of the preamble.

[163] See, e.g., Council Common Position of 11 June 2001 on the International Criminal Court, *OJEC* [2001] L 155/19, as amended by Council Common Position of 20 June 2002 amending Common Position 2001/443/CFSP on the International Criminal Court, *OJEC* [2002] L 164/1 and by Council Common Position of 16 June 2003 on the International Criminal Court (2003/444/CFSP), *OJEC* [2003] L 150/67. According to Art. 1(1) of the latter common position, 'The International Criminal Court [...] is an essential means of promoting respect for international humanitarian law and human rights, thus contributing to [...] security [...] as well as [...] to the preservation of peace and the strengthening of international security'. The conflict prevention objective of the International Criminal Court is also recognised in its Statute (Rome Statute of the International Criminal Court, Rome, 17 July 1998, 37 *ILM* (1998) pp. 998-1069, also available at <http://www.un.org/law/icc/statute/romefra.htm>): see the 3rd in conjunction with the 5th consideration of the preamble.

[164] This practice was initiated pursuant to the 1991 Declaration on Human Rights (*supra* n. 153), which, *inter alia*, stated that 'Through their policy of cooperation and by including clauses on human rights in economic and cooperation agreements with third countries, the Community and its member States actively promote human rights and the participation [...] of all individuals or groups in the life of society.' See also the Communication from the Commission on the inclusion of respect for democratic principles and human rights in agreements between the Community and third countries, COM(1995)216, 23 May 1995, available at <http://europa.eu.int/comm/external_relations/human_rights/doc/com95_216_en.pdf>.

[165] See generally <http://europa.eu.int/comm/external_relations/human_rights/eu_election_ass_observ/index.htm>.

[166] E.g., Common Position of 25 May 1998 defined by the Council on the basis of Article J.2 of the Treaty on European Union, concerning human rights, democratic principles, the rule of law and good governance in Africa (98/350/CFSP), *OJ* 1998 L 158/1.

[167] The Commission's Communication on the European Union's Role in Promoting Human Rights and Democratisation in Third Countries, COM(2001)252, 8 May 2001, available at <http://europa.eu.int/comm/external_relations/human_rights/doc/com01_252_en.pdf>.

[168] (General Affairs) Council Conclusions on the European Union's role in promoting human rights and democratisation in third countries, Luxembourg, 25 June 2001, available at <http://europa.eu.int/comm/external_relations/human_rights/doc/gac_conc_06_01.htm>.

2.2.3 *Development*[169]

A comprehensive security concept also covers development, as is illustrated by the current practice of the Organisation for Economic Cooperation and Development ('OECD'), the World Bank, the G8 and the UN. First of all, the interrelationship between conflict prevention and development was recognised in the framework of the OECD, in particular within the Development Assistance Committee ('DAC'). In 1995 the DAC established a special Task Force to develop guidance on conflict prevention in the wake of increased attention for conflict-related development assistance, which continues today as the DAC Network on Conflict, Peace and Development Cooperation.[170] In 1997, the DAC published the important DAC Guidelines on Conflict, Peace and Development Cooperation on the Threshold of the 21st Century, which were supplemented in 2001 by the DAC Guidelines on Helping Prevent Violent Conflict: Orientations for External Partners.[171] Similarly, the World Bank became involved in conflict prevention in the mid-1990s, initially mainly by way of post-conflict reconstruction, but later more generally, *inter alia*, through its Conflict Prevention and Reconstruction Unit.[172] A third international initiative in this respect is the G8 Initiative on Conflict and Development, which is part of the G8 Miyazaki Initiatives for Conflict Prevention (*supra*) and focuses on '(a) promoting the consideration of conflict prevention in development assistance strategies, (b) focusing assistance to ensure quick action to prevent conflict, and (c) ensuring a smooth transition from emergency humanitarian assistance to development assistance in the post-conflict stage'.[173] Fourthly, this interrelationship was pointedly expressed by the UN Secretary General in his 2000 Millennium Report, according to which 'every step taken towards reducing poverty and achieving broad-based economic growth [...] is a step towards conflict prevention'.[174] It was also recognised on several occasions by the EU.[175]

---

[169] See generally <http://europa.eu.int/comm/development/>. On conflict prevention and development, see Chapter 9 in this volume.

[170] OECD, *DAC Guidelines. Helping Prevent Violent Conflict* (2001, OECD), available at <http://www.oecd.org/dataoecd/15/54/1886146.pdf>, at p. 3.

[171] Both the 1997 and 2001 guidelines are published in *DAC Guidelines. Helping Prevent Violent Conflict*, *supra* previous note.

[172] See Chapter 22 in this volume. The website of this unit is at <http://lnweb18.worldbank.org/ESSD/sdvext.nsf/67ByDocName/ConflictPreventionandReconstruction>.

[173] *Supra* n. 130, Part II.2.

[174] We the Peoples: The Role of the United Nations in the 21st Century, UN Doc. A/54/2000, Part. IV, p. 45, available at <http://www.un.org/millennium/sg/report/>. This statement was also cited with approval in the influential Report of the Panel on United Nations Peace Operations (the 'Brahimi Report'), UN Doc. A/55/305-S/2000/809, 17 August 2000, para. 29, available at <http://www.un.org/peace/reports/peace_operations>.

[175] See the Commission Non Paper on Conflict Prevention of July 1998, para. 3, previously available at <http://europa.eu.int/comm/development/development_old/lex/en/1998/non_98_preventation.htm>, which, *inter alia*, refers to the Council Resolution on the Coherence of the EC's Development Co-operation with its other policies of 5 June 1997, Part III.A (*supra* n. 96).

Even before the Maastricht Treaty, the EC had already taken various measures in the field of development cooperation.[176] The Maastricht Treaty codified this practice by inserting a specific title on development cooperation in the EC Treaty,[177] the first Article of which (which has not been altered since) states that Community policy in the sphere of development cooperation shall not only foster sustainable development, integration of developing countries in the world economy and the combating of poverty, but shall also contribute to 'the general objective of developing and consolidating democracy and the rule of law, and to that of respecting human rights and fundamental freedoms'.[178] As we have argued above, these aims indeed also contribute to conflict prevention. In fact, the link between democracy, human rights and development had already been recognised by a 1991 resolution of the Member States meeting in the Council.[179]

We will only point to some aspects of the EU's development policy which are of particular relevance to conflict prevention. In its 1997 Resolution on the Coherence of the EC's Development Cooperation with its other policies,[180] the Council recommended a number of measures designed to enhance the role of development cooperation as a tool of conflict prevention. In 1998, it stressed quite rightly that development alone would not prevent violent conflict.[181] One may recall that the link between conflict prevention and development was also affirmed in the EU's approach towards conflict prevention in Africa (*supra*). Furthermore, in 1999 the Council adopted a resolution on conflict prevention, management and small arms and weapons,[182] which specifically recommends small arms issues to be taken into account in development cooperation.[183] In the same year, the Commission adopted a communication on cooperation with ACP Countries involved in armed conflicts, *inter alia*, aimed at preventing the diversion of Community funds for belligerent purposes.[184] In 2001, the European Council 'note[d] with

---

[176] See *supra* n. 5.

[177] Title XVII, Arts. 130u-130y, now Title XX, Arts. 177-181.

[178] Ibid., Art. 130u, now Art. 177.

[179] Resolution of the Council and of the Member States meeting in the Council on human rights, democracy and development, 28 November 1991, available at <http://europa.eu.int/comm/ external_relations/human_rights/doc/cr28_11_91_en.htm> ('[...] human rights and democracy form part of a larger set of requirements in order to achieve balanced and sustainable development').

[180] *Supra* n. 96.

[181] See the Council Conclusions on the role of development co-operation in strengthening peacebuilding, conflict prevention and resolution of 30 November 1998, para. 4, available at <http:// europa.eu.int/comm/development/body/theme/prevention/conclusions-1998.htm>.

[182] Council resolution of 21 May 1999 on conflict prevention, management and small arms and weapons, 21 May 1999, available at <http://www.webarchive.org/web/20030625170159> and <http://www.ib.be/grip/bdg/g1787.html>.

[183] Ibid., para. 5.

[184] Communication from the Commission on Co-operation with ACP Countries involved in armed conflicts, COM(1999)240, 19 May 1999, especially p. 3, available at <http://europa.eu.int/ comm/external_relations/human_rights/doc/acp_conficts.pdf>. See also the Conclusions of the Development Council of 30 May 2002 on this topic (EU Doc. 9693/02, 7 June 2002, available at <http:/ /register.consilium.eu.int>).

satisfaction the Council's [...] commitment to continuing its efforts to improve development cooperation instruments, particularly in the countries affected by crisis or conflict'.[185]

Despite these efforts, considerable problems remain. In order to ensure genuine coherence in its external policies, the EU will have to take the external effects of some of its internal policies into account. It is, for instance, well documented that the EU's export subsidies for its farmers have a negative effect on development in a number of developing countries, which is arguably inconsistent with the objectives stated above. This illustrates that difficult choices may have to be made in order to reconcile development and conflict prevention policy objectives with other policy objectives. When conflict prevention will be 'mainstreamed' (see *infra*), such conflicts of objectives may arise more often.

2.2.4 *Conflict diamonds*

International and EU concern for 'conflict diamonds' is a fairly recent phenomenon and results from the finding that the wars in Angola and Sierra Leone were (co-)financed by such diamonds. At the UN level, the Security Council imposed a certification scheme for diamonds in respect of both Angola in 1998 and Sierra Leone in 2000.[186] Also in 2000, and partly with the aim of enhancing the implementation of these Security Council sanctions, the Kimberley process (concerning a Certification Scheme for Rough Diamonds) was launched. This process was actively supported by the EU[187] and resulted, on 5 November 2002, in the Interlaken Declaration on the Kimberley Process Certification Scheme for Rough Diamonds, which provides for the simultaneous launching of the certification scheme on 1 January 2003.[188] This outcome was welcomed by the Security Council,[189] while it received WTO approval in 2003[190] and was implemented by the EU.[191]

---

[185] Presidency Conclusions, Laeken European Council, 14-15 December 2001, para. 54.

[186] See respectively UN Documents S/RES/1173 (12 June 1998), para. 12(b) and S/RES/1295 (18 April 2000) on the one hand, and S/RES/1306 (5 July 2000), S/RES/1343 (7 March 2001), S/RES/1385 (19 December 2001) and S/RES/1408 (6 May 2002) on the other. The measures in respect of Sierra Leone expired on 4 June 2003, see UN press release SC/7778 AFR/634, 5 June 2003.

[187] See Council Common Position of 29 October 2001 on combating the illicit traffic in conflict diamonds, as a contribution to prevention and settlement of conflicts (2001/758/CFSP), *OJEC* [2001] L 286/2.

[188] See <http://www.kimberleyprocess.com>.

[189] UN Doc. S/RES/1459 (28 January 2003).

[190] The WTO General Council granted requesting Members a waiver for trade measures taken under the Kimberley Process Certification Scheme for Rough Diamonds on 15 May 2003, see WTO Doc. WT/L/518, 27 May 2003, available at <http://www.wto.org>.

[191] See Council Regulation (EC) No. 2368/2002 of 20 December 2002 implementing the Kimberley Process certification scheme for the international trade in rough diamonds, *OJEC* [2002] L 358/28 as repeatedly amended, *inter alia*, by Council Regulation (EC) No. 254/2003 of 11 Febru-

2.2.5 *Terrorism*

Another recent example where the EU has stressed the importance of conflict prevention is the fight against international terrorism. In particular, the EU has repeatedly stressed the importance of tackling the root causes of this scourge, including by preventing and stabilising conflicts. For instance, the conclusions of the extraordinary European Council of 21 September 2001 in Brussels state that '[t]he fight against terrorism requires of the Union that it play a greater part in the efforts of the international community to prevent and stabilise regional conflicts' and that '[t]he integration of all countries into a fair world system of security, prosperity and improved development is the condition for a strong and sustainable community for combating terrorism'.[192] This was repeated on the first anniversary of 'September 11': 'We will [...] seek to build a just international order that promotes peace and prosperity for all'.[193] In this context, the EU has committed itself to enhance the cultural dialogue with other civilizations[194] and to 'devoting greater efforts to conflict prevention'.[195]

3.   TOWARDS A SYSTEMATIC AND COHERENT APPROACH TO CONFLICT PREVENTION

There were some early attempts at creating or facilitating a more systematic approach to conflict prevention by the EU. For instance, in 1995 the European Parliament called for the establishment of a European Union Analyses Centre for Active Crisis Prevention.[196] While such a Centre was not established, a policy planning and early warning unit was set up within the General Secretariat of the Council of the EU by virtue of the Treaty of Amsterdam and was, *inter alia*, tasked with 'providing timely assessments and early warning of events or situations which may have significant repercussions for the Union's foreign and secu-

---

ary 2003 amending Regulation (EC) No. 2368/2002 implementing the Kimberley Process certification scheme for the international trade in rough diamonds, *OJEC* [2003] L 36/7 and by several Commission Regulations. See also <http://europa.eu.int/comm/external_relations/cpcm/cp/ip02_1205. htm> and Chapters 10, 12 and 25 in this volume.

[192] Conclusions of the Extraordinary European Council of 21 September 2001.

[193] Declaration by the Heads of State and Government of the European Union, the President of the European Parliament, the President of the European Commission, and the High Representative for the Common Foreign and Security Policy, 11 September 2002, <http://europa.eu.int/comm/ external_relations/110901/jnt_dec_09_02.htm>.

[194] Ibid.

[195] See para. 7 of the Declaration on the Contribution of CFSP, Including ESDP, in the Fight against Terrorism, Annex V to the Seville European Council Presidency Conclusions (21-22 June 2002).

[196] Resolution on the establishment of a European Union Analyses Centre for Active Crisis Prevention, 14 June 1995, *OJEC* [1995] C 166/59.

rity policy, including potential political crises'[197] and the Commission launched and funded a Conflict Prevention Network in 1997.[198] Furthermore, the Council restated in 1998 that 'the approach to peace-building, conflict prevention and resolution that has been developed within the Union, mainly in view of the African continent, should be extended to all developing regions'.[199]

However, it appears that increased action concerning conflict prevention mainly coincided with, and perhaps resulted from, the development of the (Common) European Security and Defence Policy since the Cologne European Council of June 1999. The European Council Declaration on Strengthening the Common European Policy on Security and Defence, annexed to the conclusions of the Cologne European Council, *inter alia*, stresses that the EU 'should have the ability to take decisions on the full range of conflict prevention and crisis management tasks'.[200] The Union's responsibility for conflict prevention was subsequently repeated in the EU's Millennium Declaration, adopted at the Helsinki European Council.[201] Nevertheless, as we will see below, the Commission has also played a significant role in the development of a more comprehensive EU approach to conflict prevention exceeding CFSP.

Once more, the EU's efforts run largely in parallel with those of other international organisations in this period, in particular the UN and the G8. While it is difficult to pinpoint an exact starting point in time for this increase in efforts at conflict prevention, one can probably trace it back to 1998 and, more specifically, to two reports published by the UN Secretary General in that year. The first of these is the Report of the Secretary General on the Causes of Conflicts and the Promotion of Durable Peace and Sustainable Development in Africa.[202] The second is the 1998 Annual Report of the UN Secretary General on the Work of the UN. This report devotes considerable attention to conflict prevention and states, *inter alia*, that '[c]onflict prevention [...] should be one of the [UN's] deepest commitments, yet there is still too little emphasis on preventive action'.[203] Con-

---

[197] Declaration (No. 6) on the Establishment of a Policy Planning and Early Warning Unit, attached to the Treaty of Amsterdam (*supra* n. 24), *OJEC* [1997] C 340/132, para. 2(c). See also Chapter 2 in this volume.

[198] It appears that this project was terminated in late 2001. Nevertheless, it lives on to some extent in the form of the Conflict Prevention Associates (see <http://www.conflict-prevention-associates.org/>).

[199] Conclusions of the Development Council of 30 November 1998, *supra* n. 181, para. 2.

[200] Annex III to the Conclusions, dated 3-4 June 1999, para. 1. See also para. 2 ('We are convinced that to fully assume its tasks in the field of conflict prevention and crisis management the European Union must have at its disposal the appropriate capabilities and instruments') and para. 3.

[201] See Annex I to the Presidency Conclusions on this European Council, dated 10-11 December 1999 ('The Union shares a growing global responsibility for promoting wellbeing, preventing conflicts and securing peace').

[202] *Supra* n. 97.

[203] UN Secretary General, Annual Report of the Secretary General on the Work of the Organisation, UN Doc. A/53/1, 27 August 1998, available at <http://www.un.org/Docs/SG/Report 98/con98.htm>, para. 25.

flict prevention also figures prominently in the UN Secretary General's Millennium Report.[204] In the Millennium Declaration, world leaders committed themselves 'to make the United Nations more effective in maintaining peace and security by giving it the resources and tools it needs for conflict prevention, peaceful resolution of disputes, peacekeeping, post-conflict peace-building and reconstruction'.[205] Conflict prevention (including its post-conflict dimension) also became the subject of a number of Security Council Presidential Statements[206] and one specific resolution (Resolution 1366 (2001))[207] and was taken up by the General Assembly, which passed a resolution on conflict prevention in 2003.[208] At the level of the G8, the main development is the G8 Miyazaki Initiatives for Conflict Prevention, adopted by the G8 Foreign Ministers' Meeting in Miyazaki (Japan) on 13 July 2000[209] and its follow-up.

Returning to the EU, we see that in May 2000, a Committee for civilian aspects of crisis management was established.[210] Subsequently, the June 2000 Santa Maria da Feira European Council requested the Secretary General/High Representative and the Commission to 'submit to the Nice European Council, as a basis for further work, concrete recommendations on how to improve the coherence and the effectiveness of the European Union action in the field of conflict prevention'.[211] The Presidency Conclusions of this European Council also set goals for the development of civilian crisis management capabilities[212] and recognised that these capabilities, and also the military capabilities,[213] may serve conflict prevention purposes.[214] In December 2000, at its next meeting, and after a joint report

---

[204] *Supra* n. 173, ch. IV (at pp. 43-53).

[205] *Supra* n. 97, para. 9.

[206] See UN documents S/PRST/1998/38 (29 December 1998); S/PRST/1999/21 (8 July 1999); S/PRST/1999/34 (30 November 1999); S/PRST/2000/10 (23 March 2000) and especially S/PRST/2000/25 (20 July 2000) and S/PRST/2001/5 (20 February 2001), all available at <http://www.un.org/documents/pstatesc.htm>. See also the Presidential statements on specific topics such as small arms, e.g., UN Documents S/PRST/1999/28 (24 September 1999), S/PRST/2001/21 (31 August 2001) and S/PRST/2002/30 (31 October 2002).

[207] UN Doc. S/RES/1366, 30 August 2001. See also UN Doc. S/RES/1327 (13 November 2000), Part V. See also a number of resolutions on specific issues such as small arms, e.g., UN Documents S/RES/1209 (19 November 1998) and S/RES/1467 (18 March 2003).

[208] UN Doc. A/RES/57/337, 18 July 2003.

[209] *Supra* n. 130.

[210] Council Decision of 22 May 2000 setting up a Committee for civilian aspects of crisis management (2000/354/CFSP), *OJEC* [2000] L 127/1.

[211] Presidency Conclusions, 19-20 June 2000, Annex I, Part IV, para. 3.

[212] Ibid., para. 11 and Annex I, Part III and Annex 1, Appendices 3 and 4.

[213] The potential of military capabilities for conflict prevention is clearly illustrated by the EU's military operation in Macedonia (see *supra* n. 89 and the accompanying text).

[214] *Supra* n. 211, Annex I, Appendix 3, A: 'The Union should seek to enhance its capability in civilian aspects of crisis management [...], with the objective of improving its potential for [...] *preventing further escalation*, [...]. The reinforcement of [these] capabilities [...] should, above all, provide it with adequate means to face complex political crises by: – *acting to prevent the eruption or escalation of conflicts*; – consolidating peace and internal stability in periods of transition;' [empha-

by the Commission and the SG/HR,[215] the European Council stressed that the EU 'must [...] develop a coherent European approach to crisis management and conflict prevention' and welcomed the requested report, highlighting that the discussion about conflict prevention needed to continue and invited the Presidency, in association with the Secretary General/High Representative, 'to implement the measures necessary for [...] the definition of proposals for improving the cohesion and effectiveness of Union action in the sphere of conflict prevention'.[216]

This further work also received input from a Communication on Conflict Prevention by the Commission,[217] which, *inter alia*, stressed the role of 'Country (or Regional) Strategy Papers'[218] and the development of a 'check list for root-causes of conflict'.[219] In doing so, the Commission broadened the concept of conflict prevention, in line with international developments (see *supra*), and thus helped to contribute to a more comprehensive and coherent approach that covers measures which had mostly not previously been qualified as conflict prevention.[220] This resulted in the adoption of the European Union programme for the prevention of violent conflicts by the Göteborg European Council in June 2001, which 'will improve the Union's capacity to undertake coherent early warning, analysis and action'.[221] At this meeting, the European Council also decided that '[c]onflict prevention is one of the main objectives of the Union's external relations and

---

sis added]. This relevance to conflict prevention was later repeated: see, e.g., the Presidency Conclusions of the Nice European Council, 7-9 December 2000, Annex II to Annex VI.

[215] Improving the Coherence and Effectiveness of European Union Action in the Field of Conflict Prevention: Report by the Secretary General/High Representative and the Commission, EU Council Doc. 14088/00, 30 November 2000, available at <http://register.consilium.eu.int>.

[216] Presidency Conclusions, Nice, 7-9 December 2000, Annex VI, resp. Parts II, VII and VIII.

[217] Communication on Conflict Prevention, COM(2001)211, 11 April 2001, available at <http://europa.eu.int/comm/external_relations/cfsp/news/com2001_211_en.pdf>. For the European Parliament's reaction, see European Parliament Resolution of 13 December 2001 on the Commission communication on Conflict Prevention, *OJEC* [2002] C 177/E/291. See also European Parliament Resolution of 15 March 2001 on developing the Union's capabilities in conflict prevention and civil crisis management, *OJEC* [2001] C 343/261.

[218] COM(2001)211, *supra* previous note, at pp. 11-12. For a list of these strategy papers, see <http://europa.eu.int/comm/external_relations/sp/index.htm>.

[219] This check-list is available at <http://europa.eu.int/comm/external_relations/cpcm/cp/list.htm>. See also Chapter 1 in this volume.

[220] Interestingly, as was noted by S. Duke (*The EU and Crisis Management. Development and Prospects* (Maastricht, EIPA 2002), p. xiv-xv) the Commission's development website contained, until late 2002, a list of definitions which contrasted 'conflict prevention' (defined as 'Actions undertaken over the *short term* to reduce manifest tensions and/or to prevent the outbreak or recurrence of violent conflict') with 'peace-building' (defined as 'Actions undertaken over the medium and longer-term to address root-causes of violent conflicts *in a targeted manner*') (this page is archived at <http://web.archive.org/web/20021220072907/http://europa.eu.int/comm/development/prevention/definition.htm>). However, it was clear that in spite of this, the Commission and the Council did include long-term actions under conflict prevention, see the review of Duke's book by F. Naert in 9 *Maastricht Journal of European and Comparative Law* (2002), 311, at pp. 312-313.

[221] *Supra* n. 3.

should be integrated in all its relevant aspects, including the European Security and Defence Policy, development cooperation and trade.' It invited future Presidencies, the Commission and the Secretary General/High Representative to 'promote the implementation of the programme and to make recommendations for its further development'.[222] As part of this mainstreaming of conflict prevention in all the EU's external relations, the Commission is systematically reviewing Country (or Regional) Strategy Papers from a conflict prevention angle. On the basis of this analysis, the Commission attempts to target underlying causes of conflict. In particular, it is putting more emphasis on strengthening the rule of law, support to democratic institutions, the development of civil society and the reform of the security sector ('structural conflict prevention').[223] The Council also decided to reinforce cooperation between the EU and the UN, *inter alia*, in the field of conflict prevention.[224] Earlier in 2001, the Council had established a rapid reaction mechanism (also referred to as 'rapid reaction facility'), which was 'designed to allow the Community to respond in a rapid, efficient and flexible manner, to situations of urgency or crisis or to the emergence of crisis'.[225]

The implementation of this programme is still very much in progress. As the various aspects of this implementing process are discussed in other contributions to this book, we will end our overview here. For a general overview of the progress achieved, we refer especially to the relevant reports to the Seville[226] and Thessaloniki[227] European Councils.[228] Given the importance of both civilian and

---

[222] Göteborg Presidency Conclusions, *supra* n. 3, para. 52.

[223] See the section 'Mainstreaming of conflict prevention in the EU policies and instruments' at <http://europa.eu.int/comm/external_relations/cpcm/cp.htm>. On the notion of structural conflict prevention, both generally and within the EU, see Chapter 7 in this volume.

[224] Ibid., para. 53. The General Affairs Council adopted more detailed Conclusions on EU-UN cooperation in conflict prevention and crisis management on 11-12 June 2001 (available at <http://ue.eu.int>). See also EU Council Secretariat, Relations between the European Union and the United Nations in crisis management and conflict prevention, EU Council Doc. 12969, 7 November 2001, available at <http://register.consilium.eu.int> and the Commission communication on building an effective partnership with the United Nations in the fields of Development and Humanitarian Affairs, COM(2001)231, 2 May 2001, available at <http://europa.eu.int/eur-lex/en/com/cnc/2001/com2001_0231en01.pdf>. For a more detailed discussion, see Chapter 16 in this volume. EU-UN relations are developing ever more closely. For the latest developments, see European Commission, The European Union and the United Nations: The Choice of Multilateralism, COM(2003)526, 10 September 2003, especially pp. 11-12, available at <http://europa.eu.int/comm/external_relations/un/docs/com03_526en.pdf> and European Parliament, European Parliament resolution on the relations between the European Union and the United Nations, 29 January 2004 and the corresponding Report on the Relations between the European Union and the United Nations, A5-0480/2003, 16 December 2003, both available at <http://www.europarl.eu.int>.

[225] See Art. 1 Council Regulation (EC) No. 381/2001 of 26 February 2001 creating a rapid-reaction mechanism, *OJEC* [2001] L 57/5.

[226] See EU Council Doc. 9991/02, 18 June 2002, available at <http://register.consilium.eu.int>.

[227] See EU Council Doc. 10680/03, 18 June 2003, Annex, available at <http://register.consilium.eu.int>.

[228] See also the Note from the EU Council Presidency, Implementing the Göteborg EU Programme for the Prevention of Violent Conflicts: a Systematic Approach to Conflict Prevention,

military crisis management capabilities for conflict prevention, the progress on both of these capabilities should also be taken into account.[229]

4. CONFLICT PREVENTION IN THE DRAFT CONSTITUTIONAL TREATY

To conclude, we should briefly mention the role of conflict prevention in the final draft Constitutional Treaty[230] produced by the Convention on the Future of Europe.[231]

Apart from the general objective of the EU to 'contribute to peace, security, the sustainable development of the earth, solidarity and mutual respect among peoples, free and fair trade, eradication of poverty and protection of human rights and in particular the rights of the child, as well as to strict observance and development of international law, including respect for the principles of the United Nations Charter' (Art. I-3(4)), the draft Constitution explicitly mentions the aims to 'preserve peace, prevent conflicts and strengthen international security' in one of the general provisions of its title on the EU's external action (Art. III-193(2)(c)). More specifically, the draft Constitution envisages the use of EU military and civilian crisis management capabilities for 'missions outside the Union', *inter alia*, for 'peace-keeping' and 'conflict prevention' (Art. I-40(1)). This is also made explicit in Article III-210(1):

'The tasks referred to in Article I-40(1), in the course of which the Union may use civilian and military means, shall include joint disarmament operations, humanitarian and rescue tasks, military advice and assistance tasks, conflict prevention and peace-keeping tasks, tasks of combat forces undertaken for crisis management, including peace-making and post-conflict stabilisation.'

The explicit inclusion of conflict prevention as one of the EU's overall external policy objectives in the EU's draft Constitution is undoubtedly an important step forward and may be seen as a constitutional culminating point of a long process. Admittedly, the overview which we have presented in this contribution makes it clear that the lack of a specific legal or constitutional basis has not really proven to be a handicap for the development of the EU's conflict prevention policies.

EU Council Doc. 8410/02, 30 April 2002, available at <http://register.consilium.eu.int> and Commission, One Year On: the Commission's Conflict Prevention Policy, March 2002, <http://europa.eu.int/comm/external_relations/cpcm/cp/rep.htm>.

[229] Here too, we refer to the relevant reports to the different European Councils, most of which are available at <http://ue.eu.int/cms3_applications/applications/newsRoom/loadBook.asp?BID=76&LANG=1&cmsid=347>.

[230] EU Doc. CONV 850/03, *OJ* 2003 C 169/1. We cite the version edited by legal experts and contained in IGC Doc. 50/03, 25 November 2003, available at <http://ue.eu.int/cms3_fo/showPage.asp?id=251&lang=EN&mode=g>.

[231] The Convention's website is at <http://european-convention.eu.int>. See also <http://europa.eu.int/futurum/index_en.htm>.

However, a stronger constitutional underpinning is definitely welcome with a view to consolidating and mainstreaming these policies and keeping them high on the EU's political agenda.

Chapter 4
THE EU'S INVOLVEMENT IN CONFLICT PREVENTION – STRATEGY AND PRACTICE

by Reinhardt Rummel[1]

1.   TAKE-OFF FOR EU CONFLICT PREVENTION?

The European Union (hereinafter the 'EU' or 'Union') is both a pioneer of and a latecomer in conflict prevention. It is a pioneer with regard to advancing the idea of conflict prevention among the European nation states. In fact, the main purpose of the fifty year old unification process in Europe was to bind France and Germany as well as other states of the continent together in order to ensure that they would not go to war again as in the centuries before. By pooling their sovereignty around a supranational core the Member States of the EU decided to entangle their future in commonly agreed rules and institutions and to invite other European states to join the enterprise. The EU has grown to fifteen and will witness the accession of ten more members in 2004, increasing the population of the EU to almost half a billion.[2] Thus, European states have turned from a tradition of belligerency and repeated fighting to a culture of cooperation and peaceful conflict resolution among themselves.

Now that the European Project is so advanced, many wonder whether the Union can reproduce such a success story beyond its borders. Here one can notice that the EU is also a latecomer to conflict prevention. Brussels is not yet well enough equipped to reliably assume such international security tasks. The EU's security policy pales in comparison with the EU's status as a world trade power,

---

[1] Senior Research Associate, German Institute for International and Security Affairs, Stiftung Wissenschaft und Politik (SWP), Berlin, and Conflict Prevention Associates (CPA), Brussels. The author is grateful to Samantha Mafchir, SWP, for editing the chapter and providing research assistance. Part of this contribution has been adapted from a earlier article by the author: see R. Rummel, 'Advancing the European Union's Conflict Prevention Policy' in J. Kirton and R.N. Stefanova (eds.), *The G8, the United Nations and Conflict Prevention* (Ashgate, Aldershof 2004), pp. 113-139.

[2] Already the announcement and the expectation of the enlargement of the EU are regarded as producing a moderating effect that reduces the inclination toward the use of force. See Reinhardt Rummel, 'Conflict Prevention in Central and Eastern Europe: Concepts and Policies of the European Union', in Wolfgang Heinz (ed.), *Human Rights, Conflict Prevention and Conflict Resolution* (Brussels, 1996) pp. 51-78. See for the next enlargement round Antonio Missiroli, 'EU Enlargement and CFSP/ESDP', 25 *European Integration* (2003), pp. 1-16.

V. Kronenberger and J. Wouters, eds., The European Union and Conflict Prevention
© 2004, T·M·C·ASSER PRESS, The Hague, The Netherlands

who has a weighty common currency, an environmental policy with clear contours and whose legal policy positions have proved to be enforceable. In addition,
as one of the world's major donor organisations, the Union has obtained the image of a humanitarian superpower. Thus, the Union's weak record in managing
conflicts, in defending itself and in establishing violence-free zones outside of
Europe is all the more astonishing.

Policies such as the Common Foreign and Security Policy (CFSP) and the European Security and Defence Policy (ESDP) have been created in part to remedy
the above-mentioned shortcomings. However, their creation has been more a formal than a substantial step forward. It remains uncertain whether the Franco-Ger-
man plans for a European Security and Defence Union and the respective
suggestions made at the European Convention for a Constitution for Europe will
substantially change the situation and give the Union a higher degree of independence. Furthermore, attempts to incorporate the concept of international conflict
prevention into the Union have also been disappointing. In 2000/2001 the preventative approach was programmatically launched with much optimism and integrated in small operative steps into the Union's foreign, development and
security policy activities. But neither have there been many instances of success
nor has the EU's international standing changed. Finally, the 'partnership for global prevention', announced during the Swedish presidency, has not yet materialised.

However, this does not necessarily mean that the direction of development is
misguided. Rather, a global 'culture of conflict prevention' (Kofi Annan) is desirable, and the EU remains basically predestined to make a leading contribution.
The EU could create for itself an unmistakable profile in this area and thus tip the
international strategic scales' balance further towards Europe. The EU's tendencies and tasks allow it neither to remain a civil power nor to become a military
superpower.[3] Nevertheless, the EU must make its mark internationally. For this
to happen, the EU and its Member States must become more decisively committed to preventive policy. Conflict prevention should be anchored in the future
Constitution for Europe as a goal and task, efficiency in decision-making should
be ensured through qualified majority voting, and actions should be supported by
a foreign minister, who has the right of initiative, along with the ability and the
necessary staff to carry out actions.[4] When this happens, prevention will no

---

[3] Hans-Georg Ehrhart, 'What model for CFSP?', 55 *Chaillot Paper* (2002).

[4] For detailed policy recommendations see EPLO position paper on the European Convention
and Conflict Prevention. 'Building conflict prevention into the future of Europe'. (Brussels, European Peacebuilding Liaison Office 2002) available at <http://www.eplo.org/convpaperfin.doc>. For
a detailed discussion of possible priorities for the various Council Presidents see: 'Towards a coherent EU conflict prevention policy in Africa'. Challenges for the Belgian presidency. Conference report and policy recommendations - 17 September 2001, (Brussels, European Peacebuilding Liaison
Office in cooperation with the Heinrich Böll Foundation 2001), available at <http://
www.international-alert.org/pdf/publI/EPLOconfreport.pdf>; 'Putting conflict prevention into practice'. Priorities of the Spanish and Danish EU presidencies 2002. (Oxfam (and others) in association

longer simply be a label of European foreign and security policy, indeed prevention will then move forward to become the Union's trademark. But is Brussels really moving in this direction? Will EU conflict prevention take off? For the time being the EU is considering preventive engagement rather than practising it. The EU will have to raise the stakes and shift to more risk-taking policies if it really wants to make an impact.

2. CONSIDERING PREVENTIVE ENGAGEMENT

Despite its well accepted plausibility the concept of conflict prevention remains at the margins of the EU's external relations and CFSP. Technically, some rhetoric, goals and measures of prevention have been introduced but the subject has not yet been politically mainstreamed. The concept of prevention has not yet been internalised by EU policy makers. Conflict prevention is not a (let alone *the*) dominant strategic approach. To the extent that proactive activities are launched under the heading of conflict prevention, they are driven by missed opportunities, by financial considerations, and by competition among major actors inside and outside the EU.

2.1   Driven by opportunities missed: Too big to opt out

Today's EU approach to conflict prevention dates back to two main sources. One is connected to developments in the mid-1990s when the EU witnessed mass killings in regions like the Western Balkans as well as in sub-Saharan Africa. Although these conflicts had been recognised as critical cases before they truly ignited, the international community, including the EU and its Member States, did not intervene early enough to avoid genocide and massive destruction. The other development that acted as an impetus to the current EU approach towards conflict prevention is more recent and stems from the EU's experience both in the Kosovo war and after September 11, when Washington dominated international crisis management to such an extent that the Europeans had no choice but to follow the lead of the United States. In the most recent case of Iraq, Washington did not manage to get all the Europeans on board, but, here too, the US created a situation within which – this time after the war – the Europeans seemed to have no option but to join America in rebuilding law and order in the country.

An evaluation of the events that took place since the early 1990s made the EU and its Member States feel that, had they only acted earlier, they could have made

---

with the European Platform for Conflict Prevention and Transformation and the European Peace-building Liaison Office (EPLO) 2002), available at <http://www.international-alert.org/pdf/publII/eupres2002.PDF>; and 'Ensuring progress in the prevention of violent conflict'. Priorities for the Greek and Italian EU presidencies (London, Saferworld, International Alert 2003) available at <http://www.saferworld.org.uk/Presidency%20rep.pdf>.

a difference by reducing the large scale of human suffering. Likewise, they could have protected their investments in foreign and development aid, which were eventually wiped out within days or weeks by civil war and transborder fighting. It was decided that the human and the material cost of doing 'too little too late' required a change in the EU's approach to the developing world as well as to the states in transition in the Balkans, in Eastern Europe, and in the former Soviet Union.

The opportunities missed in Kosovo to stop the escalation of the conflict between the Serbs and the Albanians and the subsequent military intervention including the heavy bombing of Serbia made the Europeans think twice. It is difficult to see how a European civilian approach could have changed Mr. Milošević's mind, just as it is inconceivable how an EU policy could have neutralised the Bin Laden driven terrorism or could have driven Saddam Hussein from his authoritarian throne. But European capitals and publics were deeply concerned by the course of these three events, which all led to massive military responses carried out primarily by the United States.

The failure of the United States to obtain a UN mandate for the invasion of Iraq is symptomatic of the aversion that certain EU Member States feel towards simply rubber-stamping American military action. America's decision to proceed anyway reinforced the pre-existing notion in Europe that another approach to crisis management was necessary. This view also prevails in those European Capitals that had opted to support Washington's military approach. Hence the logical conclusion was made that the EU must act earlier, in more forceful, and in better targeted, ways. Brussels was encouraged in these conclusions by the wider debate on the international stage, particularly on the level of the G-8 nations and within the UN.[5] These bodies advocated a shift in emphasis from crisis management and postwar reconstruction to early action and the prevention of violent conflict.

One could see this change in policy in its embryonic stage, far before the Iraq crisis began, when looking at various policy papers written by those responsible for EU foreign policy. Shortly after the end of the Kosovo war, the heads of state and government assigned the Presidency, the Secretary General of the Council/ High Representative of CFSP (SG/HR) and the European Commission the task of developing a comprehensive conflict prevention policy. As a result, three policy papers were published in short succession:

–   *Joint report* of the SG/HR and of the EU Commissioner for Foreign Relations (November 2000);[6]

---

[5] *Brahimi Report* (New York, United Nations 2000) <http://www.un.org/peace/reports/peace_operations/>.

[6] See Joint Report of the Commission and the Council of 30 November 2000 on Improving the Coherence and Effectiveness of European Union Action in the Field of Conflict Prevention (Doc. No. 14088/00).

- *Communication* of the European Commission on Conflict Prevention (April 2001);[7]
- *EU Programme* for the Prevention of Violent Conflicts (June 2001), passed by the European Council during the Swedish EU presidency.[8]

Although each of these papers looked at conflict prevention from a different perspective, certain themes – such as efficient institutional cooperation, a need to strengthen the available instruments, and the involvement of Member States – were prevalent.[9]

After recognising the new strategy that has developed in the Union, it is important to determine to what extent the EU is capable of taking action. What are its constraints and what remains unknown. As mentioned above, the Union is not a superpower in the real sense of the word, and must therefore determine where and how it can most effectively intervene. Thus, those responsible within the Union have the task of selecting from the list of conflicts, those that are most relevant for the EU and then deciding what approach should be taken. For example, an intranational and potentially violent conflict such as that in Algeria demands a different approach than the increasing number of long-term regional conflicts (such as in Central Africa) or the growing situations of postwar support (such as in Kosovo). At the same time, it does not suffice to devote the Union's attention to single critical countries; as long as 'violence-prone' areas are expanding the so-called new risks are increasing on a global dimension, and the exact sources of the most dangerous forms of international terrorism remain diffuse. The EU needs a broader strategy.

In Brussels, the choice of means is undertaken according to Member States' interests and their ability to push through these interests at the EU level, which cannot always be generically determined. Only when confronted with a concrete situation will it become evident in how far the European actors feel affected, to what degree they want to become involved and what efforts they are actually capable of making. As is always the case, the ability to move forward on integration is dependent upon the Member States' political will.

In addition to the Member States however, one must also recognise how the agenda and priorities of the EU are often compelled by external circumstances. These circumstances include such diverse factors as the dramatic situation in the conflict area itself, media influences, campaigns of non-governmental actors and inquiries to 'Europe' by third parties, which the Brussels institutions and some of

---

[7] European Commission Communication of April 2001 concerning conflict prevention, COM (2001) 211 final. <http://europa.eu.int/comm/external_relations/cfsp/news/com2001_211_en.pdf>.

[8] Swedish Ministry of Foreign Affairs, EU Programme for the Prevention of Violent Conflicts, Stockholm, June 2001. Art. No. UD 01.038 <http://www.utrikes.regeringen.se/prefak/files/EUprogramme.pdf>.

[9] See, in particular, the chapters by S. Duke and J. Niño-Pérez in this volume.

the more influential EU capitals cannot ignore. Furthermore, global (UN, World Bank) and regional (OSCE, Council of Europe) organisations to which the EU itself belongs force the EU's hand, and that includes pressure on the part of the USA and other close partners. They all assume that the EU has a potentially strong intervention capability and can thus make a major European contribution to help alleviate international violent conflicts. Because of the numerous expectations, Brussels is relieved of the task of setting its own agenda, for the agenda is already overly full. Adhering to this agenda allows the EU to increase its efficiency while pleasing third parties.

Finally, it becomes noticeable when considering conflict prevention activities that the Union's foreign and security policy is still in an initial and experimental phase. Thus topics on the EU agenda and what happens to them often (inadvertently) become test cases for Europeans' political unanimity, their decisiveness of action, their material independence and the professional execution. For some time, the area of conflict prevention[10] has been developing and is being tested as a new area of European security policy. What have the EU and its Member States set out to accomplish and how far do their ambitions reach?[11] These questions are not only of empirical interest. As such diverse events as the forced regime change in Iraq and the debate in the European Convention demonstrate, the EU's image and influence in the rest of the world are at stake: *Brussels cannot opt out.*

2.2   Financial motivation: protecting the EU's investments

Contrary to common wisdom, conflict prevention is expensive, at least in all those cases where structural prevention is required and certainly in those cases where one wants to be sure that conflict prevention is successful. Is the EU prepared to accept that conflict prevention policy requires 'double' funding: first, for the build-up of those preventive capacities that the EU still lacks, and, second, for running the agenda of day-to-day cases of prevention? Looking at the huge cobweb of financial relations which the EU has built up over the last decades, it seems that both the money and the procedures are in place to support extensive policies of EU conflict prevention.

---

[10] In this study the term conflict prevention refers to efforts to restrain and prevent violent conflicts, before, during and/or after the outbreak of combat. According to this definition preventive policy is carried out through military and/or non-military means. Furthermore, conflict prevention is distinguished from the term crisis management which is used here so as to include military activities during the war-like phase of a conflict. In EU political practice, this distinction is not consistently used. Even if an EU action is primarily devoted to conflict prevention, it is often described (inaccurately) as crisis management. Military actions classifiable *as pre-emptive strikes* belong in their own category of conflict policy which for the purposes of this article is considered neither as conflict prevention nor as crisis management.

[11] For a detailed answer to this question, see Arzu Hatakoy, 'Konfliktprävention und Krisenmanagement in der Europäischen Union', 27 *Aktuelle SWP-Dokumentation, Reihe D* (2002).

As the 2001 Report of the European Commission points out, financial assistance to third countries is one of the central components of the Union's external action, alongside trade policy and political dialogue.[12] It is thus an important tool for promoting the fundamental values of the EU and for meeting the global challenges of the twenty-first century, such as conflict prevention and peace building. Brussels is one of the major actors in international cooperation and development assistance, donating just over 8 billion EUR per year since 2001 (see the Overview 'External Action and Pre-accession Aid Budget'). Protecting that investment is an additional motivation for the European Union to be involved in conflict prevention, and in part, it counteracts the huge cost of involvement. Referring to Table 1 below, one can see that the vast majority of the External Action and Pre-accession Aid Budget is dedicated to regional cooperation and assistance, while a little less than a fourth of the Budget is reserved for food and humanitarian aid or other more general cooperation measures, such as the European initia-

Table 1: External Action and Pre-accession Aid Budget

External Action	Amount *(Million EURO)*		
	2001	2002	2003
Action defined by geographical area			
Pre-accession strategy	3 240.0	3 328.0	3 386.0
Pre-accession aid (Mediterranean Countries)	19.0	21.0	174.0
Co-operation with the Balkans	839.0	765.0	684.6
Co-operation with Mediterranean third countries and the Middle East	896.3	861.3	753.9
Assistantship to partner countries in Eastern Europe and Central Asia	469.3	473.9	507.4
Co-operation with Asia	446.0	488.0	562.5
Co-operation with Latin America	336.3	346.7	337.0
Co-operation with southern Africa and South Africa	122.0	124.8	127.0
Food aid and humanitarian aid operations			
Food aid and support operations	455.0	455.0	425.6
Humanitarian aid	473.0	441.8	441.7
General Co-operation Measures			
Other co-operation measures	389.5	419.6	505.5
International fisheries agreements	273.4	193.2	192.5
External aspects of certain Community policies	71.8	78.7	79.9
European initiative for democracy and human rights	102.0	104.0	106.0
Reserve for administrative expenditure			4.4
CFSP (Common Foreign and Security Policy)	36.0	30.0	47.5
Total	**8168.7**	**8 131.0**	**8 335.4**

Source: EU Budget 2001, 2002 and 2003

---

[12] Commission Report of 17 September 2002 on the Implementation of the European Commission's External Assistance (Doc. No. 12104/02). This document brings together for the first time all the actions taken within the framework of the different external aid programmes of the Commission in 2000, except pre-accession instruments, macro-financial aid, CFSP and the Rapid Reaction Mechanism.

tive for democracy and human rights. Another interesting perspective that can be gained by looking at the chart is the fact that more than a third of the entire Budget is allotted to the Pre-accession strategy and aid. Resolving problems in those countries that may one day be members of the Union takes priority. Finally, the further away a region is from Europe, the less that region obtains in aid. In reality, the reverse should be true, given that the costs of stabilisation grow with the distance from Brussels.

Just like other international donors the EU is faced with the challenge of increasing the quality, focus, and impact of its financial assistance throughout the world. This challenge, along with the new focus on conflict prevention, is the main reason why the Commission launched a fundamental reform of its external assistance in 2001. This included concentrating development assistance on a limited number of priority areas with the overriding objectives of poverty reduction in developing countries worldwide and better integration of the partner countries into the global economy. In parallel, the Commission embarked on an ambitious programme of measures to make significant improvements in the quality and the timely delivery of projects while ensuring robust financial management. This reform has been driven further to include security policy goals in EU programmes.

Late in 2001 the Commission adopted a Communication which proposes to improve the procedures for funding civilian crisis management under the CFSP. The Commission aimed to circumvent the financial constraints and procedural obstacles to CFSP operations by establishing a new flexibility instrument for funding civilian crisis interventions and facilitating recourse to the current emergency reserve. In parallel, an inter-institutional agreement was concluded with the Budgetary Authority regarding three categories of crisis management operations that can be financed by the EU:

–   Operations carried out in the framework of a Community instrument under the first pillar (mine-sweeping, emergency civilian aid, civil protection aid, human rights, strengthening institutions, election observation missions, food aid, rebuilding infrastructure and economic aid);
–   CFSP operations without any military or defence implications that are funded from the CFSP budget line (the Council decides on common action and the budget, while the Commission makes commitments, signs contracts and releases funds); and
–   CFSP operations with military or defence implications that do not fall under the EU budget (like the deployment of the Rapid Reaction Force).

The Commission concluded that the budgetary procedures applying to CFSP operations are too cumbersome and that the CFSP budget would be insufficient if the EU were to decide to extend, for example, the surveillance mission in the Balkans or to launch a huge policing operation. The Commission suggested to the Council the use of a new crisis flexibility instrument which makes it possible to mobilise funds even when there is no budget latitude left and, more importantly, without having to change the Financial Perspectives in the framework of the habitual Community budget. Thus, it tried to counter the option being examined by the Council (which had the support of a range of Member States) of funding civilian CFSP operations in a crisis situation through a new *ad hoc* fund having recourse to funding from the Member States.

Funding via Member States may appear attractive, but it raises a number of questions:

- the Treaty does not cover the issue of how such a fund would be managed and controlled (unless it were managed by the Commission, like the European Development Fund);
- the lack of parliamentary control would raise serious doubts concerning the obligation to be accountable for the breakdown of responsibility between the two branches of the Budgetary Authority; and
- an *ad hoc* fund outside the regular budget might be seen as a way of getting round the normal budget procedures.

The Commission demonstrated that even if the funding of such operations from the existing budget procedure has been over-bureaucratic in the past, the Community's budget remains the best way to fund operations because it is the best way of ensuring good governance and transparency and the coherence of the EU's actions under both the CFSP and the Community itself.[13] The question of financing may at first appear minute and simply a matter of bureaucratic reshuffling, but it is actually a matter of how projects should best be organised internally, so that they are efficient and well targeted externally.

In fact, good financial governance may well drive the EU's conflict prevention strategy and future agenda. Budget constraints are likely to raise more fundamental questions regarding alternative spending. EU governments may invest in de-escalation measures rather than crisis intervention or postwar reconstruction. They may want to launch prevention policies as a protection against capital loss of aid in case of civil war and devastation in developing countries.

2.3 Stimulated by competition – Inside and outside the Union

To have more influence in the day-to-day developments in conflict areas, however, the EU must expand its sphere of influence beyond that of humanitarian and financial assistance. This will prove more complicated than one would hope. The complexity of the EU's conflict prevention policy was alluded to earlier, when both the interest of the Member States and that of external actors were cited as

---

[13] Antonio Missiroli, 'Euros for ESDP: financing EU operations', 45 *Occasional Paper* (2003) (EU Institute of Security Studies).

sources of influence for the EU's conflict prevention policy. Coordinating both
internally and externally is a difficult assignment, and one that the Communitarian institutions of the Union have not yet been able to fulfil.

To date, the developments in conflict prevention constitute a noteworthy expansion of the intergovernmental structures within the EU and thus more responsibility for Member States. The Communitarian institutions, the Commission and
Parliament seem to have missed the opportunity to develop more strongly their
positions in the new areas of conflict prevention and crisis management. Telling
is the development of the High Representative's role, as his function could have
been interpreted and shaped as Communitarian. Instead, due to the lack of support from Commission driven external relations and development policy, the SG/
HR *Javier Solana* oriented himself towards the Council committees, the foreign
ministers and the presidency rather than towards the Commission and Parliament.[14] This institutional shift has had positive effects on the EU's visibility and
its will to act, but this runs to the detriment of wide political acceptance and the
Europe-wide democratic legitimisation of the often cost-intensive and politically
controversial EU interventions.[15]

The EU needs to take its fate into its own hands, but it does so only to a limited extent. The EU is aware of this deficiency, but sometimes hides behind the
alleged lacking willingness to integrate on the part of some Member States. One
can also observe finger-pointing among the EU internal actors, both at the EU
level between institutions and between the European and Member State levels.
No wonder that the EU is being pressured from the outside to take more initiative
and shoulder more responsibility and burdens in this field of external relations.

The Belgian and Spanish presidencies have not noticeably furthered the conflict prevention dossier of the Swedish presidency. Madrid's annual report on EU
conflict prevention, presented in June 2002 in Seville, is flimsy.[16] The Danish
presidency, too, did not contribute much, and the Greek presidency did not seem

---

[14] J. Solana refutes the broad assessment that his office will lead directly to an expansion of intergovernmental structures in the EU: '... the function of the High Representative, whose conventional description as "intergovernmental" is, in my view simplistic, and simply wrong'. See: Address
of Javier Solana to the External Action Working Group of the Convention of 15 October 2002, p. 9.
(Convention Doc. No. S0186/02) <http://europa.eu.int/futurum/documents/speech/sp151002_
en.pdf>.

[15] 'The shifting of key responsibilities to the CFSP sector suffers from the serious drawback that
these areas of policy are largely outside of the control of Europe's citizens: the European Parliament
has effective mechanisms of control available for dealing with the EU Commission, but in the CFSP
domain it has only consultative rights and no say in decision-making. Up to now, the degree of accountability and control, which security and military policy have been subject to, has been minimal
– restricted, in fact, to the domain of budget proposals. The democratic deficit must be made good'.
Tobias Debiel and Martina Fischer, *Crisis Prevention and Conflict management by the European
Union* (Berlin, Berghof Report No. 4, 2000).

[16] See: Presidency Conclusions, Seville European Council, 21 and 22 June 2002. Press Release:
Seville (24/10/2002) No. 13463/02; Implementation of the EU Programme for the Prevention of
Violent Conflicts, Press Release: Brussels (18/6/2002) No. 9991/02; Presidency Report on European

to do any better.[17] Both Commission representatives and the Council administration bemoan the Member States' hesitant attitude, their lack of consensus and political will. It has been claimed that the effectiveness of EU initiatives, especially prevention measures, has been decisively weakened.[18]

The shift of the main prevention activities from communitarian policies to CFSP/ESDP gives the Member States a larger share of the responsibility and the burden. They do not yet rise to the occasion. Recently, some have worked at making progress on their own, single state prevention policy.[19] But it is those Member States which have not yet declared the prevention of violent conflicts a foreign, security and development policy priority which present a problem. Their participation in improving conflict prevention policy at the EU level leaves much to be desired. They have no understanding whatsoever of the policy area, they have shown a lack of commitment in the wake of several critical cases, and they do not support EU institutions in the new and difficult field.

However, one must recognise that a certain reorientation has occurred. Some Member States have taken the Göteborg Appeal seriously and have allocated funds of their own for conflict prevention (Belgium, France, Austria, Italy, Spain), others have increased existing budgets (Great Britain, the Netherlands, Germany, Sweden, Finland). Although individual Member States have done more for their prevention policy, this change is hardly noticeable at the EU level, except in the building of ESDP capacities.[20] Not enough momentum has been built to overcome the EU's various structural weaknesses (finance volume, HR/Commission relationship, the use of military/non-military instruments, and points of intersection with the international community).

Security and Defence Policy Press Release: Brussels (22/6/2002) No. 10160/2/02. <http://ue.eu.int/en/info/eurocouncil/>.

[17] See: Presidency Conclusions, Thessaloniki European Council – 19 and 20 June 2003, Press Release: Thessaloniki (20/6/2003). No. 11638/03 <http://ue.eu.int/en/info/eurocouncil/>.

[18] In its report, the Commission repeatedly refers to the Member States' obligation (loc. cit. n. 12). Commissioner Nielson supported this view in a speech delivered in London. 'We cannot have a High Representative on the basis of a low common denominator. The 'C' in CFSP stands for 'Common' not 'Convenient'. A main obstacle to a credible European contribution to conflict prevention are the barely co-ordinated views expressed by member states. I would not be honest with you if I did not point to this obvious lack of political will in member states to accommodate the unity in messages which is absolutely crucial to the credibility of Europe's common foreign policy'. (Speech by Mr Poul Nielson, European Commissioner for Development Cooperation and Humanitarian Aid. *Building Credibility: The Role of European Development Policy in preventing conflicts* Foreign Policy Centre London, 8 February 2001). The HR articulates similar sentiments: 'Efficient structures, access to suitable resources, institutional clarity count little in the absence of real political will on the part of our Member States.' (Address of Javier Solana, loc. cit. n. 14, p. 5).

[19] See Luc van de Goor/Martina Huber (eds.), *Mainstreaming conflict prevention. Concept and practice* (Berlin, SWP-Conflict Prevention Network 2001).

[20] For a closer look at the matter, see Reinhardt Rummel, 'From Weakness to Power with ESDP?', 7 *European Foreign Affairs Review* (2002), pp. 453-471.

How can Member States be moved to assume more collective responsibility? Political will certainly cannot be forced through majority decisions in the Council, even though this path – especially in the light of an enlarged EU – should be widened wherever possible. It is more likely, however, that progress can be expected through an increased participation of national representatives in the decision and implementation process in Brussels. That means that the foreign and security policy tasks will be fulfilled more and more on a European and less on a national level. That would fit with the ideas discussed in the European Convention and partly represented in the draft EU Constitution, namely the establishment of a foreign policy bureaucracy within the Council as a quasi-EU Foreign Ministry in conjunction with the aforementioned combination of the functions of the External Relations Commissioner and the HR.

As long as the EU and its Members States are not able to take conflict prevention initiatives or conduct them autonomously, the cooperation with Third Countries and international organisations offers a solution. But such partnerships do not come about by themselves, unless the EU restricts itself to financially supporting other actors' measures. Rather, the overriding experience has been that the various actors in conflict prevention are active without any coordination among each other. They coordinate neither the development of prevention strategies nor their execution.[21] Concerted action can most likely be found among declarations of intent. The EU runs into international competition when trying to raise its international status.

The EU has supported the UN Secretary General and participated in the dialogue with representatives of the UN system. This dialogue has been encouraged during the last decade primarily with the international financial institutions (World Bank, IMF), but has also always dwindled again. Reasons can be found on both sides. Currently it does not seem like the HR or the Commission will be able to sustain and substantiate this dialogue. This is to a large extent, but not entirely, a question of external representation and of the international legal personality of the EU – an issue that was rightfully taken up at the Convention and is evident in the draft EU Constitution. The international financial institutions are partially not capable of prevention because their bylaws explicitly forbid them from intervening in political conflicts, leaving them to concentrate on reconstruction.

On a positive note, the EU has successfully used the G8, in which the EU is represented several-fold (four Member States, presidency, Commission) as a fo-

---

[21] The heads of state and government have realised ever since passing the European Programme that the EU must seek cooperation with other international actors: 'The EU must build and sustain mutually reinforcing and effective partnerships for prevention with the UN, the OSCE and other international and regional organisations as well as civil society. Increased co-operation is needed at all levels, from early warning and analysis to action and evaluation. Field co-ordination is of particular importance. EU action should be guided by principles of value added and comparative advantage'. (European Programme, loc. cit. n. 8, p. 10).

rum for the definition and promotion of the preventative concept, but also for concrete issues (small firearms control, the diamond trade, child soldiers, etc.). Thanks primarily to the EU representatives, the G8 heads of state and government present new initiatives year by year (from Okinawa to Genoa, from Kananaskis to Evian) reminding those in power that worldwide conflict prevention needs improvement, emphasising the role of the UN Charter and advocating the sustainable strengthening of democracy, human rights and the rule of law. Although the G8 regularly goes through the agenda of the most important regional crises, there was little inclination on the part of the participating EU Member States and the Commission to give the group an operative conflict prevention task.[22]

In the EU dialogue with regional organisations modest progress has been made, especially within Europe (OSCE, Council of Europe) and in terms of experience exchange and training. Less successful is the attempt to institutionalise an EU-NATO dialogue which, in addition to crisis management tasks, could also address questions of mutual support during prevention operations. Maybe the new Berlin-Plus-Agreement will change this. On the other hand, there are already existing forms of pragmatic cooperation in the field (Western Balkans). Whether the EU's intent to strengthen the prevention capabilities of regional (ASEAN, SARC, AU) and sub-regional (SADCC, ECOWAS, IGAD) organisations with an expandable mandate for conflict prevention can be realised, seems questionable for the time being.

Nevertheless, this direction of increasing local actors' own responsibility in the conflict areas should be supported wholeheartedly. One should not expect miracles from these efforts, especially not in terms of directly taking weight off the EU's shoulders. The HR and the Commission have tried beyond the state level to intensify contact with relevant NGOs, academic institutions and the private sector to promote the cause of conflict prevention. This has been most successful with NGOs, which were assigned tasks within EuropeAid projects including contacts with non-governmental organisations and groups in the conflict region. A similarly close relationship with the private sector and the academic world has not materialised.[23]

The improvement of EU bodies in jointly tackling the task of conflict prevention is only a relative progress. The historically ingrained dysfunctional institutional structures are too deep-rooted as that one policy area could make them more flexible. The Member States are reluctant to give up competencies and ca-

[22] R. Rummel, 'Advancing the EU's conflict prevention policy', in J. Kirton and R.N. Stefanova (eds.), *Conflict Prevention: G8, United Nations, and EU Governance* (Aldershot 2004), pp. 224-255. See also the chapter by J. Kirton in this volume.

[23] The European NGOs specialising in conflict prevention formed the European Peacebuilding Liaison Office (EPLO) in Brussels in the year 2000 for lobbying and to serve as a contact for the EU institutions. EPLO itself has not yet intervened in conflict regions to support local NGOs there or to assume prevention tasks themselves.

pabilities to Brussels, but do not take over themselves. The EU and its Member States have a wide range of international partners, but the cooperation is sporadic and cannot be concentrated strategically. Among EU institutions and among international actors we still find complacency and competition rather than commitment and cooperation that characterises conflict prevention policies. Which preventive achievements can be realised under these circumstances?

3.   PRACTISING CONFLICT PREVENTION

Since its programmes were announced in 2000/2001, all foreign, security and development policy activities of the EU have been under the heading of conflict prevention. The official catalogue of tasks with the express objective of prevention is discussed at the beginning of each new presidency. The list is compiled by the Policy Unit with the help of Council bodies, the Commission and the Member States. *Ex post* these topics appear in the presidency's annual report, augmented with conclusions for the further development of the EU's prevention policy. The topic list is treated confidentially for good reason, even though conclusions can be made from current EU activities to the operative agendas.

This helps one to obtain an idea of the extent and ambition of EU activities from a variety of sources, such as Council meeting agendas, missions from HR Javier Solana, the introduction of country strategy papers by the Commission and the official reports and hearings of the European Parliament on foreign policy issues.[24] The parliamentary controlling activities, including budgetary debates, offer hints about the effectiveness of EU policy. These need also to include field reports and research analyses in order to assess the contribution of EU measures to the reduction of violent conflicts. Such an evaluative analysis would necessitate extensive investigations which cannot be conducted within the framework of this article. Instead, an overview of recent EU activity concerning acute, regional, and structural cases should help to make a preliminary assessment.[25]

3.1   **Immediate reward: Rapid Reaction Mechanism**

When the first efforts of conflict prevention were mounted on the ground, it soon became apparent that the EU did not so much suffer from a lack of funding as

---

[24] For a detailed account of some concrete EU prevention activities, see Renata Dwan, in *SIPRI Yearbook* (Stockholm 2002). For a description of the range of EU conflict prevention activities, see also Reinhardt Rummel, 'EU-Friedenspolitik durch Konfliktprävention: Erfahrungen mit dem Conflict Prevention Network (CPN)', in Peter Schlotter (ed.), *Macht-Europa-Frieden*, Band 30 AFK-Friedensschriften (Hamburg 2003), pp. 178-211.

[25] The evaluation of the effects of preventive activities is a difficult task. Neither scholars nor practitioners have been able to develop satisfactory approaches. For an overview of approaches from an EU perspective see Michael Lund/Guenola Rasmoelina (eds.), 'The Impact of Conflict Prevention – Cases, Measures, Assessment', in *CPN Yearbook 1999/2000* (Baden-Baden, Nomos 2000).

from the red tape involved in accessing it as well as the unavailability of qualified intervention personnel. As *Chris Patten* phrased it: 'The important thing about conflict prevention is that it should be quick and effective, and I repeat the word "quick".'[26] Already in December 1999, the European Council of Helsinki assigned the Commission the task of setting up a framework for immediate action. Quite some time later, in February 2001, the General Council accepted an agreement for such an immediate action fund. Since then, the Rapid Reaction Mechanism (RRM) has been used both for necessary immediate action in acute crisis situations (such as in Macedonia in late 2001) and for start-up financing for programmes needing more long-term follow-up measures (such as in Afghanistan in early 2002 and in Central Asia in July 2003). RRM provides quickly accessible funds to help alleviate crisis situations (like in Nepal in August 2002) as well as to support peace initiatives (such as in Congo-Brazzaville and Sri Lanka in 2003).

Since its launching in 2001, RRM has been deployed in numerous situations around the globe. In its first year, RRM was deployed on a total of four occasions, that number more than doubled in 2002 and will again be amply used in 2003 (see Table 2 'Deployment of RRM in 2001-2003'). RRM measures should contribute to creating specific conditions to ensure greater success for EU prevention policy and its cooperation and development programmes.[27] The edge that RRM has over the previously deployed EU instruments lies in its quick and flexible deployment which allows it to react to tense situations immediately before, during and after crises occur. Or as Commissioner *Patten* emphasised: 'In times of urgent needs we cannot anymore afford the luxury to be bogged down by bureaucratic constraints and deliver Community instruments with unnecessary delays.'[28] RRM can be deployed worldwide and – in combination with other measures – it can be tailored to the demands of a specific crisis situation. The EU and especially the Commission, which administers the fund, are now in a better starting position. Not only can they act quickly by avoiding bureaucratic hurdles, they can also make their other traditional instruments more effective.

However, the financial resources are still modest. The total budget for RRM in 2001 was EUR 20 million, of which 18 million were actually spent. The yearly budget was increased to EUR 25 million in 2002 and will remain at this level until 2006. The main purpose of the funds will be to enable quick stabilising mea-

---

[26] Chris Patten, Remarks made in the European Parliament, Brussels, 17 January 2001, available at <http://europa.eu.int/comm/external_relations/news/patten/rrf_17_01_01.htm>.

[27] The RRM was created by Council Regulation (EC) No. 381/2001 of 26 February 2001, *OJEC* [2001] L 57/5. Potential areas of intervention are: alleviation of financial crises, human rights work, election monitoring, institution-building, support of independent media, border security, humanitarian aid, clearing landmines, police force training, providing police equipment, emergency aid, reconstruction measures, resettlement, conflict mediation.

[28] European Commission, Council adopts Rapid Reaction Mechanism, Press Information, 26 February 2001, available at <http://europa.eu.int/comm/external_relations/cfsp/news/ip_01_255.htm>.

Table 2: Deployment of RRM from 2001 to 2003

Time period	Target region	Objectives and measures taken	Costs
August 2001	Macedonia	Programme of trust-building measures Reconstruction of houses destroyed in combat in the regions near Tetovo and Skopska Crna Gora	€ 2.5 Mil.
October 2001	Macedonia	Programme of trust-building measures to support Ohrid Agreement - Improving the infrastructure - Clearing landmines - Other trust-building measures on the civil society level and in the media - Reform of public administration and support of police reform	€ 10.3 Mil.
2001	Democratic Republic of Congo	- Facilitating inter-Congolese dialogue - Measures to support the reintegration of child soldiers - Support of independent media - Other trust-building measures	€ 2.0 Mil.
December 2001	Afghanistan	Programme for initiating the political, social and economic reconstruction of Afghanistan - Technical assistance to enable the interim administration to begin work - Support of United Nations efforts, especially those of Special Representative Brahimi - Landmine clearing, support of independent media, support of civil society in Pakistan - Contribution to the preparation of the donor nation conference in Brussels (20./21. December 2001) - Identification of further possible measures in Afghanistan and neighbouring countries	€ 4.9 Mil.
January 2002	Nepal	Financing an evaluation mission to ascertain possibilities of short and long-term conflict prevention strategies	€ 2.5 Mil.
Early 2002	Papua New Guinea, Solomon Islands, Fiji Islands	Financing an evaluation mission to ascertain possibilities of short and long-term conflict prevention strategies	
May 2002	Sri Lanka	Financing an evaluation mission to ascertain possibilities of RRM aid in the peace process	
April 2002	Afghanistan	Financing a series of studies (secure nourishment, gender relations and equality, urban reconstruction, education and governance) to gain up-to-date and in-depth knowledge about the situation in Afghanistan and to develop a strategy for peace consolidation	
October 2002	Indonesia	- Supporting Indonesia in the war against terrorism - Financing a group of experts	
April 2002	Afghanistan	Technical assistance to support the interim administration in its anti-drug policies and strengthen law enforceability	€ 0.5 Mil.
May 2002	Afghanistan	Promoting public support of the Afghani interim administration - Technical assistance for Afghani authorities for the co-ordination of support (AACA) - Strengthening the role of the Afghani interim administration in big cities - Support of print media - Financial contribution for civilian tasks carried out by ISAF (reconstruction of vital infrastructure)	€ 5.9 Mil.
May 2002	Horn of Africa	Support of the peace initiatives in the Horn of Africa - Financing the conference on Somalia's future - Contribution to the UN fund for border demarcation between Eritrea and Ethiopia - Landmine clearing in the Nuba mountains in Sudan	€ 2.6 Mil.

Table 2: Continued.

Time period	Target region	Objectives and measures taken	Costs
June 2002	Palestinian Authority	Emergency aid to restore administrative capacities of the Palestinian Authority which is to guarantee the implementation of other EU programmes	€ 5.0 Mil.
August 2002	Nepal	Alleviation of effects incurred by the current conflict on the long-term EU aid programmes - Promoting local mediation efforts in Midwest Nepal - Sustenance of marginalised social groups in the Midwest and Terai - Guaranteeing access of groups affected by conflict to objective information broadcasting and cable radio	€ 0.615 Mil.
September 2002	Sri Lanka	Financing measures to implement key provisions of the cease-fire and to build trust in the peace process - Reconstruction of infrastructure - Financial contribution to the peace secretariat - Support of measures of the human rights secretariat	€ 1.8 Mil.
December 2002	Indonesia	Support for the implementation of the peace agreement between the Government of Indonesia and the Free Aceh Movement (GAM): financing of up to 50 international peace monitors for a period of six months.	€ 2.3 Mil.
December 2002	Central African Republic (CAR)	Support to the mediation efforts of the African Union (AU) in the Central African Republic: - Funding for an AU special envoy and for setting up an AU liaison office in Bangui for a period of six months.	€ 0.4 Mil.
April 2003	Congo-Brazzaville	Disarmament, demobilisation and reintegration (DDR) of the so-called Ninja Rebels in the Republic of Congo after the signing of a cease-fire agreement between the rebels and the government in March 2003.	€ 0.713 Mil.
June 2003	Sri Lanka	Support of the peace process: - Support for the monitoring of the Cease Fire Agreement - Rehabilitation of electricity lines at the northern	€ 3.27 Mil.
		checkpoints to improve movement of people between the former conflict zones - Support for the Peace Secretariat in order to facilitate the dissemination of information concerning developments related to the peace process to key stakeholders and the population. - A contribution of € 2.35 million to the North East Reconstruction Fund.	
June 2003	Liberia	Funding for the immediate launching of comprehensive Round-table discussions on Liberia with the former Nigerian President Gen. Abdulsalami Abubakar acting as mediator. The main goal of these discussions is to initiate a comprehensive peace process including a cease-fire agreement.	€ 0.390 Mil.
July 2003	Central Asia	- To 'kick start' the first phase of the EC's borders management in Central Asia programme (BOMCA) - To contribute to the police assistance programme in Kyrgyzstan, which was set up by the OSCE.	€ 2.5 Mil.

Source: Information from the European Commission, Directorate-General External Relations

sures to be undertaken, usually preceding longer-term aid measures. The concert of RRM and of reconstruction efforts (as in the case of Sri Lanka) promises to become a successful pattern of response.

It is important to distinguish between the application area of RRM and the humanitarian aid guidelines of the EU. Intervention on the basis of RRM occurs with the objective of maintaining and rebuilding social structures necessary for political, social and economic stability. While ECHO, the European Commission Humanitarian Office, is politically neutral, RRM acts in crises situations and pursues specific political goals. Thus the EU does not merely continue in its well-established role as a donor organisation; instead, it, too, becomes a 'player' expressing an interest in shaping the situation. In addition to this politicisation of RRM, the 'Secrecy Code,' which could possibly impede access to written documents concerning 'military or non-military crisis management operations,' causes some to question the level of transparency of RRM-sponsored measures.[29] Yet those who initially worked on the concept shared this fear: 'There is a need for maximum transparency in all matters concerning the implementation of the Community's financial assistance as well as proper control of the use of appropriations'.[30] This discrepancy is undoubtedly one of the disadvantages of the acceleration process for RRM interventions, but is it a cause for concern?

The EU has not yet undertaken a systematic evaluation of its interventions, thus making it difficult to assess the performance of the Rapid Reaction Mechanism. The Spanish presidency's statements about EU conflict prevention policy are hesitant and even concede that not all EU efforts were successful.[31] Yet this is far from damning. A true evaluation should be undertaken to determine how effective current EU action is and how it can be improved. Until then, providing the EU with the opportunity to gain experience with this mechanism seems appropriate. Within very tight financial restraints the EU can and should be able to test its ability to respond (early warning plus early action). If the experiences are positive, an increase of funds could be taken into consideration, and, possibly, the SG/HR could then be given direct access to the fund as the European Convention and the draft EU Constitution suggest.

3.2 Regional prevention activities: building local ownership

As the Overview shows, the lion's share of prevention cases dealt with by the EU were intranational conflicts with escalatory tendencies, possibly expanding to neighbouring states. For an example thereof one should note the EU intervention in Kosovo and in Montenegro, to save the Western Balkans from an expansion of the conflict. Without the conflict containment in Macedonia (including the EU-led mission Concordia), possibly the entire Balkans would have turned into a war zone. South Ossetia, Abchasia, Nagorny Kharabach and Javakhetia appeared to pose similar dangers for the Caucasus region. By intervening in the Fergana valley, the EU tried to prevent an expansion of violent conflicts in Central Asia.

---

[29] Jane Backhurst, 'The Rapid Reaction Facility: good news for those in crisis?', *World Vision*, available at <http://www.oneworld.org/voice/jane2b.html>.

[30] Council Regulation No. 381/2001, *OJEC* [2001] L 57/5.

[31] Spanish Presidency Report on Implementation of the EU Programme for the Prevention of Violent Conflicts, (18/6/2002) No. 9991/02. <http://register.consilium.eu.int/pdf/en/02/st09/09991en2.pdf>.

For the same motives, the EU is engaged in the Democratic Republic of Congo (including the EU-led mission Arthémis in 2003), and in Ethiopia, in order to not allow the Great Lakes region or the Horn of Africa to be sucked entirely into the conflicts' vortex. By contrast, this fate looms over Western Africa, where EU efforts in Nigeria, Liberia and Côte d'Ivoire have remained without any notable success. Acute cases of violent escalation such as Angola, Zimbabwe and Aceh were on the EU's prevention list as were regions where cooperative structures and democracy were being developed in order to inhibit the use of violence as a means for particular groups to assert their interests. In some cases, the necessity for acute prevention fell together with the necessity for long-term stabilisation, especially in Afghanistan and in Iraq[32] (after the military intervention), in the Western Balkans (stability pact) and in the Middle East (Palestine). The EU's goal is to participate in the stabilisation process of the country and to counter local violent conflicts early on (*post-conflict conflict prevention*).[33]

The EU's influence seems to be greatest if the country of intervention has some justifiable hope of joining the EU one day. That is certainly the case in the Western Balkans, and this can especially be seen in Macedonia, where the distant hope of future EU membership was paired with well developed prevention and crisis management.[34]

Case Study: **Macedonia**

When ethnic Albanian rebels attacked a Tetovo police station in January 2001, it became clear that the country could expect even more serious ethnic conflicts than was previously indicated by its struggles for independence in 1991 and the shadow of heavy fighting in the neighbourhood. Between February and August 2001, Macedonia became embroiled in escalating violent conflict between the ethnic Albanian extrem-

---

[32] In the case of Iraq, the EU's support for the stabilisation process is more conditional than was the case for Afghanistan, with very much depending upon the final draft of a possible UN Resolution. See <http://www.un.org/apps/news/infocusRel.asp?infocusID=50&Body=Iraq&Body1=inspect #> for the most recent developments in the UN.

[33] In this context, a statement made by Commissioner Patten in the aftermath of September 11th is telling: 'We can and should aim to facilitate a political settlement and having facilitated it we then walk away. We have to make sure that a better government which will emerge from that sad embittered country will be able to count on the long-term support of the international community to rebuild in the ruin of the medieval ferocity which has been unleashed on Afghanistan for the last few years', see: European Commission Statement on the Situation in Afghanistan, 2 October 2001. On 13 December 2001, the Commission decided a financial package of EURO 4.9 Million as a RRM to begin the political, economic and social (re)construction in Afghanistan and affected neighbour states. In the spring of 2002, EU representatives in Afghanistan were faced with the task of sensibly using EUR 200 million collected from different programmes. The funds were allocated for reconstruction programmes and the support of social networks to prevent fighting from breaking out again and to dry out a source of international terrorism.

[34] See Marie-Janine Calic, 'The EU and the Balkans: From Association to Membership?', *SWP Comments* (7 May 2003).

ists (UCK) and regular Macedonian troops. The conflict began with local skirmishes before growing to civil war proportions. Together with other actors, the EU contributed to stopping the escalation and introducing a process of stabilisation. Most of the instruments, procedures and infrastructure that Brussels had developed for crisis prevention was used here.

As a more in-depth analysis of the EU's function in the Macedonia conflict shows, the EU, thanks to Solana and his staff, could for the first time assume both in Brussels and in the field decisive coordinating and mediation tasks.[35] Supported by a special envoy and equipped with a flexible mandate from the Member States, Solana was able to assert the EU's authority towards the conflicting parties and in its cooperation with other actors, especially NATO and the USA. Weaknesses of earlier prevention attempts were also overcome in this case. Via RRM, immediate action resources were available. There was the necessary coordination between the short-term diplomatic missions of the Council and the long-term economic-financial measures of the European Commission. The HR and the responsible member of the European Commission worked well together and developed a joint policy, which maintained a clear division of labour, where Solana acted as crisis manager and Patten provided the structural and diplomatic support. The prospect of joining a region of prosperity, stability and balanced interests was an important element of reassurance for all conflict parties, especially during the escalation phase and the uncertain period during the implementation of the Ohrid agreement. It was a blessing for all concerned that Brussels had already initiated the stabilisation and association process for Southeastern Europe (including Macedonia) back in early 1999 and that the EU representation in Skopje had been elevated to the status of permanent delegation of the European Commission in March 2000. The continuous support of this rapprochement and elevation process in parallel with the critical developments in Macedonia was highly effective. In June 2000, the European Council emphasised in Santa Maria da Feira that the EU was still striving for the broadest possible integration of that region's countries into the European economy and political structure and confirmed that 'all the countries concerned are potential candidates for EU membership'.

After the negotiations were closed at the Zagreb summit in November 2000, the Stability and Association Agreement (SAA) as well as an interim agreement were decided on in Luxembourg in April 2001. The interim agreement allowed the trade and trade-related passages of SAA to go into effect as of June 2001. On 3 October 2001, the European Commission decided to implement a trust-building programme in Macedonia with the help of RRM. The primary goal of this programme allocated with EUR 10.3 million was to offer quick support for the guidelines accompanying the Ohrid Agreement, which was signed on 13 August 2001 by the most important politi-

---

[35] For a detailed account of the preventive operation in Macedonia see Ulrich Schneckener, 'Theory and Practice of European Crisis management: Test Case Macedonia', in 1 *European Yearbook of Minority Issues* (2001/2), pp. 131-154.

cal leaders in the government coalition. It was imperative to support the agreement immediately in order to reduce interethnic tension and prevent an escalation of the conflict or it spreading to neighbouring regions. The package was subject to all the constitutional additions being ratified and a new law concerning local administration passed.[36]

The NATO engagement helped the conflicting parties overcome daunting obstacles in a similar fashion, that is by disarming the UCK, securing the borders to neighbouring states and maintaining law and order. The EU's cooperation with other multilateral organisations, primarily NATO, but also the OSCE and the World Bank was just as significant during the critical phase of the conflict as the access to EU subsidy measures. While in many prevention cases not even the exchange of information between the involved international institutions is guaranteed, in the case of Macedonia, there was a basis of a common assessment of the situation and a consensus of goals. The cooperation and joint appearances of HR Solana and NATO General Secretary Robertson in the field contributed to urging the conflicting parties to accept compromise, especially in military matters. The concerted action of the World Bank and other donor organisations can be assessed similarly. In all of these cases, the influence potential of the EU was increased through conditioned offers to the conflicting parties.

The lessons learned from postwar situations in Bosnia and Kosovo could also be applied by the EU to the preventive activities in Macedonia: an important prerequisite for successful intervention is that the international actors have a coherent concept, coordinate their efforts and use their respective strengths in a division of labour.[37] Finally, a 'lead agency' which takes the initiative and keeps the process going seems to be indispensable.

However, conditions like those in Macedonia probably cannot be found or created easily in other situations. The EU realistically accepts that there are many intranational violent conflicts which are not easily accessible from the outside. The situations in Chechnya and Tibet are among them, but also the warlike conflicts in parts of India or the archaic situation in North Korea and Algeria. In some of those difficult cases the EU has tried either to use pressure or give incentives in order to make governments shift toward more peaceful ways of solving local conflict. Individual states have been warned against reverting back to civil

---

[36] Source and further information <http://europa.eu.int/comm/external_relations/see/news/ip01_1368.htm>.

[37] 'The Macedonian crisis (...) showed that the EU has to act in concert with other actors, most notably with NATO, the OSCE and the US. Without these combined efforts which significantly increased the external pressure upon the local parties, the settlement and the implementation of the agreement would not have been possible. Here again, the course of the crisis highlighted the serious dangers if these actors are not willing to co-operate, to share information and resources as well as to develop a common platform for action'. Ulrich Schneckener, 'Developing and Applying EU Crisis Management – Test Case Macedonia', *European Centre for Minority Issues*, Working Paper 14 (Flensburg 2002), p. 37.

war (Vietnam), taking repressive measures too far (Myanmar) or repressing self-determination rights of ethnic groups with violence (Indonesia). In other cases the EU has threatened to introduce sanctions (Zimbabwe) or to discontinue contractual relations (Iran). All of this has been done with no convincing immediate success, but with the hope of obtaining incremental influence over time.

With the instrument of group dialogue, the EU has forged a path that is also viable for conflict prevention, but this path has of yet been little travelled. The ASEAN countries also see themselves as a security policy group, but they have not yet internalised the concept of prevention. The EU's recommendation is that experiences gained in the OSCE could bring about progress here. The trade and cooperation treaty between the EU and the Andean Group has been restricted to economic goals for too long without addressing the privatisation of violence and the influence of the drug Mafia. Non-state violence and drug Mafia power are neither restricted to Colombia nor the Andes region. The EU, usually craving the blessing of regional cooperation, has not fully used this instrument for prevention purposes. Yet the regional approach to conflict prevention seems to be a valuable one as it can combine both the geographical and the functional approach.

3.3   Functional prevention activities: building international regimes

As when dealing with regional prevention cases, the EU approaches horizontal tasks by concentrating on a few selected areas. In these cases, it is more difficult to determine the degree of success. It may already be considered a success that the EU best recognises the common causes of individual instances of violent escalation and the factors regularly responsible for the outbreak of civil wars, the proliferation of militant rebellion and repression and that in some regions, these phenomena cannot be stopped. The EU devotes itself less systematically here to fighting the root causes than it does when dealing with local and regional conflicts. This is indicated by the fact that there is no urgent agenda at the presidency level for horizontal issues. Nevertheless, EU activities in this field are both quantitatively and qualitatively quite impressive. They should be seen as the functional correlation to the list of individual conflict cases (see above).

The list of functional problem areas that the EU has recently devoted itself to includes: the scarcity of certain resources (land, fuel, water), inequalities of economic distribution (relative poverty, social injustices, underdevelopment), illicit trade (in human beings, drugs, diamonds, arms), child soldiers, money laundering, *war entrepreneurs* and international terrorism. Escalatory conflict factors as determined by the EU include insufficient rights of ethnic and religious minorities, the weakness of government systems and the dominance of non-democratic, often quasi-military leadership elites. In addition to the most notorious outbreak factors for armed conflicts, such as the treatment of refugees and the clarification of border disputes, the EU has also included little discussed developments like the privatisation of violence as an issue for preventive measures.

The EU rightly assumes that these horizontal factors cannot be combated only on a regional level but must be dealt with globally. There are a number of plausible explanations for this. Beyond merely treating the symptoms that arise in conflict areas, it is desirable to bring about sustainable changes specifically in the structure of the governments, in the society and furthermore in the conflicting parties' attitudes. Without such a frame of reference, it would be impossible to obtain support from such international organisations as the World Bank. However, influencing the dynamics of the local conflict area alone is not enough; in order to achieve long-term reorientation, the immediate environment of the region must be addressed. Some basic causes of conflict are understandable simply on a larger scale and not reducible to local phenomena. And combating conflict causes on a case-by-case basis is not always efficient and should be complemented by legal-structural measures (international regimes). But experience and knowledge gained from individual cases can be used to generally improve the EU's prevention policy.

Standards have been set for dealing with subjects like the rule of law, good governance, illicit trade (in human beings, drugs, weapons, precious metals, diamonds, among others), and child soldiers. The Kimberley Accord on the diamond trade and the Small Arms Convention[38] have allowed us to learn lessons in reducing the destabilising and escalation effects of trade. More sensitive is the trade in enriched uranium or biological and chemical substances, which can be used – possibly by terrorists or unauthorised governments – to produce weapons of mass destruction. The strengthening of non-proliferation regimes (including missile capability) has recently been moved to the top of the EU's agenda.[39]

Case Study: Small Arms Regimes

A typical horizontal task is regulating the proliferation of small arms, and the EU is intensively committed to this task. Unlike arms control regimes which largely originated in the Cold War era, there is no long-standing tradition of contractual commitment and verification for controlling small arms ('micro-disarmament'). Possession and use of small arms can traditionally be traced to non-governmental actors who use them for illegal deals, criminal purposes or for some sort of political motivation. They contribute to the destabilisation of entire regions and can, in special cases, be the decisive factor for the violent escalation of political conflicts, as seen by the armament of the UCK in Macedonia. On the other hand, small arms in the hands of state security bodies can be important prerequisites to enforce law and to create domestic secu-

---

[38] Joint Action 1999/34/CFSP of 17 December 1998 adopted by the Council on the basis of Article J.3 of the Treaty on European Union on the European Union's contribution to combating the destabilising accumulation and spread of small arms and light weapons, *OJEC* [1999] L 9/1.

[39] Council of the European Union, 10 June 2003, regarding the Basic Principles for an EU Strategy against Proliferation of Weapons of Mass Destruction, Doc. No. 10352/03. In addition, see the Action Plan for the implementation of the Basic Principles, 13 June 2003, Doc. No. 10354/1/03.

rity. Where these elements are absent, there is the danger that citizens will resort to self-defence and want to use weapons of their own.

A series of guidelines and decisions of the EU Council as well as countless reports of the European Commission and resolutions of the European Parliament have addressed the uncontrolled trade of small arms for many years.[40] The EU as a whole has taken the lead in the fight against the destructive effects of the small arms trade, for example with the code of conduct[41] for export to Third Countries, (already passed in 1998), and with a Joint Action of the Council of Ministers,[42] which declares war on the destabilising proliferation and agglomeration of small arms. In terms of prevention policy, the small arms trade is named in the *Joint Report* as a central, long-term priority (see Paragraph 19).

These activities have made the EU one of the most active members of the UN Conference on small arms and light weapons[43]; thanks to the Joint Action, the EU could assume a clear and well-defined position. The EU is striving for legally binding measures which would allow export control criteria, the labelling and search for arms as well as information exchange, and these measures would take into consideration ways and means to prevent overproduction and other market controlling measures. Brussels is pushing for a continuation of the activities initiated at the UN Conference. In the EU's view, the import and customs sectors in conflict-prone countries deserve special attention as trade, also small arms trade, can be best regulated from there. The EU has concentrated on critical countries and regions in order to enforce control based upon UN and OSCE standards as well as its own code of conduct. In Bosnia, one of the most efficient EU programmes has devoted itself to establishing the Customs and Fiscal Assistance Office (CAFAO), not least to keep the uncontrolled flow of small arms better in check. Despite the positive examples, it has become clear that the internal obstacles within the EU still present an even bigger problem.

---

[40] Second Annual Report on the implementation of the EU Joint Action of 12 July 2002 on the European Union's contribution to combating the destabilising accumulation and spread of small arms and light weapons (2002/589/CFSP) and repealing Joint Action 1999/34/CFSP, and the EU Programme on illicit trafficking in conventional arms of June 1997 (8 October 2002). The Rt. Hon Chris Patten, Commissioner for External Relations: Commission statement on arms exports, European Parliament – Plenary session Strasbourg, 2 October 2001. Gary Titley, Report on *the Council's Third Annual Report according to Operative Provision 8 of the European Union Code of Conduct on Arms Exports* (European Parliament, Committee on Foreign Affairs, Human Rights, Common Security and Defence Policy), 10 September 2002.
[41] European Union Code of Conduct on Arms Exports 5 June 1998 No. 8675/2/98 REV 2 <http://ue.eu.int/pesc/ExportCTRL/en/8675_2_98_en.pdf>.
[42] Joint Action 1999/34/CFSP of 17 December 1998 adopted by the Council on the basis of Article J.3 of the Treaty on European Union on the European Union's contribution to combating the destabilising accumulation and spread of small arms and light weapons, *OJEC* [1999] L 9/1.
[43] Herbert Wulf, 'Kleinwaffen – die Massenvernichtungswaffen unserer Zeit. Die Bemühungen der Vereinten Nationen um Mikroabrüstung'. 49 *Vereinte Nationen* (2001), pp. 174-178. United Nations Conference on the Illicit Trade in Small Arms and Light Weapons in All Its Aspects. New York, 9-20 July 2001, available at <http://disarmament.un.org/cab/smallarms/>.

Experiences from such initiatives at functional conflict prevention have also proven valuable for all other horizontal activities. Part of the lessons learnt is the sober fact that the good intentions connected with conflict prevention may turn out to be untrue or may lead – in some cases – to a negative impact. Even the panacea of democratic development[44] must be re-evaluated in terms of whether it does not actually accentuate the conflicting parties' antagonisms towards each other instead of leading them towards peaceful competition. Similarly, the effect of the media in conflicts can be ambivalent; at times it can glorify violence, but also, as independent sources of information, it can guarantee transparency. It can dangerously exaggerate ethnic differences but also foster dialogue between different ethnic groups. Even more critical is the question, or even unspoken reproach, that the EU's development policy could itself contribute to the escalation of local conflicts. The notorious incompetence of local partners gives birth to the justified fear that Brussels could inadvertently help anchor repressive structures in certain countries because of the necessity of cooperating with whoever is in power. That is why the issues of good governance and the emphasis of participatory politics are increasingly significant.

Pitfalls and deficiencies of the above-mentioned kind are not only limited to functional conflict prevention. It must be assumed that they occur in cases of acute and regional preventative activities as well. This is not a motivating environment. Disillusionment must be considered as a limiting factor when planning to extend investments in conflict prevention. It would be wrong to conclude that prevention does not work, rather the lessons should be used to do better and to improve the record. Prevention is a profession with a long learning curve.

4. RAISING THE STAKES AND MAKING USE OF THE UNION'S ASSETS

As the results of the first phase of targeted prevention activities show, the EU is still in the infant stages of a learning process in terms of a systematic and successful conflict prevention policy. Although it has introduced the concept of conflict prevention into all its institutions and was able to shorten the span from conflict warning to early action, the measures taken and their actual effects remain modest. Either the measures were taken in geographical proximity (the Balkans) or they affected horizontal issues of a limited range (small arms code of conduct). An intensive examination of each case and topic that the EU has dealt with in the context of conflict prevention could help the EU to more selectively

---

[44] This is not the place to evaluate individual human rights or other programmes. But it is necessary to mention at least in passing that some of these programmes have become alarmingly reduced to rote, assembly-line activities. The often cited example of Brussels' praised first measure for the democratisation of Congo – the purchase of several hundred ballot boxes – is no exaggeration. Naturally, a group of merchants has emerged, specialised in the market these 'immediate actions' have created.

widen the arsenal of conflict prevention instruments and to develop a more efficient prevention strategy in the future.

The rather chequered balance sheet could also be due to the fact that it is simply too early, and the fruits of the most recent reforms still have to grow before
progress is more recognisable. On the other hand, it cannot be denied that introduced internal changes are too weak for a number of reasons to consistently re-
tool the EU as a conflict prevention actor and prepare it for an internationally
significant role. The creation of capabilities, procedural agreement, joint declarations and actions of the Fifteen are already hailed as successes. The actual effects
of these achievements in the conflict areas themselves is a different story. Indeed,
the EU shies away from the difficult violent conflicts (such as Chechnya) or curb-
ing the proliferation of weapons of mass destruction (as in North Korea).

It seems that the arsenal of motivation which drives the EU to run more ambitious conflict prevention activities is not strong enough to allow for wider risk
taking and to focus more on the outcome than on the output of its policies. From
the start, the EU has set its sights on a lower level of addressing international
conflict. Brussels did not aspire to the role of a leading power in the area of conflict prevention. It seems driven by the restrictions of its operative options rather
than by the strategic reach of its responsibilities. The Union talks abundantly
about its particular assets, but it forgets to use them.

Chapter 5
EU INSTRUMENTS FOR CONFLICT PREVENTION

by Javier Niño Pérez[1]

1. INTRODUCTION

The European Union (EU) has at its disposal a large and formidable array of tools and mechanisms in the field of conflict prevention. The number, nature and scope of these instruments have significantly evolved over time to take account of the constant developments within the European integration process and notably the increasingly important role of the EU in the area of foreign policy. Annex A provides a non-exhaustive list of the most significant EU frameworks, activities and instruments in this area together with an outline of the conflict cycle specifying the immediate aims and adequate combination of the instruments for each phase (Annex B).[2]

The many tools which the EU can bring into play to address the prevention, management and resolution of violent conflict could be examined from different angles using a number of diverse conceptual categories. This chapter will herewith contrast, on the one hand, short-term and long-term instruments and, on the other, EU and EC ones and look in particular at the case of sanctions and military preventive deployments. This approach has the advantage of allowing us, whilst examining these instruments, to address three challenges of paramount importance with which the EU is currently confronted pertaining to the need to: (i) approach, in an effective manner, the whole range of conflict prevention and crisis management strategies; (ii) ensure the coherence and consistency of the complex institutional framework in which work in this field is carried out and (iii) integrate in its overall preventive strategy the new instruments introduced by the Common Foreign and Security Policy (CFSP) and the European Security and Defence Policy (ESDP).

---

[1] Administrator, European Commission, DG External Relations, Conflict prevention, crisis management and ACP political issues unit. All the views expressed are those of the author only.

[2] Communication from the Commission to the Council on the issue of Conflicts in Africa: Peacebuilding, Conflict Prevention and Beyond, 6 March 1996, SEC (96) 332.

V. Kronenberger and J. Wouters, eds., The European Union and Conflict Prevention
© *2004,* T·M·C·ASSER PRESS, *The Hague, The Netherlands*

2.   SHORT-TERM INSTRUMENTS AND LONG-TERM INSTRUMENTS WITHIN
     THE EU

EU policy in this field deviates from the linear approach to violent conflict,
which suggests that only efforts to forestall the outbreak of violence and thus
keeping the conflict latent, are regarded as prevention. The EU has acknowledged
that the rather cyclical and recurrent nature of conflict implies the need to devise
and utilise instruments aimed at addressing:

- the social, economic and political circumstances underpinning conflicts,
  namely their 'root-causes' as well as;
- the most 'proximate causes' that could lead to the outbreak or violent escalation of a conflict.

Thus, both the Göteborg Programme for the Prevention of Violent Conflict and
the Communication from the Commission on Conflict Prevention refer to two
categories of instruments. With a similar approach, the former differentiates between structural long-term and direct short-term preventive actions and the latter
refers to long-term prevention ('Projecting stability') and short-term prevention
('Reacting quickly to nascent conflicts') tools. Similarly a communication by the
Swedish government[3] also refers to structural and direct measures in accordance
with their respective long or short-term impact on a given conflict.

2.1   Long-term instruments

Structural or long-term instruments, which contribute to conflict prevention, fall
primarily under the area of economic assistance or cooperation.[4] These are measures that 'strengthen the society socially and economically, which may have a
stabilising effect in situations where there is a tangible risk of armed conflict
breaking out'.[5] Among the most relevant instruments available to the EU in this
area we must cite development cooperation, trade, human rights/democratisation,
environment policies, electoral observation and arms control. A few words on
these areas are necessary. However, some of these areas will be dealt with more
extensively in other chapters of this book.[6]

---

[3] *Preventing Violent Conflict, Swedish policy* (Stockholm, Government Communication 2000/
2001 No. 2, 19 October 2000), p. 11.
[4] It may be argued that any assistance aimed at increasing social and economic well-being within
societies is relevant to conflict prevention, since it reduces social and economic tensions in the recipient country, provided that it is distributed equally within the societies concerned.
[5] *Supra* n. 3, p. 30.
[6] See, in particular, the chapters by A. Rossi, B. Martenczuk, S. Fries and A. Weiss.

Development assistance has been rightly described as 'the most important contribution that can be made to preventing conflicts'.[7] The EU, which provides approximately half of the total financial assistance to developing countries covering all geographical areas of the world, has recognised the linkages between development, poverty and conflict and the paramount role of development cooperation in conflict prevention in a number of policy statements.

The EU's approach in this area is aimed at mainstreaming conflict prevention throughout the whole range of aid sectors – including transport, education, water, budgetary and macro-economic support – that can help to achieve structural stability, moving away from viewing conflict prevention as a distinct 'sector' requiring special projects or linked solely to specific areas of intervention such as the security sector.

In the context of the inevitable and dramatically hasty globalisation process, the EU *trade and economic cooperation policies* as the driving force of economic growth and poverty reduction, can also play a major role in contributing to conflict prevention. This can be done through strengthening regional cooperation as a tool to reduce political tensions, to increase economic interdependence and to create mutual trust between countries[8] and through capacity building and increasing market access (e.g., GSP, everything but arms initiative).

The link between conflict prevention and *human rights and democracy* is abundantly clear. Just as denying basic rights can fuel violent conflict, helping to guarantee those rights can prevent conflict arising in the first place. The EU is also providing significant assistance in this area.[9] Increasing attention in this area is being given to *environmental policies* including management and access to natural resources as well as environmental degradation. These issues are being addressed primarily through regional and bilateral programmes, the implementation of Multilateral Environmental Agreements or specific initiatives like the Kimberley Process dealing with the illegal trade in diamonds.

Finally, electoral observation and assistance and arms control/destruction activities can also play a very valuable role in avoiding violent conflict. A well-run election observation mission can reduce the opportunity for intimidation and conflict. The interest of utilising instruments against the multiplication of both small and mass destruction arms is self-evident given the destructive influence on political and social structures.

Whilst it has been acknowledged that economic assistance and cooperation instruments are the ones which have a more significant impact on a long-term ap-

---

[7] Speech by Commissioner P. Nielson, 'Building Credibility: The role of European Development Policy in preventing conflicts', Foreign Policy Centre, February 2001.

[8] The EU's support to regional organisations such as Mercosur, the Andean Pact, the Gulf Cooperation Council, ASEAN, ECOWAS or SADC can be described as relevant examples.

[9] The European Commission's European Initiative on Democracy and Human Rights has its own funded projects amounting to Euro 400 million for the last five years; see <http://europa.eu.int/comm/europeaid/projects/eidhr/index_en.htm>.

proach to conflict prevention, one should not obscure the role that could be played by other measures relating to:

a) Political dialogue: A long-term dialogue on political issues, including human rights and democratisation can have an early warning role by highlighting problems which could in the future lead to violent conflicts as well as contributing to their early resolution. In this respect, new emphasis is being placed on the activities of special representatives and heads of EU diplomatic missions.

b) Tackling organised crime, drug trafficking and money laundering: These activities, which fall under the heading of Justice and Home Affairs (see below), have the long-term effect of creating greater stability. In the face of the increasing attention devoted to terrorist activities a number of initiatives have been undertaken in recent years in the UN, G8 and other contexts. The challenge for the EU now is to 'develop policy-making mechanisms which allow it to integrate these initiatives into its overall political approach to specific countries and regions, to assess their respective benefits, and to set priorities for the future'.[10]

2.2 Short-term instruments

In situations where preventive measures have either failed or where they have not been applied in the first place, there is a need to resort to short-term actions with the threefold objective of:

– reducing manifest tensions and/or preventing the outbreak or recurrence of violent conflict;
– preventing the vertical (intensifying of violence) or horizontal (territorial) escalation of existing violent conflict; and
– ending violent conflict.

These situations are often characterised by their complexity and rapid change and therefore necessitate flexible and speedy instruments.

The EU also has a broad range of diplomatic, economic and humanitarian instruments for short-term prevention. These include: political dialogue, sanctions, advocating specific measures and/or solutions, deployment of observers, preventive military intervention, support for peace initiatives, peace enforcement, demobilisation and disarmament, repatriation and reintegration, demining, post-conflict relief and humanitarian aid, confidence-building measures, conflict resolution initiatives, rebuilding government structures, etc.

A conceptual distinction should be made between crisis management activities as a general category and the disbursement of humanitarian aid to crisis areas.

---

[10] Report by the High Representative /Commission on improving the Coherence and effectiveness of EU action in the field of conflict prevention, December 2000 <http://ue.eu.int/solana/details.asp?BID=111&DocID=65350>. See also the contribution by. L. Benoit in this volume.

While the former constitutes an openly political activity, the provision of emergency relief for civilian populations affected by armed conflicts is inherently apolitical[11] and cannot be considered to be a conflict prevention tool.

The EU policy in this area initially focused on emergency and transitional relief measures including rehabilitation, food aid and food security, mine action, civil protection, the rule of law and democratisation, assistance to refugees and their host communities and exceptional financial assistance. This aid is delivered through a combination of specialised sectoral as well as long-term geographic instruments.

But the initial approach to crisis response was dramatically modified by the development of a Common and Foreign Security Policy (CFSP) and, within this, the emerging European Security and Defence Policy. Thus, within the framework of the CFSP, a series of tools can be activated. These include: *soft*

a) A number of diplomatic measures undertaken either within the framework of a Common strategy[12] or of a Common position[13] on their own: declarations, *démarches*, high-level visits, Special Envoys, supporting action by other international organisations, diplomatic recognition, peace proposals, sponsoring peace conferences, etc. *soft*

b) The political dialogue to be carried out within the set of agreements concluded between the EU/EC and a number of third countries. These agreements often provide – in addition to development and cooperation assistance, trade, research and cultural cooperation issues – explicit references to human rights, the rule of law and democratisation, as well as terrorism and they provide mechanisms for addressing disputes between the parties. *economic*

c) Finally, sanctions (other than those in the agreements), which will be dealt with more extensively in point section 4 below, can also be used as a valuable tool to prevent conflict.

New actions relating to crisis management have also been introduced within the context of the European Security and Defence Policy (ESDP). Thus, the Cologne European Council meeting in June 1999 placed crisis management tasks at the heart of the process of strengthening the ESDP. These are also known as the Pe-

---

[11] 'Humanitarian aid, the sole aim of which is to prevent or relieve human suffering, is accorded to victims without discrimination on the grounds of race, ethnic group, religion, sex, age, nationality or political affiliation and must not be guided by, or subject to, political considerations' (Preamble to Council Regulation (EC) No. 1257/96 of 20 June 1996 on humanitarian aid, *OJEC* [1996] L 163/1).

[12] Common strategies are one of the frameworks of actions under the CFSP Pillar. They are aimed at establishing long-term and comprehensive strategies for the Union towards a certain third country or region, or a given issue (e.g., Common Strategies on Russia and the Ukraine, respectively adopted in June 1999 (*OJEC* [1999] L 157/1) and December 1999 (*OJEC* [1999] L 331/1)).

[13] According to Article 15 of the Treaty on European Union, common positions describe the EU's approach to a particular matter of a geographic or thematic nature (see, e.g., the Council's Common Position of 2 June 1997 on conflict prevention and resolution in Africa, *OJEC* [1997] L 153/1).

tersburg tasks, named after the place where the Western European Union (WEU) Ministerial Council that formulated them was held in June 1992. They are humanitarian and rescue tasks, peacekeeping tasks and combat-force tasks in crisis management, including peacemaking.

As far as military capabilities are concerned, in December 1999, the Helsinki European Council decided to create a rapid reaction force of up to 60,000 troops capable of carrying out the full range of Petersburg tasks. The EU also decided to develop the civilian aspects of crisis management in four priority areas defined by the Feira European Council in June 2000: police, strengthening the rule of law, strengthening civilian administration and civil protection.[14]

The first ESDP operation was launched on 1st January 2003: the European Union Police Mission (EUPM) in Bosnia and Herzegovina, which follows on from the UN's International Police Task Force established under the Paris/Dayton Agreement in 1995. On 18 March 2003, the Union decided to launch its first military operation. The aim of the EU-led Military Operation in the former Yugoslav Republic of Macedonia (FYROM), which follows on from NATO's 'Allied Harmony' operation, is to contribute to a stable secure environment in FYROM, thus facilitating the implementation of the Ohrid framework agreement that is pivotal to the effort of the international community in FYROM. Initially expected to last for a period of six months, it was agreed by the Council on 21 July to extend it until 15 December 2003, in line with the request made by the FYROM government to the EU.

In May 2003 the EU decided to launch the first EU-led military intervention outside Europe, Operation ARTEMIS to Bunia (Democratic Republic of Congo). The operation was conducted in accordance with the United Nations (UN) Security Council Resolution 1484 (30 May 2003) and the Council's Joint Action adopted on 5 June 2003.[15] The Operation officially ended on 1st September 2003. The European military force worked in close cooperation with the United Nations Mission in DRC (MONUC). It was aimed, *inter alia*, at contributing to the stabilisation of the security conditions and the improvement of the humanitarian situation in Bunia.

As requested by the Helsinki European Council, the Commission also set up a Rapid Reaction Facility, called the Rapid Reaction Mechanism[16] which will, for

---

[14] Concrete targets have been defined in those areas: Member States should be able to provide, in the field of the police, 5,000 officers for international missions and to deploy 1,000 of them within less than 30 days, 200 experts in the field of Rule of Law, a pool of experts covering a broad spectrum of functions in civilian administration and, for civil protection, 2 or 3 assessment teams that could be dispatched within 3-7 hours as well as intervention teams of up to 2,000 persons for deployment at short notice.

[15] *OJEC* [2003] L 143/50.

[16] Council Regulation (EC) No. 381/2001 of 26 February 2001 creating a rapid-reaction mechanism, *OJEC* [2001] L 57/5, also available at <http://europa.eu.int/eur-lex/en/archive/2001/l_05720010227en.html>.

the short period of 6 months, untie the strings around Community instruments and will release their potential and focus where urgent conditions require quick action. The basis of the Mechanism is existing Community instruments capable of providing a large spectrum of actions and reactions. Community instruments will, in turn, remain the key for any possible follow-up measure, which might be required, after the first emergency operation has ended.

Initially (during 2001 and early 2002), RRM mainly focused on post-conflict stabilisation efforts. During 2002 and 2003, RRM programmes broadened in scope adding activities linked to conflict prevention and the fight against terrorism. Several missions and initial studies were launched in these fields and the conclusions were fed into the Commission's Country and Regional Strategy Papers as well as specific programmes of action financed by RRM or other Community instruments. In becoming a more complete tool, RRM has taken on a more structured approach, integrating a wider range of actions at regional, national and local levels. This wider range of actions can be said to cover six major aspects of EU crisis intervention:

- assessment of possible Community responses to a crisis;
- conflict prevention in countries and regions showing significant signs of instability;
- acute crisis management;
- post-conflict reconciliation;
- post-crisis reconstruction;
- the fight against terrorism.

It is also worth noting that RRM has supported actions in all four areas of civilian crisis management as identified by the Feira European Council (June 2000): *police, the rule of law, civilian administration* and *civil protection*.[17]

2.3   Long-term versus short-term instruments

It should no longer be necessary to argue the merits of an approach to conflict prevention based primarily on long-term preventive action. A comprehensive preventive strategy 'must first focus on the underlying political, social, economic, and environmental causes of conflict'.[18] Indeed, it is better to prevent a conflict than to be forced to try to control it, when it fails to deal with consequences. The annual costs to the international community of military and civilian measures in former Yugoslavia are estimated at not less that USD 7 billion, roughly the same

---

[17] More detailed information on RRM activities can be found at <http://europa.eu.int/comm/external_relations/cfsp/news/ip_01_255.htm>.
[18] Commission on Global Governance, 1995.

amount of money the EC disbursed as development assistance to Sub-Saharan Africa in 2001.[19]

This approach to conflict prevention is also acknowledged in the new EU conceptual framework to conflict prevention. As stated by the Greek Minister of Foreign Affairs, Georgios Papandreou, 'the only way to deal with conflict is to address effectively the root causes through a long-term structural prevention policy'.[20]

A strategy focused primarily on long-term prevention should logically privilege long-term instruments as they are best placed to address the root-causes of conflict action and therefore to have a more significant and sustainable impact on peace-building strategies.

However, from a peace-building perspective, this strategy should also take due account of the very important role to be played by short-term instruments bearing in mind that:

• Although short-term instruments cannot provide sustainable solutions to violent conflict, they can contribute to stability for long-term conflict prevention work to take root;

• Preventive and reactive instruments frequently coincide, since preventing the (re)escalation of a conflict may also be understood in terms of reacting to a conflict *ex post facto*. This is particularly relevant in post-conflict situations. Measures such as the deployment of civil police are at the same time intended to both 'manage' the outcome of a violent conflict – restore order – and prevent the recurrence of an armed conflict by maintaining order and by allocating resources to institution-building, for example, to the strengthening of civilian administration.[21]

Ultimately, in a long-term, holistic approach, short-term/crisis management instruments are to be intrinsically linked with long-term/conflict prevention and peace building tools and therefore it is necessary to developed detailed approaches and ensure all synergies across the whole range of long-term conflict prevention and short-term crisis management strategies and actions.

---

[19] Annual report on EC development policy and external aid, 2001. <http://europa.eu.int/comm/europeaid/reports/index_en.htm>.

[20] EU Conference on Conflict Prevention in Helsingborg, August 2002.

[21] Saferworld/International Alert, *Ensuring progress in the prevention of violent conflict: Priorities for the Greek and Italian Presidencies* (2003), available at <http://www.international-alert.org/publications.htm#eu>.

3.   EU and Community Instruments and Their Relationships

In the context of the disintegration of the former Soviet Union and the end of the Cold War, the Maastricht Treaty signed in February 1992 and which entered into force in November 1993, significantly altered the nature and institutional framework of the European integration process by (i) creating the European Union and (ii) introducing new and more tangible and effective forms of cooperation in the fields of foreign and security policy and justice and home affairs. The principles and structures defined by the new Maastricht Treaty were to be further refined by the Treaties of Amsterdam and Nice which entered into force in May 1999 and February 2003 respectively.

As a result, the new institutional setting of the EU is fragmented across three pillars or systems of cooperation:

-   Pillar I: The European Community, including trade and development cooperation;
-   Pillar II: Common Foreign and Security Policy, and
-   Pillar III: Justice and Home Affairs.

Each pillar has its own decision-making procedures and assigns different roles and responsibilities to the three main EU institutions – the Council of Ministers, the European Commission and the European Parliament. Decisions regarding Pillar I are normally adopted on a qualified majority basis whereas those concerning Pillars II and III are taken on an unanimity basis. As far as the role of the institutions is concerned, the Commission has more power in Pillar I than in Pillars II and III, the latter two covering areas where Member States have been traditionally less willing to surrender sovereignty to the EU than in others.

The instruments of Pillar I – The European Community – are referred to as EC or Community instruments as opposed to the European Union (EU) instruments, which are those used in the areas covered by Pillars II and III. The different instruments used by the EU to address policy-making/implementation of issues on external relations/foreign policy are scattered across the three pillars. Hence the same applies to conflict prevention related activities

3.1   Pillar I – EC instruments

The European Community pillar covers the vast majority of the measures available in the field of the EU's external action. Thus, the so-called Community instruments relate to areas including trade, social, economic and environmental measures, humanitarian aid and development assistance.

The greater part of Community instruments have three distinct features.

-   They have a predominantly economic nature, bringing into play substantial material resources;[22]
-   They are primarily aimed at addressing the root-causes of conflict and are to be placed in a long term/structural perspective;
-   They have an exclusively 'civilian' nature as opposed to some of the new instruments being developed within the framework of the ESDP-Pillar II.

But EC instruments can also have a more political nature and/or a short-term impact. Electoral observation and assistance activities, implemented by the European Commission, are a good example of Community actions having a predominantly political dimension. This is an interesting example of a conflict prevention instrument which previously fell under Pillars I and II (the political decision was often taken in the CFSP framework and the financing decision in the Community and/or CFSP context) and has become an exclusive Pillar I action. RRM actions, on the other hand, are a relevant case of short-term interventions equally implemented under Pillar I.

Community instruments confer a privileged role on the European Commission as this institution has the exclusive right to formally initiate proposals in this area and is primarily responsible for the definition and implementation of the corresponding actions. Nevertheless, it should be borne in mind that the Commission's proposals have generally to be submitted to the Council of Ministers – which takes the ultimate decision – and the European Parliament – which shares the power of co-decision in most areas and has to be consulted in others.

3.2   Pillars II and III – EU instruments

Although the tools to implement actions falling under both Pillars II and III are commonly referred to as EU instruments, each one of these frameworks has its own specifics linked to the corresponding areas of intervention.

Pillar II instruments cover the implementation of all CFSP and the majority of ESDP activities. In other words, these are the instruments relating to political dialogue (declarations, *démarches*, high-level visits and Special Envoys) and some of the new crisis management activities developed under the ESDP.[23]

As opposed to Pillar I instruments, they:

-   Have a predominantly political component which is aimed at giving expression and substance to the increasingly important and active EU role in international relations;

---

[22] The EU's budget for external actions in 2001 amounted to more than Euro 8 billion.

[23] The RRM and certain civilian crisis management activities relating to the Petersburg Tasks, are implemented by the European Commission and hence fall under the First Pillar's decision-making rules in spite of being placed in the broader context of the ESDP-II Pillar.

– Focus primarily on short-term activities relating to ongoing or imminent crises; and

– Can incorporate both a civilian and a military dimension.

Nevertheless, as was the case with Pillar I actions, there are a number of exceptions to the general rule. Thus, Pillar I economic instruments like development cooperation programmes could be used in order to reprioritise or suspend activities and to mobilise funds relatively quickly if a political need arises. Pillar II instruments such as Special Envoys can have an equally long-term structural approach when their work is framed in a comprehensive common strategy.

The use of measures that fall under the CFSP pillar remains contingent on agreement between Member States in the Council. This reflects the reluctance of the Member States to surrender national sovereignty in such a critical field as foreign policy. The Commission's role within the CFSP pillar is more limited than in the European Community pillar as it does not have the sole right to submit proposals (cf., Article 22 TEU). The European Parliament's role is also limited, as the Council Presidency merely consults it concerning the main aspects of CFSP (cf., Article 21 TEU).

3.3 Pillar III instruments

The Justice and Home Affairs instruments (JHA) pillar is also relevant to the field of EU external relations and is increasingly being incorporated in the formulation of EU policies with third countries. Matters of relevance in this pillar include:

1. judicial cooperation in criminal matters;
2. customs and police cooperation for the purposes of preventing and combating terrorism, unlawful drugs, people and arms trafficking and other serious forms of international crime;
3. asylum policy;
4. crossing of external frontiers and border controls; and
5. immigration policy.

In the 'post-September 11 world', where conflict prevention is often being replaced on the agenda by the narrower prevention of terrorism, this area is becoming increasingly important in a peace building perspective.

So far, activities in this Pillar have been dominated by the strengthening of law enforcement responses together with significant efforts to enhance cooperation with other relevant international organisations and institutions. Within this Pillar, the Council takes the lead and it is the Member State holding the Presidency that takes the initiatives. The Commission's involvement with the JHA pillar was initially limited but has progressively increased in scope. The European Parliament plays no role at all in the JHA decision-making process and is simply informed after the adoption of initiatives by the Council.

Notwithstanding the above, it is worth noting that the Treaty of Amsterdam introduced a new title called 'Visas, asylum, immigration and other policies related to free movement of persons' in the Treaty establishing the European Community. Areas like controls on external borders, asylum, immigration and judicial cooperation in civil matters all now come under the first pillar and are governed by the Community method. Cooperation in criminal matters remains under the third pillar, to which the Amsterdam Treaty has added 'preventing and combating of racism and xenophobia'.

3.4   The instruments' relationships

A number of elements pertaining to the EU's current institutional framework hinder the consistency and coherence of existing instruments and activities in the field of external relations, where conflict prevention related activities are designed and carried out. Among these elements, one could cite the following:

1. There are different perceptions as to the exact nature of the different instruments. Whilst the proposal to negotiate a Free Trade agreement with a country like Iran is a Pillar I Community instrument (trade policy), it would be difficult to challenge the fact that the foreign political implications of such a proposal are extremely significant and probably outweigh many of the CFSP instruments that might be mobilised by the EU in its dealings with that country.
2. Members States' bilateral policies still play a very significant role in the areas corresponding to Pillars II and III. The recent Iraq crisis has regrettably proved how decision-making processes and diverging Member States' interests and priorities in the field of CFSP sometimes makes it difficult to obtain common approaches to crisis situations.
3. Some of the conflict prevention/crisis management activities to be implemented under the emerging ESDP have a military dimension, often necessitating *ad hoc* arrangements with other existing international bodies dealing with security affairs (i.e., UN, NATO) and impeding the smooth inter-Pillar flow of information due to the confidential nature of many of these issues.
4. Finally, the quick (6 monthly) rotation of the EU Presidency can be detrimental to coherence and continuity. The priorities of each Presidency concerning conflict prevention rarely coincide, thereby hindering any follow-up to previous initiatives.

These challenges have been recognised and the EU has made a number of formal commitments to address these issues. Three documents ought to be mentioned:

- *The resolution on Coherence (section Peace-Building, Conflict Prevention and Resolution), adopted by the Development Council on 5 June 1997.*

This text highlights the need to ensure:

Horizontal Consistency (i.e., between pillars): the Union's external activities must be consistent in the sense that measures taken must be compatible and, ideally, mutually reinforcing.

Vertical Consistency (i.e., between the EU and national levels): this refers to the need for conformity between the actions and positions of the Member States and those of the EU and explains why formulating an effective common EU foreign policy can be challenging.

Coherence: account should be taken of the EU's development cooperation objectives in the formulation and implementation of other policies that affect developing countries, especially those in the fields of: peace-building, conflict prevention and resolution, food security, fisheries and migration.

- *The Guidelines for strengthening operational coordination between the Community represented by the Commission and the Member States in the field of external assistance, adopted by the Council on 22 January 2001.*

In this document, the Commission points to the need to enhance coordination and to better ensure the flow of information between the Commission and the Member States in the area of development cooperation.

- *The Göteborg Programme for the prevention of violent conflicts adopted in June 2001.*

This programme calls upon the Council to 'pursue coherent and comprehensive preventive strategies, using appropriate existing instruments and taking into account ongoing actions, in order to identify challenges, set clear objectives, allocate adequate resources and ensure cooperation with external partners'. More importantly, it indicates that 'COREPER [the Committee of Permanent Representatives within the Council] will continue to ensure coherence between different policy areas of the Union, paying specific attention to the question of coherent preventive activities'. Thus, notwithstanding the role to be played in this area by the Political and Security Committee, which has the mandate to develop and monitor conflict prevention policies within the Common Foreign and Security Policy, COREPER is mandated to ensure the consistency of the EU across Pillars – policy and activities in the field of conflict prevention.

Although these initiatives have undoubtedly contributed to a better coordination of existing conflict prevention instruments across the three Pillars, much remains to be done to develop all possible synergies among all existing instruments, thus ensuring the coherence and consistency of all the EU's external actions in this area.

Some of the proposals of the Draft Treaty establishing a Constitution for Europe (e.g., the merging of the posts of High Representative for CFSP and the Commissioner for External Relations or the proposal for a permanent EU President that would do away with the current 6-monthly Presidency rotation), could potentially help achieve these objectives. Nevertheless, there is still no final agreement on the institutional setting in the area of external relations.

Beyond possible changes in the decision making process, ultimately, only the political will to ensure enhanced consistency would allow more effective conflict prevention policies

4. THE CASE OF EU/EC SANCTIONS AND MILITARY CAPABILITIES (PREVENTIVE DEPLOYMENTS): CAN THEY PREVENT CONFLICTS?

The means of preventive action can also be divided into positive strategies (i.e., promises, persuasion, and rewards) and negative strategies (i.e., threats, coercion and punishments).

Whilst positive strategies tend to be implemented through either political or economic actions, negative strategies can rely on all three different types of instruments, i.e., political, economic, and military ones and constitute what is called 'coercive diplomacy', the aim of which is to produce positive results by targeting the relevant actor with a specific demand, a time-limit for compliance, and a credible threat of punishment.

In 'coercive diplomacy', political tools are derived mostly from diplomatic practice: fact-finding, monitoring, mediation, influence, promises, and threats. Economic tools rely on the manipulation of material costs and benefits by cutting off economic ties, promising their re-establishment, or providing outright rewards. Finally, military instruments boil down to the use of force or the threat thereof when the parties continue to escalate the confrontation.

Both sanctions and preventive military deployments can be described as active negative strategies.

4.1 Sanctions

Sanctions constitute a foreign policy instrument, not involving the use or threat of military force, employed by a state, a group of states or a regional or international organisation to induce a state or sometimes a rebel movement, to comply with international legal norms or to bring a course of action to an end.

It is important to differentiate between the concept of a sanction and that of conditionality as the latter can also play a role in conflict prevention strategies. Whilst both conditionality and sanctions are used to enforce compliance by their

target with certain criteria, unlike sanctions, which are usually implemented reac-
tively, conditionality imposes only a *threat* of punishment.

Sanctions have been described as a 'complex, flawed, but indispensable
tool'[24] and they have, by most assessments, demonstrated at best a mixed track
record of effectiveness in influencing their targets and advancing international
peace and security. One of the most vexing questions about sanctions concerns
their externalities or unintended effects. While sanctions may well impose palpable punishments for illicit behaviour, they have also resulted in significant
costs for those who impose sanctions both in economic terms[25] and in human suffering.[26] Yet another level of complexity is added by the difficulties of measurement. The frequent imprecision of the goals of sanctions complicates the task of
setting standards for gathering and evaluating evidence of their success or failure.
Further complicating matters, sanctions have become controversial to an extraordinary extent in recent years. Both the partisans and critics of sanctions share
some responsibility for permitting this diplomatic instrument to become the ob-
ject of sloganeering. Such an environment is not at all conducive to objective assessments concerning sanctions, either in terms of the past impacts or the future
potential.

Nevertheless, in spite of the complicating factors outlined above, it has been
demonstrated that, when implemented on the basis of an international consensus
and when credibly and effectively imposed, these instruments can indeed redress
and deter grievous wrongs.

To some observers, the most sustained and ultimately successful modern example of sanctions have been the ones employed against the apartheid regime in
South Africa. In this case, the initial mandatory UN Security Council – imposed
arms embargo and the voluntary General Assembly – recommended oil embargo,
were coupled with the financial sanctions that were imposed by the Commonwealth, the EC and many individual countries and the informal restrictions imposed by the international financial community.

In order to address the many challenges above, the focus has been progressively placed on the so-called 'smart sanctions'. This term is used to describe targeted instead of comprehensive sanctions. These targeted sanctions are designed
to put pressure directly on those who are deemed to pose a threat to international
peace or to human rights. Travel restrictions, bank account freezing and the like,

---

[24] Keynote Address by Jayantha Dhanapala, Under-Secretary General for Disarmament Affairs,
United Nations, Final Expert Seminar on Smart Sanctions – The Next Step: Arms Embargoes and
Travel Sanctions (Bonn International Centre for Conversion, Germany 3-5 December 2000).

[25] On 12 October 2000, Bulgaria informed the Sixth (Legal) Committee of the UN General Assembly that its costs as a third State affected by Security Council sanctions were over $10 billion.

[26] It should be noted that economic sanctions are also regularly – if not necessarily successfully –
complemented by exemptions which are applicable to exports of food and medical supplies in order
to prevent the suffering of the civilian population in the target country.

directed at particular individuals in a leadership echelon are good examples of 'smart sanctions'. Because they are formulated in such a way as to minimise their impact upon the well-being of the civilian population, the concept of 'smart sanctions' has won favour with development organisations and international agencies.

Sanctions – other than those regarding the suspension of agreements between the EC and third countries – currently available to the EU fall under three (partly overlapping) categories:

– Political and diplomatic sanctions: reduction of the scale of diplomatic representation, the severance of all diplomatic relations, suspension of official visits and reduction/suspension of cultural and sports contacts or scientific cooperation;

– Restrictions imposed on cultural contacts and transport: flight bans and visa restrictions;

– Commercial/economic and financial sanctions: embargoes (either general or arms embargoes), the freezing of funds, restrictions on payments and capital movements and import and export restrictions.

EU sanctions can be adopted under the umbrella of a UN Security Council Resolution or autonomously. The legal nature of the measure adopted depends on the area covered. Thus, measures falling under Community competence are taken by an EC Act, whereas measures falling under Members States' competence are adopted by a Common position.

The EU has made extensive use of this instrument and as many as 18 countries have been subject to sanctions over the years:[27]

Afghanistan	FRY	Myanmar
Angola	Indonesia	Nigeria
Belarus	Iraq	Sierra Leona
DRC	Liberia	Somalia
Eritrea	Libya	Sudan
Ethiopia	Moldova	Zimbabwe

Given the economic importance of the EU, commercial and economic sanctions constitute the weightiest instruments of conflict prevention. In addition to economic sanctions, EU Member States can impose financial sanctions, namely bans on the movement of capital and on payments.

---

[27] An overview of the measures already adopted can be found at <http://europa.eu.int/eur-lex/en/lif/reg/en_register_18.html>.

In line with the predominant doctrine, the EU policy in this area has evolved progressively to (i) privilege the use of smart sanctions – thus the EC/EU may impose financial sanctions selectively with a view to punishing specific individuals in a third country by freezing their personal funds abroad (e.g., Zimbabwe)[28] – and (ii) incorporate this instrument in more comprehensive conflict prevention strategy (e.g., FRY).[29]

It is difficult to anticipate, at this point in time, the potential and possible use of 'smart sanctions'. Thus, it is worth mentioning that, in the context of Regulation (EC) No. 881/2002 of 27 May 2002, aimed at freezing funds and economic resources belonging to, or owned or held by persons and entities associated with Osama bin Laden, the Al-Qaida network and the Taliban – the competence of the EC to impose sanctions on individuals and entities who are not necessarily linked with governments or regimes of third countries has been challenged. This issue is currently being considered by the Court of First Instance of the European Communities.[30]

From a general point of view, the main challenges concerning the use of sanctions remain:

1. the need to design sanctions in such a way as to ensure that they are properly targeted to achieve their political ends;
2. their enforcement;
3. the putting in place of an effective regime to monitor implementation; and
4. to devise mechanisms permitting an evaluation of their impact.

4.2 Preventive deployments

Preventive military deployment can be defined as the deployment of military personnel with the intention of preventing a dispute (or, in some cases, an emerging threat) escalating into armed conflict. Such deployment could occur on one side of border-internal or national crises – at the request of the State feeling threatened or on both sides, or in inter-state disputes, at the request of one or more of the parties concerned.

---

[28] Council Common Position of 18 February 2002 concerning restrictive measures on Zimbabwe, (2002/145/CFSP), *OJEC* [2002] L 50/1, modified and extended by a Council Common Position of 18 February 2003, *OJEC* [2003] L 46/30, available at <http://www.mfsc.com.mt/mfsa/sanctions/313R.03.pdf>.

[29] The series of sanctions initiated against the Federal Republic of Yugoslavia (FRY) from 1998-2000 was a concerted effort to support external relations policy with the range of economic levers at the EU's disposal. The measures adopted included an embargo on the sale and supply to the FRY of petroleum and certain petroleum products; a ban on trade and investments; freezing the assets of close Miloševiæ associates in addition to visa restrictions; and a ban on international flights to and from Yugoslavia.

[30] Cf., Case T-306/01, *Aden and others* v. *Council and Commission*, pending.

Preventive deployment differs from traditional peacekeeping which typically supports or enforces a political solution that has already been reached. Preventive deployment, on the other hand, usually occurs without a settlement to govern the deployment of the multinational force. The tasks of a preventive deployment force may include:

- Acting as an interpositional force to forestall violence;
- Protecting the local delivery of humanitarian relief;
- Assisting local authorities to protect and offer security to threatened minorities, to secure and maintain essential services (water, power) and to maintain law and order.

Preventive deployment is a deterrent normally not designed to take on an attack. It provides conflicting parties with a solution that can be mutually acceptable and in some cases face-saving. Preventive deployment is most effective if it occurs along conflict fault lines; the clearest of these are international boundaries but they can also be internal conflict lines.

The United Nations Preventive Deployment Force (UNPREDEP) in the former Yugoslav Republic of Macedonia is a good example of a preventive deployment and the first mission in the history of United Nations peace-keeping to have a preventive mandate. UNPREDEP's unique preventive mandate was derived from several Security Council Resolutions since December 1992. The mission's aim was to prevent disputes in its mandate area from turning into serious conflicts. UNPREDEP used a variety of means to accomplish this task, including troop deployment, mediation, negotiation, conciliation and other peaceful means.

UNPREDEP contributed to stabilise the host country's security situation through patrolling its northern and western borders. The mission has been recognised as a significant instrument for facilitating dialogue, restraint and practical compromise between different segments of society. In the words of Secretary General K. Annan,[31] UNPREDEP was '*a demonstration of what can be accomplished in the realm of conflict prevention when good offices and troop deployment are put to effective use*'.

Although preventive deployment can – provided, it is done at the right time and with a clear mandate – be an effective form of peace-keeping and that results can be achieved even with a small, almost symbolic deployment of peace-keepers, this instrument also has a number of shortcomings.

Preventive deployment does not address a conflict's structural causes. A multinational force's stabilising and reassuring presence may push conflicting parties toward intransigence, delaying a political settlement. Additionally, preventive de-

---

[31] International Workshop, *An Agenda for Preventive Diplomacy: Theory and Practice* (Skopje, 16-19 October 1996).

ployment requires a high degree of political will on the part of troop-contributing nations and can be difficult to sell to domestic constituencies precisely because there is no crisis that appears to warrant the expense. This limits its use. Furthermore, preventive deployment can undermine conflict resolution if it is not linked to diplomatic activity and the preventive force might become involved in the conflict, often on the side of the weaker side. For many analysts, economic and in particular military means have a limited validity, even though they may have to be used when political and diplomatic tools fail to achieve the desired results.[32]

4.3   The EU and preventive military deployments

The initially exclusive economic and civilian nature of the European integration process limited *de facto* for many years the range of preventive-coercive means at the disposal of the EU in the political and economic area. Preventive military deployments should potentially be considered as new activity for the EU, to the placed in the broader context of the ESDP instruments. The ESDP is a relatively new component of the EU's CFSP. It was not until 1998, partly due to the Kososvo conflict and the realisation of Europe's dependence on the US in defence matters, that the Union seriously started to address its defence complement.

At a summit in Cologne in June 1999, EU leaders laid the foundation of the ESDP by agreeing that 'the EU must have the capacity for autonomous action, backed by the credible military forces, the means to decide to use them and the readiness to do so, in order to respond to international crisis without prejudice to actions by NATO'.

Subsequently, the Helsinki and Feira European Councils established that EU military capabilities should cover the 'full range of conflict prevention and crisis management tasks defined in the EU Treaty'. Although in the Treaty there are no agreed procedures for the use of preventive military deployments in most circumstances usually identified with the term, according to a number of commentators, the Cologne/Feira mandate includes the option of resorting to preventive military deployments by positioning forces along the borders of two states between which tension is rising or within a country when two or more sides oppose one another and the risk of violent conflict is evident.

To date, the only EU attempt to carry out an operation of this nature occurred in 1997. At the time, no agreement could be reached on the deployment of police assets to Albania as part of a stabilisation package requested by the OSCE Representative, even after the EU had informally agreed to send a high-level inspection mission which recommended the despatch of a multinational protection force. Ul-

---

[32] J. Leatherman, 'Making the Case for Cooperative Security', Book Review Essay, 31 *Cooperation and Conflict* (1996), pp. 129-142. On the other hand, the fact that political means, sometimes utilizing symbols and values, can seldom be used in isolation from economic and military instruments indicates a need to look at the interfaces of different strategies of influence.

timately, Italy obtained a UN Security Council mandate and implemented a stabilisation programme, Operation Alba, supported by a joint force of some 7,000 soldiers drawn from Austria, Denmark, France, Greece, Italy, Romania, Spain and Turkey.

It is difficult to anticipate how regularly the EU will resort to this instrument as a crisis response tool in the future. Nevertheless, it would be reasonable to affirm that it will be difficult to forge an agreement on preventive deployment where there are complex political circumstances in a country at risk. In the case of 'high-end' operations involving combat forces, EU preventive deployment of military forces is not likely to have its desired political impact without a clear determination by the EU and the participating Member States. Other reactive instruments such as the deployment of civilian police and measures taken in the field of the rule of law or non-military sanctions should precede military action, which is only to be used under extreme circumstances. And when resorting to military actions, ESDP should primarily be defined in terms of preventive defence – that is actions taken to prevent the conditions of conflict and to create conditions of peace.

4.4 Sanctions and preventive deployments as effective conflict prevention instruments

In spite of the efforts to limit the means and to clarify the messages of coercive diplomacy, it contains a risk of escalation, which can damage its original constructive purpose. Moreover, it is difficult to gain international acceptance for unilateral pre-emptive actions unless there is strong proof available that the target is a genuine threat to international peace and security.[33] Recently, it has been increasingly stressed that positive incentives are probably a more effective mode of influence than coercive punishments, although they may also be more expensive because their costs cannot be substituted. But coercive diplomacy can work, as it has been proved in the past and, on occasion, is truly the last resort to be activated in order to impede a crisis. Nevertheless, whenever resorting to negative or punitive measures, it should be borne in mind that these instruments:

- work more effectively if they are placed in a wider conflict prevention strategy. In the words of Alexander L. George, the founding father of the concept: 'whether coercive diplomacy will work in a particular case may depend on whether it relies solely on negative sanctions or combines threats with positive incentives and assurances'. A combination of carrots and sticks may achieve outcomes not obtainable solely by punishments or their threats;
- should contain pauses and controls that give the target time and opportunities to understand the preventive motives behind the tools used and the salient

---

[33] Richard N. Haas, 'Military Force. A User's Guide', 96 *Foreign Policy* (1994), pp. 21-37.

limits to honour if it wants to bring the preventive coercive action to an end. In addition, the terms of the preferred settlement of conflict must be clearly spelled out. This includes specific terms for ending the conflict, and provisions for their verification and enforcement to ensure that both parties abide by their commitments;

– appear to be more effective if applied in an instrumental and moderate way to achieve limited goals rather than used harshly and comprehensively to publicly humiliate the target.[34]

5. SHOULD THERE BE A CONSISTENT CLASSIFICATION OF CONFLICT PREVENTION INSTRUMENTS WITHIN THE EU (SHORT-TERM *v.* LONG-TERM, EU *v.* EC INSTRUMENTS, CIVIL *v.* MILITARY)?

Many conceptual categories can be used to examine all the existing instruments in the field of conflict prevention: passive/active, positive/negative, economic/legal/political/military, institutional stability/ physical security, etc.

In the case of the EU, the interest in contrasting between long-term and short-term and EC and EU instruments relates to the need to broadly consider the conflict cycle and the current EU institutional framework respectively. As the EU expands its fields of intervention to defence (ESDP) related areas, it also becomes necessary to address the role of the emerging military instruments as opposed to the civilian tools that the EU has been using since its inception. This also helps to clarify the roles of the different actors involved and the different elements relating to the decision-making process. Nevertheless, whatever the interest of categorising conflict prevention tools and activities might be, rigid distinctions should be avoided as they might be misleading and may hinder the development of all the possible synergies.

Many instruments can fall into different categories: thus, development cooperation can be a tool in a long-term peace building strategy through comprehensive aid programmes but can equally be activated in a short-term perspective by rapidly reprioritising funds. Similarly, civilian crisis management tools can be labelled as either EU or EC instruments depending on the funding source. A given instrument (e.g., electoral observation and assistance) can evolve from one category (Pillar II) to the other (Pillar I).

Alexander L. George has pointed out that theory and generic knowledge are usually more helpful in the diagnosis of specific problems than in providing prescriptions for action. Theory and knowledge may, however, contribute to policy prescriptions when couched in terms of conditional generalisations which iden-

---

[34] Iva Eland, 'Economic Sanctions as Tools of Foreign Policy', in D. Cortright and G.A. Lopez (eds.), *Economic Sanctions. Panacea or Peace-building in a Post-Cold War World?* (Boulder, Westview 1995), pp. 29-42.

tify: '(1) the conditions that favour successful use of each particular instrument and strategy and (2) other conditions that make success very unlikely'.

Beyond the categorisation of existing instruments, what ought to be borne in mind is that, ultimately, only 'multifaceted action',[35] i.e., the employment of several diverse instruments in a coordinated way, provides a basis for an effective strategy of conflict prevention. Thus, the key to an effective policy remains good coordination of both the instruments of prevention and the policies of the actors and structures which govern them. In the case of the EU, this is quite a formidable challenge considering the rather unique and complex institutional setting in which these different instruments operate and the fact that they must be used for partly new objectives that have only recently been incorporated in the area of preventing violent conflict (organised crime, terrorism, exploitation of natural resources, etc.).

Multifaceted action and the combination of existing instruments should be guided by a number of considerations:

–   Long-term, structural instruments can have a more significant impact on a comprehensive approach to conflict prevention than short-term ongoing/imminent crisis-oriented tools. The most successful peace-building strategy ever pursued by the EU has been the enlargement process. A proactive policy towards violent conflicts requires the EU to shift its focus from crisis management to conflict prevention, using primarily structural preventive measures.
–   The EU has endorsed an enlarged concept of security that transcends military security and an 'integrated' approach to conflict prevention. This concept entails the use of a combination of economic, political, legal and military instruments.
–   Military instruments can play a useful role in specific situations but ought to be considered as a last resort and be placed in a 'defence as a peace building factor' perspective. Moreover, military operations alone will achieve little beyond temporary containment of a situation unless the conditions for the pursuit of broader objectives by civil actors are created.
–   There is a need to match resources to ambitions. There should be a narrowing of focus and a visible sequencing in the development of instruments.
–   A balance should be found between devoting resources to developing generic

---

[35] Michael S. Lund, *Preventing Violent Conflicts. A Strategy for Preventive Action* (Washington, D.C., United States Institute of Peace Press 1996), pp. 85-86. The author considers that 'preventive diplomacy requires not just a strong enough combination of carrots and/or sticks but also the sum of a variety of actions and instruments to address the various facets of a dispute. These actions must be closely coordinated among the third parties participating in the preventive efforts'. Multifaceted action is one of the five 'more or less manipulable' factors that are often present in situations where emerging political disputes are handled through peaceful means. The other four are: third-party timing, support from major players to mediation efforts, moderate leadership of leaders of disputing groups and state autonomy.

frameworks for conflict prevention and resources devoted to preventing the outbreak of actual conflicts in specific countries and localities. Working on early warning mechanisms can be as effective or even more effective than addressing given crisis situations.

– All EU external tools – and not only those traditionally labelled as conflict prevention oriented – can play a valuable role in order to prevent or manage conflict. Conflict prevention should be mainstreamed across all sectors and activities of the EU.

– The use of conflict prevention instruments should not be limited to the economic sphere and regions closest to the EU. Beyond moral imperatives, in an increasingly interconnected world, there is a need to develop a peace-building strategy without geographical boundaries.

– Given the key role that Members States will continue to play in the area of external relations and particularly in the field of CFSP, ensuring good coordination between the instruments of the EU and those of the Member States individually, will constitute one of the key elements to success in this area.

ANNEX A

- **FRAMEWORKS OR PROCESSES THROUGH WHICH THE UNION MAY INFLUENCE THIRD COUNTRIES FOR THE PURPOSE OF CONFLICT PREVENTION**

  EU Membership perspective
  Contractual relationships
  Regional cooperation and stability
  Financial assistance
  Market access

- **ACTIVITIES AND MEASURES EMPLOYED BY THE UNION IN THE FIELD OF CONFLICT PREVENTION**

  EU diplomacy/political dialogue
  EU and Member States' participation and coordination in international organisations or
       forums
  Early warning
  Fact-finding
  Actions, contribution to or participation in organisations dealing with non-proliferation
       and arms destruction
  Humanitarian Assistance
  Support (financial and other) to electoral process, government, peace process, multiracial
       process, etc.
  Human rights promotion
  Security Institution building
  Fight against terrorism
  Monitoring
  Sanctions: general embargoes, arms embargoes, specific measures such as investment
       prohibition, the freezing of assets, restrictions on persons' movements, etc.
  Convoying of Humanitarian Aid
  Participation in structures implementing peace agreements
  Mine Action
  Action against proliferation of small arms and light weapons
  Police training and monitoring
  Border Control
  etc.

- **ACTORS AND INSTITUTIONS WHICH THE UNION CAN USE FOR CONFLICT PREVENTION**

  Presidency and Troika
  Secretary General/High Representative, Council Secretariat and PPEWU
  Commission
  Special Envoys and Special Representatives
  HOMs

ANNEX B

Use of EU conflict prevention instruments throughout the conflict cycle

A. Situation without obvious tension

Situation where a country is seemingly stable and largely quiet but where (structural) causes of potential conflict may be discerned.

Instruments: Targeted assistance, democracy-building, good governance and civil society, institution-building, political dialogue, etc.

B. Situation of tension

Situation where conflict in society becomes apparent and the gravity of which depends on certain events as well as existing political power.

Instruments: Political dialogue, sanctions, advocating of specific measures and/or solutions, deployment of observers, humanitarian/relief aid.

C. Open conflict

Situation of sustained fighting between organised forces, which often continues until a stalemate is reached.

Instruments: threat of sanctions, political dialogue, (advocating of) preventive military intervention, observer missions, support for peace initiatives, peace enforcement.

D. Post-conflict situation

Situation where there is no longer any organised armed violence and a cease-fire or peace agreement might or might not have been signed.

Instruments: demobilisation and disarmament, repatriation and reintegration, demining, post-conflict relief and humanitarian aid, confidence-building measures, conflict resolution initiatives, rebuilding government structures.

Chapter 6
THE INSTITUTIONAL AND FINANCIAL DIMENSIONS OF CONFLICT PREVENTION

by Simon Duke[1]

1. INTRODUCTION: WHAT IS CONFLICT PREVENTION IN THE EUROPEAN CONTEXT?

According to the Commission, conflict prevention (CP) is 'actions undertaken in the short term to reduce manifest tensions and/or to prevent the outbreak or recurrence of violent conflict'.[2] However, the development of CP, and ongoing thinking within the Commission, suggests that conflict prevention is in fact much more. The Commission refers to those instruments directly or indirectly relevant to CP as: development cooperation and external assistance, economic cooperation and trade policy instruments, humanitarian aid, social and environmental policies, diplomatic instruments such as political dialogue and mediation, as well as economic and other sanctions, and ultimately the new instruments of ESDP (including information gathering for anticipating potential conflict situations and monitoring international agreements).[3] In this case the problem is often that of deciding what does *not* fall under the rubric of conflict prevention. The pervasive nature of conflict prevention was also underlined by the Conflict Prevention Network (CPN) who urged that the 'concept must be integrated into *every* facet of EU activity' and 'mainstreamed into development and foreign policies, as well as into political dialogues from the lowest to the highest levels, into cultural exchanges, even into trade relationships'.[4]

In addition to the apparently all-encompassing reach of CP, there is also the question of time span. In spite of the fact that the Commission's working definition stresses the short term, the Commission also acknowledges the 'need to take

---

[1] Associate Professor. European Institute of Public Administration, Maastricht, the Netherlands.

[2] This definition, and others pertaining to conflict management, may be found at <http://europa.eu.int/comm/development/prevention/definition.htm>.

[3] Communication from the Commission on Conflict Prevention, COM (2001) 211 final, Brussels, 11 April 2001, p. 6.

[4] *Conflict Prevention, Crisis Management and the European Union: A CPN Commentary* (Berlin, Stiftung Wissenschaft und Politik (SWP), 23 February 2001), p. 2 (emphasis added).

V. Kronenberger and J. Wouters, eds., The European Union and Conflict Prevention
© 2004, T·M·C·ASSER PRESS, *The Hague, The Netherlands*

a long-term and genuinely integrated approach, which will address all elements of structural stability in countries at risk'.[5] In the Commission's important April 2001 communication on CP it was agreed that the long-term prevention efforts are those geared to project stability, while the short term concentrates on reacting quickly to nascent conflicts. The inclusion of 'short' and 'long' term aspects of CP also appeared in a joint report by the Commission and the Secretary General/ High Representative (SG/HR) to the 2000 Nice European Council.[6] More recently, Javier Solana presented a draft European Security Strategy to the European Council in Thessaloniki in June 2003, in which he observed that Europe 'faces new threats which are more diverse, less visible and less predictable'. This led him to conclude that 'conflict prevention and threat prevention cannot start too early'.[7] The conclusions of the Greek Presidency gave prominence to CP and those aspects that secure and defend regional and global security (the promotion of justice and sustainable development were specifically mentioned).[8]

2.   FROM CONCERN TO FIXED PRIORITY

As a concern, CP is relatively new to the EU – although it can legitimately be claimed that many activities of the Community in the 1970s and 1980s certainly had relevance to CP, even if it was not called that explicitly. The EU first grappled with CP explicitly in 1995 with reference to Africa, followed in 1997 by a resolution on CP in Africa.[9] Interestingly, CP awareness arose as a result of the efforts of the Commission's DG Development and not RELEX (External Relations). Based on these first efforts, we have to accept that, in practice, the EU already practised a broad approach to CP prior to the Commission's more recent communication and those of the SG/HR. The development of CFSP and ESDP over the course of the last decade or so has however changed the context, if not the meaning, of CP in the EU. This is manifest in two main ways. The first is the 'securitisation' of many of what were, until recently, assumed to be the type of programmes that one would expect of a pre-eminent 'civilian power'. The incorporation of so many instruments into the CP remit raises legitimate concerns of focus and selection.

The second issue is where CP hands over to crisis management (CM) and, bearing in mind that CP also applies to those efforts to prevent the recurrence of

---

[5] COM (2001) 211 final, p. 4.

[6] *Improving the coherence and effectiveness of EU action in the field of conflict prevention*, Report presented to the Nice European Council by the SG/HR and the Commission, Brussels, 30 November 2000, Doc. No. 14088/00.

[7] *A Secure Europe in a Better World*, speech by Javier Solana, EU High Representative for CFSP, to the European Council, Thessaloniki, S0138/03, 20 June 2003, pp. 4 and 11.

[8] Presidency Conclusions, Thessaloniki European Council, 19-20 June 2003, paragraph 54.

[9] See <http://europa.eu.int/comm/development/prevention/index_en.htm>

violence, when does it reappear in the post-crisis context?[10] Ideally, CP and CM should be a continuum. For analytical purposes, though, it creates problems since the main objective of this chapter is to consider the institutional aspects and financial aspects of CP and not CM as such. The focus on CP is also merited since the military aspects of CM (and to a lesser extent the civilian aspects of CM) have generally received more attention, whereas CP is less apparent to the European citizen (but not, one hopes, to a wider international audience). It is assumed therefore that there is no need to rehearse the CM institutions that are evolving in the CFSP/ESDP setting. The institutional linkages between CP and CM will however be noted.

The preliminary definitional points above have an important bearing on the discussion in this chapter, which is concerned with the institutional and financial aspects of EU CP. With regard to the short-term aspects of CP, the responsibility is clearly shared by the Council and the Commission. Their joint involvement goes back to the invitation extended to the Secretary General/High Representative (SG/HR) and the Commission at Feira under the Portuguese Presidency, where they were invited to submit proposals to improve the coherence and effectiveness of EU conflict prevention. A joint report was duly presented to the Nice European Council, with the recommendation that CP should be a 'fixed priority of EU external action' and that the EU should be more 'proactive and less reactive'.[11] The Commissioner for External Relations, Chris Patten, also noted the need to 'harness the strengths of the European Community in the service of European foreign policy' – thus underlining the clear need for consistency across the pillars.[12]

The horizontal sharing of EU CP responsibilities was borne out by the EU Programme for the Prevention of Violent Conflicts, adopted at the Göteborg European Council 15-16 June 2001, which called on 'all relevant institutions of the Union [to] mainstream conflict prevention within their areas of competence'.[13] The cross-pillar nature of the EU's CP efforts creates the obvious challenge of forging links, harmonising working and reporting practices, and maximising the effectiveness of CP with minimum delay and duplication. As will be explored later, it also creates serious issues when it comes to the financing of CP actions. A formidable set of challenges indeed.

---

[10] The terms 'nation building', 'state building' or 'post-conflict reconstruction/stabilisation' are often applied to post-crisis scenarios. Nevertheless, the specific mention by the Commission of efforts to stop the reoccurrence of violent conflict makes it a legitimate part of CP in the EU context.

[11] *Improving the coherence and effectiveness of EU action in the field of conflict prevention*, op. cit. n. 6.

[12] Quoted in S. Duke, *The EU and Crisis Management: Development and Prospects* (Maastricht, EIPA 2002), p. 209.

[13] *Presidency Conclusions*, Göteborg European Council, 15-16 June 2001, available at <http://ue.eu.int/en/info/eurocouncil/index.htm>.

Turning to the first task at hand, the institutional aspects of CP will be addressed in four sections:

i)   The first considers the *conflict prediction* aspects of CP. The emphasis here is more upon the Council, although the Commission's role is obviously important for the coherence of the EU's overall CP/CM efforts.
ii) The longer-term aspects of CP are primarily the responsibility of the Commission and its instruments. Since the focus is upon the institutional aspects, the main emphasis will be upon assessing the *coordination mechanisms* between the DGs involved.
iii) The Member States also play an important role in the EU's CP efforts. A brief assessment of *EU and Member State CP* is therefore appropriate.
iv) Lastly, the EU is not an island when it comes to CP since there are many other governmental and non-governmental organisations involved. Of interest to this section is how *EU CP measures are coordinated with the field actors*.

Following the examination of these four aspects of EU CP, an assessment of the potential changes introduced as a result of the Convention on the Future of Europe and the resultant Draft Treaty establishing a Constitution for Europe will be considered. The final institutional shape of EU CP will depend upon the Intergovernmental Conference (IGC) but it is already apparent that a number of recommendations, if accepted, could have quite far-fetching institutional effects on CP. For instance, the appointment of a President of the European Council, a Union Foreign Minister complemented by a European External Action Service, as well as the assumption by the EU of legal identity, could all have profound ramifications for the Union's international actions and profile. Whatever the final shape of the constitution and its institutional manifestations, it is unlikely that the horizontal responsibility for CP will be entirely assumed by the Commission. CP will therefore remain an inter-pillar activity with all of the political (and financial) tensions that have traditionally been associated with that.

The final section will consider the financial aspects of CP. Again, with definitional vagaries in mind, the amounts spent on CP are difficult to ascertain with any accuracy. It is nevertheless apparent that the amounts spent are less important that the way in which decisions on expenditure and disbursement are made. In this regard, there is ample room for concern, especially as the EU is assuming an active international profile which includes an increasing assumption of responsibility for a number of CP/CM actions.

2.1   Conflict prediction

The first phase of any effective conflict prevention is conflict *prediction* or, in EU parlance, early warning. The Commission works with the SG/HR to prepare a broad assessment of potential conflict issues which are then submitted to the EU General Affairs and External Relations Council at the start of each Presidency.[14] As has been noted, this procedure is likely to change in light of the generally agreed need to overhaul the cumbersome sixth-month rotating presidency system. The outcome of the 2004 IGC will determine what type of President, Foreign Minister, Commission Vice President and External Relations Commissioner, these assessments should be directed towards. At any rate, the assessment derives from a variety of sources within the Commission and the Council.

Within the Commission a variety of early warning mechanisms exist. In the first place, the Commission has developed indicators for the root causes of conflict. The early warning/root cause indicators have been developed mainly through the Conflict Prevention Network (CPN), initially backed by Michel Rocard, which was designed to provide the Commission with analyses of potential crises and trouble spots. The CPN is a 'network of independent research institutes, think tanks and NGOs that should assist the Commission to tap, rapidly and systematically, existing information and analysis on specific countries or issues.'[15] The CPN was, from 1997 until recently, coordinated by the Stiftung Wissenschaft und Politik (SWP) in Berlin, and it was through this network that much of the development of conflict indicators for the EU institutions was conducted.[16] The conflict indicators, or 'check-list of root causes of conflict', are widely distributed within the Commission, among the geographical desks, as well as to the External Service.[17] The Conflict Prevention Associates (CPA) evolved partially from the CPN in 2002 which, like its successor, undertakes policy-oriented research aimed at providing policy-makers with enhanced CP tools and practice.[18]

The Commission's 128 delegations, of which 123 are country or region based and the remainder missions to international organisations, are in many senses the eyes and ears of the Commission's early warning mechanism. The delegations report back regularly to the desk officers as well as to the SG/HR with the overall objective of indicating to EU decision-making bodies which countries or regions are at risk of conflict, or the re-emergence thereof. The information coming in from the delegations, combined with the expertise of the desk officers, is then

---

[14] The General Affairs and External Relations Council was, until the conclusions of the Spanish Presidency in June 2001, known as the General Affairs Council.

[15] João de Deus Pinheiro, 'Can EU development assistance contribute to peace'. Contribution to CESD/ISIS Conference on 'The Future of the EU's Security Policy', Brussels, 24 September 1998, available at <http://europa.eu.int/comm/speeches/en/980924.htm>.

[16] Relations between the SWP and the Commission became increasingly strained, with the result that the collaboration with the SWP was concluded at the end of 2001. A revised version of the CPN will nevertheless continue. For details see <http://www.swp-berlin.org/cpn/main/new.htm>.

[17] For a summary of the conflict indicators involved, see *European Commission Check-List for Root Causes of Conflict*, at <http://europa.eu.int/comm/external_relations/cpcm/cp/list.htm>. See also, chapter 1 in this volume.

[18] See <http://www.conflict-prevention-associates.org/>.

consolidated into a Country Strategy Paper (CSP) or its regional counterpart (RSP). Since 2001 considerable effort has been made to routinely include conflict prevention assessments in the CSP/RSPs. Within the CSPs more emphasis is now being placed on 'cross-cutting' issues (such as the Kimberley process aimed at establishing controls for the import or export of rough diamonds), early warning mechanisms and cooperation with other international organisations. The CP elements within these reports also apply to post-conflict situations where the emphasis is placed on 'DDR' programmes (demobilisation, disarmament and re-integration).

The reporting process also has the effect of enabling the EU to ensure that its policies are targeted towards potential risk areas (which, in most cases, implies Commission programmes but also has relevance for EU Member States' bilateral programmes). The assessment of potential conflict indicators will eventually be made in all CSPs. Although it is early days, desk officers and delegations alike 'express satisfaction with the usefulness of this tool and it has been an effective means for raising awareness of the conflict prevention approach'.[19] There is nevertheless plenty of work remaining to be done in 'mainstreaming' CP practices since reporting and monitoring practices still have to be refined, as does the mainstreaming of CP into a 'horizontal issue in all common or sectoral policies of the Union'.[20]

With a few exceptions, the delegations are often small in size and many of the *fonctionnaires* are technical or assistance specialists. The scope of the CSP/RSPs go well beyond this to include issues concerning the legitimacy of the state, the operation of civil society, relations between identity groups, the soundness of economic management to arbitration procedures. The type of experience necessary to identify, communicate and understand what may be quite subtle indicators has been compounded by the lack of a systematic professional and training structure for RELEX (until recently those coming back from delegations could go back to any part of the Commission and there was no compunction for officials in RELEX in the A-grade to serve overseas). The lack of a career structure and supporting professional training for the External Service meant that, in many cases, vital depth of knowledge was lost.

On the positive side, the delegations also employ locally engaged staff, whose knowledge could be of considerable importance. Knowing what to look for is obviously a challenge for the delegations, as well as for the desk officers, and requires training. This is currently being developed through the Conflict Prevention Unit (within DG RELEX) and in conjunction with other organisations such as the OSCE (see below). Conflict prevention teams may in future enhance early warning mechanisms within the Commission. These teams will be drawn from a wide

---

[19] 'One Year On: The Commission's Conflict Prevention Policy', March 2002, at <http://europa.eu.int/comm/external_relations/cpcm/cp/rep.htm>.
[20] Ibid.

variety of backgrounds and they will be instrumental in reaching an overall CP picture for the country or region in question, as well as assisting in the development of medium-term CP strategies.

The other interesting point to note in passing, regarding the role of the delegations, is that the incorporation of CP indicators in CSP/RSPs takes the delegations into an inherently more political sphere. This factor, along with the recommendation of the Convention's Working Group on Legal Identity for the EU to be accorded legal identity and for the creation of a European External Action Service, could have a significant broadening effect on the mandate, structure and size of the delegations (see below). It will also increase the overlap with what is traditionally seen as CFSP's more political concentration.

Based on the CSP/RSPs, the next stage is to ascribe countries a risk-assessment 'score' and those that appear higher on the list are placed on a confidential 'watch list'. This list is obviously subject to constant revision. The preoccupation at any one time is nevertheless reasonably easy to predict by monitoring the declarations or statements emanating from the Commission, Presidency or the General Affairs and External Relations Council.

The Commission's conflict prediction role is complemented by the Council's activities. The Policy Planning and Early Warning Unit (Policy Unit) is a small body, of twenty-five, that falls under the responsibility of the SG/HR. It was established by a declaration attached to the Amsterdam Treaty.[21] The unit, which draws its personnel from the General Secretariat, the Member States and the Commission, is divided into seven task forces, four of which are regional in orientation, one concentrates on ESDP, one for administration and security, and the final one for liaison with the Joint Situation Centre (SITCEN) within the Council Secretariat. The role of the Commission and the Member States are significant since the aim is to ensure 'full coherence' with the Union's external economic and development policies. The tasks of the unit include, as the name suggests, 'timely assessment and early warning of events or situations which may have significant repercussions for the Union's CFSP, including *potential* political crises' (emphasis added).

The Commission and the Member States are committed to 'assist the policy planning process by providing, to the fullest extent possible, relevant information, including confidential information'.[22] The fact that the Policy Unit reports to the SG/HR, along with the *political* aspects of the delegation's reporting, means that there is a need for constant exchange of information between the Secretariat and Commission on CP. The representation of the Commission at numerous levels in CFSP, along with amicable relations between the Commissioner for External Relations, Chris Patten, and the SG/HR, Javier Solana, means that there is a regular exchange of information. There are, though, two problems with the Policy Unit.

---

[21] Declaration No. 6, on the establishment of a Policy Planning and Early Warning Unit.
[22] Ibid., paragraph 5.

The first problem stems from the considerable expectations created by the mandate and the small size of the unit. This results in a 'lack of capacity to undertake analysis on the basis of information received from a wide range of conflict-affected regions, tending rather to focus on areas of immediate strategic interest to the EU. There is a real danger that it will be overloaded by the current focus on Afghanistan, Central Asia and the Middle East at the expense of attention on regions such as Africa'.[23] The obvious solution is therefore to increase the size of the Policy Unit so that routine, in-depth monitoring is possible without chronic overload.

The second problem, by no means only confined to the Policy Unit, is that CP relies heavily on open sources. The lack of an autonomous EU intelligence source for CP and crisis management is a potential drawback and has led to demands for more formal intelligence sharing arrangements. The possible exception to this point is the Satellite Centre in Torrejon, Spain. The centre was originally under the Western European Union (WEU) but became an Agency of the EU in July 2001.[24] The centre, as suggested by Jacques Chirac, could be the underpinning of 'closer cooperation between European Member States [of the EU] who are willing to contribute to it. It could later become the foundation for an autonomous European intelligence capability'.[25] Although the level of military intelligence sharing between the Council Secretariat and the Member States has increased since '9-11', there is still a discernible reluctance to share intelligence on a systematic basis.

Enhanced links between the EU Military Staff's (EUMS) intelligence branch (as well as the Europol anti-terrorist task force) and the Policy Unit might also improve CP generally. The EUMS is divided into five divisions, under the Director-General of the EUMS and his deputy. Aside from situation assessment and strategic planning, the EUMS's role includes early warning. In this regard, the role of the intelligence division is significant. The Intelligence division falls under a Dutch one star general (the Director-General and Deputy being a French three star and a Belgian two star respectively), with a German deputy in charge of Policy issues, an Irish officer in charge of requirements and an Austrian officer in charge of the Production branch.[26] As has been noted, the exchange of intelli-

---

[23] *Putting Conflict Prevention into Practice: Priorities for the Spanish and Danish EU Presidencies*, Joint report by Intermon Oxfam, International Alert and Saferworld, (European Platform for Conflict Prevention and Transformation and the European Peace-building Liaison Office, January 2002), p. 24 available at <http://www.international-alert.org/publications.htm#eu>.

[24] For a comment on the transformation and the legal status of the centre, see V. Kronenberger, 'La naissance d'établissements publics de l'Union européenne: réflexions à propos de l'institut d'études de sécurité et du centre satellitaire', 3 *Europe* (2002), pp. 5-7.

[25] Jacques Chirac, 'La Politique Étrangère et de Défense de L'Union Européenne: Un Projet Fondamental pour l'Europe', 8 *Les Dossiers de Abécédaire parlementaire: L'Europe de la défense* (2002), p. 19.

[26] The four other divisions in the EUMS are Policy and Plans, Operations and Exercises, Logistics and Resources and Communications and Information.

gence between the Member States is in most respects wanting, except for military intelligence where there has been an improvement since '9-11'.

Since the definitions of CP also include efforts to prevent the *recurrence* of violent conflict, several other early warning 'institutions' are relevant. In the specific case of the Western Balkans, the EU Monitoring Mission (EUMM) can monitor what is happening on the ground, gather information and assist with analysis.[27] The EUMM is tasked by the SG/HR, but the Council may also elaborate upon its mandate. The EUMM is comprised of around 120 international monitors and 75 locally engaged personnel and is headquartered in Sarajevo. The unarmed members of the EUMM monitor a broad range of political and security issues, as well as border monitoring, inter-ethnic questions and refugee returns. The EUMM reports to the Council through the SG/HR (and is thus considered more of a CFSP instrument). The EUMM also coordinates closely with other international organisations (such as the OSCE's Kosovo Verification Mission).

The Special Representatives, of which there are currently seven, are appointed with a mandate for specific countries or areas.[28] Although they are often appointed to post-crisis countries or regions, they clearly have an important role to play in preventing the recurrence of violent conflict. Their mandates, at present, are not only circumscribed by the reporting mechanisms to Brussels, but the CP elements of their posts are not fully exploited. The provision of clear and comprehensive mandates could assist significantly in enhancing the EU CP capacity.

2.2   Longer-term aspects of conflict prevention

The primary, but not exclusive, responsibility for the longer-term aspects of CP, outlined above, centres on the Commission since the main tools are economic in nature. The Council nevertheless plays a valuable role in the political sphere. The Commission has the right of initiative in the first pillar and this right is shared with the Member States in CFSP. This obviously puts the onus on consistency and coordinated responses which, as Patten has observed, is not always the case:

'There is an unresolved tension between the intergovernmentalism and Community powers (e.g., in mixed agreements). The welcome creation of the CFSP High Representative doubling as the Council Secretary General has not helped to resolve this tension. Indeed it has given rise to some new institutional complications. It may also have increased the tendency for CFSP to usurp the functions which should be the responsibility of the Commission (e.g., the EC Monitoring Mission to the Balkans, which was

---

[27] The EUMM originally started life as the European Community Monitoring Mission (ECMM) in July 1991 and became the EUMM in December 2000 as a result of a Joint action (2000/811/ CFSP).

[28] The Special Representatives are Soren Jessen-Petersen (FYROM), Francesc Vendrell (Afghanistan), Lord Ashdown (Bosnia and Herzegovina), Erhard Busek (Stability Pact for South East Europe), Heikki Talvitie (South Caucasus) and Mare Otte (Middle East Peace Process).

dreamt up by CFSP and then left as an expensive baby on the Commission's door-step)'.[29]

The Council's role, as observed above, is primarily oriented towards CM, although there are institutions with CP relevancy. The Policy Unit has already been discussed. With reference to longer-term CP, the Presidency (operating, if need be, as the *troika*) or the General Affairs and External Relations Council may adopt CFSP instruments that will communicate the Union's position. In addition the Political and Security Committee (PSC), established as a permanent institution by the Council on 22 January 2001, has as one of its duties the development of a 'consistent European approach to crisis management and conflict prevention'.[30] The PSC also keeps track of the 'international situation in areas falling within CFSP, help define policies by drawing up "opinions" for the Council, either at the request of the Council or at its own initiative, and monitor the implementation of agreed policies'. In a crisis, the PSC is the 'Council body which deals with crisis situations and examines all the options that might be considered as the Union's response within the single institutional framework and without prejudice to the decision-making and implementation procedures of each pillar'.[31]

The Council and the PSC's roles are primarily framed in terms of responses to an existing 'crisis situation' but the ability to respond to a broad range of international events that fall within the second pillar, certainly opens up the scope for declarations, common positions or even joint actions that may have broad implications for the Commission in the CP context. Since the Commission is represented on the PSC, the response to a looming crisis is unlikely in most cases to represent only the interests of the Member States, to the exclusion of the Community. The role of the SG/HR is obviously also of significance to longer-term CP since it is he, more often than not, who is seen as the public face of the EU. Attempts at diplomatic intercession are therefore likely to rely heavily on the High Representative and, in future, the Union's Foreign Minister.

It is important to acknowledge the role that CFSP plays in CP but, when it comes to longer-term CP, its role is limited. This is mainly due to rather obvious factors, such as CFSP's limited budget (discussed in more detail below) which is extremely modest compared to *billions* of Euros that the Commission oversees that could be used for CP-related activities. The Commission's ability to assess and respond to brewing crisis scenarios and, most importantly, its ability to harness the reporting and observation capacities of the Community's External

---

[29] *Bulletin Quotidien Europe*, 'Communication from Chris Patten to the European Commission aimed at Engaging a Debate on the EU's External Relations', No. 2193, 10 June 2000, paragraph 5.
[30] *OJEC* [2001] L 27/2.
[31] Ibid., p. 3.

Service makes its role paramount.[32] Although new institutions within the Commission have been created with a specific CP mandate, the emphasis has been on the ability of the Commission to adapt its existing structures and practices to CP roles.[33] The Commissioner for External Relations, Chris Patten, was very quick to see the potential to 'mainstream' CP to a wide variety of programmes and activities which include regional cooperation programmes – CARDS, MEDA, ALA, PHARE, TACIS and the Cotonou Agreement – as well as the pre-accession strategies and stabilisation, association and cooperation agreements with third countries.[34]

The scope of longer-term CP is spread across a number of programmes, as indicated, as well as at least four Directorate-Generals (DGs) and six external components. The Commissioner for External Relations, Chris Patten, is responsible for the coordination of all of the Commission's external activities and Commission delegations in non-member countries. He is also responsible for the Commission's CFSP linkages and chairs the board of EuropeAid, although actual decisions regarding EuropeAid are shared with DG Development. The Commissioner for Development and Humanitarian Aid, Poul Nielson, bears responsibility for relations with the African, Caribbean and Pacific (ACP) countries and is also responsible for the EC Humanitarian Aid Office (ECHO), which coordinates the Commission's humanitarian aid programmes. Commissioner Pascal Lamy heads the Trade DG, with broad responsibility for negotiating and concluding international trade agreements. Finally, Günther Verheugen heads the Enlargement DG that oversees relations with the candidates.

How harmonious is this collaboration? At the moment the response has to be 'not particularly' since the Commission suffers from the lack of an integrated CP strategy. There have been a number of suggestions to improve this based on the findings of the relevant Working Groups within the Convention and the proposals to create a European External Action Service (linking elements of the current RELEX to the Council and national diplomatic representations). For the moment, though, the Commission will have to struggle on in the absence of an integrated external service. What does this imply in practice?

The organisation of RELEX is broadly speaking along geographical lines, with a few exceptions (such as relations with international organisations, CFSP and administration). Since the restructuring of DG RELEX in 1998-2000 the Conflict Prevention and Crisis Management Unit is the only dedicated CP unit in

---

[32] The External Service comprises the 128 Commission delegations in third countries or to organisations. The delegations are, technically, only entitled to represent the Commission although the proto-diplomatic structure and titles employed by delegations, often lead them to be identified as 'EU' missions.

[33] See *Communication from the Commission on Conflict Prevention*, COM (2001) 211 final, 11 April 2001.

[34] Speech by Chris Patten, 'Debate on conflict prevention/crisis management', European Parliament Plenary, Strasbourg, 14 March 2001, SPEECH/01/123.

the Commission. Prior to the restructuring, a small unit had addressed CP issues in the ACP countries but this aspect has been transferred to DG Development, although plans are afoot to increase the competence of the Conflict Prevention Unit to include some ACP issues. However, it remains the case that one of the most volatile areas in the world (Africa) is not an area of concentration for RELEX. The danger of Africa being under-represented in the EU's CP efforts may, as has already been noted, have been enhanced by '9-11' and the subsequent focus on Afghanistan, Central Asia and the Middle East, although *Operation Artemis* in the Democratic Republic of the Congo from June to September 2003 may have focussed more attention on broader issues of peace and stability on the continent. The emphasis in the Commission's aid and assistance programmes may not always reflect CP priorities either. For instance, in contrast to Central and Eastern Europe where there are relatively few crisis-related concerns but substantial assistance programmes, the Mediterranean only has two relatively small sections in two directorates addressing their affairs. The small size of the staff also meant that the majority of the (€ 1.9 billion for 2001) MEDA budget was unused.[35] DG RELEX also lacks senior experts on Israel and the Mashrek,[36] the Maghreb[37] and region-wide issues. Following '9-11' efforts are underway to correct this imbalance.

The restructuring of DG Development, DG RELEX and the establishment of EuropeAid, reforms in aid programming, country and regional support strategies all provide the potential for 'mainstreaming' CP within a broad range of programmes.[38] However, this is a process that has its risks since, as one report observes:

'It is possible that, despite the best efforts of the crisis management unit in DG Relex, mainstreaming conflict prevention will receive less priority in DG Development. The split of responsibilities for the development of country strategies and policy and the programming and implementation process between EuropeAid, DG Relex and DG Development also have the potential to hinder the process of mainstreaming conflict prevention 'downstream' within sectoral and geographical units and at a delegation level where programme development and implementation takes place'.[39]

---

[35] Relevant expertise is in Directorate F, DG RELEX, and Directorate B of EuropeAid. Only two of the five full-time posts in the former are filled while the latter has roughly 100 officials overseeing 8,000 contracts in 12 different countries. See Simon Coss, 'Med states treated as poor relations for too long', *European Voice*, 11-17 October 2001, p. 9.

[36] Egypt, Jordan, Palestinian Authority, Lebanon and Syria.

[37] Algeria, Morocco and Tunisia.

[38] It should be noted that major changes in the EU's external services are likely due to proposals advanced in the Convention on the Future of Europe to create a European External Action Service.

[39] *Putting Conflict Prevention into Practice: Priorities for the Spanish and Danish EU Presidencies,* 2002, op. cit. n. 23, pp. 23-24.

The role of the Commission has been hampered not only by structural issues but also the ineffective administration of aid and assistance, overly bureaucratic procedures and long delays.[40] These shortcomings were acknowledged by the Commission in its White Paper on Reforming the Commission as well as its May 2000 *Reform of the Management of External Assistance*.[41] Five innovations were set into motion as a result of the Commission's restructuring that have a direct bearing on CP.

First, the excessively slow and bureaucratic administration of aid and assistance was obviously detrimental to CP/CM efforts. A Council regulation of 26 February 2001 addressed this with the creation of a Rapid Reaction Mechanism (RRM) which was designed to allow the Community to 'respond in a rapid, efficient and flexible manner, to situations of urgency or crisis or to the emergence of crisis'.[42] Although more an instrument than an institution, it is nevertheless worth noting. The fund (of €20 and €25 million for 2001 and 2002 respectively) will enable short-term (up to six months) interventions to be carried out immediately prior to, during, or after crises.[43] The RRM is designed to pave the way for longer-term assistance programmes in the context of CP/CM and is not intended to trespass on ECHO's humanitarian role, but to assist the stability of civic structures. It has been used in the Former Yugoslav Republic of Macedonia, Afghanistan and the Democratic Republic of the Congo. Part of the significance of the RRM lies in the fact that it allows the full range of EU sectoral and geographical competencies to be used when, in nearly all cases (with the exception of Cotonou which has a clause on 'peace building'), there is no specific provision for CP in bilateral or regional agreements.

Second, the issue of coordination in crisis scenarios had also surfaced on a number of occasions, especially at headquarter level. The establishment of a Conflict Prevention and Crisis Management Unit and, within that, a Crisis Management Cell (CMC), is intended to enhance the coordination of various Community initiatives. The CMC provides the logical point of contact for SITCEN in the Council's Policy Unit which operates on a 24-7 basis and is a joint civilian-military centre. The SITCEN monitors global hotspots and executes early warning and support functions for the High Representative. The SITCEN is also a common platform for collecting information from national intelligence, military intelligence and national reports. However, to complicate matters, the SITCEN can also establish an ad hoc Crisis Management Cell within the Council Secretariat to address the everyday aspects of CM.

---

[40] *Special Report No. 21/2000 on the management of the Commission's external aid programmes*, European Communities Court of Auditors, *OJEC* [2001] C 57/1.

[41] *White Paper on Reforming the Commission*, COM (2000) 200 final, 5 April 2000.

[42] Article 1 of Council Regulation (EC) No. 381/2001 of 26 February 2001 creating a rapid-reaction mechanism, *OJEC* [2001] L 57/5.

[43] The RRM was used in Afghanistan, the Democratic Republic of the Congo and FYROM in 2001.

Third, coordination was further enhanced by the creation of the EuropeAid Cooperation Office on 1 January 2001. The office is designed to speed up the implementation of Commission development and assistance projects and to simplify the procedures involved.[44] The EuropeAid office coordinates development projects on behalf of both DG RELEX and DG Development, which are funded from the EC budget and the European Development Fund (EDF) and collectively account for around 10% of worldwide investment in development.

Fourth, ECHO was created in 1992 and has existed for much of its existence to date under Emma Bonino (1994-99). It is primarily responsible for the coordination of humanitarian aid programmes, disaster relief and support for disaster preparedness action, operating mainly through Framework Partnership Agreements (FPAs) with international organisations and over 200 NGOs. Almost 69% of its funding was channelled through NGOs in 2000.[45] As with other aid and assistance programmes, ECHO has been beset by chronic delays in the transferral of humanitarian aid (especially when compared to other agencies like USAID) and occasional instances of fraud. It has also suffered from mission creep, away from its humanitarian assistance role, into more political roles (especially in post-crisis reconstruction). Criticisms have also been voiced regarding the high percentage of support awarded to European countries (primarily Albania, FYROM and Yugoslavia). Following the creation of the EuropeAid Cooperation Office in 2001 the bulk of the aid and assistance projects are now handled through this office, leaving ECHO with the clearer goal of providing short-term humanitarian assistance. However, there is still need for further coordination of effort between ECHO and other instruments (such as the RRM) as well as the difficulties of making cool assessments of need in crisis scenarios that are often heavily politicised.[46]

Finally, the CP and CM tasks of the Commission also rely heavily upon the External Service for information and first hand coordination. The emphasis now is upon deconcentration of the External Service which means, in practical terms, the transfer of responsibilities to all delegations managing aid by the end of 2003 (86 delegations in all).[47] The deconcentration exercise will also involve additional posts, infrastructure reforms in the External Services, the reallocation of personnel to the delegations, the creation of a 'deconcentration network' within EuropeAid and the creation of a Harmonised Operational Deconcentration Concept. Deconcentration will eventually be applied to all External Services by the

---

[44] It should be noted that EuropeAid does not handle pre-accession programmes (DG Enlargement), humanitarian assistance (ECHO), CFSP or RRM payments.

[45] *The European Humanitarian Aid Office (ECHO): Crisis Response in the Grey Lane*, IGC EU Brief, 26 June 2001 (Brussels: International Crisis Group, 2001), p. 3.

[46] For a thought-provoking assessment of ECHO, see *The European Humanitarian Aid Office (ECHO): Crisis Response in the Grey Lane*, op. cit. n. 45.

[47] See *Communication from the Commission to the Council and the European Parliament: The Development of the External Service*, COM (2001) 381 final, 3 July 2001.

end of 2004. Deconcentration will be accompanied by a parallel process of regionalisation, which involves the regrouping in one Delegation of a 'significant number of qualified officials giving it adequate means to service the Countries to which the regional Head of Delegation is accredited'.[48] The effects of this on CP are uncertain but, in principle, deconcentration should strengthen the role of the delegations while regionalisation may give them the depth they require to carry out the increasing number of tasks that befall them, including conflict assessments.

The longer-term aspects of EU CP therefore call, once again, for close collaboration between the Council and Commission and, when it comes to funding, with the European Parliament. Further reforms, adaptations and innovations may be expected, especially as a result of the Convention and the Draft Treaty establishing a Constitution for Europe (see below), but it is evident that the range of CP activities currently tends to be generic rather than part of an integrated strategy with clear prioritisation. The welcome prominence given to CP by Javier Solana in his outline for a EU Security Strategy to the Thessaloniki European Summit, may also assist in the prioritisation process so that CP becomes a 'fixed priority' in deed and not only word.

2.3 Conflict prevention and the Member States

The EU Member States are involved at a number of levels, some of which have already been mentioned above. This short section will not reiterate the involvement of the EU Member States (and indeed candidates) in the Council and the various CP and CM institutions. The main point to be stressed in relation to the Member States is the importance of sharing information in order to maximise effectiveness. In some specific areas, such as the fight against terrorism or organised crime, the exchange of relevant information is already well established. With regard to CP specifically, there would seem to be a need for improvement.

The sharing of information on CP between the EU and the Member States was supposed to be facilitated in a number of ways. One idea was to establish an Electronic Bulletin Board to connect the geographical desks in the Commission to their counterparts in the Member States. The concentration of resources on the development of the RELEX Crisis Room (see above) means that little progress has been made on the Board. The publication of the final version of the CSPs on the Commission's web site is nevertheless a commendable way of sharing information beyond the Member States with a variety of interested parties (NGOs, academics and so forth).

The Commission's own verdict on the sharing of information indicates that it is clearly the Member States who need to improve the exchange of information:

---

[48] Ibid.

'It remains the case that despite the injunction in the Göteborg Programme that there should be a mutual exchange of CSPs and the Member States' equivalent documents, the flow of information has tended to be one-way; few, if any, Member States have volunteered to share their national strategies with each other or with the Commission'.[49]

The exchange of information between the EU and the Member States is of importance since this underpins other forms of cooperation, such as the framework agreements with Member States for the deployment of civilian personnel in CM operations. The expansion of the EU's civilian CM role in the couple of years also highlights the importance of joint training and exercises between the Member States and with the EU.[50] Although these points apply primarily to CM, the same need for information sharing and joint training applies with equal validity to CP.

Finally, the role of the Member States in CP will again be influenced heavily by the outcome of the Convention. In particular, the adaptation of the role of the SG/HR will be significant *vis-à-vis* the Commissioner for External Relations. The appointment of a President of the Council or a 'Union Foreign Minister', who should incorporate the current role of the SG/HR, will enhance the intergovernmental aspects of CP and CM and thus the onus on collaboration between the Member States, the EU and the Community.

2.4 EU conflict prevention and field actors

International organisations, regional actors and NGOs have become increasingly important for CP and CM. The EU collaborates with a wide variety of actors, most notably the UN, the Council of Europe and the OSCE, regional actors such as Mercosur, the African Union and the ASEAN regional forum, as well as NGOs such as Oxfam and Saferworld. The benefits and challenges of this collaboration are discussed in Part III of this volume. The important point here is to understand the institutional coordination mechanisms within the EU.

The EU's relations with the UN have only been intensified fairly recently, with a series of meetings between the Troika and the UN Secretary General (UNSG). The UN is considered to be a 'key partner' in CP.[51] The EC and the UN signed a framework agreement in 1999 and it supports the Trust Fund for Preventative Action which is designed to strengthen the preventative capacity of the UNSG and his early warning capacities. The Commission also exchanges its CSPs with the UN's own Common Country Assessments. In June 2001 an agree-

---

[49] *One Year On: the Commission's Conflict Prevention Policy*, Commission, March 2002, at <http://europa.eu.int/comm/external_relations/cpcm/cp/rep.htm>.

[50] Concrete proposals for the administration of common courses and training were presented to the Member States at a conference in Madrid in March 2002.

[51] COM (2001) 211 final, p. 26.

ment was signed between the EU and UN on crisis prevention and crisis management which, amongst other things, agreed that, 'The Council underlines the commitment of the EU as well as of its Member States to contribute to the objectives of the UN in conflict prevention and crisis management, noting the United Nations' primary responsibility for the maintenance of international peace and security'.[52] The agreement sets out a 'platform for the intensified cooperation by facilitating guidance, continuity and coherence at all levels'.

The EC has maintained delegations (in New York and Geneva) to the UN since 1974 and it enjoys observer status at the General Assembly and many of the specialised agencies. The EU is also unique in that it is the only non-state party to around fifty multilateral agreements. France and the United Kingdom are also permanent members of the UN Security Council and, as such, carry considerable weight. The question of whether, in the light of the Convention Working Group on Legal Identity's recommendations, there will be pressure to have alternative representation in the UN Security Council may resurface. More generally, the issue of how the EU and the Member States are represented at international organisations (since it is inconsistent at present) may also arise.

The OSCE regards itself as 'a primary organisation for the peaceful settlement of disputes within its region and as a key instrument for early warning, conflict prevention, crisis management and post-conflict rehabilitation'.[53] The Commission has a 'continuing and permanent' dialogue with the OSCE Chair as well as the Secretariat.[54] The Commission cooperates with the Conflict Prevention Centre in Vienna where members of the Conflict Prevention Unit (DG RELEX) have been trained since 2001 on the Rapid Expert Assistance and Cooperation Teams (REACT) system. In addition to a number of joint activities in the Balkans and the Caucasus, the Commission also supported a Regional EU Conference on Conflict Prevention in August 2002 to which the OSCE, UN, Council of Europe and others were invited.[55]

The Council's coordination with the field actors tends to apply more to CM, although the coordination mechanisms could have applicability to CP. The two central actors are the PSC and the Committee for the Civilian Aspects of Crisis Management (CIVCOM), established on 22 January 2001 and 16 June 2000 respectively. Amongst the functions of the PSC is that of exercising 'political and strategic direction of crisis management operations'.[56] The PSC is the linchpin of

---

[52] *EU-UN cooperation in conflict and crisis management*, Annex: Draft Council conclusions on EU-UN cooperation in Conflict Prevention and Crisis Management, 6 June 2001, Brussels, CL01-021EN.

[53] Charter for European Security, OSCE, Istanbul, November 1999 at <http:///osce.istanbul-summit.org/charter_for_european_security.htm>. See further on the OSCE in this volume, chapter 18 (E. Bakker).

[54] COM (2001) 211 final, p. 27.

[55] See <http://www.ud.se/inenglish/projects/partners_ip/>.

[56] See Article 25(2) of the Treaty on European Union.

EU CM and, as such, it coordinates the civilian and military instruments and co-operates closely with CIVCOM, COREPER and the EU Military Committee and Military Staff. There is also provision for the SG/HR to chair the PSC, with the agreement of the Presidency, in crises.

CIVCOM reports to COREPER formally but, in practice, the link with the PSC is of greater importance. CIVCOM's role is to give information, formulate options and give advice to the relevant Council bodies. It is currently developing an inventory of resources required for non-military CM and CP within EU organisations as well as within the Member States. This inventory includes a database for judicial and penal personnel, civilian administration experts, survival and civil protection experts, all of whom should be available at short notice to support EU operations, those of other organisations or NGOs. CIVCOM will also be instrumental in establishing selection and training procedures as well as liaison with other bodies such as the OSCE and the Council of Europe.

3. CONFLICT PREVENTION AND THE DRAFT TREATY ESTABLISHING A CONSTITUTION FOR EUROPE

The deliberations of the Convention on the Future of Europe led to the presentation of a Draft Treaty establishing a Constitution for Europe to the Thessaloniki European Council in mid-June 2003.[57] The draft Constitution is notable in several aspects in so far as CP is concerned.

The first notable development is that 'conflict prevention' is specifically mentioned in the treaty, whereas before it was not but was assumed to be incorporated as an integral part of CFSP which covers 'all areas of foreign and security policy'.[58] The Petersberg tasks, currently Article 17 of the Treaty establishing the European Union, have also been expanded in the draft constitution to include, explicitly, CP.[59] Moreover, CP is mentioned in the context of an overall common security and defence policy, thus stressing the need for close linkage between CP and other aspects of CM.

The second innovation is the institutional arrangements that will affect CP as well as other areas of CFSP. The main change is the recommendation that an EU Minister for Foreign Affairs, incorporating the current roles of the SG/HR and the Commissioner for External Relations, should be appointed.[60] The Foreign Minister, who shall also be a Vice-President of the Commission shall be 'responsible there for handling external relations and for coordinating other aspects of

---

[57] The version referred to, however, is that of 18 July 2003, CONV 850/03.

[58] *Draft Treaty establishing a Constitution for Europe*, CONV 850/03, 18 July 2003, Article I-40 (1), *OJEC* [2003] C 169/1.

[59] Ibid., Article III-210 (1).

[60] Ibid., Article III-197.

the Union's external action'.[61] The EU Minister for Foreign Affairs should also chair the Foreign Affairs Council, which consists of the External Relations component of the current General Affairs and External Relations Council (see above). In a further significant change, the Foreign Affairs Council will *not*, for the most part, fall under the rotating Presidency system.

In fulfilling his or her mandate, the Union Minister for Foreign Affairs shall also 'be assisted by a European External Action Service'. Again, bearing in mind the important role currently played by the (Commission) delegations in CP, this is a potentially significant development for CP. In a declaration attached to the draft constitution 'the Convention agrees on the need for the Council of Ministers and the Commission to agree, without prejudice to the rights of the European Parliament, to establish under the Minister's authority one joint service (European External Action Service) composed of officials from relevant departments of the General Secretariat of the Council of Ministers and of the Commission and staff seconded from national diplomatic services'.[62]

It remains ambiguous whether the European External Action Service will build upon the existing RELEX and External Service in the Commission, creating a 'super-RELEX', or whether the intention is to create an autonomous service comprising former Commission and Council officials, as well as national diplomats, reporting to the Union Foreign Minister. On the former the assumption by key Convention players, such as Michel Barnier and António Vitorino, was that the European External Action Service would be built around the 'famille RELEX' (including DG RELEX and its External Service, DG Trade; DG Development; DG Enlargement; the EuropeAid Cooperation Office; the European Humanitarian Aid Office; and some external aspects of DG Economic and Financial Affairs.[63] On the Council side the Service would incorporate those services currently working for the High Representative, including the Policy Unit, the SITCEN, and the DG-E (External Relations) of the Council Secretariat. This assumption was shared by Guiliano Amato, Elmar Brok and Andrew Duff who wished to see the European External Action Service established as an integral part of the Commission administration, but that the administration shall work as mandated by the Council without prejudice to the competences of the Commission.[64]

The possibility of an autonomous European External Action Service emerging is somewhat unlikely, especially since its final administrative shape will be subject to agreement between the Council, the Commission and the Parliament. This

---

[61] Ibid., Article I-27 (3).

[62] Ibid. *Declaration on the Creation of a European External Service.*

[63] See the *Contribution by Mr. Barnier and Mr Vitorino to the Members of the Convention, 'Joint External Action Service'*, CONTRIB 375, 30 June 2003, p. 4.

[64] See the Proposal by Amato, Brok and Duff, *Declaration on the Creation of A European External Action Service*, at european-convention.eu.int/Docs/Treaty/pdf/ 873/Art%20III%20225a% 20Amato%20EN.pdf .

does not preclude the possibility of existing parts of the 'famille RELEX' being made into agencies, such as EuropeAid. Whatever the shape of the Service, it will be a potent tool for the Union Foreign Minister and give him the potential, within one administrative entity, to mainstream CP in a way that is difficult at present. This of course applies with equal force to other currently inconsistent aspects of EU external action.

The draft Constitution does not, however, suggest that the potential EU Foreign Minister should have exclusive competence in external affairs since this is clearly shared by the new European Council chair and, to a lesser extent, the President of the Commission. The President of the European Council shall 'in that capacity ensure, at his level, the external representation of the Union on issues concerning its Common Foreign and Security Policy, without prejudice to the responsibilities of the Minister for Foreign Affairs'.[65] The key phrases are clearly 'in that capacity' and at 'his level' since, otherwise, the potential for territorial transgressions between the two posts is evident. It remains to be seen how this is interpreted in practice. It also remains unclear whether, in particular cases, a revised rotating Presidency will be able to resist straying into external affairs, especially given the General Affairs and Legislative Council's charge to ensure consistency in the Council's work.

A number of other suggested changes will have significance for CP, such as the revised decision-making procedures, the 'solidarity clause' and financing arrangements (see below). However, most of these areas still evidently require further honing, especially the currently convoluted decision-making procedures. The recommendation that the 'Union shall have legal personality' (Article 1-6) may also have potentially far-reaching consequences for CP, especially since it will *per force* lead to a revision of the Community's External Service into something more closely resembling a professional EU diplomatic service, with closer links to the diplomatic representations of the Member States.

As it stands, the draft Constitution, along with the EU Security Strategy initiated by Solana in June 2003, bodes well for CP. The presence of a key figure to represent the EU in external relations, who will also incorporate the *communautaire* as well as intergovernmental aspects of CP, is welcome in principle. The potential for turf-wars and bureaucratic delays should be reduced while a clearer, more consistent, policy on CP and security more generally should emerge from a European External Action Service under the European Foreign Minister. Some vagaries remain, however, such as the Minister's potential relations with the President of the European Council, as well as more detailed questions of how the current CFSP/ESDP structures in the Council Secretariat should be incorporated into a European external action service. A further issue, to which we turn briefly, concerns the financing of CP.

---

[65] See n. 58, Article 1-21 (2).

4. FINANCING CONFLICT PREVENTION IN THE EU

One of the problems of assessing CP-related expenditure has already been touched on above. Namely, the expandable definitions of CP makes it difficult to pin-down exactly what is CP-related expenditure and what is more generally part of the Union's effort to foster regional and global stability. For instance, the efforts to 'mainstream' CP into a variety of regional programmes, such as MEDA or PHARE, may lead to inflated (or meaningless) figures for CP expenditure, or arbitrary exercises in determining what is and what is not CP-related expenditure. For example, an expansive definition of CP, including long and short-term aspects, would include a considerable number of geographical area actions, food aid and humanitarian programmes, as well as a number of general cooperation measures (falling under Heading 4 of the EU budget addressing external action generally). The incorporation of all items falling under B7 (see Annex I) gives a largely meaningless idea of actual CP expenditure, although the overall figures do give an impression of the Union's considerable leverage as an international actor as well as the relatively small amount dedicated to CFSP (a mere 30 million EUR in 2002).

The concentration will therefore be upon B8 (of Heading 4) which deals with CFSP and includes a specific category for conflict prevention and crisis management (see Annex II). Again, the divisions give a slightly misleading impression since, as will be explained, the categories are highly porous and the practice is often that of robbing Peter to pay Paul. Even within the specific category for CP and CM it is difficult to assess what is spent on the former and the latter, although the assumption is that, given the recent commitments of the EU in Bosnia Herzegovina, the Former Yugoslav Republic of Macedonia and the Democratic Republic of the Congo, much of the expenditure is actually dedicated to CM (this also accounts for the increase in the overall CFSP budget for 2003 over the previous year).

The original budgetary arrangements for CFSP merely stated that 'administrative' expenditure would be charged to the EU budget, while 'operating' expenditure would either follow the same schema or be charged to the Member States on a scale 'to be decided' (Article J.11). The obvious question of where 'administrative' and 'operational' expenditure fell became an issue in 1994 with EU involvement in the administration of Mostar which led to disputes between the Council and Parliament over who should be charged what.

Under the Amsterdam Treaty, which now included the Petersberg tasks in the funding equation, it was agreed (with the Mostar experience in mind) that 'administrative' expenditure would be charged to the EU budget under a Community instrument while 'operational expenditure' could either be charged to the EU budget (under the CFSP heading), except expenditure having military or defence implications or those cases where the Council unanimously decides otherwise. In cases where expenditure is not charged to the Union budget, it is charged in ac-

cordance with a GDP scale, or as determined by the Council (see Annex III). The
GDP scale, which inevitably places most of the financial burden on Germany, the
United Kingdom, France and Italy (in that order) has led to successive disagreements, especially since the larger countries are most likely to contribute appre-
ciable personnel, thus contributing to not only 'common' costs but 'individual'
ones as well. Understandably, this has made Germany in particular wary of attempts to extend the GDP formula.

In broad terms, the above arrangement is retained in the draft Treaty establishing a Constitution for Europe.[66] To complicate matters, the bulk of external action is undertaken by the Community in budgetary terms and this includes
matters which superficially might appear to be CFSP concerns (such as mine
clearance, civilian emergency assistance, human rights, election monitoring, the
consolidation of democracy and the rule of law). Hence expenditure on external
action could actually be accounted for through the EU budget (a Community action), the EU budget under the CFSP heading, by the Member States applying a
GDP scale, or other arrangements as agreed by the Council unanimously. As the
former Chair of the EU Military Committee, General Gustav Hägglund has noted,
'It is, perhaps, controversial that the Council is heavily dependent on Commission funding in the execution of its crisis management activities'.[67]

The unhappy Amsterdam formula was supplemented by an Inter-Institutional
Agreement (IIA) of 6 May 1999 which is of some importance regarding CP.[68]
Under the agreement, when CFSP 'non-compulsory' expenditure is charged to
the general budget of the EU under Article 28 of the Treaty on European Union,
the amount is determined by a separate co-decision procedure between the European Parliament and the Council, based on a preliminary budget drawn up by the
Commission. It was also suggested that within the CFSP budget chapter, the articles into which the CFSP actions should be entered should include prevention of
conflicts (see Annex II).

The IIA included a number of agreed consultation mechanisms, including substantial obligations on the part of the Council Presidency to inform the Parliament
on a regular (often quarterly) basis of the basic choices of the CFSP, budgetary
implications, the implementation of CFSP actions, estimates of costs envisaged
and so forth. However, the 'Council and all Council Presidencies systematically
ignored their obligations' until December 2002'.[69] A number of factors led to sig-

[66] *Draft Treaty establishing a Constitution for Europe*, CONV 850/03, 18 July 2003, Article III-
215, *OJEC* [2003] C 169/1.

[67] Intervention of General Gustav Hägglund, Chairman European Union Military Committee at
the Seminar on Crisis Management and Information Technology, Helsinki, 30 September 2002, p. 3
at <http://www.itcm.org/seminar/presentations/Hagglund_EUMC.pdf>.

[68] *OJEC* [1999] C 172/1.

[69] *Working Document on the financial aspects of the common foreign and security policy: State
of Play*, Committee on Budgets, Rapporteur Armin Laschet, DT/486596EN.doc, 18 February 2003,
p. 5.

nificant changes in cooperation but the main catalyst was the decision by the EU in 2002 to assume the functions of the UN International Police Task Force in Bosnia Herzegovina (which became the EU Police Mission on 1 January 2003).

The prospective EU Police Mission, which entailed an increase of 10 million EUR in the CFSP appropriations for the 2003 budget, led to closer cooperation between the European Parliament and the Council, the outcome of which was a Declaration on the Financing of the Common Foreign and Security Policy in accordance with the May 1999 IIA. The declaration, dated 25 November 2002, saw agreement between the European Parliament, the Council and the Commission on the 'need to ensure the necessary funding for common foreign and security policy within the framework of the financial perspectives and in respect of the provisions of the Treaty, taking into account that the development of the common foreign and security policy is a priority for the European Union'.[70] Under the IIA, as well as the agreement above, the Council is obliged to inform the Parliament 'immediately and in each case' of an 'estimate of costs envisaged', 'whenever the Council adopts a decision in the field of CFSP involving expenditure'. It is worth stressing that this applied to *all* CFSP-related decisions entailing expenditure, not only expenditure from the EU budget. However, the Council interpretation of this, based on the Presidency's failure to inform the Parliament of the budgetary implications of the Joint Action of 27 January 2003 by which the EU would assume NATO's 'Allied Harmony' responsibilities in the Former Yugoslav Republic of Macedonia, was that the agreements referred to above 'applied in principle only to EU funds'.[71]

The commencement of the EUPM in Bosnia Herzegovina, the EU mission in the Former Yugoslav Republic of Macedonia (*Operation Concordia*) and, shortly thereafter, a military mission to the Democratic Republic of the Congo (*Operation Artemis*), underline the growing scope of CFSP/ESDP activities. It is therefore imperative that clear and transparent budgetary procedures are followed, along with adequate guidelines for joint costs (to be borne by the EU budget) and individual costs (to be borne by the Member States). Other issues, such as the possible use of NATO assets and capabilities by the EU, the political grounds for which were solidified by the Danish Presidency in December 2002, remain ambiguous from the budgetary perspective. The possibility of emergency, parallel and *ad hoc* CFSP funds has also been raised in the Convention, but it is far from clear who, if anyone, would scrutinise such funds. Even in those cases where there are apparently clear budgetary guidelines, such as for the funding of EU Special Envoys, the funding is actually cobbled together from the B8 budget allo-

---

[70] *Declaration of the European Parliament, Council and Commission on the financing of the common foreign and security policy in accordance with the interinstitutional agreement of 6 May 1999*, adopted 19 December 2002, quoted in full in DT\486596EN.doc, pp. 13-15.

[71] Quoted in DT\486596EN.doc, pp. 8-9.

cation, a variety of regional programmes and national contributions (see Annex II).

The budgetary travails of CFSP/ESDP seem likely to continue, in part due to the inter-pillar nature of the activities that fall under the rubric. However, the need for rapid action on the part of the Council (often in response to an urgent requirement) and the ponderous workings of the B8 budgetary line has exacerbated problems; hence the provision in the draft Constitution for (as yet) unspecified 'rapid access to appropriations in the Union budget'.[72] Even if a *modus operandi* is established between the European Parliament and the Council in the context of the Inter-Institutional Agreement, ultimate budgetary responsibility lies with the Commission. This is of course contrary to the prevailing intergovernmental ethos of CFSP. The consequence of this has been for the Parliament to whittle the B8 line down to levels that, in some cases such as the Special Envoys, leaves little choice but to resort to creative solutions by funding from multiple sources.[73] The problems with funding the launch of the EU Police Mission to the Former Yugoslav Republic of Macedonia remain instructive and worrying, especially since the EU has it in mind to possibly assume NATO's duties in SFOR after 2004. This could well involve funding arrangements for over 10,000 personnel and equipment, which will not be amenable to improvised arrangements of the EUPM or *Concordia* variety. Nor can the larger Member States expect much alleviation of their GDP-based shares with the prospect of enlargement. If anything, this will only exacerbate existing tensions.

5. CONCLUSIONS

The institutional dimensions of CP have evolved rapidly within the EU; less so the financial aspects. The analysis has attempted to trace the growing importance of CP to the EU, not the least through the institutional adaptations. The considerable importance attached to CP has resulted in a number of potentially far-reaching changes presented by the Convention in their draft constitution. There are, though, no institutional panaceas and attention should be paid to three more general challenges to EU CP.

The first is the issue of consistency and, more specifically, how the various elements of CP and CM should be woven together into a seamless cross-pillar whole. The initial emphasis upon the military elements of CM, although understandable as a reaction to successive shocks in the Balkans, has been rectified somewhat by the promotion of CP as a 'fixed priority' and the development of the civilian aspects of CM as well. Further thought has to be given to build upon

---

[72] *Draft Treaty establishing a Constitution for Europe*, Article III-215 (3), *OJEC* [2003] C 169/1.

[73] See S. Duke, 'The Rhetoric-Resources Gap in EU Crisis Management', 3 *EIPASCOPE* (2002), pp. 2-9.

the Community's institutional CP structures and those of the Council, so that duplication can be avoided and rapid response assured. This will be no easy task as the precise relations between the Union Foreign Minister, the European External Action Service, the Council, the Commission and the President of the European Council are grappled with.

The second challenge is really one of focus. The discussion above commenced with a few comments on the difficulty of understanding what exactly CP is in the EU context. The Commission is quite right to claim a role of *primus inter pares* but the promotion of almost every aid or assistance programme as having a CP role raises its own problems. In this regard the draft of a Security Strategy Paper by the HR/SG is an important step forward, especially since CP features prominently in its priorities. Nevertheless, in subsequent iterations of the strategy the natural concentration on Central Asia and the Middle East in the aftermath of '9-11' may have some potentially distorting effects to the detriment of the considerable CP challenges that remain in Africa. The cross-pillar efforts need to be complemented by enhanced coordination with other international organisations with a CP mandate, most notably the OSCE. The obvious requirement for EU CP is to avoid any needless duplication of effort and resources through sharing arrangements. Progress has been made in this regard, but there is also evidence of duplication.

The third set of issues related to the 'ears and eyes' of the EU's CP. Although several sources of early-warning have been identified above, emphasis needs to be given to the role of the nascent European External Action Service which has to be backed by adequate training and staffing for CP and other roles. There is also the need to underline the early-warning aspects of CP through greater reliance on autonomous intelligence assets since, generally, the exchange of information and intelligence between the EU's CP bodies and the Member States is less than it might be.

Finally, the financing arrangements for CP and, more generally CM, are clearly wanting. In all likelihood this problem will get worse, not better, with the prospect of further enlargement and the assumption by the EU of complicated CP/CM missions that are neither clearly civilian nor military in nature. The current funding arrangements for CP/CM lack coherence, and are often politically divisive and ponderous. Given the likely unwillingness of the EU Member States to contribute to an EU budget for actions with military or defence implications, it would make sense to think of a common reserve fund (consisting of actual funds and in-kind contributions) for EU CP/CM operations which could be drawn upon for EU sanctioned actions. The EDF, which falls outside the EU budget and utilises a special 'key' for Member State contributions, could serve as an interesting prototype for such an arrangement.[74] The remaining civilian aspects of CP/

---

[74] This idea is explored in Antonio Missiroli, *Euros for ESDP: Financing EU Operations*, 45 Occasional Papers (European Institute for Security Studies, Paris 2003), pp. 24-27.

CM should be addressed through the EU budget, including the civilian aspects of missions. The key difference between the current system and that proposed in the draft Constitution is that a Union Foreign Minister would have a vested interest in improving the current system to reduce inconsistency and to reduce inter-institutional tensions. The Foreign Minister will inevitably become the linchpin of the Union's CP efforts, building upon but also adjusting existing CP capacities.

ANNEX I

General Expenditure External Action and Pre-Accession Aid (Budget 2002)

External action Amount %	(EUR million)	
Action defined by geographical area		
Pre-accession strategy (B7-0)	3 328,0	40,9 %
Pre-accession aid (Mediterranean countries) (B7-0)	21,0	0,2 %
Cooperation with Mediterranean third countries and the Middle East (B7-4)	861,3	10,6 %
Assistance to partner countries in Eastern Europe and Central Asia (B7-5 2)	473,9	5,8 %
Cooperation with Asia (B7-3 0)	488,0	6,0 %
Cooperation with Latin America (B7-3 1)	346,7	4,3 %
Cooperation with southern Africa and South Africa (B7-3 2)	124,8	1,5 %
Cooperation with the Balkans (B7-5 4)	765,0	9,4 %
Food aid and humanitarian aid operations		
Food aid and support operations (B7-2 0)	455,0	5,6 %
Humanitarian aid (B7-2 1)	441,8	5,4 %
General cooperation measures		
Other cooperation measures (B7-6, B7-5 1, B7-5 3)	419,6	5,2 %
International fisheries agreements (B7-8 0)	193,2	2,4 %
External aspects of certain Community policies (B7-8 1 to B7-8 7)	78,7	1,0 %
European initiative for democracy and human rights (B7-7)	104,0	1,3 %
CFSP (Common foreign and security policy) (B8-0)	30,0	0,4 %
Total	**8 131,0**	**100,0 %**

Source: European Commission, at <http://europa.eu.int/comm/budget/publfin/data/x_en21.pdf>.

ANNEX II

External Policies: CFSP Expenditure 1999-2003

Line	Title (HEADING 4 - EXTERNAL ACTIONS / PART B COMMISSION)	1999 commitments	1999 Payments	2000 commitments	2000 payments	2001 Commitments	2001 payments	2002 commitments	2002 payments	2003 commitments	2003 payments
B8	COMMON FOREIGN AND SECURITY POLICY										
B8-01	Common Foreign and Security Policy										
B8-010	Conflict prevention and crisis management	12.000.000	10.000.000	15.250.000	10.000.000	10.600.000	8.000.000	8.000.000	9.000.000	7.500.000	10.000.000
B8-011	Non-proliferation and disarmament	5.750.000	3.000.000	2.250.000	1.200.000	9.000.000	12.000.000	8.000.000	10.000.000	8.500.000	11.500.000
B8-012	Conflict resolution, verification, support for the peace process and stabilisation			12.500.000	9.500.000	10.000.000	7.500.000	8.000.000	10.300.000	27.000.000	26.000.000
B8-013	European Union special envoys	5.000.000	3.300.000	6.500.000	4.750.000	900	3.000.000				
B8-014	Emergency measures	4.250.000	4.250.000	9.000.000	3.800.000	5.000.000	4.000.000	5.300.000	5.000.000	4.000.000	2.000.000
B8-015	Preparatory and follow-up measures			1.500.000	750	500	500	700	700	500	500

Total B8	27.000.000	20.550.000	47.000.000	30.000.000	36.000.000	35.000.000	30.000.000	35.000.000	47.500.000	50.000.000
Total Heading 4	4.672.538.300	3.325.690.000	4.825.070.000	3.642.572.279	4.928.672.000	4.370.997.000	4.873.000.000	4.665.439.500	4.949.362.000	4.843.756.000
Share of CFSP expenditure under heading 4	0,58%	0,62%	0,97%	0,82%	0,73%	0,80%	0,62%	0,75%	0,96%	1,03%
Total B8 in 1999 prices	27.000.000	20.550.000	46.217.852	29.501.426	34.669.483	33.705.701	28.134.619	32.823.783	43.755.028	46.057.480

Source: Working Document on the financial aspects of the common foreign and security policy (CFSP) – State of Play, Committee on Budgets, European Parliament, Rapporteur, Armin Laschet, DT\486596EN.doc, 18 February 2003, p. 15.

ANNEX III

GDP shares of contributions to the EU budget (2003)

Country	%
Austria	2.31
Belgium	2.95
Denmark	2.01
Finland	1.50
France	16.39
Germany	22.75
Greece	1.58
Ireland	1.19
Italy	13.83
Luxembourg	0.23
Netherlands	4.96
Portugal	1.36
Spain	7.46
Sweden	2.69
United Kingdom	18.78
TOTAL	100.0

Source: European Commission

PART TWO

EU CONFLICT PREVENTION STRATEGY AND PRACTICE SO FAR

PART TWO B

TOWARDS A STRUCTURAL CONFLICT PREVENTION

Chapter 7
EU STRUCTURAL FOREIGN POLICY AND STRUCTURAL CONFLICT PREVENTION[1]

by Stephan Keukeleire[2]

1. TRADITIONAL VERSUS STRUCTURAL CONFLICT PREVENTION

Traditionally, conflict prevention aims to prevent the escalation of conflicts at the moment a conflict starts to escalate, threatens to take a violent turn, or has already taken a violent turn. It focuses on a specific stage of the conflict dynamic in which, at short notice, conflict prevention tools have to be used in order to stop or limit the escalation of the conflict. The traditional conflict prevention tools, which in the short term should lead to results, are aimed at convincing the parties involved to change their behaviour. Examples of these conflict prevention instruments are: diplomatic pressure, mediation, peace negotiations, (promising) financial, economic, military or any other form of support, (threatening with) diplomatic, economic or other sanctions, an arms embargo, and sending civilian observers or military personnel as peace monitors or peace keepers.

This traditional approach to conflict prevention is, as such, important and necessary: the use of short-term conflict prevention instruments is often essential to prevent a conflict from escalating or taking a violent turn. However, the limitations of this approach are more and more visible and lead to an increasingly critical assessment of this traditional conflict prevention.

Firstly, traditional conflict prevention is *de facto* often *reactive* rather than *proactive*. Proactive conflict prevention refers to efforts which are made before a conflict has escalated. Reactive conflict prevention means that conflict prevention activities are initiated after a conflict has escalated and started to become vio-

---

[1] This chapter on 'structural conflict prevention' forms part of an ongoing research project on 'structural foreign policy'. As both concepts are still 'under construction', critical comments are welcome <Stephan.Keukeleire@soc.kuleuven.ac.be>. For previous publications on structural foreign policy, see nn. 5 and 27. The author is grateful to Jennifer MacNaughtan for her useful comments and suggestions.

[2] Professor at the Katholieke Universiteit Leuven (Institute for International and European Policy), EHSAL (Brussels) and the College of Europe (Bruges).

V. Kronenberger and J. Wouters, eds., The European Union and Conflict Prevention
© 2004, T·M·C·ASSER PRESS, *The Hague, The Netherlands*

lent.[3] The predominance of reactive conflict prevention in the practice of conflict prevention implies that efforts to tackle a conflict are often no longer to be considered as conflict prevention efforts, but rather as conflict *management* efforts. Many so-called conflict prevention actions thus start late, rendering it more difficult to avoid a further escalation, to address the conflict effectively and to limit the costs.

Secondly, traditional conflict prevention efforts often have only limited effects because of the complexity of the situation and because of the relationship with other fundamental problems, such as the failure of the state system, undemocratic governance, systematic oppression of part of the population, ethnic or religious antagonism, poverty, lasting economic problems, proliferation of arms, environmental problems or demographic pressure. Furthermore, even when conflict prevention actions are successful in preventing or limiting the escalation of a conflict and in limiting the intensity, duration and geographic spill-over of a conflict, this success is often limited in time and proves to have no lasting effects when the related or underlying fundamental problems are not addressed and resolved.

These weaknesses of traditional conflict prevention are leading to a gradually increased attention in academic literature and in documents of some international governmental and non-governmental organizations to the need to address the root causes of a conflict. Long-term conflict prevention actions are necessary in order to tackle the root causes of a potential conflict and to achieve lasting and sustainable results. Long-term conflict prevention can help to avoid the need for short-term conflict prevention, or can act as a necessary complement. The need to address the root causes of a conflict was recognized much earlier with regard to 'peace-building' *after* a violent conflict occurred and after this conflict was managed or resolved. The experience in conflict arenas such as Bosnia or Kosovo indeed demonstrated that conflict management or conflict resolution efforts can only have lasting effects where they are followed by long-term efforts which function as 'sustainable peace-building' in the post-conflict stage.[4] However, in general there has been much less attention to the need to tackle the root causes of a potential conflict *before* a potential conflict comes to the fore or escalates.

A critical examination of the possible root causes of a (potential) conflict – poverty, the marginalization of countries or societies, poor governance, the discrimination of minorities, etc. – indicates that they are very often closely related to problematic structures, organizing principles or 'rules of the game' that characterize a country, society or region. Long-term conflict prevention efforts that address the root causes of a potential conflict must therefore address these

---

[3] L. Reychler, *Democratic Peace-building and Conflict Prevention: The devil is in the transition* (Leuven, Leuven University Press 1999), p. 11.

[4] On sustainable peace-building, see L. Reychler and T. Paffenholz (eds.), *Peacebuilding. A Field Guide* (Boulder, Lynne Rienner Publishers 2001), in particular its Chapter 1: 'From Conflict to Sustainable Peacebuilding: Concepts and Analytical Tools', at 3-20.

structures particularly. And to relate this to the first-mentioned criticism of the re-active nature of traditional conflict prevention: in order to avoid the need of using traditional short-term conflict prevention tools, proactive conflict prevention has to address the root causes of a potential conflict by improving, reinforcing or changing the underlying structures and the rules of the game.

This need to tackle these problematic structures lies at the heart of the term *structural conflict prevention*. This term points to the core of what long-term con-flict prevention is really about: influencing or shaping the structures which are at the basis of a potential conflict or which provide a fertile breeding ground for a conflict. Using the term 'structural conflict prevention' is therefore more illumi-nating and more precise than the more frequently used concept 'long-term con-flict prevention'. The latter term correctly points to the time dimension, but fails to point to its specificity in terms of substance.

As structural conflict prevention is a specific dimension of a *structural foreign policy*, the next section of this chapter elaborates in more detail the concept of a 'structural foreign policy'. This will clarify the various dimensions of structural conflict prevention, place structural conflict prevention within the broader con-cept of structural foreign policy, and facilitate a critical evaluation of the EU's structural conflict prevention policy in the last section of this chapter. It can also contribute to a critical assessment of the development cooperation, trade policy, human rights policy and other policies of the EU, which are dealt with in the fol-lowing chapters of this book.

2. STRUCTURAL CONFLICT PREVENTION: A SPECIFIC DIMENSION OF A STRUCTURAL FOREIGN POLICY

The concept structural foreign policy refers to a foreign policy which, in the long-term, is aimed at influencing or shaping viable and sustainable political, socio-economic and security structures as well as 'mental structures' under which states and societies, relations between states and societies, the position of individuals within the states and societies, and the international system as a whole operate.[5] As structures consist of semi-permanent organizing principles and 'rules of the game', they will generally change only gradually and over a longer period of time.[6] This also implies that a structural foreign policy is focused on influencing long-term changes, long-term developments and processes. This is in contrast to a

---

[5] For a theoretical analysis of the 'structural foreign policy' concept, see S. Keukeleire, "Reconceptualizing (European) Foreign Policy: 'Structural Foreign Policy'" (Paper for the 1st Pan-European Conference on EU Politics, Bordeaux, 26-28 September 2002 <http://www.wmin.ac.uk/csd/rw/TMP1005915395.htm>), pp. 1-12.

[6] Exceptions are structural changes as a result of revolutions (such as in Russia in 1917) or mili-tary defeats (such as in Germany and Japan after the Second World War).

traditional foreign policy, which *de facto* pays more attention to events and actions, crises and conflicts. In view of their semi-permanent quality, influencing or changing the structures within which other actors operate is more difficult and challenging than influencing or changing the specific actions of these actors or the behaviour of such actors in specific cases. However, if successful, the efforts to influence or change these structures can have a significantly more profound and enduring impact than efforts to influence or change the specific actions or behaviour of these actors or than efforts to tackle specific events, crises or conflicts in an isolated way.

Central features of a structural foreign policy are (1) the long-term perspective and the focus on sustainability, (2) the interrelatedness of the various structures (the political/legal, socio-economic, security and mental structures) and (3) the interrelatedness of the various levels (individual level, society, state level, relations between state and societies, global level) (see Table 1). Within the scope of this chapter, it is not possible to analyse every dimension of the structural foreign policy concept. Neither is it possible to discuss every section of Table 1. The analysis in this section will in particular focus attention on three aspects: the importance of two levels that usually receive less attention (the societal level and the individual level), the importance of a comprehensive approach as a result of the interrelatedness of the various structures and levels, and the 'sustainability' requirement and its link to mental structures.

Table 1. Structural foreign policy: structures and levels[7]

LEVEL STRUCTURES	Individual level	State level	Societal level[8]	Inter-state/society level	Global level
Political and legal structures	Human rights; Civil liberties; ...	Democracy; Rule of law; ...	Recognition of and respect for religious and ethnic groups; ...	Friendly relations; Mutual respect; Cooperation; Integration; ...	Legitimacy and effectiveness of multilateral regimes and IO; ...
Socio-economic structures	Human security (freedom of want); ...	Economic development; Macro-economic situation; ...	Welfare; Social safety nets; ...	Trade relations; Cooperation; Integration; ...	Legitimacy and effectiveness of multilateral regimes and IO; Welfare; ...
Security structures	Human security (freedom of fear); ...	Internal security; Internal order;	Societal security; ...	Mutual trust; Peaceful relations; Security community; ...	Legitimacy and effectiveness of multilateral regimes and IO; Peace; ...
Mental structure	Interiorization; Identity; ...	Interiorization; Identity; ...	Interiorization; Identity; ...	Interiorization; Identity; ...	Interiorization; Identity; ...

---

[7] This table provides, by way of illustration, a limited number of options in the squares at the intersection between the various structures and levels and is thus not exhaustive. ('IO' = 'international organisations').

[8] Societies can be situated within one state or can be transnational.

2.1 Two neglected levels: the societal level and the individual level

Before explaining the interrelatedness of the various structures and levels, it is useful to pay some attention to the explicit incorporation of the societal level and the individual level in the definition of structural foreign policy. This is particularly valuable in view of the traditional focus on the state, inter-state and global level in Western foreign policy and academic research in the international relations field. This section focuses on the security dimension of both levels and elaborates the concepts 'societal security' and 'human security'. Both dimensions of security have been largely neglected by the Western foreign policy elite as a result of the traditional attention to 'national' security, which has usually been defined in territorial and military terms.

The concept 'human security' refers to the 'freedom of fear' (of violence, violations of human rights, crime) and the 'freedom of want' (of hunger, poverty, disease, environmental degradation) of individual people.[9] It refers to an objective of foreign policy which has generally been disregarded in the conceptualization of foreign policy goals (in contrast to the more limited objectives of 'human rights' or 'humanitarian aid'). However, human security is of vital importance not only for the individuals concerned, but also in terms of achieving other essential foreign policy aims on other levels and within other structures.[10] Major Western foreign policy goals, such as peace, stability, human rights and democratization, cannot be achieved except in a context in which the human security of individuals is guaranteed. The example of the Balkans and of other conflict areas has demonstrated that improving the human security situation is an essential factor in order to achieve foreign policy objectives such as sustainable economic development and stable and sustainable military or territorial security. An illustration of this interrelatedness is the relationship between the lack of human security in Northern or Sub-Saharan African countries, the problems of governance on a national level in several of these states, the growing strength and popularity of radical fundamentalist groups within society, the expanding recruitment basis for terrorist groups, and the growing insecurity for the West that arises

---

[9] UNDP, *Human Development Report 1994. New dimensions of human security* (New York, United Nations Development Programme 1994). For an assessment of the different interpretations of this concept, see R. Paris, 'Human Security', 26 *International Security* (2001), pp. 87-102; G. King and C. Murray, 'Rethinking Human Security', 116 *Political Science Quarterly* (2002), pp. 585-610.

[10] For an analysis of the interrelationship between 'human security' and other levels and structures, see for instance: C. Thomas, *Global Governance, Development and Human Security* (London, Pluto Press 2000); A. Suhrke, 'Human Security and the Interests of States', 30 *Security Dialogue* (1999), pp. 265-276; A.W. Nafziger, et al. (eds.), *War, Hunger, and Displacement* (Oxford, Oxford University Press 2000); W.T. Tow and R. Trood, 'Linkages between Traditional Security and Human Security', in W.T. Tow, et al. (eds.), *Asia's Emerging Regional Order: Reconciling Traditional and Human Security* (Tokyo, United Nations University Press 2000).

from the increasingly popular fundamentalist movements and terrorist groups.[11] From the perspective of structural conflict prevention, this implies that the probability of conflict arising can be diminished when conflict prevention strategies consider the human security dimension as a priority of conflict prevention and foreign policy, and not just as a dimension that is to be dealt with merely within the context of development aid or humanitarian aid. The choice of the terminology – human *security* – serves to emphasize the urgency and importance of this dimension.

The concept 'societal security' refers to the ability of a society (mostly defined on an ethnic or religious basis) 'to persist in its essential character under changing conditions and possible or actual threats. More specifically it is about the sustainability, within acceptable conditions for evolution, of traditional patterns of language, culture, association, and religious national identity and custom'.[12] Societal insecurity can be the result of internal pressure within a state or of direct external pressure from other states or societies. The problems of the Kurds, Armenians, Huttis/Tutsis, Tamils, Sinhalese, Bengalis, Bosnians, Kosovars, Palestinians, Sunnists, Shiites, Jews and other ethnic and religious groups are to a greater or lesser extent an illustration of this kind of internal or external pressure. Societal insecurity can also be the result of indirect external pressure from the international system. A major example of the latter is the potential threat to societies resulting from the 'Westernization' and homogenising impact of globalization and of the free-market economy. As Buzan argues, a global free-market economy undermines cultural distinctiveness in several ways. It generates global products, attitudes and values, and styles that erode the distinctiveness (and in some cases the viability) of national, ethnic or religious cultures. It reinforces this with ever higher intensities of interaction across a broad spectrum: exchange of goods, movement of individuals, multiple channels of communication, and mass linkage of information and transportation networks.[13] The latter also explains the growing interrelatedness of the various levels and of the various levels of security and insecurity. The identification of societies with a specific religion and/or ethnicity explains the often large capacity of mobilization among the members of this society, including the capacity to mobilize against the (perceived or real) threat or

---

[11] For an empirical analysis of the interrelationship between social and economic development and (the fight against) terrorism, see: K. Cragin and P. Chalk, *Terrorism and Development. Using Social and Economic Development to Inhibit a Resurgence of Terrorism* (Santa Monica, Rand 2003).

[12] O. Waever, 'Societal security: the concept', in O. Waever, et al., *Identity, Migration and the New Security Agenda in Europe* (London, Pinter Publishers 1993), p. 23.

[13] B. Buzan, 'Societal security, state security and internationalisation', in O. Waever, et al., *Identity, Migration and the New Security Agenda in Europe* (London, Pinter Publishers 1993), p. 52. See also: Waever, op. cit. n. 12, at 21-23 and S. Latouche, *The Westernization of the World. The Significance, Scope and Limits of the Drive Towards Global Uniformity* (Cambridge, Polity Press 1996).

enemy. It also provides a deep and durable foundation to compete with the existing territorial state as a political organizing principle.[14]

The relevance for foreign policy is quite obvious. More extensively: problems resulting from societal insecurity can be considered as being at the basis and at the heart of many of the current international problems and crises. First of all, a large proportion of the conflicts at the start of the 21st century are related to conflicts between societies and to societal insecurity. Most conflicts in the world are not conflicts between states, but conflicts within states and between societies. This indicates the importance of conflict prevention policies paying much more attention to this societal level. This also makes explicit the relevance of the concept 'societal security', and questions what remains the predominant focus on states in Western foreign policy.[15]

Secondly, the sense of societal insecurity, which is felt in several parts of the world as a result of the processes of globalization and Westernization, indicates that an effective Western foreign policy requires that Western countries seriously assess the potentially negative external effects of the Western system and of the process of globalization on other societies. An effective structural conflict prevention policy implies that the West not only tries to influence and shape the structures in other parts of the world, but also seriously investigates the external effects of its own structures and of the structures which the West promotes or creates on a global level. It implies that the West examines what adaptations are required in these structures in order to diminish the potentially negative effects on societal security in other parts of the world. This is not just a matter of altruism; it is also of vital importance in terms of simple Western self-interest. The (correct or incorrect) perception in other regions of the world that the West is at the origin of increasing societal insecurity can lead to a mobilization of forces against the West and against the structures, values and organizing principles that are promoted by the West. The current challenges of radical religious fundamentalism and of global terrorist movements are two illustrations of this danger.

2.2 Interrelatedness and comprehensiveness

The analysis of human security and societal security has already provided some examples and indications of the interrelatedness of the various levels and structures in the concept of structural foreign policy. This interrelatedness indicates why, in a structural foreign policy, a comprehensive approach is essential to achieve lasting effects, as the neglect of one level or one structure can undermine the achievements obtained by foreign policy efforts on other levels and struc-

---

[14] Waever, op. cit. n. 12, at 22-23.

[15] T.B. Seybolt, 'Major armed conflicts', in *SIPRI Yearbook 2002. Armaments, Disarmament and International Security* (Stockholm, SIPRI 2002), pp. 21-62. See also, M.E. Brown, *The International Dimension of Internal Conflict* (Cambridge, Massachusetts, MIT Press 1996).

tures. However, too often, the tendency in the foreign policy of the West is to focus attention on only certain structures and levels, and to disregard others. This
selectivity in Western foreign policy conceptualization explains the sometimes
disappointing effects of foreign policy efforts and the often unexpected or negative side-effects of this policy.

In this context, it is essential to emphasize that the selectivity in Western foreign policy conceptualization not only impedes the effectiveness of specific foreign policy actions, but can also undermine the credibility of Western foreign
policy in general, of Western values and ultimately of the West as such. Some
examples will illustrate this selective and restrictive Western foreign policy
conceptualization and its potentially negative effects in terms of credibility and
legitimacy. First, the Western emphasis on human rights is, in itself, positive, and
can be motivated by a real concern for the situation of individual people in other
regions of the world. However, it can also be perceived as lacking credibility for
as long as the West does not place the same priority on the human security situation of individuals in other parts of the world, for whom the access to goods such
as clean water, food and medicines is at least as essential for their survival as the
respect of human rights. Or to formulate the problem in an other way: to what
extent can the West expect that its emphasis on human rights is both taken seriously and accepted generally as long as it does not accept, for instance, that access to clean water is also a 'human right'?[16]

Secondly, the Western efforts to promote democracy as the basic organizing
principle of the political structures in countries all over the world can, again, be
considered to be positive. However, these efforts can equally be perceived as
lacking plausability as long as the West only aims to introduce democracy on the
state level and is not willing to introduce the principles of democracy on a global
level within the various international organizations and forums that it dominates
(the UN Security Council, the WTO, the IMF and World Bank, and the G7/
G8).[17] Thirdly, the West promotes the introduction of free-market economy principles within other states and within the world economy as a whole. This can be
motivated by an honest belief that in the long-term this will better the situation of
people in other countries. However, the West meanwhile neglects the potential
negative effects which this policy has on the individual level and societal level, as
this also leads to problems in terms of human security and societal security in
various countries in Africa, Latin America and Asia.[18]

---

[16] The importance of the human security situation of individuals for their actual survival becomes clear when comparing the statistics for the various human security indicators with the statistics on life expectancy (with, for instance, life expectancy in Sub-Saharan Africa being lower than
50 years) (see the yearly *Human Development Report* of the United Nations Development
Programme, published by Oxford University Press).

[17] See D. Held, *Democracy and Global Order* (Cambridge, Polity Press 1995); A.G. McGrew
(ed.), *The Transformation of Democracy? Globalization and Territorial Democracy* (Cambridge,
Polity Press 1997).

[18] See Latouche, op. cit. n. 13; Buzan, op. cit. n. 13, at 41-58.

2.3   Sustainability, internalization and 'mental structures'

A central feature of a structural foreign policy is that it is aimed at achieving *lasting* results. The objective is to influence, shape or create structures that are not only viable in the short-term, but that are equally sustainable in the long-term. In view of the semi-permanent character of structures, a structural foreign policy can indeed only be successful if it succeeds in influencing and shaping structures in such a way that the adapted or new structures become relatively permanent as well.

An important factor to achieve this sustainability is the above-mentioned comprehensiveness of a structural foreign policy, which takes into account the inter-relatedness of the various levels and structures. Another central element is the extent to which the various structures are part (or become part) of the mindset, mental framework or 'mental structure' of the people concerned (population as well as elites). This means that these structures are (or become) internalized and are considered (or are gradually considered) to be part of one's identity, culture, traditions and value system – in short, as something that is evident. To indicate the importance of this dimension of a structural foreign policy, the 'mental structure' is added to the political, socio-economic and security structures that are to be dealt with in a structural foreign policy. The sections in Table 1 at the intersection between 'mental structure' and the various 'levels' refer to the extent to which the features of the various structures within the various levels (such as 'democracy', 'human rights') are internalized and considered part of one's own identity.[19]

The extent to which a structure is, or can be, internalized and becomes part of the 'mental structure' is to a large extent depending on the method through which these structures are created, influenced or stimulated: as the result of coercion or force by an external actor who left no other option than accepting these structures; as the result of a rational choice in which a cost-benefit calculation and self-interest made an actor accept these structures and in which this acceptance is the acceptable price to be paid to gain specific advantages (in this case, they may not always be considered legitimate or positive as such); or as something which is self-evident as these structures are considered, by the people concerned, as legitimate in and of themselves (which implies that these structures are accepted not because of compulsion or self-interest, but because they are legitimate and constitute part of one's own identity).[20] The internalization of structures will in general be facilitated – and their sustainability strengthened – the more these structures

---

[19] On the phenomenon of internalization, see A. Wendt, *Social Theory of International Politics* (Cambridge, Cambridge University Press 1999), at pp. 250, 266-278.

[20] The difference between these three pathways is not always that clear, which implies that in practice they are to be seen as more of a continuum. For an analysis of the different pathways towards internalization, see Wendt, op. cit. n. 19.

are considered legitimate rather than the result of a pure cost-benefit calculation, or the more they are seen as the acceptable result of a cost-benefit calculation rather than as the unavoidable result of force or coercion by external actors.

The importance of the internalization of structures for achieving lasting and sustainable results also explains why a structural foreign policy will generally have for a heightened probability of success if there exists an indigenous base for the structures that are promoted, if the impetus for change (also) comes from within a state or society, if the structures, at least to some degree, concur with traditions or currents within these states or societies, and if the specific circumstances and values in the state, society or region concerned are taken into account. The failure of the West to systematically take into account the importance of internalization and of the factors that facilitate internalization, explains part of the failures of Western foreign policy towards other regions of the world. Western countries try to transpose (dimensions of) their own political, legal, socioeconomic and other structures onto other regions and countries, however often without a critical evaluation of the appropriateness of these structures and, in particular, of the Western way of operationalizing these structures. To what extent do the necessary material and immaterial foundations exist in these countries to apply those structures (and, especially, to apply them in the particular manner in which the West operationalizes them)? What conditions have to be fulfilled to make the introduction or adaptation of structures a success? What are the potential side-effects and costs, and how can they be off-set or entirely avoided? To what extent can alternative indigenous structures be used, or can indigenous methods be applied to make new structures operational?

The West has proven itself to be very reluctant to consider the plausible utility of indigenous structures or to recognize the value of 'deviant' ways to operationalize organizing principles such as 'democracy', 'justice' or 'social protection'. Some concrete examples will illustrate the previous points. A first example of a structure with an indigenous basis is the *Gacaca* jurisdictions in Rwanda. These are elected juries inspired by a traditional Rwandan justice system which were established after the 1994 genocide. These *Gacaca* jurisdictions have provided a solution for the inadequacy of the judicial system which, due to a lack of capacity and an excessive case load, has been unable to deal with all genocide cases. The introduction of the *Gacaca* system (as a complement to the existing judicial system) was also important for its central role in the crucial reconciliation process in Rwanda after the genocide. Indeed, this social and psychological reconciliation process is at least as important for the reconstruction of Rwandan society as the judicial dimension. However, it was only after long hesitation and still with a great deal of reluctance that the international community has embarked on the *Gacaca* process. This has been the case primarily for two reasons. Firstly, it did not fit within the Western conception or 'template' of a judicial system and, secondly, the West did not sufficiently understand the crucial role of the reconciliation process. Nevertheless, it was clear from the outset that the Western conception of a judicial structure would never be able to cope with the problems in Rwanda.[21]

A second example is the promotion of democratic structures by the West.[22] We will elaborate more extensively on this example, because it elucidates the crucial dimension of sustainability in structural foreign policy. Western countries have been quite active in supporting the transition towards a democratic system in other countries in the world, through financial or technical assistance for democratic elections, for the creation of a parliamentary system, etc. However, evidence from case-studies indicates that external actors and factors are rarely, if ever, crucial to the progress towards democratic consolidation in the post-transition phase. In his study on democracy in the developing world, Haynes demonstrates that once democratic transitions were complete (as marked by the first free elections) then both the ability and the desire of foreign governments and other international actors to influence democratic progress seemed to become less significant.[23] This underlines the importance of indigenous bases for developing democratic structures. However, these indigenous bases are often considered by Western actors as alien, undemocratic or threatening, principally since they often fit uneasily within Western templates and the Western methods of operationalizing democratic principles.

This paradox is illustrated quite well by the democratization process in Iran.[24] Firstly, from a sustainability and internalization perspective, it can be argued that a gradual, difficult and ambiguous process towards democratization such as in Iran (which is to a large extent the result of indigenous developments) is preferable to the formal democratization process in several developing countries, which result mainly of Western pressure and support. As the Iranian political transformation is embedded in existing domestic trends, the opportunity for sustainable democracy will be stronger in Iran than in countries where the democratic system has been imposed or steered by external actors. Secondly, it can be argued that sustainable democratic structures in Muslim countries require that, to some extent, they be rooted in or based on Islamic traditions, discourse and theology. This argument validates the criticism (formulated in the West as well as in Iran)

---

[21] S. da Câmara Santa Clara Gomes, 'The European Union's Political and Development Response to Rwanda', 27 *ECDPM Discussion Paper* (Maastricht, ECDPM – European Centre for Development Policy Management 2001), pp. 8, 26-27.

[22] For critical assessments of this issue, see R. Pinkney, *Democracy in the Third World* (Boulder/ London, Lynne Rienner Publishers 2002); J. Haynes, *Democracy in the Developing World – Africa, Asia, Latin America and the Middle East* (Cambridge, Polity Press 2001); H. Smith (ed.), *Democracy and International Relations: Critical Theories/Problematic Practices* (London, Macmillan 2000).

[23] Haynes, op. cit. n. 22, at 205.

[24] See J. Amuzegar, 'Iran's "Virtual Democracy" at a Turning Point', 20 *SAIS Review* (2000), pp. 93-109; A.W. Samii, 'Iran's Guardians Council as an Obstacle to Democracy', 55 *Middle East Journal* (2000), pp. 643-662; R. Jahanbegloo, 'Pressures from Below – The Deadlock in Iran', 14 *Journal of Democracy* (2003), pp. 126-131.

of ongoing undemocratic practices and in particular of the power of the religious Guardians Council. However, it also indicates that the demand to stop any interference by religion in politics may run counter to the objective of promoting sustainable democracy. This because, in some cases, it can undermine the internal legitimacy and the possibility of internalizing democratic structures.[25] As such, if the West is really concerned about promoting democracy in Muslim countries, it might have to accept that religious values and actors will play a role in operationalizing democratic structures in these countries. In this context, it is useful to emphasize that Western acceptance of 'deviant' or 'alternative' methods to make democratic (and other 'Western') structures operational, can be facilitated when Western leaders and researchers cast a critical eye on democracy in the West, and recognize that also the Western translation of democracy contains 'undemocratic' elements.[26]

3.   THE EU AND STRUCTURAL CONFLICT PREVENTION

The structural foreign policy concept provides a useful prism to conceptualize conflict prevention and to evaluate the conflict prevention policy of international actors. It emphasizes that the root sources of conflicts must be tackled and that these sources can often only be tackled seriously by changing the structures under which a state, society or region operates. The structural conflict prevention concept underlines that traditional conflict prevention efforts, which are mostly aimed at achieving results in the short-term, are in most cases insufficient to guarantee lasting effects, as structural changes are also required. It also makes clear that, in particular cases, structural conflict prevention measures may even render the traditional conflict prevention measures redundant. Structural conflict prevention also provides a prism to foresee potential conflicts before they actually arise, as it allows one to detect and tackle potentially problematic structures. With its emphasis on the various interrelated structures (political, socio-economic, security, mental) and levels (state, society, individual, inter-state, global) and its focus on sustainability and interiorisation, it helps to place a conflict in a

---

[25] For a similar argument with regard to Indonesia, see M. Woodward, 'Indonesia, Islam, and the Prospect for Democracy', 21 *SAIS Review* (2001), pp. 29-37.

[26] One example can illustrate the need for some more critical self-reflection. The presidential elections in Iran in 2001 demonstrated that Iran did have democratic elections, despite the remaining power of the religious Guardians Council in supervising the elections and in approving the candidates. The population indeed had the possibility to choose between various candidates, which promoted very different models of society. One of the questions which may be formulated in this regard is, for instance, why the West accepts within Western democracies a strong link between politics and financial-economic power (cf., the major impact of financial and economic groups on the presidential elections in the US), but would not accept a link between politics and religious groups (including a major impact of religious groups on the democratic election of political leaders).

broader context and underlines the necessity of a comprehensive conflict prevention policy which encompasses various levels and structures.

What does the prisma of a 'structural conflict prevention' teach us about the conflict prevention policy of the EU? The following section analyses the development of a EU long-term conflict prevention policy, followed by a critical assessment in the subsequent sections.

3.1 Structural stability and the long-term conflict prevention policy of the EU: an overview

Since the early 1990s, in its foreign policy towards other regions in the world the EU (and in particular the European Commission) has been paying a great deal of attention to the structural dimension.[27] This structural approach was first evident in the policy towards the Central and Eastern European countries, but was also followed from 1995-96 onwards in the policy towards the Mediterranean countries (and to a more limited extent also in the EU policy towards other regions in the world).[28]

With regard to conflict prevention, the structural dimension came to the forefront for the first time in the Communication of the European Commission of March 1996 on *The European Union and the issue of conflicts in Africa: Peace-building, conflict prevention and beyond.*[29] In this communication, the Commission pointed to the importance of 'structural stability' as the ultimate policy goal of all conflict prevention activities. The Commission defines structural stability as 'a situation involving sustainable economic development, democracy and respect for human rights, viable political structures, and healthy environmental and social conditions, with the capacity to manage change without [having] to resort to conflict'.[30] The Commission emphasized the importance of the capacity of political analysis, not only of events, but also of the political and socio-economic

---

[27] For an analysis of the structural foreign policy of the EU in the 1990s, see S. Keukeleire, *Het buitenlands beleid van de EU* [The foreign policy of the EU] (Deventer, Kluwer 1998), pp. 363-447. For a more recent evaluation, see S. Keukeleire, 'Au-delà de la PESC: la politique étrangère structurelle de l'UE', *Annuaire français de relations internationales 2001*, Vol. II (Brussels, Bruylant 2001), pp. 536-551; S. Keukeleire, 'The EU as a Diplomatic Actor: Internal, Traditional and Structural Diplomacy', 14 *Diplomacy & Statecraft* (2003), pp. 31-56.

[28] For the EU policy towards the Central and Eastern European countries and the Mediterranean countries, see: K. Smith, *The Making of EU Foreign Policy: The Case of Eastern Europe* (Basingstoke, Palgrave 1999); M. Maresceau and E. Lannon (eds.), *The EU's Enlargement and Mediterranean Strategies. A Comparative Analysis* (Basingstoke, Palgrave 2001). For an overview of the policies towards other regions, see H. Smith, *European Union Foreign Policy. What it Is and What it Does* (London, Pluto Press 2002).

[29] European Commission, *Communication from the Commission to the Council – The EU and the issue of conflicts in Africa: Peace-building, conflict prevention and beyond,* SEC (96) 332 final, 6 March 1996.

[30] SEC (96) 332 final, p. 2.

structures. Such an analysis should help to detect major obstacles to the viability of a state and/or policy mechanisms that carry the seeds of violent conflicts. A country-by-country and region-by-region analysis resulting in the establishment of comprehensive policy frameworks should point to priority areas and in particular to long-term options. For the Commission, peace and security are closely interrelated with economic and social development. This implies that an adequate combination of political, economic, legal, social, environmental and military measures of stabilization has to be considered within these comprehensive policy frameworks, in terms of fully appreciating their potential for addressing the root causes of violent conflicts have to be taken fully into account.

This communication by the Commission was a first indication of a structural approach towards conflict prevention by the EU. In the second half of the 1990s, such an approach lay at the heart of the EU's post-war peace-building policy towards the Balkans, within the framework of the Stability Pact for South Eastern Europe. However, the structural approach had not yet been translated into the conflict prevention policy of the EU. This was to a large extent due to the rather limited interest in conflict prevention, to the fact that conflict prevention was still closely tied to the idea of short-term, military-related actions, and to the limited strategic view of the various intergovernmental actors that were responsible for the EU's CFSP. It took until 2001 before the EU developed a comprehensive approach towards conflict prevention. This new priority was crystalized in the *Communication from the Commission on Conflict Prevention* of April 2001 and in the *EU Programme for the Prevention of Violent Conflicts*, which was adopted by the Council and endorsed by the European Council in Göteborg in June 2001.

In its *Communication on Conflict Prevention*[31] the Commission distinguished between long-term conflict prevention (labelled 'Projecting stability') and short-term conflict prevention ('Reacting quickly to nascent conflicts'). The major part of the document focused on long-term conflict prevention. It emphasized the need to take a genuinely long-term and integrated approach which addresses all aspects of structural stability in countries at risk and which aims at tackling the root causes of conflict. The various sections of the chapter on 'Projecting stability' deal with: strengthening regional cooperation, building trade links, promoting a sound macro-economic environment, supporting democracy, the rule of law and civil society, reforming the security sector (police forces, the armed forces and democratic control over the security forces), support for rehabilitation and reintegration programmes, managing access to natural resources such as clean water, fighting human trafficking and drugs, fighting small arms proliferation, and fighting environmental degradation and the spread of communicable diseases. The integrated approach also emerged in the list of EU instruments directly or indirectly relevant to the prevention of conflict: development cooperation and external as-

---

[31] European Commission, *Communication from the Commission on Conflict Prevention*, COM (2001) 211 final, 11 April 2001.

sistance, economic cooperation and trade policy instruments, humanitarian aid, social and environmental policies, diplomatic instruments, economic and other sanctions, and the new instruments created within the European Security and Defence Policy (ESDP). Within this context, the many agreements and cooperation programmes with other countries and regions in the world were pointed to as the most powerful instruments at the Community's disposal. The new system of *Country Strategy Papers*, which are elaborated for each country receiving EC assistance, became the key tool to ensuring an integrated approach to conflict prevention. Together with the check-list for root causes of conflict (which looks at issues such as the balance of political and economic power, the control of the security forces, the ethnic composition of the government in ethnically-divided countries, the human rights situation and environmental problems), these Country Strategy Papers answered the need for information and analysis emphasized in the 1996 communication by the Commission.[32]

The merely 5-page long *EU Programme for the Prevention of Violent Conflicts*, endorsed by the Göteborg European Council,[33] to a large extent reflected the contents of the Commission's Communication on Conflict Prevention. It emphasized the need to address the root causes of conflicts, it made the same distinction between 'instruments for structural long-term and direct short-term preventive actions', and enumerated the same EU instruments for conflict prevention. In addition, the Council paid some more attention to the need to ensure early warning and policy coherence, and indicated that it would examine how instruments for disarmament, arms control and non-proliferation, including Confidence and Security-Building Measures, can be used more systematically for preventive purposes (which reflected the specific competences of the EU's CFSP). The Council also foresaw a yearly follow-up of the EU programme to maintain the new dynamic that was created with regard to conflict prevention. In this context, it is interesting to note that the 2002 report on the *Implementation of the EU Programme for the Prevention of Violent Conflict* explicitly used the term 'structural conflict prevention'.[34]

The two basic documents from 2001 provided, on the one hand, an overview of policy instruments that already existed or of policy initiatives that were already adopted. On the other hand, they provided a solid basis for the subsequent development of a more comprehensive, more targeted and more integrated long-term

---

[32] For an overview of the available Country Strategy Papers, see <http://europe.eu.int/comm/external_relations/sp/index.htm>. The European Check-list for Root Causes of Conflict can be found on <http://europe.eu.int/comm/external_relations/cpcm/cp/list.htm> (both accessed on 6/8/2003).

[33] *Presidency Conclusions, Göteborg European Council*, 15 and 16 June 2000, p. 12. *EU Programme for the Prevention of Violent Conflicts*, Press Release (Brussels, 7/6/2001) No. 9537/1/01.

[34] Report of the Presidency to the European Council of Seville on the *Implementation of the EU Programme for the Prevention of Violent Conflict* of 18 June 2002 (Council of the European Union, 9991/02) p. 5.

conflict prevention policy and for giving a greater priority to conflict prevention in the various sectoral policy fields of the EU. Most of the dimensions of this long-term EU conflict prevention policy are analysed in more detail in various other chapters of this book.[35] This chapter formulates some general observations and critical remarks from a structural conflict prevention perspective.

An analysis of the 2001 documents, and of the policy developed since then, indicates that the EU's long-term conflict prevention policy can, to a large extent, be considered as a structural conflict prevention policy. The EU, and in particular the European Commission, pays increasingly attention to the root causes of conflicts, and increasingly focuses its policy on developing, shaping and adapting the various political, socio-economic and security structures on the various levels. This was not only obvious in the promotion of human rights, democracy and good governance, or in the support for regional integration and cooperation in other parts of the world (which since a long time have been major dimensions of the EU's foreign policy). It also emerged in initiatives such as the 'everything-but-arms' (EBA) initiative (increasing the possibility for developing countries to export their products to the EU), the Kimberley process (which aims at cutting a source of revenue to rebel groups by establishing an international control regime for the import and export of rough diamonds), the support for the creation of the International Criminal Court and support for the Highly-Indebted Poor Countries (HIPS) initiative (which is designed to help these countries to deal with the burden of their debts). Also the new policy on the non-proliferation of weapons of mass destruction might point in the direction of a more structural approach.

In pinpointing the root causes of conflicts and to the need for a long-term approach towards conflict prevention, the EU proved its added-value *vis-à-vis* the conflict prevention policies of the Member States. The magnitude of the challenges with regard to structural conflict prevention explains why on many issues only a larger entity, such as the EU, is able to have any effect, as the capabilities and influence of the individual Member States (even the larger ones) is in most cases too limited. This also makes the conflict prevention policy of the EU important for individual Member States: they are able to bring some of their national priorities with regard to long-term conflict prevention on to the European agenda and, when gaining support from the Commission and other Member States, they can see these priorities elaborated within the framework of the EU conflict prevention policy. The development of a rather comprehensive conflict prevention policy in just a few years is indeed the result of interplay between several elements. Notably, the dynamic policy of the European Commission, the engagement of the Swedish presidency of the Council in 2001, the strong interest of individual Member States in developing specific issues on the EU's conflict pre-

---

[35] See in particular the chapter on 'EU instruments for conflict prevention' above and the various chapters on specific EU policies (trade policy, development cooperation, human rights, etc.) below.

vention agenda, and the new policies that were developed within the context of the ESDP.

In view of the rather recent prioritization of structural conflict prevention and the fact that several initiatives are still in the initial implementation stage, it is too early to give a well-founded critical assessment of the structural conflict prevention policy of the EU. Nevertheless, some general comments can already be formulated.

3.2 Comprehensiveness, interrelatedness and consistency

Criticisms to new policy

A first fundamental criticism is that the EU does not sufficiently use its power in the two policy fields where it could have the highest leverage to change the structures under which other countries in the world operate, namely its trade policy and agricultural policy. In its Communication on Conflict Prevention, the Commission argues that the many agreements and cooperation programmes with other countries and regions in the world provide the most powerful instruments at the Community's disposal.[36] This statement is incorrect. Structural changes in the EU's agricultural and external trade policies combined with the active support for more fundamental reforms within the WTO, IMF, World Bank and G7/G8 framework, would lead to much more profound changes for other countries and regions in the world than most of the structural conflict prevention measures in the EU's agreements and cooperation programmes with other countries. The above-mentioned initiatives – such as the EBA initiative and the HIPS initiative – are useful initiatives. However, their critical scrutiny reveals that they do not focus on changing the structures under which developing countries are to operate. They are, in the first place, aimed at removing the most negative and most criticized effects of these structures and at providing some relief to those countries that have most problems in surviving within the existing structures. The EU's capacity to use the international financial and economic organizations as a leverage to obtain more far-reaching structural reforms is, moreover, also impeded by the limitations of the EU's external competences. The adamancy of the Member States with regard to their competences and prerogatives within the international financial organizations precludes a common EU policy therein.[37]

A second, related critical remark is that the EU neglects the interrelatedness of the various structures and levels, and in particular neglects the impact of its trade and agricultural policy on other countries – on the individual level, as well as on

---

[36] European Commission, COM (2001) 211 final, p. 4.

[37] For the failure of the EU to translate its economic power and its voting power within the various multilateral institutions into real political influence, see M Van Reisen, *EU Global Player. The North-South Policy of the European Union* (Utrecht, International Books 1999). See also B. Gavin, *The European Union and Globalisation. Towards Global Democratic Governance* (Cheltenham, Edward Elgar 2001); T.L. Brewer, P.A. Brenton and G. Boyd (eds.), *Globalizing Europe. Deepening Integration, Alliance Capitalism and Structural Statecraft* (Cheltenham, Edward Elgar 2002).

the state and inter-state level. An example of this is the promotion by the EU of a free-trade area and of free-trade agreements with the Mediterranean countries, while disregarding its negative socio-economic impact of a free-trade system for parts of the population in the Northern African Mediterranean countries.[38] The EU underestimates the negative effects of its trade policy in terms of both human security and societal security. It also undervalues the danger of undermining the existing political structures, in view of the plausible linkage between growing social and economic disparities and problems and increasing radicalism and violence. Disruptive effects in terms of human security and societal security are potentially more significant than the positive effects of EU policies aimed at strengthening the human security situation in these countries (such as through the promotion of human rights). To exemplify this point, there is a clear contradiction between, on the one hand, for instance, the philosophy behind the *Country Strategy Papers* and the *check-list for root causes of conflict* with their concern for human security, and, on the other hand, the EU trade and agricultural policies which largely disregard this dimension. In this context, it is remarkable that so little attention is given in EU policy to societal security and to the disruptive effects of societies that are disintegrated or that feel themselves to be threatened or marginalized as a result of the external pressure of globalisation and 'Westernization'. This neglect of the societal level (even in the *check-list for root causes of conflict*) mirrors the general neglect of this dimension in Western foreign policy. The policy of the EU towards the Mediterranean is also illustrative of the EU's attempts to transfer its own structures and organizing principles to other regions, without sufficiently considering whether the necessary foundations exist in these countries to interiorize these structures and to operate within those structures. Eventually this undermines the legitimacy, viability and sustainability of the structures that are promoted.

The interrelatedness of the various structures and the resulting need for a consistent as well as comprehensive policy leads to the question whether the recent proposals on the reform of the EU will have positive effects. At the first glance, the proposals aimed at abolishing the pillar-structure of the EU and creating a new function of a EU Minister for Foreign Affairs seem to be positive (this new function would replace the functions of High Representative for the CFSP of the EU and of the Commissioners for External Relations and for Development). This reform should in theory lead to a greater coherence and consistency in the policy of the EU. The separation between the first and second pillar would disappear, as well as the problems and internal conflicts which arise when different actors and different bureaucratic entities are responsible for one policy field. However, from the perspective of a long-term structural conflict prevention policy there are sev-

---

[38] B. Khader, 'The Economic, Social and Political Impact of the Euro-Mediterranean Partnership', in M. Maresceau and E. Lannon (eds.), *The EU's Enlargement and Mediterranean Strategies. A Comparative Analysis* (Basingstoke, Palgrave 2001), pp. 3-28.

Why these new abolition of pillar system [handwritten annotation]

eral reasons why these reforms do not necessarily constitute an improvement of this policy and why the result could even be negative. The main reason is that the EU Minister for Foreign Affairs will probably focus on the most sensitive and visible political dimensions of his or her job (external political and military crises, ESDP, short-term conflict prevention), and might be unable or unwilling to devote the equivalent time and energy in developing a structural conflict prevention policy as the Commissioners have done in the past. Since the Commission has previously demonstrated its credentials as the most dynamic actor in developing a structural approach towards conflict prevention, this is naturally problematic. A further reason is that trade and agriculture will remain outside the competence of the EU Minister for Foreign Affairs and, more importantly, will still have more weight within internal EU deliberations than foreign policy concerns. When combined with the fact that the EU will not obtain additional competences in terms of representation in the multilateral international economic and financial institutions, it becomes evident that the solutions to the various problems which have been discussed in this section will probably remain elusive.

3.3 Symbolism or substance?

The EU's reports and documents on conflict prevention seem to be very ambitious and promising, but are with regard to several issues little more than enumerations of existing EU instruments and good intentions. More detailed scrutiny of several dimensions of the EU's long-term conflict prevention policy reveals policy to be rich in symbolism and intensions, yet often lacking in substance.[39] At first sight, various policy initiatives are indeed aimed at promoting, changing or influencing the structures in other regions of the world. However, in substantive terms, their potential impact is often rather limited. This results from a limited endowment of political energy and financial or other resources. Two examples can illustrate this. *concentration too limited* [handwritten annotation]

Firstly, consider the important and well-elaborated set of EU activities aimed at encouraging democracy, good governance and the rule of law. A critical assessment of these programmes indicates that efforts are mainly focused on one dimension of the process of democratization, namely the preparation, organization and observation of elections. Efforts aimed at other dimensions of democratization are often limited to providing financial support to rather small-scale NGO projects. Youngs in his analysis of the European Union democratization policies (in Northern Africa, the Middle East and East Asia), points to both the major asset and the major failure of the EU. The EU has developed a distinctive bottom-up philosophy, aimed at constructing the socio-economic and ideational

---

[39] For an account of the development of the EU's external policies from the perspective of 'substance and symbolism', see I. Manners, *Substance and Symbolism. An anatomy of cooperation in the New Europe* (Aldershot, Ashgate 2000).

foundations for political liberalization. However, in practice, it has failed to develop a fully comprehensive and coherent democracy promotion strategy.[40] Formulated in a different way: the EU's democratization policies are clearly driven by a structural foreign policy perspective, but the EU fails to generate a foreign policy output and impact which in a similar way reflects this structural approach.[41]

Secondly, consider the case of the EU's support for 'disarmament, demobilization and reintegration' programmes (also labelled *DDR*), aimed at the disarmament, demobilization and reintegration of combatants in civil society. The EU documents on conflict prevention invariably refer to the EU's support for *DDR*. In many countries and regions, these *DDR*-projects are indeed a crucial, but often also neglected dimension of long-term conflict prevention. This implies that EU attention for *DDR* should be considered positively. However, a critical assessment indicates that the EU's activities are in practice very limited, with limited resources, limited internal coordination, and with most work being done by other organisations (such as NGOs and in particular the World Bank). Whilst it may be footing the bill, the EU's influence in this field remains negligible.[42]

3.4   Coordination and complementarity

The previous examples illustrate a further point. Hill correctly emphasizes that it is not inherently constructive to load the tasks of conflict prevention on to every aspect of the EU's external relations. The EU should thus distinguish between what can seriously be expected of it, and what cannot – which is also important to avoid an ever growing capability-expectation gap.[43] The implication of this comment is that, despite the inherent strength of a comprehensive and integrated structural conflict prevention policy, defining a more limited number of priorities is advantageous, instead of giving the impression that the EU is, or can be, active in all the policy fields mentioned in the various conflict prevention documents. This becomes particularly pertinent if the EU is not able or willing to add substance to symbolism, and to bear the financial and internal political costs which

---

[40] R. Youngs, *The European Union and the Promotion of Democracy – Europe's Mediterranean and Asian Policies* (Oxford, Oxford University Press 2002). For a more fundamental criticism on the EU's democratization policy, see H. Smith, 'Why is There no International Democratic Theory', in H. Smith, loc. cit. n. 22, at 28-29.

[41] A similar conclusion can be formulated with regard to other policy fields, such as the EU's human rights policy. See T. King, 'Human Rights in European Foreign Policy: Success or Failure for Post-modern Diplomacy?', 10 *European Journal of International Law* (1999), pp. 313-337.

[42] J. MacNaughtan, *Understanding the cycle in Sub-Saharan Africa. The role of demobilisation, disarmament and reintegration programmes and the EC's conflict prevention capabilities* (College of Europe, Thesis presented for the Degree of Master of European Studies, 2003).

[43] C. Hill, 'The EU's Capacity for Conflict Prevention', 6 *European Foreign Affairs Review* (2001), at pp. 332-333. See also C. Hill, 'The Capacity-Expectation Gap, or Conceptualizing Europe's International Role', 31 *Journal of Common Market Studies* (1993), pp. 305-328.

would accompany more structural reforms in, for instance, its trade or agricultural policies.

This points to one of the dilemmas of a structural foreign policy approach. On the one hand, comprehensiveness is a principle feature of structural conflict prevention and is necessary in view of the interrelatedness of the various structures and levels. On the other hand, the evident limitations in terms of resources and policies make it impossible for any international actor to develop and implement an all-encompassing structural conflict prevention policy. This underlines the importance, not only of Member States acting together within the EU, but also of the EU systematically both coordinating its policies and developing a clear division of labour with other international actors (such as the various specialized agencies of the United Nations, the World Bank, other states, etc.). Recognizing this need, the EU is gradually developing framework agreements with relevant UN organizations and other international organizations to enhance this cooperation, with conflict prevention being one of the priority areas in this process of coordination.[44]

One final critical comment is related to the complementarity between the EU's structural and traditional conflict prevention policies. A fundamental problem is that the efficiency of the EU's structural conflict prevention efforts is sometimes undermined by the lack of effective short-term conflict prevention capabilities. A good illustration of this problem was the EU policy towards Sub-Saharan Africa. On paper the EU possessed quite an impressive range of structural conflict prevention instruments to tackle the structural problems on this continent. However, in several instances the use of these instruments has not lead to any positive and sustainable effect since the EU lacked an effective or credible capacity for short-term conflict prevention (notable, no military instruments to guarantee a modicum of security and stability).[45] This points to the value of the first small-scale military operation by the EU in Africa in mid-2003 (operation *'Artemis'* in Congo), which served as a kind of test-case.[46] More in general, it indicates the importance of the EU further developing and operationalizing the ESDP. Just as a *traditional conflict prevention policy* needs to be complemented by a structural conflict prevention policy in order to be effective, also a *structural conflict pre-*

[44] *Presidency Conclusions – Göteborg European Council (15 and 16 June 2001)*, p. 12; 'Draft Council Conclusions on EU-UN cooperation in conflict prevention and crisis management' (Press Release, Brussels (07-06-2001) – No. 9528/2/01); *Joint Declaration on UN-EU Cooperation in Crisis Management*, 24 September 2003. See also, European Commission, *Communication from the Commission to the Council and the European Parliament – The European Union and the United Nations: The choice of multilateralism*, COM (2003) 526 final, 10 September 2003.

[45] See W. Brown, *The European Union and Africa. The Restructuring of North-South Relations* (London, I.B. Tauris Publishers 2002); P. Magalhães Ferreira, et al., 'The EU's Common Foreign and Security Policy: Opportunities for a more Effective EU Response to Crisis-Affected Countries in Africa', 22 *ECDPM Discussion Paper* (2001).

[46] C. Mace, 'Operation Artemis: Mission improbable?', 18 *European Security Review* (2003), pp. 5-6.

vention policy in many cases can only be effective if it is complemented by a traditional short-term conflict prevention policy. And this will depend on the ability of the EU Member States to overcome their differences in interests, strategic cultures and world views, and to develop a comprehensive *common foreign policy* which allows the EU to take the necessary preliminary political decision.[47]

[handwritten annotation:] ⟳ need cooperation on the part of M.S. to develop com. for. pol.

---

[47] S. Keukeleire, 'European Security and Defence Policy without a European Foreign Policy?', in H.-G. Ehrhart (ed.), *Die Europäische Sicherheits- und Verteidigungspolitik* (Baden-Baden: Nomos 2001), pp. 231-242; S. Keukeleire, 'Directorates in the CFSP/CESDP of the EU', 6 *European Foreign Affairs Review* (2001), pp. 75-101.

Chapter 8
EU REGIONAL TRADE AGREEMENTS' ROLE IN THE PREVENTION OF CONFLICT AND IN INCREASING (INTRA-REGIONAL AND GLOBAL) SECURITY AND STABILITY: AN ECONOMIC PERSPECTIVE

by Andrea Rossi[1]

1. INTRODUCTION

The European Union (EU)[2] is widely recognised as being one of the world's key players in trade matters. It is one of the leading participants in international trade, accounting for 19% of world merchandise trade, and 24% of world trade in services in 2002.[3] It is also the largest source and one of the largest destinations of Foreign Direct Investment, accounting for 20% of total world inflows and 45% of total world outflows in 2001. Globalisation, a process of rapid integration of markets and societies fuelled by changes in technology and increases in trade and economic links, and its consequences is clearly a development that affects the EU directly.

In order to address the globalisation challenge, harness its potential for economic growth, while pursuing the goal of sustainable development, multilateral and regional trade liberalisation have been used in EU trade policy as mutually supportive policy tools.

The multilateral route and therefore the ongoing Doha Development Agenda (DDA) negotiations are the overriding priority for EU trade policy in the coming years. The World Trade Organisation (WTO) provides us with the ground rules (the 'bedrock') for international trade, together with a permanent framework for negotiation.

---

[1] The author works at the European Commission, DG Trade, Trade Analysis Unit. The views expressed in this paper are those of the author only and should not be attributed to the European Commission. The author wishes to thank Gustavo Martin-Prada for his useful comments.

[2] For the sake of simplicity the term EU will here be used unless, legally speaking, the term EC (and its Member States) is felt to be more appropriate.

[3] These figures do not include intra-EU trade and flows.

V. Kronenberger and J. Wouters, eds., The European Union and Conflict Prevention
© 2004, T·M·C·ASSER PRESS, *The Hague, The Netherlands*

WTO-compatible[4] regional trade agreements (RTAs, i.e., Free Trade Areas or Customs Unions) are nevertheless recognised by the EU as a useful policy tool, not an alternative but instead a complement to multilateral rule making and liberalisation.[5] Indeed, the EU itself is a clear success story for regional trade integration, from which non-European partners have also benefited. The EU is an integrated single market, open to international trade and investment, its increased prosperity, peace and stability being also advantageous to partner countries.

The EU has developed its approach to regional integration over half a century of integration. In a nutshell, it is based on an integrated market; the harmonisation of regulations affecting the movement of goods, services, people and capital; solidarity; and, where necessary, common policies, among them trade and competition policies. In the EU, economic integration has even led to a single currency.

The EU has clearly been an active user of RTAs over time and it is currently negotiating a series of important regional initiatives to which it is committed (e.g., the launch of Economic Partnership Agreements (EPAs) with Africa, Caribbean, Pacific (ACP) countries and negotiations with Mercosur, and the Gulf Co-operation Council (GCC) members).

The legal basis for concluding trade agreements with third parties is Article 133 of the EC Treaty, whereby the European Commission makes recommendations to the Council of Ministers, and the latter authorises the Commission to open the necessary negotiations. The Commission conducts the negotiations within the framework of the Council's mandate and in consultation with a special committee appointed by the Council to assist the Commission in this task. Once the negotiations with the third party are completed, it is the Council that concludes the agreement, normally voting by qualified majority. The recent amendments to the text of Article 133 introduced by the Treaty of Nice have further aligned the decision-making process for external trade negotiations on internal decision-making rules (e.g., in the area of services and intellectual property rights). Therefore the qualified majority in the Council applies for international trade negotiations covering areas of the Community's internal competence,[6] whereas unanimity is required for agreements that include provisions for which unanimity is needed for the adoption of internal rules.[7] This 'principle of parallelism' explains why international agreements relating for example to trade in cultural and audiovisual services, educational services, and social and human health services fall within the shared competences of the Community and its Member

---

[4] See Article XXIV of the GATT 1994, and the 'Understanding on the Interpretation of Article XXIV of the GATT 1994', in an annex to the Marrakech Agreement establishing the WTO.

[5] See also OECD, *Regionalism and its Place in the Multilateral Trading System* (Paris, OECD Documents 1996).

[6] With the area of investment remaining a major exception.

[7] Or where it relates to a field in which the Community has not yet exercised the powers conferred upon it by the EC Treaty by adopting internal rules.

States. Agreements covering these areas require the common accord of the Member States, and are concluded jointly by the Community and the Member States.

In practice, the RTAs the EC has negotiated tend to cover much more than just trade issues, such as provisions on political dialogue for example. In these cases the legal basis for negotiations is Article 300 EC on negotiations of international agreements, which also reflects the above described 'principle of parallelism'.[8]

To clarify the relationship between conflict prevention and EU policy on RTAs, a key issue is to identify the reasons behind the launch of EU RTA negotiations, the objectives pursued, and the impact of such policy.

This chapter analyses how EU Trade Policy has interacted with and may promote conflict prevention, looking in particular at the roles which the EU's RTAs have played and play in the prevention of conflict and the increase in (intraregional and global) security and stability.

It focuses on the economic perspective, rather than on the political dimension, and argues that the impact of EU RTAs on competitiveness and growth, full integration in the international trade system, and the promotion of sound domestic policies that are essential for development and regional cooperation and interdependence have a central role in conflict prevention.

2.   REGIONAL TRADE AGREEMENTS IN EU TRADE POLICY

The EU is the participant in the largest number of preferential trade agreements notified to the WTO. Following the 2004 EU enlargement, the EU contractual reciprocal trade agreements currently in force number 22 with 5 more being negotiated (counting country groupings with which the EU already has or is currently negotiating agreements as a single partner). If the individual country membership of these regional groupings – Mercosur (4 members), ACP (76) and the GCC (6) – were counted in full, the total number of countries potentially linked to the EU in this way rises to 108. While comparisons with other WTO members based only on the number of bilateral/regional trade agreements is clearly misleading,[9] the sheer number of RTA partners is an apparent indicator of the relevance of the RTA policy instrument for the EU.

---

[8] For international agreements establishing an association involving reciprocal rights and obligations, common action and special procedures, Article 310 EC applies to the decision-making procedure. For international agreements in the field of transport Article 300 EC and the provisions of Title V of the EC Treaty apply.

[9] The US has 'just' 5 RTAs, and 6 more are being negotiated (including the FTAA). Nevertheless, the share of trade with reciprocal preferential partners for the EU25 is significantly smaller than for the US. Imports from current RTA (FTAs + CUs) partners accounted for 23.5% of EU25 imports in 2002, but for 32.7% of US imports in the same year. In terms of exports the difference is even more striking. Exports to current RTA partners amounted to 26.2% of total EU25 exports in 2002, but reached 42.2% of US exports in the same year. Taking into account the RTAs being negotiated does not change the overall picture.

In negotiating these bilateral trade agreements, the EU/EC has responded to a combination of geopolitical as well as purely commercial objectives, including: preparing countries for Union *membership* (as in the case of the Europe Agreements[10] with Central and Eastern European Countries (CEECs)), providing close and stable economic relationships with immediately neighbouring countries (European Economic Area (EEA)[11], Euro-Mediterranean Agreements[12]), supporting *development* (Yaoundé, and Lomé Conventions and currently the Cotonou Agreement[13] that foresees the negotiation of EU-ACP Economic Partnership Agreements), responding to external *political developments* with a positive indication of support for particular countries (e.g., Stabilisation and Association Agreements[14] with the countries of the former Yugoslavia) or achieving *mutually beneficial reciprocal market opening* (e.g., agreements recently concluded with Mexico,[15] Chile[16] and South Africa[17] and the ongoing negotiations with the GCC states and Mercosur).

This multiplicity of objectives pursued through EU RTAs, suggests that the main driver of a number of regional agreement is actually political, trade often being considered as a means to a end. The EU itself is the prime example of realising the political objective of reducing the risk in future of war between Member States through economic and commercial cooperation and integration. Other EU objectives include regional stability and development.

Besides, the EU experience shows that regional integration has the potential to yield significant economic gains: it can pave the way for enhanced competitiveness and growth deriving from efficiency gains in the regional market (e.g., Europe Agreements), it can be used as a building block towards full integration in the international trade system and to promote sound domestic policies which are

---

[10] *OJEC* [1994] L 358 (Bulgaria); *OJEC* [1994] L 360 (Czech Republic); *OJEC* [1998] L 68 (Estonia); *OJEC* [1993] L 347 (Hungary); *OJEC* [1998] L 26 (Latvia); *OJEC* [1998] L 51 (Lithuania); *OJEC* [1993] L 348 (Poland); *OJEC* [1994] L 357 (Romania); *OJEC* [1994] L 359 (Slovak Republic); *OJEC* [1999] L 51 (Slovenia).

The text of the Europe Agreements is available at <http://europa.eu.int/comm/enlargement/pas/europe_agr.htm>. For a comprehensive study of these agreements, see A. Ott and K. Inglis (eds.), *Handbook on European Enlargement* (The Hague, TMC Asser Press 2002).

[11] The text of the EEA agreement can be found at <http://secretariat.efta.int/Web/LegalCorner/>.

[12] *OJEC* [2000] L 147 (Israel); *OJEC* [1998] L 97 (Tunisia); *OJEC* [2000] L 70 (Morocco); *OJEC* [2002] L 129 (Jordan); *OJEC* [2002] L 262 (Lebanon); *OJEC* [1997] L 187 (Palestinian Authority).

The text of the Euro-Mediterranean Association Agreements is available at <http://europa.eu.int/comm/external_relations/euromed/med_ass_agreemnts.htm>.

[13] The text is available at <http://europa.eu.int/comm/development/body/cotonou/agreement_en.htm>.

[14] See note 28 below.

[15] *OJEC* [2000] L 276.

[16] *OJEC* [2002] L 352.

[17] *OJEC* [1999] L 31.

essential for development.[18] The review of existing agreements highlights that there has been a marked evolution in EU RTA policy over the past decade. This evolution is characterised by:

- an increase in the number of agreements concluded and the range of partners;
- the conclusion of RTAs with non-neighbouring countries (e.g., South Africa, Mexico, Chile);
- a greater degree of reciprocity;
- greater coverage of agriculture;
- inclusion of trade in services;
- strong encouragement for parallel regional integration between EU RTA partners.

In recent years a general trend has emerged for EU regional trade arrangements to go beyond 'border measures', and include elements of *deep integration*, i.e., efforts to agree to common disciplines for regulatory regimes, involving different degrees of regulatory intervention covering 'new subjects' and other rules and disciplines (services, investment, intellectual property rights (IPR), government procurement, competition policy, etc).[19]

This trend is visible in the EU arrangements with candidate countries in Central and Eastern Europe, with Mexico, Chile and Turkey[20] that increasingly cover services and other regulatory areas. Outside the EU such a trend also concerns Mercosur which has aspirations to become a single market and the North America FTA (NAFTA) agreement, as well as the 'export' of the NAFTA model in particular by Mexico and Canada in their FTAs with third countries; and now through the Free Trade Area of the Americas negotiating process.[21]

Such a trend is explained by the fact that the simple removal of tariffs at the border while other regulatory obstacles within the economy remain in place is not sufficient to fully achieve the potential gains from RTA participation. In particular the *dynamic gains from competition and scale effects* for RTA members might not be achieved unless other factors causing segmentation of markets were removed. Theoretical and empirical economic impact assessments of existing and potential RTAs tend to agree that these dynamic effects dwarf the purely static

---

[18] OECD, *Regional Integration: Observed trade and Other Economic Effects* (TD/TC/WP (2001)19/FINAL).

[19] G. Sampson, S. Woolcock, et al. (eds.), *Regionalism, Multilateralism and Economic Integration: the Recent Experience* (Tokyo, UN University Press 2003).

[20] *OJEC* [1973] C 113 (text of the Association Agreement), *OJEC* [1996] L 35/1 (Decision No. 1/95 of the EC-Turkey Association Council of 22 December 1995 on implementing the final phase of the Customs Union).

[21] See OECD, *Regional Trade Agreements and the Multilateral Trading System: Consolidated Report* (TD/TC(2002)8/FINAL).

ones that result from shallow integration, limited to the removal of barriers at the border (i.e., tariffs and quotas).[22]

Once more, the European experience of RTAs shows that the most successful preferential agreements are those where the process of regional economic integration has been deep and comprehensive, involving the regulatory integration of domestic markets. There is little empirical evidence that shallow FTAs in goods have a substantial trade impact. On the contrary, they may even have an ambiguous effect upon the economic welfare of their members. However, deep RTAs like the EU itself or the ones with the EEA or with the candidate countries do show clear evidence of a substantial positive trade and investment impact. In other cases of preferential treatment, results are still limited (ACP, Mediterranean) or it is too early to say (Mexico, South Africa, Chile). This is confirmed by the available quantitative studies, that consistently find much higher economic benefits (increase in welfare, production, exports) for EU deepest integration agreements.

As for regional integration between EU RTA partners, the EU is increasingly looking for relations around the world on a 'region-to-region' basis, be it in ongoing FTA negotiations (Mercosur, GCC, EPAs) or other forms of relations (Andean Community, Central America, the Association of South-East Asian Nations (ASEAN)). Such an approach has the potential to generate more economically viable and interesting results, since regional integration on the partners' side increases the market potential and makes more 'cost-effective' efforts in the regulatory area. Ultimately this approach should facilitate economic development and growth.

3.   WHAT IS THE RELEVANCE FOR CONFLICT REDUCTION, SECURITY AND STABILITY OF THESE RESULTS?

3.1   Regional integration as a tool for (South-South) cooperation and interdependence

Developing countries' non-reciprocal access to developed countries' markets through unilateral trade preferences has not been sufficient to ensure that poorer countries share in the wealth being generated by globalisation. RTAs have long been seen as a useful instrument for supporting developing countries' participation in the international trade system.[23] RTAs amongst developing countries that create an open trade regime both among participants and with the rest of the world can contribute to their participation in the global economy and reinforce

---

[22] See World Bank, *Trade Blocs. A World Bank Policy Research Report* (Washington, 2000).

[23] *Inter alia*, political economy reasons may make it easier for countries to liberalise trade on a regional basis than unilaterally or through the multilateral process.

the multilateral trade system provided they are outward-oriented and lead to lower external trade barriers.[24] In this respect over the last decade RTAs between developing countries have moved in the direction of outward looking, less defensive and more comprehensive approaches.

On the basis of economic analysis and historical experience it is often argued that for most developing countries and especially for the poorest ones, a North-South RTA with a large industrial country is likely to be superior to a South-South RTA among developing countries,[25] provided the right design encourages the necessary domestic reforms.[26]

The EU approach is different, because in most initiatives it promotes a South-South-North model (with Mediterranean partners, Mercosur, GCC, and now EPAs with ACP countries), which is aimed at combining the strong points of North-South RTAs (locking in reforms, credibility, good governance, access to large markets, FDI incentives, technology transfers, etc.) with the positive aspects of South-South agreements (economies of scale, bargaining power, markets large enough to attract Foreign Direct Investment, etc.). Therefore North-South and South-South integration are seen as complementary.

This approach is particularly conducive to conflict prevention purposes. Indeed it can be argued that South-South trade integration can help achieve some political objectives that are supportive of conflict prevention aims, including *increasing security* among members (on the basis that increased trade among RTA members would reduce the risk of intraregional conflict, and/or increase extraregional security helping members to unite in facing a common external threat); *enhancing interregional cooperation* (when neighbouring countries share resources, such as rivers, fishing grounds, etc., or when they face common problems, such as pollution and transport bottlenecks);[27] *increasing bargaining power* (e.g., smaller countries can wield more influence in international forums if they learn to act or negotiate in a group with their neighbours or with other countries of like interests, than if they pursue their interests individually).

These results are of course dependent on the capacity and willingness of EU RTA partners to enter into dialogue with each other, but a trade agreement with the EU can provide powerful incentives through the opportunity of gaining free access to a wide and integrated market.

---

[24] *Trade and development: assisting developing countries reap the benefits of open trade*, Communication from the Commission to the Council and the European Parliament, COM (2002) 513 final.

[25] World Bank, op. cit. n. 22.

[26] But see Lucian Cernat, 'Assessing Regional Trade Arrangements: Are South-South RTAs more trade diverting?', 16 *UNCTAD Policy Issues in International Trade and Commodity Study Series* (2001).

[27] See also Maurice Schiff and L. Alan Winters, *Regional Cooperation, and the role of International Organisations and regional Integration* (World Bank Policy Research Working Paper No. 2872, July 2002).

An important example of a concrete effect of such a North-South-South regional integration approach of EU RTAs which comes to mind is that of the Western Balkans (WB), where the Stabilisation and Association Agreements within the framework of the Stability Pact promoted a network of bilateral free trade agreements among WB countries.[28] In this area the progress achieved to date can be considered remarkable, in particular with reference to the network of bilateral FTAs in the region that is now complete, and is fostering economic cooperation, trade integration and political dialogue also among WB states. This is quite an achievement, given the recent bloody conflicts in the WB area.

Other major examples of the impact of the EU region-to-region approach include the EU-Mediterranean Association Agreements, with the Agadir Process[29] launched in May 2001 the latest tangible step towards South-South market integration in the Mediterranean area, and the ongoing negotiations of Economic Partnership Agreements with the ACP countries, that are strengthening the emergence of self-defined ACP sub-regions. It can be argued that also the Europe Agreements with Central and Eastern European Countries which were not formally based on a region-to-region relationship, have helped to foster cooperation among these countries (e.g., with the negotiation of a Central European FTA) and prevent conflict – for example concerning the treatment of minorities – notably through a moral suasion mechanism.

In the case of Mercosur, the EU has had more of an indirect effect, first as a model of successful regional cooperation and integration, and then as a catalyst for its own integration process through the ongoing negotiation of an FTA framed on a region-to-region basis. The perspective of an agreement with the EU is also for Mercosur countries a way to counterbalance a potential participation in the FTAA, and improve their bargaining power in the negotiations with the US. The EU negotiations with the Gulf Cooperation Council countries concerning a comprehensive Free Trade Agreement with the GCC, has also been instrumental in accelerating the constitution of a GCC internal Customs Union, whose entry into force was advanced from 2005 to 1 January 2003.

To the extent that these South-South regional integration projects are conducive to increased economic stability and prosperity, improved security and the prevention of conflict, the negotiation of an RTA with the EU will have strongly contributed to achieving such a sought after effect.

---

[28] See the relevant documents at <http://europa.eu.int/comm/external_relations/see/docs/index.htm#sap> and the Stabilisation and Association Agreement between the European Communities and their Member States, on the one part, and the Republic of Croatia, on the other, Commission of the European Communities, COM (2001) 371 final, at <http://europa.eu.int/comm/external_relations/see/croatia/com01_371en.pdf>; and the Stabilisation and Association Agreement between the European Communities and their Member States, on the one part, and the former Yugoslav Republic of Macedonia, on the other, at <http://europa.eu.int/comm/external_relations/see/fyrom/saa/saa03_01.pdf>.

[29] See also <http://europa.eu.int/comm/trade/issues/bilateral/regions/euromed/index_en.htm>.

3.2 Regional integration as a tool for fostering domestic reforms, good governance and the rule of law

The link between trade, economic development and poverty reduction is complex. The recent historical experience shows that trade openness and market access are a necessary but not a sufficient condition for economic development and poverty reduction. Only if supported by proper domestic institutions and policies, good governance and the expansion of human freedoms will they lead to true development. Trade and trade liberalisation is more likely to promote growth and poverty reduction when mutually supportive domestic policies, adequate infrastructure and sound institutions are present. Therefore trade cannot be looked at in isolation but as an element of a more general policy context.

In this respect RTAs with a developed partner such as the EU can be used through their regulatory content to promote sound domestic policies and institutions which are essential for development.

By 'locking in' reforms through mutual commitments – in the area of politics, such as for democracy and the rule of law, and in the area of economics, such as for trade policy reforms – EU regional trade agreements help to enhance the credibility and transparency of the partner's domestic policy reforms and thus support the creation of an environment conducive to trade and investment, and in the process sustainable development.[30] EU RTAs provide a framework for governance which is more stable, enhancing predictability for investors and economic operators. It is expected that the process will increase competitiveness and investment and ultimately accelerate development in the EU RTA partners.

Moreover, also the (South-South) regional integration dimension of EU RTAs can provide a further incentive to adopt sound policies – for example for macroeconomic stabilisation, social protection and conflict resolution – and build the necessary institutions and regulatory environment that could otherwise be difficult, or even unfeasible to achieve at the national level. It is therefore possible to save resources when institutions and capacity building can be set up at the regional level. This applies to many trade-related areas such as standards, intellectual property protection and the whole range of trade facilitation measures, including customs procedures.[31]

Increasingly RTAs can provide the opportunity to reinforce regional cooperation on regulatory policies, including on the environmental and social dimensions of sustainable development. This regulatory cooperation is becoming more important in RTAs, particularly in a North-South context.

---

[30] See M. Shiff. and L.A. Winters, *Regional Integration and Development* (Washington and Oxford, World Bank and Oxford University Press 2003), pp. 188-192.
[31] COM (2002) 513 final.

The European Commission has been active in encouraging the inclusion of a stronger governance element in EU trade-related agreements with third countries. This activity will be strengthened in future agreements further to the Commission's commitment in its Communication 'Towards a global partnership for sustainable development'[32] to 'strengthen the sustainability dimension of bilateral and regional agreements by including a commitment to sustainable development and establishing a dialogue to enable exchange of best practices'.

The EU aims to better integrate sustainable development and governance in all of the current trade agreements in negotiations, for instance through the setting up of a regular dialogue on sustainable development between trade partners. Such a dialogue will address how best to support sustainable development through appropriate policies and institutional structures.

A clear example of the impact of EU RTA policy instruments on good governance and domestic policy reforms in the EU partners is represented by the Europe Agreements between the EU and Central and Eastern European Countries, that covered trade-related issues, political dialogue, legal approximation and other areas of cooperation, including industry, the environment, transport and customs. They aimed progressively at establishing a free-trade area between the EU and the associated countries over a given period, on the basis of reciprocity but applied in an asymmetric manner (i.e., more rapid liberalisation on the EU side than on the side of the associated countries). It is nevertheless unclear to what extent the Europe Agreements would have had such a strong and deep impact on the domestic policy reforms of the CEECs independently from the accession perspective that was linked to the candidate status.

At the centre of the EU-Mediterranean Association Agreements is a similar virtuous process of domestic policy reforms and institutional and regulatory upgrading, upheld by the incentive of improved market access and the prospect of increased growth and prosperity thanks to the increased attractiveness of domestic and foreign investment. Admittedly – though – in this latter case much still remains to be done, because many of the EU-Mediterranean agreements are very recent, and their full potential in terms of supporting regulatory convergence and good governance is still to be exploited.

Among the RTAs currently being negotiated by the EU, the most integrated approach to development and trade is to be found in the ACP-EU negotiations of Economic Partnership Agreements. Here there will be a strong link to economic governance in ACP countries and regions. EPAs will be aimed at improving and modernising the economic environment in the ACP through addressing bottlenecks to trade such as tariffs, non-tariff barriers and deficiencies in all relevant trade-related areas. Trade in goods, trade in services and the whole regulatory framework (import/export procedures, sanitary and phytosanitary measures, tech-

---

[32] COM (2002) 82 final. This constituted a major part of the Commission's input at the World Summit on Sustainable Development (WSSD) in Johannesburg 2002.

nical barriers to trade, investment rules, etc.) will be the subject of discussions and will be addressed on a regional level.

The objective is to strengthen and accelerate regional integration, creating larger harmonised regional markets. In addition, by 'locking in' reforms through mutual commitments, the agreements will provide more a framework for governance which is more stable, enhancing predictability for investors and economic operators. It is expected that the process will increase competitiveness and investment and ultimately accelerate development in ACP countries.

3.3 Regional integration as part of a policy mix: trade/aid/dialogue

As seen above, it is clear that the positive effect of trade integration can only be realised when the overall policy framework and the governance and institutional conditions are conducive. But it is also evident that addressing these constraints requires considerable resources.

In an RTA context, to ensure a significant economic impact, ambitious regulatory convergence is required (both South-South and North-South), in other words a substantial depth on the part of the agreement in terms of non-tariff and regulatory aspects (i.e., rules content) and a sufficient width in its scope (inclusion of provisions on services, intellectual property and investment). The experience of the EU and Candidates, and the US and Mexico with NAFTA are the most successful examples in this respect. This immediately raises the question of which developing partners are willing and, especially, able to embark upon such a complex process.

The costs of adjustment to trade liberalisation are a significant challenge to developing countries. The inclusion in RTAs of efforts to reform domestic policies, agreeing to common disciplines for regulatory regimes, and to strengthen institutional capacity, exacerbates such a problem. To develop flanking policies, such as substantial external financial and technical assistance, is therefore paramount to support the economic transition in the Partners and to help offset the significant loss of government tariff revenue, the increasing opportunity cost of administering RTA rules and for addressing the social and economic consequences of this reform process. That is why EU RTAs are never limited to trade issues, but crucially include aid in the form of financial and technical assistance and political dialogue.[33]

Bilateral and regional dialogue typically covering the political and security dimension is indeed an essential element of this policy mix of which regional economic integration is a part.

---

[33] For an overview of the objectives, the financial envelope and the workings of the MEDA programme – the principal financial instrument of the EU for the implementation of the Euro-Mediterranean Partnership, see <http://europa.eu.int/comm/external_relations/euromed/meda.htm>; for EU financial assistance to the countries of the Western Balkans, and the Stabilisation and Association Agreements countries in particular, see <http://europa.eu.int/comm/external_relations/see/>.

For example, within the Barcelona process – whose aim is to create an integrated area of peace and prosperity on both sides of the Mediterranean – the participants agreed 'to conduct a strengthened political dialogue at regular intervals, based on observance of essential principles of international law, and reaffirm a number of common objectives in matters of internal and external stability'.[34] The dialogue element is also aimed at promoting understanding between cultures and rapprochement of the peoples in the partners as well as to develop free and flourishing civil societies (social, cultural and human partnership). In all of these areas, as in the trade and economic integration field, the regional cooperation dimension complements and reinforces the bilateral approach. It should also be noticed that all EU RTAs contain a 'conditionality clause' stating that respect for the *democratic principles* and *fundamental human rights* established by the Universal Declaration of Human Rights shall inspire the domestic and external policies of the Community and the partner country and shall constitute an essential element of the Agreement.[35]

If these principles are not respected, this clause could be used for suspending the application of a EU RTA *vis-à-vis* a given partner. To date, though, this possibility has not been used (even if in the case of Israel, a demand for suspension was presented in the European Parliament). These clauses allow the EU to exert a 'moral suasion' effect on the RTA partner, whose extent has in practice been fully appraised in the context of the bilateral dialogue more than in actual suspension measures of preferential treatment.[36]

Recently, in negotiating new trade agreements the EU has been considering the inclusion of a Weapons of Mass Destruction (WMDs) non-proliferation clause, fostering cooperation to counter the proliferation of WMDs. Such a clause would foresee the possibility of suspending or terminating the RTA agreement in the case of non-compliance by one of the parties to the agreement with the commitments undertaken under the non-proliferation clause. A recent development is also the negotiation of a specific provision in new RTAs whereby the parties reaffirm the importance of the fight against terrorism, and agree to cooperate in the prevention of and the fight against terrorist acts, in accordance with international conventions and with their respective legislation and regulations.[37]

---

[34] See the text of the Barcelona Declaration at <http://europa.eu.int/comm/external_relations/euromed/bd.htm>.

[35] See, as an example, Article 2 of the Euro-Mediterranean Agreement establishing an Association Agreement between the European Communities and their Member States, on the one part, and the Kingdom of Morocco, on the other, *OJEC* [2000] L 70.

[36] But see M. Shiff and L.A. Winters, op. cit. n. 30, at 198-201.

[37] See information document on the conclusion of the negotiations at the technical level for an EU-Syria Association Agreement at <http://europa.eu.int/comm/external_relations/syria/intro/index.htm>. See also the GCC-EU 13th Joint Council and Ministerial Meeting report, March 2003, at <http://europa.eu.int/comm/external_relations/gulf_cooperation/intro/13jc.pdf>. These issues play an important role also in the current negotiation of an EU Trade and Cooperation Agreement with Iran; see <http://europa.eu.int/comm/external_relations/iran/intro/gac.htm#iran171103>.

Summing up, EU RTAs – through this policy mix based on trade integration, financial and technical assistance, and political dialogue – have a very important role to play in helping to prevent conflict, diffusing tension following conflict (e.g., Western Balkans) and upholding and improving security and stability in partner countries.

4. CONCLUSION

Historically the EU has been a major user of Regional Trade Agreements (Free Trade Areas and Customs Unions). While the EU's priority is and remains multilateral trade liberalisation and rule making within the WTO system, RTAs are seen as a potentially useful policy instrument for trade liberalisation and economic development when used as a complement to this multilateral priority.

The conditions that need to be met to ensure such complementarity are full WTO compatibility, a high degree of regulatory convergence and rule making going beyond the basic multilateral rules, and – in most cases – effective regional integration among the EU's partners themselves.

The most recent FTAs concluded by the EU have shown a steady evolution in terms of their scope and level of ambition. This reflects the EU view that an FTA must go beyond the WTO in order to make sense: the WTO sets the ground, an FTA builds on it, both in terms of goods and services liberalisation and rule-making and regulatory harmonisation or cooperation. This also reflects the EU view that preferential trade agreements should include elements of 'deep integration' involving common disciplines for a broad range of regulatory areas (customs procedures, standards, sanitary questions, competition, services, government procurement, etc.), the simple removal of barriers at the border not being sufficient to ensure a significant economic impact.

In so doing, EU RTAs encourage and support the adoption of sound domestic institutions and policies, good governance and the expansion of human freedoms that – beyond trade liberalisation, competition and market openness – have proved to be necessary conditions for sustainable development and poverty reduction.

Besides, the EU is increasingly looking for relations around the world on a 'region-to-region' basis, be it in ongoing FTA negotiations (Mercosur, GCC, EPAs) or other forms of trade cooperation relations (e.g., with ASEAN). Such an approach has the potential to generate more economically viable and interesting results, since regional integration on the partners' side increases the market potential and makes efforts in the regulatory area more 'cost-effective'. Ultimately, this should lead to stability, development and growth.

Overall EU RTAs, through their impact on partners' competitiveness and growth, full integration in the international trade system, the promotion of sound domestic policies that are essential for sustainable development and regional cooperation and interdependence, plus technical and financial assistance and political dialogue, have had a very important role in helping to diffuse conflict and to uphold and improve security and stability in many partner countries. This has been more immediately visible in neighbouring countries, such as the CEECs, the Western Balkans, and the Southern Mediterranean countries, where the goal of the EU policy was more directly oriented at preparing accession to the Union (CEECs), at creating an integrated area of peace and prosperity (Mediterranean) or at ensuring peace and stability, by anchoring the region to the EU and its values and ensuring its economic development (Balkans). In all these cases trade liberalisation and economic integration was a central element in the process.

The Economic Partnership Agreements being negotiated between the EU and the ACP countries also aim to have a large impact on stability, security and conflict reduction, through their integrated approach to development and trade, a strong link to economic governance in ACP countries and regions, and support for regional integration, coupled with political dialogue and financial assistance. It is expected that the process will increase competitiveness and investment and ultimately accelerate development in ACP countries.

A more indirect, 'mirror' effect can instead be identified in the case of other RTAs being negotiated by the EU, such as those with Mercosur and GCC countries, where the EU has acted first as a model of successful regional cooperation and integration, and then as a catalyst for their own trade integration process through the ongoing negotiation of an FTA framed on a region-to-region pattern. Indirectly, then, the ongoing FTA negotiations with the EU contribute significantly to achieving the objectives of South-South regional integration: increased economic prosperity and stability, improved security and the prevention of conflict.

Even for those FTAs with distant partners that were mainly dominated by market access considerations, it can be argued that the agreement with the EU helped to underpin a delicate economic and political transition process (South Africa), and to support domestic policy reforms and economic development (Mexico, Chile), thus contributing to the partner's economic and political stability.

Indeed the agreements entered into, or under discussion, between the EU and third countries have often been instrumental to the desire to strengthen political relations and thereby to promote and facilitate the achievement of the EU's geopolitical objectives. These, in very general terms, are to secure a stable and prosperous external environment, with all countries and regions firmly placed on a path of sustainable development. The recent Commission Communication on 'Wider Europe'[38] is inscribed in this context, where the EU, following the next

---

[38] Communication from the Commission, *Wider Europe – Neighbourhood: A New Framework for our Eastern and Southern Neighbours*, COM (2003) 104 final.

enlargement, has clearly much to gain, economically and politically, from the improved economic, social and political conditions of its Eastern and Southern neighbours.

Clearly in many of the EU Regional Trade Agreements geopolitical considerations have been central or even dominant, so much so that Trade Policy in the form of (reciprocal or unilateral) trade preferences has often been seen in the past as the principal instrument available to the EU for pursuing foreign policy objectives.

Nevertheless, recognising the impact of EU RTAs on security and stability, and conflict prevention, is not the same as seeing EU RTAs as a policy instrument that should be driven solely by political considerations. Establishing stronger economic links through trade and investment liberalisation, the promotion of sound domestic policies and good governance, should not be seen as automatically ancillary to prevailing political objectives.

In general the strengthening of political links may or may not require stronger economic links and, if it does, an RTA may or may not be a useful and appropriate way of doing this. The issue is then whether creating an FTA or a CU is the most appropriate policy instrument given the political aims in mind and the existing constraints. In some cases other instruments may be preferred. The criteria against which to undertake such an assessment include a careful evaluation of the potential economic effects, in order to avoid that the political momentum behind integration will lead to counterproductive economic decisions.[39]

---

[39] World Bank, op. cit. n. 22.

Chapter 9
COMMUNITY COOPERATION POLICY AND CONFLICT PREVENTION

by Bernd Martenczuk[1]

1. INTRODUCTION

Since the end of the cold war, the number of countries involved in violent conflict has risen sharply. At the same time, the forms of violent conflict have changed, with internal and notably ethnic conflicts becoming more and more frequent. Whether internal or external, violent conflict frequently not only affects the countries directly involved, but may destabilise entire regions, and pose a threat to international peace and security. As a consequence, conflict prevention has become a major concern for the international community in general, and for the European Union in particular.

This new focus on conflict prevention has also left its mark on the cooperation policies of the European Community (hereinafter 'EC' or 'Community'). Whereas EC development cooperation traditionally focused on long-term structural assistance, Community cooperation policy increasingly follows a 'deep' approach, which permits the Community to address the underlying causes of poverty and underdevelopment, such as political and social instability, a lack of adequate institutional and administrative structures, and insufficient respect for democratic principles, human rights and the rule of law.[2] The increasing number of conflicts involving the EC's partner countries has provoked a further deepening of the EC's approach to development cooperation. It has become clear that traditional development assistance is no longer sufficient where the bases for development cooperation are being eroded by armed conflict or civil strife. This shift in priorities is reflected in a joint declaration of the Council and the Commission on the development policy of the European Community, which identifies conflict pre-

---

[1] Doctor of Law, MPA. Member of the Legal Service of the European Commission, Brussels. This article expresses the personal views of the author only, and does not necessarily reflect the position of the European Commission.

[2] See the Commission's communication on the Community's development policy, which defines institutional support, good governance and the rule of law as a priority area for Community development cooperation, COM (2000) 212 final, pp. 30-31.

V. Kronenberger and J. Wouters, eds., The European Union and Conflict Prevention
© *2004, T·M·C·ASSER PRESS, The Hague, The Netherlands*

vention and crisis management as a horizontal aspect which requires systematic attention.[3] More recently, the European Commission adopted a Communication on conflict prevention, which stressed in particular the need to integrate conflict prevention into the EC's cooperation programmes.[4]

It is against this background that the present contribution will examine to what extent conflict prevention can be addressed with the tools available to the European Community in the context of its cooperation with developing and developed third countries. The article will also address the question of how EC cooperation policies in this area relate to the competences of the European Union (hereinafter the 'EU') under its second pillar, the Common Foreign and Security Policy (CFSP). The contribution's focus will therefore be mainly on questions of EU law, including the question of EC v. EU competence. In contrast, questions of the effectiveness of conflict prevention measures are not the primary focus of the present contribution. This notwithstanding, it is hoped that an improved understanding of the Community's powers and procedures may also contribute to a more effective formulation of EU responses to conflict.

2. SOME DEFINITIONS

At the outset, a number of clarifications and definitions may be necessary. First of all, the geographic scope of the analysis should be defined. Whereas for a long time, cooperation with developing countries was at the forefront of the Community's activities, this focus has equally shifted since the end of the cold war. For instance, the Community now undertakes extensive cooperation activities with the countries of the former Soviet Union, as well as with those of South Eastern Europe, which the EC has not traditionally considered as developing countries. As shown by the case of the former Yugoslavia, conflict prevention is also a major concern with respect to some of these countries. For this reason, the contribution will examine the Community's cooperation both with developing and with developed countries, and examples will be drawn from all geographical regions where conflict has been a major issue.

Second, it should be noted that the contribution will only deal with conflict prevention through 'cooperation measures'. The term 'cooperation' is used in both Articles 177 and 181a EC, but is not further defined in the Treaty. For present purposes, we can understand cooperation measures as any measures

---

[3] Declaration of 3.11.2000, paragraph 21.

[4] COM (2001) 211 final (notably p. 9 et seq.). See also the contribution from EC External Relations Commissioner Chris Patten, 'Prévention des conflits, gestion des crises: une contribution européenne', 66 *Politique étrangère* (2001) at 648. More generally, cf., also Carlos Santiso, *The Reform of EU Development Policy – Improving Strategies for Conflict Prevention, Democracy Promotion and Governance Conditionality* (Brussels, CEPS Working Document No. 182 March 2002).

through which the EC supports developments in the beneficiary country or region. Such support will usually take the form of targeted financial or technical assistance. In contrast, the present contribution is not concerned with the numerous other tools which the EU may have at its disposal for the purposes of conflict prevention, such as declarations, political dialogue, special representatives, sanctions, or the use of other sectoral policies, such as trade policy or environmental policy.[5]

Finally, the difficult task of defining the notion of 'conflict prevention' remains. From a general perspective, all measures of cooperation policy might be argued to contribute to conflict prevention by stimulating growth, reducing poverty, reducing inequality, or improving governance, and thus reducing the potential for conflict. However, for the purposes of the present contribution, it appears appropriate to use a narrower definition, which focuses on cooperation measures directly linked with the prevention of conflict, and notably of armed conflict. Some examples of issues addressed by cooperation measures which the EC or EU has undertaken in the recent past would be the following:

- small arms collection and landmine clearing;
- demobilisation and reintegration of combatants;
- mediation, facilitation and conciliation efforts;
- stabilisation and peace-keeping activities;
- police missions and support in the field of the maintenance of law and order;
- election observations and election support;
- assistance to refugees and displaced persons;
- minority rights, ethnic questions;
- human rights;
- institutional support when referring to the above.

Such cooperation measures at the borderline of technical cooperation and political stabilisation are a relatively new development in EC cooperation policies. At the same time, they frequently generate difficult issues of competence and procedure between the first and the second pillars of the EU. For this reason, they shall be the main focus of the following contribution. In contrast, the present contribution does not distinguish between pre-conflict and post-conflict measures. Although a pre-conflict approach is clearly the preferable form of conflict prevention, conflict prevention may also sometimes require the post-conflict easing of tensions in order to prevent the resurgence of conflict. In contrast, to what extent Community or EU cooperation can also contribute to the ending or containment of ongoing conflict is a different question which will be addressed later.

---

[5] On these, see respectively the contributions by J. Niño Pérez, A. Rossi and A. Weiss in this volume.

3.   Cooperation Policy, Conflict Prevention, and the EC Treaty

The EC Treaty does not contain any specific provisions on conflict prevention. However, the EC Treaty gives the Community the power to conduct a policy in the field of development cooperation (Article 177 EC). Since the Treaty of Nice, the EC Treaty also contains a specific legal basis on economic, financial and technical cooperation with third countries (Article 181a EC).[6] This section shall examine to what extent these provisions enable the EC to address issues of conflict prevention through its cooperation policies.

3.1   Development cooperation

The objectives of development cooperation are defined in Article 177(1) EC. These objectives include notably the sustainable economic and social development of the developing countries, and more particularly the most disadvantaged among them; the smooth and gradual integration of the developing countries into the world economy; and the campaign against poverty in the developing countries.

The description of these objectives is relatively wide, and therefore leaves the Community a margin of appreciation for the definition of the actual content of its cooperation with developing countries.[7] In particular, cooperation measures may also concern areas which internally fall under other fields of Community policy. As the Court of Justice of the European Communities has held for a cooperation agreement with India based on the Community's powers in the field of development cooperation, the outer limit is that cooperation agreements must not impose on the Community 'such extensive obligations concerning the specific matters referred to that those obligations in fact constitute objectives distinct from those of development cooperation'.[8] In concrete terms, this means that the Community can provide funding and assistance to developing countries in all fields which are relevant for their development, be they economic, social, cultural, or political. In contrast, it is not decisive whether the Community could legislate internally in the field concerned by the cooperation measures.

---

[6] The legal bases for development cooperation and cooperation with other third countries have been integrated into the Draft Treaty establishing a Constitution for Europe elaborated by the European Convention (cf., Articles. III-218 to III-220 and III-221 to III-222), published in *OJEC* [2003] C 169/1.

[7] On the following, see also Bernd Martenczuk, 'Cooperation with Developing and Other Third Countries', in Stefan Griller/Birgit Weidel (eds.), *External Economic Relations and Foreign Policy in the European Union* (Vienna/New York, Springer 2002), p. 385, 392.

[8] Case C-268/94, *Portugal* v. *Council* [1996] ECR I-6177, paragraph 39. On this case, cf., Steve Peers, 'Fragmentation or Evasion in the Community's Development Policy? The Impact of Portugal v. Council', in Alan Dashwood/Christoph Hillion (eds.), *The General Law of E.C. External Relations* (London, Sweet & Maxwell 2000), p. 100.

It is noteworthy that under Article 177 EC, development cooperation is not limited to questions of economic or social development. Rather, Community development cooperation may address all the 'root causes' of poverty and underdevelopment, including questions related to the political system of the developing countries, including the potential for violent conflict. The importance of political considerations for development cooperation is illustrated by Article 177(2) EC, which provides that Community policy in this area 'shall contribute to the general objective of developing and consolidating democracy and the rule of law, and to that of respecting human rights and fundamental freedoms'. The Court held on this basis that the inclusion of a human rights clause in the cooperation agreement with India had been in accordance with the objectives of Community development policy.[9]

The fact that unlike democracy, the rule of law, and human rights, the prevention of conflicts is not specifically referred to in Article 177 EC does not exclude conflict prevention from the scope of possible measures under this provision. First of all, it is unlikely that democracy, the rule of law and human rights can flourish in a political system which is afflicted by violent conflict. The same can also be said of the broader objectives of Article 177(1) EC, notably the sustainable economic and social development and the campaign against poverty in developing countries. In many developing countries, violent conflict is one of the main causes of underdevelopment and poverty. In such a situation, development cooperation would fail its objectives if it did not attempt to contribute actively to the re-establishment of a stable and peaceful political system, which is one of the preconditions for sustainable development.

In this context, it is also worth noting that, according to Article 3(2) EU, the Union shall ensure the consistency of its external activities as a whole, including its development policy. Since one of the objectives of the Union according to Article 11(1) EU is to contribute to international peace and security, it would be strange if the Community could not contribute to this objective through the means at its disposal, notably development cooperation. In this sense, conflict prevention is a concern which is structurally similar, but even more fundamental than democracy, the rule of law and human rights. Accordingly, conflict prevention is a transversal issue of development cooperation under Article 177 EC.

3.2 Cooperation with other third countries

Until the entry into force of the Treaty of Nice, the EC Treaty did not contain any specific provisions on cooperation with non-developing third countries. In the absence of a specific legal basis, and to the extent that such measures did not fall under other areas of Community policy, such measures had to be based on Article 308 EC. Since the Treaty of Nice, Article 181a EC now empowers the Commu-

---

[9] Case C-268/94, *Portugal* v. *Council* [1996] ECR I-6177, paragraph 29.

nity to adopt economic, financial and technical cooperation measures with third countries which are not necessarily developing countries.[10]

As the conflicts in the former Yugoslavia, but also in certain areas of the former Soviet Union and in the Middle East have illustrated, violent conflict is not necessarily limited to countries which have traditionally been considered as 'developing countries'.[11] For this reason, the question to which extent cooperation measures under Article 181a EC may address issues of conflict prevention arises in the same way as it does for developing countries. Article 181a EC does not explicitly define the objectives of cooperation under this provision. Rather, the reference to 'economic, financial and technical cooperation measures' in Article 181(1) EC could be interpreted as indicating a more technical and non-political character of the measures to be adopted under this provision.

However, such a narrow reading would ignore that Article 181a EC was essentially intended to replace recourse to Article 308 EC for cooperation measures with third countries. As will be seen below, the EC has, notably with respect to the former Yugoslavia, adopted a number of measures with a strong emphasis on conflict prevention. Since Article 181a EC was not intended to limit, but rather to facilitate the exercise of Community competence, it can therefore be assumed that it continues to cover conflict prevention as a cross-cutting concern. This is also supported by the second sentence of Article 181a(1) EC, which provides that measures under this provision shall be 'consistent with the development policy of the Community'. Moreover, like Article 177(2) EC, the second subparagraph of Article 181a(1) EC provides that Community cooperation with third countries shall contribute to democracy, the rule of law, and respect for human rights and fundamental freedoms. Like for developing countries, a stable and peaceful political and institutional system is therefore recognised as one of the preconditions for cooperation under Article 181a EC.

Without prejudice to the differences between developing and other third countries, which may affect the actual content of cooperation measures, Article 181a EC therefore permits the Community to address concerns of conflict prevention to the same extent as does Article 177 EC.

4. COMMUNITY COOPERATION INSTRUMENTS AND CONFLICT PREVENTION

On the basis of the EC Treaty, the Community has adopted a number of measures which institute cooperation programmes with third countries,[12] and which to a varying degree cover aspects of conflict prevention. The present section will no-

---

[10] In more detail on this new legal basis, see Martenczuk, op. cit. n. 7, pp. 405-410.

[11] On the notion of developing country, see Martenczuk, op. cit. n. 7, pp. 389-392.

[12] On the EC's cooperation programmes generally, see Martenczuk, op. cit. n. 7, p. 396, 402.

tably examine the scope of the geographical instruments, which cover cooperation with a particular third country or region. We shall also briefly look at the thematic instruments, which cover cooperation with third countries with respect to a specific issue or concern. In a further step, we shall analyse the procedures for the implementation of Community assistance, with specific attention to the problems of conflict prevention. Finally, we shall examine the recently created Rapid Reaction Mechanism (RRM), which is a new instrument of great relevance for conflict prevention.

4.1 Geographic instruments

In the following, we shall look at a number of cooperation programmes where conflict prevention is a particular concern, notably the Cotonou Agreement covering the ACP countries, and the CARDS, MEDA, ALA and TACIS regulations.

4.1.1 The ACP countries

The basic framework for cooperation between the EC and the 77 countries of Africa, the Caribbean and the Pacific (ACP) is the Cotonou Agreement, which has replaced the previous Lomé Conventions.[13] Notably in Africa, violent conflict has embroiled many countries, and hindered the attainment of the objectives of the Community's development policy. Already during the negotiations of the Cotonou Agreement, there was awareness that peace and political stability are an essential precondition for a fruitful cooperation with the ACP countries, and that the future partnership would have to reflect this fact. As a consequence, in a set of guidelines adopted in 1997, the Commission identified the reinforcement of the political dimension of the partnership as a key objective for the negotiations.[14] In this context, the Commission notably advocated that more resources should be devoted to conflict prevention.[15]

This new focus is clearly reflected in the text of the Cotonou Agreement, which distinguishes itself from its predecessors by its strong emphasis on peace building and conflict prevention. According to Article 1(1), the basic objective of the Partnership is 'to promote and expedite the economic, cultural and social development of the ACP States, with a view to contributing to peace and security and to promoting a stable and democratic political environment'. More impor-

---

[13] *OJEC* [2000] L 317/1. After a period of transitional application, the Cotonou Agreement has definitely entered into force on 1st April 2003. For more detail on the Cotonou Agreement, see B. Martenczuk, 'From Lomé to Cotonou: The ACP-EC Partnership Agreement in a Legal Perspective', 5 *European Foreign Affairs Review* (2000) at 461. Cooperation with South Africa is covered by a separate regulation (Regulation No. 1726/2000, *OJEC* [2000] L 198/1).

[14] Guidelines for the negotiation of new cooperation agreements with the African, Caribbean and Pacific (ACP) countries, COM (97) 537 final, p. 3.

[15] Idem, p. 11.

tantly still, aspects of peace building, conflict prevention and resolution are specifically addressed in Article 11 of the Agreement. According to Article 11(1),
the Parties shall pursue 'an active, comprehensive and integrated policy of peace-
building and conflict prevention and resolution within the framework of the Partnership'. This policy shall focus in particular 'on preventing violent conflicts at
an early stage by addressing their root-causes in a targeted manner, and with an
appropriate combination of all available instruments'. Article 11(2) goes on to
state that the activities in this field 'shall in particular include support for balancing political, economic, social and cultural opportunities among all segments of
society, for strengthening the democratic legitimacy and effectiveness of governance, for establishing effective mechanisms for the peaceful conciliation of
group interests, for bridging dividing lines among different segments of society,
as well as support for an active and organised civil society'. Article 11(3) lists a
number of activities that shall be supported by the Parties with a view to peace
building, conflict prevention and resolution. This includes actions such as support
for mediation, negotiation and reconciliation, for effective regional management
of shared, scarce natural resources, for the demobilisation and reintegration of
former combatants into society, for addressing the problem of child soldiers, for
suitable action to set responsible limits to military expenditure and the arms trade,
for the fight against anti-personnel landmines, as well as against the spread, illegal trafficking and accumulation of small arms and light weapons. Finally, according to Article 11(4), in situations of violent conflict the parties shall take all
suitable actions to prevent an intensification of violence, to limit its territorial
spread, and to facilitate a peaceful settlement of the existing disputes.

   Article 11 of the Cotonou Agreement contains an almost comprehensive
programme of peace-building and conflict prevention, which applies to all the activities governed by the Partnership Agreement. In particular, Article 11 also
opens the possibility of financing of such operations under the Partnership Agreement.[16] On this basis, the EC has already, in the relatively short time since the
provisional application of the Cotonou Agreement, contributed to a number of activities falling under Article 11(3). For instance, in the Democratic Republic of
Congo, the EC has financed the mediation effort in the context of the Lusaka
Peace agreements, as well as a number of other activities concerning the reconstruction of this war-torn country with a specific emphasis on refugees and displaced persons. In the Horn of Africa, the EC has supported an OAU conflict
prevention and crisis management mechanism, targeting in particular the conflict
between Eritrea and Ethiopia. In Tanzania, the EC has financed a small-arms collection programme, and also supported the implementation of the 'Muafaka'
Political Agreement for Zanzibar. In West Africa, the EC has supported the

---

[16] Whereas Article 220 Lomé IV contained a detailed list of objectives for development finance
cooperation, Article 55 of the Partnership Agreement merely contains a reference to the objectives of
the Agreement.

development of a conflict prevention and crisis management mechanism of the Economic Community of West African States (ECOWAS). Finally, in a recent development, the EC is preparing to finance the deployment of Nigerian peace-keepers in Liberia after the departure of former President Taylor.[17] This will constitute the first time that EDF funds are used to finance peace-keeping activities by a third country.

4.1.2   The Western Balkans

Cooperation with the countries of the former Yugoslavia and Albania is covered by the CARDS regulation.[18] Following the painful experience of the conflicts in the former Yugoslavia, this regulation places a very strong emphasis on conflict prevention. According to Article 2(1) of the Regulation, the main purpose of the Community assistance 'is to support participation by the recipient countries in the stabilisation and association process'. Community assistance shall, *inter alia*, cover reconstruction, aid for the return of refugees and displaced persons, and stabilisation of the region (Article 2[2][a]), the creation of an institutional and legislative framework to underpin democracy, the rule of law, and human and minority rights, reconciliation and the consolidation of civil society, the independence of the media and the strengthening of legality and of measures to combat organised crime (Article 2[2][b]), or the development of closer relations among the recipient countries covered by the regulation (Article 2[2][e]). Even though conflict prevention is not explicitly mentioned as an objective, it clearly underlies the various activities envisaged in the regulation. On the basis of a separate Council Regulation,[19] the EC also contributes to the United Nations Interim Administration Mission in Kosovo (UNMIK), where the EC is responsible for 'Pillar IV', which is in charge of economic reconstruction. Even though the focus of the EC's activities is on issues directly related to economic reconstruction and development, these remain intimately linked with the overall mission of UNMIK, which is the stabilisation and reconstruction of the Kosovo. On the basis of the same regulation, the EC also contributes to the Office of the High Representative in Bosnia and Herzegovina, who is responsible for the monitoring of the imple-

---

[17] See on this Council Decision 2003/631/EC adopting measures concerning Liberia under Article 96 of the ACP-EC Partnership Agreement in a case of special urgency, *OJEC* [2003] L 220/3. In the annex to this decision, it is indicated that the balances remaining for Liberia from the 8th EDF may be used for 'support to the peace process in Liberia that could include support to a peacekeeping operation in Liberia'. The financing decision implementing this support will be adopted by the Commission.

[18] Regulation No. 2666/00, *OJEC* [2000] L 306/1. The Regulation covers Albania, Bosnia and Herzegovina, Croatia, the Federal Republic of Yugoslavia (now Serbia and Montenegro), and the Former Yugoslav Republic of Macedonia. The Regulation does not apply to Slovenia, which as a candidate for accession falls under the Phare regulation (Regulation No. 3906/89, *OJEC* [1999] L 375/11).

[19] Regulation No. 1080/2000, *OJEC* [2000] L 122/27.

mentation of the Dayton Peace Agreements. More recently, the Commission has proposed to the Council to amend the regulation to also cover the support for to the Stability Pact for South Eastern Europe, which has so far been financed from the CFSP budget.[20] Overall, it is fair to say that the prevention of any resurgence of conflict has become a central theme of all Community assistance to the Western Balkans.

4.1.3   North Africa and the Middle East

The legal basis for cooperation with the countries of North Africa and the Middle East is provided by the MEDA Regulation.[21] This regulation specifically identifies in its Article 2(1) 'the reinforcement of political stability and of democracy' as one of the three sectors of the Euro-Mediterranean partnership eligible for support, and thus at least partially allows the financing of activities relevant for conflict prevention. A particularly thorny conflict for the region is obviously the one between Israel and its neighbours, and most importantly in the Occupied Territories. Support for the Palestinian Administration of the Occupied Territories is based on a specific Council regulation, which generally refers to the aim of aiding their sustainable economic and social development, but also foresees assistance for the proper working of the public administration and the advancement of democracy and human rights.[22] As with the Community support to UNMIK, the focus is thus primarily on questions of economic development, but this assistance is intimately linked with the need to remove the social and economic root causes of conflict. Worth mentioning in this context is also the EC assistance to the United Nations Relief and Works Agency for Palestine Refugees (UNRWA). Although this assistance has a strong humanitarian component, it is also motivated by the desire to contribute to the stabilisation of the situation in the Middle East.[23]

---

[20] COM (2003) 389 final.

[21] Regulation No. 1488/96, *OJEC* [1996] L 189/1, as last amended by Regulation No. 2698/00, *OJEC* [2000] L 311/1.

[22] Regulation No. 1734/1994, *OJEC* [1994] L 182/4; as amended by Regulation No. 2840/98, *OJEC* [1998] L 354/14. The political sensitivity of this support is illustrated by a recent case brought against the Commission before the Tribunal of First Instance by several victims of a Palestinian suicide bombing. The plaintiffs alleged that the EC's support to the Palestinian Authority, and notably to the Palestinian education system, which in turn they alleged fostered hatred of Israel, had contributed to the attacks. By order of the Court of First Instance of the European Communities of 23 April 2003 (Case T-73/03, *Zaoui* v. *Commission*, not yet published), the actions were dismissed as manifestly unfounded, since the plaintiffs had not shown that the Commission's support had in fact been the cause of the attacks.

[23] See in this sense explicitly the third recital of Council Decision 2002/817 on the conclusion of the Convention between the EC and UNRWA for 2002 to 2005 (*OJEC* [2002] L 281/10). It is interesting to note that the corresponding recital of the decision concluding the Convention for the years 1999 to 2001 (*OJEC* [1999] L 261/36) does not yet include a reference to the aspect of stabilisation, but only to sustainable economic and social development.

4.1.4   Latin America and Asia

Cooperation with the developing countries of Latin America and Asia is based on the ALA Regulation.[24] This Regulation, which dates from 1992, is one of the older regional cooperation instruments of the Community. As a consequence, it does not explicitly address issues of conflict prevention, but refers more broadly to questions of human development, including support for democracy, good governance and human rights. Of course, the relative silence of the ALA regulation on these issues does not mean that actions of conflict prevention are excluded from financing, if they fall under the general objectives of the regulation. In fact, conflicts like the one in Colombia, and in certain parts of Asia (e.g., Cambodia, Indonesia, East Timor) show that in these regions, support for conflict prevention and peace-building may be necessary. As a consequence, the Commission proposal for a successor regulation to the ALA regulation now mentions 'measures aiming at confidence-building and conflict prevention', and measures 'to support rehabilitation, reconstruction and aid to uprooted people' explicitly as sectors for cooperation with the countries of Latin America and Asia.[25] Currently, actions to support uprooted people in Latin America and Asia, including the reintegration of former combatants, are the subject of a separate regulation,[26] which will, however, be merged with the new ALA regulation once it has been adopted.

4.1.5   The former Soviet Union and Mongolia

A specific programme has also been established for the countries of the former Soviet Union and Mongolia (TACIS).[27] However, even though conflict prevention is an issue for this region, as evidenced for example by the conflict in Chechnya, conflict prevention is not well reflected as an area for support in the TACIS regulation. In fact, the TACIS regulation follows a narrower approach in the definition of the activities to be supported than the programmes which have been discussed so far. The central objective of TACIS is to promote the transition to a market economy and to reinforce democracy and the rule of law (Article 1). The regulation lists in an annex a number of sectoral areas which are eligible for cooperation, including support for institutional, legal and administrative reform, and provides that cooperation with each partner country shall cover at most three of these areas (Article 2). The sector of institutional, legal and administrative reform may also cover some activities relevant from the point of view of conflict prevention, but this does not appear to be a main focus of the regulation. It be-

---

[24] Regulation No. 443/92, *OJEC* [1992] L 52/1.
[25] COM (2002) 340 final, Articles 2(2)(d) and (f).
[26] Regulation No. 2130/2001, *OJEC* [2001] L 287/3.
[27] Regulation No. 99/00, *OJEC* [2000] L 12/1. The regulation does not apply to the Baltic countries, which as candidates for accession fall under the Phare regulation (op. cit. n. 18).

comes obvious, therefore, that the extent to which Community programmes cover conflict prevention does not just depend on the Community's powers, but is also a matter of political choice and expediency: in the case of the former Soviet Union, the particular historical and social context, as well as the still predominant role of Russia in the region, may have induced the Community to be more selective in its cooperation programmes than it has been in other regions.

4.2 Thematic instruments

Supplementing the geographic instruments described above, the Community has also adopted a number of thematic cooperation programmes. Some of these thematic instruments are interesting from the point of view of their relevance for conflict prevention. However, since a number of these instruments are the subject of specific contributions elsewhere in this book, the following discussion shall be brief.

One instrument to be mentioned is the regulation on humanitarian aid, which constitutes the basis for the Commission's humanitarian activities worldwide.[28] Since the humanitarian aid regulation covers assistance in case of man-made disasters, notably wars, and also operations for short-term rehabilitation and reconstruction, it is a very valuable tool for the Community to assist in immediate post-conflict situations. However, due to its focus on humanitarian concerns, the regulation cannot generally address long-term issues of reconstruction and conflict prevention.[29]

Directly relevant with respect to conflict prevention is the regulation concerning rehabilitation and reconstruction in developing countries.[30] This regulation, which dates from 1996, was rather progressive for the time of its adoption. Notably, in its Article 2.2, it identifies as priorities the relaunch of production on a lasting basis, the physical and operational rehabilitation of basic infrastructure, including mine clearance, social reintegration, in particular of refugees, displaced persons and demobilised troops, and the restoration of the institutional capacities needed in the rehabilitation period, especially at local level, and thus a number of activities closely linked to conflict prevention. Nonetheless, the instrument has gradually fallen into disuse, and its budgetary allocation has shrunk. Currently, the regulation covers only assistance in a limited number of cases, notably East Timor and Afghanistan, where other instruments have not been sufficient. Presumably, this gradual erosion of the rehabilitation regulation reflects the stronger

---

[28] Regulation No. 1257/96, *OJEC* [1996] L 163/1. The Community's humanitarian aid policy is implemented by the European Commission Humanitarian Aid Office (ECHO), which is a service of the Commission.

[29] On this issue, cf., the Commission Communication on *Linking Relief, Rehabilitation and Development*, COM (2001) 153 final.

[30] Regulation No. 2258/95, *OJEC* [1996] L 306/1.

integration of rehabilitation and conflict prevention into the geographic cooperation programmes, which has made a separate legal instrument on rehabilitation
dispensable.

Of great relevance from the point of view of conflict prevention are the two
regulations concerning operations which contribute to the general objective of
furthering democracy, human rights, and the rule of law.[31] Most of the activities
under these regulations contribute in some way to the stability of the political system, and thus to the prevention of conflicts. However, the regulations also specifically provide for support for a range of measures to 'promote respect for
human rights and democratisation by preventing conflict and dealing with its consequences', which are targeted directly at conflict prevention and resolution.[32] Finally, worth mentioning from the point of view of conflict prevention are also the
two regulations concerning action against anti-personnel landmines.[33] Undoubtedly, the motivation of these regulations is partially humanitarian; however, both
regulations acknowledge that anti-personnel landmines 'obstruct [...] reconstruction and rehabilitation and the restoration of normal social conditions',[34] and
therefore can partially be seen as measures of conflict prevention and peace
building.

4.3 Implementing procedures

All assistance under the programmes described above is in principle financed
from the General Budget of the European Union, and is implemented by the European Commission in accordance with Article 274 EC. The only exception is cooperation under the Cotonou Agreement, which is financed not from the budget,
but from the European Development Fund (EDF), which is established by an internal agreement of the Member States.[35] Partially as a consequence of the extra-
budget status of the EDF, the Cotonou Agreement has traditionally been a mixed

---

[31] Regulation No. 975/99, *OJEC* [1999] L 120/1, which covers cooperation with developing
countries, and Regulation No. 976/1999, *OJEC* [1999] L 120/8, which covers other third countries.
On the reasons for this split, see Martenczuk, op. cit. n. 7, pp. 400-401.

[32] Article 2(3) of Regulation No. 975/1999, Article 3(3) of Regulation No. 976/1999. In more
detail on these regulations, see the contribution by S. Fries in this volume.

[33] Regulation No. 1724/2001, *OJEC* [2001] L 234/1, covering actions in developing countries;
Regulation No. 1725/2001, *OJEC* [2001] L 234/6, covering actions in other third countries.

[34] See the second recital of both regulations.

[35] Currently in force is the Internal Agreement of the 9th EDF, *OJEC* [2000] L 317/355. In the
context of the European Convention, it has been proposed to integrate the EDF into the General
Budget of the EU (Final Report of the Working Group on External Action, CONV 459/02, paragraph
56). In accordance with this proposal, Article 179(3) EC, which provides that EC development cooperation measures do not affect cooperation with the ACP countries, is not contained in the corresponding provision of the Draft Constitution prepared by the European Convention (cf., Article
III-219).

agreement of the Community and its Member States.[36] In a judgment from 1994, the Court of Justice confirmed the legality of this practice under the EC Treaty. However, in this judgment, the Court also held that the provision of financial assistance under the Convention was a joint obligation of the Community and its Member States.[37] Moreover, it should be noted that the Internal Agreement mandates the Commission to implement the financial assistance in a way which is similar to the implementation mechanisms under the other Community cooperation instruments.[38] Accordingly, it should be stressed that despite the special status of the EDF, finance cooperation under the Cotonou Agreement is a Community competence, albeit shared with the Member States. This therefore also applies with respect to the activities regarding peace-building, conflict prevention and resolution described in Article 11 of the Cotonou Agreement.

The implementation procedures for each Community programme vary according to the provisions of each specific instrument. Nonetheless, a number of general features can be distinguished. Under all geographic instruments, it is by now required that assistance is programmed through country strategy papers and national indicative programmes. Such programmes are normally elaborated in cooperation with the recipient country and define the priorities of cooperation for a certain period of time. Similar programming mechanisms also exist for most of the thematic instruments. In all cases, it is important that conflict prevention is already given due attention at the programming stage, and that appropriate activities are foreseen where there is a potential for conflict. For this reason, the Commission now systematically uses country strategy papers to analyse the potential for conflict in a given country, and to elaborate appropriate responses.[39] Obviously, given the sometimes sudden nature of conflict, the Community also needs to keep a certain flexibility to react as and when conflict occurs. Tools to provide for such flexibility would be envelopes of national programmes reserved for 'unforeseen events',[40] the underprogramming of envelopes, or – as a last resort – budgetary transfers.

Within the framework of programming, it is the Commission that decides on individual actions to be financed. Frequently, the underlying legal basis provides that before taking the financing decision, the Commission must consult a committee composed of representatives of the Member States. With some rare exceptions,[41] the respective legal bases do not take into account the urgency of the measure in question. Rather, the need for committee consultation is frequently

---

[36] In more detail on the mixed nature of the Cotonou Agreement and its implications see Martenczuk, op. cit. n. 13, p. 484.

[37] Case C-316/91, *Parliament* v. *Council* [1994] ECR I-625, paragraph 33.

[38] See notably Article 11(1) of the 9th EDF Financial Agreement (op. cit. n. 35).

[39] See the Commission's Communication on conflict prevention, COM (2001) 211 final, pp. 11-12.

[40] As foreseen under the Cotonou Agreement, Annex IV, Article 3(2)(b).

[41] In particular, the humanitarian aid regulation (op. cit. n. 28), Article 13.

determined on the basis of the financial amount to be committed. The financial threshold for consultation may vary strongly from instrument to instrument; for instance, under the EDF, committee consultation is required for projects with a value of more than € 8 million, whereas under ALA, the threshold is still € 1 million. Under the thematic instruments, the threshold is generally relatively low; for instance, under the human rights regulation, it is € 1 million, under the demining regulations, € 3 million. It is clear that the requirement of committee consultation considerably slows down the process, and may negatively affect the Commission's ability to respond quickly to situations of crisis. This problem may also arise where, as for instance is the case under the CARDS, MEDA and TACIS regulations, commitments are generally made in the form of annual programmes, and not in the form of project-specific decisions.

An important aspect from the point of view of conflict prevention is also the degree of involvement of the beneficiary country in the decision-making process. A relatively extreme case in this regard is the Cotonou Agreement, where the agreement of the ACP country is required both at the programming and the project identification stage. Most other geographic instruments require coordination with the beneficiary country at least at the programming stage, but leave the Commission more flexibility in defining itself the actions to be financed. The thematic instruments, finally, generally do not require the agreement of the beneficiary country, even though this may of course practically remain necessary for the implementation of a project in the beneficiary country. It is clear that in conflicts where the government of the beneficiary country is itself a party, a strong involvement on the part of that government in the decision-making and implementation process may be undesirable. Presumably for this reason, electoral observation projects have generally been financed under the human rights regulation, which allows a distance to be kept from the government concerned, whereas electoral support activities are normally financed under the geographic instruments, and implemented in cooperation with the beneficiary country.

Finally, an interesting question is also who actually implements cooperation projects. Under the geographic programmes, and notably under the Cotonou Agreement, it is frequently the partner country that is responsible for project implementation. However, for politically sensitive operations, it may be more preferable to have recourse to implementing partners independent of the government, e.g., non-governmental organisations or international organisations.[42] Similarly, difficulties may also occur where, due to conflict, the partner country in question no longer has the capacity to implement projects itself. In such situations, the Commission may have no choice but to resort to other implementing partners, or to exceptionally assume implementation itself. An interesting varia-

---

[42] However, Article 58(2) of the Cotonou Agreement allows implementation by non-state actors only with the consent of the ACP country concerned.

tion of the latter case is the Community's assistance to the Western Balkans, for which a European Agency for Reconstruction was set up, to which the Commission has delegated the implementation of assistance under the CARDS regulation, including support to UNMIK and the OHR. This creation of a specialised agency was presumably motivated by the great volume and long-term character of the Community's assistance; it remains to be seen whether this will be followed by other examples.[43]

4.4   The Rapid Reaction Mechanism

Despite the multitude of tools available to the Community, the Union's response to crisis has frequently been criticised as being too slow and ineffective. As a consequence, the Helsinki European Council of 10 and 11 December 1999 called, *inter alia*, for the establishment of a non-military crisis management mechanism to allow a speedier Union response in situations of crisis.[44]

As a response, the Rapid Reaction Mechanism (RRM) was created in 2001 by a Council regulation based on Article 308 EC.[45] According to Article 1 of the Regulation, the RRM is designed to allow the Community to respond in a rapid, efficient and flexible manner, to situations of urgency or crisis or to the emergence of crisis. According to Article 2.1, the RRM builds upon all the existing Community legal instruments which are listed in an Annex to the Regulation; this Annex includes most of the instruments discussed above which were already in force at the time of the adoption of the Regulation.[46] According to Article 2.2, an action may be undertaken under the RRM if it would 'under normal circumstances fall within all the regulations and programmes listed in the Annex', if the action is intended to be immediate and cannot be launched within a reasonable time-limit under the existing legal instruments, and if the action is limited in time, which according to Article 8.2 means that the action should normally not exceed a period of six months.

According to Article 3(1) of the Regulation, the mechanism may be triggered 'when in the beneficiary countries concerned there occur situations of crisis or emerging crisis, situations posing a threat to law and order, the security and safety of individuals, situations threatening to escalate into armed conflict or to destabilise the country and where such situations are likely to jeopardise the ben-

---

[43] A recent Council Regulation (No. 58/2003, *OJEC* [2003] L 11/1) empowers the Commission to set up agencies, to which it may entrust certain tasks relating to the management of Community programmes.

[44] Paragraph 28 of the Presidency Conclusions.

[45] Regulation No. 381/2001, *OJEC* [2001] L 57/5. Since the entry into force of the Nice Treaty, it would appear that this regulation would be covered by Articles 179 and 181a EC.

[46] A notable exception is the humanitarian aid regulation. This is due to the fact that according to Article 2(3) of the RRM Regulation, humanitarian operations shall not normally be financed under the RRM.

eficial effects of assistance and cooperation policies [...]'. All action under the RRM shall be implemented by the Commission. It is noteworthy that the Commission may take action without recourse to any committee; it is however required to inform the Council before taking a decision, and must 'duly take into account the approach adopted by the Council, in the interest of the cohesion of EU external activities' (Article 4[2] of the Regulation).

As a crisis response instrument, the RRM is of course not exclusively focused on conflict prevention. However, many of the interventions of the RRM, particularly where they attempt to prevent the deterioration or resurgence of conflict, have a conflict prevention component. Compared to the existing EC cooperation instruments, the RRM has a number of advantages. First of all, despite its link with the existing EC cooperation tools, the RRM is an independent instrument with its own budget line.[47] Moreover, the scope of application of the RRM is wider than that of each of the instruments mentioned in its annex. This follows from Article 2.2, which says that the operations must normally 'fall within all the regulations and programmes' ('relèvent de l'ensemble des règlements et programmes') listed in the Annex. This wording, even though it is somewhat imprecise, was intended to mean that whenever an action is possible under any of the geographical or thematic instruments listed in the annex, it may be undertaken under the RRM, provided that the other conditions are fulfilled. This means, for instance, that an action can be carried out in a TACIS country even if the action by its nature would not be possible under the TACIS regulation, but is possible under another geographic or thematic regulation.[48]

The second main advantage of the RRM is speed. Since the Commission does not have to first consult a committee, it can react to a nascent crisis within a relatively short time frame. The prior information of the Council foreseen in Article 4.2 does not require the Commission to delay the implementation of its operation, even though it should of course, as follows already from Article 3.2 EU, take due account of any decisions that the Council may have taken in the context of the CFSP.

On the basis of the RRM, the Commission has already decided on interventions in a number of crises, including Congo-Brazzaville, the Democratic Republic of Congo, Burundi, Indonesia (Aceh), Sri Lanka, Nepal, Palestine, the Horn of Africa, Afghanistan, and the Former Yugoslav Republic of Macedonia. It may still be too early to evaluate the effectiveness of the RRM as a new crisis response tool of the Community. However, it can already be said that the RRM has confirmed the central importance of crisis management and conflict prevention for the Community's cooperation policies.

---

[47] The 2003 appropriations for the RRM amount to € 30million (budget line B7-67 of the General Budget of the European Union for the Year 2003).

[48] This is overlooked by Felix Nkundabagenzi/Caroline Pailhe/Valérie Peclow, *L'Union européenne et la prévention des conflits* (Bruxelles, GRIP 2002), p. 41.

5. COMMUNITY CONFLICT PREVENTION AND CFSP

As was shown in the preceding sections, Community cooperation policy – in particular cooperation with developing countries – is no longer limited to addressing the symptoms of poverty and underdevelopment. Rather, the Community follows a 'deep approach' to cooperation policy, in which it increasingly addresses the root causes of conflict and political instability, which in turn contribute to the persistence of underdevelopment and poverty in the affected countries. Almost all important EC instruments of development cooperation now include conflict prevention among their objectives. Moreover, with the RRM, the Community has established a mechanism which is specifically geared towards crisis management and conflict prevention and resolution. Accordingly, it can be said that conflict prevention has become an important cross-cutting theme for EC cooperation policies.

Inevitably, many Community measures in the field of conflict prevention also have political implications. Therefore, the question of the relationship of Community cooperation policy with the CFSP arises. The question of the dividing line between Community competence and CFSP is by no means a theoretical question. First of all, CFSP measures are financed from a separate title of the EU budget, which is relatively limited.[49] More importantly still, the distinction between Community competence and CFSP has important institutional implications. Under most Community instruments, it is the Commission, where appropriate after consultation of a committee composed of representatives of the Member States, which approves the measures to be taken. In exchange, it is the Council which decides on actions in the context of CFSP in accordance with the requirements of Article 23 EU, which will normally require unanimous voting. Finally, it should be noted that the distinction between Community competence and CFSP is also amenable to judicial review. As the Court has already held, Article 46 EU does not exclude its competence to interpret the final provisions of the EU Treaty, including the provision of Article 47 EU, concerning the relationship between the Community and the second and third pillar.[50] As a consequence, should the Council, acting within the framework of CFSP, adopt an act falling under Community competence, the Court would have jurisdiction to review such an act under Article 230 EC.

In practice, however, conflict prevention is still to a certain extent a 'grey area' where activities of the first and the second pillar sometimes seem to overlap. Despite the increased activities of the Commission in the area, certain types of conflict prevention measures are still the subject of CFSP instruments. To start

---

[49] For 2003, Title B8-0 foresees an overall amount of appropriations of € 47.5 million, out of which € 7.5 million for conflict prevention and crisis management, and € 27.5 million for conflict resolution and related activities.

[50] Case C-170/96, *Commission* v. *Council* [1998] ECR I-2763, paragraphs 14-17. This case law is reflected in Article III-209 of the Draft Constitution prepared by the European Convention.

with, the Council has occasionally adopted common positions stating the EU position on aspects of conflict prevention in a specific country or region.[51] More frequent still have been joint actions or decisions supporting specific activities aiming at conflict prevention or crisis management in a particular country. Recent examples would include small arms collection projects in a number of countries[52] and police missions and support for the establishment of viable police forces.[53] Within the context of CFSP, the Union has also provided for support to ongoing negotiation, mediation, and facilitation processes, in particular in the Balkans,[54] South Ossetia,[55] and Togo.[56] Finally, CFSP measures have also decided the financing of monitoring missions[57] and exceptionally also missions with a peace keeping component.[58]

---

[51] Common Position 2001/374/CFSP concerning conflict prevention, management and resolution in Africa, *OJEC* [2001] L 132/3; Common Position 2003/203/CFSP concerning European Union support for the implementation of the Lusaka Ceasefire Agreement and the peace process in the Democratic Republic of the Congo (DRC), *OJEC* [2003] L 115/87; Common position 2000/420/CFSP concerning EU support for the OAU peace process between Ethiopia and Eritrea, *OJEC* [2000] L 161/1; Common Position 1999/479/CFSP concerning support for the popular consultation of the East Timorese people, *OJEC* [1999] L 188/1.

[52] Decision 2003/543/CFSP on a EU contribution to combating the destabilising accumulation and spread of small arms and light weapons in Latin America and the Carribean, *OJEC* [2003] L 185/59; Decision 2003/276/CFSP on a EU contribution to the destruction of ammunition for small arms and light weapons in Albania, *OJEC* [2003] L 99/60; Decision 2002/904 concerning an EU contribution to combating the destabilising accumulation and spread of small arms and light weapons in Cambodia, *OJEC* [2002] L 313/1; Decision 2002/842/CFSP on an EU contribution to the fight against the destabilising accumulation and spread of small arms and light weapons in South-East Europe, *OJEC* [2002] L 289/1. These decisions are all based on Joint Action 2002/589/CFSP on the European Union's contribution to combat the destabilising accumulation and spread of small arms and light weapons, *OJEC* [2002] L 191/1.

[53] Joint Action 2002/210/CFSP on the European Police Mission in Bosnia and Herzegovina, *OJEC* [2002] L 70/1; Joint Action 1999/189/CFSP concerning a contribution by the EU to the re-establishment of a viable police force in Albania, *OJEC* [1999] L 63/1. Related is also Joint Action 2000/298/CFSP on a European Union assistance programme to support the Palestinian Authority in its efforts to counter terrorist activities from the territories under its control, *OJEC* [2000] L 97/97.

[54] Joint Action 1999/480/CFSP in relation to the holding of a meeting of the Heads of State and Government in Sarajevo, Bosnia, and Herzegovina, concerning the Stability Pact for South-Eastern Europe, *OJEC* [1999] L 188/2; Council Joint Action 2001/915/CFSP appointing the Special Representative of the EU to act as Coordinator of the Stability Pact for South-Eastern Europe, *OJEC* [2001] L 337/62. Initially, this also included support to the structures of UNMIK, see Joint Action 1999/522/CFSP concerning the installation of the structures of the United Nations Mission in Kosovo (UNMIK), *OJEC* [1999] L 201/1.

[55] Joint Action 2003/473/CFSP regarding a contribution from the European Union to the conflict settlement process in South Ossetia/Georgia, *OJEC* [2003] L 157/72.

[56] Decision 2001/375/CFSP implementing Common Position 98/350/CFSP with a view to a European Union contribution to a mission to facilitate dialogue in Togo, *OJEC* [2001] L 132/7.

[57] Cf., Joint Action 2000/811/CFSP on the European Union Monitoring Mission, *OJEC* [2000] L 328/53; Joint Action 2002/373/CFSP regarding a contribution of the European Union towards reinforcing the capacity of the Georgian authorities to support and protect the OSCE observer mission on the border of Georgia with the Ingush and Chechen Republics of the Russian Federation, *OJEC* [2002] L 134/1.

[58] E.g., Joint Action 2001/801/CFSP regarding European Union support for the establishment of an interim multinational security presence in Burundi, *OJEC* [2001] L 303/7.

This side-by-side practice of Community cooperation and CFSP in the field of conflict prevention is legally not without problems. The central provision governing the relationship between the Community and CFSP is Article 47 EU,[59] which provides that nothing in the EU Treaty shall affect the EC Treaty.[60] In concrete terms, this means that no measure adopted in the context of the second (or third) pillar may affect the competences of the EC under the EC Treaty. However, Community competence would necessarily be affected if the Council were to adopt an act or measure which could also have been adopted on the basis of the EC Treaty. As a consequence, the second pillar has a residual character: only where action is not possible on the basis of the EC Treaty may CFSP instruments be used. Concretely speaking, this has meant that since the entry into force of the Human Rights regulations, electoral observation missions are no longer adopted through CFSP actions, but are financed and organised by the Commission acting on the basis of these regulations.[61] Similarly, since the entry into force of the demining regulations, demining operations are no longer decided and financed in the framework of CFSP, but on the basis of the regulations.

However, despite the gradual extension of Community competence, there remain a number of problematic fields. For instance, it is not quite clear why demining operations are now the subject of a Community regulation, but small-arms collection projects continue to be anchored in CFSP. This situation has become further complicated by the fact that Article 11 of the Cotonou Agreement specifically mentions the campaign against small arms, as a consequence of which small-arms projects in ACP countries are now financed by the Commission, whereas the Council continues to finance such projects within the framework of the second pillar for other countries and regions. Similarly, support for mediation and conciliation efforts continue to pose difficulties. In the Balkans, it is not obvious why support to UNMIK and the OHR has been financed by the Community, but the Special Representative for the Stability Pact continues to be financed from the CFSP budget.[62] An even more problematic case is the CFSP support for the facilitation effort in Togo, which could have been financed both under the Cotonou Agreement or the Human Rights regulation. The fact that the Commission, for political reasons, did not consider the financing to be opportune, does not justify the recourse to CFSP financing.[63]

---

[59] A corresponding provision is contained in Art. III-209 of the Draft Constitution prepared by the European Convention.

[60] On the relation of Community competence and CFSP, see in more detail Ramses A. Wessel, *The European Union's Foreign and Security Policy* (The Hague, Kluwer Law International 1999), pp. 56-58.

[61] In this sense, see the Commission''s communication on EU Election Assistance and Observation, COM (2000) 191 final, p. 11.

[62] But see now the Commission proposal referred to *supra* n. 20, which envisages the 'communitarisation' of this support.

[63] *Supra* n. 56. However, at the time of the adoption of this decision, it was agreed that this would remain exceptional, and any continuation of the mission would take the form of special repre-

As can be seen, the gradual evolution of Community cooperation policy in the field of conflict prevention has important implications for the scope of the second pillar. Where a specific conflict prevention measure can be financed under an EC instrument, it may no longer be the subject of CFSP financing. This does not only apply with respect to Joint Actions, but should also be respected in the drafting of Common Positions. Whereas Common Positions define the approach of the Union to a particular matter of a geographical or thematic nature (Article 15 EU), they should not go so far as to prejudge the Commission's discretion to decide on particular actions to be supported or not supported on the basis of the applicable Community instruments.

Overall, the dividing line between Community competence and CFSP is not easy to trace in general terms. It essentially depends on the reach of the instruments of the Community, and therefore keeps evolving. However, with the risk of a certain generalisation, it can be said that most measures addressing the root causes of conflict, including certain measures of civilian crisis management, for instance through mediation, conciliation, and negotiation, now can be supported on the basis of geographic and thematic EC instruments. This tendency has been further confirmed by the adoption of the RRM. A core residual competence of CFSP, in contrast, seem to be measures which involve a potential use of force, and notably measures with military implications. This would notably seem to include the 'Petersberg tasks' mentioned in Article 17.2 EU, namely humanitarian and rescue tasks, peacekeeping tasks and tasks of combat forces in crisis management, including peace-making, which frequently will have a military implication.

It would appear that the Draft Constitution prepared by the European Convention will not entirely remove this ambiguous status of conflict prevention within the European Union. The Draft Constitution envisages the creation of a European Union with a single legal personality, and thereby abolishes the current pillar structure. It also contains major institutional innovations such as the creation of a European Foreign Minister as a Member of the Commission with responsibility for CFSP. However, CFSP is maintained as a specific policy area of the Union with procedures which are essentially equivalent to those currently valid under the second pillar.

Article III-193(2)(c) of the Draft Constitution provides that it is an overall objective of the external action of the European Union 'to preserve peace, prevent conflicts and strengthen international security'. This will also apply with respect to development cooperation and cooperation with other third countries, the legal bases for which provide that these policies will be conducted in accordance with the 'principles and objectives of the Union's external action'. This would seem to confirm the relevance of conflict prevention as an objective for future EU cooperation policies.

---

sentatives of the Council pursuant to Article 18(5) EU. The facilitation mission in fact ended and EU support was not continued.

At the same time, Articles I-40(1) and III-210(1) mention conflict prevention as a task of the future common security and defence policy. It is interesting to note that a similar reference is not contained in the provisions regarding the general aspects of the foreign and security policy. While it may still be too early for a final appraisal of the results of the Convention, this might be seen as a certain confirmation of the above interpretation according to which CFSP is primarily focused on the aspects of conflict prevention having military and defence implications.

6. CONCLUSION

Conflict prevention has become an essential part of EC cooperation policy. Almost all cooperation programmes of the EC foresee activities relating to conflict prevention. On this basis, the Commission finances an increasing number of activities relevant to conflict prevention in almost all partner countries and regions of the EU. Recently, the RRM has further reinforced the Commission's capacity to react rapidly to emerging situations of conflict and crisis.

The flipside of this increasing 'communitarisation' of the cooperation aspect of conflict prevention is a reduction of the scope of CFSP. Despite the persistence of a 'grey zone' between the first and second pillars, CFSP is increasingly limited to the overall coordination of external activities, and to the support and organisation of measures having directly or potentially military implications. This development should be welcomed and reinforced. Whereas Community measures may also not always be effective or optimally managed, it is beyond doubt that the Community method is more effective than the intergovernmental method of CFSP for the management of cooperation activities in the field of conflict prevention. Indeed, it is difficult to see why a small-arms collection project in a third country, or the financial and administrative support for a negotiation process, requires a decision in a Council of Ministers soon composed of 25 Members. Such an institutionally heavy procedure would seem appropriate only for measures of great political significance, which cooperation measures typically do not have.

Of course, even if the above delimitation of competences between the current pillars is accepted, there will remain a potential for problems of coherence and interinstitutional conflicts. For this reason, it is highly important that the institutional differences between the pillars be reduced. Certain of the proposals contained in the Draft Constitution prepared by the European Convention, such as a single personality for the Union, the abolition of the pillar structure, the increase of majority voting in the field of CFSP, and the creation of a European Foreign Minister as a Member of the Commission with a right of proposal in the field of CFSP, lead in this direction. Nevertheless, even in a future Union with a single legal framework, cooperation policy and foreign and security policy are likely to remain side by side as distinct policy areas of the Union with different procedural arrangements. The questions discussed in this contribution are therefore likely to remain relevant for some time to come.

Chapter 10
ENVIRONMENTAL POLICY AND CONFLICT PREVENTION

by Andrea Weiss[1]

1. INTRODUCTION

The security dimension of environmental stress and natural resource degradation and scarcity has been emphasised and conceptualised by environmentalists mainly since 1972.[2] For peace and security research and policy, however, 'environmental conflict', 'environmentally-induced conflict', 'ecological security', 'environmental security' or 'environment and security' are rather new topics and concepts which developed in the 1990s. The EU has participated in such studies and discussions mainly through the Conflict Prevention Network (CPN) and through international forums, namely OECD, OSCE and NATO.[3] The Community has adopted a wide notion of 'human security'. It includes a focus on the intricate sets of relationships between the environment (including natural resources) and society. These general linkages and their security dimension are equally reflected in the EC's approach to conflict prevention and its environmental policy. The latter is firmly rooted in international environmental law and policy. Its main instruments are multilateral environmental agreements (MEAs), multi-year Environmental Action Programmes (EAP) and Community environmental legislation. Since the causes and effects of environmental and resource degradation and scar-

---

[1] Officer at the EFTA Surveillance Authority in Brussels. The article expresses the personal view of the author only. The internet site citations refer to their status on 18 November 2003.

[2] 1972 report of the Club of Rome, D.L. Meadows, et. al., *The Limits of Growth* (New York, Universe Books 1972), 1987 Brundlandt report of the World Commission on Environment and Development, *Our Common Future* (Oxford, University Press 1987); 1992 Rio United Nations Conference on Environment and Development (UNCED), *inter alia*, Rio Declaration of Principles, 31 *ILM* (1992), p. 876.

[3] See for key documents G. Dabelko, et al., *State-of-the-art Review on Environment, Security and Development Co-operation* (Gland, IUCN/OECD 1999); K.M. Lietzmann and G.D. Vest, *Environment & Security in an International Context,* Report No. 232 (Berlin, Rotadruck Armin Weichert 1999) commissioned by NATO's Committee on the Challenge of Modern Society; OSCE Economic Forum, preparatory seminars <http://www.osce.org/eea/seminars/archive/> and conference reports, *inter alia*, of the 10th Meeting (May 2002) 'Water and Security' (EF.GAL/13/02) and the 7th Meeting (May 1999) 'Security Aspects in the Field of the Environment' (EF.GAL/3/99). Cf., Joint UN-OSCE initiative for security and environment for Central Asia and South-Eastern Europe.

V. Kronenberger and J. Wouters, eds., The European Union and Conflict Prevention
© 2004, T·M·C·ASSER PRESS, *The Hague, The Netherlands*

city are distinct in time and space, the internal dimension of the Community's environmental and resource policy is an essential contribution to combating environmental causes of conflict in other parts of the world. The present chapter, however, will concentrate on the Community's external relations. Article 174(4) EC explicitly lists environmental cooperation with third countries and international organisations as Community activity. The Community's external powers flow from Article 175 EC, the principle of implied powers and the case law of the Court of Justice of the European Communities on parallelism of internal and external powers.[4] The Community's substantive scope of powers is defined by its tasks laid down in Article 174(1) EC. They encompass preserving, protecting and improving the quality of the environment, protecting human health, the prudent and rational utilisation of natural resources, and the promotion of measures at the international level to deal with regional and worldwide environmental problems. Since environmental problems and resource management are of a horizontal nature involving a vast variety of tools rooted in other sectoral policies, the right choice of the legal basis for Community actions is one of the most disputed legal issues of EC environmental law. In particular the access to and the use and management of natural resources fall rather under policies and the legal basis dealing with the specific resource concerned (e.g., fisheries or agricultural policies) or the special tool employed (e.g., trade policy). The protection and conservation of natural resources, on the other hand, may be directly addressed by measures based on Article 175 EC or as an integral part of other policy measures. Article 6 EC obliges the Community to integrate environmental protection requirements in the definition and implementation of all its policies and activities in particular in view of sustainable development. Environmental and resource protection has become but one pillar of the Community's broader concept of sustainable development.[5] As a result, the Community's environmental cooperation with less developed countries is mostly embedded in a broader development cooperation context aiming at the sustainable management and use of the natural environment and resources. These features of environmental policy are reflected in the Commission's Communication on Conflict Prevention.[6] First, the Communication requires integration of the concept of conflict prevention in sectoral policies including the environment. Second, it follows from the concept of structural stability and Article 6 EC that environmental policy and conflict prevention need to be mainstreamed within Community actions rooted in other policies, especially the EC's development cooperation which shall focus on addressing the root

---

[4] See in particular Case 22/70 *AETR* [1971] ECR 263; Opinion 2/92 *OECD* [1995] ECR I-521; Opinion 1/94 *WTO* [1994] ECR I-5267.
[5] Göteborg European Council, Presidency conclusions, paragraphs 19 et seq.; COM (2001) 264 final 'A sustainable Europe for a better world: an EU strategy for sustainable development', *Bull.* 2001/5 1.4.32.
[6] COM (2001) 211 final *Bull.* 2001/4 1.6.2.

causes of conflict in an integrated way. Third, and while reinforcing the latter aspect, cross-cutting issues such as the management of natural resources and environmental degradation shall be tackled in a more efficient way. This calls for a holistic approach to identified priority problems such as, for example, conflict diamonds, water and forest management. International cooperation to all these ends shall complement the Community's efforts. The present contribution will examine the achievements made by the Community to attain the objectives set in the given order. To start with, however, an outline of the definitions and approaches used by the Community when linking environmental policy and conflict prevention seems to be necessary.

2. LINKING ENVIRONMENTAL POLICY AND CONFLICT PREVENTION: DEFINITIONS AND APPROACHES

The check-list for root causes of conflict comprises environmental degradation as well as access to and use of natural resources. They are addressed in a governance and economic management context rather than as concerns in their own right. Their concrete security relevance is a case-by-case assessment in the light of the given social, economic and political conditions, a task taken up in the EC's Regional and Country Strategy Papers. The Community appears to recognise, in a flexible manner, that environmental degradation may trigger, fuel, catalyse or even directly cause conflicts depending on the specific contextual situation. It acknowledges that environmental change and degradation (e.g., climate change, ozone depletion, loss of biodiversity, desertification, deforestation, etc.) may have negative repercussions on quality, scarcity, inequitable distribution and non-sustainable use of natural resources (e.g., croplands, forests, fisheries, potable water, minerals, etc.) and life support systems for man and ecosystems. Targeting global environmental problems is, therefore, the Community's priority under both its environmental and conflict prevention policy. Among the most important consequences of and, at the same time, the reasons for aggravating environmental stress, are poverty, food insecurity, poor health conditions, migration or refugee movements, a lack of (environmental) governance and the disruption of social and political institutions. They in themselves constitute threats of conflict addressed through other Community policies' instruments. Recently, natural and man-made disasters (floods, droughts, forest fires, pollution incidents, etc.) have been added to the list of consequences attributable – at least in a multi-causal context – to environmental changes and to the catalogue of destabilising factors. The terminology used in EC documents to express the linkages between the environment and conflict is far from consistent or clear. It appears that notions such as, *inter alia*, 'environment and security', 'environmental security', 'environment-related security' or more specifically 'water security' are overlapping or are used partly interchangeably.[7] Resource, i.e., 'water', 'energy', etc. security appears to describe qualitative and quantitative security in resource supply[8] which overlaps with a broader approach to resource management. 'Environment and security' appears to cover any possible linkage including 'water use and conflict prevention, environmental terrorism, environmental disasters, environmental impact of war', etc.[9] Other terms are not defined. Their use might be partly seen as a reflection of insecurities resulting from continued debates in academia and (inter)governmental forums as to whether environmental change and degradation are to be recognised as immediate threats to national, regional and global security, i.e., as direct causes of conflict.

2.1 Institutional approach

The starting point for conflict prevention is information gathering, situation analysis, and policy planning, the key tool for which are the Community's Regional and Country Strategy Papers (CSP). The new CSPs for 2002-2006 show improved quality in describing a country's environmental and natural resource situation in terms of quantity, quality and governance, the social and economic dependencies on environmental assets and competition over access thereto and control thereover. By setting up a network of environmental focal points for each geographical region and thematic external policy units, DG External Relations has taken an important step to better integrate environmental information and analysis in these papers. The focal points are intended to maintain open channels of communication with DG Environment and other relevant DGs, in particular DG Development and the EuropeAid Co-operation Office.[10] Trade issues have not been integrated in this organisational set-up. Their interplay with the environment is rather dealt with in a separate unit in DG Trade. Within the external relations services, thematic and regional experts shall work in close cooperation to ensure that cross-cutting issues such as environment/development/security/conflict prevention are reflected in regional and country policy planning and in political dialogue. It is important that the cooperation will work two ways in order to ensure that DG Environment acts consistently with conflict prevention considerations within the sphere of its external competences. The Commission's inten-

---

[7] E.g., Commission Communication COM (2002) 82 final 'Towards Global Partnership for Sustainable Development', *Bull.* 2002/1/2 1.4.44, equally refers to 'environmental security' and 'environment and security' without specification. The Commission Staff Working Paper SEC (2002) 271 'Environmental Integration in the External Policies of the General Affairs Council' uses terms such as 'environment-related security threats' 'environmental threats', 'environmentally related causes of conflict', or 'environment and security'.

[8] See, e.g., definition in Annex I to COM (2002) 132 final 'Water Management in Developing Countries: Policy and Priorities for EU Development Cooperation', *Bull.* 2002/3 1.6.47.

[9] SEC (2002) 271 final, p. 9.

[10] Idem, p. 15.

tion to internally and externally involve environment officials where environmental expertise might be requested, e.g., by including them in negotiation teams with third countries or at international forums, is a positive contribution to an inter-services approach to cross-cutting issues. The Commission suggested and started to establish an experts' network under the aegis of the Presidency composed of environment and foreign policy officials from the Commission and the Member States to promote informal cross-fertilisation between policy areas. This approach may help to achieve mutually supportive actions across the sectors in the EU, and across actors (the Commission and the Member States) in bi- or multilateral relations. The Community's approach is supported by diplomatic tools. The Thessaloniki European Council (June 2003) reaffirmed its commitment to 'green diplomacy' by promoting a European diplomacy on the environment and sustainable development.[11]

2.2 Short-term prevention

Conflict prevention has initially been defined by the EU as actions undertaken over the short-term to reduce manifest tensions and/or to prevent the outbreak or recurrence of violent conflict. This narrow notion has been abandoned in the Commission's Communication on Conflict Prevention which rather distinguishes between short-term (acute) and long-term (structural) prevention with a strong focus on the latter. The Commission specifies short-term prevention as 'reacting quickly to nascent conflicts'. The delimitation of proactive short-term prevention and reactive crisis management thereby seems blurred. This is reinforced by post-conflict rehabilitation being part of the EC's conflict prevention approach and long-term development and cooperation assistance being a tool of crisis management.[12] Hence, crisis management tools like the Community's Rapid Reaction Mechanism (RRM)[13] shall equally be used in a short-term prevention context. The RRM, designed to quickly react to crisis or pre-crisis situations, encompasses environmental measures through integration especially in rehabilitation and development initiatives.[14] At the same time, the Göteborg European Council

---

[11] Presidency conclusions, paragraph 76. For EU Member State cooperation cf., 3rd Conference of EU Foreign Ministers on Environmental Foreign Policy, 'Confidence Building in Climate Protection' (Berlin, 15-16 May 2003), succeeding previous meetings on topics such as 'Environmental Foreign Policy' or 'Environment and Security'.

[12] On the interaction between conflict prevention and crisis management, cf., European Commission Conflict Prevention and Crisis Management Unit, *Civilian instruments for EU crisis management,* April 2003, published at <http://europa.eu.int/comm/external_relations/cfsp/doc/cm03.pdf>.

[13] Council Regulation (EC) No. 381/2001 of 26 February 2001 Creating a Rapid-Reaction Mechanism, *OJEC* [2001] L 57/5.

[14] Regulation (EC) No. 2493/2000 of the European Parliament and of the Council of 7 November 2000 on Measures to Promote the Full Integration of the Environmental Dimension in the Development Process of Developing Countries, *OJEC* [2000] L 288/1.

(June 2001) stressed the key role of the Community mechanism to facilitate reinforced cooperation in civil protection assistance interventions[15] in the implementation of civil crisis management targets. The Council Decision is based on
Article 308 EC; it falls within the responsibility of DG Environment and is available for use under the Common Foreign and Security Policy (CFSP) subject to
conditions to be determined.[16] The mechanism makes available the necessary operational resources in cases requiring an immediate response to natural (floods,
earthquakes, landslides, storms, forest fires), technological (biological, chemical,
nuclear) and environmental (marine pollution) disasters, including bio-terrorism.
Based on a first specification of procedures, the Member State entrusted with the
Presidency of the Council of the European Union may, on behalf of the Council
and following consultations with the Member States and the Commission in the
appropriate Council bodies, request civil protection assistance under Title V of
the EU Treaty.[17] Further specifications on civil protection interventions as part of
EU crisis management operations is, however, required. Practice has to show
how the civil protection mechanism will be efficiently embedded in the wider
conflict prevention, relief, rehabilitation and long-term assistance. Another contribution to short-term prevention in an environment/conflict context is the joint
initiative of the Commission and the European Space Agency on a Global Monitoring for Environment and Security (GMES). It may provide an important input
for an effective early warning system by submitting security-relevant environmental data related to global change, environmental stress and natural and man-
made disasters.[18] The initiative which has been launched in 2000 will, however,
not be operative before 2008.

2.3 Long-term prevention

The Community's emphasis in conflict prevention lies on the concept of structural stability. This is defined as comprising the characteristics of 'sustainable
economic development, democracy and respect for human rights, viable political
structures and healthy environmental and social conditions, with the capacity to

---

[15] Council Decision 2001/792/EC, Euratom of 23 October 2001, *OJEC* [2001] L 297/7, based on
Commission proposal COM (2000) 593 final, *OJEC* [2001] C 29 E/287; Commission Communication COM (2001) 707 final on Civil Protection and Bio-terrorism. *Bull.* 2001/11 1.4.46.

[16] The draft Treaty establishing a Constitution for Europe provides a separate legal basis for civil
protection in its Article III-184.

[17] General Affairs Council of 17 June 2002, attachment Presidency Report on European Security
and Defence Policy (Annex III) of 22 June 2002 (Doc. No. 10160/2/02, COSDP 188).

[18] Commission Communication COM (2000) 597 final 'Europe and Space: Turning to a new
chapter', *Bull.* 2000/9 1.3.57; Commission Staff Working Paper SEC (2001) 993 final 'A European
Approach to Global Monitoring for Environment and Security (GMES): Towards Meeting Users'
Needs'; Commission Communication COM (2001) 609 final 'Global Monitoring for Environment
and Security (GMES) – EC Action Plan (2001-2003)'.

manage change without having to resort to conflict'. As a result the key tool of conflict prevention is a long-term task of 'mainstreaming' policies, i.e., an integrative approach.[19] Such an approach appears, however, rather to qualify as 'peace building', initially defined by the Community as actions undertaken over the medium or longer term to address root causes of violent conflicts in a targeted manner. Indeed, the Community explicitly emphasises the important role of environmental and natural resource cooperation for confidence building between communities and across borders.[20] This is particularly valid for cooperation on access to, use and protection of water which has been identified in the past as a catalyst for regional cooperation and security.[21] The Community's conflict prevention concept appears to extend even further: Based on the presumption that better management of the environment and natural resources, in particular in a socio-economic context, automatically contributes to the overall objective of peace and stability, conflict prevention refers to a long-term structural approach to promote common stability through sustainable development.[22] It is true that sustainable development and environmental policy by their very nature target root causes of conflict and are capable of doing so at a very early stage. By equating 'conflict prevention' with (environmentally) 'sustainable development' the Community risks, however, that its conflict prevention policy becomes a loose concept without contours or specific orientation. In more specific terms of conflict prevention goal-setting, the Commission has committed itself to address issues of natural resources and environmental degradation through its bilateral and regional programmes, to enhance support for the implementation by partner countries of Multilateral Environmental Agreements and to give high priority to environmental rehabilitation projects in post-conflict programmes.[23]

---

[19] EU Programme for the Prevention of Violent Conflicts, Göteborg European Council, Presidency Conclusions (15/06/2001).

[20] COM (2001) 211 final *Bull.* 2001/4 1.6.2, p. 18.

[21] 'Petersberg Declaration: Global Water Politics' of March 1998 (published at <http://www.dse.de/ef/petersb.htm>), jointly drafted by the participants of the First Petersberg Dialogue on 'Global Water Policy' organised by the Development Policy Forum (Entwicklungspolitisches Forum – EF) and the German Foundation for International Development (Deutsche Stiftung für Internationale Entwicklung – DSE). For empirical studies on water conflict/cooperation from 1948-1999 see A.T. Wolf, et al., 'International Waters: Identifying Basins at Risk', 5 *Water Policy* (2003) pp. 29-60; cf., also P. Gleick, 'Water Conflict Chronology', September 2000 Version, published at <http://www.worldwater.org/conflictchronologychart.PDF>.

[22] Improving the Coherence and Effectiveness of European Action in the Field of Conflict Prevention. Report Presented to the Nice European Council by the Secretary General/High Representative and the Commission (30 November 2002, Doc. No. 14088/00), point 17 (published at <http://register.consilium.eu.int/pdf/en/00/st14/14088en0.pdf>).

[23] COM (2001) 211 final *Bull.* 2001/4 1.6.2, p. 18 et seq.

3. INTEGRATING CONFLICT PREVENTION IN ENVIRONMENTAL POLICY

The Community's concept of 'integration' addresses two main aspects: the impact of environmental measures on conflict prevention efforts and the use of environmental instruments to achieve conflict prevention objectives. The first aspect is one of coherence: EC activities adopted under the Community's environmental policy shall not run counter to the EU's conflict prevention efforts. The General Affairs Council stressed the need for a two-way mainstreaming of conflict prevention and environmental requirements striving for an 'early collaboration between environmental departments and external relations officials on many ostensibly "EU-internal" environment-related proposals if their external policy implications are to be picked up at an early stage'.[24] The first achievements to this end may be seen in the new institutional approach, including interservices' communication channels. Furthermore, the Community has committed itself to submit all measures to sustainability assessment encompassing, *inter alia*, the effects of internal policies in third countries.[25] Finally, the 6th EAP[26] ensures the programmatic coherence of priorities set under the EC's environmental and conflict prevention policy. The second aspect has been defined as making use of EU instruments in a more systematic and coordinated manner in order to get at the root causes of conflict.[27] This aspect so far seems to have been within the focus of the EC's integration efforts. The principal environmental instruments available for the purpose of conflict prevention are MEAs, regional or bilateral environmental cooperation and LIFE-Third Countries, the Community's financing instrument specifically directed at technical assistance activities for promoting sustainable development in eligible third countries (States of South Eastern Europe, the Mediterranean and Russia). Other geographical cooperation instruments (e.g., CARDS, MEDA or TACIS regulations) provide for specific support to environmental cooperation programmes.

3.1 The 6th Environmental Action Programme

The Community has achieved considerable coherence in setting goals and priorities in its environmental and conflict prevention policies. The 6th EAP explicitly refers to conflict prevention and environmental security. It assumes the Community's responsibility as 'major contributor[s] to global environmental

---

[24] SEC (2002) 271 final p. 35.

[25] COM (2002) 82 final *Bull.* 2002/1/2 1.4.44, p. 14.

[26] Commission Communication COM (2001) 31 final 'Environment 2010: Our future, Our choice', *OJEC* [2001] C 154 E/218, adopted by Decision No. 1600/2002/EC of the European Parliament and of the Council of 22 July 2002 laying down the Sixth Community Environment Action Programme, *OJEC* [2002] L 242/1.

[27] 'One Year On: the Commission's Conflict Prevention Policy', published at <http://europa. eu.int/comm/external_relations/cpcm/cp/rep.htm>.

problems such as greenhouse gas emissions' and a consumer of a considerable 'share of the planet's renewable and non-renewable resources, such as minerals, fish, and timber'. The EC's environmental priorities set for 2001 to 2010 are climate change; nature and biodiversity; environment and health and quality of life; and natural resources and wastes. They shall be complemented by thematic strategies, including one on the sustainable use of natural resources.[28] This is the Community's internal contribution to global sustainability and resource protection. It aims to review production and consumption patterns in the light of the environment's carrying capacity. At the international level, the Community is committed to more sustainable agriculture, forestry, fishing, mining and oil extraction and other economic activities. The main tool by which to achieve these aims is a horizontal approach, i.e., 'integration': the EC's trade, development and aid policies shall take up nature and biodiversity issues 'with full and serious environmental assessments of aid projects'. Poverty reduction strategies, environmental security, sustainability and conservation of natural resources and biodiversity shall play a key role in such an approach addressing the root causes of conflict such as, *inter alia*, climate change, desertification, deforestation, water and sustainable management of natural resources.

3.2 Multilateral Environmental Agreements

MEAs are the only adequate answer to tackle global environmental and resource problems and to address transboundary environmental impacts by submitting the international community to commonly agreed concepts, principles, rules, norms and practices. Some MEAs provide for legally enforceable rules on the right of access to and the use of natural resources. They may be deemed to have immediate conflict resolving or preventing potential by addressing these specific root causes of tension. Most MEAs, however, provide for obligations of a 'soft' nature. Their effectiveness depends on the willingness and the capability of the State concerned to implement measures translating environmental commitments into action. It is the EC's stated objective to encourage signature/ratification of MEAs and to support and enhance their implementation by partner countries.[29] The Community's efforts cover industrialised partners such as the United States of America[30] and developing countries alike. Contractual commitments to sign

---

[28] Commission Communication COM (2003) 572 final 'Towards a Thematic Strategy on the Sustainable Use of Natural Resources'.

[29] COM (2001) 211 final, *Bull.* 2001/4 1.6.2, p. 18 et seq.; COM (2001) 31 final, *OJEC* [2001] C 154 E/218, p. 58 et seq.

[30] Cf., the EU's unsuccessful efforts to persuade the USA, the world's biggest greenhouse gas producer, to sign the 1997 Kyoto Protocol to the Framework Convention on Climate Change, the Biosafety Protocol to the Convention on Biological Diversity, or the Basel Convention on the Control of Transboundary Movements of Hazardous Wastes and their Disposal.

MEAs have been incorporated into development cooperations (e.g., Cotonou Agreement), Stability Pacts (e.g., South Eastern Europe) or environmental partnerships (e.g., NIS). There are, however, clear limits to the effectiveness of this tool. Among these is the unclear relationship between trade rules under the World Trade Organisation (WTO) and MEAs which may risk depriving MEAs of their efficiency. The EC has taken and still takes a lead in this debate.[31] The Doha mandate[32] initiated negotiations to this end. However, it fell short of the Community's intentions. It excluded the issue of applying trade measures to non-parties to MEAs and is restricted to specific trade obligations,[33] hence excluding MEA-implementing measures which are not mandatory or are not clearly defined in the MEA in question.

3.3   Regional and bilateral environmental cooperation

In compliance with the priorities set under its conflict prevention and environmental policy as laid down in the 6th EAP and on the basis of the CSPs, the EU has recently further developed security-relevant cooperation with the Newly Independent States (NIS) and the Mediterranean countries in the context of regional processes. The EU actively participates in the two components of the 'Environment for Europe' process of the UNECE: the political framework for pan-European environmental cooperation including the negotiation of legal instruments, and the Environmental Programme with long-term environmental priorities and corresponding activities in a pan-European context. At the 2003 Kiev Conference,[34] the EU refocused its future cooperation on NIS. Convergence of environmental policies and laws with EU environmental standards is the EU's 'stick' in its wider Partnership and Co-operation Agreements (PCA) with the Western NIS and the Caucasus when offering the 'carrot' of strengthening their economic links with the EU.[35] The EU goals of cooperation with all NIS countries have been identified in the context of the EU's broader objectives of its international environmental commitments and in the light of conflict prevention objectives. Especially environmental cooperation with countries of Central Asia (in particular

---

[31] See the submission by the European Community to WTO on 19 October 2000 Doc. WT/CTE/W/170 (published at <http://www.ictsd.org/English/WT-CTE-W-170.htm>).

[32] Ministerial Declaration WT/MIN(01)/DEC/1 adopted on 14 November 2001 at the 4th Ministerial Conference in Doha, paragraph 31(I).

[33] Examples are the Montreal Protocol for the Protection of the Ozone Layer, the Basel Convention on Transboundary Movement of Hazardous Wastes, the Convention on International Trade in Endangered Species (CITES) and the Rotterdam Convention on Trade in Hazardous Chemicals (PIC).

[34] Ministerial Declaration ECE/CEP/94/Rev.1 adopted at the UNECE Ministerial Conference in Kiev on 21-23 May 2003.

[35] Cf., e.g., Commission Communication COM (2001) 772 final EU-Russia Environmental Co-operation; Common Strategy of the European Union on Russia (1999/414/CFSP).

water and energy) shall first and foremost serve the promotion of democracy, security and conflict prevention.[36] The security focus on nuclear safety, environmental security, and the sustainable management of shared natural resources have been fully taken into account, *inter alia*, in the EU-NIS Water Partnership and TACIS funding. These efforts could be reinforced by the EU's participation in the joint UNEP/OSCE/UNDP 'Environment and Security' initiative.[37] In line with the need to strengthen regional and sub-regional cooperation, the Commission's Strategic Considerations (2002-2006) and Indicative Programme (2002-2003) for TACIS Regional Cooperation – although not strictly following the CSPs – is extensively dedicated to the transboundary management of natural resources and the environment in priority concerns such as water.[38] TACIS has an important role in supporting environmental programmes for Regional Seas. The Aral Sea Basin, an area affected by dramatic environmental decline and tensions over water, is among the cooperation priorities as are other regional seas, namely the Black and Caspian Seas (TACIS focus for 2002-2003) and the Baltic Sea. This is supported by other EU efforts in particular within the UNECE and the OSCE and within sub-regional forums.[39] As regards the Mediterranean region, DG Environment contributes to environmental protection and sustainable development through participation in multilateral programmes and through its own initiatives and instruments, namely the Mediterranean Action Plan (MAP), the Mediterranean Commission for Sustainable Development (MCSD), the Mediterranean Technical Assistance Programme (METAP), LIFE-Third Countries and the Short and Medium-Term Priority Environmental Action Programme (SMAP). SMAP is the framework programme that constitutes the basis for common actions in environmental priority issues in the Mediterranean, comprising both policy and funding orientation.[40] It clearly focuses on identified threats to stability and security in the region caused by water shortage, waste, polluted areas and

---

[36] Commission Communication COM (2003) 62 final 'Pan-European Environmental Co-operation after the 2003 Kiev Conference', *Bull.* 2003/1/2 1.4.38.

[37] Launched in the autumn of 2002, the initiative promotes environmental management as a strategy for reducing insecurity in South Eastern Europe and Central Asia by defining and mapping environment/security linkages in the regions and, based thereon, by implementing responses; the first results were presented at the Kiev Conference 2003; on behalf of UNEP, OSCE and UNDP see A. Carius, *Environment and Security Initiative: Addressing Environmental Risks and Promoting Peace and Stability – The post Kiev process* (24 April 2003), published at <http://www.iisd.org/pdf/2003/envsec_post_kiev.pdf>.

[38] Tacis Regional Cooperation: Strategic Considerations 2002-2006 and Indicative Programme 2002-2003 of 27 December 2001.

[39] E.g., Danube-Black Sea Task Force, EU Northern Dimension, Council of the Baltic Sea States (CBSS), Helsinki Commission for the Protection of the Marine Environment of the Baltic Sea Area (HELCOM), etc. For the latest EU Action Plan for the Northern Dimension see COM (2003) 343 final 'The Second Northern Dimension Action Plan 2004-2006' endorsed by the Brussels European Council on 16/17 October 2003.

[40] Full text published at <http://europa.eu.int/comm/environment/smap/program.htm>.

threatened biodiversity, endangered coastal areas and desertification.[41] The main financial instrument to implement SMAP is the Mediterranean Development Programme (MEDA). However, only 10% of the funding is invested in regional cooperation whereas nearly 90% of the resources are dedicated to National Indicative Programmes (NIP).[42] In the light of the new EU Regional Strategy Paper (2002-2006) transboundary cooperation, including at the regional and sub-regional levels, needs to be strengthened. This concerns water management in particular. An important existing security-related MEDA-financed project for sub-regional cooperation is the Israeli-Jordanian-Palestinian cooperation on water management (EXACT).

4. MAINSTREAMING CONFLICT PREVENTION AND ENVIRONMENTAL REQUIREMENTS IN EXTERNAL POLICIES

The Community has reiterated its commitment that environmental requirements shall be fully and properly integrated into all aspects of the Community's external relations, encompassing the EU's overall policies on conflict prevention and resolution, including under the Common Foreign and Security Policy.[43] To this end and complementing sectoral integration processes, the General Affairs Council (GAC) and the Development Council adopted their strategies for integrating environmental requirements in their fields.[44] It is their aim to ensure that all external measures, namely those relating to trade, development, environment and conflict prevention, are mutually supportive. Internationally, the Community promotes a mainstreamed integration of environmental requirements and conflict prevention in international organisations and forums. It adopted a concerted approach to Doha,[45]

---

[41] For the security relevance of environmental degradation in the region and the need for related preventive actions, see also Commission Communication COM (1999) 543 final 'Europe's Environment: What directions for the future? The Global Assessment of the European Community Programme of Policy and Action in relation to the environment and sustainable development, "Towards Sustainability"', *Bull.* 1999/11 1.3.104.

[42] See the Commission report for 1997-2001 <http://europa.eu.int/comm/environment/smap/home.htm>.

[43] Göteborg European Council, Presidency Conclusions; COM (2001) 31 final, *OJEC* [2001] C 154 E/218, p. 58 et seq., in particular p. 60; SEC (2002) 271 final, p. 16 et seq.

[44] SEC (2002) 271 final 'Environmental Integration in the External Policies of the General Affairs Council' has been endorsed by the Barcelona European Council (March 2002); this paper complements earlier works, namely the Commission Staff Working Paper SEC (2001) 508 final 'Integrating the environment into external relations policies' and an informal paper on 'Sustainable Trade' by DG Trade; Commission Staff Working Paper SEC (2001) 609 final 'Integrating the Environment into EC Economic and Development Co-operation'.

[45] 4th WTO Ministerial Conference at Doha (Qatar), 9-14 November 2001, to facilitate access of developing countries to the international market and to participate in trade.

Monterrey[46] and WSSD[47] in order to shape a global partnership for sustainable development, including the 'greening' of trade, investment and finance at the international level. At the Johannesburg World Summit on Sustainable Development (WSSD), following up the Community's commitments at the 1992 Rio UNCED[48] and the 2000 UN Millennium Summit,[49] the EC did not achieve all its objectives. The Community intended to use the WSSD to address the potential threat of conflict due to environmental pressure and to place environmental protection at the heart of preventive security policy making.[50] The official Conference documents address the environment/conflict nexus mainly under the aspect that conflicts are detrimental to the environment and sustainable development and that conflict prevention is a precondition for environmental protection and sustainable development cooperation.[51] Yet, the EU's emphasis given to combating security threats related to illegal logging, water resources or land degradation received broad support.[52] Furthermore, the Johannesburg Plan for Implementation recognised the need for conflict prevention policies. It called in particular for support for Africa's efforts to prevent, resolve, manage and mitigate conflicts, to respond early to emerging conflict situations and to deal efficiently with natural disasters and conflicts including their environmental impacts. In the light of these objectives, the EU might, however, risk depriving its structural conflict prevention policies of its efficiency if military assistance like the EU 'African Peace Facility' for African-led peacekeeping operations was financed by means of the European Development Fund.[53] This would result in cutting back the main financial

---

[46] International Conference on Financing for Development at Monterrey, 18-22 March 2002, launching the process of harmonising donor practices and procedures at the international level including replenishing of the Official Development Assistance (ODA); confirmed by the High Level Forum of Rome – Declaration on Harmonisation, Rome, 24-25 February 2003; see Commission Staff Working Document SEC (2003) 569 'Follow-up to the International Conference on Financing for Development (Monterrey – 2002) – Monitoring the Barcelona Commitments'.

[47] World Summit on Sustainable Development (WSSD) at Johannesburg, from 24 August to 4 September 2002.

[48] 1992 Rio United Nations Conference on Environment and Development, cf. <http://www.unep.org>.

[49] Convened on 6 September 2000 at the United Nations Headquarters in New York on the basis of General Assembly Resolutions GA/53/202, GA/53/239 and GA/54/254 and under the title 'The Role of the UN in the twenty-first century'. It was launched in order to meet ambitious goals on poverty eradication, sustainable development and development partnerships.

[50] COM (2001) 53 final 'Ten Years after Rio: Preparing for the World Summit on Sustainable Development in 2002', *Bull.* 2001/1/2 1.4.30, p. 16. Cf., also to the Commission's report 'One Year On: The Commission's Conflict Prevention Policy'.

[51] UN Report of the World Summit on Sustainable Development A/CONF.199/20.

[52] Published at <http://www.johannesburgsummit.org/html/documents/summit_docs/plan_final 1009.doc>.

[53] A draft decision to this effect has been approved by the General Affairs Council on 17 November 2003.

instrument for the ACP countries to the detriment of civil measures combating, *inter alia*, environment and resource related root causes of conflict.

4.1 Regional and bilateral cooperation

It is against this background, namely the WSSD, that the Community's economic and development cooperation and the integration of environmental and conflict prevention considerations has been built. The Community's strategy 'Towards global partnership for sustainable development' provides for the general framework of cross-sector development cooperation.[54] Geographic and thematic instruments at the regional level form the umbrella for more specific bilateral cooperation and aid projects based on CSPs. Thematic policy orientation papers cover priorities for development cooperation concerning climate change,[55] forests,[56] rural development,[57] water resource management,[58] fisheries,[59] and trade,[60] including the financing of the environmental dimension of development processes.[61] The EU Partnerships on poverty, water and energy launched at the WSSD are examples of combining priority objectives of sustainable development, environmental policy and conflict prevention. For instance, the EU Poverty Partnerships address in a systematic and comprehensive manner rural development concerns including their environmental dimension, i.e., environmental and natural resource degradation.[62] This takes account of the intricate relations between poverty reduction and environmental degradation, on the one hand, and of

---

[54] COM (2002) 82 final, *Bull.* 2002/1/2 1.4.44.

[55] Doc. VIII/279/99-EN of 03.11.1999 'EC Economic and Development Co-operation: Responding to the New Challenges of Climate Change'.

[56] COM (1999) 554 final 'Forests and Development: the EC approach', *OJEC* [1999] C 327/2.

[57] COM (2002) 429 final 'Fighting Rural Poverty: European Community policy and approach to rural development and sustainable natural resources management in developing countries', *Bull.* 2002/7/8 1.6.86.

[58] COM (2002) 132 final 'Water Management in Developing Countries Policy and Priorities For EU Development Cooperation'.

[59] COM (2000) 724 'Fisheries and Poverty Reduction', *Bull.* 2000/11 1.6.45.

[60] COM (2002) 513 final 'Trade and Environment – Assisting developing countries to benefit from trade', *Bull.* 2002/9 1.6.47.

[61] Regulation (EC) No. 2493/2000 of the European Parliament and of the Council of 7 November 2000 on Measures to Promote the Full Integration of the Environmental Dimension in the Development Process of the Developing Countries, *OJEC* [2000] L 288/1; Regulation (EC) No. 2494/2000 of the European Parliament and of the Council of 7 November 2000 on Measures to Promote the Conservation and Sustainable Management of Tropical Forests and Other Forests in Developing Countries, *OJEC* [2000] L 288/6. These Regulations set the framework for the management of budget line B7-6200, the most specific instrument available to the EC in the context of its development cooperation policy in the environment sector. For Strategic Guidelines and Priorities for Interventions financed by the budget line in 2002-2003 see Doc. DEV2790/2002 and DEV2792/2002.

[62] COM (2002) 429 final, *Bull.* 2002/7/8 1.6.86.

poverty and conflict, on the other.[63] Similarly, the EU Energy Initiative[64] strives for poverty reduction through access to energy supply, use of renewable energy resources and enhanced energy efficiency. It involves both genuine environmental issues (pollution prevention, deforestation, climate change, natural resource depletion and degradation) as well as potential root causes of conflict (e.g., competition over resources such as water, oil, gas, forests, etc.). Without diminishing the prominent importance of the Community's achievements, it may, however, be questioned whether these partnerships qualify as direct tools of conflict prevention as seems to be argued by the Community. The same question arises concerning geographical instruments, among which the Cotonou Agreement stands as an example of an ambitious model for cross-cutting the application and integration of 'principles of sustainable management of natural resources and the environment [...] at any level of the partnership'.[65] Specific measures are envisaged to address selected environmental problems of potential security relevance, such as, e.g., tropical forests, water resources, soils, biodiversity, energy, desertification or deforestation. Moreover, the Agreement employs, *inter alia*, dialogue on environmental issues as a means of contributing to peace, security and stability in the regions through an integrated peace building and conflict prevention policy. It should be noted, however, that, irrespective of the importance given by the Community to environmental considerations in a conflict prevention and sustainable development context, environmental commitments are not essential elements of the Agreement in the meaning of Article 9 thereof. They cannot be enforced, e.g., by selective withdrawal or coercive use of EC financial aid under Article 96 of the Cotonou Agreement.

4.2   Common Foreign and Security Policy (CFSP)

While Article 6 EC on environmental integration applies to the EU's conflict prevention policy to the extent that it is an integrated objective of measures clearly falling within the Community's competences (e.g., trade, development), Article 6 EC cannot bind the EU's second pillar (Common Foreign and Security Policy).

---

[63] See the conclusions of the Development Council (31 May 2001) on Conflict Prevention and Development addressing environmental requirements in an integrated manner (Doc. No. 885/01), Press 19. Cf., also 'Linking Poverty Reduction and Environmental Management', jointly prepared by the Commission/DG Development, United Nations Development Programme (UNDP), The World Bank, and the UK Department for International Development as a contribution to the Johannesburg WSSD Summit, published at <http://europa.eu.int/comm/development/body/publications/docs/full_linking_poverty_en.pdf#zoom=100>.

[64] 'Energy Initiative for Poverty Eradication and Sustainable Development' based on Commission Communication COM (2002) 408 final 'Energy Cooperation with the Developing Countries', *Bull.* 2002/7/8 1.6.85.

[65] Articles 1, 8(3), 11, 20, 30, 32 and 49 of the Cotonou Agreement, Final Act, *OJEC* [2000] L 317/3.

The draft Treaty establishing a Constitution for Europe,[66] however, suggests that in future Article III-4, replacing Article 6 EC, shall apply to the Union and all its policies, including the CFSP. The GAC's priorities set for integrating environmental requirements in the CFSP focus on post-conflict actions including rehabilitation measures. Previous efforts to integrate environmental considerations in landmine clearance, disarmament, non-proliferation of arms and their disposal, destruction and related waste management shall be continued. The achievements attained to this end encompass two Council Regulations requiring that any action concerning landmine clearance and hazardous debris of war shall be consistent with the local environment and the sustainable development of the affected region.[67] For the disposal and destruction of nuclear, biological or chemical weapons, however, no explicit environmental impact provisions have so far been adopted or included in existing instruments such as, for example, the EU Joint Action on non-proliferation and disarmament in Russia.[68] As regards reconstruction and rehabilitation actions, regional environmental or resource cooperation are among the principal tools for confidence and peace building. The Stability Pact for South Eastern Europe is a successful example of a structural post-conflict approach with a substantial environmental dimension through the Commission's initiative for the Regional Environmental Reconstruction Programme (RERP). RERP, co-financed by Community instruments such as CARDS (Community Assistance for Reconstruction, Development and Stabilisation),[69] LIFE-Third Countries and ISPA (Instrument for Structural Policies for Pre-accession),[70] provides the framework for environmental actions coordinating various donors and countries engaged in the region. It comprehensively addresses environmental governance and civil society, environmental capacity and institution building, trans-boundary cooperation through management of shared resources, accession to MEAs, the set up of national environmental laws and sustainability strategies to combat environmental pollution and biodiversity loss, etc.[71]

---

[66] Of 18 July 2003 (Doc. No. CONV 850/03).

[67] Council Regulation (EC) No. 1724/2001 of the European Parliament and of the Council of 23 July 2001 concerning action against anti-personnel landmines in developing countries, *OJEC* [2001] L 234/1; Council Regulation (EC) No. 1725/2001 concerning action against anti-personnel landmines in third countries other than developing countries, *OJEC* [2001] L 234/6.

[68] Council Joint Action of 17 December 1999 (1999/878/CFSP), *OJEC* [1999] L 331/11, provides generally for environmentally sound dismantlement and/or reconversion of infrastructure and equipment, and establishes an environmental monitoring mechanism as a confidence building measure. According to Council Decision of 25 June 2001 (2001/493/CFSP), *OJEC* [2001] L 180/2, an environmental impact assessment is explicitly foreseen only for waste containing weapons-grade plutonium.

[69] Council Regulation (EC) No. 2666/2000, *OJEC* [2000] L 306/1.

[70] Council Regulation (EC) No. 1267/1999, *OJEC* [1999] L 161/73.

[71] For detailed information see <http://www.rec.org/REC/Programs/REREP/>.

5. TACKLING PRIORITY CROSS-CUTTING ISSUES

A 'cross-cutting issue' has become the catchword for 'horizontal concerns'. It seems to refer to complex multi-causal and interacting problems involving many actors in different sectors and requiring various responses rooted in different policies. Environmental problems and resource management as well as conflict prevention are typical cross-cutting issues recognized as such by the EU. The use of the term by the Community is, however, less clear. Under the heading of 'cross-cutting issues', the Commission's Communication on Conflict Prevention lists the trade in rough diamonds on an equal footing with such multidimensional issues as sharing of water resources or forest loss. Whereas control over geological resources and trade in legally or illegally produced commodities play a key role in conflicts, e.g., in Africa, they are but one root cause in a more complex causality web. When tackling conflict diamonds as 'cross-cutting issue', the Community, however, appears to suggest, as priority action, a rather one-dimensional trade approach. In contrast, water and forest management are examples of intricate relations of access rights, environmental protection and conservation as well as sustainable resource use and management, on the one hand, and poverty reduction, energy supply, sanitation, urban development, land use, waste and industry management, on the other. All these aspects need to be addressed in a comprehensive manner.

5.1 Conflict diamonds

Internal armed conflicts in Angola, Liberia or Sierra Leone for instance have been fuelled for years by the trade in rough diamonds, profits from which have been used by rebel groups to obtain or produce weapons. Diamonds thereby nourished armed conflicts and contributed to continued human rights violations.[72] The European Community is by far the largest trader in rough diamonds with more than 60% of the global annual production passing through it. The participation of the EU in the so-called Kimberley Process is therefore a priority in the EU's conflict prevention efforts in the region. To this end, the Göteborg European Council gave the Commission the mandate to negotiate, on behalf of the Community, an agreement establishing an international certification scheme for rough diamonds.

---

[72] For background information see, e.g., Global Witness, *A Rough Trade: The Role of Companies and Governments in the Angola Conflict* (London, 1998) and *For a Few Dollars More* (London, April 2003); I. Smillie, et al., *The Heart of the Matter: Sierra Leone, Diamonds and Human Security* (Ottawa, Partnership Africa Canada 2000).

5.1.1   The Kimberley Process

Following embargoes adopted by the UN Security Council on all (non-certified) diamonds from Angola and Sierra Leone in 1998 and 2000, respectively,[73] the Kimberley Process was launched in May 2000 upon the initiative of Southern African diamond producing countries.[74] This consultation process involves governments of diamond importing and exporting countries, the diamond industry represented by the World Diamond Council[75] and representatives of civil society.[76] It is directed towards developing minimum international standards for national certification systems relating to the trade in rough diamonds. The process has been endorsed by and extended following UN General Assembly Resolution 55/56 which was adopted unanimously on 1 December 2000.[77] So far, the Kimberley Process has resulted in the adoption by its participants of a recommendation on a Certification Scheme in November 2002.[78] The Scheme was supposed to be launched on 1 January 2003. It is based on national laws and practices meeting internationally agreed minimum standards on certification and import/export control. It includes a voluntary industry self-control system and a dispute prevention mechanism. Upon the request of, *inter alia*, the EU, the WTO granted a waiver to the Kimberley Scheme, thereby ensuring its compatibility with WTO rules.[79]

5.1.2   Council Regulation 2368/2002

Based on Article 133 EC, on 20 December 2002 the Council adopted Regulation 2368/2002 implementing the Kimberley Process Certification Scheme for the international trade in rough diamonds. It fully entered into force on 1 February

---

[73] UN Security Council Resolutions adopted under Chapter VII of the UN Charter including, *inter alia*, Resolutions 1173 (1998), 1295 (2000), 1306 (2000) and 1343 (2001) published at <http://www.un.org/documents/scres.htm>. The European Community implemented the Security Council's Resolutions against Sierra Leone by Council Regulations 1745/2000 and 303/2002.

[74] For detailed information cf. <http://www.kimberleyprocess.com>.

[75] The World Diamond Council, created in July 2000 as a reaction to the role of diamonds in internal conflicts in Africa, is composed of representatives of the diamond industry, governmental institutions and the banking sector. For further information, see <http://www.worlddiamondcouncil.com>.

[76] The extended Kimberley process comprised 38 governments. At the plenary meeting of the Kimberley Process on 28-30 April 2003, the list of participating States was reviewed, and it now includes 58 States.

[77] The key UN GA Resolutions as well as other official documents of the Kimberley process are published at <http://www.kimberleyprocess.com/bulletinboard.asp>.

[78] Interlaken Declaration of 5 November 2002. The final scheme was based on the detailed proposal of the ministerial meeting in Garbarone on 29 November 2001, endorsed by UN GA Resolution 56/263 adopted on 13 March 2002 (A/RES/56/263), published at <http://www.un.org/documents/resga.htm>.

[79] WTO General Council Decision of 15 May 2003.

2003.[80] The Regulation sets up a Community Certification System and import/ export controls. Producer countries are responsible for controlling the production and transport of rough diamonds from the mine to the point of export. The EU Member States of import will verify through national authorities – designated as Community authorities for this purpose and listed in Annex III to the Regulation – that imports arrive in sealed containers accompanied by a Kimberley Process Certificate and that only such certified rough diamonds are re-exported accompanied by a Community certificate. Non-certified imports are prohibited as are exports to non-participants of the Kimberley Process. Based on specified minimum requirements implementing a system of warranties and industry self-regulation, organisations representing diamond traders may apply to the Commission to be listed in Annex V to the Regulation. If an exporter is a member of a listed organisation, the Community authorities may accept as conclusive evidence of lawful import into the Community a signed declaration by the exporter to that effect. The Regulation includes other measures such as information and reporting obligations towards the Commission, consultation mechanisms with participants of the Kimberley Process and statistical data collection. The Regulation has in the meantime been amended on several occasions, mainly updating the Annexes. On 1 September 2003, about 40 countries were listed as participants in Annex II. 'Participants' in the Kimberley Process are defined as any State, regional economic integration organisation, WTO member or separate customs territory that fulfils the requirements of the Kimberley Process Certification Scheme, that has notified that fact to the Chair of the latter and is listed in Annex II. This open access approach is an important prerequisite in moving towards a global agreement which is open to all States and organisations in compliance with WTO rules. The Regulation's efficiency depends on the quick and full implementation of the Process in the EU Member States and on the national implementation of the Kimberley Process in other participating countries. The EU's efforts to consolidate the Kimberley Process in an international agreement with enforcement mechanisms should, however, continue. Moreover, control over and trade in 'conflict diamonds' is but one aspect of the tensions and conflicts in the countries concerned. Care should be taken that, as a result of the Kimberley Process, 'conflict diamonds' are not substituted by 'conflict timber' or other conflict-stricken natural resources.[81]

---

[80] *OJEC* [2002] L 358/28.

[81] On the role of timber (e.g., Liberia) in financing conflicts (e.g., in Sierra Leone) cf., I. Smillie, 'Diamonds, Timber and West African Wars' published at <http://www.iisd.org/pdf/2002/envsec_ diamonds_timber.pdf>. See also the reports by Global Witness, *The Logs of War: The Timber Trade and Armed Conflict* (London, March 2002) and *The usual suspect* (London, March 2003).

5.2   Forest management

There is no specific provision on forestry policy in the EC Treaty. The protection
and sustainable development of forests is part of different Community policies
such as, e.g., the environment, agriculture and rural development, industry, energy, research or, specifically for external relations, development cooperation and
trade. The EU's main international environmental commitments related to forests
are notably the 1992 UNCED, the Framework Convention on Climate Change
(FCCC), the Convention on Biological Diversity (CBD) and the Convention to
Combat Desertification (CCD). Specific recommendations have been made by
the Intergovernmental Panel on Forests (IPF) and its successor the Intergovernmental Forum on Forests (IFF) as well as the International Tropical Timber
Agreement. The Ministerial Conference for the Protection of Forests in Europe
(MCPFE) established a platform to work towards the sustainable management
and protection of forests in a pan-European context. The Community participates
in all the named forums. Forests are linked to security and conflict prevention in
many ways because of their ecological, social and economic value.[82] They are
threatened, *inter alia*, by climate change, desertification, fires, pollution, unsustainable forest exploitation and management or illegal logging, factors which
mostly interact through feedback loops. While illegal logging means the harvest
of timber in breach of national legal requirements, most other factors rather refer
to a lack of adequate national environmental or forestry laws and practices ensuring protection, conservation and the sustainable use of forests. The EU's answer
to the quest for sustainable forest management in third countries is its forest strategy and related instrument.[83] It combines in a comprehensive approach all management aspects from forest conservation to use and trade. So far, however, there
has not been an adequate response to illegal logging which has directly been associated with corruption, organised crime and violent conflicts. In Central African States such as Liberia, for example, profits from illegal logging and related
trade have financed arms and fuelled violent disputes for many years. Although
the problem has been addressed in many international forums such as the UN Security Council, G8, the International Tropical Timber Council, the UN Forum on
Forests or the Johannesburg WSSD, so far no multilateral approach has been
taken. In the past, CITES and the EU implementing Regulation played an important role in controlling the trade in endangered timber species.[84] It is a genuine

---

[82] For an overview, see, e.g., J. McNeely, 'Biodiversity, Conflict and Tropical Forests', in M.
Halle, et al., *Conserving the Peace: Resources, Livelihoods and Security* (IISD 2002), pp. 29-55.

[83] COM (1999) 554 final 'Forests and Development: the EC approach', *OJEC* [1999] C 327/2;
Regulation (EC) No. 2494/2000 of the European Parliament and of the Council of 7 November 2000
on Measures to Promote the Conservation and Sustainable Management of Tropical Forests and
Other Forests in Developing Countries, *OJEC* [2000] L 288/6.

[84] 1973 Washington Convention on Trade in Endangered Species (CITES), Council Regulation
(EC) No. 338/97 of 9 December 1996 on the Protection of Species of Wild Fauna and Flora by

tool for nature conservation based on Article 130s EC Treaty and needs to be complemented by measures addressing trade in non-protected species. Following the EU's commitment under paragraph 45c of the WSSD Plan of Implementation, the 6th EAP and the Community's strategy on a global partnership for sustainable development, the Commission has recently adopted a proposal for an Action Plan on Forest Law Enforcement, Governance and Trade (FLEGT). It is directed at combating illegal logging and associated illegal trade and strengthening international cooperation to address violations of forest law, and forest crime.[85] The Commission's action plan suggests a holistic approach encompassing development cooperation, trade in timber, public procurement, private sector initiatives (Tropical Forest Trust), and financing and investment safeguards (e.g., money laundering). Bilateral or regional Forest Partnership Agreements shall support timber-producing countries in forest law enforcement and governance and establish monitoring systems covering certification, licensing and verification of timber and wood product import/exports. 'Conflict timber' loosely defined as 'timber traded by armed groups, the proceeds of which are used to fund armed conflicts', still needs more specific measures which can be effectively applied in crisis or pre- and post-conflict situations. The Commission's efforts are still at an initial stage, seeking cooperation at the international level, in particular for defining 'conflict timber'. The EU should take a leading role and urge multilateral actions for both 'conflict timber' and 'illegal logging'. The EU's efforts to this end, using the Kimberley Certification Scheme as model, should continue.

5.3 Water management

Water – ground, surface, coastal and marine water – is a key natural resource which is vital to sustain life, ecosystems and economic development. The management and conservation of water falls within the EC's environmental policy, whereas specific uses such as, e.g., shipping or fisheries, including their external relations, are dealt with under the Community's Transport or Common Fisheries Policy respectively. In its external relations with less developed countries, the EU tackles water management mainly under its development cooperation competences. Whatever the specific problem linked to water in a given country or region (pollution, aridity, access, upstream/downstream sharing, etc.), it results in competition for (clean) water among different users/needs (households, industry,

---

Regulating Trade therein, *OJEC* [1997] L 61/1; Commission Regulation (EC) No. 1808/2001 of 30 August 2001 Laying Down Detailed Rules Concerning the Implementation of Council Regulation (EC) No. 338/97 on the Protection of Species of Wild Fauna and Flora by Regulating Trade therein, *OJEC* [2001] L 250/1.

[85] COM (2003) 251 final, endorsed by the Environment Council on 12 June 2003. Cf., the International Workshop on FLEGT organised by the Commission in 2002, the contributions to which are published at <http://europa.eu.int/comm/external_relations/flegt/workshop/index.htm>.

agriculture/irrigation, ecosystems/habitats, etc.) within a country or across borders, thereby constituting a potential threat of conflict.[86] The quality and quantity of water are interdependent issues and must be dealt with as such in a conflict prevention context. Therefore, the structural distinction drawn in the Commission's Communication on Conflict Prevention between support for regional collaboration as regards 'sharing and fair management of water resources' and cooperation on resource management and environmental degradation may be questioned. Transboundary questions of access rights and management of the shared resources are linked to national water policy and problems and need to be dealt with in a common approach. There are, however, different priorities in water cooperation depending on the EC's partners. Whereas especially in less developed countries the main focus lies on acute supply (scarcity) and sanitation (poverty) issues, the conflict potential in transitional and industrial countries rather relates to transboundary water management (access and utilisation rights concerning rivers, regional seas, etc.), water quality (pollution) and water quantity (consumption).

5.3.1   *Regional and bilateral cooperation in sharing and fair management of water resources*

An important basis for water cooperation is the UNECE Convention on the Protection and Use of Transboundary Watercourses and International Lakes (Helsinki Convention), its Protocols and supporting soft-law recommendations, guidelines and specific action plans.[87] With the Water Framework Directive[88] the European Community established a model for implementing and strengthening the Convention in the territory of the EU Member States and even beyond.[89] In view of the enlargement of the European Union, it may provide an important contribution to preventive conflict policies with the NIS.[90] The reason for this is that the Directive is based on a river basin management approach dealing with natural geographical and hydrologic units rather than areas defined by administrative or political boundaries. Many of the European rivers are international, crossing territorial borders. Cooperation with riparian States which are not Members or future

---

[86] For a comprehensive overview of water use and management in the light of conflict prevention cf., A. Talsma (ed.), *Water and Development in developing countries* (Luxembourg 2000).

[87] 31 *ILM* (1992), p. 1312.

[88] Directive 2000/60/EC of the European Parliament and of the Council of 23 October 2000 establishing a framework for Community action in the field of water policy, *OJEC* [2000] L 327/1.

[89] See the conclusions of the Second International Conference on Sustainable Management of Transboundary Waters in Europe, ECE/MP.WAT/8 of 12 June 2002.

[90] Cf., also J. Hafemann, 'Preventive conflict management in the context of implementing the EU Water Framework Directive in the Oder River system', in: F. Bernardini, et al. (eds.), *Sustainable Management of transboundary waters in Europe*, Proceedings of the second international conference on the UNECE Convention on the Protection and Use of Transboundary Watercourses and International Lakes (Poland, Com Graph 2003).

Members of the European Union is therefore crucial. The importance of the Water Framework Directive beyond the Community's boundaries has also been emphasised by the UNECE: activities under the Helsinki Convention and the Protocol on Water and Health should be closely linked to the implementation of this piece of supranational legislation.[91] Supported by the EU, the OSCE – under security aspects – assists projects to implement the Water Framework Directive in OSCE countries such as the Ukraine.[92] Complementary efforts are being undertaken by the EU, among which the Environmental Cooperation in the Danube-Black Sea Region is an ambitious example of the EU's 'environment and security' approach.[93] It brings together the States of the Danube river basin encompassing EU Member States, accession countries, South-Eastern European and NIS countries. Through the DABLAS Task Force the EU provides for a continuous platform for cooperation for the protection of water and water ecosystems, for coordinating the activities and actors (donors) in the region and for dialogue.[94]

5.3.2   *Water cooperation in a development context*

The Community is a signatory to and a participant in numerous international agreements, processes and organisations concerning water management.[95] Among the global landmarks developing water policies and principles are the Dublin International Conference on Water and Environment (1992), the 1992 UNCED in Rio (see in particular Agenda 21, Chapter 18), the Action Plan on freshwater resources drafted by the UN Commission on Sustainable Development, or the Bonn International Conference on Freshwater (2001). The Community works with international networks, e.g., with the Water Supply and Sanitation Collaborative Council (WSSCC), the Global Water Partnership and the World Water Forum which foster the coordination of activities in the field of water management at the international level. The central Community instrument addressing 'water and security' is the EU Initiative 'Water for Life' launched at the 2002 Johannesburg WSSD. There, Strategic Partnerships have been initiated

---

[91] Cf., UNECE Doc. ECE/MP.WAT/8, para. 14 (cf., n. 89).

[92] OSCE Annual Report 2002. In July and November 2002 round-table conferences on the water management were held in the Ukraine. Also Moldova showed interest in a project on implementing the Water Framework Directive.

[93] Commission Communication COM (2001) 615 final 'Environmental Co-operation in the Danube – Black Sea Region' *Bull.* 2001/10 1.4.47.

[94] Memorandum of Understanding between the International Commission for the Protection of the Black Sea (ICPBS) and the International Commission for the Protection of the Danube River (ICPDR) on common strategic goals; Declaration on Water and Water-related Ecosystems in the Wider Black Sea Region; both published at <http://europa.eu.int/comm/environment/enlarg/danubeblacksea_en.htm>.

[95] For a compilation of legal documents, water law, and resources related to water policy see the International Water Law Project at <http://www.internationalwaterlaw.org>.

with Africa and the NIS, with more concrete proposals having been presented at the World Water Forum in Kyoto in March 2003 and the Ministerial Conference 'Environment for Europe' in Kiev in May 2003 respectively. Partnerships with the Mediterranean countries and Latin America followed at the end of 2002 as well as the establishment of the EU-ASEM Waternet Multi-Stakeholder Platform. The first 'design' phase of the initiative will continue until the end of 2004 and it is preparing, by means of concrete situation analysis, project coordination and monitoring mechanisms, for the subsequent second 'implementation' phase. The EU Water Initiative is an open cooperation and coordination process at all geographical levels, committed to a demand-driven, multi-stakeholder approach and based on the principle of ownership by development partner countries. It comprises three key tasks: water supply, sanitation and integrated water management by encompassing research, governance and concrete projects (including funding, namely through ODA). It involves governments, water agencies, water users, civil society and private investors. The participation of the latter group has been criticised in light of the dominance of European multinationals on the international water services market. This is particularly true in light of the EU's position in WTO/GATS negotiations promoting the inclusion of water supply services as environmental services for liberalisation and free trade which might run counter to the initiative's objectives.[96] In many developing countries it is questionable whether the necessary structures exist to ensure stakeholder and civil society participation, on the one hand, and the privatisation of water supply services which is successful in the light of conflict prevention and sustainable development, on the other. Yet, from an ecological and security point of view, the initiative has the potential of successfully addressing the increasing water-related threats of conflict in a national and regional context by employing a river basin management approach.

6. CONCLUSION

It is against the Community's commitment to a common but differentiated responsibility to conserve, protect and restore the Earth's ecosystem[97] that the EC's environmental policy and its interface with conflict prevention is built. Based on precaution, prevention and an ecosystem approach, the EC's environmental policy is a predestined long-term tool to minimise environmental problems *before* they give rise to tensions and conflicts. Environmental and sustainability impact assessments have proved in the past to be important tools to ensure the integration of environmental requirements in other policies. The experiences gained may

---

[96] See the consolidated position submitted to the WTO on 29 April 2003, published at <http://europa.eu.int/comm/trade/index_en.htm>.

[97] Principle 7 of the Rio Declaration, 31 *ILM* (1992), p. 876.

be employed for a conflict prevention impact assessment in order to improve the efficient integration of conflict prevention in other policies including the environment. The Community has achieved considerable progress in addressing the environment/conflict nexus in long-term bilateral and regional environmental or development cooperations with third countries and in international forums. However, a more clearly and narrowly defined scope of 'conflict prevention' would be desirable.[98] An analytical approach to 'environment and conflict' would help to identify the environmental problem, its link to conflict and the available responses in a specific time and space relationship, hence, to promote structural stability.

---

[98] See, e.g., the definitions suggested in the Swedish Action Plan by the Swedish Government Communication 2000/01:2 'Preventing Violent Conflict – Swedish Policy for the 21st Century' (Ministry of Foreign Affairs, Stockholm 2001), p. 20. Under 'conflict prevention' it comprised measures taken (i) before a conflict or dispute escalates into acts of violence, (ii) in order to prevent an ongoing violent conflict from spreading to other areas, (iii) to prevent the resurgence of violence after the parties have reached a peace agreement, an armistice, etc.

Chapter 11
CONFLICT PREVENTION AND HUMAN RIGHTS

by Sybilla Fries[1]

1. INTRODUCTION

Let us start by admitting that the above title is not quite correct. This chapter not only concerns conflict prevention and human rights, it is also about conflict prevention and democracy and about conflict prevention and the rule of law. These three principles are inextricably linked. They constitute the very foundations of the Union itself and have been made an objective of the Union's policy *vis-à-vis* third countries.[2] Indeed, their trinity seems so natural, at least in the EU context, that whoever speaks of human rights in that context, is certain to be referring to the above broader meaning. That explains not only the title, but also the possible 'short cut' references in the following pages.

The following pages will explore how conflict prevention and human rights (and democracy and ...) relate to each other in the context of EU policies. Two different perspectives will be taken. One, the perspective of the EU's conflict prevention policy. What role are human rights seen to play in that policy? How are they to be addressed as a measure of conflict prevention? And two, the perspective of the EU's human rights policy. How does that policy take account of the necessity to prevent conflicts? And through what measures does it propose to address the issue?

In addressing these questions, the analysis will focus on the 'first pillar' dimension of the EU's policies. That having been said, some of the considerations might also be of value for the 'second pillar' initiatives in this field.[3]

---

[1] Member of the Legal Service of the European Commission. The views expressed in this article are personal and do not necessarily reflect the position of the EU institutions.

[2] See Article 6 of the EU Treaty, on the one hand, and Article 11 of the EU Treaty as well as Articles 177(2) and 181a of the EC Treaty, on the other. See also below section 3.1.

[3] 'First pillar' is a reference to the EC Treaty, through which competences have been transferred from the Member States to the Community, while the 'second' and 'third pillar', i.e., under the EU Treaty policies (the Common Foreign and Security Policy and the Justice and Home Affairs Policy) have remained 'intergovernmental' in nature.

V. Kronenberger and J. Wouters, eds., The European Union and Conflict Prevention
© 2004, T·M·C·ASSER PRESS, *The Hague, The Netherlands*

2. HUMAN RIGHTS IN EU CONFLICT PREVENTION POLICY

In this section, the perspective of the EU conflict prevention policy is taken. The section will describe how EU policy documents in this field view the role of human rights and what measures they prescribe to contribute to the objectives of a conflict prevention policy. The EU policy documents on conflict prevention and their history have been described in more detail elsewhere in this book.[4] The following analysis, while taking all of them into consideration, primarily focuses on the Commission's 2001 Communication on Conflict Prevention.[5]

2.1 The root causes of conflict – human rights and the concept of structural stability

Perhaps the role that the EU policy documents on conflict prevention attribute to human rights and democracy is best summarised in the words of the Commissioner for External Relations Christopher Patten:

> 'The link between conflict prevention and the promotion of human rights and democracy is abundantly clear. Just as denying basic rights fans the flames of conflict, helping to guarantee those rights can prevent conflict arising in the first place'.[6]

The EU policy documents translate this wisdom into the concepts of root causes and structural stability. A root cause is described as a factor which produces or exacerbates violence.[7] Lack of respect for human rights and sometimes more specifically the violation of certain human rights such as non-discrimination and freedom of speech, are said to constitute such root causes.[8] Poverty and a lack of good governance are identified as other root causes.[9]

In order to prevent conflict from arising the EU policy documents state that it is necessary to address these root causes. The Communication on Conflict Prevention sees this as a task of creating, enhancing or consolidating structural stability. Conflicts do not arise, according to the underlying belief, where societies are built on a number of basic elements which act as guarantors for stability. The

---

[4] See, e.g., the contribution by J. Wouters and F. Naert in this volume.

[5] COM (2001) 211final, available at <http://europa.eu.int/comm/external_relations/cfsp/news/com2001_211_en.pdf>.

[6] Opening address at the Human Rights Forum, Brussels, 28 and 29 May 2001 'The Role of Human Rights and Democratisation in Conflict Prevention and Resolution'.

[7] See the Report presented to the Nice European Council by the Secretary General/High Representative and the Commission, at point 28.

[8] See the Report of the Secretary General/High Representative and Commission, op. cit. n. 7, at point 21.

[9] See the EU Programme for the Prevention of Violent Conflicts, available at <http://www.eu2001.se/static/eng/pdf/violent.PDF>, point 12.

Commission has described the concept of structural stability elsewhere in the following words:

> 'Structural stability is to be understood as a term denoting a dynamic situation, a situation of stability able to cope with the dynamics inherent in (emerging) democratic societies. Structural stability could thus be defined as a situation involving sustainable economic development, democracy and respect for human rights, viable political structures, and healthy social and environmental conditions, with the capacity to manage change without having to resort to violent conflict. Working towards structural stability would mean the targeted reinforcement of those factors that enable peaceful change'.[10]

Thus, the concepts of root causes and structural stability seem to be juxtapositioned. Where the basic structural elements are in place, there are no factors that produce or exacerbate violence. Conversely, addressing such factors, where they exist, means working on ensuring that the basic structural elements are put in place. In this perspective, therefore, addressing the lack of respect for human rights and democratic values contributes to enhancing structural stability and thereby to preventing the outbreak of violent conflicts in the long-term. The Communication highlights a number of EU initiatives in this regard which it considers to be of particular value for conflict prevention such as election observation and measures to ensure freedom of expression and the independent media.[11]

Conflict prevention on the level of structural stability is quite an indirect form of prevention policy compared to, say, mediation between warring parties. A direct link to a given conflict does not seem necessary. On the contrary, it would seem that measures focusing on structural stability should ideally address problems long before they have led to the outbreak of violent conflict. Because of its remoteness from a given (or potential) conflict, it is also more difficult to measure the success of such a policy other than through the absence of conflict.

2.2 Mainstreaming conflict prevention in EU policies and instruments

In order to address the root causes of conflict, the Communication on Conflict Prevention proposes an integrated approach, that is to say, a more systematic and coordinated use of EU instruments.[12] Making more systematic and coordinated use of EU instruments translates into mainstreaming conflict prevention in the EU policies and instruments. While this is supposed to apply to all EU policies

---

[10] See the Communication from the Commission to the Council of 6 March 1996, *The European Union and the Issue of Conflicts in Africa: Peace-building, Conflict Prevention and Beyond*, SEC (1996) 332, point 1.

[11] See the Communication on Conflict Prevention, op. cit. n. 5, p. 13.

[12] See the Communication on Conflict Prevention, op. cit. n. 5, at 10.

concerning or affecting third countries, it is seen to be of particular relevance for EU development cooperation and other external assistance.[13]

2.2.1 Overview of instruments for EU development cooperation and other external assistance

A brief overview of the instruments for EU development cooperation and other external assistance allows one to have a better understanding of how mainstreaming is supposed to work. EU development cooperation and other external assistance, as described in more detail elsewhere in this book,[14] are based on both geographical and thematic instruments.

The geographical instruments are mainly Council regulations, on the basis of which the Community funds cooperation projects with given third countries, usually in a broad range of areas. Such regulations exist for the Western Balkans,[15] for North Africa and the Middle East,[16] for Latin America and Asia,[17] and for the former Soviet Union and Mongolia.[18] By contrast, cooperation with the African, Caribbean and Pacific countries is based not on a regulation, but directly on an association agreement, the so-called Cotonou Agreement.[19]

Funding activities under these geographic instruments are programmed with the help of so-called Country Strategy Papers (CSPs). CSPs provide an analysis of the political economic and social situation of a given country with the political analysis focusing on assessing democratic participation, human rights and the rule of law.[20] More specifically, the human rights analysis, in this context, requires an examination of the adherence to and the implementation of commit-

---

[13] See Report prepared by Commission services *One year on: the Commission's Conflict Prevention Policy*, available at <http://europa.eu.int/comm/external_relations/cpcm/cp/rep.htm>, at point 1.1.

[14] See the chapter by B. Martenczuk in this volume.

[15] Council Regulation (EC) No. 2666/2000 of 5 December 2000 on assistance for Albania, Bosnia and Herzegovina, Croatia, the Federal Republic of Yugoslavia and the Former Yugoslav Republic of Macedonia, repealing Regulation (EC) No. 1628/96 and amending Regulations (EEC) No. 3906/89 and (EEC) No. 1360/90 and Decisions 97/256/EC and 1999/311/EC, *OJEC* [2000] L 306/1.

[16] Council Regulation (EC) No 1488/96 of 23 July 1996 on financial and technical measures to accompany (MEDA) the reform of economic and social structures in the framework of the Euro-Mediterranean partnership, *OJEC* [1996] L 189/1.

[17] Council Regulation (EEC) No. 443/92 of 25 February 1992 on financial and technical assistance to, and economic cooperation with, the developing countries in Asia and Latin America, *OJEC* [1992] L 52/1.

[18] Council Regulation (EC, Euratom) No. 99/2000 of 29 December 1999 concerning the provision of assistance to the partner States in Eastern Europe and Central Asia, *OJEC* [2000] L 12/1.

[19] 2000/483/EC: Partnership agreement between the members of the African, Caribbean and Pacific Group of States of the one part, and the European Community and its Member States, of the other part, signed in Cotonou on 23 June 2000, *OJEC* [2000] L 317/3.

[20] See Guidelines for Implementation of the Common Framework for Country Strategy Papers (Commission Staff Paper), available at <http://europa.eu.int/comm/external_relations/reform/document/iqsg_04_01.pdf>.

ments under international human rights Treaties and Agreements, the protection of civil liberties including freedom of speech and of assembly, and the effective operation of human rights monitoring.

On the basis of this analysis a funding strategy is determined in line with co-operation objectives and the policy agenda of the beneficiary country. The government of the beneficiary country is involved to a varying degree, depending on the instrument in question, in determining what is to be funded. Funding decisions are adopted by the Commission, which is usually assisted by a (management) Committee of representatives of the Member States (and, in the case of the Cotonou Agreement, of the associated states as well).

As regards human rights and democracy, the geographic instruments usually provide for the possibility to fund projects in these areas. Thus, for example, the so-called ALA Regulation for Asia and Latin America[21] provides in its Article 5 that

'Aid should [...] be allocated, *inter alia*, to specific projects for the spread of democracy, good governance and human rights'.

Thematic instruments, on the other hand, are Council regulations that address issues of cooperation in a horizontal manner. These range from environmental issues[22] to issues such as gender equality,[23] demographic policies[24] or drug problems.[25] Many of these instruments were adopted in the specific context of cooperation with developing countries.[26] More recent legislative initiatives have led to the adoption of twin regulations for certain subject-matters, with one covering developing countries and one covering third countries other than developing countries.[27] Funding under the thematic instruments is also subject to a programming exercise. Contrary to the geographic instruments, however, the government of the beneficiary country is not involved in the decision-making process. Indeed, funding usually goes directly to non-governmental or international organisations.

---

[21] Op. cit. n. 17.

[22] Regulation (EC) No. 2493/2000 of the European Parliament and of the Council of 7 November 2000 on measures to promote the full integration of the environmental dimension in the development process of developing countries, *OJEC* [2000] L 288/1.

[23] Council Regulation (EC) No. 2836/98 of 22 December 1998 on integrating of gender issues in development cooperation, *OJEC* [1998] L 354/5.

[24] Council Regulation (EC) No. 1484/97 of 22 July 1997 on aid for population policies and programmes in the developing countries, *OJEC* [1997] L 202/1.

[25] Council Regulation (EC) No. 2046/97 of 13 October 1997 on north-south cooperation in the campaign against drugs and drug addiction, *OJEC* [1997] L 287/1.

[26] That is to say, on the legal basis of Article 179 of the EC Treaty.

[27] See for example Regulation Nos. 1724/2001 and 1725/2001 of the European Parliament and of the Council of 23 July 2001 concerning action against anti-personnel landmines, *OJEC* [2001] L 234/1 and 6.

Among the thematic regulations there are the so-called Human Rights Regulations.[28] These twin regulations, one adopted for developing and one for other third countries, provide the legal basis for funding activities relating not only to the promotion of respect for human rights but also (see the above-mentioned 'trinity') to the development and consolidation of democracy and the rule of law. The two regulations constitute one of the main pillars of the EU Human Rights Policy. This is why they will be described in more detail in the third section of this article.

2.2.2 *Human rights and democracy issues as conflict indicators*

Mainstreaming means systematically giving consideration to the issue of conflict prevention in other policies. For the EU's cooperation policy with third countries the Commission, in its Communication on Conflict Prevention, proposes to achieve such a systematic inclusion with the help of the above-mentioned Country Strategy Papers. Thus, an automatic check of certain risk factors – or potential conflict indicators – listed in a 'check-list for root causes of conflict'[29] is built into the process of drafting a CSP.

Human rights and democracy issues are on this check-list. Points 1 to 4 raise a series of questions regarding the legitimacy of the state, the rule of law, respect for fundamental rights and civil society and the media. These questions refine and go beyond the standard political analysis carried out in CSPs (see above). Compared to, for example, the relatively broad standard CSP analysis on human rights, as described above, the check-list analysis requires the following detailed questions to be examined:

'Are civil and political freedoms respected?: Respect of right to vote/eligibility, protection of civil liberties including freedom of speech and of assembly, free and fair elections respecting the rights of the opposition.

Are religious and cultural rights respected?: Punition by law of religious, ethnic or cultural discrimination, recognition of minority languages, e.g., in education, definition of the state with no reference to a dominant religious/cultural identity.

Are other basic human rights respected?: Prosecution of human rights violations (torture, illegal detention), gender equality, freedom of private practices (dress codes, private life, etc.), adherence to and implementation of commitments under international

---

[28] Council Regulation (EC) Nos. 975/1999 and 976/1999 of 29 April 1999 laying down the requirements for the implementation [..] operations [..], which contribute to the general objective of developing and consolidating democracy and the rule of law and to that of respecting human rights and fundamental freedoms, *OJEC* [1999] L 120/1 and 8.

[29] Available at <http://europa.eu.int/comm/external_relations/cpcm/cp/list.htm> and annexed to J. Niño-Pérez's contribution (chapter 1) in this volume.

human rights treaties and conventions, effective operation of human rights monitoring by NGOs and/or international organisations'.

A first observation, therefore, would be that given its broader scope, it would seem that the human rights and democracy analysis required under the check-list for root causes has replaced the one normally required under the CSPs as it has been described above under section 2.2.1.

A second observation would be that there does not seem to be a hierarchy of human rights issues. All seem to matter equally for the purposes of conflict prevention. Thus, say, a systemic gender equality problem in a given country, on the basis of this list, is as much an indicator of conflict as, for example, the systematic persecution of an ethnic minority. This would seem to be in line with the above concept of structural stability, under which respect for human rights (democracy and the rule of law) is generally to be ensured.

The mainstreaming exercise is supposed to result in a better focus for the activities that external aid is to target in order to contribute to effective conflict prevention. For human rights, democracy and the rule of law, funding should focus on these issues if and where problems have been identified on the basis of the above list. Given the latter's nature, from the point of view of conflict prevention, all human rights and democracy issues equally deserve to be addressed through funding.

This was the perspective that the EU's conflict prevention policy takes on human rights, democracy and the rule of law. Let us now look at the opposite perspective, i.e., that which the EU's human rights policy takes on conflict prevention.

3. CONFLICT PREVENTION IN EU HUMAN RIGHTS POLICY

This section will thus look at how EU policy documents on human rights view the issue of conflict prevention and how they propose to address that issue through human rights policy measures. Let it be said once again that the concept of a 'human rights policy' in this context is to be understood in a broad sense encompassing the promotion of democracy and the rule of law. As seen above this 'trinity' is established by the Treaties themselves and forms the basis of the major policy and legislative 'human rights' instruments as they will be described in this section. Before entering into an analysis of the role of conflict prevention in these instruments, however, it would seem appropriate to briefly recall the foundations and main aspects of the EU human rights policy.

3.1 Origin and instruments of EU human rights policy

Although the appearance of human rights and democracy issues in the EU's policy *vis-à-vis* third countries dates back much further,[30] it was at the beginning of the 1990s that an actual EU human rights (foreign) policy came into being. A central feature of that process was the introduction of the so-called human rights clauses into the Community's trade and cooperation agreements with third countries. On the basis of such a clause, which has become a standard clause in Community agreements, it is possible to suspend or terminate an agreement with a third country that is guilty of grave breaches of human rights obligations.[31] The same possibility has been introduced in the Community's unilateral trade instruments.[32] The introduction of the human rights clause was motivated by the realisation/belief that human rights issues cannot and should not be separated from economic (or other) relations with third countries, but that such relations can only prosper if they are built on the foundations of respect for human rights and democratic values. Through the 1993 Maastricht Treaty this belief was explicitly laid down in the Treaty. The objective of promoting respect for human rights, democracy and the rule of law was made an explicit objective of the Community's cooperation policy with developing countries.[33] The same was done for the newly institutionalised EU Common Foreign and Security Policy (CFSP).[34] Over the following years, in addition to the human rights clauses, EC funding activities (see below) as well as diplomatic tools such as human rights dialogues and *démarches* on specific human rights topics were developed and intensified.

In its Communication of May 2001 on the European Union's Role in Promoting Human Rights and Democratisation in Third Countries (hereinafter 'the Communication'),[35] the Commission reviewed its human rights policy with a view to enhancing its impact. Two issues are prominent in this Communication and will be discussed in the light of what they mean for conflict prevention.

---

[30] In particular the European Parliament had committed itself to a systematic scrutiny of the human rights situation in third countries from the late 1970s/early 1980s onwards. On the role of the European Parliament in this regard see Rack/Lausegger 'The Role of the European Parliament: Past and Future' in Alston/Bustelo/Heenan (eds.), *The EU and Human Rights* (Oxford, Oxford University Press 1999), p. 801.

[31] For an overview of human rights clauses, see Riedel/Will 'Human Rights Clauses in External Agreements of the EC' in Alston/Bustelo/Heenan (eds.), *The EU and Human Rights* (Oxford, Oxford University Press 1999), p. 723.

[32] For an overview of human rights conditionality in autonomous trade instruments, see Brandtner/Rosas, 'Trade Preferences and Human Rights' in Alston/Bustelo/Heenan (eds.), *The EU and Human Rights* (Oxford, Oxford University Press 1999), p. 699.

[33] See Article 177(2) EC Treaty. Note that with the Nice Treaty of 2000, a new legal basis for cooperation with third countries other than developing countries has been introduced into the Treaty in Article 181a. It refers to the objective of promoting human rights, democracy and the rule of law in an identical way to Article 177(2).

[34] See Article 11 of the EU Treaty.

[35] COM(2001) 252 final, available at <http://europa.eu.int/comm/external_relations/human_rights/doc/com01_252_en.pdf>.

3.2 Mainstreaming déjà vu – human rights as a horizontal objective of EU policies

The first prominent issue in the Communication is the call for the mainstreaming of human rights and democracy in all EU external policies. In fact, it was not new to say that human rights should be an integral consideration of all policies. Indeed, it follows from the Treaties themselves that human rights and democracy are a horizontal objective. As seen above, they constitute fundamental principles of the European Union and, as such, have found expression as an objective of external policy both in the CFSP and in the EC cooperation policy. Consistent with the latter all of the EC's geographical instruments on development cooperation, as also discussed above, have, in one way or another, the objective of promoting respect for human rights and democratisation built into them. However, it was felt that there was room for improvement and that better use could be made of existing instruments.

The Communication sets out how this is to be done.[36] Human rights and democracy issues are to be included in the planning, design, implementation and monitoring of policies and programmes. The role of Country Strategy Papers is central in that they are to provide an analysis of the human rights situation and constitute the focal point for coordination and complementarity between different instruments. While mainstreaming is to apply to all policies – including also dialogue at all levels – particular importance is attached to the EC's cooperation policy and other external assistance.

All of this sounds familiar. Indeed, as seen above, for the purpose of mainstreaming conflict prevention, CSPs are also being relied upon. As part of the check-list for conflict indicators a human rights analysis is to be carried out. On the basis of the check-list analysis, funding activities are to be better focussed on the issues identified. The cooperation instruments are to be used for funding.

Arguably, therefore, the conflict prevention mainstreaming exercise (to the extent that it concerns human rights) and the human rights mainstreaming exercise present a complete overlap; they are actually the same exercise.

3.3 European Initiative for Democracy and Human Rights – conflict prevention times two

The second prominent issue in the Communication on Human Rights is the European Initiative for Democracy and Human Rights (EIDHR).

---

[36] See the Communication, op. cit. n. 35, at point 3.2.

3.3.1   EIDHR – origin and method of implementation

The EIDHR goes back to an initiative of the European Parliament which, in 1994, introduced it as a new chapter (B7-7) in the budget. In 1999, the Council adopted the above-mentioned two 'human rights regulations' providing the basic act for the EIDHR.[37] The human rights regulations are thematic regulations in the field of development cooperation and other external assistance as described above. On the basis of these regulations, Community funding can be provided to operations aimed at promoting and defending human rights as well as developing and consolidating democracy and the rule of law.

Funding under the EIDHR is meant to be complementary to the other instruments of development cooperation and other external assistance. Contrary to these latter instruments, which provide for the funding of activities through the government of the third state, the human rights regulations primarily serve to directly fund the activities of NGOs. Needless to say, this advantage of not depending on the consent of the government opens the way for a whole range of other human rights activities – all those sensitive enough to encounter little willingness on the side of the government concerned to agree on funding schemes.

The Communication on Human Rights makes the EIDHR a prominent issue in proposing a new approach to the method of its implementation.[38] In fact, the funding policy of the Commission under the EIDHR had in the past sometimes been criticised for lacking focus and not being sustainable. The Communication addresses this issue by proposing to adopt a more strategic approach to EIDHR funding. The approach consists of establishing, in a longer term perspective, priorities both in terms of themes to be addressed and countries to be targeted. As regards the *thematic priorities*, the Communication identified the following four:

- 'Support to strengthen democratisation, good governance and the rule of law;
- Activities in support of the abolition of the death penalty;
- Support for the fight against torture and impunity and for international tribunals and criminal courts, and
- Combating racism and xenophobia and discrimination against minorities and indigenous people'.

As regards the *focus countries*, the Communication proposed to select them 'primarily on the basis of the analysis and priorities identified in CSPs and Accession

---

[37] See n. 28 above.

[38] Note that under Article 110 of the (new) Financial Regulation (Council Regulation (EC, Euratom) No. 1605/2002 of 25 June 2002 on the Financial Regulation applicable to the general budget of the European Communities), *OJEC* [2002] L 248/1, all EU grants are subject to an annual work programme.

Partnerships, so as to ensure coherence and complementarity with other instruments and the establishment of a critical mass of EC support'.[39]

As the Communication explains, the priority-focused approach is not to apply to urgent and unforeseen needs, in response to which the EC should preserve its flexibility.

Following the Communication, a programming document was issued in December 2001. It covers the period of 2002 to 2004 and has been updated once so far (2003). The programming document spells out in more detail the specific objectives and key activities proposed to implement the four thematic priorities and it identifies 31 focus countries. It was decided that the first thematic priority, i.e., the support to strengthen democratisation, good governance and the rule of law, was to be implemented primarily in the focus countries, leaving the possibility for funding outside these countries only for regional projects.[40] Implementation takes place through calls for proposals.

As an issue apart, i.e., outside the priority approach, the Programming document defines the funding of election assistance and observation, explaining that 'election programming is a more flexible, ongoing process, given that an election observation mission will be inserted in the yearly programming only when, following and exploratory mission, the political decision to observe that election is taken'.[41] The Programming document provides that EIDHR funding is to concentrate on funding EU election observation missions (as opposed to giving financial assistance directly to the third country's government, as can be done on the basis of the above geographic instruments) and establishes a rolling calendar of elections for which EIDHR funding is to be considered.

Against this background, the following sections will describe the role which is given to conflict prevention in the implementation of the EIDHR. In fact, it would seem that conflict prevention is given a role on two levels.

3.3.2   *Conflict prevention as an objective of human rights policy*

The first role is explicitly addressed in the Human Rights Regulations. Article 3.3 of Regulation No. 976/99 and Article 2.3 of Regulation No. 975/99 stipulate that technical and financial aid is to be provided for operations aimed at

'support for measures to promote the respect for human rights and democratisation *by preventing conflict* and dealing with its consequences in close collaboration with relevant competent bodies, in particular' [emphasis added].

---

[39] See the Communication, op. cit. n. 35, at point 4.2.2.

[40] See the Commission Staff Working Document *European Initiative for Democracy and Human Rights Programming Document 2002-2004*, available at <http://europa.eu.int/comm/external_ relations/human_rights/doc/eidhr02_04.pdf>, point 2.

[41] See the Commission Staff Working Document, op. cit. n. 40, point 1.

Notably, the perspective taken here is quite different from the one taken above in the context of a conflict prevention policy. As seen above, from a conflict prevention point of view, human rights violations are seen to be a *cause of conflict*. Here, on the other hand, human rights violations are seen to be a *consequence of conflict*. Indeed violent conflicts often give rise to human rights violations on a massive scale and more generally undermine the enjoyment of human rights by the individual. From this perspective, to prevent the outbreak of conflicts (or to end a conflict as quickly as possible) thus becomes an objective of a human rights policy.

The activities to be supported through funding, from this perspective, are mostly focused on addressing issues directly related to potential, actual or recent conflicts. As stated in the Regulation they cover:

- 'supporting capacity-building, including the establishment of local early warning systems;
- supporting measures aimed at balancing opportunities and at bridging existing dividing lines among different identity groups;
- supporting measures facilitating the peaceful conciliation of group interests, including support for confidence-building measures relating to human rights and democratisation, in order to prevent conflict and restore civil peace;
- promoting international humanitarian law and its observance by all parties to a conflict; and
- supporting international, regional or local organisations, including the NGOs, involved in preventing, resolving and dealing with the consequences of conflict, including support for establishing ad hoc international criminal tribunals and setting up a permanent international criminal court, and support and assistance for the victims of human rights violations'.

On the basis of these provisions, a number of projects have been funded in the past.[42] While a few of them directly addressed conflict or post-conflict situations (e.g. peace negotiations in Burundi, post-war reintegration and rehabilitation of women and children in Mozambique), the majority were aimed more broadly at education and capacity building in civil society (e.g., the human rights educational programme in Burkina Faso, a civic education project in Somalia, the creation of legal clinics in Niger). Finally, on the basis of this provision considerable funding was provided to measures supporting the establishment of the International Criminal Court.[43]

---

[42] Overview of EIDHR-funded projects available at <http://europa.eu.int/comm/europeaid/projects/eidhr/documents_en.htm>.

[43] Between 1995 and 2002 a total of 7 million Euro has been provided in grants to support the ICC, see at <http://europa.eu.int/comm/europeaid/projects/eidhr/pdf/cpi-initiatives-commission_fr.pdf>.

3.3.2.1 Programming conflict prevention

Under the new programming exercise, support for activities in this area has been somewhat reorganised. For one thing, as seen above, support for the ICC or other international criminal tribunals has been made a thematic priority in itself. Furthermore, other aspects of conflict prevention were taken up under the (first) priority 'support to strengthen democratisation, good governance and the rule of law'. Under this priority conflict prevention is explicitly identified as one of the sub-areas, alongside other sub-areas such as governance, legal system and strengthening institutions and human rights education and training. Compared to the activities envisaged in the above Articles 2.3 and 3.3 of the Human Rights Regulations, the programming document somewhat narrows the field of intervention as regards conflict prevention. The specific objectives in this regard are:

- 'early warning, mediation, reconciliation and confidence-building measures from grass roots and international NGOs developed;
- common training modules for civilian staff to be deployed in international missions promoted;
- capacity of international regional or local organisations involved in conflict prevention strengthened'.

As seen above, the funding of activities relating to the first priority and, therefore, also to conflict prevention, under the programming document, is only available for regional projects and projects in focus countries. That having been said, it is still possible, on the basis of the Human Rights Regulations, to fund conflict prevention measures in non-focus countries on an *ad hoc* basis: the programming document has set aside 6% of the yearly budget to respond to urgent and unforeseen needs.

Under the updated programming document of 2003 conflict prevention is explicitly foreseen as a sub-priority only for four countries, namely, Angola, Cambodia, Indonesia and Nepal.[44] In other countries, and namely in Colombia, Eritrea, Fiji, Guatemala and Zimbabwe, the document identifies areas of intervention that are also directly related to conflicts.[45]

---

[44] For Colombia: Contribution to the Negotiated Political Solution of the Armed Conflict. For Eritrea: Strengthen independent civil society involvement in the democratic development of the country, including support for the implementation of programmes for peace and confidence building and programmes fostering a culture of peace. For Fiji: Promotion of dialogue and reconciliation between ethnic groups. For Guatemala: National reconciliation is improved as a result of a more effective fight against impunity. For Zimbabwe: Promotion and protection of human rights and reconciliation at local level limited to a number of pilot districts. See the Commission Staff Working Document 'European Initiative for Democracy and Human Rights Programming Update 2003', available at <http://europa.eu.int/comm/external_relations/human_rights/doc/prog03_en.pdf>, Annex II.

[45] Idem.

3.3.2.2   Programming implemented

Setting specific objectives at the programming stage and achieving those objectives are two different things given that the Commission neither plans nor implements any operations itself, but depends entirely on what NGOs and other actors (e.g., international organisations) propose in terms of projects. Such projects are selected primarily on the basis of a call for proposals.[46] Thus, on the basis of the last call for proposals, whose results were published in the summer 2003, of the four focus countries identified above, only Indonesia will be the target of a project specifically addressing conflict prevention ('Women transforming conflict in Indonesia', project to be funded by the EC to the amount of € 786,282). Of the countries for which conflict related sub-priorities had been identified, specific projects could only be selected for Fiji ('Democratisation, Human Rights and Ethnic Group Reconciliation', project to be funded by the EC to the amount of € 813,648) and Guatemala ('Justice and Reconciliation Programme', project to be funded by the EC to the amount of € 800,000). Projects in other focus countries relating to thematic priorities other than conflict prevention, on the other hand, will have a 'conflict' focus (Nigeria: 'Management and Resolution of Sharia influenced conflicts in Communities in Northern Nigeria', to be funded by the EC to the amount of € 749,732 or Burundi: 'Province Governance and Conflict Management Project' to be funded by the EC to the amount of € 698,777).[47]

Finally, whether those projects, while fitting the specific objectives, will actually achieve those objectives remains an open question. In fact, the debate on how to measure the success of the project is currently in full swing and Commission services are working on developing 'impact indicators' to assess the efficiency of human rights projects.

As has been seen in this section, conflict prevention is an objective of the EC human rights policy. To achieve that objective, the EC human rights policy focuses on funding activities that are directly related to an impending or ongoing conflict such as mediation or reconciliation initiatives. From this perspective, in other words, EC human rights policy has a direct role in the prevention or resolution of an actual conflict. Compared to the perspective that the conflict prevention policy takes on human rights as seen above, this is clearly a different role.

---

[46] Under the new Financial Regulation, the possibilities to fund projects outside a call for proposals are limited to exceptional circumstances, see Article 110 of the Financial Regulation (see above n. 38).

[47] The results of the Call for Proposals are published on the internet at <http://www.europa. eu.int/comm/europeaid/projects/eidhr/projects_2003_themes_en.htm>.

3.3.3   Conflict prevention as a cross-cutting theme?

Beyond its role as an objective of human rights policy, however, conflict prevention (and resolution) is given an additional dimension not in the Regulations themselves, but in the recent programming documents. Thus, it is stated:

> 'Conflict prevention and resolution is a crucial element of many different areas including addressing impunity through strengthening civil society. The international Tribunals and ICC is also important to preventing, resolving and delaying with consequences of conflicts. Truth commissions and other human rights institutions can contribute in a meaningful way to conflict prevention and resolution. Developing an International Penal Code and a pool of crisis response experts, as described in the section on rule of law, also corresponds to this area. The human rights education of relevant officials and public awareness-raising corresponds to this theme, as do the rule of law aspects of ensuring compliance with international instruments'.[48]

This selection of other highlighted human rights activities that contribute to conflict prevention, seems somewhat arbitrary. Why would, say, human rights education of relevant officials be any more contributory to preventing conflicts than, for example, the fight against discriminatory treatment of minorities? Indeed, was the latter not explicitly seen as a key to a conflict prevention policy in the EU policy documents on conflict as was, for example, the assistance and observation of elections which is also not mentioned in the above statement?[49] In fact, it would seem that the above statement is an attempt to demonstrate that conflict prevention – as stipulated in the Communication on Conflict Prevention – has also been mainstreamed into EU Human Rights Policy. Arguably, however, there is no need for that. From the point of view of structural conflict prevention, as understood in this article, all measures focused on promoting the overall respect for human rights, democracy and the rule of law, contribute to the goal of preventing conflict. Thus, the EIDHR, in all its aspects – in other words, the EIDHR, as such – constitutes a contribution to that goal.

4.   CONCLUSION

This chapter has looked at the relationship between conflict prevention and human rights from two opposite angles, namely from the point of view of the EU's conflict prevention policy and from the point of view of the EU's human rights policy. From the conflict prevention point of view, the lack of respect for human rights, democracy and the rule of law is a root cause of conflict. Helping to ensure that respect means enhancing structural stability which will, in the long-

---

[48] See Programming Document, op. cit. n. 44, Annex 2, point 2.
[49] See the Communication on Conflict Prevention, op. cit. n. 5, p. 13.

term, prevent violent conflict from arising. As a matter of conflict prevention, therefore, the overall human rights situation in a given country is to be closely monitored and possible problems have to be identified with the help of a check-list. Such problems need to be addressed through all the policies available and in particular through the EU's policy of cooperation and other external assistance. This kind of integrated approach – or mainstreaming exercise – is also viewed, in turn, as necessary from the point of view of the EU's human rights policy. As regards the question of mainstreaming human rights in all EU policies, therefore, the EU's conflict prevention and the EU's human rights policy use an identical approach. Apart from that overlap, however, the EU's human rights policy perspective on conflict prevention is somewhat different. First and foremost, if, under the above concept of structural stability, protecting human rights is a means to prevent conflict, from a human rights point of view, conflict prevention is an objective to protect human rights by preventing those massive scale human rights violations that conflicts usually bring with them. Furthermore, it is (arguably) incorrectly assumed that only certain aspects of the EU's human rights policy contribute to the goal of conflict prevention. If the concept of structural stability is to be accepted as valid, then the EU human rights policy as such, and indeed its very existence, is a contribution to that goal.

Chapter 12
THE PREVENTION OF CONFLICTS AND COMBATING TRAFFICKING (HUMANS, DRUGS, FIREARMS, WEAPONS ...) AND TERRORISM

by Loïck Benoit[1]

1. INTRODUCTION

In its communication of 11 April 2001 on conflict prevention, the Commission mentioned the necessity to '*address cross-cutting issues which may contribute to tension and conflict. The most important ones concern drugs, small arms, (...) population flows, human trafficking*'.[2] If this document had been written after the 11 September attack, the Commission would probably have added terrorism to this enumeration. Without detracting from the extent of these phenomena and their treatment by international law,[3] it is appropriate to stress the similarities and the differences between those two subjects. Obvious links join trafficking and terrorism, the former financing and sometimes motivating the latter. Legally, the European Union (EU) refers to all these phenomena by one single expression: crime. Article 29 of the Treaty on the EU (TEU), the aim of which is to offer a high level of protection to citizens in an area of freedom, security and justice, refers expressly to the crime, which includes notably terrorism, human trafficking and crimes against children and drug trafficking. However, in spite of these analogies, a concomitant study of trafficking and terrorism is a difficult task. On the one hand, the multifaceted trafficking – drugs, arms, human beings, diamonds... – have mobilized institutions and Community instruments. On the other hand, combating terrorism, considered as an internal State matter for so long, has become the EU's priority since the destruction of the Twin Towers, so much so that it has pushed the other activities into the background.[4] For all that, under the

---

[1] Lecturer at the University of Tours, France; Member of GERCIE (Groupe d'Études et de Recherches sur la Coopération Internationale et Européenne). The author is grateful to Johanna Lecler for her contribution to this article.

[2] COM (2001) 211, 11 April 2001, p. 4.

[3] On this point, cf., D. Ascensio, E. Decaux and A. Pellet, *Droit international pénal* (Paris, Pedone 2000).

[4] A terrorist act has been defined by the Council since November 2001 during the negotiations on the future framework decision 2002/475/JHA of 13 June 2002 relating to the fight against terror-

V. Kronenberger and J. Wouters, eds., The European Union and Conflict Prevention
© 2004, T·M·C·ASSER PRESS, *The Hague, The Netherlands*

prism of conflict prevention, fighting against trafficking and terrorism proves that the EU is preparing to face these two scourges.

The basis of the Union's preventive action appears from Article 2 TEU, according to which it 'shall set itself the following objectives : (...) to maintain and develop the Union as an area of freedom, security and justice, in which (...) the prevention and combating of crime is assured ...'. Naturally, the provisions relating to the Police and Judicial Penal Cooperation (Title VI TEU) confirm and list this desire for prevention. However, because of the pillar structure of the EU and of the transversal feature of its aims, the two components which consist of the Common Foreign Security Policy (CFSP) and the community pillar, are applied. A Resolution of December 1998 and a 'Strategy' of May 2000 have prepared the ground for the prevention of this kind of crime by using a declaring and programming method.[5] Since then, heads of government and statesmen have taken advantage of their summit meetings to assert their backing for the prevention of criminal phenomena.[6]

The interest of this contribution consists of scrutinizing the combating of trafficking and terrorism. These themes frequently catch the attention because they are at the core of the Member States' policy and judicial concerns in a repressive setting. What does the EU do to prevent these phenomena, before they bring violence, terror or death? The Council has estimated that, since December 1998, combating crime requires efficient repression but also a large panel of measures with regard to prevention. Efforts undertaken by the EU in this matter have to be evaluated especially because this fight is not limited solely to the European territory. According to the EU programme for the prevention of violent conflicts confirmed by the European Council, *'conflict prevention calls for a co-operative approach to facilitate peaceful solutions to disputes and implies addressing the root-causes of conflicts'.*[7] With cooperation in the background, the EU has decided to combat trafficking and terrorism at a dual level. On the international scene, the Union can pride itself on having developed the preventive aspect of its external action (section 2.). Within the Community, the fight against criminality

---

ism (*OJEC* [2002] L 164/3). By 'terrorist offences', the EU means intentional acts that can seriously damage a country or an international organisation when committed in three possible cases. The first two hypotheses mention acts which are accepted by the UN conventions as seriously intimidating a population or unduly compelling a Government or international organisation to perform or abstain from performing any act. The third motivation contemplated, and which is totally original, concerns seriously destabilising or destroying the fundamental political, constitutional, economic or social structures of a country or an international organisation.

[5] Cf., European Parliament Resolution of 21 December 1998 relating to the prevention of organized criminality in order to establish a global strategy to fight against this crime, *OJEC* [1998] C 408/1 – Prevention and control of the organized crime: a European Union strategy for the next millennium, *OJEC* [2000] C 124/1.

[6] The European Councils of Tampere (October 1999), Göteborg (June 2001) and Seville (June 2002) provide accurate illustrations.

[7] Cf. <http://ue.eu.int/Newsroom/LoadDoc.asp ?BID=75&DID=66832&from=&LANG=1>.

amounts to the preventive aspect for an area of freedom, security and justice (section 3.).

2. International Cooperation, Trafficking and Terrorism: The Preventive Part of the External Action of the European Union

In its communication on conflict prevention, the Commission considers that *'whatever form international co-operation takes, therefore, it must address the need to spot potential outbreaks of conflict at the earliest possible stage'.*[8] The list of the EU's instruments which have a direct or an indirect role in conflict prevention is long: cooperation for development and external assistance, economic cooperation and trade policy, humanitarian aid, diplomatic instruments such as political dialogue and mediation, economic sanctions without forgetting the new tools of the European policy for security and defence. In the scope of international cooperation, the political impulse has turned out to be decisive. First of all, the preventive part of the EU's external action is based on principles determined by European diplomacy. Thanks to these concrete material and financial measures, the Union is obviously equipping itself in order to achieve its aim. So, the EU has defined guidelines as part of its preventive diplomacy (section 2.1) and makes use of them thanks to implementation measures (section 2.2).

2.1 Preventive diplomacy

Within partnerships, strategies and more generally political dialogue, the EU supports reformation processes undertaken by third countries and discusses with them various international events. Therefore, all these forums constitute places where opinions may be exchanged and discussed places where themes relating to trafficking and terrorism are regularly tackled. These questions of Justice and Home Affairs (JHA) are then integrated into the European international action (section 2.1.1). The EU and its Member States have also undertaken innumerable political initiatives with States which are, or are not, as the case may be, signatories to an international treaty to combat terrorism and trafficking in order to promote this objective, to reinforce the existing system or to perpetuate the universal character of these commitments (section 2.1.2).

2.1.1 *The international feature of Justice and Home Affairs issues*

Pragmatism gives life to the diplomacy of the Fifteen: initially confined to combating trafficking (drugs, human beings), the cooperation has quickly been ex-

---

[8] COM (2001) 211, 11 April 2001, p. 28.

panded to the whole criminal spectrum, including terrorism. From now on, all the aspects of JHA are tackled in the conventional and international relationships of the EU. The latter seeks to contain trafficking and terrorism in its own backyard or which have their origins in more remote regions (transnational mafia, cocaine or heroin routes). Even if some countries like China or African States do not yet appear on the European agenda, the EU reinforces political dialogue and coopera-tion with the Mediterranean countries within the scope of the Barcelona process (section 2.1.1.1), but also with the countries of the old Eastern bloc (section 2.1.1.2), without forgetting Asian and Latin American countries (section 2.1.1.3).

2.1.1.1 Cooperation with Mediterranean countries

Inaugurated in the Catalan capital in November 1995, the Barcelona process regularly reunites the representatives of twelve countries which are either Medi-terranean[9] countries or members of the EU. Basing themselves on this partner-ship, in June 2000 the Fifteen adopted a CFSP Common Strategy concerning the Mediterranean region,[10] which dedicates several points to terrorism and combat-ing crime. The political and security part thereby insists on the reinforcement of *'the co-operation against global challenges to security, such as terrorism, organised crime and drug trafficking'*. Regarding JHA, the EU asserts its inten-tion to set up an efficient cooperation mechanism for combating illegal immigra-tion networks, in particular against human trafficking. The evaluation of this CFSP Common Strategy remains particularly modest insofar as the priority for Europeans is restricted to organising meetings dedicated to these subjects. As a result of the attacks of 11 September 2001, the EU Council has decided to rein-force provisions regarding the JHA in the scope of its conventional relationships. Some of the Mediterranean association agreements now contain an article relat-ing to the prevention of organised crime. The Parties have agreed to cooperate in order to prevent organised crime, especially concerning human trafficking, ex-ploitation for sexual purposes, trafficking illegal products and weapons traffick-ing. Combating drugs and drug addiction also have a predominant place in these agreements since the aim of the cooperation is to improve the efficiency of poli-cies and implementation measures to prevent the culture, the production, the of-fer, the consumption of and trafficking in drugs.

The greatest innovation consists of being able to insert an anti-terrorist clause in these agreements. This clause encourages the exchange of experiences, re-search and a common analysis for preventing terrorism. It also enables a system-atic reassessment of the relationships between the EU and the third countries, in

---

[9] Algeria, Cyprus, Egypt, Israel, Jordan, Lebanon, Malta, Morocco, Palestinian Authority, Syria, Tunisia and Turkey.

[10] Common Strategy 2000/458/CFSP of 19 June 2000 on the Mediterranean region, *OJEC* [2000] L 183/5.

the light of the support that could be provided to terrorism by these countries. Such a clause was tested during the signature of the agreement with Algeria in December 2001 and it appears in the Egyptian and Lebanese agreements as well. However, even if this clause is legally binding, it is not an essential element, unlike the 'human rights' clauses contained in the agreements on cooperation, development, association or partnership. Hence, the non-respect of commitments relating to terrorism cannot lead to the suspension of the agreement. Furthermore, the content of this anti-terrorist clause turned out to be fairly watered down. Its legal form only gives rise to some satisfaction because it should promote the emergence of the legal personality of the EU. Instead of inserting the clause in the agreement itself or drafting a joint declaration, the Parties can enter into an agreement by exchanging letters concerning cooperation in combating terrorism. This option, which was applied in the case of Lebanon, is based on Article 24 TEU and illustrates the ability of the EU to assert itself at the international level. Even if the EU does not have an express international legal status, the agreement is nevertheless approved in its name and is binding. By its will to organise an elaborate dialogue and increased cooperation with countries and regions from which terrorism and trafficking emanate, the EU also pays particular attention to the countries of the old Eastern bloc.

2.1.1.2 Cooperation with Eastern European countries

Apart from the pursuit of political dialogue relating to terrorism within the scope of the CFSP, the collaboration with the Kiev authorities concerns the exchange of information between experts.[11] In accordance with the Action Plan of the Union in the scope of JHA in the Ukraine (10 December 2001), the Fifteen have decided to prevent and to combat cross-border organised crime, in particular human and drug trafficking. At the end of the first joint ministerial meeting concerning JHA on 11 November 2002, the partners agreed to push the prevention of children's sexual exploitation and paedo-pornography to the forefront.

In the same vein, since the summit between Russia and the European Union on 3 October 2001, Presidents of the European Council, the Commission and the Russian Federation have firmly expressed their will to intensify their relationships in combating terrorism and international crime. Many initiatives are taken to prevent these phenomena, especially through information exchange and training. An agreement between Europol and the Russian Federation should reinforce this cooperation. On the fringe of the part specifically dedicated to combating terrorism, the EU presidency wishes to intensify cooperation in the non-proliferation area. Therefore, it proposes to set up an information exchange scheme on the

---

[11] This exchange concerns the activities of individuals or groups considered to be in league with terrorist networks, the trade in weapons, explosives, double use materials and also new forms of terrorism (chemical, biological and nuclear threats).

various kinds of terrorism which imply the use of weapons of mass destruction.

Then, the CFSP common strategies concerning these countries or the Cooperation and Partnership Agreement (CPA) insist on the common interest to reinforce cooperation, especially its preventive aspect for combating drugs. According to the geostrategic magnitude of Russia and the Ukraine, the EU reinforces its cooperation with these two states as a priority and to the detriment of the other countries of the Community of Independent States. This favourable treatment is the same for European countries which are geographically near the EU's territory and are potential EU candidates, such as Croatia or Albania. The stability and association agreement negotiated with Croatia comprises an article entitled 'Preventing and combating crime and other illegal activities'. The preventive cooperation which consists of consultations and coordination between the parties deals with human, drug and weapons trafficking or terrorism. Negotiations on a similar agreement with Albania mention concerns inherent in crime since the trafficking in humans, drugs, weapons and other goods is prevalent in Albania. Within the scope of prevention, European institutions consider that Albania should create a cooperation framework in order to prevent and to combat delinquency and illegal activities. In targeting its diplomacy towards the most sensitive regions, the EU is quite selective in conflict prevention. This method is strictly applied as regards Latin American and Asian countries where drug trafficking and terrorism are flourishing.

2.1.1.3   Cooperation with Asian and Latin American countries

Soon after the attacks perpetrated in October 2002 in Bali (Indonesia), the EU re-iterated its will to reinforce its role within the international community in order to prevent and restrain regional conflicts. According to the conclusions of the Council on General Affairs, the intensification of the political dialogue with Indonesia is becoming a priority in order to include the combating of terrorism.[12] However, before the events that occurred in Bali, the EU had developed a strategic framework to reinforce relations within the partnership between Europe and Asia. By conflict prevention, the EU wants to intensify its dialogue and its cooperation with Asia on JHA issues. In concrete terms, common efforts are expected in order to combat international crime (drug, human, weapons trafficking, exploitation of migrants).[13] China, which has also been approached in the light of the EU's Strategy, is particularly requested to continue and extend political dialogue on combating illegal immigration and human trafficking. In addition, the Fifteen also propose to introduce cooperation in order to combat organised crime.[14]

---

[12] 2458th Council session, 13330/02, 6 February 2003.

[13] COM (2001) 469, 4 September 2001, *Europe and Asia: A strategic framework for enhanced partnerships*, p. 18.

[14] COM (2001) 265, 15 May 2001, *EU strategy towards China*, pp. 10-11.

Preventing drug trafficking also mobilizes the European diplomacy in Latin America. Thanks to the impulse of the European Council of Madrid (December 1995), the EU, Latin America and the Caribbean have set up a coordination and cooperation mechanism to prevent and combat drugs. This mechanism constitutes a forum for reflection and consultation concerning worldwide drugs issues. Within the scope of this political dialogue, various agreements have been concluded. Some of them concern the precursors and other chemical substances frequently used for illegal manufacture of drugs or psychotropic substances.[15] Since no drug can exist without precursors, the Community and the other countries control these chemical products, thereby preventing their diversion. The prevention of drug trafficking is also possible thanks to association agreements. Chile, for example, has agreed to cooperate in combating drugs in accordance with a clause which is now considered to be classic. According to Article 47 of this agreement, the Parties coordinate and reinforce *'their efforts aimed at preventing and reducing the production, trade and the consumption of illegal drugs, and also laundering benefits resulting from drugs trafficking'*. The practical steps are various: training programmes, survey and research, information exchange, measures to prevent the diversion of precursors, etc. In sum, JHA issues occupy an increasingly important place in the preventive diplomacy of the EU. This projection of European internal security on the international scene is coupled with numerous diplomatic actions.

2.1.2   *Actions in international forums*

Within the United Nations, negotiations have led to the signature of a convention against transnational organised crime and of three protocols relating to trafficking.[16] In connection with, or independent from, the United Nations' work, the EU has undertaken diplomatic preventive actions against terrorism and trafficking in weapons and diamonds.

As far as terrorism is concerned, the main diplomatic pressure being exerted relates to countries around the Mediterranean Sea. In the CFSP Common Strategy of June 2000 regarding the Mediterranean region, the EU asserts that it *'will continue to encourage Mediterranean partners to adhere to the UN's international conventions on terrorism'*.[17] During the Euro-Mediterranean conference in Brus-

---

[15] Nine states including six Latin American countries are bound by such agreements: Bolivia, Chile, Colombia, Ecuador, the United States, Mexico, Peru, Venezuela. Turkey has also been bound by this kind of agreement with the European Community since March 2003.

[16] Cf., the three protocols concerning the fight against trafficking in humans, immigrants and weapons. For a comment on the UN Convention and its Protocols, see C. Rijken and V. Kronenberger, 'The United Nations Convention Against Transnational Organised Crime and the European Union', in V. Kronenberger (ed.), *The European Union and the International Legal Order: Discord or Harmony?* (The Hague, TMC Asser Press 2001), pp. 481-517.

[17] Common Strategy 2000/458/CFSP, op. cit. n. 10, p. 9.

sels on 5 and 6 November 2001, the ministers promised to accelerate the signature, the ratification and the application by their States of all the United Nations conventions, especially the one from December 1999 on the suppression of the financing of terrorism. Furthermore, in the half-yearly updating of the activity table for scrutinizing the progress made in the creation of an Area of Freedom, Security and Justice, the Commission reiterates the continuous support of the EU for the second stage of negotiations to establish a convention against international terrorism.[18] Diplomatic *démarches* turned out to be even more numerous in the fight against trafficking of weapons.

Chronologically, the Programme of 26 June 1997 for preventing and combating conventional weapons trafficking is the first major initiative of the EU in this area. Among the three identified aspects, the second encourages the EU to assist certain third countries in preventing and combating weapons trafficking. In line with this programme, a CFSP Common Action has, since December 1998, organised the EU's contribution to the fight against the destabilising accumulation and diffusion of small arms and small calibre firearms.[19] By this text, the Union has determined three objectives: combating the destabilising accumulation and diffusion of small arms; helping to reduce existing stocks of arms and ammunition; helping to solve problems caused by the accumulation of these stocks. Prevention then lies at the heart of the EU's diplomatic initiatives because in pursuing these objectives it *'shall aim at building consensus in the relevant international forums, and in a regional context as appropriate, (...) to prevent the further destabilising accumulation of small arms'*. In concrete terms, the EU has participated in the preparation of a United Nations conference on all aspects of the illegal small arms trade.[20]

In order to make European initiatives more consistent, the Council has adopted a JHA Common Position on 31 January 2000 relating to negotiations in progress which required from the Member States that they should reach a common definition of firearms and to exclude such arms from the (at the time future) protocol to the UN Convention on transnational organised crime.[21] Following all these actions, the Community and the Member States have signed this protocol.[22] This preventive diplomacy, which sometimes amounts to good offices, also enables the EU to state with satisfaction: *'working towards the elimination of this*

---

[18] COM (2002) 738, 16 December 2002, p. 86.

[19] Common Action 1999/34/CFSP, *OJEC* [1999] L 9/1. Cf., its abrogation and its replacement by common action 2002/589/CFSP of 12 July 2002, *OJEC* [2002] L 191/1.

[20] It has made numerous proposals such as control and criteria applicable to exports, markings and drawings, stock control, disarmament and veterans' rehabilitation.

[21] Common Position 2000/130/JHA of 31 January 2000, *OJEC* [2000] L 37/1.

[22] On the respective competences of the Community and the Member States to sign this protocol, see C. Rijken and V. Kronenberger, op. cit. n. 16, pp. 512-516.

source of destabilisation and conflict will be a great contribution to preventing future conflicts'.[23]

The final open diplomatic action on the part of the EU concerns trafficking in diamonds. In one CFSP common position of 29 October 2001 on combating the trafficking in diamonds, the Council considered that *'conflict diamonds fuel some of the bloodiest conflicts in Africa. There is a clear need for measures to be taken to help prevent and resolve conflicts'.*[24] In accordance with Article 1 of this common position, the EU and its Member States support efforts by the international community to break the existing link between diamonds and conflicts, including the financing of armed conflicts. According to the framework for small arms, the EU and its Member States will use all their diplomacy to combat this trafficking. So they raise the diamonds issue within their bilateral and multilateral relationships; they consult each other, especially within the United Nations and the forums concerned, on the most efficient means in attaining this objective; finally, they invite the countries mainly concerned to join the multilateral agreement elaborated in the so-called Kimberley process.[25] Within the EU, the first realisation of these diplomatic initiatives consists of a Community Regulation of 20 December 2002 in order to set up a certification system for the origin of diamonds.[26] Although the EU has not been able to eliminate conflicts stemming from natural resources, the EU combats trafficking of such resources with its diplomatic armaments. However, in this area just like in the case of terrorism or other forms of trafficking, the EU's statements are frequently turned into action since it complements its diplomacy by numerous implementation measures.

2.2 Implementation measures

Among all the instruments which are at the EU's disposal for implementing its diplomacy, some are particularly worth scrutinizing. Conflict prevention is carried out thanks to various implementation measures which explore all the cooperation features. It is thereby not surprising that in the preventive aspect of external action, emphasis is sometimes placed on commercial and economic instruments (section 2.2.1), sometimes on the confiscation of products resulting from trafficking and the financing of terrorism (section 2.2.2) or technical and financial aid programmes (section 2.2.3).

---

[23] Second annual report on the application of the European Union common action of 12 July 2002, *OJEC* [2002] C 330/18.

[24] Common Position 2001/758/CFSP of 29 October 2001, *OJEC* [2001] L 286/2.

[25] On 11 and 12 May 2000, the Kimberley (South Africa) process commenced in order to scrutinize and to set up measures which might eliminate conflict diamonds from the market, mainly by introducing a certification system for the origin of diamonds. On this process, see the chapters of A. Weiss and V. Kronenberger in this volume.

[26] Regulation (EC) No. 2368/2002, *OJEC* [2002] L 358/28.

2.2.1   *Commercial and economic instruments*

As the Commission notes, '*the EU seeks to project stability in supporting re-gional integration and in building trade links. (...) Development policy and other co-operation programmes provide the most powerful instruments at the Community's disposal for treating the root causes of conflict*'.[27] Commercial Community relationships are, however, instrumented in order to prevent con-flicts: sometimes they support the economic expansion of third countries (section 2.2.1.1) and sometimes they penalize some of the States which indulge in traf-ficking or in terrorist actions (section 2.2.1.2).

2.2.1.1   Supportive commercial actions

As a commercial incitation, the GPS (Generalized Preferences System) is a par-ticularly efficient tool. It affords pricing preferences at variable rates. The Com-munity then offers a privileged access to the European market for most products coming from developing countries. As far as drugs are concerned, additional preferences are granted to a dozen Latin American countries which are commit-ted to combating drug production and trafficking.[28] On the Commission's initia-tive, the last regulation implementing a GPS for the years 2002-2004 has included Pakistan in the list of beneficiaries of this particular system.[29] The Drugs GPS constitutes an important advantage in the effort to suppress illegal cultures and to create jobs without any connection to drugs production and traf-ficking. More generally, it is likely to stabilize the social and economic structures of beneficiary countries and to consolidate State rights. However, commercial aid is granted by the Community in return for the necessary cooperation because the Commission controls and evaluates the effects of the special drugs policy. Natu-rally, some States can have their preferences suspended in order to prevent the development of conflict and they can even be subject to commercial sanctions.

2.2.1.2   Sanctions

The EU attempts to prevent trafficking and terrorism by threatening, in a round-about manner, the guilty States with commercial retaliatory measures. The EU has established a procedure for revising and modifying the relationships between third countries in connection with combating terrorism, including contractual re-lationships. In parallel, in its conclusions of 13 June 2002 on the applicable mea-

---

[27] COM (2001) 211, op. cit. n. 2, p. 4.

[28] They are the following States: Bolivia, Columbia, Costa Rica, Ecuador, Guatemala, Honduras, Nicaragua, Peru, Panama, El Salvador, Venezuela. They benefit from an exemption of rights in all industrial products that come under the GPS general system as well as many agricultural products.

[29] Regulation (EC) No. 2501/2001 of 10 December 2001, *OJEC* [2001] L 346/1.

sures for preventing and combating illegal immigration and trafficking in immigrants and the maritime slave trade,[30] the Council insists on various preventive measures. Countries where boarding, leaving and transit on boarded vessels occur have to adopt measures which are necessary for preventing and combating trafficking and the slave trade. If such a system has not been adopted by these countries and they are not justified in doing so, the EU has retained the possibility to adopt political retaliatory measures. It sometimes crosses the Rubicon and imposes commercial penalties on some countries. Based upon self-limitation rules in the code of conduct relating to the export of armaments,[31] the EU regularly determines CFSP common positions prohibiting the export of weapons to regions suspected of participating in terrorist actions. Since the beginning of the conflict in Kosovo, the EU has firmly applied its code of conduct and has developed a regulation prohibiting the provision of material likely to be used for terrorist purposes to the Federal Yugoslav Republic. The Yugoslavian precedent, which unfortunately did not prevent the army and Serbian militias from committing atrocities, now allows the EU to react quickly in cases of serious violations of human rights and international humanitarian law. Hence, independently of any United Nations Resolution, the EU has imposed sanctions against Indonesia (September 1999) and Burma (April 2000) in an attempt to bring an end to the repression of civil and political rights. During the long Afghan crisis, the EU decided, in November 1999, on an embargo on flights to and from the Community by Taliban aircraft. A CSFP Common Position of February 2001 having determined additional restrictive measures,[32] the Community successively enacted nine Regulations which, in addition to the prohibition on flights and the freezing of funds, also prohibited some the export of certain goods, the provision of technical advice or training and ordered the closure of Taliban offices as well as those of Ariana Afghan Airlines.[33]

Since July 2000, the import of rough diamonds from Sierra Leone has been forbidden in the Community, in accordance with the United Nations Resolution 1306 (2000). However, this embargo has pointed out the limitations of economic sanctions in relation to conflict prevention, since they are imposed after the start of the conflict and are usually only partly effective. An additional implementation measure is aimed at suppressing terrorist financing sources and trafficking profits.

---

[30] Conclusions of 13 June 2002, JHA 142, p. 2.

[31] Code of conduct, 2097th session of the 'General Affairs' Council, Brussels, 25 May 1998.

[32] Common Position 2001/157/CFSP of 26 February 2001, *OJEC* [2001] L 57/1.

[33] Cf., Regulation (EC) No. 467/2001 of 6 March 2001, *OJEC* [2001] L 67/1. Cf., also Regulation (EC) No. 205/2002 of 18 January 2002, *OJEC* [2002] L 17/52.

2.2.2   *Suppressing the profits from terrorism and trafficking*

The prevention of criminal activity can best be achieved by suppressing and seizing the financial profits of terrorists and traffickers. After the Fifteen froze the funds and other financial resources which the Taliban held abroad in November 1999,[34] the destruction of the Twin Towers gave rise to a CFSP common position in order to organise the application of specific measures to combat terrorism.[35] This intergovernmental text reveals the EU's determination to tackle terrorism's financing sources. The method consists of establishing a common list of individuals, groups and entities involved in terrorist actions for which funds and assets have to be frozen.

Since cross-border organised crime is usually lucrative, the Council wants to prevent this phenomenon by focusing its efforts on the detection, the seizure and the confiscation of criminal means. The draft JHA Framework Decision on this subject[36] aims to guarantee that all Member States have efficient regulations in place in order to be able to confiscate the products of crime.[37] To simplify the decision to freeze assets or evidence, another proposal for a framework decision is being investigated concerning the mutual recognition of decisions relating to the confiscation of the products of crime and the distribution of assets. These texts, once they will be transposed in national legal systems, will constitute important tools for the prevention of all trafficking (drugs, human beings, including immigrants, etc.) and terrorist attacks. Money laundering which is at the core of organised crime is also dealt with. Directive 91/308/EEC on the prevention of the use of the financial system for the purpose of money laundering, only applies to money laundering in connection with drug trafficking. Thanks to Directive 2001/97/EC of 4 December 2001, which amends Directive 91/308/EEC, the lacuna is now filled. The text indeed modifies the definition of criminal activity, so that all kinds of organised crime are covered by the prohibition on money laundering.[38] In its fight against trafficking and terrorism, the EU then alternates between incentive and coercive measures. However, it could be said that generosity characterizes the EU's international cooperation because its main implementation measures focus on technical and financial aids.

---

[34] Common Position 1999/727/CFSP of 15 November 1999, *OJEC* [1999] L 294/1.

[35] Common Position 2001/931/CFSP of 27 December 2001, *OJEC* [2001] L 344/93.

[36] Cf., 'Projet de décision relative à la confiscation des produits, des instruments et des biens en rapport avec le crime', 23 January 2003, 5299/03.

[37] Especially concerning the burden of proof regarding the origin of assets held by an individual considered to be guilty of an offence connected with organised crime.

[38] Directive 2001/97/EC of 4 December 2001, *OJEC* [2001] L 344/78.

2.2.3   Technical and financial aids

These aids contribute to the application of the EU's political objectives and provide an operational feature for preventive diplomacy. The assistance is first
organised in a geographical manner. Mediterranean countries benefit from financial and technical implementation measures in accordance with the MEDA
programme which is the main financial instrument of the partnership. The support for a lasting social and economic development notably includes cooperation
and technical assistance in order to combat organised crime and human trafficking. A similar legal framework exists for Asian and Latin American countries in
accordance with Regulation (EEC) No. 443/92 of 25 February 1992. In a recent
proposal, the Commission intends to replace this old standard and to determine
rules for a programme on Community cooperation with these regions.[39] The aim
of these aids is notably to support the fight against organised crime, money laundering, terrorism, drugs, illegal immigration and human trafficking and also to
enact measures for conflict prevention. The assistance is then organised along the
lines of various themes.

Concerning the prevention of terrorism, the implementing measures chiefly remain at the negotiation stage. Analyses of the terrorist threat have been established concerning some countries and regions which are particularly interesting in
this respect. They should provide a useful basis for future operational measures.
The Commission has already identified the areas in which technical assistance
could generally be provided. For prevention, the following themes are pertinent:
ratification of international conventions, combating the financing of terrorism,
and border controls. The Commission considers that Indonesia, Pakistan and the
Philippines should have priority as regards pilot projects.[40] The CFSP common
actions relating to combating the accumulation and the spread of small arms is
explicitly considering financial and technical aid for some projects, consisting of
collecting weapons, reforming the security area and demobilization. Within this
scope, implementing decisions follow each other concerning Albania,
Mozambique, Cambodia, South Ossetia, Latin America and the Caribbean. These
projects, which mainly focus on the collection and the destruction of arms, cost
between EUR 90,000 and 500,000 each.[41] The prevention of drug trafficking
benefits for its part from particularly favourable treatment, especially thanks to
important financial efforts. The budget for preliminary actions in a programme to
combat drug trafficking (B5 831) allocated one million of euros for this purpose

---

[39] COM (2002) 340, 2 July 2002.

[40] Cf., 'Projet de rapport sur les activités de l'Union en matière de lutte contre le terrorisme', 4
December 2002, 15211/02, p. 11.

[41] For an exhaustive presentation of these various actions, cf. respectively the annual reports on
the implementation of the EU common action of the EU published in *OJEC* [2001] C 216/5 and
OJEC [2002] C 330/6.

in 2001. This has financed projects whose aim was, for example, the reinforcement of control instruments for chemical precursors, the prevention of money
laundering, setting up an Union action plan against organised crime and the promotion of substitute development methods. As for cocaine (Latin America) and
heroin (Central Asia, the Caucasus), the Community's technical and financial assistance is very extensive. However, combating trafficking and terrorism would
be insufficient if it would be confined to international cooperation and would certainly not eliminate criminal phenomena threatening the Old World. The EU is
therefore actively developing the prevention of trafficking and terrorism on its
own territory.

3.   COOPERATION WITHIN THE COMMUNITY, TRAFFICKING AND
     TERRORISM: THE PREVENTIVE ASPECT OF AN AREA OF FREEDOM,
     SECURITY AND JUSTICE

The Vienna Action Plan of 3 December 1998 already invoked preventive crime
measures in the five years after the Amsterdam Treaty came into effect.[42] Subsequently, the European Council in Tampere (October 1999) concluded that it was
necessary to intensify cooperation for the purpose of crime prevention. All these
measures have received a favourable response from the JHA ministers. In order
better to tackle trafficking and terrorism, the Council has clearly defined the aim
of prevention: it 'covers all measures that are intended to reduce or otherwise
contribute to reducing crime and citizen's feeling of insecurity, both quantitatively and qualitatively, either through directly deterring criminal activities or
through policies and interventions designed to reduce the potential for crime and
the causes of crime'.[43] The development of an area of freedom, security and justice (AFSJ) constitutes a preference for preventive actions against trafficking and
terrorism. The success of this preventive aspect is evidenced by the
harmonisation of legislation and national practice in Europe. The rapprochement
between the rules and their standardization remains an absolute necessity for
combating criminal activities. At the EU level, none of the Member States should
be considered by criminals as a relative haven for their illegal activities. While
the EU was setting up an area of freedom, security and justice, the Fifteen wished
to prepare future Member States for combating terrorism and trafficking by re-
newing the aims of JHA (section 3.1). The Member States wish to demonstrate
unambiguously their willingness to introduce strict sanctions that are likely to de-

---

[42] 2001/427/JHA: Council Decision of 28 May 2001 setting up a European crime prevention network.
[43] Cf., Decision 2001/427/JHA setting up a European crime prevention network, *OJEC* [2001] L
153/2.

ter criminals and, consequently, to prevent trafficking and terrorist activities (section 3.2).

3.1 The acceptance of Justice and Home Affairs aims and *acquis* by candidate States

The future members of the EU pose the risk of introducing internal security problems. It has to be admitted that some Central and Eastern States provide departure, transit or destination points for several forms of trafficking and a growth in crime is thereby a threat. This is the reason why the acceptance of JHA aims and *acquis* by candidate States lies at the core of the expansion negotiations.

Combating trafficking has given rise to the first harmonisation of national practices through previous JHA programmes (STOP, Hippocrate, Oisin, Falcone or Odysseus), to which all the candidate States were naturally associated. Once the JHA *acquis* has been identified, the Council proposes all relevant instruments to candidates which must, in concrete terms, sign and/or ratify about sixty agreements and protocols, subscribe to about thirty actions and common positions, one hundred unnamed acts and all the regulations adopted within the third pillar since the Amsterdam Treaty entered into force. Regarding conflict prevention, the Commission oversees the pursuit of combating trafficking in human beings and drugs. The Commission checks whether a national regulation partially or totally falls into line with this aim. If not, the Commission will persuade the State to take action in this respect. However, none of the 2002 reports on the progress made by each candidate State mentioned any legislative insufficiency in trafficking matters. While the ten new Member States seem to be ready to prevent serious aspects of crime, the terrorist attacks on the US have given rise to a renewal of cooperation in combating terrorism.

Since combating terrorism is one of the EU's priorities, it encourages candidate countries to adopt the necessary legislative measures. A firm message is consequently delivered to candidates who must strictly follow the new evolution of the *acquis*. However, the EU wishes to assist the efforts made by the candidate States. They are therefore supported so that they can comply with the EU's measures and other international instruments in combating the financing of terrorism and money laundering. There is no doubt that the cooperation between the EU and the candidate countries is reaching a *crescendo*. Following the extraordinary European Council of Brussels (September 2001), the President of the Council welcomed the ambassadors of the thirteen candidate countries in order to request that they support the Summit conclusions. The ambassadors all provided a favourable reply and decided to fall into line with the EU position. Subsequently, it has been the EU's inclination to express itself in the name of twenty-eight countries. This implies real discipline because the policy lead by the States – members of the EU or not – must comply with the EU's decisions. The rallying of these countries to combat terrorism reinforces the significance of European actions and provides an additional echo for Europe in international relationships. While awaiting an expanded Europe, the Fifteen are also combating trafficking and terrorism by imposing sanctions which are likely to deter criminals.

3.2 Deterrent sanctions

Since December 1998, the Action Plan on how best to implement the provisions of the Amsterdam Treaty on an area of freedom, security and justice (AFSJ) has evoked the resumption of harmonious relations as far as the Member States' criminal laws are concerned.[44] Efforts intended to reach an agreement on definitions, accusations and common sanctions should concern human trafficking and trafficking in children for sexual purposes, drug trafficking, crime using advanced technologies and terrorist actions. These priorities which have certainly not remained a dead letter have been complemented with other initiatives according to new AFSJ new requirements.

As far as the prevention of trafficking is concerned, in January 2001, the Commission proposed to adopt two Framework Decisions for combating human trafficking and trafficking in children for sexual purposes.[45] The first proposal was quickly adopted because intergovernmental texts already existed on this matter. A framework decision of 19 July 2002[46] currently defines the slave trade and imposes sanctions which are severe enough to stop these practices. Each Member State is required to take the necessary measures to render the following acts punishable: recruitment, transport, transfer, subsequent reception of a person, including entry and the transfer of control exercised over that person, and also participation, complicity or an attempt to do so. In line with the judgment delivered by the Court of Justice in the case of 21 September 1989 *Commission* v. *Greece*,[47] these infractions must be subject to effective sanctions, which are proportioned and dissuasive; the maximum punishment cannot be less than eight years imprisonment.

The second proposal relating to combating the trafficking in children for sexual purposes and paedo-pornography has been subject to a political agreement within the Council in October 2002. The Ministers decided that each Member State will take the necessary measures to punish certain forms of intentional behaviour[48] by penalties which are effective, proportionate and dissuasive and amount to custodial sentences from one to eight years. These two texts should contribute to preventing the trafficking in individuals because they destroy the

---

[44] Action Plan of 3 December 1998, *OJEC* [1999] C 19/13.

[45] COM (2000) 854, 22 January 2001.

[46] Framework Decision 2002/629/JHA of 19 July 2002, *OJEC* [2002] L 203/1.

[47] Case 68/88 *Commission* v. *Greece* [1989] ECR p. 2965 s.

[48] The following forms of behaviour are punished: forcing a child to prostitute itself; to recruit a child for prostitution purposes or for its participation in pornographic shows; to engage in sexual activities with a child.

feeling of impunity that has prompted some criminals to embark upon this illegal activity. The prevention of drug trafficking is in keeping with the same penal logic. In this matter, the Commission has again used its right of initiative in proposing a Framework Decision concerning the establishment of minimum provisions relating to the constitutive elements of criminal acts and penalties in the field of illicit drug trafficking.[49] According to the Commission, this trafficking should be considered as a criminal offence and should be subject to penalties which are effective, proportionate and dissuasive. So far, the adoption of this text is not on the agenda because discussions have become bagged down as regards the level of penalties. The prevention of terrorist attacks is, however, the subject of much greater success.

The harmonisation of penalties for combating terrorism constitutes a strong signal that potential terrorists and silent partners who want to attack European territory cannot ignore. The Framework Decision of 13 June 2002[50] should erase the serious legislative disparities between the Member States. This intergovernmental act has set itself a double objective: to define the goal of and terrorist offences on the one hand, to set up sanction thresholds for these various kinds of offences on the other. Three types of penalties are contained in the Framework Decision: the first type is accompanied by a minimum of an eight years imprisonment and concerns offences relating to the participation in the activities of a terrorist group. The second type, liable to a minimum of fifteen years imprisonment, concerns the direction of a terrorist group. The third, and final one, covers all those offences for which each Member State will have to implement, in its criminal code, harsher sentences than when such offences have been committed without any terrorist motive. If the harmonisation seems to be incomplete, one can notice that the EU wishes to eradicate sanctuary States from its territory. The Fifteen have therefore decided to '*tolerate that only very serious behaviours defined in common should be liable to sentences varying sometimes in very important proportions*'.[51] Furthermore, the Council has once again embarked upon a 'high' degree of harmonisation of penal codes. The traditional requirement for penal sanctions that are effective, proportionate and dissuasive is maintained. But far from contenting itself with sentences that could justify an extradition or with sentences ranging from one to eight years as in previous framework decisions, the June Framework Decision has now reached a degree of sanction harmonisation never equalled in the EU by requiring a fifteen-year prison sentence for the direction of a terrorist group. In addition, the Commission wishes to prevent the cyber-

---

[49] COM (2001) 259 final, 23 May 2001.

[50] Framework Decision 2002/475/JHA of 13 June 2002 on combating terrorism, *OJEC* [2002] L 164/3.

[51] E. Barbe, 'Une triple étape pour le troisième pilier de l'Union Européenne. Mandat d'arrêt européen, terrorisme et Eurojust', 454 *Revue du Marché Commun et de l'Union européenne* (2002), p. 9.

terrorist threat. Therefore, a final proposal for a Framework Decision relating to attacks aimed at information systems[52] will consider harmonising the Member States' criminal law relating to computer crime. In February 2003, the Council has reached a common agreement on the adoption of this new act which also provides for efficient, proportionate and dissuasive sanctions.

4. CONCLUSION

Combating trafficking and terrorism, from the angle of conflict prevention, completes the EU's measures for combating criminal activities. The approach being turns out to be global and multidisciplinary since all the components of the EU – the Community pillar system, CFSP and PJCC – act jointly at the European and international level. However, in looking at the EU's Official Journal, a careful reader cannot fail to have noticed the imbalance between the prevention of trafficking and terrorism on the one hand, and the combating these crimes on the other hand. The latter is undeniably in the scope of competence of the Member States. Naturally, the die hard development of the prevention is not a panacea. However, the search for a median way has to be explored because an increase of efficient preventive measures would enable the reduction of repressive measures. In an area of freedom, security and justice which has become obsessed with security since the terrorist attacks on the US, citizens would certainly not be disadvantaged by a reinforcement of the whole range of preventive measures as long as fundamental human rights are taken into account.

---

[52] COM (2002) 173, 19 April 2002.

Chapter 13
PULLING UP CONFLICTS BY THE ROOTS: TOWARDS A
CONFLICT PREVENTION ASSESSMENT OF EU POLICIES

by Joost Lagendijk and Ute Seela[1]

1. INTRODUCTION

'Conflict prevention is one of the core tasks of European foreign policy',[2] declared the European leaders in 2001 in Göteborg. Likewise, conflict prevention is
explicitly mentioned in the proposed EU constitution prepared by the Convention
on the Future of Europe as part of the Common Foreign and Security Policy. This
pulling of conflict prevention towards the centre is a major step forward. While
still some years ago, organisations and political parties like ours were being
laughed at when they reiterated, once again, the importance of conflict prevention, it is now 'bon ton' to repeat the mantra that violent conflicts can better be
prevented than be allowed to escalate. Especially after September 11, Europe has
tried to find its own answer to the feeling of threat and instability caused by terrorism and weapons of mass destruction. The paper outlining the framework of
Europe's security strategy that Javier Solana proposed to the European Council in
June 2003 very clearly stresses this concept of Europe as a 'civil superpower'
preferring the use of non-violent means to solve conflicts.[3] Contrary to the 'sable
rattling' in Washington, Brussels underlines the need to address the causes of
radical discontent that leads to violence both by state and non-state actors. The
European Commission itself calls it the 'dark side of globalisation': the divide
between the rich and the poor, environmental degradation, organised crime and
trafficking in human beings that we should be aware of to really have an opportunity to tackle current and future threats.[4]

---

[1] Joost Lagendijk is a Member of the European Parliament for the Dutch Green Left, Chairman
of the Turkey delegation of the European Parliament and a speaker on security issues and the
Balkans for the Green/EFA Group in the European Parliament. Ute Seela is Policy Adviser on Foreign Affairs and Enlargement for the Dutch Green Left Party. This article has been written with the
cooperation of Ivo Schutte.

[2] See, e.g., the Conclusions of the European Council in Göteborg, June 2001.

[3] European Council Secretariat: 'A safer Europe in a better world' Draft June 2003.

[4] See the European Commission's Report: 'One Year On: the Commission's Conflict Prevention
Policy', March 2002.

V. Kronenberger and J. Wouters, eds., The European Union and Conflict Prevention
© *2004, T·M·C·ASSER PRESS, The Hague, The Netherlands*

Yet, while some diligent civil servants have ploughed through more than 120 'Country Strategy Papers' to check whether there was reason to expect some crisis to break out, so far there is no general vision on where and when the EU might itself have a harmful impact on weaker countries. That vision should ideally lead to a major overhaul of all of Europe's policies (think of economic policy, trade or agriculture) to make sure that we are not ourselves directly or indirectly contributing to (causes of) conflict. The European Parliament called this 'the need for a "conflict prevention assessment"'.[5]

2.   WHAT IS MEANT BY CONFLICT PREVENTION ASSESSMENT?

Western democracies have been part of violent conflicts in Africa, Asia, the Middle-East and Latin America throughout the post-Second World War era. Certainly, most interference has come from the two super powers, the United States and the Soviet Union. Most of the time they deemed intervention to be necessary for the sake of bipolar stability. Remember the Vietnam War when the US sent forces to prevent communist groups from setting up a communist state that would naturally become another Russian ally. Or take the Afghan civil war in the 1980s where Soviet troops invaded to prevent the Marxist regime from collapsing (and where the American secret service in turn trained and funded Osama bin Laden to fight against the Russian army). Yet also European powers like France, Britain or Belgium have played their role in local conflicts, especially in their former African colonies. Often they supported authoritarian regimes that would be most inclined to safeguard their economic and political interests. Even today, the access to crucial natural resources like oil, gas, minerals or timber is a considerable factor in countries' overall policy towards other parts of the world. It is, therefore, not a wild guess that Europe might not only 'do good'.

A conflict prevention assessment would be a method of raising the level of awareness as to the cause-effect relationship of European Union policies and the economic, social and ecological structure of third countries. Such an understanding would first be needed on the level of broad policy fields. Therefore, screening is necessary, in order to answer questions like the following: does the lack of legally binding restrictions on the weapons trade contribute to the availability of arms to fighting factions in conflict-ridden areas? Does the fight against terrorism (like blacklisting so-called terrorist organisations) help governments to crackdown on unwanted liberation movements in their own country? Does trading with a regime that has a negative human rights record provide that government with additional means to pursue suppressive policies? However, conflict prevention

---

[5] European Parliament, Report on the Commission communication on Conflict Prevention (rapporteur J. Lagendijk), 13 December 2001, p. 8.

should also be seen in a wider picture. One of the most important root-causes for conflicts is poverty and an unequal repartition of wealth. Which effect does the EU's protectionist agricultural policy have on the economy of a country that is dependent on the export of food? What do patent rights for medicines mean for developing countries' access to drugs against AIDS or malaria? And will the privatisation of the water sector in poor countries help to provide more people with clean drinking water?

In the following pages we will examine potentially 'harmful' policy fields – describing the possible effects of EU actions on the break-out, continuation or re-emergence of conflicts. We will classify the different policy fields following the level of directness of their impact on conflicts, we will indicate to which extent the EU already takes conflict-preventing measures, and finally we will provide some suggestions for improvement.

The aim of such an analysing exercise should be to distil, firstly, whether there are any EU policies that are the absolute opposite of conflict prevention – in other words, that incite a dispute through direct political or financial support for one side or the other. Next in line on the scale of incompatibility would be policies that allow private and public undertakings to pursue their commercial interests disregarding them playing into the hands of suppressive regimes or violent groups. More indirectly, yet still relevant would be EU actions that do not con-tribute to conflicts in the first place but to potential causes of conflict like poverty or social and regional inequalities – also the downsides of globalisation. If global competition is given free rein to allow for a 'race to the bottom' of workers' – and consumers' rights, to undermine public services and to dictate trade policies and financial markets, it will be the poor and voiceless in developing countries that suffer the most.

This exercise should not be misunderstood as a rallying cry against globalisation. Neither should a whole institution be kept busy with introducing another chapter into the EU's policy documents. Instead, a conflict prevention as-sessment would be comparable with the integration of environmental factors into decision making – a process that has started with the Rio Earth Summit of 1992. In parallel, the evolving 'culture of conflict prevention' should contribute to a deeper reflection of the priorities of the European Union: Which world, which globalisation do we want?

3.   EU POLICIES THAT CAN HAVE A DETRIMENTAL IMPACT ON PEACE
      AND STABILITY IN THIRD COUNTRIES

3.1   **Direct impact (contributing to conflict)**

3.1.1   *Sending troops, weapons or money for the purpose of fighting the
        opponent*

The direct, open involvement of a Western power in a conflict elsewhere, for instance by sending troops, weapons or money to a government, has become less
and less accepted in international politics. With the end of the Cold War, the
overriding concern of a conflict between the two superpowers has vanished as a
rationale for interference. International law and the need for a mandate by the
United Nations Security Council when using force have become driving forces
for the European Union's foreign relations. Interference by the EU as a whole or
by a Member State would have to be very well founded as serving a just cause to
obtain the support of national parliaments and the population in general. The reluctance of EU Member States to be dragged into a conflict has become apparent
by their attempts to keep Turkey from occupying Kurdish areas in Northern Iraq
during the American intervention in the spring of 2003. While different European
countries had sent *weaponry* and personnel to protect Turkey from Iraqi retaliatory action, some threatened to withdraw this support should Ankara proceed
with moving troops into Iraq. Such occupation, motivated by the fear of an independent Kurdish state, would run the risk of renewed violent clashes between
Kurdish factions and the Turkish state.

3.1.2   *Political alliance with a country in conflict*

An often cited example in this respect is the EU's close relationship with Russia
despite the country's conflict with rebels fighting for the independence of
Chechnya. While the EU has often expressed its concern about the human rights
and humanitarian situation in Chechnya, it has failed to exert any meaningful influence on the Russian authorities to refrain from violence against civilians.[6]
With the fight against terrorism becoming a global objective and Chechnya
turning out to be a meeting place of internationally networking terrorist groups,
Moscow has received sympathy for its struggle rather than condemnation. Furthermore, Europe needs a friendly relationship with Russia in order to tackle a
whole range of issues: the new security architecture of Europe through the integration of former Soviet allies in EU and NATO, the problem of unsafe nuclear

---

[6] See, e.g., Human Rights Watch, 'Into Harm's Way: Forced Return of Displaced People to
Chechnya' (New York, 2003).

energy and obsolete weapons that might fall into the hands of terrorist organisations, natural resources (especially gas) that the EU would like to have access to, the common border that Russia and the EU will soon have, the problem of Kaliningrad, etc. Yet trying to help solve the conflict in Chechnya is not only a responsibility of the EU according to its conflict prevention policy, but it is also in its own interest, considering the fact that instability in Europe's future backyard will threaten Europe's own security.

With a conflict prevention assessment the EU would have to weigh the importance of its diplomatic relationship against co-responsibility for the prolongation of a conflict. In a sense, the EU's difficult relationship with the United States in the light of the American attack on Iraq can be interpreted in those terms. Because of the enormous implications of this crisis, one can be sure that such an assessment has been made in various prime ministers' offices and European crisis-teams.

3.1.3 *Combating terrorism*

The so-called fight against terrorism can also turn into a stimulant for conflicts in third countries. As part of a conflict prevention assessment, the EU should examine whether the specific measures it intends to apply against groups and individuals on the list of terrorist organisations[7] do not give governments the moral backing to fight legitimate political organisations. Several countries with secessionist movements have tried (and partly succeeded) to get international recognition for an indiscriminate crackdown on groups seeking more rights, autonomy or independence. In Turkey for instance, the EU's decision in 2002 to place the PKK (Kurdish Workers Party) on the blacklist has been followed by renewed military operations in Kurdish areas, the arrest and alleged torture of people applying for Kurdish lessons and the request by the Turkish Foreign Ministry to the EU to close down several hundred civil society groups on the grounds of being terrorist organisations. The issue at stake in this case is not so much whether the PKK has in the past committed terrorist attacks – at the time of blacklisting, the PKK had already been dissolved and its successor KADEK has not been put on the list. In taking such decisions, the EU was well advised to equally consider wider implications for the legitimate struggle of moderate Kurdish activists for more political and cultural rights.

Similar criticism has been voiced against the placement of the Philippine New Peoples Army and the Communist political leader Jose Maria Sison on the list which seems not to have been preceded by sufficient investigations as to whether this group is indeed involved in terrorist activities. Economic or strategic consid-

---

[7] The list is being updated regularly, see Council Common Position 2002/976/CFSP of 12 December 2002, *OJEC* [2002] L 337/93 and Council Decision 2002/974/EC of 12 December 2002, *OJEC* [2002] L 337/85.

erations should not determine the composition of the list and there should be ways to appeal against unjustified blacklisting.

3.1.4 *Trading agreements with countries despite conflict/human rights violations*

Trade is the *raison d'être* of the EU, between its Member States but also as regards its relations with the rest of the world. Human rights organisations and other NGOs working on conflict prevention have criticised the EU for concluding trade agreements without sufficiently addressing the concerned governments' responsibility for human rights and a peaceful settlement of disputes. Most recently the protest concerned the EU's failure to insist upon a conflict management strategy and the elimination of torture and 'disappearances' by the Egyptian and Algerian authorities which have both been fighting against Islamic forces in their country for the last ten years and longer. Similarly, the resumption of a structural relationship with Iran has been questioned since the country has been very indifferent in the past to calls to improve its human rights record.

Both the Israeli and the Palestine lobbies have attacked the EU on its trade (and aid) relationship with the other side. Despite an unequivocal human rights clause in its Association Agreement with Israel and the United Nations condemning Israel's policy of extra-judicial killings of alleged terrorist leaders, the EU refrains from making these violations a subject of debate in the framework of the Association Treaty. EU member countries have suspended the supply of weapons or parts of weapon systems to Israel. A weapons embargo has so far not gained EU-wide support. The Member States do not agree on whether there is reason to assume that their weapons are being used against the Palestine population.

In all these cases, the economic interests of the EU as a whole are not terribly strong. The negotiation of trade agreements with these countries is rather seen as a means of integrating its neighbours into the European tried and tested system of economic interdependence. Involving these countries simultaneously in a political dialogue (focusing on the respect for human rights and democracy), Brussels believes, will increase the chances of converting them into peaceful, stable societies. Nevertheless, the EU is well advised to regularly examine whether these policy objectives are being achieved, and to actually use the instruments it created to enforce respect for human rights.

3.1.5 *Development cooperation with countries in crisis*

Countries with the potential of violent conflict as well as post-war societies are most in need of international aid. While, in the first case, help from outside is needed to tackle the root causes of conflict, the second requires external assistance for reconstruction. Yet the effectiveness of more than half a century of development aid is still an area of uncertainty. As James K. Boyce puts it: 'Aid does not necessarily act like water on the embers of conflict, effectively helping to extinguish further hostilities. It can add fuel to the fire'.[8] This can be the case when former fighting parties become part of the political establishment, thereby perpetuating old divisions. On the other hand, excluding formerly powerful players from a post-conflict settlement can also result in them rejecting the agreement and taking up arms once again.

While decisions in the policy areas mentioned so far are primarily determined by Europe's own interests, with development cooperation this is much less the case. Although donors also pursue economic interests with a great part of their aid (so-called tied aid – recipient countries are obliged to hire companies from the donor country to realise a contract), development aid is generally well intended. Still, donors need to ask themselves whether the kind of aid they give, the channels through which they work and the conditions they attach (or fail to attach) to their aid are the most effective in the light of preventing the outbreak or re-emergence of conflict.

Aid runs the risk of reinforcing illegitimate political structures and to cement existing socio-economic divisions.[9] In Rwanda, for instance, intensive development cooperation over decades has supported authoritarian regimes that were based on ethnic, regional and social exclusion. The ethnic conflict between the Hutu and the Tutsi that led to the slaughter of up to one million people has been blamed in part on the political blindness of the donor community.[10] In Somalia, humanitarian aid for the victims of drought and war actually subsidised the warring factions.

On the other hand, engagement in conflict-affected regions can also bring about leverage to support the peace process. Aid bound to certain conditions can serve as a 'carrot' to encourage specific actions by the recipient. The European Union has applied this peace-conditionality extensively in post-war Bosnia and uses comparable methods (now working with the perspective of European integration) in the whole Balkan region. While this sort of engagement works in more subtle ways than simply turning the tap 'on' or 'off', the freezing or discontinuation of the aid flow needs to be a viable option.

Mainstreaming conflict prevention in development programmes therefore does not primarily mean to retarget aid to all kinds of specific conflict prevention activities, but to assess who benefits from the aid relationship in order to prevent the misuse of funds and other negative political effects. Broadly, one can say that in its aid policy, the EU is already on the right track. In 1999 the Commission

---

[8] James K. Boyce, *Investing in Peace: Aid and Conditionality after Civil Wars* (London, International Institute for Strategic Studies 2002), p. 8.

[9] For a list of risks and opportunities concerning development aid in conflict-affected areas see Manuela Leonhardt, *The Challenge of Linking Aid and Peace building* (London, International Alert 2000), p. 2.

[10] See Peter Uvin, *The Role of Development Aid in the Creation of Conflict in Rwanda* (Providence, Brown University 1996).

developed scenarios laying down what steps have to be taken when conflict breaks out in one of the countries where the EU runs large development programmes. According to the gravity of the situation, those scenarios stipulate when to freeze or discontinue programmes, when to initiate special consultation procedures or impose sanctions.[11] Conflict prevention has also been added as an objective in the Country Strategy Papers which the Commission prepares. This means that the Commission will encourage initiatives that strengthen the rule of law and democratic institutions, support the development of civil society and the reform of the security sector. So-called 'conflict prevention teams' are being deployed in external services and delegations of the Commission. These pools of experts with different backgrounds, but all with a conflict prevention perspective, give advice on how to develop conflict prevention strategies.

Furthermore, a checklist for root causes of conflict/early warning indicators has been developed which is used by the desk officers of the Commission and the General Affairs Council. The checklist contains questions such as: How inclusive is the political power of the state? Is corruption widespread? Does unlawful state violence exist? Can civil society operate freely? Are there uncontrolled flows of migrants? How robust is the economy? How are social and regional inequalities tackled? Countries receive a score on every question and the highest scoring countries will be included in a 'watch list' which the General Affairs Council discusses. Up until now, it is not clear, however, what action the Council then takes with regard to the countries on this list.[12]

Finally, the Commission very well realises that aid disbursed via sectoral programmes, like transport, rural development, energy, environment, health, research and education programmes, must not create or stir up conflicts. Therefore, the EC plans to develop a 'Conflict Prevention Handbook' to help programmers analyse possible cause-effect relationships. This would mean an important step in the direction of an overall conflict prevention assessment.

3.1.6   Regulating foreign activities of European companies

The trade in natural resources such as oil, gems, minerals or timber has fuelled violent conflicts, especially in Africa. According to a World Bank study,[13] developing countries that are dependent on the export of one primary commodity are more likely to be prone to conflicts than other developing countries. This applies above all to civil wars (rather than wars between countries) when rebel

---

[11] Communication of the Commission to the Council and the European Parliament *Co-operation with ACP Countries Involved in Armed Conflicts*, COM (1999) 240 final.

[12] 'One Year On: the Commission's Conflict Prevention Policy', available at <http://www.europa.eu.int/comm/external_relations/cpcm/cp.htm>.

[13] Paul Collier, *Economic Causes of Civil Conflict and their Implications for Policy* (Washington, D.C, World Bank 2000).

organisations engage in conflicts because they can do well out of a war. Primary commodity exports can be easily taken over by rebels because assets are long lasting, production is bound to a certain area and transport routes cannot be easily changed – the product needs to get to the port to be shipped out of the country. Rebels can choose to control the production site itself or demand illegal taxes on the route. This does not mean that conflict is motivated exclusively by economic interests – often enough grievances of an ethnic or kin group like inequality, injustice or exclusion from political power do play a role. Yet trade in these resources makes the conflict possible – by supplying the financial means to buy weapons and provide rebel leaders with considerable wealth that makes conflict worthwhile.

Needless to say, this equation only works out if there is a market where rebels can sell the looted products. Examples are numerous where European companies are involved in such illegal trade. The non-governmental organisation Friends of the Earth UK,[14] for instance, estimates that around half of all tropical timber imports to the European Union stem from illegal logging in war zones like Liberia or Cambodia. Civil wars in Angola, Congo, Nigeria, the Central African Republic, Sudan, Sierra Leone and several other countries are being funded by the export of oil, diamonds, minerals (like coltan or copper) and timber. Multinationals based in European Member States are involved in this trade – both in extraction and as brokers, both supplying governments and rebels. Some industries have set up self-regulation systems or codes of conduct, yet there are still no binding rules. Much effort has been put into the regulation of the trade in rough diamonds. Three million people have allegedly died as a result of diamond-funded wars. In 2003 the EU implemented the so-called *Kimberley process*, stipulating that only those diamonds for which sellers can guarantee that they come from a conflict-free source can be bought and resold in Europe. These diamonds receive a 'Kimberley certificate'. Producer countries must control production and transport from the mines to the point of export, and have to set up, in cooperation with the buying countries, a monitoring system. Countries in conflict are automatically excluded from the Kimberley certification. This initiative has the potential to stop the trade in blood diamonds, yet in practice it lacks the necessary teeth. The scheme builds, at this moment, on self-regulation by the diamonds industry. Research has proved this system to be inadequate, as still a significant proportion of the diamonds industry remains unaware of the suffering caused by the trade in conflict diamonds.

European companies also play a role in the direct supply of weapons to countries in crisis. British, French, German, Spanish, Italian and Swedish manufacturers export – with the authorisation of their respective governments – small arms

---

[14] Cited by Global Witness, *The Logs of War. The Timber Trade and Armed Conflict* (London, Global Witness Reports 2002), available at <http://www.globalwitness.org/reports/>, p. 59.

and light weapons to war countries and regimes accused of massive human rights violations.[15] According to the non-governmental organisations CIDSE, Caritas Europa and Pax Christi International, Western companies have even established weapons factories in Africa so as to circumvent EU and other international legislation and control.[16] Worldwide, the EU Member States together account for 40% of the trade in arms. This makes the EU a key player in the armament sector, and offers the opportunity for the EU to play an important role in regulating the global arms market.

In 1998, the EU Member States agreed on a *Code of Conduct for Legal Arms Trade*. This Code of Conduct provides detailed export criteria which must guide decisions by the Member States to grant or refuse an application for an arms export licence. These criteria concern human rights, regional and international security as well as development considerations. Furthermore, the text calls on the Member States to encourage other arms exporting countries to adopt similar Codes of Conduct. Unfortunately, the interpretation of the criteria between the Member States differs widely. The Commission can only advise, but has no official voice in this matter, as it is an agreement between the 15 countries. Thus, every Member State applies this code as it pleases and there is no institution that controls the decisions taken within the framework of the Code of Conduct. Up until now there are no viable results available to establish to what extent the Code has contributed to reducing the arms trade to conflict-ridden areas. A very important problem which the code fails to resolve is that of arms brokers, who can freely operate between Europe and other parts of the world. As Oxfam puts it: 'The EU regulates everything from beaches to bananas, but not arms brokers'.[17]

Taking conflict prevention seriously also brings about the responsibility to regulate international trade and investment in such a way that it does not have undesired consequences. As part of a conflict prevention assessment, the EU should examine which trade areas are most likely to fuel conflict, whether the measures taken are effective and whether they are the maximum that politics can do without dictating the market. In 2001, a European Commission *Green Paper on Corporate Social Responsibility* opened the discussion on social and environmental responsibilities of European enterprises. The European Parliament, in its reaction to the Green Paper, has asked that conflict prevention be added to these duties, including sanctions for companies that contribute to conflicts.

---

[15] See, e.g., Amnesty International, 'Germany, small arms and Africa' and 'Britons involved in Africa gun-running', available at <www.amnesty.org>.

[16] Position Paper of CIDSE, Caritas Europa and Pax Christi International in preparation of the EU-Africa Summit, *From Cairo to Lisbon: The EU and Africa Working Together for a New Partnership*, 4-5 April 2003, p. 12, available at <http://www.caritas-europa.org/code/EN/publications. asp>.

[17] Oxfam GB, *Regulating Weapons Deals. The Case for European Controls on Arms Brokers* (London, Oxfam Briefing Papers Feburary 2003), available at <http://www.oxfam.org.uk/what_we_ do/issues/conflict_disasters/bp39_weapons.htm>, summary report, p. 1.

3.2   Indirect impact (contributing to causes of conflict)

A conflict-sensitive approach is not only required in matters of foreign affairs but in all common policies of the Union. This is in fact the same plea that development organisations have put forward regarding the responsibilities of rich countries towards the development of the poor. Development cooperation is not enough when trade restrictions bar developing countries from international markets and agricultural subsidies harm farmers from the third world. When policy makers are asked to bear in mind the possible effects of the European agricultural policy on the emergence of conflicts in developing countries, the underlying rationale is that the same agricultural policy might make poor people poorer and therefore more prone to conflict. The conflict prevention assessment which we propose thus only adds an extra dimension to the need to reform trade, agriculture and liberalisation policies.

The relationship between poverty and inequalities on the one hand and the likeliness of conflict on the other has not only been emphasised by academic studies but is in fact the basis of the European Union itself. Its founders have deliberately promoted economic cooperation and integration so as to increase welfare and interdependence that would keep countries from engaging in war with each other.

3.2.1   *Trade policy*

International trade has a great potential to increase welfare. Poor countries like Vietnam, Brazil or Bangladesh that were open to trade (meaning that they increased their exports but also reduced import barriers) grew six times faster than closed countries.[18] They benefited much more from trade than from aid. Yet compared to the poorest countries in Africa, the success stories of Vietnam, India and Mexico had a more favourable start: their infrastructure (in terms of transport, communication technologies and micro-credit systems), education and health standards were high enough to enable the local people to take part in the opening of their economies. Besides, their governments were able to regulate foreign investment to a certain degree (for instance by opening their markets gradually and by requiring multinationals to source products locally) – possibilities which are currently being removed in the World Trade Organisation (WTO). The current conditions which poorest countries face in the trade sector do not help them out of poverty.[19]

---

[18] Jeffrey Sachs and Andrew Werner as cited by Philippe Legrain, *Open World: The Truth about Globalisation* (London, Little Brown 2002), p. 50.

[19] See Oxfam International, *Rigged Rules and Double Standards: trade, globalisation, and the fight against poverty*, (London Oxfam International Policy Papers, 2002) available at <http://www.oxfam.org/eng/policy_pape.htm#2002>. The report has inspired the European Commission to write a lengthy reply: EU welcomes Oxfam campaign to Make Trade Fair, while setting the record

Although the European Union claims to pursue policies that help developing countries to become better integrated in the world economy, within the WTO its role is clearly driven by its own interests. African, South Asian and Latin American countries have great problems selling their goods, especially agricultural products and textiles, on the European market. Their access is still greatly limited by tariffs and quotas. On the other hand, developing countries are more or less forced (by the World Bank and the International Monetary Fund (IMF), but also the liberalisation policy of the rich countries within the WTO) to open up their own markets to foreign products and investors. Most of the time, local producers are not competitive enough to survive the price fluctuations.

Also foreign investment does not always work to the benefit of the people. Although it brings about employment and tax income, the transfer of skills and technologies and the involvement of local firms as suppliers often turns out to be less than what was hoped for. At the same time, the local workforce is often left with poor employment conditions – creating new dependencies and grievances.[20] Low and unstable prices for primary commodities form an additional problem to exporters from developing countries. Many of the world's poorest countries are dependent on the export of primary commodities such as sugar, coffee, bananas and cotton. Coffee is about the only product that countries like Uganda, Ethiopia and Burundi export, making their economies highly vulnerable to falling prices. Due to structural over-supply (dating back to colonial times), the world market price for coffee is already so low that small farmers cannot cover their production costs. International coffee traders (multinationals like Nestlé and Douwe Egberts) take advantage of the competition between producers by trying to play them off against each other. Often producers are also forced to turn to the traders for loans to buy equipment – again for lower purchase prices in return.

Of course developing countries have their own share of responsibility to make trade work for the poor. It is in the first place their own public spending that needs to be directed at poverty reduction. Investments in infrastructure, education and health, access to land, financial resources and marketing infrastructure, and not in the last place reducing corruption are essential steps to be taken. To get there, development assistance is necessary. Equally so is the insight on the part of the Western countries – including the European Union – that agreements within the World Trade Organisation must not damage developing countries, and create hot-beds for conflicts.

Thanks to the pressure of various players like the anti-globalist movement and left-wing political parties, the European Union has started to change its stance.

---

straight on its contribution to maximising the benefits of trade for the poor (Memorandum, Brussels, 22 April 2002).

[20] The different workers' rights which companies apply in countries outside the EU is the subject of the discussion on Corporate Social Responsibility.

A cornerstone in this respect is the 'Everything but Arms' initiative.[21] Since March 2001, the 49 least developed countries (LDCs) no longer need to pay duties for most products to be sold on the European market, except arms. For three commodities – bananas, sugar and rice – transition periods apply. Unfortunately, for many developing countries these are the most important export products. For developing countries other than the LDCs, namely all Latin American countries and many Asian countries, tariffs and quotas continue to apply. Also, rules of origin do not allow the duty-free export of semi-manufactured and manufactured products if part of the product does not come from a LDC.

Commissioner Lamy recently congratulated himself on the EU having imported around € 432 billion from developing countries in 2000.[22] Yet, by far the largest part of these imports are not from LDCs, but from the 'better off' developing countries, which means the Indian sub-continent and Latin America. It must be acknowledged that developing country exports to the EU have indeed increased since 1995, and the EU does relatively more for developing countries than other major trading partners, like the US, Japan and Canada. Whether this is all that can be done should be questioned. In January last year the Commission announced a 'radically better deal for developing countries'. It meant a proposal for more market opening and less trade distorting support in the field of agriculture. The press release that accompanied the proposal expressively tempered too high expectations by putting as a condition: 'providing there is fair burden sharing from other developed countries in particular'.[23] The EU indeed takes a social attitude when it comes to international trade – as long as this does not hurt.

3.2.2 Agricultural policy

The need to reform the European Union's common agricultural policy (CAP) has been evident for several years. Motives to change the system of subsidies are diverse, the fact that they are way too expensive ranking first. Direct income support for farmers that is linked to production capacity has stimulated over-production which harms the environment and threatens animal welfare. Equally important, that same over-production contributes to very low prices for these products on the world market. Farmers from developing countries cannot sell their products at the same low prices. Even though the market may formally be open to them, practically speaking, they do not have a fair opportunity.

Additionally, European farmers receive export subsidies to sell their products outside the European Union. Food producers in developing countries cannot com-

---

[21] European Commission, 'Generalised System of Preferences. EU approves "Everything But Arms" trade access for least developed countries' March 2001.

[22] See the Commission's reaction to Oxfam's policy report, as cited above n. 19.

[23] European Commission, 'WTO and Agriculture: European Commission proposes more market opening, less trade distorting support and a radically better deal for developing countries', December 2002.

pete with the dumping prices of European companies and are driven out of their own markets. This is not only harmful to a few farmers. It makes developing countries dependent on European imports that might suddenly become much more expensive (thereby threatening food security), but also contravene people's own nutritional, cultural and environmental norms.

Consciousness as to the damaging potential of the CAP is growing. Within the framework of the WTO negotiations on agricultural products the European Commission has recently come up with proposals for a better market access for developing countries.[24] However, one should not expect too much from these proposals as nothing has yet been decided and unilateral action by the EU (in the face of a more protectionist American agricultural policy) is unlikely. Recent Commission proposals for a reform of the CAP have looked hopeful, but the Member States, under pressure from a very strong agribusiness lobby in Germany and France, seem to be more than reluctant to adopt these reforms.

3.2.3   Intellectual property rights

Multinationals have an enormous influence in safeguarding their own interests through the rules of the WTO. One recent example is the regulation of intellectual property rights in an agreement called TRIPs (Trade-Related Aspects of Intellectual Property Rights). It enables companies to claim a global patent over an 'innovation', be it a technical device, a drug or even a plant. The patent forbids the production or import of the good without paying royalties to the patent holder.

The idea of patents arose long ago to encourage invention by providing a return for the costs involved in research. The protection of an innovation, however, has to be balanced against the need to spread its benefits as widely as possible. In an area such as health, patents on drugs mean that medicines cost a lot more than the production price and are thereby unaffordable to people in poor countries. This is especially true for AIDS patients. The cocktail of patented drugs they need to survive costs as much as 15, 000 Euro a year. An Indian company has calculated that it would be able to supply generic copies of these medicines for 350 Euro a year.[25] Yet, under the rules of the WTO, it is not allowed to do so – because big, mainly American, pharmaceutical companies have the patent on AIDS treatment drugs. In the preparation for the WTO summit in Cancún, diplomats from the key WTO member countries tried to reach a compromise on the export of generic copies of medicines. Countries like India and Brazil were to be allowed to export these drugs to countries with a public health crisis, yet permission would have to be granted by the WTO – providing that the pills would for

---

[24] European Commission op. cit. n. 23.

[25] Legrain op. cit. n. 18, p. 256.

instance not resemble the more expensive original by producers such as Pfizer and Merck. [26]

TRIPs also allows multinationals to claim a patent on plant varieties and plant DNA. In the search for new products with a special taste or potential health effects, agrochemical corporations take seeds from plants in developing countries, grow them at home and sell them as their own innovation. This way the people of India and Pakistan have been robbed of their basmati-rice, the San bushmen of the Kalahari desert (southern Africa) of the hoodia cactus, Zimbabwe of its snake-bean tree and the Philippines of its ilang-ilang plant, amongst others.[27] The people who have used these plants for centuries in their own countries usually do not get a share of the financial benefits. Instead, farmers might have to pay royalties to the patent holder for growing their own crops, they might be denied the right to save, grow and sell their seeds and they might be forced to buy new seeds every year (and the chemicals that go with them) if 'gentech' corporations modify the crops in such a way that only one harvest is possible. EU Commissioner Lamy for External Trade has announced that the position should be taken in TRIPs so that patents on plants are possible, but should not apply to farmers rights to use, save and sell their seeds. Also people who used these plants before must be able to share the profit generated through the sale of the patented product.

This position is a step in the right direction. Although WTO agreements are a matter of international negotiation, the European Union is one of the strongest players in this system. Surely, the biggest pharmaceutical and agrochemical companies have their home in the United States – which they have successfully lobbied to draft the rules that fit their commercial interests. Yet, in the light of an integrated conflict prevention approach, the EU has the responsibility to do all it can to reform these rules and to combat the 'bio-piracy' of poor countries' resources as well as to counter drug patents that cost the lives of millions.

3.2.4   Liberalisation of the water sector

The World Bank Vice President Ismail Serageldin once stated that in the 21st century wars would not be fought over oil, but over water. Water is a basic necessity, and should be available to everyone at low cost or free of charge. The European Union urges the WTO to open up the global market of drinking water for private companies. In that scenario it will be no longer the state that provides drinking water. It will be private corporations like Suez or Vivendi, most of them based in the EU, that take over the responsibility for water provision. These private corpo-

---

[26] At the time of writing, this compromise has again been turned down and a solution is not expected before the Cancún meeting.

[27] See John Madeley (ed.), *Crops and Robbers* (London, ActionAid 2001) available at <http://www.actionaid.org/resources/foodrights/trips.shtml>.

rations claim to be able to provide better quality and to work more efficiently than state suppliers. Moreover, they claim that they invest in additional capacity and adapt quickly to changing demands.

As water is a basic necessity, privatisation puts too much power into the hands of private companies. There are also practical objections. Poor people in third world countries will rather use water form rivers and ponds than spend the little money that they have on water – possibly with serious health effects. Likewise, although 90% of the poor in developing countries live in rural areas, the water services of private providers will concentrate on urban areas.

In Johannesburg, the EU committed itself to halve the number of people without access to clean drinking water by 2015. Whether liberalisation of the water sector will help to reach this goal is doubtful. On the contrary, it will increase the conflict-sensitiveness of water. Therefore it would be wise to reconsider the EU input in the WTO negotiations on the liberalisation of services from a conflict prevention point of view.

3.2.5   *Debt relief and regulating international finance*

The debt-ridden economies of developing countries are very sensitive to economic and financial fluctuations. The burden of debt keeps lesser developed countries hostage within a vicious circle of poverty and conflict. EU Member States are important creditors to developing countries. With the so-called 'Millennium Goals' the EU pledged itself to important debt relief by 2015. The current trend shows that this goal will not be met, as even the HIPC countries (Highly Indebted Poor Countries) will only have about 30% of their debts written off.

Likewise, the ups and downs of the financial markets can have devastating consequences for developing countries, as the case of Argentina shows. To protect vulnerable economies from financial fluctuations the financial markets should become more stable. The idea to tax speculative capital flows, in the form of simple sales taxes on currency trades across borders (the so-called Tobin Tax) could help to control financial fluctuations and to use the yield to combat poverty. The Commission, the European Parliament and the Member States have conducted feasibility studies on the Tobin Tax.

Although the EU as such is not competent in these matters, common initiatives can be taken at the EU level in the shape of voluntary commitments by the Member States. This could concern writing off debts, or the introduction of a Tobin Tax, which of course will only work if decided internationally.

3.2.6   *Other policies that might have an indirect impact on conflicts*

Finally, policies can indirectly and in spite of their intentions have an impact on the outbreak or the perpetration of conflicts by creating social or numeral inequalities between potentially or historically adversary groups. Examples are large infrastructure projects, like dams or irrigation projects, that can lead to forced migration of the population, and thus to conflicts over property rights or scarce resources. In Sri Lanka, a large-scale irrigation project brought about Sinhala settlements in a zone where Tamils used to be in the majority, and thus played an important role in the Sri Lankan interethnic conflict.

Also the hastened and badly prepared return of refugees can contribute to the reappearance of recently tempered conflicts. Direct causes can be unresolved property issues or the fact that perpetrators of crimes are still in powerful positions, which can lead to the flaring up of old tensions. Examples are Bosnia and Afghanistan, where EU countries sometimes decided too soon that 'the situation was under control' and that refugees could return. It would be extremely important to take these policies into account in a conflict prevention assessment.

4.   WHAT COULD AND SHOULD BE DONE?

Over the past few years, the awareness of Europe's responsibilities in promoting human rights, fair trade and environmental sustainability has grown. This development must at the very least be attributed to active lobbying from NGOs, movements like the anti-globalists and political parties like the Greens. Joschka Fischer's influential contributions to the Convention on the Future of Europe have permitted conflict prevention to find a prominent role in the proposals on the Common Foreign and Security Policy.

4.1   European interests should be redefined

Now the time has come to move on towards a broader vision. European policymakers have to decide which world they want, being conscious of the consequences of their actual policies. Awareness building must make clear that actively including conflict prevention in our decision making does not mean broaching a totally new question. On the contrary, with most of our current policies, be it agriculture or fisheries, we passively and unconsciously decide daily on the shape of the world. That is why it is so important to establish the cause-effect relationship between EU policies, on the one hand, and poverty or conflicts in other parts of the world, on the other.

A think-tank could therefore be set up to analyse the consequences of the current EU policies. The composition and working methods of such a think tank could be comparable to the Convention, comprising representatives from EU institutions, from Member States' governments and from parliaments, but also scientists, experts from developing countries and representatives of the civil society like delegates of NGOs and trade unions. This think tank should develop principles to which all European policies have to conform. To crystallise these principles, on the basis of the above-mentioned analyses, will be a long and labour-intensive task. Very generally speaking, these principles would boil down to the idea that poor countries should not be harmed in any way by EU policies. In the European Parliament, on the occasion of the latest resolution on the EU stance in the WTO, the Greens have tried to adopt this notion, but, as yet, they have not convinced a majority of the EP.

4.2 Indicators

The check-list for root causes of conflict which the European Commission has developed could very well be used as indicators to assess which impact the EU, its Member States or private enterprises have on conflict-prone countries. Running down this list the EU would have to analyse whether its policies and actions have any detrimental effect on the legitimacy of the State, the rule of law, respect for fundamental rights, civil society and the media, the relations between communities, sound economic management, social and regional inequalities and finally the geopolitical situation.[28]

Lessons on the dynamics of conflicts and the impact of outside interventions can be learnt from assessment studies within the field of development policy. Academics like Mary Anderson[29] and Luc Reychler,[30] and International Alert representative Manuela Leonhardt[31] have listed the risks and the opportunities (Anderson calls them 'dividers' and 'connectors') for development aid in conflict-affected regions. On the micro level they prescribe the steps that have to be taken before launching (or continuing) a specific development project in a conflict prone environment. They range from conflict and stakeholder analysis to drawing up objectives (based on a clear definition of 'peace') and conditions that have to be met in order to achieve them.

4.3 Integrating indicators into decision-making

Much can be learnt from the process of integrating environmental considerations into other policy areas, and to a lesser degree from the so-called gender mainstreaming. Both show the complexity of such an undertaking. It took the European institutions ten years (having started after the Rio Earth Summit in 1992) from the writing of an internal note to the development of comprehensive strate-

---

[28] European Commission's 'EC Check-list for Root Causes of Conflict', available at <http://www.europa.eu.int/comm/external_relations/cpcm/cp.htm>.

[29] Mary B. Anderson, *Do Not Harm: How aid can support peace – or war* (Boulder, Lynne Rienner Publishers 1999).

[30] Luc Reychler, 'The Conflict Impact Assessment System (CIAS): A Method for Designing and Evaluating Development Policies and Projects', in Peter Cross/Guenola Rasamolina (eds.), *Conflict Prevention Policy of the European Union* (Baden Baden, SWP 1999), pp. 144-162.

[31] Manuela Leonhardt, *Conflict Impact Assessment of EU development cooperation with ACP-countries. A review of policy, literature and practice* (London, International Alert/Saferworld 1999).

gies to integrate the environment in the different policy-fields (transport, energy, agriculture, development, trade, etc.). Furthermore, the focus still lies on what the EU can do additionally in a specific field to advance environmental protection, and much less on how current policies have an impact on the environment. In the field of economics and finance for example, an emission trading system was elaborated long before it was decided that the phasing out of environmentally harmful subsidies would be necessary to make economic policy compatible with environmental concerns.

Apart from this, the measures proposed in the different fields varied widely. DG Development, for instance, has developed, as early as 1997, a complex 'Environmental Integration Manual' with certain procedures to follow when developing cooperation policies, formulating country or sector programmes and deciding on projects. DG Trade, on the other hand, has announced that it will hire external experts to carry out 'Sustainability Impact Assessments' of all trade agreements between the EU and other countries. Yet, these assessments expressly do not have as their objective 'to assess the desirability of further liberalisation overall', but rather 'to provide elements of information on the range of possible impacts' and 'to accompany and optimise their implementation'.[32]

With a conflict prevention assessment, these weaknesses must be overcome. Council formations should not again focus on the potential *positive* effects they could have, by adding another policy area to their work. By doing so they run the risk of closing their eyes to the potentially *negative* effects they are already producing. It is a lengthy process: political will is vital and capacity within the Commission is needed. Awareness is increasing – the different initiatives laid down in the preceding pages demonstrate this. In its latest communication on conflict prevention the Commission admitted that it had managed to integrate conflict prevention into some external policies (especially external aid) but much less in sectoral Community policies. A start should be made by including conflict prevention as a factor in the reform of the Common Agricultural Policy and in trade negotiations within the WTO. To speed up the process, the Commission should be obliged to report to the Parliament on the steps it has taken. At a later stage the results of the assessment need to be made public as well. If conflict prevention really is the core task of EU external policies, Europe has to deliver on all fronts.

---

[32] See Commission Staff Working Paper 'Environmental Integration in the External Policies of the General Affairs Council', March 2002.

PART TWO

EU CONFLICT PREVENTION STRATEGY AND PRACTICE SO FAR

PART TWO C

SELECTIVE GEOGRAPHICAL CASE STUDIES

Chapter 14
EU CONFLICT PREVENTION IN THE WESTERN BALKANS

by Steven Blockmans[1]

1. TOWARDS AN INTEGRATED APPROACH TO THE WESTERN BALKANS

It is almost banal to repeat that the Balkans have been seen by many as a powder-keg, a black hole, a troublesome corner of Europe, a region with more history than it can cope with, and other negative stereotypes. Yet, the fact remains that, whether or not they have been directly involved in conflict during the last decade, the post-communist societies of the Balkans face widespread criminalization, high levels of unemployment, and waves of ethnic violence. While the worst affected area is Bosnia and Herzegovina (BiH, alternatively Bosnia), nowhere in the region is untouched by the social distortion that has accompanied the disintegrative violence of the Yugoslav wars of the 1990s.[2] Bosnia can be described as the epicentre. Its 'gangster economy' has radiated outwards through networks of refugees, arms smugglers, drug traffickers, money launderers, and black market traders, to name just a few. Bosnia is surrounded by concentric circles of more or less affected societies. Hence, there is an inner ring of Croatia, Serbia and Montenegro, and the Former Yugoslav Republic of Macedonia (FYROM, alternatively Macedonia[3]) which are similarly war affected; then Slovenia, where, after 'only' ten days of war, transition by peaceful means and political consolidation has gone further; then Albania, Romania, and Bulgaria, where the conse-

---

[1] Researcher in European Union Law, T.M.C. Asser Institute, The Hague. The research came to an end on 8 September 2003. I would like to thank Dr. Frank Hoffmeister (Legal Service, European Commission) and the editors of this book for their helpful comments on a draft of this contribution.

[2] This kind of fragmentation has been referred to as 'balkanisation' or 'balkanism'. For a critique of the use of both this generic term and of the theory behind interventionism, see J. Stilhoff Sörensen, 'Balkanism and the New Radical Interventionism: A Structural Critique', 9 *International Peacekeeping* 2002, pp. 1-22. For a more nuanced analysis of the perspectives of both 'Atlantic Europe' and the Balkan peoples on intervention in the region, see I. Kadare, 'The Balkans: Truths and Untruths', in D. Triantaphyllou (ed.), 'The Southern Balkans: Perspectives from the Region', 46 *Chaillot Papers* (Paris, ISS 2001), pp. 5-16.

[3] The term 'Macedonia' is used here as an informal name. Greece believes that the name Macedonia should properly be applied to its own northern region with origins dating from the time of Alexander the Great. Similarly, the name 'Kosovo' is used here in spite of the Albanian and Serb appellations for the region, respectively 'Kosova' and 'Kosovo-Metohija'.

V. Kronenberger and J. Wouters, eds., The European Union and Conflict Prevention
© 2004, T·M·C·ASSER PRESS, *The Hague, The Netherlands*

quences of the wars have only later become visible; and, finally, there is an outer least affected ring consisting of Hungary, Turkey, and the Member States of the European Union, most notably Greece and Germany, which have not been able to prevent the influx of refugees and the spread of organized crime.[4]

The disintegrative violence mentioned above is difficult to contain in either time or space. Up to the present, no single international or European organization has been capable of preventing or solving a conflict in the Balkans by itself. So far, this has only been achieved through cooperation between several functionally specialized organizations. The United Nations (UN), the North Atlantic Treaty Organization (NATO), the Western European Union (WEU), the European Union (EU), the Organisation for Security and Cooperation in Europe (OSCE), and, to a lesser extent, the Council of Europe, have all made mutually reinforcing contributions towards creating a stable and secure environment in South Eastern Europe. But, sadly, cooperation between the European security organizations has not prevented the outbreak of two of Europe's gravest conflicts since the end of WW II, namely Bosnia and Kosovo.[5] Neither has NATO's single-handed armed intervention in Kosovo eliminated any of the fundamental socio-economic and political threats to the stability of South Eastern Europe. While it did bring a temporary conclusion to the ten-year ethnic-territorial decomposition of Yugoslavia, it unfortunately also gave rise to new security threats for certain countries as well as for the region as a whole. There is evidence that a splitting of the rump-state of Serbia and Montenegro and a further crumbling of Serbia should not be ruled out. The crises in Kosovo and Macedonia equally suggest that, in view of Albanian nationalists' aspirations for unification, the whole region's recomposition should not be excluded.[6] Hence, the critical mass for security stabilization in the Balkans lies at the junction of Serbian-Albanian interests.[7]

---

[4] See M. Kaldor, V. Bojicic and I. Vejvoda, 'Reconstruction in the Balkans: A Challenge for Europe?', 2 *EFA Rev.* (1997), pp. 329-350.

[5] For an analysis of the effectiveness of the European security architecture in these crises and proposals to improve the functioning of the system, see J. Wouters and F. Naert, 'How Effective is the European Security Architecture? Lessons from Bosnia and Kosovo', 50 *ICLQ* (2001), pp. 540-576; and H. Neuhold, 'Collective Security After 'Operation Allied Force'', in J. Frowein and R. Wolfrum (eds.), *Max Planck Yearbook of United Nations Law* (2000), pp. 73-106.

[6] Recent developments reflect a growing consensus that any stable, long-term settlement in the Western Balkans will not be possible until all territorial disputes are resolved. At the EU-Western Balkans Summit in Thessaloniki on 21 June 2003 it was agreed that the EU and the US would back direct talks between Serbia and Kosovo that could eventually lead to an agreement on how the two could peacefully separate from each other, with internationally recognized borders (see the summary of the results of the summit at <http://www.eu2003.gr/en/articles/2003/6/23/3138/print.asp>, reaffirmed in the GAERC conclusions of 21 July 2003, Press Release No. 11439/03 (Presse 209)). However, such talks could open a Pandora's box, since Albanian nationalists might use the possibility of an independent Kosovo as a vehicle to create a greater Albania, as could the ethnic Albanians in neighbouring Macedonia. The fact that the final status talks could unravel the tenuous union forged between Serbia and Montenegro by the EU is perhaps of lesser concern, for both parties seem to be in favour of dismantling the union. See *infra*, n. 88 and accompanying text.

[7] See M. Hadzic, 'Kosovo and the Security Stabilization of South-East Europe', 7 *International Peacekeeping* 2000, pp. 83-94; D. Triantaphyllou (ed.), 'What Status for Kosovo?', 50 *Chaillot Pa-*

The determinants of security stabilization in the Balkans are not just political. An integrated approach towards reconstruction is central to the efforts geared at stabilizing the region. A strategy for lasting peace has to aim at the creation of an opposite logic to that of war. This implies the establishment of autonomous societal spheres and the creation of legal and new or reformed administrative structures which guarantee the rule of law instead of the 'law of the ruler'. But there is more than that. The establishment of effective democratic structures has to go hand in hand with macroeconomic stabilization, liberalization, and privatization. Finally, a good approach will adapt to local and regional differences. This is the consequence of disintegration and fragmentation. The situation in Tuzla, Mostar, Sarajevo, Krajina, Macedonia, Kosovo, and Albania will be different in each case. Hence, what is needed is a flexible, multilayered approach that recognizes these specificities and provides a form of assistance which is designed to encourage political, economic, and social integration in the Balkans and in Europe, a process that would render states and borders relatively unimportant.[8]

The adoption of a regional approach towards the Western Balkans on 29 April 1997 by the EU General Affairs Council seems to represent just that: the first step towards a multiple strategy designed to favour a progressive process of stabilization and association of Albania, Bosnia and Herzegovina, Croatia, Serbia and Montenegro, and the FYROM.[9] Add to this the recent establishment of a real and credible Common Foreign and Security Policy (CFSP) towards the Western Balkans and the launching of the first ever EU missions within the framework of the European Security and Defence Policy (ESDP), and every self-declared Europhile would be tempted to conclude that what we are witnessing in 2003 is nothing less than the emergence of the first international organization that is able to adopt a comprehensive strategy by itself. If this were really the case, then this would of course be a welcome development in the improvement of the European security architecture, especially in cases where other international organizations or single countries such as the United States are unwilling or unable to act.

The present contribution will not repeat what has been exhaustively dealt with elsewhere concerning the 'Yugoslav crises' of the 1990s,[10] nor will it give a de-

---

pers (Paris, ISS 2001); and P. Jurkovic (ed.), *Building Stability in Weak States: The Western Balkans* (Vienna, National Defence Academy 2002).

[8] M. Kaldor, V. Bojicic and I. Vejvoda, op.cit. n.4, at 344-346. The authors call this approach 'reconstruction assistance', a category of assistance between humanitarian assistance and the kind of assistance that is predicated on a successful transition as conventionally defined and applied in, e.g., Central and Eastern European countries.

[9] GAC conclusions on the principle of conditionality governing the development of the EU's relations with certain countries of South East Europe, *Bull. EU* 4-1997, point 2.2.1.

[10] See, e.g., D. Owen, *Balkan Odyssey* (London, Harvest 1995); UN, *The Blue Helmets. A Review of United Nations Peace-keeping* (Washington, United Nations 1996), pp. 487-509; D. Bethlehem and M. Weller (eds.), *The 'Yugoslav' Crisis in International Law: General Issues* (Cambridge, Cambridge International Documents Series 1997); M. Glenny, *The Balkans, 1804-1999, Nationalism, War and the Great Powers* (New York, The Modern Library 1999); and M. Mazower, *The*

tailed account of the institutional changes of the Union's CFSP and ESDP as a result of these crises.[11] Rather, this chapter will examine a variety of legal and political aspects of the European Union's current actions to prevent the outbreak of conflicts in the five countries of the Western Balkans.[12] For the purpose of this contribution, the term 'conflict prevention' will be used to include any action taken to prevent conflicts (i.e., armed conflict as understood in international law and/or large-scale violent human rights violations) from arising and/or existing conflicts from escalating or spreading. The term also covers post-conflict action, for suitable and structural peace-building measures can simultaneously serve as a means to prevent conflicts.[13] When looking at the EU's role in the Western Balkans, it becomes clear how strongly intertwined its conflict prevention activities and post-conflict reconstruction assistance are. This is best illustrated in Macedonia, where the EU has deployed a military operation to prevent the outbreak of new ethnic violence, while it continues to provide financial assistance for the reconstruction of houses and public facilities through the European Agency for Reconstruction.

In what is to follow, the role of the EU is providing short-term conflict prevention assistance to prevent renewed fighting in the Western Balkans will be examined first. Particular attention will be paid to the recent actions which have been undertaken within the framework of the ESDP. Next, the Union's long-term approach towards projecting stability in the region will be investigated.[14] The Stabilisation and Association Process (SAP) will be analyzed, as well as more specific efforts to integrate each of the Western Balkan countries into the European Union. Finally, some conclusions will drawn.

Balkans, A Short History (New York, Random House 2000). For an analysis of the political impact of the EU on the conflicts in ex-Yugoslavia from 1991 to 1995, see R. Ginsberg, *The European Union in International Politics* (Lanham, Rowman & Littlefield Publishers 2001), pp. 57-104.

[11] See, e.g., S. Duke, 'From Amsterdam to Kosovo: Lessons for the Future of CFSP', 2 *Eipascope* (1999), pp. 2-15; and C. Piana, 'The EU's Decision-making Process in the Common Foreign and Security Policy: The Case of the Former Yugoslav Republic of Macedonia', 7 *EFA Rev.* (2002), pp. 209-226.

[12] For an analysis of the EU's more traditional transition strategies towards Bulgaria, Romania, Slovenia, Turkey, and other acceding and candidate countries, see M. Maresceau (ed.), *Enlarging the European Union – Relations Between the EU and Central and Eastern Europe* (London, Longman 1997); A. Ott and K. Inglis (eds.), *Handbook on European Enlargement – A Commentary on the Enlargement Process* (The Hague, TMC Asser Press 2002); and M. Cremona (ed.), *The Enlargement of the European Union* (Oxford, Oxford University Press 2003). Like in the policy documents of the EU, the terms 'Western Balkans' and 'South Eastern Europe' will be used interchangeably throughout this contribution.

[13] See UN, *An Agenda for Peace*, UN Doc. A/47/277-S/24111, 17 June 1992, paras. 21 and 57.

[14] The distinction between long-term and short-term prevention has an operational assumption. See European Commission, *Conflict Prevention*, COM (2001) 211 final, Brussels, 11 April 2001.

2. SHORT-TERM CONFLICT PREVENTION

2.1 Reacting quickly to nascent conflicts

History has shown that rogue leaders with bad intentions only understand the language of diplomacy backed by force.[15] Since the entry into force of the Treaty of Amsterdam, the Member States of the European Union have actively used the *diplomatic* structures with which they had endowed their CFSP. Much to his credit, Javier Solana, Secretary General/High Representative for the CFSP (SG/HR), supported by his staff at the Council, has made the most of the cautious wording of his tasks in Article 26 of the EU Treaty. The EU, by way of its SG/HR, has brokered a peace deal between the government and the Albanian separatists in Macedonia,[16] and it has forced a new Constitutional Charter and Implementing Law upon Serbia and Montenegro.[17] But it remains doubtful whether these diplomatic constructs can sustain the disintegrative forces mentioned earlier. For a long time it has been clear that the EU is in need of other, more persuasive machinery to force parties (that have the intention of) fighting each other in an armed conflict not to commit heinous crimes such as ethnic cleansing, religious persecution, and racial discrimination, and to settle their differences in a peaceful manner. This need has become apparent, first with the crisis in Bosnia, next in Albania, and then in Kosovo. In all of these crises the European Union was plainly embarrassed at how little it could contribute to the prevention and 'management' of conflicts on its doorstep.[18] Reliance upon US diplomacy and NATO's military strength condemned the Union to 'paying the bills' while not moving the emphasis to short-term conflict prevention and crisis management. Frustration at such inadequacies has led the EU to take its *military* emancipation more seriously. In subsequent steps, the European Councils of Cologne, Helsinki, Feira, Nice, and Göteborg have established that the European Union should de-

---

[15] See R. Holbrooke, *To End a War* (New York, Random House 1998), at 146.

[16] The Ohrid Framework Agreement of 13 August 2001.

[17] The Constitutional Charter was adopted and proclaimed on 6 February 2003 by the Parliament of Serbia and Montenegro. See GAERC Conclusions of 24 February 2003, Doc. No. 6604/03 (Presse 52). The Constitutional Charter is underpinned by the Belgrade Agreement of 14 March 2002, see W. van Meurs, 'The Belgrade Agreement: Robust Mediation Between Serbia and Montenegro', in D. Lopandic and V. Bajic (eds.), *Serbia and Montenegro on the Road to the European Union – Two Years Later* (Belgrade, European Movement in Serbia and Friedrich Ebert Stiftung 2003), pp. 192-194.

[18] For an analysis of the role which the EU played in the crises of Bosnia and Kosovo, see J. Wouters and F. Naert, *supra*, n. 5. Although the crisis which erupted in Albania in the wake of the collapse of the 'pyramid' speculation systems would have lent itself *par excellence* to a so-called 'Petersberg mission' of the EU, the principal responsibility for managing the chaos and violence in Albania was left to a military operation launched by a 'coalition of the willing' under Italian leadership and the OSCE (Operazione Alba). See, e.g., G. Kostakos and D. Bourantonis, 'Innovations in Peace-keeping: The Case of Albania', 29 *Security Dialogue* (1998), pp. 49-58; and E. Foster, 'Ad hoc in Albania: Did Europe Fail? A Rejoinder', 29 *Security Dialogue* (1998), pp. 213-219.

velop an ability of its own to undertake the full range of conflict prevention and crisis management tasks defined in Article 17 of the Treaty on European Union (the so-called 'Petersberg tasks') through the development of the necessary civilian and military means, To this end, dedicated structures for crisis management have been put in place within both the Council of Ministers and the European Commission and new procedures have been elaborated.[19] The European Security and Defence Policy was – somewhat prematurely – declared operational at the European Council of Laeken on 14 and 15 December 2001.[20] Since then, the European Union has reaffirmed its operational capability by launching three ESDP operations: EUPM in Bosnia-Herzegovina, Concordia in Macedonia, and Artemis in Bunia (Democratic Republic of Congo). As this contribution only focuses on the Western Balkans, the latter operation will remain outside the scope of the following analysis.

2.2   Operation Concordia

It can be said that the new institutional framework for the CFSP and the ESDP allowed EU action in Macedonia to produce a more positive outcome than was the case in previous Balkan crises. Nonetheless, in terms of conflict prevention *stricto sensu*, the Union failed to identify, let alone address, some of the early signs which pointed to the possibility that a crisis might emerge in the FYROM, long before it actually did in March 2001.[21] First, the growing problem of Albanian refugees from Kosovo in Macedonia, following Milošević's crackdown on Albanians in Kosovo and NATO's air campaign in March-June 1999. Repeatedly, the Macedonian government warned the international community that it could not allow more refugees on its soil, both for economic reasons and for fear of disrupting the fragile ethnic fabric of the country. Second, there was a great deal of evidence pointing to massive arms smuggling activity in the northern re-

---

[19] For an overview of the Union's efforts to build an ESDP, see, e.g., R. Wessel, 'The EU as a Black Widow: Devouring the WEU to Give Birth to a European Security and Defence Policy', in V. Kronenberger (ed.), *The European Union and the International Legal Order: Discord or Harmony?* (The Hague, T.M.C. Asser Press 2001), pp. 405-434; and A. Deighton, 'The European Security and Defence Policy', 40 *Journal of Common Market Studies* (2002), pp. 719-741. This process is far from over, considering the ongoing work on the Union's own overall strategy in the field of foreign and security policy and the plans to create an intergovernmental agency in the field of defense capabilities development, research, acquisition, and armaments in the course of 2004. *Infra*, note 45.

[20] *Bull. EU* 12-2001, points I.5.6 and I.28. The Thessaloniki European Council of 19 and 20 June 2003 admitted recognized shortfalls in the Union's operational capability across the full range of Petersberg tasks, but considered that they can be alleviated by the further development of the EU's military capabilities. See <http://eu2003gr/en/articles/2003/6/23/3135/print.asp>.

[21] See, e.g., S. Clément, 'Conflict Prevention in the Balkans: Case Studies of Kosovo and the FYR of Macedonia', 30 *Chaillot Papers* (Paris, ISS 1997), at 13-16 and 24-27. Clément draws the same conclusion concerning the limited preventive measures adopted by the international community, 'in particular the European Union', in the case of Kosovo; at 21-23.

gions of Macedonia bordering Kosovo and southern Serbia. Reports showed that Albanians in the Macedonian border villages were preparing themselves for an armed uprising. Finally, the EU failed to establish a link between the crisis of the Presevo Valley and a possible crisis in Macedonia. The attention of the Union, indeed of the international community as a whole, was focused on Kosovo and Serbia, while Macedonia was regarded as a relatively stable country in the Western Balkans. While it is true that the European Commission, in the months preceding the crisis, was engaged in Macedonia with different projects (e.g., by providing support to strengthen the administrative and judicial capacities and by contributing financial means to the South East Europe University in Tetovo, the first official university institution providing tuition in the Albanian language, as well as Macedonian and English), these actions did not prevent the eruption of the conflict between the state authorities and the Albanian rebels.

To a large extent, the Union's success in preventing the further escalation of violence and in suppressing the conflict, is thanks to its 'preventive' diplomacy and the leading role played by Javier Solana. The SG/HR travelled to Skopje on countless occasions, sometimes accompanied by Chris Patten, the Commissioner for External Relations. Ably supported on the ground by François Léotard, the EU's resident envoy, and José Pinto Teixeira, Head of the Commission Delegation, the SG/HR put considerable pressure on both the Macedonian and the Albanian sides to engage in dialogue.[22] The looming signature of the Stabilisation and Association Agreement between the EU and the FYROM was certainly the strongest incentive at Solana's disposal to pressurize the two parties in the conflict to arrive at an agreement by political means.[23] To this end, the Commission's brandnew Rapid Reaction Mechanism (RRM) was also utilized.[24] It is thanks to the combination of first pillar incentives and second pillar pressure that the EU managed to broker a peace deal at Ohrid on 13 August 2001. The Ohrid Framework Agreement brought an end to several months of violence between ethnic Albanian groups and the state security forces and provided for a decentralized

---

[22] See N. Whyte, N. Arbatova and D. Allin, 'The Macedonian Crisis and Balkan Security', *ESF Working Papers* (2001).

[23] On Stabilisation and Association Agreements, see *infra*, para. 3.2.

[24] Council Regulation (EC) No. 381/2001 creating a rapid-reaction mechanism, *OJEC* [2001] L 57/5. The RRM allows the Commission to dispatch Community funds rapidly in case of an emergency. It can be used both to conduct one-off actions arising out of a crisis situation, and to 'kick-start' projects or programmes which will require longer-term follow-up through other assistance instruments. The RRM funds measures aim at restoring the conditions of stability under which the main Community cooperation programmes can achieve their objectives. These can include measures to restore the rule of law, promoting democracy and human rights, peace-building and mediation initiatives, the demobilization and reintegration of combatants, the reconstruction of infrastructure and the strategic planning of the economic, administrative and social rebuilding of countries affected by crisis. The funds available through the RRM were € 20 million for 2001 and € 25 million for 2002. The RRM was first used in March 2001 to pay for the reconstruction of houses destroyed or damaged by the fighting in the areas of Tetovo and Skopska Crna Gora.

government, an equitable representation for ethnic Albanians in the Macedonian state structures, and the recognition of the Albanian language and culture. Additional economic and financial incentives were necessary to persuade the former rivals to stick to their commitments. In October 2001, for example, the Commission adopted a decision to finance a Confidence Building Programme for the FYROM, including the use of funds of the RRM. This package worth €10.3 million was inextricably linked to the full ratification of all the amendments to the Macedonian Constitution, as well as a new law on local government, as requested in the Ohrid Framework Agreement.

As a complement to the ongoing political dialogue, the assistance programmes, and the trade and cooperation agreements, the EU recently adopted yet another technique to contribute further to a stable and secure environment in the FYROM. On 31 March 2003 the EU launched its inaugural military operation 'Concordia', officially at the request of the Macedonian authorities in order to ensure the follow-up from NATO's operation 'Allied Harmony'.[25] The European Union had hoped to already take over from NATO in Macedonia when the mandate of the alliance's operation 'Amber Fox' came to an end in December 2002. However, the EU-led operation could not go ahead until an agreement was reached with Turkey, within NATO, on EU access to NATO assets (the so-called 'Berlin Plus' arrangements). The negotiations between the EU and Turkey were deadlocked for months, until a breakthrough finally came on 12 December 2002, when the European Council of Copenhagen agreed that Berlin Plus arrangements and the implementation thereof would 'only apply to those EU Member States which are also either NATO members or parties to NATO's "Partnership for Peace", and which have consequently concluded bilateral security agreements with NATO'.[26] This formulation, which effectively excludes Cyprus (and Malta) from taking part in EU military operations using NATO assets, was sufficient to overcome Turkish objections and to secure access to NATO assets.[27] At the same summit, the European Council confirmed the Union's readiness to take over the military operation in the FYROM based on UN Security Council Resolution 1371. The Union's wish eventually became a reality at the end of March 2003. At the time of writing, a total of 27 countries (13 EU Member States[28] and 14 non-

---

[25] Council Joint Action 2003/92/CFSP on the European Union military operation in the Former Yugoslav Republic of Macedonia, *OJEC* [2003] L 34/26.

[26] *Bull. EU* 12-2002, points I.9.27 and I.17.

[27] The finalization of the Berlin Plus arrangements was concluded with the signing of a Security of Information Agreement between the EU and NATO on 14 March 2003. See Council Decision 2003/211/CFSP hereto, *OJEC* [2003] L 80/35. The Agreement itself is not publicly accessible.

[28] Denmark does not participate in the elaboration, implementation, and financing of decisions and actions of the EU which have defence implications. The Irish government has decided that it is unable to contribute personnel to Concordia due to the lack of *explicit* UN Security Council authorisation for the operation. Nevertheless, Ireland is contributing to the mission's joint costs and will play a full role in the Committee of Contributors.

EU countries[29]) are contributing to a force of 350 soldiers and support staff.[30] The mission carries out classical peacekeeping tasks such as patrolling Macedonia's crisis areas, mostly near the Kosovo border.[31] Initially expected to last for a period of six months, it was agreed by the Council on 29 July 2003 to extend Operation Concordia for an additional period until 15 December 2003, in line with the request made to the EU by the government of the FYROM.[32] The command and control arrangements for Operation Concordia have been drawn up in accordance with the Berlin Plus arrangements so as to create an EU chain of command which recognizes the need for coordination with NATO.[33] As a military operation, Concordia receives no funding from the Community budget and is entirely financed by the Member States (with the exception of Denmark) and participating third countries.[34]

In terms of crisis management, the European Union has – so far – fared well in the case of Macedonia. While it is true that, overall, the situation in the FYROM is relatively straightforward when compared to other Balkan conflicts, the security situation in Macedonia nevertheless remains precarious. Incidents which took place at the beginning of 2003 and that apparently were the work of ethnic Albanian extremists unhappy with the Ohrid Framework Agreement, serve as a reminder of the potential for a resurgence of ethnic violence in the country. Although Concordia is a relatively small force, its deployment will prove an important test for both the Union's military crisis management capabilities and the Berlin Plus arrangements.

2.3   EU Police Mission to Bosnia and Herzegovina

On 1 January 2003, the EU launched its firstever civilian crisis management operation within the framework of the ESDP: the EU Police Mission (EUPM) in

---

[29] Bulgaria, Canada, the Czech Republic, Estonia, Hungary, Iceland, Latvia, Lithuania, Norway, Poland, Romania, Slovakia, Slovenia, and Turkey.

[30] The status of the EU-led forces in the FYROM is the subject of an agreement between the EU and the government of the FYROM, concluded on the basis of Article 24 TEU. See Council Decision 2003/222/CFSP, *OJEC* [2003] L 82/45, to which the so-called SOFA is annexed.

[31] Already ten weeks after the EU launched Operation Concordia, President Trajkovski of the FYROM has suggested that the force may need to be transformed into one that advises on border controls and the police. See E. Jansson, 'Macedonia Seeks Greater Role for Balkans', *Financial Times*, 9 June 2003.

[32] Council Decision 2003/202/CFSP relating to the launch of Concordia, *OJEC* [2003] L 76/43, and Council Decision 2003/563/CFSP on the extension of the EU military operation in the FYROM, *OJEC* [2003] L 190/20.

[33] For a detailed description, see C. Mace, 'European Union Security and Defence Policy Comes of Age in the Balkans', *EPC Working Papers* (2003), available at <http://www.TheEPC.be>.

[34] Joint costs totaling € 6.2 million will be funded by the Member States according to a formula based on GDP. The remaining costs will be funded by participating states on a 'costs lie where they fall' basis.

Bosnia and Herzegovina.[35] The EU thereby provided a follow-on mission to the United Nations International Police Task Force (IPTF). The aim of EUPM, which has an expected duration of two years, is to consolidate the achievements of the IPTF and the international community's work to establish sustainable policing arrangements under Bosnian ownership in accordance with best European and international standards.[36] This overall goal is to be achieved in particular through monitoring, mentoring, and inspecting BiH police at the appropriate level, as well as through training and technical support.[37] Understandably, EUPM does not have a mandate to enact legislation nor to enforce the law in Bosnia and Herzegovina. To possess either would be to undermine the principle of an independent, non-politicized police service that the international community is seeking to instill seven years after the war.

A total of 33 countries (the 15 EU Member States and 18 third countries[38]) are contributing to a force of 508 police officers and support staff. In accordance with the Nice Treaty, the Political and Security Committee (PSC, most commonly referred to by its French acronym COPS) is tasked to exercise political control and strategic direction of the mission. The EUPM Commissioner is in operational control of the mission, reporting to the SG/HR through the EU Special Representative (EUSR) in Bosnia.[39] In order to support the domestic police forces in their work, EUPM has co-located over 400 of its officers with BiH officers at medium and senior levels in all the police forces of BiH, i.e., in the police forces of the two entities which make up BiH, the Federation (FBiH) and Republika Srpska (RS), and the independently administered Brcko District.[40] It is the officers' joint task to implement EUPM's seven core programmes in crime

---

[35] Before that, the EU had already conducted civilian crisis management missions in cooperation with both the WEU (police cooperation in Albania (MAPE) and the administration of the city of Mostar) and the UN (the EU is still leading one of the pillars of UNMIK and is engaged in reconstruction efforts as well as institution-building, support to local administration and civil society). EUPM is the first operation for which the EU alone assumes leadership and responsibility.

[36] Council Joint Action 2002/210/CFSP on the EUPM, *OJEC* [2002] L 70/1.

[37] The total cost of EUPM amounts to € 38 million per year. Member States are funding € 18 million through staff secondment. The remaining € 20 million in operational costs is financed through the Community budget. In order to secure the necessary funding for EUPM, the European Parliament approved an increase of € 47.5 million in the CFSP budget for 2003-5. At the same time the EP, Council, and Commission agreed a declaration on the financing of CFSP, which states that if the Council foresees a joint action that will require an increase in the CFSP budget during the current financial year, the Council will enter into dialogue with the EP on the matter without delay.

[38] In addition to the third countries also involved in Operation Concordia, Cyprus, Russia, Switzerland, and the Ukraine have contributed police officers to EUPM.

[39] Paddy Ashdown, who is currently the international community's High Representative to BiH, was named EUSR to BiH in March 2002. It was hoped that this 'double hatting' would facilitate the coordination of the rule of law reform programmes.

[40] The present structure of the State of Bosnia and Herzegovina was established under the General Framework Agreement for Peace, initialled in Dayton on 21 November 1995 and signed in Paris on 14 December 1995, 35 *ILM* (1996), p. 75.

policing, criminal justice, internal affairs, police administration, and public or-der.[41] Each programme is implemented through a number of concrete projects, such as the Major and Organized Crime project and the Fight and Intervention against Human Trafficking project. In the field of internal affairs, one of EUPM's main tasks is to encourage the domestic authorities to deal with cases of non-compliance such as obstruction of EUPM, failure to adhere to the terms of the Dayton Agreement, or failure to uphold democratic policing principles. Only if the local authorities are seen to be failing in their duty to properly apply the disci-plinary procedures will the matter be taken up by EUPM. In the last instance, the EUPM Commissioner can recommend the removal of non-compliant officers to the SG/HR. Any officer so removed would be barred from any future service in the police.[42]

It is difficult to objectively assess how successful EUPM has been in the per-formance of its tasks in the first eight months since its inception. On the basis of official press releases it seems that EUPM is 'learning by doing'.[43] It has in-creased border security after the assassination of the Serbian Prime Minister Djindjic, it has raided night clubs after reports of human trafficking, and it has increased surveillance after indications of smuggling activities via the beaches at Neum. Eight months down the road, the time has come for EUPM to move be-yond responding to violent incidents after they have occurred and to formulate a security doctrine which will enable it to prevent the eruption of renewed violence. It is clear that a stable and secure environment in Bosnia and Herzegovina, under-pinned by a military presence, is an essential element for the success of EUPM. As long as the EU remains dependent on the military presence of NATO/SFOR to secure this environment, close consultation between EUPM and, *inter alia*, SFOR will be imperative to establish the rule of law in Bosnia and Herzegovina.[44] Continued dialogue between the EU and non-governmental orga-

---

[41] On the activities of the EUPM in BiH, see the Agreement of 4 October 2002 between the EU and BiH, annexed to Council Decision 2002/845/CFSP, *OJEC* [2002] L 293/1. In coordination with the HR/EUSR, international organizations in BiH, as well as with senior BiH police authorities, EUPM's Police Head of Mission, Commissioner Sven Christian Frederiksen, has set two priorities for the EU mission, namely combating organized crime and guaranteeing the safe return of refugees and internally displaced persons, particularly those who return to an area where the ethnic group to which they belong is in the minority. It has been acknowledged that EUPM's priorities will develop and adapt over the course of the mission.

[42] C. Mace, op.cit. n. 33.

[43] See also A. Nowak, 'L'Union en action: la mission de police en Bosnie', Occasional Papers (Paris, ISS 2003), available at <http://www.iss-eu.org>.

[44] To this end, Council Joint Action 2003/188/CFSP amending Joint Action 2002/210/CFSP, *OJEC* [2003] L 73/9 was adopted to amend the original mandate of EUPM to give the SG/HR the authorization to release classified information and documents up to the level 'CONFIDENTIEL UE' to NATO/SFOR, to the host state, and to the third parties associated with the EU Joint Action, and up to the level 'RESTREINT UE' to the Office of the High Representative, to the UN, and to the OSCE.

nizations is also vital if the ESDP is to be a force for the protection and enforcement of human rights and fundamental freedoms.

2.4 Future developments

At the Copenhagen European Council in December 2002, the EU stated its willingness to follow on from a strong NATO-led military operation in Bosnia and Herzegovina by the middle of 2004. This ambition was restated by President Chirac and Prime Minister Blair at the Franco-British summit in Le Toucquet in February 2003. SFOR, which operates under a United Nations mandate, was set up in Bosnia in 1996 following the Dayton Accords that ended the civil war in the republic. It has a mandate to provide security and stability as well as to capture alleged war criminals and transfer them to the International Criminal Tribunal for the former Yugoslavia (ICTY) in The Hague. SFOR consists of 13,000 troops (reduced from 40,000 seven years ago and from 19,000 in January 2003 as part of a restructuring exercise), with European states contributing the majority of the force and the US providing 1,500. Yet, leading an operation of this size would certainly represent a major task for the EU. The United States had initially given a cautious welcome to the Union's proposal, emphasizing the need for a successful initial military operation in Macedonia before any takeover from SFOR could be considered. At the beginning of June 2003, however, the US put the brakes on the EU's plans to take over the large NATO-led mission, citing security reasons, the complexity of the mission, and continuing problems with the transfer of war criminals to the ICTY. It seems that high-level EU diplomats may still need to be persuaded that, by postponing the take-over by the EU of NATO's mission, the US is rendering the Union a favour and not bidding to thwart their efforts at giving its ESDP real visibility – which the mission in Bosnia certainly would provide.[45] Discontentment over the spat between the US and a divided Europe over the latest war in Iraq has certainly fuelled the Union's eagerness to prove its military capabilities by taking over some of the tasks performed by NATO and the UN, especially in the nearby Western Balkans. Yet, as most of the

---

[45] See J. Dempsey, 'A Case of Overloaded Agendas', *Financial Times*, 3 June 2003, in which the author points to the overloaded agenda from which the EU is currently suffering: it is, *inter alia*, going through the most ambitious enlargement process in the history of European integration; it is involved in one of its most intense treaty amendment debates; it is working on its own 'security doctrine'; it is faced with a new dilemma on whether the EU defence structures should or should not rely on NATO; and increasingly, the EU is being asked to 'intervene' in places throughout the world. From 12 June until 1 September 2003, the EU dispatched French peacekeeping troops, under UN Security Council Resolution 1484, on a high-risk mission to the Democratic Republic of Congo (Operation Artemis; see Council Joint Action 2003/423/CFSP, *OJEC* [2003] L 143/50; and Council Decision 2003/432/CFSP, *OJEC* [2003] L 147/42). In July, it was asked by the OSCE to send peacekeeping forces to Transdniestria (where pro-Russian nationalists have attempted to break away from Moldova), concerning which it has already held exploratory talks with NATO. See S. Spiteri, 'EU ponders peace-keeping mission to Moldova', *euobserver.com*, 15 July 2003.

region increasingly sheds its dependency on large international military forces (13,000 NATO-led troops in Bosnia, up to 25,000 in Kosovo, and a few hundred in Macedonia) and slowly moves to state- and institution-building, the need is growing to have professionally trained police forces capable of providing security. Military missions can neither be open-ended nor carried out in isolation of building civilian structures, such as the police, otherwise they become self-defeating exercises. In Bosnia, security has been provided by the military since the 1995 Dayton Accords that ended the civil war, and in Kosovo since the end of the 1999 NATO bombing campaign against Serbia. With plans to further reduce the number of troops in Bosnia to around 8,000 by the end of 2003, the desire to do the same in Kosovo, and the time to shift the emphasis in Macedonia away from military peace-keeping, we are bound to witness a reinforced role for the European Union in police reform, in particular integrating the police forces, improving training, and overhauling the judiciary and penal systems.

Maintaining the 'negative peace' (absence of hostilities) is a necessary condition for establishing and maintaining a 'positive peace' in Bosnia, Kosovo, and Macedonia; it does not, on its own, deal with the underlying causes and conditions of the symptoms of violent conflict in the whole of the Western Balkan region. To fill the relative 'Hobbesian void' in South Eastern Europe with conflict controlling and resolving mechanisms, the European Union has, for some years now, engaged in longer-term conflict prevention, for which it is far better equipped: long-term conflict prevention capitalizes on the EU's greatest asset, i.e., the promise of association and future membership.[46]

3. THE UNION'S LONG-TERM APPROACH TO THE WESTERN BALKANS

3.1 Important part of a wider international effort to project stability in the region

The dreadful consequences of the Yugoslav crises necessitated a comprehensive and encompassing approach to deal with the plethora of issues in South Eastern Europe. The international community's approach towards the region was unveiled as the 'Process for stability and good neighbourliness in South Eastern Europe'. It was inaugurated at the Royaumont summit of 13 December 1995 and brought together the ministers of foreign affairs of the EU Member States, repre-

---

[46] The short-term interests of EU involvement in the Western Balkans are obvious. The EU does not want instability that leads to hundreds of thousands of refugees fleeing to EU countries as happened during the three Balkan wars of the 1990s. Neither does the EU want the exportation of other problems, such as organized crime, with which the societies of the Western Balkans are faced. The long-term interests of the Union are about creating a belt of security, stability, and prosperity, stretching from Albania in the west to Turkey in the east, thereby unlocking geographically-isolated Greece. That stability could be anchored on EU membership.

sentatives of former Yugoslav countries (BiH, Croatia, the Federal Republic of Yugoslavia (FRY, now Serbia and Montenegro) and the FYROM), representatives of neighbouring countries in the region, including Albania, delegations from the US and Russia, as well as representatives of NATO, OSCE, and the Council of Europe.[47] The Kosovo crisis of 1999 showed the shortcomings of the Royaumont Process in addressing the complex and volatile situation in the Western Balkans and triggered a response by the international community. At the Cologne European Council of 10 June 1999, the day that NATO's 78-day bombing campaign of Serbia ceased, the instigators of the Royaumont Process adopted an inclusive regional approach in the form of the 'Stability Pact for South Eastern Europe'.[48] The Stability Pact is aimed at supporting the implementation of the Dayton Agreements, facilitating political stability and economic prosperity, improving coordination, and, as a result of this, the efficiency of the instruments of all of the actors in the region.[49] The Pact represents an ambitious attempt to deal with the Western Balkans on a *regional* basis, recognizing that all political units and conflicts in the region are interconnected components of a larger whole: to deal effectively with any one unit or conflict means that, ultimately, the others have to be dealt with as well, if not simultaneously, then certainly in sequence. Although the aim of the Pact was never to put the Yugoslav jigsaw back together, betting on the results of a regional approach for the Western Balkans was extremely risky at the time of its adoption. For no sooner had each breakaway Yugoslav Republic become independent – in essence given *itself* a new identity – that it needed to integrate again on a regional basis and eventually become a member of a new larger entity. Indeed, one of the purposes of the Stability Pact is to move all five states of the Western Balkans forward on their way to the European Union.[50] Hence, the Stability Pact was rather pompously compared to a combination of the Marshall Plan that facilitated the rebuilding of Western Europe following the end of WW II, and the European integration process, which civilized relations between all of the former adversaries of that war, notably

---

[47] *Bull. EU* 1/2-1996, point 1.4.108.

[48] *Bull. EU* 6-1999, point I.26.71.

[49] See L. Friis and A. Murphy, '"Turbo-charged negotiations": The EU and the Stability Pact for South Eastern Europe', 7 *Journal of European Public Policy* (2000), pp. 767-786; M. Cremona, 'Creating the New Europe: the Stability Pact for South Eastern Europe in the Context of EU-SEE Relations', in A. Dashwood and A. Ward (eds.), *The Cambridge Yearbook of European Legal Studies – Volume 2, 1999*, (Oxford, Hart Publishing 2000), pp. 463-506; D. Papadimitriou, 'The EU's Strategy in the Post-Communist Balkans', 3 *Journal of Southeast European and Black Sea Studies* (2001), pp. 69-94; F. Cameron and A. Kintis, 'Southeastern Europe and the European Union', 2 *Journal of Southeast European and Black Sea Studies* (2001), pp. 94-112; and P. Jurkovic (ed.), *The Stability Pact for South East Europe – Dawn of an Era of Regional Co-operation* (Vienna, National Defence Academy 2002).

[50] See P. Pantev, 'Security Risks and Instabilities in Southeastern Europe', in W. van Meurs (ed.), *Beyond EU Enlargement, Volume 2: The Agenda of Stabilisation for Southeastern Europe* (Gütersloh, Bertelsmann Foundation Publishers 2001), pp. 118-138.

France and Germany.[51] In spite of the fact that the Stability Pact has created expectations that, in view of the available resources, it cannot hope to meet, it nevertheless remains one of the most enigmatic political inventions for South Eastern Europe in the last century.[52]

As part of the negotiations leading to the adoption of the Stability Pact, the EU leaders agreed that the European Union would build on its existing set of policies towards the Western Balkans by implementing a so-called 'Stabilisation and Association Process' (SAP) for those countries in South Eastern Europe that had not yet signed an association agreement with the EU, namely Albania, Bosnia and Herzegovina, Croatia, the FRY, and the FYROM.[53] Here, the Commission argued that the conclusion of so-called Stabilisation and Association Agreements (SAAs) would provide an appropriate alternative to the Europe Agreements (EAs), which are regarded as leading to EU membership, and the Partnership and Cooperation Agreements (PCAs), which have been concluded with almost all the successor states to the Soviet Union and have far less ambitious goals.[54] To a large extent, the SAP indeed follows the 'evolutionary' approach taken towards the integration of the twelve countries from Central and Eastern Europe, and Turkey. Based on political and economic conditions corresponding to the values and models underpinning the Copenhagen criteria as laid down in Articles 49 and 6 of the EU Treaty,[55] and adapted to the situation of each country,[56] the emphasis of

---

[51] For an exploratory assessment of the effectiveness of the Stability Pact to serve as a conflict prevention or, as the case may be, a management regime, see D. Sandole, 'The Balkans Stability Pact as a Regional Conflict Management and Prevention "Space": An Evaluation', in P. Jurkovic (ed.), op. cit. n. 49, pp. 20-36. On the basis of his 'three pillar comprehensive "mapping" of conflict and conflict resolution' framework methodology, Sandole draws the conclusion that, being a mere three years old, the Stability Pact has offered a great deal in terms of peacemaking through governmental and IGO diplomacy, advocacy, and funding activity, but not too much in terms of reconciliation through professional conflict resolution, commerce, and citizen-to-citizen interaction.

[52] See W. van Meurs, 'The Stability Pact Beyond EU Enlargement', in D. Lopandic (ed.), *Regional Cooperation in South Eastern Europe – Conference Proceedings* (Belgrade, European Movement in Serbia 2002), pp. 39-45.

[53] European Commission, *The Stabilisation and Association Process for Countries of South-Eastern Europe*, COM (1999) 235 final, Brussels, 26 May 1999.

[54] On EAs, see M. Maresceau (ed.), *Enlarging the European Union: Relations between the EU and Central and Eastern Europe* (London, Longman 1997). On PCAs, see C. Hillion, 'Institutional Aspects of New Partnership between the European Union and the Newly Independent States of the Former Soviet Union: Case Studies of Russia and the Ukraine', 37 *CML Rev.* (2000), pp. 1211-1235.

[55] *Bull. EU* 6-1993, at 13: stability of institutions guaranteeing democracy, the rule of law, human rights, and the respect for and protection of minorities; the existence of a functioning market economy; the capacity to cope with competitive pressure and market forces within the Union; and the ability to take on the obligations of membership, including adherence to the aims of political, economic, and monetary union.

[56] *Bull. EU* 4-1997, point 2.2.1. The conditions include respect for democratic principles, human rights, and the rule of law; protection of minorities; return of refugees; the implementation of the Dayton Agreements, including full cooperation with the ICTY; market economy reforms; and regional cooperation.

the SAP is placed on differentiation according to the specific needs and situations of each country as well as on improvements in the relations within the entire region. The application of conditionality has to be seen as a progressive process, the start of the SAA negotiations requiring 'a lower level of compliance than the conclusion of the agreements'.[57] Although anchored to a common set of political and economic conditions, the approach of the SAP is thus flexible enough to allow each country to move ahead at its own pace.[58] Ultimately, the SAP is designed as the framework for preparation for the full integration of the Western Balkan states into the EU. The explicit offer of future EU membership for these countries was first made by the Feira European Council of 19-20 June 2000.[59] The 24 November 2000 Zagreb Summit of heads of state and government of EU Member States and SAP countries set the seal on the SAP by gaining the region's agreement to the above-mentioned set of objectives and conditions.[60] At the 21 June 2003 EU-Western Balkans Summit in Thessaloniki, it was acknowledged that the SAP will remain the framework for the European course of the Western Balkan countries, 'all the way to their future accession'.[61] Indeed, the SAP and the prospects it offers serve as the anchor for reform in the Western Balkans, in the same way as the accession process has done in Central and Eastern Europe. In the light of the latter, the European Council endorsed 'The Thessaloniki Agenda for the Western Balkans: Moving Towards European Integration' to further strengthen and enhance the political visibility of the SAP by, *inter alia*, launching the high-level multilateral EU-Western Balkans Forum, European Integration Partnerships, as well as the decisions for enhanced cooperation in the areas of political dialogue and the Common Foreign and Security Policy, parliamentary cooperation, support for institution-building, and the opening of Community programmes.[62] The European Integration Partnerships are no doubt the most important 'enrichment' of the SAP and are clearly inspired by the pre-accession process.[63] It is the Commission's intention to tailor them to each Western Balkan

---

[57] E. Lannon, K. Inglis, and T. Haenebalcke, 'The Many Faces of EU Conditionality in Pan-Euro-Mediterranean Relations', in M. Maresceau and E. Lannon (eds.), *The EU's Enlargement and Mediterranean Strategies – A Comparative Analysis* (Basingstoke, Palgrave 2001), pp. 97-138.

[58] An annual review mechanism assesses each country's performance in meeting the conditions. The recommendations contained in the Commission's – 'progress' – reports, as well as the Council's annual assessment are intended to help the SAP countries focus their attention for the year ahead on specific priority areas.

[59] *Bull. EU* 6-2000, point I.49.67.

[60] *Bull. EU* 11-2000, point I.6.57. For the full text of the declaration of the Zagreb Summit, see <http://europa.eu.int/comm/external_relations/see/sum_11_00/statement.htm>.

[61] For the full text of the declaration of the EU-Western Balkans Summit at Thessaloniki, see <http://www.eu2003.gr/en/articles/2003/6/23/3135/print.asp>.

[62] For the text of the Thessaloniki Agenda, see Annex A to the GAERC Conclusions of 16 June 2003, Press Release No. 10369/03 (Presse 166).

[63] See European Commission, *The Western Balkans and European Integration*, COM (2003) 285 final, Brussels, 21 May 2003.

country's needs, identifying, on a regular basis, priorities and obligations to be fulfilled. Each country will then be expected to draw up an action plan for the implementation of the partnerships. Essentially, the partnerships will reflect the particular stage of development of each country and will serve as a timetable and checklist against which to measure progress, and to provide guidance for Community and Member State financial assistance.

On the basis of the foregoing, one cannot help but noting that the Stability Pact stresses a regional approach and multilateralism, whereas the SAP, and the SAAs and the future partnerships in particular, are based on conditionality and bilateralism.[64] This structural tension between the principles of regionalism and conditionality may endanger the coherence of the international approach towards a region still known to many as a powder-keg. For, the best pupils of the class will – in line with the conditionality of EU (pre-)accession – 'leave' the region by acquiring a different contractual status in their relations with the Union, thereby increasing rather than reducing the disparities within the region.[65] While official EU documents have always shunned a prioritization between the Stability Pact and the SAP, it is clear that, in practice, the SAAs (as part of the SAP) are seen, both by the countries in the region and the international community, as the most important instruments to achieve a lasting solution to the current problems in the Western Balkan countries, because they offer the prospect of European integration. Thus, priority is given to conditionality where appropriate and to regionalism where possible.

3.2 Stabilisation and Association Agreements

3.2.1 *A distinct type of association agreement*

Article 310 TEC, which has seen a revival over the last fifteen years with the establishment of the European Economic Area in 1994 and the conclusion of Europe Agreements with the countries from Central and Eastern Europe, has provided the legal basis for the SAAs which the EU is offering to countries in the Western Balkans.[66] Content-wise, the SAAs are also based on the existing EAs, even if they include new elements respecting the specific situation of the Western Balkan countries.[67] Nonetheless, the Commission was keen to differentiate be-

---

[64] Even though regional cooperation is one of the formal conditions in the bilateral relationships between each of the five Balkan countries and the EU, it is difficult to assess and enforce as a condition.

[65] W. van Meurs, op. cit. n. 52, at 41.

[66] See D. Phinnemore, *Association: Stepping-Stone or Alternative to EU Membership?* (Sheffield, Sheffield Academic Press 1999).

[67] This was to be expected given the short period of time that the Commission had to develop the SAAs. In crisis situations, the EU traditionally acts conservatively and instinctively falls back on an existing policy approach, even where this is no longer appropriate (so-called 'path dependency

tween this 'new type of contract' and the EA.[68] As Phinnemore explains, the reasons were essentially twofold. First, the challenges in the Western Balkans went beyond those concerning economic and political transition which had been posed by the Central and Eastern European countries over the last decade. Therefore, a new and dedicated type of relationship responding to the particular needs of the Western Balkans was deemed necessary. Second, by the spring of 1999 the EU was making headway towards realizing its most ambitious enlargement to date. The prospect of up to 12 new entrants over the next few years was unprecedented. Added to this was the question of admitting Turkey into the accession process. Faced with such an overwhelming enlargement agenda, there was little enthusiasm for widening it further by offering EAs to the countries of the Western Balkans, thereby raising expectations of pre-accession aid and encouraging membership applications. Mindful of this and anxious to cause concern among the candidate countries about their position in the enlargement process, the EU had to avoid any formulation which might raise objections and potentially undermine reform efforts in those countries. This was recognized in the title of the SAAs: their purpose was not just association but, in the short-term at least, stabilization.[69]

Before negotiations for the conclusion of an SAA can start, a certain level of progress must be made. The Commission observes and evaluates the situation in the country, in particular the fulfilment of key conditions, such as the presence of functioning democratic structures, respect for human rights, fundamental freedoms and the rule of law, as well as the cooperation with neighbouring countries. Observation and evaluation are based on reports of international organizations, committees, or institutions which are active in the region, such as NATO, the OSCE, and the Council of Europe. The results are published in so-called 'feasibility reports'. On the basis of a positive evaluation of the political stability and progress on reforms, negotiations on an SAA with Albania were opened by the Commission on 31 January 2003. The substantial completion of the so-called 'road-map' for Bosnia and the establishment of the first elected government for a four-year term were rewarded by the Commission with the launching of a feasibility study in June 2003. Nevertheless, in its second annual review of the SAP, the Commission demanded further political and economic reform and progress towards making the country a self-sustaining state based on the rule of law before negotiations on the SAA would be considered.[70] Problems surrounding the en-

---

behaviour'). See J. Peterson, 'The European Union as a Global Actor', in J. Peterson and H. Sjursen (eds.), *A Common Foreign Policy for Europe?* (London, Routledge 1998), pp. 3-17.

[68] COM (1999) 235 final, Brussels, 26 May 1999.

[69] Analysis of the two SAAs shows considerable similarities with the earlier EAs. See D. Phinnemore, 'Stabilisation and Association Agreements: Europe Agreements for the Western Balkans?', 8 *EFA Rev.* (2003), pp. 77-103, at 79-81.

[70] European Commission, *The Stabilisation and Association Process for South East Europe: Second Annual Report*, COM (2003) 139 final, Brussels, 26 March 2003. According to Eric Jansson, to

dorsement of the Internal Market and Trade Action Plan by the State Assembly of Serbia and Montenegro had to be solved with a view to a rapid launching of a feasibility study for an SAA with that country. SAAs have already been signed with the FYROM (on 9 April 2001)[71] and with Croatia (on 29 October 2001).[72] SAAs, like EAs, are mixed agreements. Hence, to enter into force they require the assent of the European Parliament (Article 300(3) TEC), as well as ratification by all EU Member States and the non-Member State concerned.[73] In anticipation of the full ratification of the two existing SAAs, the trade provisions have entered into force via interim agreements and political dialogue has been established.[74]

3.2.2   General principles

Both SAAs make reference to the importance of the agreement for stability within South Eastern Europe and set out various principles to which the parties are committed.[75] These include such 'essential elements' as the respect for democratic principles and human rights, the principles of the free market economy and of free trade, the rights of persons belonging to minorities, and the constituent documents of the UN and the OSCE. Unlike the EAs, 'respect for international law principles and the rule of law' are also mentioned among the general prin-

---

people who see their country dominated, for better or worse, by foreign masters, the EU's demands ring hollow. In this NATO-occupied protectorate, locally-elected leaders are routinely overruled and sometimes sacked by international fiat. This tends to embolden EU-friendly reformers, but it also undermines popular faith in democracy. Lord Ashdown is fond of warning that in Bosnia defeat could still be 'snatched from the jaws of victory' unless the international community's commitment remains strong. His realistic view clashes seriously with the EU's newly unveiled policy of optimistic patience, for in fact Bosnia, as indeed the whole region, lags far behind the poorest EU accession states. See E. Jansson, 'Are the Balkans European?', *Financial Times*, 6 July 2003. See also D. Triantaphyllou (ed.), op. cit. n. 2.

[71] COM (2001) 90 final, Brussels, 19 February 2001.

[72] COM (2001) 371 final, Brussels, 9 July 2001.

[73] Ratification in both FYROM (12 April 2001) and Croatia (5 December 2001) followed shortly after the respective agreements were signed. The EP was also quick to give its assent to the agreements (3 May 2001 and 12 December 2001 respectively). Like mixed agreements, SAAs are open to national interpretation. While a majority of the EU Member States have ratified the SAAs, the Netherlands and the UK have so far withheld ratification of the Croatian SAA because of their negative perception of Croatia's willingness to cooperate with the ICTY. This raises the question whether individual Member States should maintain the power to introduce, unilaterally and at such a late stage, political conditionality upon SAA candidates. One would think that such action undermines the authority of the Commission to evaluate the fulfilment of the key conditions for association and that it blocks the Union's efforts to build a common policy to engage candidate associates.

[74] SAA-FYROM, *OJEC* [2001] L 124/2; and SAA-Croatia, *OJEC* [2001] L 330/3. The interim agreements entered into force on 1 June 2001 and 1 March 2002 respectively.

[75] For an analysis of the two existing SAAs, see J. Marko and J. Wilhelm, 'Stabilisation and Association Agreements', in A. Ott and K. Inglis (eds.), *Handbook on European Enlargement – A Commentary on the Enlargement Process* (The Hague, TMC Asser Press 2002), pp. 165-174.

ciples of the SAAs. In the case of Croatia, a commitment to the right of return for all refugees and compliance with the 1995 Dayton Agreements is also reaffirmed. The preamble and Article 2 of both sets of agreements describe the objectives of the associations being created: essentially, the establishment of an appropriate framework for political dialogue between the associate and the EU, the approximation of the associate's legislation to that of the EU, the development of a climate conducive to increased trade and investment, the transition of the associate's economy into a market economy, EC support for reform, and regional cooperation in all fields covered by the SAA.

Whereas regional cooperation was encouraged among the countries that signed an EA with the Union, it was never made a distinct feature of their associations. In the case of the SAAs, it is viewed as key to stabilization in the Western Balkans and made an explicit condition before the likes of Croatia and the FYROM can join the EU (Article 3). However difficult it is to enforce this additional conditionality, the importance attached to it has been underlined by the Commission which noted, in bold type, in its first annual report on the SAP: 'Integration with the EU is only possible if future members can demonstrate that they are willing and able to interact with their neighbours as EU Member States do'.[76] In Article 4, the FYROM and Croatia commit themselves to 'continue and foster cooperation and good neighbourly relations' with the other countries in the region. The SAAs explicitly refer to such relations covering the movement of people, goods, capital, and services, as well as the development of projects of common interest. In the case of the SAA with Croatia, specific examples are given: refugee return and combating organized crime, corruption, money laundering, illegal migration and trafficking. To achieve regional cooperation on these issues, the FYROM and Croatia are expected to conclude conventions between each other within two years after the entry into force of the second SAA (Article 12). SAA signatories are also obliged to engage in regional cooperation with the other countries covered by the SAP (Article 13). The political dialogue, held within a multilateral framework (Articles 7 and 8), shall also contribute to the development of regional cooperation and good neighbourly relations. It seems that these provisions are codifying a proliferation process which was already underway in South Eastern Europe. Among those initiatives for multilateral cooperation in the region worth mentioning are the Central European Initiative (CEI), the Black Sea Economic Cooperation (BSEC), the Central European Free Trade Association (CEFTA), the South East Europe Cooperation Process (SEECP), the Southeast European Cooperation Initiative (SECI), and the Adriatic-Ionian Initiative (AII).[77] The greatest achievement of these initiatives is without doubt the

---

[76] European Commission, *The Stabilisation and Association Process for South East Europe: First Annual Report*, COM (2002) 163 final, Brussels, 4 April 2002, at 11.

[77] For an overview and analysis of these initiatives, see D. Lopandic, *Regional Initiatives in South Eastern Europe* (Belgrade, European Movement in Serbia 2001).

sustainable political dialogue between the countries involved in these frame-works. But with partly overlapping memberships and agendas indicating a lack of complementarity, competitiveness is growing among them. Many regional initia-tives have been criticized because of the modesty of their objectives and the lim-ited concrete results they have yielded. Moreover, most of them only address the immediate post-conflict situation, and all but the SEECP have been created as a consequence of external incentives by resuscitating and broadening existing ini-tiatives. It seems that, in the search for the most appropriate regional initiative, valuable resources are being wasted.[78]

The approximation of the associate's legislation to that of the EU is another important aspect of the SAAs as far as the perspective of future integration is concerned. The existing SAAs define the rules of the internal market as priorities for legislative approximation by the associates. The focus on internal market law bears a risk of an unbalanced situation in the approximation process, leaving be-hind other essential areas such as social or environmental policy. Yet, it is a criti-cal component within the SAA, essentially extending the EU's own philosophy to the Western Balkans that the adoption of the hard core of economic standards based on a free market economy is a route to national as well as regional peace, stability, and growth and that such integration serves the mutual interests of all countries concerned.

The SAA with Croatia declares that this legislative approximation process shall be fully implemented within six years, starting from the date of signature (Articles 5 and 69). In the case of the FYROM, the approximation shall take place within a time frame of ten years divided into two successive stages (Ar-ticles 5 and 68). In the first phase of implementation of this SAA, the approxima-tion shall cover fundamental elements of the internal market *acquis* and other trade-related areas. This includes competition law, intellectual property law, stan-dards and certification law, public procurement law, and data protection law. During the second phase, the remaining elements shall be covered. The reasoning behind the shorter time frame and the absence of stages in the case of the SAA with Croatia reflects the belief among the EU Member States that Croatia is in a better position, both economically and politically, to meet its obligations under the SAA.

3.2.3   'Potential' membership

In contrast to the preambular reference to accession in the Europe Agreements, the preambles of the SAAs recall not simply the EU's readiness to integrate the FYROM and Croatia 'to the fullest possible extent' into the 'political and eco-nomic mainstream of Europe', but also the status of the two associates as 'poten-

---

[78] See J. Minic, 'Summary and Recommendations of the Conference', in D. Lopandic (ed.), op. cit. n. 52, pp. 9-17.

tial' candidates for European Union membership. The membership perspective is set out in the final recital of the preamble to the two existing SAAs:

'[the contracting parties recall] the European Union's readiness to integrate to the fullest possible extent the [associate] into the political and economic mainstream of Europe and its status as a potential candidate for EU membership on the basis of the Treaty on European Union and fulfilment of the criteria defined by the European Council in June 1993, subject to successful implementation of this Agreement, notably regarding regional cooperation'.

From the wording of the recital as well as its *travaux préparatoires* it becomes clear that the inclusion of the membership perspective came against a background of reticence towards any firm commitment to admit the SAA countries into the EU at a future date.[79] This is very apparent in the Commission's May 1999 communication on the SAP which made no mention of membership at all, referring instead to the SAAs 'draw[ing] the [Western Balkan] region closer to the perspective of full integration into EU structures'.[80] One month later, the Cologne European Council agreed to a similar wording but acknowledged that this would be done 'with a prospect of European Union membership on the basis of the Amsterdam Treaty and fulfilment of the criteria defined at the Copenhagen European Council in June 1993'.[81] In the course of drawing up the SAAs, the EU watered down the strength of the commitment.[82] The actual wording of the recital followed declarations which were made at the June 2000 Feira European Council and at the Zagreb summit of EU leaders and their counterparts from South Eastern Europe in November 2000 that the Western Balkan countries are 'potential candidates' for EU membership.[83] Although this notion has no official definition and does not confer on the holder a legally enforceable right to membership, politically speaking, the term 'potential candidate' recognizes the Union's willingness to see membership ambitions of the status holder realized in the future. In the words of Friis and Murphy:

'this promise, however vague and conditional, cannot be withdrawn (...). [I]t will force the Union to increase its level of engagement with the region and to advance the ongoing enlargement process (...). [The] genie is now out of the bottle'.[84]

---

[79] D. Phinnemore, op. cit. n. 69, at 98 with reference to R. Biermann, 'Die Europäische Perspektive für den westlichen Balkan', 51 *Osteuropa* (2001), pp. 922-937, at 926-927.

[80] COM (1999) 235 final, Brussels, 26 May 1999, at 4.

[81] *Bull. EU* 6-1999, point I.26.72.

[82] See R. Biermann, 'The Stability Pact for South Eastern Europe – Potential, Problems and Perspectives', C56 *ZEI Discussion Papers* (1999), at 15-19.

[83] *Bull. EU* 6-2000, point I.49.67; and *Bull. EU* 11-2000, point I.6.57.

[84] L. Friis and A. Murphy, 'Enlargement of the European Union: Impacts on the EU, the Candidates and the 'Next Neighbours', 14 *ECSA Rev.* (2001), cited in D. Phinnemore, op. cit. n. 69, at 102.

However half-hearted the Member States' commitment to enlarge 'their' Union with the countries of the Western Balkan region may at first have seemed, the repeated confirmation of it has provided the governments of these states with a justification for difficult political and economic reforms and a means to rally support for tough decisions at home. Croatia's recent bid for membership,[85] the expectation that Macedonia will submit its application in the nearby future,[86] the eagerness of Prime Minister Terzic to guide Bosnia into the EU by 2009,[87] and the increasingly louder calls in Belgrade and Podgorica for a peaceful separation of Serbia and Montenegro to speed up the process of European integration[88] all attest to the fact that, indeed, the only worthwhile 'carrot' the EU could offer Western Balkan countries in exchange for concerted efforts to promote peace and stability in the region was the prospect of membership.[89]

3.3   Financial and technical assistance

As an overarching, multi-country strategy, the SAP not only commits political but also financial and technical support by the Union towards the five countries of the Western Balkans. The CARDS (Community Assistance for Reconstruction, Development and Stabilisation) programme is the Community's funding instrument dedicated to the region of South Eastern Europe and supports the

---

[85] On 20 February 2003, President Mesic and Prime Minister Racan presented the application of Croatia for accession to the European Union. See doc. 6991/03 ELARG 19 COWEB 28. Despite initial objections by the Netherlands and the UK (for reasons mentioned *supra*, note 73) to ask the Commission for its opinion on the fulfilment of the membership conditions (according to the Dutch and the British, Article 49 TEU also grants full discretion to the Council itself to evaluate these conditions) the GAERC eventually decided to implement the Article 49 procedure in line with previous practice. On 14 April 2003, it invited the Commission to elaborate its opinion (see Press Release No. 8220/03 (Presse 105), at 12). The Commission may take a year or so to do so. It has handed over to the Croatian authorities a 'questionnaire' with over 2,500 questions on the political, economic, and administrative situation in the country. The answers, which are expected to be returned to the Commission in October, will form the basis for the Commission's opinion on the starting of accession negotiations. In any case, time will be very short for Croatia to catch up with Bulgaria and Romania and to conclude such negotiations by 2006 for accession in 2007.

[86] See H. Swoboda, 'Recommendation on the proposal for a Council and Commission decision on the conclusion of the Stabilisation and Association Agreements between the European Communities and the Member States, of the one part, and the Former Yugoslav Republic of Macedonia, of the other part', *European Parliament Session Document*, A5-0132 final, Brussels, 25 April 2001, point 8.

[87] *NRC Handelsblad*, 2 May 2003.

[88] P. Michielsen, 'Montenegro en Servië: hoe gaan we uiteen?', *NRC Handelsblad*, 5 August 2003.

[89] D. Phinnemore, op. cit. n. 69, at 98, with reference to L. Friis and A. Murphy, op. cit. n. 49, at 779-780.

actions undertaken within the SAP and under the SAAs.[90] Under the CARDS programme for the period 2000 to 2006, a budget of €4.65 billion has been agreed upon.[91] To achieve its objective of facilitating the SAP, CARDS assistance finances investment, institution-building, and other programmes in four major areas: (i) reconstruction, democratic stabilisation, reconciliation, and the return of refugees; (ii) institutional and legislative development, including approximation of domestic legislation with EU norms to underpin democracy and the rule of law, human rights, civil society and the media, as well as the operation of a free market economy; (iii) sustainable economic and social development, including structural reform; and (iv) the promotion of closer relations and regional cooperation among SAP countries and between them, the EU, and the new acceding Member States and candidate countries of Central and Eastern Europe.

In a Regional and five Country Strategy Papers (RSP and CSPs respectively) the Union has set its priorities for the implementation of the SAP and the legally binding bilateral agreement between the EU and each associate. The Commission has identified the RSP and CSPs as key tools to integrate conflict prevention in the programming of its development cooperation.[92] As such, they are complements to the political dialogue backed up by annual reviews of the SAP. When drafting the political analysis section of the CSPs, or as the case may be RSP, risk factors are systematically checked. For that purpose, the Commission is using the indicators developed in the so-called 'check-list for root causes of conflict'.[93] This check-list looks at issues such as the balance of political and economic power, the control of the security forces, the ethnic composition of the government for ethnically-divided countries, the human rights situation, the level of organized crime, the potential degradation of environmental resources, the level of corruption, and so forth. On the basis of this conflict analysis, attention is then drawn to conflict prevention focused activities that external aid should target.

The RSP was adopted by the Commission in October 2001 and provides a strategic framework for programming the regional envelope of the CARDS programme in the period 2002-2006.[94] Some 10% of the available CARDS budget will be directed towards raising the levels of regional cooperation between the countries of the Western Balkans. As mentioned earlier, addressing this issue is a

---

[90] Council Regulation (EC) No. 2666/2000 on assistance for Albania, Bosnia and Herzegovina, Croatia, the Federal Republic of Yugoslavia, and the Former Yugoslav Republic of Macedonia, *OJEC* [2000] L 306/1. On CARDS, see European Commission, *CARDS Assistance Programme to the Western Balkans: Regional Strategy Paper 2002-2006*, Brussels, 22 October 2001.

[91] Annex B to the first annual review of the SAP, COM (2002) 163 final, Brussels, 4 April 2002, at 23. In the 1990's, the EU's political, trade, and financial relations with the region focused on crisis management and reconstruction, reflecting the countries' emergency needs at that time. The Community's assistance programmes to these countries were substantial, totaling some € 5.5 billion.

[92] COM (1999) 235 final, Brussels, 26 May 1999.

[93] Available at <http://europa.eu.int/comm/external_relations/cpcm/cp/list.htm>.

[94] European Commission, *CARDS Regional Strategy Paper*, Brussels, 22 October 2001, IP/01/1464.

key goal within the SAP. In terms of conflict prevention, the RSP has earmarked funds for support in four priority areas: (i) integrated border management to help tackle cross-border crime, to facilitate trade across borders, and to stabilize the border regions themselves; (ii) institutional capacity building to help raise awareness of EU policy and laws that the region should increasingly be moving towards; (iii) democratic stabilisation to help cement advances on democracy and boost the involvement of civil society in the region's development; and (iv) integration of the region's transport, energy, and environmental infrastructure into the wider European networks. These areas were selected because of their contribution to regional cooperation or because the support could be best delivered at the regional level.

The CSPs provide the strategic framework in which EC assistance will be provided to each country in the period 2000-2006. Each CSP sets out cooperation objectives, policy response, and priority fields of cooperation based on a thorough assessment of the partner country's policy agenda and political and socio-economic situation. The Multi-annual Indicative Programme (MIP) attached to each CSP sets out the EU response in more detail, highlighting programme objectives, expected results, and conditionality in the priority fields of cooperation for the period 2002-2004. The malfunctioning governance, combined with organized crime, corruption, and smuggling, constitutes the most serious obstacle to a rapid improvement of the situation in most of the Western Balkan countries.[95] Within that context and taking into account the objectives of the SAP, it is notable that the EU response under the CARDS programme to the partner countries focuses on the sustainable return of refugees and displaced persons, the full integration of ethnic minorities into society, democratic stabilisation, administrative capacity building, an effective and accountable legal system, economic and social development, environment and natural resources, and justice and home affairs.[96]

3.4   Trade preferences

In addition to the significant amounts of EU aid which the countries of the Western Balkans receive, all five benefit from generous trade preferences. As part of the SAP, the Council of Ministers adopted Council Regulation (EC) No. 2007/2000, as amended by Council Regulation (EC) No. 2563/2000,[97] in order to im-

---

[95] Bosnia faces even greater challenges over the medium term, notably strengthening the State of BiH and reinforcing the administration. The CSPs for Serbia and Montenegro and the FYROM set out an approach that is designed to require the least modification possible, whatever the outcome of the final status talks.

[96] For 'facts and figures' on assistance to each of the five Western Balkan countries, see the RSP, CSPs, and MIPs available at <http://www.europa.eu.int/comm/external_relations>. See also the joint initiative of the European Commission and the World Bank in economic reconstruction and development in South East Europe, at <http://www.seerecon.org>.

[97] *OJEC* [2000] L 295/1.

prove the existing autonomous trade preferences and provide for an autonomous trade liberalization of 95% of all of the five countries' exports to the EU. Imports of all products from these countries into the EU should be admitted without quantitative restrictions or measures having equivalent effect. These arrangements are even more generous than those enjoyed by the accession and candidate countries of Central and Eastern Europe. The EU is now the region's largest trading partner, with over half of all exports going to the European market.

4. CONCLUSION

The European Union has come a long way in the Western Balkans in just a few years. Where, in the 1990s, the EU stood by and watched the Balkan wars rear their ugly heads, it was the United States, within NATO, that acted decisively to stop the Bosnian war and the conflict in Kosovo. In the aftermath of the Kosovo crisis, the Union finally found its voice to say no to violent conflict in the heart of Europe. In Macedonia, the European Union for the first time acted quickly and in a unified way to head off the plunge into inter-ethnic warfare. Since then, the Union has taken over responsibility for peacekeeping in the FYROM and for international policing in Bosnia, its firstever ESDP engagements. Thanks to its intervention, there is also peace in Serbia and Montenegro, although this loosely organized union is a protectorate rather than a state.

Despite considerable progress during the past few years, the EU needs to keep focusing on the Western Balkans. The region remains a trouble spot. It will require continued attention and support by the European Union if it is to become stable and secure. The need for further investment in conflict prevention in the Western Balkans is clear. Complicated issues need to be tackled urgently if the Union is to get a return on its investment in the region. In order to succeed, the short-term intervention actions must be underpinned by reinforced policies to address the root causes of radical discontent. Organized crime and widespread corruption need to be eradicated quickly and the sustainable return of internally displaced persons is vital for ethnic reconciliation. During the last four years, the European Union's Stabilisation and Association Process has contributed critically to progress achieved throughout the region in promoting peace and stability. The SAP is designed to encourage and support the domestic reform processes that these countries have embarked upon. It is a step-by-step reform approach based on aid, trade preferences, dialogue, technical advice, and ultimately contractual relations in the form of Stability and Association Agreements. As noted in the Commission's communication on conflict prevention, the SAAs for the Western Balkans are living examples of the possibility of EU policies contributing to tackling the root causes of conflict. SAAs have already been concluded with Macedonia and Croatia and it seems that Albania, Bosnia and Herzegovina, and

Serbia and Montenegro will soon follow suit. In the long run, the SAP offers these countries the prospect of full membership of the Union.

Regional integration remains the key to overall conflict prevention in potentially unstable regions. Nevertheless, it is clear that the European Union's regional strategy towards the Western Balkans becomes untenable with the widening differences between the countries in the region (take Croatia and Bosnia as each other's extremes). The time has come to adopt full-fledged individual country approaches, even if this creates wider differences between the five countries in the medium term. In this regard, one should welcome the fact that the SAP has recently been 'enriched' with elements from the enlargement process, so that it can better meet the new challenges as the countries move from stabilization and reconstruction to sustainable development, association, and ultimately integration into the European structures. The European Integration Partnerships could finally provide each of the five countries with a timetable and road-map towards membership. Such partnerships are necessary to measure progress and build motivation to persist with the painful reforms that are necessary to attract private domestic and direct foreign investment, help stimulate economic growth, and overcome high unemployment. The time frame will of course depend on the pace of political and economic reform in each country (the 'ownership' principle), but in view of the many unresolved issues, it seems reasonable to expect that at least another 6 to 10 years will be necessary to complete the integration process. Yet, it is important that the Union does not give the impression that membership is too distant, as this might lead to rapid domestic deterioration. Pressure and conditionality are required. The vision of full membership in itself is not enough. As part of the future partnerships, the EU should offer new forms of assistance, resources similar to that of the Marshall Plan.

It seems that the European Union is at present the only international organization capable of comprehensive action – ranging from trade, economic reform and infrastructure, humanitarian assistance, human rights and democratization, justice and the police, to crisis management and military security – to influence the political, economic, and social processes on which long-term stabilization of the Western Balkans depends. But the capacities with which history has endowed the European Union come with big responsibilities. Security risks in the Western Balkans are structural. Implementing only parts of the above-mentioned comprehensive strategy will lead to 'a false sense of mission accomplished, whereby the region would be contained by a stable physical framework within which weak states and insecurity reign supreme'.[98] The European Union is right to press the US, within NATO and the UN, for the 'Europeanisation' of security in the Western Balkans, essentially for three reasons. First, the Western Balkans is clearly an environment which very much favours an increased role for the EU in security

---

[98] See D. Triantaphyllou (ed.), op. cit. n. 2, at 66.

management. Second, the US has long supported the idea that the EU should take greater responsibility for security in Europe and increased EU-NATO coopera-tion in the Western Balkans remains in the US interest.[99] And third, by taking over SFOR's functions in Bosnia *and* Kosovo, the EU would be able to increase the horizontal coordination in the administration of its political, economic, finan-cial, and military actions in the region, thereby creating a more coherent conflict prevention strategy.

It is for these reasons that the European Union should push its full weight to resolve the conflict between Serbs and Albanians. The 'standards before status' approach with which it has so far tried to fend off claims for independence by Kosovo and Montenegro is too small a fig leaf to cover the Union's anxiety to upset the territorial and political status quo in South Eastern Europe. The union of Serbia and Montenegro was a still-born child delivered after immense pressure by Javier Solana, while Kosovo has been an international protectorate since 1999. If the Union's fundamental aim for the Western Balkans is to create a situation where military conflict is unthinkable, then it cannot expect to build a lasting peace in the region if entire societies cannot seriously exert their right to self-de-termination and consequently do not set themselves the task of state-building. The present status quo would probably not even survive the withdrawal of inter-national and European peacekeeping forces. Hence, the 'final status talks' should, sooner rather than later,[100] lead to the independence of Kosovo and the peaceful separation of Serbia and Montenegro along the lines of the 'velvet dismantle-ment' of the former Czechoslovakia. Ultimately, it is up to the UN Security Council to decide on the status of each of the constituting parts of the ex-FRY. Of course, independence should come with certain obligations, both for the Euro-pean Union and the local populations. The EU should reinforce its presence by providing a security guarantee, by working towards regional and eventual Euro-pean integration, as well as by assisting the independent elites of Kosovo, Serbia, and Montenegro to keep to their end of the bargain, i.e., state-building under the same conditions as applied to the rest of the states of the Western Balkans.

It is hoped that the European Union will seize the new momentum built up in the wake of the assassination of Serbian Prime Minister Djindjic to eliminate the root causes of conflict in the Western Balkans. Not only structural peace and sta-

---

[99] On the EU and NATO joint strategic approach for the Western Balkans, see the recently pub-lished *Framework for an Enhanced NATO-EU Dialogue and a Concerted Approach on Security and Stability in the Western Balkans*, Press Release No. 11605/03 (Presse 218), Brussels, 29 July 2003. See also C. Mace, op. cit. n. 33.

[100] An EU plan to host the first of such talks in summer 2003 between Serbian officials and Kosovo's ethnic Albanian leaders has been postponed after a new outbreak of violence in Kosovo and southern Serbia (including dozens of bombings and gun attacks against UN police, ethnic Serbs, and ethnic Albanians), following a Pristina court ruling against four senior members of the dis-banded Kosovo Liberation Army found guilty of carrying out abductions, torture, and murders. The talks may now be more than a year away. See E. Jansson, 'EU Postpones Balkan Peace Talks', *Fi-nancial Times*, 19 August 2003.

bility in the Western Balkans and Europe are at stake. The European Union itself cannot afford to fall pray to the consequences of a half-hearted policy or another 'Balkan fatigue', for the Western Balkans may offer the Union's one and only chance to develop credible and lasting foreign policy, security, and defence arrangements.

Chapter 15
STRATEGIES OF CONFLICT PREVENTION FOR
SUB-SAHARAN AFRICA

by Erik J. Eidem[1]

1. INTRODUCTION

Conflict prevention in Africa is a policy area which, over the last ten years, has been put firmly on the agenda of major international organisations, such as the UN, the World Bank, and the European Union (EU). During the same period the EU has developed policy instruments and mechanisms for conflict prevention in Africa. The intention of this chapter is not to comprehensively cover all aspects of EU-Africa relations, but to present selected policy instruments and agreements with specific reference to conflict prevention and peace-building targeting sub-Saharan Africa, and in particular the region of Southern Africa, and, within that region, Angola, which have just emerged from a three-decade long war.

The approach chosen for this chapter is to geographically zoom in on the African continent. The aim is to present an overview of EU strategies as they have evolved from the 1990s until today, and to show how the strategies chosen to respond to conflicts and their causes at the continental, regional, and state level lock into each other. It will become apparent that the EU and its African counterparts have created a framework for conflict prevention based on instruments ranging from formal international agreements to common declarations and 'soft law'. Direct intervention on the ground using military deployment, as in the case of the *Artemis* operation in Congo,[2] is the exception to the general rule that, to a large extent, the instruments still need to be applied on the ground. However, these instruments carefully lock into each other and provide the list of factors that need to be addressed in order to prevent conflicts and maintain peace in Africa, such as the eradication of poverty, human rights and democracy, integration into the world economy, and environmental protection.

---

[1] Deputy Director, EFTA Surveillance Authority, Brussels. Any views expressed in this chapter reflect the views of the author alone.

[2] See Council Joint Action 2003/423/CFSP of 5 June 2003 on the European Union military operation in the Democratic Republic of Congo, *OJEC* [2003] L 143/50 and Council Decision 2003/432/CFSP of 12 June on the European Union military operation in the Democratic Republic of Congo, *OJEC* [2003] L 147/42.

V. Kronenberger and J. Wouters, eds., The European Union and Conflict Prevention
© 2004, T·M·C·ASSER PRESS, *The Hague, The Netherlands*

In the following, the emergence of EU conflict prevention strategies toward Africa will be presented. We shall explore how the EU's policy of conflict prevention in Africa is based on the assumption that if the so-called root-causes of conflict are eliminated, peace will endure.

First, the background and guiding principles for EU conflict prevention in Africa are briefly presented. Second, strategies for the entire continent are presented, focusing on the ongoing EU-Africa Dialogue and the Cotonou Agreement in particular. Third, a regional focus is provided by an overview of policies aimed at the Southern Africa Development Community (SADC). Finally, Angola, within the SADC, will illustrate how the EU, in cooperation with national authorities and civil society, implements its guiding principles on conflict prevention through concrete projects.

In the period since the end of the Cold War, the African political landscape has changed, and so has the nature of conflicts on the continent. The Cold War led to the emergence of East-West spheres of influence in Africa. Whereas the former colonial powers, and the USA, sought to maintain their influence on the continent, a number of the post-colonial regimes sought to counterbalance the West by seeking support from the Soviet Union and its allies. Ghana, under the leadership of Nkrumah, Congo under Lumumba's leadership, or, albeit later, Dos Santos in Angola, provide examples of this. The result was a system of client-states which were rewarded for their allegiance to one or the other superpowers. Internal strife was largely ignored by the international community, and inter-state conflicts were contained. In particular, the Horn of Africa and Southern Africa were of strategic interest. As a result, the interests of the superpowers to control these strategic areas for trade and security concerning the supply of important raw materials (petroleum, diamonds) directly fuelled conflicts in these areas. To take the example of Angola, South Africa, supported by the occidental powers, intervened in Angola in 1975 to prevent the Movement for the Liberation of Angola (MPLA) coming to power. The MPLA was perceived by the Western powers as being under Communist control. The result was a civil war, fuelled by foreign intervention, which left up to one and a half million people dead and another four million displaced. In all, Cuba, supported by the Soviet Union, sent 12,000 troops to Angola. Supported by the West, which wanted to secure its own control over resources and to reduce Soviet influence, South Africa, for its part, was able to divert attention from its apartheid regime. Angola only recently emerged from a state of semi-permanent war since 1975. Another example of how the Cold War stimulated conflicts can be found in the Somali-Ethiopian war, which began in 1977. The Western support for Somalia, and the Soviet and Cuban support for Ethiopia kept the conflict going until 1990. Whereas Ethiopia regained a precarious peace, Somalia as a State, for all practical purposes, disintegrated and has not yet recovered.

Perversely, it is generally recognised that the shift in the geopolitical power balance in the late 1980s had the effect of increasing the number of conflicts in

Africa, as external support for governments dried up. However, the causes of these 'new' conflicts have been perceived to be somewhat different. Conflicts now had their roots in ethnicity, religion and personalities, rather than Cold War considerations.[3]

In the course of the past five to ten years there has been a growing and dual realisation that there were and are, for the one part, tough economic interests behind these conflicts and, for the other part, that not all the continent's conflicts are the same or have the same roots. Consequently, the approach to conflict prevention and peace-building has evolved to take into account, in addition to the international context, a whole range of elements that traditionally have been dealt with in development policies, humanitarian aid or trade policies, but not in conflict prevention strategies, e.g., the effectiveness of governance, the rule of law, access to education and health care, and access to income-generating activities.

Another feature that has increasingly come to influence foreign donors and interventionists is the participation of the African governments and peoples themselves in the formulation of policies. The new ACP-EU Agreement (hereinafter the 'Cotonou Agreement'), for example, contains very specific provisions making sure that the cooperation programmes shall be formulated through a dialogue involving state actors and civil society organisations. Indeed, it is a central feature of EU conflict prevention strategy to lend support to initiatives by Africans themselves.[4]

2. BACKGROUND

The EU seriously began to address its role in conflict prevention in Africa in the mid-1990s. A starting point was the establishment of a basic document on preventive diplomacy and peacekeeping in Africa, adopted by the European Council on 4 December 1995, and incorporated into the conclusions of the Madrid European Council of 15 and 16 December 1995.[5] The document established that the EU was ready to support African efforts in the field of preventive diplomacy and peacekeeping. It stressed that the main players at all stages must be African bodies, in particular the then Organization of African Unity (OAU), later to become the African Union (AU). The EU contribution to, and support of, African action should be based on the following principles:

---

[3] Timothy M. Shaw, *Conflict and Peace Building in Africa: The Regional Dimension*, UNU/ Wider Discussion Paper 2003/10 (Helsinki, UNI/WIDER 2003), p. 1.

[4] See, e.g., Council Common Position of 26 January 2004 concerning conflict prevention, management, and resolution in Africa (2004/85/CFSP), *OJEC* [2004] L 21/25.

[5] 'Preventive diplomacy, conflict resolution and peacekeeping in Africa' Council conclusions on preventive diplomacy, conflict resolution and peace keeping in Africa. *Bulletin of the European Union*, Bull. 12-1995, points 1.4.116 and I.78.

- increasing African involvement in the prevention and resolution of their crises;
- improving the interlocking between the efforts of the EU and those of the African countries and other members of the international community;
- harmonising in particular the efforts of the EU, including bilateral efforts by its Member States, in the light of the above;
- coordinating endeavours in this field with the development aid policy of the Community and its Member States and support for the democratization process;
- facilitating the mobilisation of African capacities and means of action. It is essential that Africans take a lead in preventive diplomacy and conflict resolution on the continent.[6]

The Council Common Position was followed up by a communication from the Commission to the Council on 6 March 1996.[7] That communication effectively sets the scene for subsequent actions by the EU relating to conflict prevention in Africa.

First, it provides a justification for EU action. It points out that, thus far, the EU has focused on responses to open civil wars or to situations where the outbreak of violence was imminent. The Commission puts forward an argument based on *efficiency* and suggests that a policy aimed at preventing conflicts would be a better one than responding to their consequences: 'As no amount of humanitarian aid and no effective peace-keeping operation will solve a crisis of peace and security, justice and resources in a sustainable way, there is a need to try to go beyond ad-hoc decisions and a policy of damage limitation'.[8] A new policy should focus on the prevention of conflicts and should be at the centre of a comprehensive EU response towards the issue of conflicts in Africa. The approach should be comprehensive in so far as the EU, within its competencies, should address the entire cycle of conflict and peace.

Second, it offers an overriding policy goal: structural stability. The term is defined as '*a situation involving sustainable economic development, democracy and respect for human rights, viable political structures, and healthy social and environmental conditions, with the capacity to manage change without to resort to violent conflict*'.[9]

Third, it stresses the importance of addressing the root-causes of conflicts. *Conflict prevention*, defined by the European Commission as actions undertaken over the short-term to reduce manifest tensions and/or to prevent the outbreak or

---

[6] Council conclusions, op. cit. n. 5, at point 3.

[7] Communication from the Commission to the Council of 6 March 1996 'The EU and the issue of conflicts in Africa: Peace-building, conflict prevention and beyond', SEC (96) 332, available at <http://europa.eu.int/comm/development/body/legislation/recueil/en/en17/en171.htm>

[8] Commission communication, SEC (96) 332, op. cit. n. 7, at Chapter I.1.

[9] Commission communication, SEC (96) 332, op. cit. n. 7, at Chapter I.2.

recurrence of violent conflict,[10] is closely linked to the concept of *peace-building*. Peace-building involves actions over the medium and longer term to address the root-causes of violent conflicts in a targeted manner. The root-causes of conflict are generally considered to comprise:

- Imbalance of political, socio-economic or cultural opportunities among different identity groups (ethnic, religious, regional, social, etc.);
- Lack of democratic legitimacy and effectiveness of governance;
- Absence of effective mechanisms for the peaceful conciliation of group interests (including democratic structures), and for bridging dividing lines between different interest groups;
- Lack of a vibrant civil society.

Policies aimed at addressing these root-causes should, therefore, be considered part of the overall conflict prevention efforts of the EU.

Finally, the Communication offered the definitions and analytical tools that have become the basis for the formulation of specific policies aimed at individual regions or countries.

The Communication provides an analytical distinction between 4 different situations of conflict or potential conflict and surveys the activities in the different situations where the EU could become involved, here taken directly from the Communication:

a) Situation without obvious tension
This is the situation where the country is seemingly stable and largely quiet but where (structural) sources of potential conflict may be discerned. For example, the constant marginalisation of an important minority or the use of repressive instruments in the absence of effective mechanisms for the peaceful conciliation of divergent group interests.

Immediate aims:
Peace-building: Establishment – subject to respect for democracy and fundamental human rights – of viable political and socio-economic structures (mechanisms for peaceful conciliation of interests, viable democratic models and so on).

Instruments:
Targeted assistance including training, education, social and economic cohesion, strengthening human and social development, democracy building, good governance and civil society, institution building, etc., political dialogue, watching changes, voicing concerns.

---

[10] Definitions and categorisation used by the European Commission are published at <http://europa.eu.int/comm/development/development_old/prevention/definition.htm>

b) Situations with tension

This is the situation where conflict in society becomes clearly apparent (social unrest, armed opposition, mass demonstrations, etc.). The gravity of the situation depends not only on the events themselves but also on the existing political and power structures: is the opposition able to present negotiable demands? Is the government in a position to fulfil them? And so on.

Immediate aims:

Conflict prevention (in the strict sense): Reduction of tension; prevention of a complete outbreak of hostilities

Instruments:

Political dialogue with the parties concerned (missions, preventive diplomacy); advocating specific measures (including preventive deployment of troops) and/or specific solutions to the problems; (the threat of) sanctions; deployment of observers; own and contribution to other humanitarian/emergency aid (also to prevent refugee flows for economic reasons). Peace-building measures could continue to apply and could even be intensified. They will have the most effect if targeted at the heart of the conflict (easing the economic situation of a marginalized group while offering assistance to the government to find a sustainable solution, for example).

c) Open conflict

Immediate aims 1:

Conflict management: Reducing the threat of vertical and horizontal escalation (including the reduction of immediate human suffering and the handling of the refugee problem).

Instruments:

Threat of sanctions (including to third countries), political dialogue, own and contribution to other humanitarian/emergency aid, (advocating) preventive military intervention, observer missions.

Immediate aims 2:

Conflict resolution: Ending the hostilities and starting peace negotiations.

Instruments:

Sanctions, political dialogue, advocating specific solutions, supporting peace initiatives, (advocating) peace-enforcement.

d) Post-conflict situation

This is the situation where there is no longer any organised armed violence. A cease-fire or a peace agreement might or might not yet have been signed. In any case, the consequences of the war are still present and obvious in a large part of the society (refugees and ex-combatants still in the progress of reintegration, etc.), and it is still uncertain if the situation will deteriorate (back to the phase of tensions or open conflict) or improve (towards a situation without obvious tensions or structural stability).

Immediate aims:
Conflict resolution/peace-building: Successful peace negotiations, return to normality.

Instruments:
Demobilisation and disarmament, repatriation and reintegration, demining, post-demining, post-conflict relief and humanitarian aid, rehabilitation, peace-building measures (see above), political dialogue, advocating specific solutions, watching changes, confidence-building measures, (support for) conflict resolution initiatives, rebuilding government structures.

The definitions, analytical tools, as well as the basic approach to conflict prevention has remained in place since this Communication, but EU action has become more targeted in its strategies. The current EU intervention in the Congo serves as an illustration of how far the EU has come since the Madrid European Council in 1995 (see above). Through the launching of the *Artemis* operation,[11] the EU is now involved in the full series of conflict situations described in the 1996 Commission Communication, employing all instruments envisaged at that time, including preventive military intervention.

Consequently, conflict prevention has been dealt with not only as a policy area in its own right, but as a horizontal policy that has been integrated into trade policies, development aid, the CFSP and the political dialogue with Africa.

3.   GUIDING PRINCIPLES

The EU today seeks to include conflict prevention and peace-building in its relations with Africa through the means at its disposal with a view to reducing the potential for violent conflicts. Initiatives are taken on the basis of its competencies in the fields of CFSP, development aid, humanitarian aid, and in its trade relations with Africa.

Since the mid-1990s, the EU has broadly based its development and peace-building policies on five principles, which remain valid to this day.

First, the principle of *ownership*. Ownership means that the Africans themselves should identify the problem and its causes and propose solutions to the problem. It has been suggested that 'outside actors, such as the EU, should abstain from prescribing blueprints for the way towards peace and democratic stability, but should actively assist Africans in taking the lead concerning the matter and help shape the environment in which effective ownership is possible'.[12] The

---

[11] See n. 2 above.

[12] João de Deus Pinheiro, 'Peace-Building and Conflict Prevention in Africa', in *CPN Yearbook 1998/99* (Baden-Baden, Nomos Verlagesgesellschaft 1999), p. 20.

Council Common Position on conflict prevention in Africa[13] states that its main objective is to contribute to the prevention of conflicts in Africa by strengthening African capacity and means of action in this field in particular through support for the OAU (later AU) and subregional organisations and initiatives, and civil society organisations.[14] In a Communication to the Council on the EU-Africa Dialogue, adopted in June 2003, the Commission stressed this approach by calling for a 'sizeable contribution'[15] in favour of the AU Peace and Security Council, set up in July 2002.

The Partnership Agreement between the ACP States and the EU (the Cotonou Agreement), which entered into force on 1 April 2003, makes specific reference to the concept of ownership, by stating that '[the policy of peace-building and conflict prevention and resolution] shall be based on the principle of ownership'.[16] The current practice under the Cotonou Agreement of producing Country Strategy Papers (CSP) including indicative programmes with each country concerned illustrates how the principle is applied.[17] Albeit 'soft law', the Country Strategy Papers are *de facto* agreements between the EU and African states in which the individual African country identifies development priorities, including those deemed to be necessary for the prevention of conflicts or the resolution of existing ones.

Second, the principle of *prevention*. For example, the EU's policy relating to conflicts in Africa should focus on preventing the outbreak and spreading of violent conflicts through early action, and on preventing the recurrence thereof. In this context the EU policy shall cover:

- Conflict prevention by seeking to target the direct causes – trigger factors – of violent conflict;
- Crisis management by addressing acute phases of conflicts, supporting efforts to bring the violence to an end;
- Peace-building by seeking to support initiatives for containing violent conflict and to prepare for, and sustain, peaceful solutions to such conflicts;
- Reconstruction by supporting the economic, political and social rebuilding of

---

[13] Council Common Position of 26 January 2004 concerning conflict prevention, management, and resolution in Africa (2004/85/CFSP), *OJEC* [2004] L 21 /25.

[14] Council Common Position 2004/85/CFSP, op. cit. n. 13, Article 1.

[15] Communication from the Commission to the Council of 23 June 2003, 'The EU-Africa Dialogue', COM (2003) 316 final, p. 9. See also *Bulletin of the European Union*, Bull. 6-2003, point I.6.124.

[16] Partnership Agreement between the African, Caribbean and Pacific Group of States, on the one part, and the European Community and its Member States, on the other, signed in Cotonou on 23 June 2000, *OJEC* [2000] L 317/3.

[17] A full list of Country Strategy Papers adopted on the basis of the Cotonou Agreement is available at <http://europa.eu.int/comm/development/body/csp_rsp/csp_en.cfm>.

post-conflict States and societies to prevent reescalation of violence and to promote sustainable peace.[18]

In the Regional Strategy Paper (RSP) for Southern Africa Development Community, for example, 'prevalence of peace in the region' is one of the stated sources of verification of success.[19]

As we shall see below, EU policy in the field of conflict prevention will often take the shape of action and aid in areas that have conventionally been branded 'development cooperation' or 'trade facilitation'. In the case of Angola, for example, areas of action defined jointly by the EU and Angola with a view to preventing further violent conflict cover not only relief, resettlement and rehabilitation of former fighters, but also food security and social policies such as health and education.[20]

Third, *mainstreaming* has become a key to implementing a policy of conflict prevention in Africa. It suffices to point to the amalgamation of development cooperation and conflict prevention to make the point. The EU seeks to support the mainstreaming of conflict prevention within the framework of its development policy and its associated country strategies.[21] Recently, EU efforts to prevent conflicts have also been linked to the threat of terrorism. The most obvious example in policy documents is to be found the 2004 Council Common Position on conflict prevention in Africa, which states that: '*The EU shall develop long-term conflict prevention and peace-building initiatives, recognising that progress in these areas is a necessary precondition also for African States to build and sustain capacity to deal effectively with terrorism*'.[22]

Fourth, *early warning* mechanisms have been considered essential to effective conflict prevention. Despite the fact that there is increased focus on actions aimed at dealing with the root-causes of conflict so as to create lasting peace and stability in Africa, the EU has maintained that the gap between analysis, early warning and action must be narrowed. The EU stays in frequent and close contact with African countries, through the Commission Delegations on the African continent, or through meetings as foreseen by its Agreements, e.g., the Cotonou Agreement, or through regular Ministerial meetings as a follow-up to the Cairo Summit (see below). The Council of Ministers has recently called for Member States and the Commission to give higher priority to country and regional strategies and risk assessment.[23] In doing so, it stated that country strategies and risk assessment

---

[18] Council Common Position 2004/85/CFSP, op. cit. n. 13, Article 2.

[19] A full list of Regional Strategy Papers adopted on the basis of the Cotonou Agreement is available at <http://europa.eu.int/comm/development/body/csp_rsp/rsp_en.cfm>

[20] Angola – European Community: Country Strategy Paper and Indicative Programme for the period 2002-2007, signed in Luanda 28 January 2003.

[21] Council Common Position 2004/85/CFSP, op. cit. n. 13, Article 5.

[22] Council Common Position 2004/85/CFSP, op. cit. n. 13, Article 1(3).

[23] Council Common Position 2004/85/CFSP, op. cit. n. 13, Article 6(3).

would benefit from greater use of local knowledge, including greater use of local experts trained in early warning and risk assessment, echoing the principle of ownership mentioned above.

Fifth, *coordination* of policies among Member States and the EU, and between the EU and other international organisations has been stressed by both the Council of Ministers and the Commission on numerous occasions. Focusing on Africa, the Council of Ministers has clearly stated that coordination and cooperation with the UN, the AU and other subregional organisations, e.g., SADC, is vital in order to maximise the opportunities for successful action and efficient use of resources.[24]

4.   CONTINENTAL FOCUS

4.1   EU-Africa Summits: dialogue for conflict prevention

Even if individual Member States of the EU have a long and significant history of relationships with the African Governments, it is only during the last part of the 1990s, that the EU made its first paths towards a *common* approach in its foreign relations towards Africa. Arguably, this was a result of the various initiatives of the Commission to keep African issues on the Council of Ministers' agenda.[25]

At the continental level, the first EU-Africa Summit was organised in Cairo on 3-4 April 2000, to provide a forum for dialogue between the European Union heads of state and African leaders, in the same way as the analogous meetings with ASEAN and Latin America. The purpose of the dialogue is first and foremost political. A second EU-Africa Summit was foreseen[26] in the course of 2003. However, a decision was taken by the EU early in 2003 to postpone the meeting. An alternative date has not been set, but the EU has indicated that it wants it to take place at 'the earliest possible date'.[27]

The Cairo Summit adopted a joint declaration and an action plan, addressing, *inter alia*, the issue of conflicts and their causes.

A Plan of Action[28] was adopted to contribute to the achievement of the principles and commitments contained in the Cairo Declaration, targeting actions in the fields of regional economic cooperation and integration, international trade

---

[24] Council Common Position 2004/85/CFSP, op. cit. n. 13, Article 6.

[25] A. Krause, 'The European Union's Africa Policy: The Commission as Policy Entrepreneur in the CFSP', 8 *European Foreign Affairs Review* (2003), pp. 221-237.

[26] Africa-Europe Summit under the Aegis of the OAU and the EU, Cairo, 3-4 April 2000: Cairo Plan of Action. Para. 130. Document 107/4/00 Rev 4.

[27] Commission Communication COM (2003) 316 final, op. cit. n. 15, p. 2.

[28] Africa-Europe Summit under the Aegis of the OAU and the EU, Cairo, 3-4 April 2000: Cairo Plan of Action. Document 107/4/00 Rev 4, available at <http://europa.eu.int/comm/development/body/eu_africa/eu_africa_en.htm>.

and debt issues, human rights, democratic principles and institutions, good gover-nance and the rule of law, peace-building, conflict prevention, and development issues. A wide range of topics were covered by these headings, *inter alia*, sustain-able development, poverty eradication, education, health, gender issues, as well as migration, and the arms trade.

On the subject of conflict prevention, the Heads of State affirmed that peace, security, stability and justice are essential prerequisites for socio-economic devel-opment and underlined that '(...) *efforts are needed to prevent violent conflict at the earliest stages by addressing their root-causes in a targeted manner and with an adequate combination of all available instruments*'.[29] The parties agreed to '*tackle the root causes of conflicts with a view to preventing further conflicts*' and '*use the experience acquired by the EU for the strengthening of OAU's sub-re-gional organisations' operation capacities*'.[30]

As a follow-up to the Cairo Summit, a biregional group of senior officials has been set up to try and develop fields of priority. Europe-Africa ministerial meet-ings were arranged in Brussels in October 2001 and Ouagadougou in November 2002, in order to monitor and to provide guidance to the follow-up.

Eight priority areas of cooperation have been identified:
1. Conflict prevention and resolution, including anti-personnel mines;
2. Cooperation and regional integration, integration of Africa in the world economy and trade;
3. Environment, including the fight against drought and desertification;
4. HIV/AIDS and communicable diseases;
5. Food security;
6. Human rights and democracy;
7. Restitution of stolen or illegally exported cultural goods;
8. Africa's external debt.

At the second ministerial meeting, held in Ouagadougou on 28 November 2002, Ministers urged the biregional group of senior officials to continue its work on the agreed areas of action, including:

- Regular exchange of information;
- Establishing an inventory of existing institutions in Africa dealing with con-flict;
- Strengthening of African institutional capacity in the area of early warning and preventive diplomacy;

---

[29] Africa-Europe Summit under the Aegis of the OAU and the EU, Cairo, 3-4 April 2000: Cairo Declaration. Recital 65. Document 06/4/00 Rev 4, available at <http://europa.eu.int/comm/develop-ment/body/eu_africa/eu_africa_en.htm>.

[30] Cairo Plan of Action, op. cit. n. 26, at Recitals 72 and 79.

- Reinforcement of good governance and rule of law as indispensable elements of conflict prevention and resolution.[31]

As follow-up to the EU-Africa dialogue, the Commission has suggested that, given the level of instability, which characterises most African regions, conflict prevention must be a top priority in this dialogue.[32]

4.2 The Cotonou Agreement and conflict prevention

The EU-ACP Partnership Agreement, signed in Cotonou, Benin, on 23 June 2000, (hereinafter the Agreement) entered into force on 1 April 2003.[33] It constitutes a partnership between the European Union and 76 ACP States.[34] The ACP states comprise 48 African states. For the purposes of this article reference shall be made to these African states, even if the provisions of the Cotonou Agreement quite obviously also apply to the Caribbean and Pacific States that are parties to the Agreement.

According to Article 1 of the Agreement, it aims to promote and expedite *'economic, cultural and social development of the ACP States, with a view to contributing to peace and security and to promoting a stable and democratic political environment.'*

It has been suggested that an overriding aim of the Agreement is essentially to accelerate the economic development of the ACP countries, by their gradual integration into the world economy.[35] As a consequence, major objectives of the Agreement are, on the one hand, the improvement of and growth in trade between the EU and the ACP countries and, on the other, the support and financing of development projects.

The Agreement provides that the partnership between the EU and African states shall centre on the objective of reducing and eventually eradicating poverty. Subsidiary areas of focus are to be taken into account at all stages of actions aimed at meeting the overriding concern of eradicating poverty. In order to achieve its goals, the Agreement lists a whole range of areas of cooperation, initiatives and concerns, including conflict prevention, that are to be taken into account, *inter alia*:

---

[31] Africa-Europe Ministerial Meeting, Ouagadougou, Burkina Faso, 28 November 2002: Final Communiqué, Council of the European Union Document No. 15197/02, 3.12.2002.

[32] Commission Communication COM (2003) 316 final, op. cit. n. 15, p. 3.

[33] Council Decision of 19 December 2002 concerning the conclusion of the Partnership Agreement between the African, Caribbean and Pacific Group of States, on the one part, and the European Community and its Member States, on the other, signed in Cotonou on 23 June 2000 (2003/159/EC), *OJEC* [2003] L 65/27.

[34] The number of ACP States having ratified the Agreement as of 7 May 2003.

[35] P. Vincent, 'L'entrée en vigueur de la convention de Cotonou', 39 *Cahier de droit européen* (2003), pp. 157-176.

- Sustainable development;
- The gradual integration of the ACP countries into the world economy;
- Sustained economic growth;
- Development of the private sector;
- Improved access to productive resources;
- Employment;
- Institution building;
- Human rights;
- Democracy;
- The rule of law, and
- Conflict prevention and resolution.

Specific reference is made to conflict prevention in Article 11 of the Agreement, which, *inter alia*, states that the parties to the Agreement shall pursue an active, comprehensive and integrated policy of peace-building, conflict prevention and resolution. It furthermore states that this policy shall be based on the principle of ownership, and shall focus on preventing violent conflicts at an early stage by addressing the root-causes in a targeted manner.

The Agreement itself also outlines, albeit in general terms, what the signatories might consider to be the relevant root-causes of conflict, *inter alia*, scarce natural resources, lack of democratic legitimacy or effectiveness of governance. Actions that the parties consider to be important to conflict prevention include mediation, negotiation and reconciliation efforts for effective regional management of shared, scarce natural resources, for demobilisation and reintegration of former combatants into the society, for addressing the problem of child soldiers, as well as for suitable action to set responsible limits to military expenditure and the arms trade, including through support for the promotion and application of agreed standards and codes of conduct.

On the basis of the Agreement, region and country-specific measures have been adopted, either in the form of so-called Regional Strategy Papers (RSP), Country Strategy Papers (CSP)[36] or Economic Partnership Agreements (EPA). The latter will not be discussed in this chapter.

The RSPs and CSPs are produced in accordance with the provisions of Annex IV to the Agreement, on the implementation and management procedures. Chapters 1 and 2 of Annex IV provide the basis for the CSPs and RSPs, respectively. Annex IV provides, *inter alia*, that operations financed by grants within the framework of the Agreement shall be programmed at the beginning of each five-year period covered by the Financial Protocol to the Agreement.[37] These

---

[36] A full list of the Regional and National Strategy Papers is available at <http://europa.eu.int/comm/development/body/eu_africa/eu_africa_en.htm>.

[37] See Article 1 of Annex IV to the Agreement for national programming and Article 9 for regional programming.

programmes shall be drawn up in accordance with the requirements of the Annex. The programmes must include at least:

a) the preparation and development of a Country or Regional Support Strategy based on the country's own medium-term development objectives and strategies;
b) a clear indication from the Community of the indicative programmable financial allocation from which the country may benefit during the five-year period as well as any other relevant information;
c) the preparation and adoption of an indicative programme for implementing the support strategies; and
d) a review process covering the support strategies, the indicative programme and the volume of resources allocated to it.[38]

Four RSPs have been signed by the EU and African sub-continental counterparts: Central Africa,[39] West Africa,[40] Eastern and Southern Africa and the Indian Ocean,[41] and the Southern Africa Development Community (SADC) (see below). Forty Country Strategy Papers for African States have been signed or adopted.

5. REGIONAL FOCUS: EU-SADC COOPERATION

The South African Development Community (SADC)[42] was established in 1992, as a successor to the Southern African Development Coordination Conference (SADCC). The SADC today comprises Angola, Botswana, DR Congo, Malawi, Mauritius, Mozambique, Lesotho, Namibia, the Seychelles, South Africa, Swaziland, Tanzania, Zambia, and Zimbabwe. The aims and objectives of the SADC largely overlap the aims and objectives contained in the Cotonou Agreement, e.g., poverty eradication, development of international trade, health, gender, governance, the rule of law, and the promotion of peace and stability in the region.

---

[38] Ibid.

[39] Represented by the Economic Community of Central African States (ECCAS) and the Economic and Monetary Community of Central Africa (CEMAC).

[40] Represented by the Economic Community of West African States (ECOWAS) and the West African Economic and Monetary Union (WAEMU).

[41] Represented by the Common Market for Eastern and Southern Africa (COMESA), the East African Community (EAC), the Intergovernmental Authority on Development (IGAD) and the Indian Ocean Commission (IOC).

[42] For further information, see <http://www.sadc.int>.

On 7 November 2002, the Southern Africa Development Community and the European Commission, representing the EU, signed a Regional Strategy Paper (RSP).[43,44] The RSP provides a comprehensive framework for EU-Southern Africa cooperation for the period 2002-2007 and makes a € 101 million initial contribution available for attaining joint objectives. The RSP contains, in its Annex I, a detailed intervention framework, and includes a detailed definition of objectives, indicators, sources of verification and a list of agreed assumptions. That intervention framework specifically foresees EU support for SADC initiatives.

In the area of conflict prevention the RSP aims to support action initiated and undertaken by SADC itself with the aim being to prevent conflicts. The specific objectives are in line with the objectives of the Cotonou Agreement, and are outlined in the Regional Indicative Programme, which is part of the RSP. The funds have been allocated from the 9th European Development Fund (EDF), which is the financial instrument of the EU-ACP Partnership Agreement.

SADC and the EU have identified the priority areas for EU support which address the major obstacles to economic development and poverty reduction.

First, support in the field of economic development and trade (€35 to €45 million of the allocation) encourages the countries in the region to continue to move towards a larger and more unified market. The fostering of the free trade area and the future creation of a customs union will increase the region's competitiveness and help to attract more investment in the productive sectors. Economic Partnership Agreements (EPAs) are meant to be given priority in the cooperation strategy as a means of assisting the region to integrate itself more successfully into the global trading system and at the same time to strengthen its own regional integration process.

Second, programmes in transport and communication (€ 35 to € 45 million) aim to reduce the costs of transport and communication mainly through improved utilisation of existing infrastructure and services and through the continued development of a regional transport and communications policy and regulatory framework.

Third, up to € 20 million of the allocation will be used to support programmes in other areas such as peace and security, the fight against HIV/AIDS and drugs control in the region.

The SADC's own regional priorities include trade facilitation, investment harmonisation, and infrastructure development aimed at reducing transaction costs within the region, and conflict prevention and resolution. The SADC Treaty, on the basis of its Article 9, foresees the establishment of an Organ on Politics, Defence and Security Co-operation. On 14 August 2001, the SADC

---

[43] South Africa is not part of the strategy paper, but is a party to a separate trade and development agreement with the EU.

[44] SADC-EU Regional Strategy Paper and Regional Indicative Programme for the period 2002-2007.

states signed a protocol (SADC Protocol 20) on Politics, defence and security co-operation. Among the specific objectives of the Organ are to prevent, contain and resolve inter-and intrastate conflicts by peaceful means. In April 2003, the SADC organised a workshop to finalise the Strategic Indicative Development Plan for the Organ (SIPO) on Politics, Defence and Security.[45]

Relating to conflict prevention the RSP sets as a specific objective the 'promotion of peace and security and the role of gender'.[46] The expected results of any action undertaken are that:

1. Operation on peace and security matters is facilitated;
2. Drug trafficking and use are reduced;
3. Levels of organised crime, money laundering, bribery and corruption are reduced;
4. Gender is mainstreamed in peace and security issues.

The indicator chosen is, *inter alia*, the ratification of the SADC protocol on defence, peace and security. The source of verification is the actual implementation of the protocol.

To meet the objectives, projects/programmes are foreseen under the following headings:

1. Capacity building for conflict prevention and management;
2. Enhancing the implementation of the protocol's control of illegal drug trafficking;
3. Implementation of the SADC HIV/AIDS Strategy and procurement policy harmonisation;
4. Gender mainstreaming, legal and policy development.

Between 15% and 25% of the financial contribution by the EU is to be allocated to these projects/programmes. According to the RSP timetable projects are to be identified and approved in the course of 2003, and a decision as to their financing is to be taken in 2004. Their implementation was to start in 2003 and will end in 2006.

6.   NATIONAL FOCUS: ANGOLA

6.1   **Introduction**

Last year (2003) officially marked the first year of peace in the 28 years of Angola's existence. Since independence from Portugal, in 1975, civil war has

---

[45] Source <http://www.sadc.int>.

[46] Annex I to the SADC-EU Regional Strategy Paper and Regional Indicative Programme for the period 2002-2007.

been the norm in Angola, often fuelled by foreign interference. The rivalry between the ruling Popular Movement for the Liberation of Angola (MPLA) and the National Union for Total Independence of Angola (UNITA) has left up to 1.5 million people dead over the last three decades. The 1994 peace agreement provided for the integration of UNITA insurgents into the government and the armed forces. A national unity government was formed in 1997, but collapsed the following year, with the resumption of serious fighting.

In February 2002 Jonas Savimbi, the UNITA leader, was killed during a gunfight with government forces. Following his death a formal cease-fire was signed in Luanda in April 2002. The coming of relative peace in Angola led the way to the lifting of sanctions with regard to Angola, and UNITA in particular – which at times has controlled large parts of Angolan territory – imposed through the UN in 1993. This has raised the prospect of creating sustainable peace in the area. The sanctions included, *inter alia*, a ban on the trade in 'blood diamonds' from Angola and a restriction on the sale of fuel and arms.

On 21 November 2002 the UN-sponsored Joint Commission for the Angolan Peace Process was dissolved marking the successful completion of the 1994 peace agreement concluded between the MPLA and UNITA. Even if the civil war appears to be over, the situation in Angola remains precarious. For example, Angola has one of the highest percentages in the world of internally displaced people (IDPs). It is estimated that more than 4 million persons, or in excess of 30% of the total population, are displaced within the country. As a result, the influx of people to urban areas has been dramatic. It has been estimated that as much as a third of this population is deprived of access to income-generating opportunities, and, therefore, is directly dependent on external aid. It is generally accepted that poverty is increasing in Angola, with almost 70% of its population living below the national poverty line. Life expectancy at birth is 47 years. Illiteracy stands at around a third of the population.

The last elections were held in 1992, and new legislative and presidential elections may not be expected to take place before 2006.[47] At a subnational level, in the provinces, and in municipalities there are currently no elected organs. The local elections and administrative decentralisation provided for in the 1992 elections are still pending. However, it is a generally accepted fact that the development potential for Angola is huge, not least because of its still largely untapped natural resources of oil, diamonds and fisheries.

According to the Country Strategy Plan (CSP) signed between the EU and Angola, on the basis of the Cotonou Agreement, a '*sustainable peace could allow Angola to fulfil its potential and become a regional economic powerhouse*'.[48]

---

[47] UN Office for the Coordination of Humanitarian Affairs (OCHA), Integrated Regional Information Networks (IRIN), press report 9 February 2004, available at <http://www.irinnews.org>.

[48] Angola Country Strategy Paper and Indicative Programme for the period 2002-2007, p. 15.

The strategy adopted by the EU appears to be one of acting to prevent future conflict by assisting the reconstruction of civilian society with a view to consolidating the peace process in Angola. This fits in with the Angolan Government's strategy to consolidate the peace process. In the short-term emphasis has been centred on the demobilisation and disarmament of UNITA soldiers, and their integration into the Angolan Armed Forces or the police force. The socio-professional reintegration of demobilised personnel remains a priority. The very recent emergence from war means that efforts directed towards Angola cannot be compared to aid programmes directed towards more stable countries. National policies have yet to be structured, whereas it is recognised that populations need immediate relief aid. Angolans cannot wait for the delivery of complete services, which is still to be planned by the national authorities.

The EU has made it clear that the satisfaction of immediate needs has to tie in with the conditions for their long-term sustainability. The EU strategy towards Angola must be seen against that background. For example, EU support for action in the social sectors and relating to food security in the medium term is meant to make a pragmatic and progressive transition from the relief and rehabilitation phases foreseen in the short-term.

6.2   New political impetus from the EU

In June 2002, following the death of Jonas Savimbi in February of the same year, the EU reviewed its policy towards Angola adopting a Council Common Position on Angola expressing its renewed '(...) *willingness to support the efforts of the Angolan people to bring lasting peace, stability and sustainable development to the country'*.[49]

In order to achieve these objectives, the Common Position on Angola stresses the cooperation of the EU with other international organisations, such as the UN, IMF, and the Partnership with the ACP countries (through references to the Cotonou Agreement). The EU shall support the process of peace, national reconciliation and democracy in Angola through the promotion of good governance and a culture of tolerance among all political parties and all sectors of civil society. It also urges the Angolan Government to intensify its efforts to relieve the very serious humanitarian situation and to favour actions for demining, social reintegration and the resettlement of all the internally displaced people and refugees and to create the necessary conditions to allow the international community to help in this regard. Furthermore, it shall encourage cooperation and understanding among the countries in the region with the aim of improving regional security and economic development. In order to further these objectives the EU will conduct a regular dialogue with the Angolan authorities as envisaged in the Cotonou

---

[49] Council Common Position 2002/495/CFSP of 25 June 2002 on Angola and repealing Common Position 2000/391/CFSP, *OJEC* [2002] L 167/9, Preamble, Recital 5.

Agreement. It shall offer to assist Angola to strengthen democratic institutions and practices so as to allow free and fair elections, respect for human rights, the rule of law and independent civil society. In cooperation with the international community and other international organisations it shall also assist the country in its fight against corruption and poverty. It shall contribute to the efforts to alleviate the humanitarian situation and the suffering of the people as a result of war, and assist the Angolan Government in its rebuilding and reconstruction of the country.

The list of objectives and priorities referred to in the Common Position in Angola is not, however, comprehensive. The Council of Ministers also gives its blessing to actions by the Commission by taking note that the Commission intends to direct its action toward achieving the objectives and priorities of the Common Position by '(...) *pertinent Community measures*'.[50]

The fact that the Council, in Article 3 of the Common Position, '*notes*' that the Commission will direct actions '*by pertinent Community measures*', effectively should mean that the EU will be holistic in its approach to Angola, and that specific policies, e.g., through the country strategy papers foreseen in the Cotonou Agreement, may seek to attain the same objectives. The objectives and priorities referred to above coincide with what the Commission considers to be the root-causes of conflict, e.g., lack of effective governance, or the imbalance of political, socio-economic or cultural opportunities among different identity groups as a result of the war. The proposed strategy, as described in the next section of this chapter, regarding Angola concerns these root-causes, and, therefore, fits within the overall approach of EU conflict prevention, e.g., as outlined in the Commission Communication on Conflict Prevention from April 2001 and the Common Position on Angola.

6.3 The Country Strategy Paper and Indicative Programme (CSP)

The CSP for Angola was signed in Luanda on 28 January 2003 and entered into force at the same time as the Cotonou Agreement, on 1 April 2003.

In accordance with the Cotonou Agreement, the CSP is aimed at defining areas of action for Community Aid in favour of Angola covering the period up to 2007. In all, € 146 million has been set aside by the 9th EDF, in addition to leftovers from previous EDFs. The CSP states that measures to promote peace and conflict resolution constitute an important priority for the EU. Consolidation of peace is defined as a necessary step towards the central objective of poverty alleviation.

The prevention strategy for Angola must fit into and pursue the link between relief, rehabilitation and development aiming to take advantage of synergies

---

[50] Council Common Position 2002/495/CFSP, op. cit. n. 49, Article 3.

between different financial instruments. This LRRD strategy proposes short, medium and longer-term interventions to contribute to:

- the furtherance of the 2002 peace process, national reconciliation and the consolidation of democracy, including the creation of conditions for free and fair elections;
- good governance and the development of civil society;
- poverty alleviation, through a gradual concentration of aid on food security and social sectors.

In the short-term, the focus will be on consolidating the 2002 peace process. An amount of € 51 million from previous EDFs is available, in addition to the money set aside by the 9th EDF. The funds will cover, as needed, gaps in the financing of the Angolan Government's plans for disarmament, demobilisation and reintegration of combatants, especially for the relief, resettlement and rehabilitation of former fighters and their families. Supporting the peace process also means that, if necessary, depending on the situation on the ground, funds are made available for medical assistance, food aid and the distribution of seeds and tools, and demining. Also in the short-term, the EU is ready to initiate support to good governance, in particular with regard to the judicial sector and the reform of the public administration. In particular, the EU has stated that it attaches great importance to promoting the development of Angolan civil society, especially in relation to democracy and human rights, as good governance constitutes a prerequisite for more sustainable development interventions in Angola. Up to € 35 million will be allocated to the promotion of good governance, through the interventions launched in the short-term to support the peace process, and continuing through the medium term to respond to the LRRD approach. This involves, for example, support for feasibility studies for the justice sector, helping to improve public finances, and the development of the private sector. The latter will focus on support for small and micro-enterprises. The approach must also address the different levels of administration. The short-term post-emergency transition programmes will look in particular at the municipal level, whereas the medium-term programmes planned must support the provincial and national levels.

In the medium and longer term, concentration will be on poverty alleviation, in particular food security and social sectors. However, the initiated actions and programmes related to good governance are meant to continue in the medium term. Areas likely to be covered include capacity building, training, technical assistance for legislation, support for the development of private services in agriculture, and agricultural pilot projects. A significant number of such actions will be developed with the participation of civil society. When the CSP was signed, it was estimated that an amount of € 40 million will be required for food security actions. In the social sector, health and education is given priority. The main thrust of health sector interventions are institutional strengthening, the physical rehabilitation and equipment of basic health units, including municipal hospitals, blood safety, support for a national pharmaceutical policy, development of human resources and the supply of essential and nutritional services. In partnership with other donors, e.g., the World Bank, the EU intends to continue its support for the education and training sector, with the specific objective of improving the level of education and access to employment through the better quality of general education, improved school infrastructure and professional training.

The main interventions foreseen are to provide continuity and sustainability to primary teacher training projects, and to extend training to second and third level teachers; to train new primary teachers; and to provide professional training, including in agriculture; to build and rehabilitate first-level schools, including equipment and educational materials; to reintegrate street children into general education; and to provide institutional support for the formulation and implementation of policies to improve general education and develop education.

7. CONCLUDING REMARKS

The European Union's policy of conflict prevention in Africa is based on the assumption that if the so-called root-causes of conflict are eliminated peace will endure. The identification of root-causes is made in cooperation with regional organisations, national authorities, and civil society to the extent possible. Notwithstanding its commitment to African ownership, the EU has, nonetheless, recently made it clear that it is prepared to become involved whenever necessary, in crisis management in Africa with its own capabilities.[51]

Development cooperation remains the instrument primarily employed by the EU to achieve its objectives in conflict prevention. However, direct political dialogue between the EU and African organisations and states appear to be gaining ground since the Cairo Summit in 2000. The EU, in addition, often channels its efforts at preventing conflicts through other international organisations, supporting their work. Poverty alleviation and sustainable development are primary objectives which appear in almost all policy documents, both within the EU and in Agreements between the EU and African organisations and states. Other favoured objectives of the EU include the gradual integration of African states into the world economy and democracy building.

The concept of conflict prevention has been positively integrated in the development strategies of the EU and appears in all policy documents at all levels. The Cotonou Agreement and the subsequent Regional and Country Strategy Papers represent the tangible attempts at mainstreaming the concept in EU-Africa rela-

---

[51] Council Common Position 2004/85/CFSP, op. cit. n. 13, Article 1(2).

tions. But mainstreaming will not be complete until the EU and its Member States fully coordinate their strategies with regard to sub-Saharan Africa. Admittedly, efforts are under way to create a common framework for actions of individual Member States,[52] but a tangible common European Foreign and Security Policy is, however, not yet a reality.

At the end of the day, the prevalence of peace remains the chief indicator of conflict prevention and peace-building. Every day, however, reports of violent conflict come out of Africa. In a country like Angola, having been in a semi-permanent state of war for the last few decades, there is, however, a hope that the efforts being put into alleviating poverty, building civil society, disarming militias and demining the countryside will act to prevent the reignition of violent conflict. If the absence of civil war is anything to go by, peace consolidation efforts seem to be paying off in Angola.

---

[52] Council Common Position 2004/85/CFSP, op. cit. n. 13, Article 1(4).

PART THREE

EXPERIENCE OF OTHER ACTORS

PART THREE A

INTERNATIONAL ORGANISATIONS

Chapter 16
INTERNATIONAL ORGANISATIONS' COOPERATION IN THE FIELD OF CONFLICT PREVENTION

by Manuel Szapiro[1]

1.   INTRODUCTION: SCOPE AND LIMITATIONS

1.1   Scope of this chapter

This chapter considers how cooperation between international organisations can be improved in order to prevent armed conflicts. For the purpose of this study, conflict prevention measures will be defined in a wide sense as measures taken to forestall violence, to limit the spread of violence and to prevent the occurrence of violence after settlement. Hence, the prevention measures concerned cover the emergence, spreading and recurrence of conflict. Conflict prevention cannot, thus, be dissociated from other stages in the life cycle of conflicts, such as crisis management, including peace-making/peace enforcement and long-term post-conflict peace-building. This study will, however, focus primarily on the prevention of emerging conflicts (preventive diplomacy, preventive deployment, etc.), rather than on the more traditional peace-making or peace-building activities.

The purpose of this chapter is to evaluate international organisations' responses to unfolding conflicts at an early stage and to examine how cooperation between international institutions should and can be strengthened in order to prevent armed conflict or mass violence from breaking out. One chapter alone would not suffice to tackle resource-allocation and political will formation issues in each international institution. Rather, a systemic approach is favoured which places the main international organisations in a larger perspective of 'interlocking'[2] versus 'interblocking' institutions. Consideration will, thus, be given to why interna-

---

[1] Member of the Task Force on the Future of the EU, Secretariat-General, European Commission, Brussels. The information, views, findings, suggestions, likely omissions and possible errors in this chapter are the full responsibility of the author alone. This chapter was finalised in January 2004.

[2] North Atlantic Council, Brussels 19 December 1991, final communiqué NACC-2(91)110, para. 8: 'The peace and security of Europe will increasingly depend on a framework of *interlocking institutions* which complement each other, since the challenges we face cannot be comprehensively addressed by one institution alone'.

V. Kronenberger and J. Wouters, eds., The European Union and Conflict Prevention
© 2004, T·M·C·ASSER PRESS, *The Hague, The Netherlands*

tional organisations have failed to act and how this situation can be remedied. This general approach may be usefully complemented by the geographical case studies above (S. Blockman's on the Western Balkans and E.J. Eidem on conflict prevention in Sub-Saharan Africa) and the institutional typology (analysis per institution) in subsequent contributions (e.g., E. Bakker on the OSCE, J. Kirton on G7/G8, I. Bannon on Financial Institutions).

1.2 **Inherent limitations**

This chapter is based on two sets of assumptions:

First, conflict prevention can help, provided there are sufficient resources and adequate instruments. The idea that the international community can remain outside 'out of area' conflicts is unsustainable.[3] We do not claim that the proposed venues would guarantee cessation of a conflict outbreak, but that the possibilities for reducing conflicts and heading towards a peaceful settlement would increase.

Second, the expectation-capability gap can be overcome by some '*ingénieurie institutionnelle*' at the multilateral level. Of course, one may argue that the approach adopted is simplistic as it only partially addresses the decisive issue of political will. Further analysis of political will formation (notably through the behaviour of the political elites), although of relevance, would have entailed political, sociological, psychological, cultural/anthropological and other considerations of domestic agendas and international negotiations, that would have gone way beyond the general scope of this chapter.

Furthermore, this chapter has focused on governmental forces within international organisations. While dealing with the division of labour between international organisations, we have not addressed the possible patterns for involving non-State actors. Prevention is more likely to be effective when it relies not upon a single, but a multi-track approach, involving local actors, external NGOs, government and international organisations. NGOs have a decisive and unique role to play in addressing the causes and symptoms of conflicts, notably via their access to local communities and indigenous institutions. The State-centric approach of this chapter should, therefore, be complemented within the framework of this volume by H. Schneider's contribution on the critical role of non-governmental actors and V. Kronenberger's examination of private sector input, *inter alia*.

2. WHY INTERNATIONAL ORGANISATIONS NEED TO COOPERATE – A GENERAL VIEWPOINT

The end of the Cold War has shifted the focus of attention of strategic thinking from inter-state ideologically fuelled conflicts to predominantly intrastate multi-

---

[3] 'In the international society of States those who can do something and choose not to are materially affecting the situation, and their actions and inactions have consequences like any other' H. Miall, et al. (eds.), *Contemporary Conflict Resolution* (Cambridge, Polity Press 1999), p. 219.

faceted crises. This lifting of the ideological veil shed a glaring light over the root causes of internal conflicts, i.e., a complex combination of degraded economic conditions, social and political instability, weak State/governance structures and (real and/or perceived) discrimination against ethnic minorities. Spill-over effects are particularly acute in relation to transnational trafficking (weapons, drugs, money laundering, etc.), to displaced populations and to environmental degradation. Civilians are no longer victims of 'collateral' damage but, rather, have become the direct targets of transnational-based conflicting parties. Terrorism has, sadly, become a case in point. The meaning of security has, thus, broadened to spread beyond the scope of collective defence (where a territorial threat *stricto sensu* proceeded from the perceived calculated aggression of a well identified third State actor) into the complex realm of 'human security' (based on the linkage between human rights *lato sensu*, democracy, peace, stability and development). The multifaceted crises and huge potential for escalation and contagion require appropriate international mechanisms to be put in place in order to prevent intrastate violence. The diverse and complex nature of post-Cold War conflicts has thus called for broad-based international community responses based on a comprehensive mix of socio-economic, institutional, political, diplomatic, humanitarian, developmental and military actions. Conflict prevention has been perceived by scholars and practitioners alike as encompassing both short-term/operational (early warning and early response; preventive diplomacy in the form of mediation, conciliation, good offices, fact-finding missions, peace conferences and envoys; preventive deployment; preventive humanitarian actions; economic measures; the use of force) and long-term/structural prevention measures (policy planning; economic measures; developmental action; preventive disarmament; peace-building measures, etc.).[4] Preventive action, indeed, aims not only to remove the symptoms of conflict so as to forestall the imminent outbreak of war (short-term/operational prevention) but also to eliminate or mitigate deep/root causes (long-term/structural preventive strategy). Just as the root causes may vary widely, the nature of appropriate implementing measures must cover a wide spectrum.

There is no single international actor capable of providing and sustaining such a large panoply of political, economic, military and socio-economic instruments. Whereas the Cold War placed NATO on a pedestal as *the* collective security/defence organisation, the new security environment would thus tend to rehabilitate cooperation between different types of international organisations, both of a mainly 'hard'/military essence (NATO) and a 'soft' power-based[5] nature (UN, EU, OSCE, Council of Europe, etc.). Current developments at the EU level marry

---

[4] Distinction made, *inter alia*, by the Carnegie Commission on Preventing Deadly Conflict, *Preventing Deadly Conflict, final report* (Washington, Carnegie Commission on Preventing Deadly Conflict 1997).

[5] J. Nye, 'Soft power', 80 *Foreign Policy* (1990), p. 153 at p. 171.

both civilian and hard/military components (see J. Nino-Perez's contribution in this volume). This two-pronged approach is essential as a means of improving the EU's credibility on the international stage: international organisations in general must be able to skilfully mix the 'carrots' of aid and cooperation development, technical and financial assistance, preferential trade agreements, diplomatic recognition, the prospect of membership, etc., with the use of political (e.g., moral condemnation of violation of human rights), diplomatic (e.g., withdrawal of diplomatic recognition), economic (e.g., sanctions, embargoes) and even military 'sticks'.

Thus, the end of the Cold War has created high expectations for international organisations to adjust to the new security environment and to cooperate, as a result, in preventing widespread conflicts. These expectations, however, have seldom been met with effective action.

3. NOT JUST WORDS, DEEDS!

The paradigmatic stance of the international community over prevention stems from the straightforward premise that preventive action is less costly than conflict management. The opportunity costs of preventive action (or costs of non-preventive action, i.e., costs of reconstruction, repatriation of refugees, etc.) have indeed proved huge in the recent past. According to M.E. Brown and R.N. Rosecrance,[6] the costs incurred by third countries in *ex post* conflict management in the case of Bosnia-Herzegovina have amounted to US $ 53.7 billion, as opposed to a US $ 33.3 billion estimate for conflict prevention (i.e., had the international community chosen to intervene preventively). This accounting does not withstand other less directly quantifiable and just as – if not more – important dimensions in terms of human, psychological and political costs (e.g., discredit for the international community at large). From the former Yugoslavia to Kosovo, there is indeed no lack of declarations to recall that conflict prevention should take precedence over crisis management in order to avoid humanitarian catastrophes.[7]

Actions speak louder than words, however, and, so far, the rhetoric has not been matched by effective action. Calls for conflict prevention are symptomatic of the failure of international organisations and major powers to provide security to States and societies at risk. The EU and the international community have failed to live up to their responsibility: nowhere are the lessons more glaring than

---

[6] M.E. Brown and R.N. Rosecrance, *The Cost of Conflict: Prevention and Cure in the Global Arena*, (Lanham, Rowman and Littlefield 1999), p. 51. Other studies comparing the costs of conflict with more modest costs of prevention include M.B. Cranna, *True cost of conflict: seven recent wars and their effects on society* (New York, the New Press 1994).

[7] K.A. Annan, *Prevention of Armed Conflict – Report of the Secretary-General* (New York, United Nations 2002), p. 2.

in the recent past, notably in Rwanda and ex-Yugoslavia (Macedonia excepted). The rarity of preventive deployments is a case in point.[8] Political leaders are generally reluctant to deploy forces in the absence of an open conflict. Western States are wary of putting into place 'out of area' operations where vital strategic interests are not deemed to be directly at stake. The qualification of a potential conflict in conflict prevention will always have, as opposed to downstream 'real' conflict management, a subjective element to it. Government representatives have an understandable tendency, being accountable to their domestic constituencies, to prioritise according to the urgency of the matter, i.e., conflict resolution over prevention.[9] The costs of prevention have to be paid immediately, while their potential benefits are only accrued in the distant future (when politicians may no longer be in power). This long-term perspective vies with the short-term electoral considerations of national governments. A successful prevention strategy further offers low exposure to elected political decision-makers. If successful, the end-result is, by definition, of little visibility (the situation does not deteriorate), especially if the crisis is addressed at a very early stage of the conflict life cycle. Prevention is, thus, a non-opportunistic process which does not cohere with many domestic political agendas. As a result, real conflict management (once violence has broken out) has always taken a clear precedence in the political mindset over preventive statecraft.

Can this be reversed? Can international organisations be of any help in fuelling the much needed conflict prevention activities?

Answering this question calls for a further diagnosis of international organisations' ability to develop well coordinated and efficient preventive strategies. As with any diagnosis, we will first assess the deficiencies/weaknesses of international organisations in the area of conflict prevention: why is conflict prevention so seldom practised and why do international organisations often fail when there is clearly the potential to avoid armed conflict? Based on this preliminary analysis, we will explore ways of enhancing opportunities for the EU and international organisations to cooperate in creating a meaningful international regime for the deterrence of mass violence.

[8] K.A. Annan, op. cit. n. 7 at 45: Preventive deployment has taken place only three times in the past decade with the United Nations Preventive Deployment Force (UNPREDEP) in the former Yugoslav Republic of Macedonia, the United Nations Mission in the Central African Republic (MINURCA) and a succession of operations in Haiti.

[9] S.J. Stedman, 'Alchemy for a New World Order: overselling preventive diplomacy', 74 *Foreign Affairs* (1995), at p. 16.

4. The Conditions for Successful Preventive Action Are Not Fulfilled

International organisations have experienced difficulties in implementing the paradigm shift from interstate deterrence to intrastate multifaceted conflict prevention.[10]

4.1 Lack of consent on the part of war protagonists and the issue of sovereignty

To be effectively implemented, prevention needs to be based on the explicit or tacit consent of at least one of the parties involved.[11] All OSCE missions are based on the prior consent of the host country.[12] This is particularly true as one moves further through the conflict life cycle: peacekeeping, to be effective, must be seen as being impartial.[13] The successful dispatching, in Macedonia, of the first ever UN preventive peacekeeping operation (UNPREDEP – United Nations Preventive Deployment Force) was made possible by the invitation and cooperation of Macedonia's President.[14]

More often than not, however, protagonists in conflicts do not wish and/or cannot be intimidated into external preventive action. Despotic leaders have, indeed, a direct interest in creating and sustaining the conditions of conflict (nota-

---

[10] The literature covers this issue at length. Interesting case studies include:
– *The Fall of Srebrenica, A/54/549 – Report of the Secretary-General Pursuant to General Assembly Resolution 53/35* (New York, United Nations, 15 December 1999);
– *Report of the Independent Inquiry into the Actions of the United Nations during the 1994 Genocide in Rwanda* (New York, United Nations, 15 December 1999);
– *Report of the Panel on United Nations Peace Operations A/55/305 – S/2000/809* (New York, United Nations, 15 August 2000), known as the 'Brahimi Report';
– M. Berdal, 'United Nations Peace Operations: the Brahimi Report in Context', in K.R. Spillmann, et al. (eds.), *Peace Support Operation: Lessons Learned and Future Perspectives* (Bern, Peter Lang 2001), p. 35 at p. 53.
Also see J. Mackinlay, 'The Development of Peacekeeping Forces', in K.R. Spillmann, et al. (eds.), op. cit. n. 10 at 57.
[11] J. Leatherman, et al., *Breaking cycles of Violence – Conflict Prevention in Intrastate Crises* (West Hartford, Kumarian Press 1999), p. 209, refer to the often cited case of Estonia, where President Meri chose to submit his country's legislation to the OSCE and the Council of Europe for comments, and to adopt international organisations' standards on citizenship and minority rights.
[12] E.g., long-term OSCE missions in Kosovo (in Sandjak and Voivodine) had to be interrupted when the host country withdrew its consent.
[13] E.g., in Bosnia, the UN Security Council refused to strengthen the United Nations Protection Force (UNPROFOR) mandate, which could have enabled more robust self-defence and protection of vulnerable populations to avoid blue helmets being seen as a party to the conflict.
[14] The same rationale applies to diplomatic missions. Special envoys cannot even enter the country to which they have been designated without the permission of the targeted government. In 1998, for instance, Milošević refused to meet Felipe Gonzalez who was appointed both Personal Representative for the FRY of OSCE Chairman-in-Office and Special EU Representative for FRY.

bly by demonising adversaries, terrorising target populations, promoting hostile/ divisive messages, etc.) and, thus, in refusing any external mediation/intervention.[15]

The issue of consent is intertwined with that of the inviolability of State sovereignty. In the case mentioned above, the fact that Macedonia was already recognised by the international community as a sovereign State also helped in the decision to deploy UNPREDEP. On the contrary, as demonstrated in Kosovo,[16] there is, traditionally, a major reluctance on the part of members of international organisations to intervene in an internationally recognised territory without the consent of the parties concerned.

The principle of State sovereignty has thus continued to prevail in the post-Cold War era over national determination considerations.

4.2 Competing international organisations

The implementation of coordinated international prevention actions is complicated by competing international organisations. Of course, not all international organisations are involved in every conflict situation, but in the course of a conflict's life cycle on the European scene, the UN, the EU, the OSCE, the Council of Europe and NATO, can all claim to have a role to play in conflict prevention. The EU shares for instance with the OSCE[17] and the Council of Europe the role of promoting democratic values and structures in Central and Eastern European countries, South East Europe and the former Soviet Union. All these organisations embark on similar (fact-finding, election monitoring, etc.) missions.

A good example of a lack of synergies is the proliferation of envoys by international organisations, thereby representing various and overlapping constituen-

---

[15] E.g., Milošević's non-cooperative stance in the Rambouillet negotiations. See R. Väyrinen, 'Challenges to preventive action', in K.R. Spillmann, et al. (eds.), *Peace Support Operations: Lessons learned and future Perspectives* (Bern, Peter Lang 2001), at p. 59.

[16] Milošević had obtained from Russia, in June 1998, a commitment that 'Kosovo was Yugoslavia's internal affairs'. As a result, the UN Security Council satisfied itself with issuing declarations against Belgrade's policy in Kosovo: in March 1998, the Security Council condemned 'the growing repression' of the civilian populations in Kosovo and demanded that the parties put an end to the violence. It was not until the conflict had escalated into mass violence, however, that the international community reacted with mediation (Rambouillet Conference) and military force (NATO bombing beginning at end of March 1999). For a detailed calendar of the Kosovo operations, see R. Väyrinen, op. cit. n. 15, p. 59.

[17] The OSCE's role is addressed elsewhere in this volume (chapter 18). It is worth mentioning, however, that the OSCE is not just a normative body but has also developed a large range of tools for field operations to prevent conflicts and promote peace-building efforts. Particularly noteworthy has been the role played in this respect by the Office of the High Commissioner on National Minorities in identifying situations of crisis and seeking solutions to prevent violence from breaking out. OSCE further has the advantage of its inclusiveness (Russia and the US are both full-fledged members).

cies. The EU itself clearly used and abused the instrument of special envoys in the former Yugoslavia.[18]

Actors can become involved in an uncoordinated manner and work at cross-purposes. This was the case in Bosnia, for instance, where NATO advocated resorting to air power, while the United Nations, on the other hand, feared that military force would jeopardise its UNPROFOR peacekeeping mission on the ground which needed Milošević's consent and cooperation to carry out its task properly.[19]

Major powers naturally favour the action of organisations where their weight is greater. Hence the US insistence on NATO's intervention in the Balkans. Another example is the Pact for Stability and Security in Europe (proposed by French Prime Minister E. Balladur in 1993), where Americans and Russians undertook to anchor the initiative to the CSCE (now OSCE) of which they are members.

Finally, a problem of diffusion of responsibility between international actors can arise, whereby each international organisation abdicates responsibility to another.[20]

The often cited lack of synergy should not, however, overshadow cases of good cooperation between international organisations.

This is particularly apparent in the international community's reconstruction/peace-building efforts. There is a plethora of examples of fruitful coordination between international organisations in this field.[21]

---

[18] In chronological order: Lord Carrington, David Owen, Carl Bildt (with three hats: UN, Contact Group and that of the EU), Carlos Westendorp, Felipe Gonzalez (OSCE and the EU), Wolfgang Petrush, Marti Ahtisaari and Panagiotis Roumeliotis.

[19] This case showed that NATO and the UN have different organisational cultures: in a nutshell, whereas the former is a military organisation, the latter is aimed at promoting conflict resolution via peaceful means. Article 51 of the UN Charter has been interpreted as permitting the use of force only in self-defence, and only 'if an armed attack occurs against a Member of the United Nations' (e.g., Iraq's invasion of Kuwait).

[20] C. Peck, *Sustainable Peace – The Role of the UN and regional Organizations in preventing Conflicts* (Lanham, Rowman and Littlefield 1998), p. 223.

[21] In the case of Bosnia, for instance, the Dayton Agreement was closely followed by a Peace Implementation Conference held in London and attended by over 50 countries and international organisations. The Stability Pact for South-East Europe (adopted on 10 June 1999 in Cologne by all Foreign Ministers from the participating countries) is yet another illustration of efforts geared at involving and coordinating financial and technical aid from a large array of actors in the regions: CEECs and South-East European countries, EU Member States, European Commission, third countries (US, Canada, Japan, Russia, Norway and Switzerland) and international organisations (UN, OSCE, Council of Europe, NATO, International Monetary Fund, European Investment Fund, Bank for Economic Reconstruction and Development, OECD).

NATO started to support UN or OSCE mandated peacekeeping/post settlement (e.g., implementation of the Dayton Agreement 1995) operations as early as 1992. It has contributed to a secure environment for other international organisations, *inter alia*, to perform their work properly. The OSCE generally works in close collaboration with the UN High Commissioner for Refugees, the UN High Commissioner for Human Rights, the UNDP, etc. The European Union provides financial and technical assistance.

Overlapping membership of different organisations also helps to promote co-operation in the area of conflict prevention and offers important inducements to prospective members to achieve the principles of good governance. The prospect of membership creates momentum for reform in candidate countries. Enlargement is seen as the best way to entrench peace, stability and democracy in a region. Parallel enlargements of the EU and NATO catalyse compliance with a set of structural standards within the realm of conflict prevention. The membership tool coheres with what Joseph Nye[22] has defined as the 'soft' rather than 'hard' power of States/international organisations. It converts the economic power of the EU[23] and the hard security/military clout of NATO into driving forces for the adoption of norms of good governance.

4.3   Lack of resources

The lack of resources has to be seen in relation to the mandate (what is commonly referred to as the 'capability-expectation' gap). For instance, UNPROFOR in Bosnia clearly lacked the necessary means to prevent massacres and deportations, let alone its own self-defence.[24] As a result of its limited resources, UNPROFOR personnel were made hostage to Bosnian-Serb forces and this aggravated the situation on the ground. Similarly, in Somalia significant UN/US casualties resulted from the discrepancy between the fairly ambitious mandate of the United Nations Operation in Somalia (UNOSOM II March 1993 – March 1995) and the limited forces made available to it.

Limited resources aggravate the dilemma between *ex ante* prevention and *ex post* management. As international organisations' resources are strained, the tendency to focus on problems that have reached the stage of open conflict, at the expense of preventive action, is exacerbated.

Although lack of funding is particularly acute in the case of the UN[25] in view of its wide-ranging commitments, it is a feature which is common to all interna-

---

[22] J. Nye, loc. cit. n. 5, p. 153 at 171.

[23] The lure of membership has become a powerful foreign policy tool for the EU, not only with its central and East European neighbours but also in relation to South-East European countries (the so-called 'Stabilisation and Association Process' offers these countries the long-term prospect of full integration into the EU).

[24] K. Talentino, 'Evaluating success and failure: conflict prevention in Cambodia and Bosnia' in D. Carment and A. Schnabel, *Conflict Prevention: Path to Peace or Grand Illusion?* (Tokyo, United Nations University 2003), p. 78. According to K.A. Annan ('The Peace-keeping Prescription' in K.M. Cahill, *Preventive Diplomacy: stopping wars before they start* (New York, Harper Collins 1997) p. 186), the UN Secretariat had asked for 34,000 troops for UNPROFOR to defend the so-called 'safe areas' and only got 7,600.

[25] K.A. Annan, op. cit n. 7, pp. 82-84. According to its Secretary General, the UN still lack the resources to embark on an effective conflict prevention strategy.

tional organisations.[26] The 'capability-expectations' gap will only be breached with appropriate resource commitments on the part of major powers within international organisations. As previously mentioned, preventive action is a time-expansive endeavour, and Member States must recognise the long-term perspective in the mandate and resources given.[27]

4.4   Lack of political will within international organisations

International organisations are member-driven. They are only as effective as their members allow them to be. In crisis situations requiring operational prevention, decisions must be taken in a speedy manner. This is anathema to the consensus-based decision-making practised by international organisations. Even though some international organisations now provide for some exceptions to the unanimity rule,[28] in practice action is taken by consensus. The ever-present possibility of a veto from one or more members (a permanent member in the UN Security Council, members of the OSCE, etc.) acts as a major brake on international intervention, especially where sovereignty is an issue.[29]

As mentioned above in the case of the UN and NATO (see *supra* n.19), divisions in international organisations are often symptomatic of diverging patterns of interests and cultures. Cultural sensitivity in particular is crucial in conflict prevention. The dilemma for democracies concerning the use of force in crisis management (beyond humanitarian-oriented deployment) is especially acute in the case of the EU, whose foundations are based on non-coercive (economic/functionalist) pacification of antagonist actors (originally France and Germany). However, not all powers and cultures take the same approach with respect to military intervention. The US public is, for instance, traditionally much more

---

[26] According to the European Commission, the current annual Community budget for CFSP (€ 30 million in 2002) needs to be increased substantially so as to accommodate future civilian management operations, notably in view of crisis management commitments (European Convention Working Group VII on External Action – Working doc. 24 from the European Commission, 11 November 2002, pp. 5-6)

[27] Peck, op. cit. n. 20, at 75: 'the organization [the UN] has simply not been given adequate resources to allow it to develop and adapt its procedure to conflict prevention ... Until member states can agree on what should be done and provide sufficient resources, this situation is likely to persist'.

[28] E.g., OSCE 'consensus minus one' for rare urgent cases, reinforced qualified majority for the adoption of EU acts of an implementing nature under CFSP, affirmative vote of nine members of the UN Security Council including the concurring votes of the five permanent members, etc.

[29] In the case of Kosovo, the UN Security Council was paralysed by Russia's unwillingness to agree on any enforcement action against Serbia (see *supra* n. 16). Different attitudes toward the use of force also account for the Security Council's failure to prevent US unilateralism in the war against Saddam Hussein's regime. Thus, in the two cases of Kosovo and Iraq, no Security Council authorisation was given for the use of force.

supportive of the use of force[30] (including ground troops, in spite of possible casualties) than EU public opinion in general.

We have undertaken this study at a time when many commentators conclude that the US is prone to reject multilateral organisations as venues for the effective promotion of US foreign policy, especially in so far as unilateral 'preventive wars' are concerned. While it is difficult to contradict this stance in the case of *Operation Iraqi Freedom*, it is also apparent that the US has always had a differentiated approach to conflict management *lato sensu*. In many policy areas the US still considers that multilateralism can help it achieve its goal, especially in so far as burden sharing is concerned, e.g., *Operation Concordia* in Macedonia where the US agreed to the dispensing of its assets in the multilateral framework of NATO so as to enable EU-led operations (see *infra* 5.3.2), or the fight against terrorism. The US stance on the use of violence can further be complementary to that of 'soft security' oriented institutions: without the threat of resorting to military action on the part of the US, Resolution 1441 (new inspection regime in Iraq) would probably never have been accepted by the Iraqis. This brings us back to the need for a wide and integrated panoply of preventive instruments.

5.   THE WAY AHEAD: A MORE FLEXIBLE DIVISION OF LABOUR BETWEEN INTERNATIONAL ACTORS

The purpose of this section is to encourage a fuller appreciation of the opportunities for the international community to cooperate in reducing the number of conflicts. We will start with general considerations that can be applied to all international organisations, before proposing a flexible allocation of tasks between the EU, the UN and NATO (the OSCE and the Council of Europe will be dealt with elsewhere in this volume).

5.1 Diffusing a culture of prevention

Introducing prevention as a central theme in all international organisations can contribute an important step towards developing a common culture of prevention. This should be done at various stages in the policy process. First of all, via the strengthening of analytical capacities (e.g., the EU Policy Planning Unit and the UN Department of Political Affairs). Furthermore, the sharing of information between various organisations may be conducive to the progressive definition of common criteria/risk indicators to be applied to unfolding crises, thus encourag-

---

[30] There does not seem to be an enduring Somalia syndrome among the US public at large (Michael J. Glennon 'Why the Security Council Failed', *Foreign Affairs* (May-June 2003); R. Foot et al. (eds.), *US hegemony and international organization* (Oxford, Oxford University Press 2003), p. 265 at 272).

ing the emergence of a community of views on the opportunity and modalities for intervention. The specific role of regional organisations with respect to information-gathering and sharing is examined below (see *infra* 5.3.1).

Another complementary way to foster a culture of prevention is via the institutionalisation of discussions at the highest political level (e.g., the UN Security Council, the European Council and the North Atlantic Council) on vulnerable situations, coupled with a consideration of possible preventive options.[31] In these high-level discussions/interactions, a notion of society-based, rather than State-based security, needs to be introduced and refined. The initiatives of some international organisations' Members or Secretariat to provide an impetus to such discussions can indeed help to undermine the Statist approach/mindset of policy-makers.[32]

5.2   The right mix of instruments: a gradual/differentiated approach

As mentioned above, any preventive action needs to include incentives for its acceptance and disincentives (in the form of gradual threats: cutting off aid, sanctions, embargoes, direct military intervention) for its rejection. An appropriate combination of positive and negative measures needs to be modulated on a case-by-case basis.

In the Bosnian case, the low-key mandate of UNPROFOR was too late and too little in view of the unfolding warfare between belligerents. Negotiations under the joint authority of the EC and the UN[33] ultimately proved ineffective due to the lack of a credible military deterrence. As previously mentioned, some nationalist political leaders have a direct interest in the worsening of situations. To come back to the issue of consent, international action should sometimes be geared towards inducing or even forcing reluctant protagonists into seek peaceful settlement. Some indigenous leaders can and should be heavily influenced to avoid violence. If they cannot be persuaded, they must be coerced into resorting to peaceful settlement. The credible threat of and/or resorting to the use of force

---

[31] Early warning *per se* does not suffice. In many conflicts (e.g., Rwanda, Kosovo) the problem was more that of early response than early warning. The international community had been alerted to the deteriorating situation in Kosovo, all through the 1990s (See M. Szapiro, 'Will the Kosovo Crisis Rejuvenate CFSP and European Defence?' in D. Mahncke, *Old Frontiers – New Frontiers* (Bern, Peter Lang 2001)). Similarly, the history of hatred politics between the Hutu and Tutsi in Rwanda was widely known. The civil war had waged since a Rwandan Patriotic Front invasion from Uganda as early as 1992. (C.P. Scherrer, *Structural Prevention of Ethnic Violence* (Houndsmill, Palgrave Macmillan 2002, p. 228)).

[32] 'The time of absolute and exclusive sovereignty has passed; its theory has never been matched by reality. It is the task of leaders for States to understand this': B. Boutros Ghali, *Addendum to the An Agenda for Peace* (New York, United Nations 1995), p. 3, para. 17

[33] 'Why are some ethnic disputes settled peacefully, while others become violent? Comparing Slovakia, Macedonia, and Kosovo' in H.R. Alker, et al. (eds.), *Journeys through Conflicts* (Lanham, Rowman and Littlefield 2001), p. 176.

is, in some cases (e.g., convincing Milošević to withdraw Serbian forces from Kosovo), the only way to force uncooperative warlords into negotiations. In the cases of Bosnia and Kosovo, the 'civilian' power-based intervention of the UN and the EU did not suffice to persuade Milošević to accept a peaceful settlement. Only military action via NATO (August/September 1995 *Operation Deliberate Force* in Bosnia, March-June 1999 *Operation Allied Force* in Kosovo) ultimately brought Milošević to the negotiating table.

However, while the credible threat of the use of force is a precondition, in many difficult cases, for the success of conflict prevention, actually resorting to the military option evidences the failure of prevention proper. Where mass violence is not imminent, 'carrots' such as preferential trade, development aid and the prospect of membership should prevail over the 'sticks'.[34] Hence there should be a graduated correlation between the mix of measures employed and the level of or potential for conflict escalation: the proportion and degree of coercive and non-coercive measures will vary according to the stages of the conflict life cycle. Military intervention should be envisaged as *ultima ratio*. NATO's military intervention at an early stage could in particular jeopardise the credibility and impartiality of preventive diplomacy/deployment.[35] As the conflict escalates the threat or actual use of force may, however, prove to be necessary. As shown in Bosnia and Kosovo, a policy of non-violence can make matters worse.

5.3 The EU in the division of labour between global and regional organisations

As mentioned above, no single multilateral organisation possesses the full range of tools required at every stage of a conflict situation. Some international organisations are better equipped to resort to the use of force while others have a comparatively well developed range of 'soft power' attributes: Whereas the OSCE relies exclusively on non-coercive means in the field of conflict prevention/management[36] (see chapter 18), it clearly lacks the institutional means to coerce or deter. On the other hand, NATO, as a military organisation, epitomises

---

[34] M.S. Lund argues, for instance, that 'rather than almost totally isolating Yugoslavia by casting it so readily as a pariah State, a more consistently vigorous strategy that maintained the prospect of positive incentives for Milošević upon good behaviour, while also supporting the strengthening of his political opposition to compete electorally, (...) may have created some brakes on the escalation' of the Kosovo conflict. M.S. Lund, *Preventing violent conflicts: a strategy for preventive diplomacy* (Washington, United States Institute of Peace Press 2001). On the graduated approach in general, see Lund, op. cit. n. 34, pp. 155-160.

[35] European contributors to UNPROFOR (UK and France) feared the use of force (air strikes) advocated by the US in NATO would jeopardise the perceived impartiality and real safety of their troops. When air power was finally used on 11 April 1994 to protect UN personnel in Goradze, Karadzić accused the UN of taking sides in the conflict.

[36] See *supra* n. 17: the OSCE is in a privileged position to embark on long-term post-conflict peace-building activities, in cooperation with the EU and the UN.

the hard/military stance in crisis management *lato sensu*. As per the EU, it has resolutely embarked on the process of complementing its panoply of civilian means with an autonomous military capacity (see *infra* 5.3.2).

Just as the appropriate combination of positive and negative measures needs to be modulated on a case-by-case basis, the optimal division of labour between international organisations will need to be case-specific. The section below only aims to offer broad guidelines to help achieve a flexible division of labour between international institutions.

5.3.1   *The UN and regional organisations (including the EU)*

The UN has the ability to focus world attention on key issues. It is the only global intergovernmental organisation founded on its members' commitment 'to take effective collective measures for the prevention and removal of threats to international peace' (UN Charter Article 1 para. 1). The UN has the legitimacy to act as a mandate organisation. According to the European Commission's Communication on the EU/UN strategic partnership of September 2003, the 'UN is the backbone of the multilateral system'.[37]

From the days of the first Secretary General, Trygve Lie, up until now, numerous UN memoranda and reports have focused on conflict prevention. This trend has intensified since the end of the Cold War. The most notable example of the strengthening of the UN mandate in conflict prevention can be found in the landmark report of the Secretary General Boutros Boutros Ghali 'An Agenda for Peace: preventive diplomacy, peacemaking and peace-keeping', notably in relation to preventive diplomacy.[38] The lifting of the ideological veil at the end of the Cold War further allowed for greater emphasis on the close links between conflict prevention and democratisation.[39] Secretary General Kofi Annan's 2002 report on the 'Prevention of armed conflict' presents the prevention of violent conflict as a resolute UN priority.[40]

---

[37] COM (2003) 526 Communication from the Commission to the Council and the European Parliament – *The EU and the UN: the choice of multilateralism*, Conclusion at p. 23.

[38] B. Boutros Ghali, *An agenda for peace: preventive diplomacy, peacemaking and peace-keeping*, Report A/47/277-S/24111 of the Secretary General pursuant to the Summit meeting of the Security Council on 31 January 1992: B. Boutros Ghali sees a continuum between what he describes as the four key roles of the United Nations: preventive diplomacy, peacemaking, peacekeeping and peace-building.

[39] B. Boutros Ghali, *Agenda for Democratization*, Supplement to Reports A/50/332 and A/51/512 on Democratization, UN, 17 December 1996, in particular para. 16 'democracy contributes to preserving peace and security' and para. 18 'democratic institutions within States may likewise be conducive to peace among States'.

[40] K.A. Annan, op. cit. n. 7: the author also commits to further UN reform in the field of conflict prevention in relation to other institutions, notably by engaging in a more active use of preventive deployment, by strengthening UN country teams, by reinforcing coordination within the UN (agencies/programmes/funds) and with other international organisations (World Bank, Monetary Fund,

Aside from declarations of intent, the UN has built up a comprehensive panoply of preventive instruments and bodies involved directly or indirectly in conflict prevention. Within the UN, the Secretary General, the Security Council and the General Assembly, *inter alia*,[41] play an important part in the peace and security fields. As the UN main decision-making body in charge of the maintenance of international peace and security, the Security Council should finally play a key role in preventing armed conflict. The Secretary General can and does make use of his 'good offices', send fact-finding and confidence-building missions, convene 'friends of the Secretary General' groups to help coordinate international response, appoint special representatives, develop regional prevention strategies, etc. He is also given powers to 'bring to the attention of the Security Council any matter which in his opinion may threaten the maintenance of international peace and security' (UN Charter Article 99), which he has also done on various occasions. The General Assembly has issued various resolutions and recommendations in relation to conflict prevention, notably based on reports from the Secretary General.[42]

Yet, as reported by Koffi Annan himself in his 2002 report on the work of the Organization, the 'UN is still an imperfect organization'.[43] The Security Council's 'focus remains exclusively on crises and emergencies, normally becoming involved only when violence has already occurred'.[44] We have already mentioned the non-opportunistic dimension of conflict prevention, which accounts for the Security Council focusing on disputes that have already escalated

---

WTO) and by arranging regional workshops to discuss the regional dimension of cooperation in conflict prevention.

[41] Many of the UN agencies and programmes and international organisations such as the United Nations High Commissioner for Refugees, the United Nations Development Programme, the United Nation's Children Fund, the World Food Programme, the World Health Organisation and the Bretton Woods Institutions contribute to conflict prevention.

[42] E.g., Resolutions A/47/120A of 18 December 1992 and A/47/120 of 20 September 1993 on the above-mentioned 'Agenda for peace' with specific recommendations geared towards its implementation (recommendation to create a working party / sub-working group on conflict prevention / preventive diplomacy, recommendation to draw up a list of personalities for fact-finding / confidence-building missions or making use of 'good offices', etc.). See also the 'Declaration on the occasion of the fiftieth anniversary of the UN' at <http://www.un.org/UNSO/dec.htm>. As underlined more recently in the July 2003 57th session of the General Assembly (Resolution A/RES/57/337 on the prevention of armed conflict, the following Secretary General's 2002 report on the work of the organization), the UN has contributed decisively to many positive outcomes in the field of conflict prevention (e.g., in Slovakia (peaceful independence), Macedonia (preventive deployment), East Timor (independence and UN membership), Afghanistan and Angola). The setting up of the International Criminal Court (ICC) in 2002 is further presented as an 'unprecedented step forward for world order and justice'.

[43] K.A. Annan, A/57/1 *Report of the Secretary-General on the work of the organization* (August 2002), introduction, para. 8.

[44] K.A. Annan, op. cit. n. 7, at 19.

into armed conflict.[45] Another reason is the composition of the Security Council: permanent members of the Security Council have little or no incentive to take, or sustain, preventive action in non-neighbouring States (e.g., the Great Lakes). As noted by many scholars,[46] there is a compelling need to enlarge the Security Council to ensure that its membership reflects the world of today rather than that of 1945.[47]

As mentioned in the European Commission's September 2003 Communication on EU/UN cooperation,[48] there are ample examples of positive cooperation between the EU and the UN in the area of conflict prevention, notably in the former Yugoslavia and in Africa. *Artemis*, the recent EU operation in the Democratic Republic of Congo (see *infra* 5.3.2), is a promising illustration of using the EU's emerging military force under a UN mandate (Security Council Resolution 1484 of 30 May 2003). Cooperation has also been stepped up at the political level, notably with twice-yearly high-level meetings.[49] However, the Commission recognises that further progress at the administrative/desk level[50] and on the ground is still much needed. This will, according to the Communication, require further 'bold steps to be taken in terms of information-sharing and the adoption of common operational standards'.

Recent institutional developments in the Common Foreign and Security Policy (CFSP)/European Security and Defence Policy (ESDP) have been acknowledged,

---

[45] Other reasons for the post-Cold War marginalisation of the UN Security Council in the case of Kosovo and Iraq have already been mentioned in the section on the lack of political will – see *supra* n. 29. In the same way, as an US rejection of multilateralism *per se* is not evident, the Security Council is not bound to fall into desuetude, especially in so far as common threats are concerned (terrorism, proliferation of weapons of mass destruction, etc.) or where permanent members can agree to mandate a coalition of the 'able and the willing' (e.g. *Operation Concordia* – see *infra* 5.3.2).

[46] E.g., B.M. Russet, *The once and future Security Council* (New York, St Martin's Press 1997); J. Morris 'UN Security Council Reform: a counsel for the 21st century', 31/3 *Security Dialogue* (2000), p. 265 at 277; J. Menkes 'Equality of UN member States', 4/1 *Polish Quaterly of International Affairs* (1995) p. 79 at 96.

[47] Pending the necessary constitutional reforms, the UN Security Council could do more, for instance, to bring regional organisations into its deliberations, by inviting representatives of regional organisations to attend and participate in issue-specific Council meetings as observers (no voting rights).

[48] COM (2003) 526 final, op. cit. n. 37.

[49] Ministerial Troïka meetings with the UN Secretary General and meetings of the EU High Representative and the Commissioner for External Relations with the UN Secretary General or Deputy Secretary General. The latter is also invited regularly to the EU Political and Security Committee (COPS).

[50] E.g., between Commission/Council/Member States officials and the UN Department of Political Affairs, with the UN Department of Peacekeeping Operations, UNDP and the UN Office for the Coordination of Humanitarian Affairs. According to the Greek Presidency's conflict prevention report of 18 June 2003, contacts at a working level have been taken between the EU and 'the UN Framework Team for co-ordination on early warning & preventive action, a structure associating all relevant UN agencies and Departments and dealing with situation analysis in a conflict prevention perspective'.

by the UN Secretary General, as contributing resolutely to reinforcing the strategic partnership with the UN in the field of conflict prevention.[51] When presenting his recommendations for a European Security Strategy to the Thessaloniki European Council, the EU High Representative for CFSP, Javier Solana, emphasised that the Union's role was to contribute actively to render multilateralism more effective, with the UN being central to such a system.[52] Ultimately, these developments, coupled with the enlargement process and expected institutional innovations in the draft Constitutional Treaty,[53] are bound to the provoke consideration of more incisive forms of participation and of the role of the EU in the UN, in particular within the framework of the Security Council.

The EU is by no means the only regional organisation with which the UN aims to develop prevention strategies. More generally, the challenge for the UN is to develop partnerships with regional players. The UN Charter sets out in Chapter VIII the need for cooperation with regional entities to address regional problems.[54] The founding acts of many regional organisations/arrangements refer

---

[51] The creation of the Conflict Prevention Network by the European Commission (1997), of the Policy Planning and Early Warning Unit (referred to as Policy Unit) under the auspices of the High Representative for CFSP Javier Solana (1999) and the adoption of an EU programme for conflict prevention (European Commission Communication COM (2001) 211 of 11 April 2001 on Conflict Prevention) endorsed by 15-16 June 2001 Göteborg European Council) have been acknowledged by the UN Secretary General as positive developments in the framework of enhanced cooperation between the two organisations. In his 2002 report (K.A. Annan, op. cit. n. 7, at 19), the Secretary General also notes the strengthening of the high-level annual dialogue between the two institutions in the area of conflict prevention (including also OSCE and the Council of Europe to rationalise a division of labour between the four institutions). Similarly, the EU's rapid reaction force (on 10-11 December 1999, the Helsinki European Council called for the establishment of a rapid reaction force of 50,000-60,000 soldiers, deployable within 60 days and sustainable for at least a year), may become a surrogate UN peacekeeping force, for low-scale operations, as in the precedent of *Operation Artemis* in the Democratic Republic of Congo (see *infra* 5.3.2 and n. 68/69).

[52] Thessaloniki European Council 19 and 20 June 2003, Presidency Conclusions para. 54 on the 'EU Security Strategy'. 'Effective multilateralism with the UN as its core' is recalled in Brussels European Council 12 December 2003 Presidency Conclusions (para. 85) in relation to its adoption of the European Security Strategy.

[53] Proposals to grant the EU legal personality (Article I-6 of the draft Constitutional Treaty) and to create the post of European Foreign Affairs Minister (Article I-27) are likely to facilitate the uniform representation of the EU at the international level. Article III-206 of the draft Constitutional Treaty provides that where the EU has defined its position in relation to an issue on the Security Council's agenda, the EU Minister for Foreign Affairs shall be asked by EU members of the Security Council to present the Union's position. Currently, representation at the UN level relies on Article 19 of the Treaty that merely commits Member States (permanent members of the Security Council and others) to coordinate their action.

[54] Greater coordination between the UN and regional organisations is high on all international/regional organisations' agendas. For instance, in recent years, the UN and all regional organisations have instituted a practice of holding biennal meetings to discuss potential violence in the regions, possible preventive strategies/guidelines for coordinated regional efforts (e.g., establishment of peace-building units, joint assessment missions to be sent to the field, etc.) but actions rarely follow suit, due to a lack of resource commitment on the part of members. A further positive step in institu-

in turn to the United Nations.[55] Regional organisations are sometimes indeed better suited (or less ill-fitted) to carry out preventive action. They possess a first-hand knowledge of the background to the conflict and a greater interest in its resolution. Such regional structures can provide possible means of alleviation/de-escalation, including providing a forum for efforts to decrease tensions. Regional organisations are better placed to bring together diverse actors and measures, due to their more focused geographical scope. Finally, with fewer items competing in principle for attention on their agenda in comparison to the UN, regional organisations may also be able to respond to crises more swiftly, provided they can equip themselves with the relevant tools.

As exemplified by the allocation of competence inside the EU between the European and national/regional/local levels on a case-by-case basis, the relationship between the global and regional level could be based on the principle of *subsidiarity* whereby the upper level would take action only if and in so far as the objectives of the proposed action cannot be sufficiently achieved at the lower level. Hence those problems that can be addressed properly by a 'lower-level' organisation should be handled at a 'higher' level. Where conflict protagonists are incapable of resolving their own dispute, assistance for prevention should first shift to the regional level.[56] The regional organisation may thus be deemed as the optimal level for conflict prevention at the early stages, where less military and political clout is needed from the international community. If regional organisations lack the capacity/ability to help provide peaceful resolutions to conflicts, then the wider international community should become involved.[57]

5.3.2   *The EU and NATO*

While the UN provides legitimacy, NATO and the EU can act as synergetic mandate carriers, providing political, economic (for the latter only) and military resources.[58]

---

tion-building, as proposed by Peck, op. cit n. 20, p. 253 and p. 227 at 248, consists of creating 'regional centres for sustainable peace to deal with assistance in dispute settlement and long-term assistance in developing good governance under the shared responsibility of the UN and the international organisation concerned'.

[55] E.g., Article 11 TEU states that the objectives of the Common Foreign and Security Policy should be: 'to safeguard the common values, fundamental interests, independence and integrity of the Union in conformity with the principles of the United Nations Charter (...); to preserve peace and strengthen international security, in accordance with the principles of the United Nations Charter, ...'

[56] Preventive diplomacy in the form of holding and mediating a conference of the parties can be best organised by regional organisations, with the help of authoritative mediators.

[57] E.g., with the Vance mission taking over from the EC special envoy Lord Carrington in the early 1990s, the EC was implicitly recognising that only the UN had the required political authority and legitimacy to respond to the crisis. For further development on this 'vertical hierarchy', the reader can refer to M.S. Lund, op. cit. n.34 at 183.

[58] 'Without the UN and the OSCE, the rule of law would be replaced by the rule of force. Without NATO and the EU, the rule of law would be powerless', W. Biermann (ed.), *Peace Support Operations: lessons learned and future perspectives* (Bern, Peter Lang 2001) p. 100.

Recent NATO/EU cooperation[59] provides encouraging *prima facie* evidence that, provided the requisite impetus is there, rhetoric can indeed be matched by effective action.

Concrete EU/NATO cooperation seems to have developed substantially in the last five years, notably under the joint action of the EU High Representative for CFSP (and former NATO Secretary General) Javier Solana, and NATO's Secretary General, Lord Robertson. The impetus for renewed cooperation was undoubtedly linked to EU political and institutional ESDP developments in relation to the 1999 Kosovo crisis[60] and the growing pressure on the US in its War against Terror since the events of 11 September 2001. The US strategic focus on Iraq, Iran and North Korea may ultimately accentuate US disengagement from the European (and Sub-Saharan African) battlefields.

Cooperation between the EU and NATO is centred on the operational concept of a 'Combined Joint Task Force' (CJTF),[61] developed by NATO to enhance the flexibility of its military structure. CJTFs would ensure the operational link between the EU's 'autonomous' capacity (3-4 December 1998 Franco-British Declaration in Saint-Malo, followed by the Cologne European Council on 3-4 June 1999, *inter alia*) and the development of a European Pillar of the North Atlantic Alliance (European Security and Defence Identity (ESDI) – Berlin 3 June 1996 North Atlantic Council). These 'separable but not separate' capabilities will enable the EU to use NATO assets on EU-led missions. CJTFs are made possible on the basis of a series of agreements between the EU and NATO on access by the former to collective assets and capabilities of the latter for EU-led operations.[62] On 13 December 2002 the North Atlantic Council made a series of landmark decisions to put in place special arrangements for NATO support to EU-led operations (know as the 'Berlin Plus' arrangement[63]). Cooperation concerns ca-

---

[59] Cooperation includes EU/NATO working group meetings, joint meetings at ambassadorial (COPS and North Atlantic Council) and Ministerial level and informal contacts and formal meetings between the High Representative for CFSP, the EU Presidency and the NATO Secretary General.

[60] For a brief account of EU developments in the civilian and military fields in relation to the Petersberg tasks and an explanation of the British u-turn and the apparent Franco-British convergence on European defence, the reader can refer, *inter alia*, to M. Szapiro, loc. cit. n. 31.

[61] On the basis of the June 1996 Berlin Ministerial Summit: 'A Combined Joint Task Force is a multinational, multi-service deployable task force generated and tailored primarily, but not exclusively, for military operations not involving the defence of Alliance territory, such as humanitarian relief and peace-keeping. It provides a flexible and efficient means whereby the Alliance can generate rapidly deployable forces with appropriate command and control arrangements'.

[62] Such agreements are adopted under Article 24 EU which allows the Presidency to negotiate on behalf of the Council.

[63] The 'Berlin Plus' (1996) agreement contains four points:
– assured EU access to NATO operational planning;
– presumption of availability to the EU of NATO capabilities and common assets;
– NATO European command options for EU-led operations, including the European role of Deputy SACEUR;
– adaptation of the NATO defence planning system to incorporate the availability of forces for EU operations.

pacity planning, modalities of access to NATO assets, mechanisms of permanent consultation between the two institutions and the security of classified information. While specific procedures and commitments had been agreed previously for the first three points[64], an agreement on the latter (confidentiality agreement) was only finally reached in March 2003[65] after two years of intensive negotiations. This agreement between the EU and NATO is the crowning achievement of efforts taken by EU institutions[66] to align the treatment and transmission of classified information with that of NATO. This level playing field for information security and exchange is an indispensable prerequisite for the efficient organisation of joint operations by the two organisations (cf., *Operation Concordia* below, which followed, by a few days, the signature of the agreement). This agreement will also foster cooperation with other international organisations (e.g., the OSCE) on the basis of strict information security standards.

The EU/NATO cooperative framework ultimately aims to allow for intervention to take place in a differentiated manner: under NATO's flagship (e.g., *Operation Allied Force* in Kosovo), under the EU flag dispensing with NATO's assets in situations where the US is reluctant to send troops (the first ever EU-led peace-keeping mission to make use of NATO's assets is *Operation Concordia* in Macedonia which took over, on 31 March 2003, from NATO's *Operation Allied Harmony*[67]); under an autonomous EU chain of command for operations where NATO would not want to be engaged. The EU French-led *Operation Artemis* in the Democratic Republic of Congo launched on 12 June 2003 is the first EU autonomous military mission under an UN mandate.[68] The last option (autonomy) is, however, only possible for low-key (thus excluding peace-making) operations.[69] For larger scale operations, any chain of command would need to involve the means and capacity of NATO (mainly that of the US within NATO), as the

---

[64] Thus, specific commitments and consultation mechanisms are foreseen at both preoperational and operational stages (including mechanisms for access to capabilities) between EU and non-EU continental NATO members (including Turkey which lifted its veto in December 2002). For a succinct account of 'Berlin Plus' implementation see J.Y Haine at <http://www.iss-eu.org/esdp/03-jyhb+.pdf>.

[65] *OJEC* [2003] L 80/36.

[66] Council Decision of 19 March 2001 adopting the Council's security regulations, *OJEC* [2001] L 101/1 and Commission Decision of 29 November 2001 amending its internal Rules of Procedure, *OJEC* [2001] L 317/1.

[67] Resolution 1371 (2003): *operation Concordia* is undertaken in agreement with the host country's government (an indispensable prerequisite, as developed above, see *supra* section 4.1).

[68] Resolution 1484 (2003): *operation Artemis* was set up on France's initiative and under its direction (General Neveux appointed EU Operation commander, the operational Headquarters located in Paris, etc.). As recognised by the 19 and 20 June 2003 Thessaloniki European Council Presidency Conclusions, this EU-led military operation has provided a strong impetus for cooperation between the EU and the UN (see section 5.3.1 above).

[69] *Operation Artemis'* mandate is limited in scale (around 1,200 soldiers in July 2003 posted in the city of Bunia whereas the entire country – which is the size of Western Europe – is subject to

EU still clearly lacks command, control, computers, intelligence, surveillance and reconnaissance capacity, plus the necessary air and sea transport capabilities.

6. CONCLUSION

As we have seen, any conflict prevention regime must be multifaceted and designed for the long term. Conflict prevention *lato sensu* strains the capacity of any single international organisation, let alone national government. To provide for the wide repertoire of political, socio-economic and military instruments required, international organisations are compelled to cooperate. Most international organisations are still ill-equipped to deal with intrastate violence, though. So far, the adaptation of mandates and mechanisms has not proved easy, especially in view of diverging cultures *vis-à-vis* preventive action and submission to the rule of law.[70] Attributes and instruments of State sovereignty, on which most international organisations are founded,[71] have proved to be unwieldy in their application to the paradigmatic shift in post-Cold War conflicts.

The EU is at an advantage in so far as it can offer a uniquely broad spectrum of instruments: as a 'civilian power', it can utilise the wide panoply of economic, diplomatic and humanitarian tools which it has developed over the years. As an embryonic military power, it may be able to deploy troops to perform Petersberg tasks.[72] These developments do not preclude interaction and cooperation with other international actors. Quite the contrary: as we have seen, a UN mandate gives legitimacy to EU operations. Moreover, lacking capabilities in terms of communication, control, command and other support functions, still render the EU highly dependent on NATO's (US) assets. The most 'atlantist' EU 'old' (UK) or 'new' (Poland) Members, have repeatedly stressed that ESDP should indeed be a means to reinforce – not rival – NATO. Hence, cooperation with NATO is, at least in the foreseeable future, required in order to strengthen ESDP. Recent EU/NATO cooperation for the EU-led operation in Macedonia is a promising example of governments' attempts to close the gap between words and deeds. See

---

civil unrest) and scope (expired on 1 September 2003 and was restricted to securing the airport of Bunia and its surroundings).

[70] From this standpoint, the setting up of the International Criminal Court (ICC) is to be welcomed. By outlawing human rights violence, it should contribute to creating a culture of accountability covering the international community. Conforming to the principle of subsidiarity mentioned above for the division of competence between the global and regional/national levels, the ICC is only empowered to act when national instances are 'unable' or 'unwilling' to prosecute.

[71] The EU political system in particular clearly departs from the realist perspective of interest and power.

[72] Adopted on the June 1992 WEU Ministerial Conference and recalled in Article 17(2) EU, the Petersberg tasks cover: 'humanitarian and rescue tasks, peace-keeping tasks and tasks of combat forces in crisis management, including peace-making'.

supra n. 3. To sustain peace-building efforts the EU also needs to interact effectively with the OSCE.

The granting of legal personality to the EU, as proposed in the framework of the Convention and confirmed by the IGC, may further act as a catalyst for changing the State-centred logic of, and eventually membership in other international/global organisations.[73] The integration of the Charter of Fundamental Rights of the European Union in the draft Treaty establishing a Constitution (Article I-7), will further provide a window of opportunity for the EU to act as a driving force in adjusting traditional international concepts of narrowly defined State sovereignty/security, and integrating the principles of respect for human rights, democracy and the rule of law in international relations.

Ultimately, discussions in international organisations should be geared towards a broader/less Statist definition of national interest and international security, notably by developing clear analogies between the domestic/community context and international ones. The weakening of the concepts of sovereignty and non-interference would need to be more explicitly acknowledged at the multilateral level in order to open further space for collective action,[74] under strict safeguards. This may take considerable time to materialise.

---

[73] In the WTO and FAO cases, the EC has already succeeded in adjusting State-based structures of international law to the needs of regional organisations.

[74] According to V.-Y. Ghebali 'Inter and intra State norms of conduct' in M. Bertrand and D. Warner (eds.), *A new Charter for a Worlwide Organisation?* (The Hague, Kluwer Law International 1997), p. 144, 'the UN Charter could state that the respect of human rights and fundamental freedoms (...) is a matter of international concern, and, consequently, does not constitute exclusively internal affairs. Second, it could commit States not to recognise as legitimate any government coming to office undemocratically, through usurpation of powers ...' Other authors (M. Bertrand, *La fin de l'ordre militaire* (Paris, Presses de Sciences Po 1996)) have in corollary advocated the abolition of veto rights in the Security Council when humanitarian catastrophes are at stake.

Chapter 17
THE UNITED NATIONS, THE EU AND CONFLICT PREVENTION: INTERCONNECTING THE GLOBAL AND REGIONAL LEVELS

by Jan Wouters[1]

> 'We are only at the beginning of a fundamental process of mobilization and of building partnerships in order to ensure that conflict prevention is made the cornerstone of the collective security system of the Organization in the twenty-first century.'

> K. Annan[2]

1.   INTRODUCTION

The United Nations (UN) occupies a special place in the family of international organisations when it comes to conflict prevention.[3] It stood at the cradle of the development of policies of conflict prevention in the early 1990s and together with its multiple organs, subsidiary bodies and specialised agencies, the organisation has gradually developed unique expertise in this area. This being said, the UN still faces a significant gap between its aspirations, on the one hand, and its capabilities or power to deliver, on the other. The present contribution looks at the evolution of UN practice in the area of conflict prevention (section 2) and at the growing cooperation between the UN and the EU in this area (section 3).

2.   THE UN AND CONFLICT PREVENTION: FROM THE UN CHARTER TO AN AGENDA FOR PEACE AND TODAY'S APPROACH

2.1   The UN Charter

Although the Charter of the United Nations (UN Charter) does not mention the words 'conflict prevention', it can be safely submitted that the prevention of

---

[1] Professor of International Law and the Law of International Organisations, KU Leuven; *Of Counsel*, Linklaters De Bandt, Brussels.

[2] Report of UN Secretary General Kofi Annan of 12 September 2003, 'Interim report of the Secretary-General on the prevention of armed conflict', A/58/365 – S/2003/888, p. 11, para. 32.

V. Kronenberger and J. Wouters, eds., The European Union and Conflict Prevention
© 2004, T·M·C·ASSER PRESS, *The Hague, The Netherlands*

armed conflicts, in particular of new worldwide armed conflicts, lies at the heart of the UN's mission and even forms the main rationale for its very foundation. In the preamble of the Charter '[w]e, the peoples of the United Nations' declare themselves 'determined to save succeeding generations from the scourge of war, which twice in our lifetime has brought untold sorrow to mankind' and, *inter alia*, to that end declare their resolve to combine their efforts 'to ensure, by the acceptance of principles and the institution of methods, that armed force shall not be used, save in the common interest'. Article 1 of the UN Charter states as the very first objective of the Organisation to 'maintain international peace and security, and to that end: to take effective collective measures for the *prevention* and removal of threats to the peace, and for the suppression of acts of aggression or other breaches of the peace, and to bring about by peaceful means, and in conformity with the principles of justice and international law, adjustment or settlement of international disputes or situations which might lead to a breach of the peace'.[4] Two forceful obligations laid down in Article 2(3) and (4) of the UN Charter are aimed at contributing to this objective and therefore to the prevention of conflicts, at least those of an international nature: all UN Member States must 'settle their international disputes by peaceful means in such a manner that international peace and security, and justice, are not endangered' (Article 2(3)) and they must 'refrain in their international relations from the threat or use of force against the territorial integrity or political independence of any State, or in any other manner inconsistent with the Purposes of the United Nations' (Article 2(4)). These core provisions make it clear that the primary obligation to prevent international con-

---

[3] See on the UN and conflict prevention, *inter alia*, E. Cousens, 'Conflict prevention', in D.M. Malone (ed.), *The UN Security Council: from the cold war to the 21ˢᵗ century* (Boulder, Rienner 2004), 101-116; C. Lekha Sriram and K. Wermester (eds.), *From promise to practice: strengthening UN capacities for the prevention of violent conflict* (Boulder, Lynne Rienner 2003); K. Aggestam, 'Conflict prevention: old wine in new bottles?', 10 *International Peacekeeping* (2003/1), 12-23; R. Bredel, 'The UN's long-term conflict prevention strategies and the impact of counter-terrorism', 10 *International Peacekeeping* (2003/2), 51-70; H.P. Langille, 'Conflict prevention: options for rapid deployment and UN standing forces', in T. Woodhouse and O. Ramsbotham (eds.), *Peacekeeping and conflict resolution* (London, Cass 2000), 219-253; O.P. Lefkon, 'Culture shock: obstacles to bringing conflict prevention under the wing of U.N. development and vice versa', 35 *New York University Journal of International Law and Politics* (2003), 671-739; A. Mack and K. Furlong, 'When aspiration exceeds capability: the UN and conflict prevention', in R.M. Price and M.W. Zacher (eds.), *The United Nations and Global Security* (New York, Palgrave MacMillan 2004), 59-74; F. Osler Hampson and D.M. Malone (eds.), *From reaction to conflict prevention: opportunities for the UN system* (Boulder, Rienner 2002); Id., 'Improving the UN's capacity for conflict prevention', 9 *International Peacekeeping* (2002/1), 77-98; F. Osler Hampson, 'Preventive diplomacy at the United Nations and beyond', in F. Osler Hampson and D.M. Malone (eds.), *From reaction to conflict prevention: opportunities for the UN system* (Boulder, Rienner 2002), 139-157; C. Lekha Sriram and K. Wermeister, 'Preventive action at the United Nations: from promise to practice?', in F. Osler Hampson and D.M. Malone (eds.), *From reaction to conflict prevention: opportunities for the UN system* (Boulder, Rienner 2002), 381-398; L.R. Sucharipa-Behrmann and T.M. Franck, 'Preventive Measures', 30 *New York University Journal of International Law and Policy* (1998), 485-538.

[4] Emphasis added.

flicts rests with States.[5] The methods provided for in Chapter VI of the UN Charter with a view to the pacific settlement of disputes follow the same logic: Article 33 obliges '[t]he parties to any dispute, the continuance of which is likely to endanger the maintenance of international peace and security, [to], first of all, seek a solution by negotiation, enquiry, mediation, conciliation, arbitration, judicial settlement, resort to regional agencies or arrangements, or other peaceful means of their own choice'. These techniques, for which States have the freedom of choice,[6] continue to have a lasting significance for conflict prevention purposes (*infra*, section 2.2). Chapter VI also brings the Security Council into the picture. Pursuant to Article 34, any 'dispute or situation [...] likely to endanger the maintenance of international peace and security' can be investigated by the Security Council,[7] which may, at any stage of such a dispute or situation, recommend appropriate procedures or methods of adjustment.[8] Any UN Member State may bring such a dispute or situation to the attention of the Security Council or of the General Assembly.[9] Should the parties to a dispute of the nature referred to above fail to settle it by the means indicated in Article 33, they must refer it to the Security Council.[10] If the latter considers that the continuance of the dispute is in fact likely to endanger the maintenance of international peace and security, it must decide whether to recommend appropriate procedures or methods of adjustment or to recommend such terms of settlement as it may consider appropriate.[11] We will not consider here the machinery of UN enforcement action provided for under Chapter VII of the UN Charter, once the Security Council has determined the existence of a threat to the peace, a breach of the peace or an act of aggression. It should be observed, though, that also at this juncture attention is given to prevention, in the sense of preventing a further aggravation of a crisis, in the form of provisional measures which the Security Council may take pursuant to Article

---

[5] See also the second principle of the 'Ten Guiding Principles for the Approach of the United Nations to Conflict Prevention' in the Report of UN Secretary General Kofi Annan of 7 June 2001 on 'Prevention of armed conflict', A/55/985 – S/2001/574, para. 169, reproduced below.

[6] See also ICJ, *Fisheries Jurisdiction* (Spain v. Canada), ICJ Rep. (1998), 432, para. 56. As to the question of whether the parties should try all these procedures one after the other if one of them has failed, see C. Tomuschat, 'Article 33', in B. Simma (ed.), *The Charter of the United Nations. A Commentary* (Oxford, OUP 2002, 2nd edn.), p. 587, para. 20.

[7] Article 34 UN Charter. However, this article 'fell asleep' in the early years of the UN and it has, because of continuing reluctance on the part of the members of the Security Council, remained in that state until now: see T. Schweisfurth, 'Article 34', in B. Simma (ed.), op. cit. n. 6, p. 607, para. 39.

[8] Article 36(1) UN Charter.

[9] Article 35(1) UN Charter. Pursuant to Article 35(2), a State which is not a UN Member State may bring to the attention of the Security Council or of the General Assembly any dispute to which it is a party if it accepts in advance, for the purposes of the dispute, the obligations of pacific settlement provided in the Charter.

[10] Article 37(1) UN Charter.

[11] Article 37(2) UN Charter.

40 of the UN Charter.[12] Measures like sanctions can also have a preventive effect.[13]

2.2   Chapter Six and a Half and an Agenda for Peace

So much for the theory. In practice, due in large part to the Cold War, the UN's record of preventive (and enforcement) action with regard to conflicts after the Second World War has been very mixed. Faced with a more or less constant stalemate in the Security Council, an alternative UN policy has developed since the 1950s for which the UN Charter did not make any provision and which has been referred to – in the words of former UN Secretary General Dag Hammarsjköld – as 'Chapter Six and a Half' action: UN peacekeeping operations.[14] Those peacekeeping operations have gradually evolved over time. Incrementally, the UN has sought to put them into use not only for the preservation of (a sometimes very fragile) peace, but also for the prevention of conflicts.[15] The Yugoslav crises in the 1990s provided an example of such use, namely UNPROFOR's preventive role in Macedonia/FYROM in 1992,[16] followed in 1995 by the deployment of a UN Preventive Deployment Force (UNPREDEP)

---

[12] Various other provisions of the UN Charter relate to preventive action by the UN and the obligations of UN Member States in this respect. Pursuant to Article 2(5) UN Charter, all Member States must give the UN every assistance in any action it takes in accordance with the Charter, and must refrain from giving assistance to any State against which the UN is taking preventive or enforcement action. Pursuant to Article 5 UN Charter, a UN Member State against which preventive or enforcement action has been taken by the Security Council may be suspended from the exercise of the rights and privileges of membership by the General Assembly upon the recommendation of the Security Council. Pursuant to Article 50 UN Charter, if preventive or enforcement measures against any State are taken by the Security Council, any other State (whether or not a UN Member State) which finds itself confronted with special economic problems arising from the carrying out of those measures has the right to consult the Security Council with regard to finding a solution to those problems.

[13] See also the third principle of the 'Ten Guiding Principles for the Approach of the United Nations to Conflict Prevention' in the Report of UN Secretary General Kofi Annan of 7 June 2001 on 'Prevention of armed conflict', A/55/985 – S/2001/574, para. 169, reproduced below. Compare the sobering statement on the preventive effect of UN sanctions in the Secretary General's report 'The causes of conflict and the promotion of durable peace and sustainable development in Africa' (1998), available at <http://www.un.org/ecosocdev/geninfo/afrec/sgreport/>, para. 25.

[14] See generally P. Lewis, 'A Short History of United Nations Peacekeeping', in B. Benton (ed.), *Soldiers for Peace* (New York, Facts on File, 1996), 25-41.

[15] See also the UN General Assembly's Declaration on the Prevention and Removal of Disputes and Situations Which May Threaten International Peace and Security and on the Role of the United Nations in this Field (attached to Res. 43/51 of 5 December 1988), para. 12: 'The Security Council should consider sending, at an early stage, fact-finding or good offices missions or establishing appropriate forms of United Nations presence, including observers and peace-keeping operations, as a means of preventing the further deterioration of the dispute or situation in the areas concerned'. See on this Declaration, T. Treves, 'La prévention des conflits internationaux dans la déclaration adoptée en 1988 par l'Assemblée générale de l'O.N.U.', 34 *Annuaire français de droit international* (1988), 436-453.

[16] See UN Doc. S/RES/795, 11 December 1992.

there.[17] Another example of preventive deployment, the first such operation in Africa, was the UN Mission in the Central African Republic (MINURCA).[18]

Meanwhile, at the request of the special Security Council summit of 31 January 1992, UN Secretary General Boutros Boutros-Ghali produced a remarkable report entitled *An Agenda for Peace* (1992).[19] The report contains an ambitious agenda for a more peaceful world and offers 'a coherent contribution towards securing peace in the spirit of the Charter'.[20] It repeatedly attaches great importance to conflict prevention, including the eradication of the root causes of conflict, and discusses various conflict prevention instruments. It stresses the need for an integrated approach, whereby the UN's aims should be

'– To seek to identify at the earliest possible stage situations that could produce conflict, and to try through diplomacy to remove the sources of danger before violence results;
– Where conflict erupts, to engage in peacemaking aimed at resolving the issues that have led to conflict;

---

[17] See UN Doc. S/RES/983, 31 March 1995, repeatedly extended. On 25 February 1999, China used its veto in the Security Council to prevent a renewal of UNPREDEP. See on this operation, *inter alia*, G. Assonitis, 'Aspects juridiques du déploiement préventif des forces des Nations Unies: le cas de l'ex-République yougoslave de Macédoine', 10 *Anuario de derecho internacional* (1994), 47-59; H.J. Sokalski, *An Ounce of Prevention. Macedonia and the UN Experience in Preventive Diplomacy* (Washington, US Institute of Peace Press, 2003); R. Väyrynen, 'Challenges to preventive action: The cases of Kosovo and Macedonia', in D. Carment and A. Schnabel (eds.), *Conflict Prevention. Path to Peace or Grand Illusion?* (Tokyo, UNU Press 2003), 47-56; A. Williams, 'The United Nations and preventive deployment in the former Yugoslav Republic of Macedonia', in W.A. Knight (ed.), *Adapting the United Nations to a Postmodern Era: Lessons Learned* (New York, Palgrave 2001), 65-76. Another example in the Balkans was operation 'Alba', i.e., the preventive deployment of troops in Albania, authorized by UNSC Res. 1101 of 28 March 1997. See M. Castillo, 'L'opération Alba: une réussite pour l'ONU, un bilan mitigé pour l'Union européenne et l'UEO', 44 *Annuaire français de droit international* (1998), 243-261; M. Favretto and T. Kokkinides, 'Anarchy in Albania: collapse of European collective security?', *Basic Papers. Occasional Papers on International Security Policy* (June 1997), also available at <http://www.basicint.org/pubs/Papers/BP21.htm>; P. Tripodi, 'Operation Alba: a necessary and successful preventive deployment', 9 *International Peacekeeping* (2002), 89-104.
[18] See UN Doc. S/RES/1159, 27 March 1998, repeatedly extended. MINURCA lasted from April 1998 to February 2000.
[19] An Agenda for Peace. Preventive Diplomacy, Peacemaking and Peacekeeping, Report of the Secretary General pursuant to the statement adopted by the Summit Meeting of the Security Council on 31 January 1992, UN Doc. A/47/277 – S/24111, 17 June 1992, available at <http://www.un.org/Docs/SG/agpeace.html>. See, *inter alia*, Y. Daudet, 'An Agenda for Peace as a new means of settling conflicts', in *Conflict Resolution: new approaches and methods* (Paris, UNESCO 2000), 21-46; D. Hamburg and K. Ballentine, 'Boutros-Ghali's agenda for peace: the foundation for a renewed United Nations', in *Boutros Boutros-Ghali Amicorum Discipulorumque Liber* (Brussels, Bruylant 1998), 489-509; Y.K. Tyagi, 'The United Nations in the New World Order: a critique of an agenda for peace', 31 *International Studies* (1994), 265-286.
[20] Ibid., para. 22.

– Through peace-keeping, to work to preserve peace, however fragile, where fighting has been halted and to assist in implementing agreements achieved by the peacemakers;

– To stand ready to assist in peace-building in its differing contexts: rebuilding the institutions and infrastructures of nations torn by civil war and strife; and building bonds of peaceful mutual benefit among nations formerly at war;

– And in the largest sense, to address the deepest causes of conflict: economic despair, social injustice and political oppression.'[21]

An Agenda for Peace contains a chapter on 'preventive diplomacy', i.e., 'action to prevent disputes from arising between parties, to prevent existing disputes from escalating into conflicts and to limit the spread of the latter when they occur'.[22] In a nutshell:

'The most desirable and efficient employment of diplomacy is to ease tensions before they result in conflict – or, if conflict breaks out, to act swiftly to contain it and resolve its underlying causes. Preventive diplomacy may be performed by the Secretary-General personally or through senior staff or specialized agencies and programmes, by the Security Council or the General Assembly, and by regional organisations in cooperation with the United Nations. Preventive diplomacy requires measures to create confidence; it needs early warning based on information gathering and informal or formal fact-finding; it may also involve preventive deployment and, in some situations, demilitarized zones.'[23]

One notices how old and new are intertwined: some of the classical instruments for the peaceful settlement of disputes, like mediation/good offices and enquiries/fact-finding[24] (*supra*, section 2.1) are made functional for a broader preventive diplomatic exercise. This being said, *An Agenda for Peace* goes beyond preventive diplomacy.[25] Its approach is a comprehensive one and it stresses the link between preventive diplomacy and other key concepts, such as peacekeeping (the utility of which for conflict prevention is stressed[26]) and post-conflict peace-building, which can prevent the recurrence of violence among nations and peoples.[27] The report also devotes a whole chapter to cooperation between the UN and regional arrangements and organisations, which has given a further in-

---

[21] Ibid., para. 15.

[22] Ibid., para. 20, first indent. Chapter III of *An Agenda for Peace* deals with preventive diplomacy (paras. 23-33).

[23] Ibid., para. 23.

[24] Fact-finding missions are an important instrument for early warning. The *Brahimi Report* (A/55/305 – S/2000/809, para. 34) supported the Secretary General's more frequent use of such commissions and stressed UN Member States' obligations, under Article 2(5) of the UN Charter, to give 'every assistance' to such UN activities.

[25] Compare the more critical assessment of A. Mack and K. Furlong, op. cit. n. 3, at 60-61.

[26] Ibid., para. 20, third indent.

[27] Ibid., para. 21.

centive to the process of regionalisation of security arrangements and organisations[28] and increasing cooperation between the UN and such regional arrangements and organisations, including the EU (see *infra*, section 3.).

Although Secretary General Boutros-Ghali undertook various initiatives to make the UN suited to this task,[29] in his 1995 *Supplement to an Agenda for*

---

[28] The literature on this process is booming. See, *inter alia*, A. Acharya, 'Regional organisations and UN peacekeeping', in R. Thakur and C.A. Thayer (eds.), *A crisis of expectations: UN peacekeeping in the 1990s* (Boulder, Westview 1995), 207-222; J. Boulden, *Dealing with conflict in Africa: the United Nations and regional organizations* (New York, Palgrave MacMillan 2003); Z. Deen-Racsmány, 'A redistribution of authority between the UN and regional organizations in the field of the maintenance of peace and security', 13 *Leiden Journal of International Law* (2000), 297-331; S. Forman and A. Grene, 'Collaborating with regional organizations', in D.M. Malone (ed.), *The UN Security Council: from the cold war to the 21st century* (Boulder, Rienner 2004), 295-310; A. Gioia, 'The United Nations and regional organisations in the maintenance of peace and security', in M. Bothe, N. Ronzitti and A. Rosas (eds.), *The OSCE in the maintenance of peace and security: conflict prevention, crisis management and peaceful settlement of disputes* (The Hague, Kluwer Law International 1997), 191-236; C. Gray, 'Regional arrangements and the United Nations collective security system', in A. Saab and others (eds.), *The changing constitution of the United Nations* (London, B.I.I.C.L., 1997), 91-116; B. Hettne, 'The United Nations and conflict management: the role of the 'new regionalism'', 4 *Transnational Law & Contemporary Problems* (1994), 643-668; B.L. Job, 'The UN, regional organizations, and regional conflict: is there a viable role for the UN?', in R.M. Price and M.W. Zacher (eds.), *The United Nations and global security* (New York, Palgrave MacMillan 2004), 227-244; R. Kern, *Global governance durch UN und Regionalorganisationen: OAU und OSZE als Partner der Weltorganisation beim Konfliktmanagement* (Baden-Baden, Nomos 2002); H. Körbs, *Die Friedenssicherung durch die Vereinten Nationen und Regionalorganisationen nach Kapitel VIII der Satzung der Vereinten Nationen* (Bochum, Brockmeyer 1997); J. Lunn, 'The need for regional security commissions within the UN system', *Security Dialogue* (2003), 369-376; M.M. MacKenzie, 'The UN and regional organizations', in E. Newman and O.P. Richmond (eds.), *The United Nations and human security* (New York, Palgrave 2001), 151-167; I. Österdahl, 'The continued relevance of collective security under the UN: the Security Council, regional organizations and the General Assembly', 10 *Finnish Yearbook of International Law* (1999), 103-140; C. Peck, *Sustainable peace: the role of the UN and regional organizations in preventing conflict* (Lanham, Rowman & Littlefield 1998); M. Pugh and W.P.S. Sidhu (eds.), *The United Nations and Regional Security. Europe and Beyond* (Boulder, Rienner 2003); B. Rivlin, 'Regional arrangements and the UN system for collective security and conflict resolution: a new road ahead?', 11 *International Relations* (1992), 95-110; U. Villani, 'Les rapports entre l'ONU et les organisations régionales dans le domaine du maintien de la paix', 290 *Recueil des Cours* (2001), 225-436; U. Villani, 'The Security Council's authorization of enforcement action by regional organizations', 6 *Max Planck Yearbook of United Nations Law* (2002), 535-557; T.G. Weiss (ed.), *Beyond UN subcontracting: task-sharing with regional security arrangements and service providing NGOs* (Houndmills, MacMillan Press, New York, 1998); G. Wilson, 'UN authorized enforcement: regional organizations versus 'coalitions of the willing'', 10 *International Peacekeeping* (2003), 89-106.

[29] This included the creation of a Department of Political Affairs (DPA) to handle a range of political functions that had previously been performed in various parts of the Secretariat and to provide early warning of impending conflicts and analyse possibilities for preventive action by the UN: see B. Boutros-Ghali, *Supplement to An Agenda for Peace: Position Paper of the Secretary General on the Occasion of the Fiftieth Anniversary of the United Nations* (UN Doc. A/50/60 – S/1995/1, 3 January 1995, available at <http://www.unog.ch/archives/agendas/supagp.htm>), para. 26. Likewise, in 1995 the UN Interdepartmental Framework for Coordination on Early Warning and Preventive Action (Framework Team) was created, which instigates and coordinates early preventive action among 23 UN agencies, departments, offices and programmes.

Peace[30] he had to point to a number of practical difficulties in implementing those objectives. He noted that it was not the lack of information, analytical capacity or ideas for UN initiatives that constituted the greatest practical obstacle, but often the reluctance of one party or another to accept UN help, rooted in strong sentiments of sovereignty and non-interference.[31] The Secretary General did not see an immediate solution to this problem;[32] he hoped for a long-term solution in which a 'climate of opinion, or ethos, within the international community' would be created in which the norm would be for Member States to accept UN good offices.[33]

It is interesting to see how the UN's thinking on conflict prevention developed since then, both under the influence of internal discussions and in reaction to some of the major humanitarian tragedies of the 1990s. Within the UN system, a thought-provoking report, entitled *Strengthening of the United Nations System Capacity for Conflict Prevention*,[34] was published by the UN's Joint Inspection Unit (JIU) in 1995. The report called for a comprehensive and structural conflict prevention strategy going beyond preventive diplomacy. It stressed in particular the need to sharpen the focus on alleviating root causes of conflicts, with special attention to be paid to building indigenous capacity (including the capacity of women and youth) for problem solving/conflict prevention and to strengthening the UN agencies' programmes and activities addressing root causes of conflicts.[35] The report identified as a key root cause poverty and underdevelopment: 'since behind many conflicts and emergencies, there lies a silent crisis of under-development, it has become increasingly clear that neither emergency relief nor fitful policy interventions are keys to averting conflicts, but a long, quiet process of sustainable human development'.[36] The JIU report gave rise to – somewhat defensive – comments by the Secretary General and the UN's Administrative Committee on Coordination (ACC) in 1997, which pointed to the impracticability of the report's recommendations in the light of UN Members' concerns over sovereignty and non-interference and of the UN's lack of resources.[37] Through this

---

[30] See n. 18.

[31] Ibid., para. 27.

[32] Ibid., para. 28, where it is observed: 'Clearly the United Nations cannot impose its preventive and peacemaking services on Member States who do not want them. Legally and politically their request for, or at least acquiescence in, United Nations action is a sine qua non.'

[33] Ibid., para. 28. In paras. 30-32 the Secretary General pointed to two other practical problems, namely the difficulty of finding senior persons with the required diplomatic skills who would be willing to serve as special representative or special envoy of the Secretary General, and the establishment and financing of small field missions for preventive diplomacy and peacemaking.

[34] H.L. Hernández and S. Kuyama, *Strengthening of the United Nations System Capacity for Conflict Prevention*, Geneva, 1995, JIU/REP/95/13, available at <http://www.unsystem.org/jiu/new/reports/1995/en95_13.pdf>.

[35] H.L. Hernández and S. Kuyama, op. cit. n. 34, at xi (recommendations 8 and 9).

[36] H.L. Hernández and S. Kuyama, op. cit. n. 34, at p. 32, para. 148.

[37] See Report of the Secretary General on the work of the Organization, A/52/184, 24 June 1997.

discussion one senses not only conceptual differences between a more 'political' and 'developmental' approach to conflict prevention, but also what some authors have referred to as bureaucratic turf wars within the UN system.[38]

However, external events in the 1990s forced the UN Secretariat to reconsider its position and to embrace a more comprehensive approach to conflict prevention. The humanitarian tragedies of Somalia, Rwanda and Srebrenica and the UN's failures in this respect painfully brought to the fore the inadequacy of UN peacekeeping operations. Faced with the reluctance of the international community – in the first place, the permanent members of the Security Council – to commit resources when no vital interests are at stake and to risk the lives of soldiers before the horror unfolds, the argument in favour of a structural prevention policy carried the day, both at the level of the UN Secretariat and, increasingly, with the Security Council, UN Member States and civil society.[39]

2.3   Today's UN practice: toward a culture of conflict prevention

The UN Secretariat's new thinking becomes clear in Secretary General Kofi Annan's 1999 report to the Organisation, *Preventing War and Disaster: A Growing Global Challenge*, in which he stresses that 'the United Nations has long argued that prevention is better than cure; that we must address the root causes, not merely their symptoms' and that '[o]ur aspiration has yet to be matched by effective action'.[40] The Secretary General's well-received *Millenium Report*[41] (2000) lays considerable emphasis on long-term conflict prevention too. In the report Kofi Annan notes that 'strategies of prevention must address the root causes of conflicts, not simply their violent symptoms'. Identifying the majority of today's wars as wars among the poor, Kofi Annan points to the lack of economic and political resources to manage conflicts in those countries, including the capacity to make financial transfers to minority groups or regions and the fragility of State apparatus which precludes it from countenancing devolution. This means, in the Secretary General's words, that 'every step taken towards reducing poverty and achieving broad-based economic growth (...) is a step towards conflict prevention. All who are engaged in conflict prevention and development, therefore – the United Nations, the Bretton Woods institutions, governments and civil society organisations – must address these challenges in a more integrated fashion'.[42] As almost invariably in poor countries at war 'the rights of subordinate groups are insufficiently respected, the institutions of government are insufficiently inclusive

---

[38] See A. Mack and K. Furlong, op. cit. n. 3, at 63.

[39] See A. Mack and K. Furlong, op. cit. n. 3, at 64.

[40] Report of the Secretary General on the Work of the Organisation, General Assembly Official Records, Suppl. No. 1 (A/54/1), para. 1.

[41] K.A. Annan, *We the Peoples. The Role of the United Nations in the 21st Century* (A/54/2000), available at <http://www.un.org/millennium/sg/report/full.htm>.

[42] Ibid., at 45.

and the allocation of society's resources favours the dominant faction over the others', the solution, however difficult to achieve in practice, is 'to promote human rights, to protect minority rights and to institute political arrangements in which all groups are represented (...). Every group needs to become convinced that the State belongs to all people.'[43] The Secretary General's recommendations received a strong endorsement in the *Brahimi Report,* the Report of the Panel on United Nations Peace Operations, of August 2000.[44] In the *Millenium Declaration*, the UN General Assembly resolved '[t]o make the United Nations more effective in maintaining peace and security by giving it the resources and tools it needs for conflict prevention, peaceful resolution of disputes, peacekeeping, post-conflict peace-building and reconstruction'.[45]

Meanwhile in July 2000 the Security Council had invited Secretary General Kofi Annan to submit a report with recommendations on the prevention of armed conflict. In his detailed report in June 2001, *Prevention of Armed Conflict,*[46] the Secretary General stressed that 'conflict prevention lies at the heart of the mandate of the United Nations in the maintenance of international peace and security, and that a general consensus is emerging among Member States that comprehensive and coherent conflict prevention strategies offer the greatest potential for promoting lasting peace and creating an enabling environment for sustainable development'.[47] The Secretary General proposed ten principles (reproduced below) which should guide the UN's approach to conflict prevention and enable it to move 'from a culture of reaction to a culture of prevention'. In its Resolution 1366 of 30 August 2001 on 'the role of the Security Council in the prevention of armed conflicts' the Security Council expressly recognized these principles.[48] Likewise, in Resolution 57/337 adopted by consensus, the General Assembly recognized these principles and it emphasized 'the importance of a comprehensive and coherent strategy comprising short-term operational and long-term structural measures for the prevention of armed conflict.'[49]

[43] Ibid.
[44] See n. 24, paras. 29 and 34.
[45] UNGA Res. 55/2 of 8 September 2000, point 9. In point 28, the UN General Assembly, addressing 'the special needs of Africa', resolved to 'encourage and sustain regional and subregional mechanisms for preventing conflict and promoting political stability, and to ensure a reliable flow of resources for peacekeeping operations on the continent.'
[46] *Prevention of Armed Conflict. Report of the Secretary General,* 7 June 2001 (A/55/985 – S/2001/574).
[47] Ibid., p. 35, para. 160.
[48] S/RES/1366 (2001).
[49] UNGA Res. 4/57/337 of 3 July 2003, 'Prevention of armed conflict', para. 2.

Ten Guiding Principles for the Approach of the United Nations to Conflict Prevention

(Report of UN Secretary General Kofi Annan of 7 June 2001 on 'Prevention of armed conflict', A/55/985 – S/2001/574, para. 169)

- Conflict prevention is one of the primary obligations of Member States set forth in the Charter of the United Nations, and United Nations efforts in conflict prevention must be in conformity with the purposes and principles of the Charter.
- Conflict prevention must have national ownership. The primary responsibility for conflict prevention rests with national Governments, with civil society playing an important role. The United Nations and the international community should support national efforts for conflict prevention and should assist in building national capacity in this field. Conflict prevention activities of the United Nations can therefore help to support the sovereignty of Member States.
- Conflict prevention is an activity best undertaken under Chapter VI of the Charter. In this regard, the means described in the Charter, for the peaceful settlement of disputes are an important instrument for conflict prevention, including such means as negotiation, enquiry, mediation, conciliation, arbitration, judicial settlement or other peaceful means, as set forth in Article 33 of the Charter. It must also be recognized that certain measures under Chapter VII of the Charter such as sanctions, can have an important deterrent effect.
- Preventive action should be initiated at the earliest possible stage of a conflict cycle in order to be most effective.
- The primary focus of preventive action should be in addressing the deep-rooted socio-economic, cultural, environmental, institutional, political and other structural causes that often underlie the immediate symptoms of conflicts.
- An effective preventive strategy requires a comprehensive approach that encompasses both short-term and long-term political, diplomatic, humanitarian, human rights, developmental, institutional and other measures taken by the international community, in cooperation with national and regional actors. It also requires a strong focus on gender equality and the situation of children.
- Conflict prevention and sustainable and equitable development are mutually reinforcing activities. An investment in national and international efforts for conflict prevention must be seen as a simultaneous investment in sustainable development since the latter can best take place in an environment of sustainable peace.
- The preceding suggests that there is a clear need for introducing a conflict prevention element into the United Nations system's multifaceted development programmes and activities so that they contribute to the prevention of conflict by design and not by default. This, in turn, requires greater coherence and coordination in the United Nations system, with a specific focus on conflict prevention.
- A successful preventive strategy depends upon the cooperation of many United Nations actors, including the Secretary General, the Security Council, the General Assembly, the Economic and Social Council, the International Court of Justice and United Nations agencies, offices, funds and programmes, as well as the Bretton Woods institutions. However, the United Nations is not the only actor in prevention and may often not be the actor best suited to take the lead. Therefore, Member

States, international, regional and subregional organizations, the private sector, non-governmental organizations, and other civil society actors also have very important roles to play in this field.

- Effective preventive action by the United Nations requires sustained political will on the part of Member States. First and foremost, this includes a readiness by the membership as a whole to provide the United Nations with the necessary political support and resources for undertaking effective preventive action in specific situations.

If anything, since the Secretary General's 2001 report the theme of conflict prevention has remained at the forefront of the UN's activities. Follow-up reports ensued in 2002 and 2003.[50] The Secretary General's 2003 interim report notes that 'some initial progress has been made in improving our capacity' but that 'this is not enough'.[51] While announcing a comprehensive report for the 2004 General Assembly in which he intends to present recommendations on how to strengthen the UN's capacity in order to ensure that conflict prevention is made the cornerstone of the UN's collective security system in the 21st century, the Secretary General identified as the key task for the UN system in the years to come 'to agree on practical measures to integrate conflict prevention further into its activities, to build a more structured link between political and socio-economic strategies and to ensure that the prevention of armed conflicts becomes a deliberate component in the planning and coordination arrangements of development programmes'.[52] In addition, the Secretary General outlined three areas to which the UN system needs to pay additional attention: (i) strengthening its capacity to help coordinate the international efforts of all actors to carry out structural prevention strategies, (ii) responding to the political economy of armed conflicts, including addressing war economies at all stages of the conflict,[53] and (iii) devoting greater attention to the potential threats posed by environmental problems, in particular international natural resource disparities.[54] Meanwhile, the Security Council has held a number of open debates on a variety of issues relating to a

---

[50] Report of UN Secretary General Kofi Annan of 5 November 2002 on 'Prevention of armed conflict: views of organs, organizations and bodies of the United Nations system', A/57/588 – S/2002/1269; Report of UN Secretary General Kofi Annan of 12 September 2003, 'Interim report of the Secretary General on the prevention of armed conflict', A/58/365 – S/2003/888, n. 2.

[51] See n. 2, p. 32, para. 32.

[52] Ibid., para. 33.

[53] See for interesting case-studies, *inter alia*, P. Andreas, 'Clandestine Political Economy of War and Peace in Bosnia', 48 *International Studies Quarterly* (2004), 29-52; B. Rubin, 'The Political Economy of War and Peace in Afghanistan', available at <http://www.eurasianet.org/resource/afghanistan/links/rubin99.shtml>.

[54] Ibid., paras. 35-37. See, e.g., on the connections between natural resources, environmental degradation and conflict, C. Koppell and A. Sharma, *Preventing the Next Wave of Conflict. Understanding Non-Traditional Threats to Global Stability* (Washington, Woodrow Wilson International Center for Scholars, 2003), at 71-92, with further references.

comprehensive conflict prevention strategy, such as the role of civil society in post-conflict peace-building,[55] the role of business in conflict prevention, peace-keeping and post-conflict peace-building,[56] cooperation of the UN with regional organisations in stabilisation processes[57] and the role of the UN in post-conflict national reconciliation.[58] The Secretary General's report of 3 August 2004 on *The Rule of Law and Transitional Justice in Conflict and Post-Conflict Societies* explicitly links this last theme to conflict prevention.[59]

In spite of this proliferation of commendable initiatives, reports, debates and statements, there are a number of practical obstacles to a more effective conflict prevention policy at UN level which should not be disregarded. First, the sovereignty and non-interference concerns of various UN Member States, in particular developing countries,[60] already voiced in the *Supplement to an Agenda for Peace* and the 1997 comments to the JIU report (*supra*, section 2.2), continue to make the UN's efforts on conflict prevention a delicate balancing act. One notices, for instance, how the Ten Guiding Principles quoted above try to meet these concerns by stressing that conflict prevention can 'help to support the sovereignty of Member States'. In any event, these sensitivities render the gathering of information – and therefore the functioning of early warning systems – more difficult and they complicate the effective engagement of UN organisations and programmes on the ground.[61] Second, the lack of political will on the part of UN Member States often leads to non-compliance with earlier commitments and problems of

---

[55] 22-23 June 2004. See S.PV.4993, S/PV.4993 (Resumption1) and Press Release SC/8128. In his statement to the debate Secretary General Kofi Annan could refer to the freshly-released report of the Panel of Eminent Persons on United Nations-Civil Society Relations, *We the Peoples: Civil Society, the United Nations and Global Governance* (A/58/817).

[56] 15 April 2004. See S.PV.4943 and Press Release SC/8058.

[57] 20 July 2004. See S.PV.5007 and S.PV.5007 (Resumption 1) as well as Presidential Statement S/PRST/2004/27 of 20 July 2004.

[58] 26 January 2004. See S.PV.4903 and Presidential Statement S/PRST/2004/2 of 26 January 2004.

[59] See *The Rule of Law and Transitional Justice in Post-Conflict Societies. Report of the Secretary General* (S/2004/616), para. 4: 'Of course, in matters of justice and the rule of law, an ounce of prevention is worth significantly more than a pound of cure. While United Nations efforts have been tailored so that they are palpable to the population to meet the immediacy of their security needs and to address the grave injustices of war, the root causes of conflict have often been left unaddressed. Yet, it is in addressing the causes of conflict, through legitimate and just ways, that the international community can help prevent a return to conflict in the future. Peace and stability can only prevail if the population perceives that politically charged issues, such as ethnic discrimination, unequal distribution of wealth and social services, abuse of power, denial of the right to property or citizenship and territorial disputes between States, can be addressed in a legitimate and fair manner. Viewed this way, prevention is the first imperative of justice'.

[60] The G-77 is an important voice for these countries. See, e.g., A. Mack and K. Furlong, op. cit. n. 3, at 63, according to whom 'G-77 objections have long prevented the Secretariat from creating any serious intelligence and analytical capacity that could be used for early-warning purposes and to create more effective prevention policies'.

[61] See the extensive analysis by O.P. Lefkon, op. cit. n. 3, at 706-723.

underfinancing.[62] Third, there are also important barriers to effective structural prevention policy within the UN system itself. Apart from a lack of analytical capacity – partly linked to the aforementioned problems – the UN's conflict prevention activities suffer from the apolitical mandates of its development agencies[63] (such as UNDP[64] and the World Bank[65]) and, as we have seen above (*supra*, section 2.2), from interdepartmental rivalries. More generally, it has been observed that the UN lacks a comparative advantage with respect to structural prevention in the light of the limited development assistance resources it has at its disposal.[66]

3.   UN-EU COOPERATION ON CONFLICT PREVENTION[67]

3.1   The UN and EU constitutional framework for EU-UN cooperation

The UN Charter pays rather scant attention to cooperation between the UN and regional organisations, except to some extent in the field of international peace and security, where such agencies or arrangements may play a role in implementing Security Council decisions (Article 48(2)). The brief Chapter VIII on 'regional arrangements' takes a somewhat reserved stand *vis-à-vis* regional organisations: they may deal 'with such matters relating to the maintenance of international peace and security as are appropriate for regional action provided that such arrangements or agencies and their activities are consistent with the Purposes and Principles of the United Nations' (Article 52(1)). In essence, the UN Charter limits their actions to the pacific settlement of local disputes (Article

---

[62] See the barely disguised criticism in the Secretary General's Report of 7 June 2001 on 'Prevention of armed conflict', A/55/985 – S/2001/574, para. 72: 'Too often, departments, agencies and programmes have found that proposals, having received political endorsements from Member States in one forum, fail to win support from the same States in other – particularly financial – forums'.

[63] See O.P. Lefkon, op. cit. n. 3, at 690-706.

[64] On UNDP's vision on (the development side of) peacebuilding, see, *inter alia*, M. Malloch Brown, 'Rebuilding peace: the development dimensions of crisis and post-conflict management', keynote address to the 2nd Committee of the 58th Session of the UN General Assembly, 4 November 2003. On UNDP's conflict prevention activities, which include the recent establishment of a Crisis Prevention and Recovery Practice Area and the development of Conflict-related Development Analysis (CDA), see <http://www.undp.org/bcpr/conflict_prevention/index.htm>.

[65] On the World Bank and conflict prevention, see Chapter 22. On the IMF and conflict prevention, see D. Rowlands and T. Joseph, 'The International Monetary Fund and conflict prevention', in D. Carment and A. Schnabel (eds.), *Conflict Prevention. Path to peace or grand illusion?* (Tokyo, UNU Press 2003), 207-230.

[66] See A. Mack and K. Furlong, op. cit. n. 3, at 71. For an argument in favour of an expansion of the international community's efforts to focus development activities through a conflict prevention lens, see, e.g., D.L. Phillips, 'Enhancing International Cooperation in Conflict Prevention Through Preventive Development', available at <http://www.cfr.org>.

[67] This part was written in cooperation with Frederik Naert, Institute for International Law, KU Leuven.

52(2)-(3)). It provides that the Security Council shall, where appropriate, resort to regional arrangements or agencies for enforcement action under its authority, but it likewise stresses that no enforcement action shall be taken without the authorisation of the Security Council (Article 53(1)). For a long time, a restrictive view was taken of what arrangements and agencies were covered by Chapter VIII. However, since the 1990s – especially since Secretary General Boutros-Ghali in *An Agenda for Peace* had recommended greater involvement of regional organisations in the peace-related activities of the UN (*supra*, section 2.2) – the UN has increasingly cooperated on a practical level with a great number of regional organisations. An ongoing practice of high-level meetings of the Secretary General with regional organisations has developed[68] with the support of the Security Council[69] and has, *inter alia*, led to a framework for cooperation in conflict prevention[70] and in peacebuilding.[71] In addition, a number of international organisations participate in the UN as observers. This also applies to the EC: since 1974 the EC has been an observer at the General Assembly.[72]

---

[68] For example, on 29-30 July 2003 the UN headquarters in New York hosted the Fifth High-Level Meeting between the UN and Regional Organisations. The regional organisations that participated were, apart from the EU (represented by the Presidency of the Council, the Council Secretariat and the European Commission), the African Union, Association of Southeast Asian Nations, Caribbean Community, Collective Security Treaty Organization, Commonwealth of Independent States, Commonwealth Secretariat, the Community of Portuguese Speaking Countries, Council of Europe, Economic Community of West African States, Interpol, the League of Arab States, NATO, Organisation Internationale de la Francophonie, OSCE, Organization of American States, Organization of the Islamic Conference, Pacific Islands Forum, and the Shanghai Cooperation Organization. The next such meeting is scheduled for mid-2005. The Security Council's Counterterrrorism Committee also collaborates closely with many regional organisations; see, for the EC/EU, Commission staff working paper, *EC external assistance facilitating the implementation of UN Security Council Resolution 1373: an overview*, SEC(2002)231, 25 February 2002.

[69] See UNSC Presidential Statement S/PRST/2004/27 of 20 July 2004 on 'Cooperation between the United Nations and Regional Organizations in Stabilization Processes'.

[70] See the statement of Secretary General Kofi Annan at the concluding session of the Third High-Level Meeting between the UN and Regional Organisations of 29 July 1998 (Press Release SG/SM/6658).

[71] See *Framework for Cooperation in Peace-Building*, Annex I to Letter of 12 February 2001 from the Secretary General to the President of the Security Council (S/2001/138). This document is the Chairman's (i.e., Secretary General Kofi Annan's) summary of the proposals presented at the Fourth High-Level Meeting between the UN and Regional Organisations that took place in New York on 6-7 February 2001.

[72] The EC was granted observer status in the General Assembly pursuant to Resolution 3208 (XXIX) of 11 October 1974, enabling the president of the European Council – these were the days of European Political Cooperation – to address the plenary session on behalf of the EC membership. See R.H. Ginsberg, *Foreign Policy Actions of the European Community. The Politics of Scale* (Boulder, Lynne Rienner 1989), 68. On the EU's role and position within the UN General Assembly, see, *inter alia*, P. Luif, *EU cohesion in the UN General Assembly* (Paris, Institute for Security Studies, Occasional Papers, No. 49, December 2003), 75 p.; J. Wouters, 'The European Union as an actor within the United Nations General Assembly', in V. Kronenberger (ed.), *The EU and the International Legal Order: Discord or Harmony?* (The Hague, Asser Press 2001), 375-404.

The relevant provisions of the Treaty on the European Union (TEU) can be found in its Title V on the EU's common foreign and security policy (CFSP). Article 11(1) TEU states, *inter alia*, that the CFSP is aimed at safeguarding 'the common values, fundamental interests, independence and integrity of the Union in conformity with the principles of the United Nations Charter' and at 'preserv[ing] peace and strengthen[ing] international security, in accordance with the principles of the United Nations Charter [...]'. This is also forcefully expressed in the EU's draft Constitutional Treaty (EU Constitution): 'In its relations with the wider world, the Union shall [...] contribute to peace, security, the sustainable development of the earth [...] as well as to strict observance and development of international law, including respect for the principles of the United Nations Charter'.[73] Consequently, the EU is obliged, under its present (and future) constitutive treaty, to develop and implement its CFSP, including its (Common) European Security and Defence Policy ((C)ESDP), in conformity with the UN Charter. Moreover, the EU Constitution instructs the EU to 'establish all appropriate forms of cooperation with the organs of the United Nations and its specialised agencies'.[74]

However, unlike the EC Treaty, Article 302 TEC of which directs the European Commission to 'ensure the maintenance of all appropriate relations with the organs of the United Nations and of its specialised agencies', the TEU does not provide for a single institution to represent the EU at the UN in CFSP matters. Instead, the representation is shared by several actors (Articles 18-20 TEU). In principle, the EU is represented by the Presidency of the Council,[75] assisted by the Secretary General/High Representative (SG/HR) (J. Solana) and, where necessary, the incoming Presidency, with the involvement of the Commission.[76]

---

[73] Article I-3(4) EU Constitution (agreed on 18 June 2004, provisional version as contained in EU documents CIG 87/04, CIG 87/04 ADD 1 and CIG 87/04, ADD 2, available at <http://ue.eu.int/cms3_fo/showPage.asp?id=251&lang=EN&mode=g>, final version to be signed in Rome on 29 October 2004). See also Article III-292.

[74] Ibid., Article III-327(1).

[75] Article 18(1) TEU.

[76] See Article 18(3) and (4) TEU. Pursuant to Article 18(5) TEU, the Council may, whenever it deems it necessary, appoint a special representative with a mandate in relation to particular policy issues. Currently these are: Michael Sahlin, EU Special Representative in the Former Yugoslav Republic of Macedonia (Joint Action 2004/565/CFSP, *OJEC* [2004] L 251/18); Marc Otte, EU Special Representative for the Middle East peace process (Joint Action 2002/965/CFSP, *OJEC* [2003] L 184/45); Heikki Talvitie, EU Special Representative for the South Caucasus (Joint Action 2003/496/CFSP, *OJEC* [2003] L 169/74, Joint Action 2003/872/CFSP, *OJEC* [2003] L 326/44); Francesc Vendrell, EU Special Representative in Afghanistan (Joint Action 2002/496/CFSP, *OJEC* [2002] L 167/12; Joint Action 2003/448/CFSP, *OJEC* [2003] L 150/71); Lord Ashdown, EU Special Representative in Bosnia and Herzegovina (Joint Action 2002/211/CFSP, *OJEC* [2002] L 70/7); Erhard Busek, EU Special Representative to carry out the tasks defined in the Stability Pact for South Eastern Europe (Joint Action 2001/915/CFSP, *OJEC* [2001] L 337/62; Joint Action 2003/449/CFSP, *OJEC* [2003] L 150/71); and Aldo Ajello, EU Special Envoy for the African Great Lakes Region (most recently, Joint Action 2003/447/CFSP, *OJEC* [2003] L 150/71).

Hence, the permanent representative to the UN of the EU Member State holding the EU Presidency is increasingly making statements in that capacity. The impact of this is enhanced when (as is often the case) such statements are also made on behalf of the accession countries (i.e., States currently negotiating accession with the EU) as well as the EFTA Member States. Furthermore, the EU Member States represented in UN organs must defend EU common positions there.[77] This also applies to EU Member States represented in the Security Council, although in respect of the (two) EU permanent members (France and the UK) there is the added proviso 'without prejudice to their responsibilities under the provisions of the United Nations Charter'.[78] This *caveat* is somewhat puzzling and one may wonder why it applies only to the permanent members.[79] Nevertheless, it appears that the EU is increasingly speaking with one voice in the Security Council, at least where there are no fundamental divisions between Member States, mostly through the EU Presidency,[80] but occasionally also through the SG/HR.[81] Finally, Commission and Member State representations to international organisations, including the UN, must 'cooperate in ensuring that the common positions and joint actions adopted by the Council are complied with and implemented'. In pursuance of this, these permanent representations consult on an almost daily basis.[82] This system will improve significantly if the EU Constitution enters into force, but, even though the function of 'Union Minister for Foreign Affairs'[83] will be created, multiple actors will still be involved.[84]

---

[77] Article 19(1) TEU.

[78] Article 19(2), para. 2, TEU.

[79] It may mean that these Member States can deviate from EU common positions when this is required by the urgency of the situation, see W. Devroe and J. Wouters, *De Europese Unie. Het Verdrag van Maastricht en zijn uitvoering: analyse en perspectieven* (Leuven, Peeters 1996), p. 636, para. 731; M.R. Eaton, 'Common Foreign and Security Policy', in D. O'Keeffe and P.M. Twomey (eds.), *Legal Issues of the Maastricht Treaty* (Chichester, Chancery 1994), 215, at 223, who with reference to Article 24 of the UN Charter observes that '[i]t is conceivable that there might be insufficient time to go back for a further CFSP decision if the requirement for prompt and effective action demanded a departure from a common position to accommodate the views of the other UNSC members and get action moving. In such a situation UN considerations would prevail over the European ones. This corresponds, in any case, to the position under Article 103 of the UN Charter. However, this is likely to be a very unusual situation.'

[80] For a list of Presidency statements at the Security Council, see <http://europa-eu-un.org/articles/articleslist_s52_en.htm>.

[81] E.g., the SG/HR briefed the Security Council on operation Artemis on 18 July 2003 and spoke on Bosnia to the Security Council on 5 March 2003.

[82] See J. Wouters, op. cit. n. 72.

[83] See Article I-28 EU Constitution. On his functions, see mainly Articles I-40, III-296, III-299, III-301-302, III-304-305 and III-227 EU Constitution. Under Article III-305(2) *in fine*, where a defined EU position exists on an issue addressed in the Security Council, the EU Security Council members shall request that the Union Foreign Minister be asked to present the EU's position.

[84] See J. Wouters, 'The Union Minister for Foreign Affairs: Europe's Single Voice or a Trojan Horse', in *Liber Amicorum Alfred E. Kellermann – The EU: An Ongoing Process of Integration* (The Hague, Asser Press 2004, forthcoming).

3.2   The evolution of the EU-UN relationship since the 1990s

The EU-UN relationship has undergone major changes since the 1990s.[85] On the occasion of the 50th anniversary of the UN in 1995, the EU strongly reaffirmed its attachment to the UN Charter and pledged to support the UN in a Declaration adopted at the Cannes European Council in June 1995, where it also stated that in the field of preventive diplomacy capacities and peacekeeping 'the UN plays an irreplaceable role, since only the UN may decide on the use of force in international relations'.

The development of ESDP since 1999 – which, as illustrated in Chapter 3 in this volume, coincides with the more systematic approach to conflict prevention in the EU – and practical cooperation in the field, such as in Bosnia,[86] Kosovo[87] and East Timor,[88] have in particular contributed to an ever closer relationship between the EU and the UN in the area of peace and security.[89] The development of ESDP was made possible by the addition of the 'Petersberg' crisis management tasks[90] to Article 17 TEU by the Treaty of Amsterdam. The decision to concretely launch ESDP was taken at the June 1999 Cologne European Council and its operational and institutional features were further specified principally at the December 1999 Helsinki European Council (the military component) and at the June 2000 Santa Maria da Feira European Council (civilian component, explicitly noting the possibility of deployment in the framework of UN operations). In Helsinki, the European Council explicitly stated: 'The Union will contribute to

---

[85] An excellent overview of the EU-UN relationship with a wealth of documents can be found at <http://europa-eu-un.org/>. See also *The Enlarging European Union at the United Nations: Making Multilateralism Matter* (2004), the chapters of which are available at the same website. See more generally on the EU-UN relationship, *inter alia*, J.-P. Cot, 'La Communauté européenne, l'Union européenne et l'Organisation des Nations Unies', in *Boutros Boutros-Ghali amicorum discipulorumque liber* (Brussels, Bruylant 1998), 327-346; B. Lindemann, *EG-Staaten und Vereinte Nationen: die politische Zusammenarbeit der Neun in den UN-Hauptorganen* (Munich, Oldenbourg 1978); F.K. Lister, *The European Union, the United Nations, and the revival of confederal governance* (Westport, Greenwood 1996); J. Wouters, op. cit. n. 72.

[86] On the EU's and the UN's role there, see J. Wouters and F. Naert, 'How Effective is the European Security Architecture? Lessons from Bosnia and Kosovo,' 50 *International and Comparative Law Quarterly* (2001), 540-576.

[87] Ibid. See also the reference to the EU in para. 17 of UN Security Council Resolution 1244 (10 June 1999).

[88] See Commission, *Communication on Conflict Prevention*, 11 April 2001, COM (2001) 211, 26.

[89] For recent analyses on EU-UN cooperation in this area, see, *inter alia*, A. Schnabel, 'The European Union, ESDP and the United Nations: competitors or partners?', in H.-G. Ehrhart (ed.), *The European Union, ESDP and the United Nations: competitors or partners?* (Baden-Baden, Nomos 2002), 304-318; T. Tardy, *L'UE et l'ONU dans la gestion de crise. Opportunités et limites d'une relation déséquilibrée* (Paris, Fondation pour la Recherche Stratégique, Recherches & Documents No. 32, May 2004).

[90] I.e., 'humanitarian and rescue tasks, peacekeeping tasks and tasks of combat forces in crisis management, including peacemaking'.

international peace and security in accordance with the principles of the United Nations Charter. The Union recognises the primary responsibility of the United Nations Security Council for the maintenance of international peace and security'.[91] The ESDP was declared operational, within limits, by the December 2001 Laeken European Council,[92] and the June 2003 Thessaloniki European Council declared that the EU 'has operational capability across the full range of Petersberg tasks, limited and constrained by recognised shortfalls, which can be alleviated by the further development of the EU's military capabilities'.[93] Finally, in the course of 2003 ESDP was put into practice and the EU conducted four crisis management operations: the EU Police Mission in Bosnia,[94] the Concordia military operation in the former Yugoslav Republic of Macedonia[95] and its follow up Proxima police mission,[96] and the Artemis military operation in the DRC.[97] In the summer of 2004 it established its first 'rule of law' mission.[98] In December 2003 the European Council also adopted a European Security Strategy, entitled *A Secure Europe in a Better World*, in which effective multilateralism, with the UN at the core, is a strategic objective.[99]

More systematic EU-UN relations in the field of peace and security were set in motion by a speech by the then French Presidency at the UN General Assembly in 2000, *inter alia*, inviting Kofi Annan to meet with EU institutions,[100] which he did that very month. The call for exploring cooperation in crisis management was taken up by the December 2000 Nice European Council. Subsequently, concrete arrangements were agreed in this field and approved by the EU General Affairs

---

[91] Annex IV, final paragraph. This was repeated several times; see the Presidency conclusions of the December 2000 Nice European Council, Annex VI and the June 2001 Göteborg European Council, para. 47. All European Council conclusions since 1994 are available at <http://ue.eu.int/presid/conclusions.htm> and in *Bulletin of the EU*, since 1996 available online at <http://europa.eu.int/abc/doc/off/bull/en/bullset.htm>.

[92] Presidency conclusions, para. 6 and Annex II.

[93] Presidency conclusions, para. 56.

[94] Established by Council Joint Action 2002/210/CFSP of 11 March 2002, *OJEC* [2002] L 70/1; see also <http://www.eupm.org and http://ue.eu.int/cms3_fo/showPage.asp?id=585&lang=en&mode=g>. The EU is also set to take over the NATO-led SFOR military peacekeeping mission in Bosnia.

[95] Established by Council Joint Action 2003/92/CFSP of 27 January 2003, *OJEC* [2003] L 34/26.

[96] Established by Council Joint Action 2003/681/CFSP of 29 September 2003, *OJEC* [2003] L 249/66.

[97] Established by Council Joint Action 2003/423/CFSP of 5 June 2003, *OJEC* [2003] L 143/50; see also <http://ue.eu.int/cms3_fo/showPage.asp?id=605&lang=en&mode=g>.

[98] Established by Council Joint Action 2004/523/CFSP of 28 June 2004, *OJEC* [2004] L 228/24; see generally <http://ue.eu.int/cms3_fo/showPage.asp?id=701&lang=en&mode=g>.

[99] Presidency conclusions of the December 2003 Brussels European Council, paras. 84-87. See, *inter alia*, S. Biscop, 'The European Security Strategy. Implementing a distinctive approach to security', available at <http://www.irri-kiib.be/papers/Artikel%20V&S%20ESS.pdf>.

[100] Speech of 12 September 2000, <http://www.un.int/france/eu/speeches/debat/0912F.htm>.

Council on 11 June 2001[101] and by the Göteborg European Council later that month.[102] These arrangements spell out three priorities: conflict prevention, civilian and military aspects of crisis management and particular regional issues (Western Balkans, Middle East and Africa, in particular the Great Lakes, Horn of Africa and West Africa). On a practical level, measures were adopted to ensure more continuous and consistent cooperation. They include meetings of the EU Ministers with the UN Secretary General, contacts between the SG/HR, the external relations Commissioner and the UN Secretary General and Deputy Secretary General, meetings of the EU's Political and Security Committee (a key CFSP body) with the UN Deputy Secretary General and Under Secretaries General and at other levels as appropriate (including with the UN Department of Peacekeeping Operations), and contacts between the EU Council Secretariat and the Commission's services, on the one hand, and the UN Secretariat, on the other.

The EU and its Member States envisage three possible ways of contributing civilian capabilities to UN operations: (i) national contributions following EU consultations aimed at, e.g., identifying opportunities to pool resources, (ii) a coordinated EU contribution, or (iii) a complete EU component in an operation under the overall direction of an international organisation. The EU will systematically assess whether it can contribute in one of these ways to each UN peacekeeping and political and peacebuilding mission. Regarding contributions by way of a complete EU component under overall UN direction, the Council invited the Presidency to submit proposals for a comprehensive Memorandum of Understanding with the UN.[103] The options for contributing military capabilities are somewhat different: 'at this stage' (June 2004), two main options have been identified: 'provision of national military capabilities in the framework of a UN operation' and 'an EU operation in answer to a request from the UN'.[104] Thus, at present, the EU appears unwilling to contribute by means of an EU military operation as part of a UN operation.

The next step was the adoption of the EU-UN Joint Declaration on cooperation in crisis management of 24 September 2003.[105] On 29 September 2003 the

---

[101] *Bull. EU*, 6-2001, para. I.31.53. For details, see the Draft Council conclusions on EU-UN cooperation in conflict prevention and crisis management, Doc. 9528/2/01 REV 2, 7 June 2001. See also Council Secretariat, Relations between the European Union and the United Nations in crisis management and conflict prevention, Doc. 12969/01, 7 November 2001. All EU Council documents cited below are available at <http://register.consilium.eu.int>.

[102] Conclusions, para. 53.

[103] EU cooperation with the UN, Practical aspects of EU contributions to civilian crisis management operations and activities led by the UN, Doc. 11022/1/03, 4 July 2003.

[104] See EU/UN cooperation in Military Crisis Management Operations – Elements of implementation of the EU/UN Joint Declaration, Doc. 9638/1/04 REV 1, 9 June 2004. Compare Doc. 12969/01, n. 101.

[105] Text at <http://europa-eu-un.org/articles/en/article_2768_en.htm>. Originally a treaty had been envisaged rather than a mere declaration, see Documents 12338/03, 8 September 2003 and 12466/03, 11 September 2003.

Council asked the SG/HR to continue talks with the UN to 'ensure that the cooperation mechanisms envisaged in the declaration [...] are swiftly put into practice'. To this end, *inter alia*, steering committees have been established to coordinate joint work between the Secretariats in crisis management.[106] Moreover, in the context of a follow-up to the European Security Strategy,[107] the EU has provided input to the UN's High Level Panel on Threats, Challenges and Change.[108]

In parallel, cooperation in the field increased. Two examples stand out. First, on 1 January 2003 the EU took over the UN's police mission in Bosnia.[109] Second, in June – September 2003 the EU helped to bridge a gap in UN capabilities in the DRC by conducting operation Artemis until the UN was able to reinforce its peacekeeping operation there.[110] On the Middle East, too, the EU cooperates with the UN, in particular in the 'Quartet', where the two organisations are joined by the US and Russia.[111]

In other areas, especially development and humanitarian affairs, but also human rights,[112] the EU (or rather: the EC[113]) has started to step up cooperation with the UN as well. For instance, the EC concluded a framework agreement with the UN in July 1999 on EC (co-)financing of UN programmes,[114] updated on 29 April 2003,[115] and the European Commission and EU Member States cooperated with the UN in drafting the UN Guidelines on the Use of Military and Civil Defence Assets in June 2003.[116] Elements of this relationship that are particularly relevant to conflict prevention are addressed below.

Finally, the increased cooperation in the area of peace and security has stimulated efforts at enhancing more comprehensive EU-UN relations.[117] In this con-

---

[106] (Draft) report to the European Council on EU activities in the framework of prevention, including implementation of the EU Programme for the Prevention of Violent Conflicts, Doc. 10327/04, 8 June 2004, 3.

[107] See n. 99.

[108] See Doc. 10327/04, n. 106, 3. The (draft) EU contribution is contained in EU Doc. 9165/04, 11 May 2004.

[109] See n. 94.

[110] See n. 97.

[111] A role recognized, *inter alia*, in Security Council Resolutions 1403 (4 April 2002) and 1515 (19 November 2003).

[112] Commission, *Communication on the European Union's Role in Promoting Human Rights and Democratisation in Third Countries*, COM (2001) 252, 8 May 2001, 18-19.

[113] Since these matters fall within EC competences.

[114] *Bull. EU*, 7-8-1999, para. 1.4.28 (not published in the *OJEC*). See also the Commission communication of 2 May 2001, *Building an effective partnership with the United Nations in the fields of Development and Humanitarian Affairs*, COM (2001) 231, 6-7.

[115] See <http://europa-eu-un.org/articles/en/article_2275_en.htm>.

[116] See <http://europa-eu-un.org/articles/en/article_2480_en.htm>.

[117] See especially European Commission, *The European Union and the United Nations: The Choice of Multilateralism*, COM (2003) 526, 10 September 2003 and the Council conclusions of 8 December 2003 on EU-UN relations. The December 2003 Brussels European Council welcomed this Commission communication and these Council conclusions, reaffirmed the EU's commitment to

text, it must be noted that the EU will succeed the EC if and when the EU Constitution enters into force[118] and will consequently take over the EC's observer status at the UN General Assembly (*supra*, section 3.1).

3.3 The main developments in EU-UN cooperation in the area of conflict prevention

As the UN and the EU both develop more comprehensive conflict prevention activities and as they enhance their cooperation generally (*supra*, section 3.2),[119] the potential for cooperation between both organisations in the field of conflict prevention obviously increases significantly. The main developments in this cooperation can be summarised as follows.

First, as mentioned above,[120] there has been an increasing number of crisis management operations comprising conflict prevention elements in their mandate in which both the EU and the UN are or were involved and have cooperated in the field, including in Bosnia and Kosovo[121] and the DRC.[122] While the practical details of these operations vary greatly, the EU is trying to develop more or less generic options for such cooperation, regarding both civilian and military operations.[123]

Second, the EU and the UN have both taken action on a number of issues that are relevant to conflict prevention. Two of these issues deserve particular attention: conflict diamonds and development. Regarding conflict diamonds, the UN Security Council took the lead by imposing certification schemes for Angola and Sierra Leone and subsequently the Kimberley Process, strongly supported by the EU, led to a generalised Certification Scheme.[124] The EC not only implemented this scheme by adopting the necessary legislation,[125] but also chaired the Working Group on Monitoring in the Kimberley Process since September 2003 and

---

'making effective multilateralism a central element of its external action, with at its heart a strong UN' and stressed the need for these conclusions, as well as the Joint Declaration on crisis management, to be translated into operative action (paras. 91-93).

[118] Pursuant to Article IV-438 EU Constitution.

[119] Moreover, the UN is enhancing its cooperation with regional organisations generally, see, e.g., the High Level Meetings between the UN and regional organisations held since 1994, including on conflict prevention (the third meeting) and peace-building (the fourth meeting), see <http://www.un.org/Depts/dpa/prev_dip/fr_un_cooperation.htm>, the April 2003 and July 2004 Security Council meetings with regional organisations (ibid., and S/PRST/2004/27, 20 July 2004) and the Security Council's Counter-Terrorism Committee's cooperation with regional organisations, see <http://www.un.org/Docs/sc/committees/1373/ctc_meeting.html>.

[120] See n. 86-88.

[121] See on this also Chapters 3 and 14 in this volume.

[122] See n. 97 and 131.

[123] See n. 103 and 104.

[124] See also Chapters 3, 10, 12 and 25 in this volume.

[125] See also Chapters 3 and 25 in this volume.

has been instrumental in introducing a comprehensive system of 'peer review'.[126] Thus one sees the EU supporting, further developing and implementing an initiative that originated in the UN.

The cooperation in the area of development is interesting because this is probably the most institutionalised field of EU-UN cooperation and an area with great conflict prevention potential. The 1999/2003 EC-UN framework agreement with the UN on EC (co-)financing of UN programmes[127] is highly relevant in this area: from 1999-2002 the EC funded UNDP-led activities with a total of 124 million euro.[128] In addition, UNDP is the first UN agency (or rather: programme) with which the EU has – very recently – concluded a strategic partnership that aims 'to strengthen both organizations' ability to deliver efficient, high quality aid to developing countries, particularly in the areas of governance, conflict prevention and post-conflict reconstruction'.[129]

Third, another – this time geographical – area of common concern and action is Africa. EU initiatives started before the UN took up the issue and focused on cooperation with the Organisation for African Unity (OAU).[130] Nevertheless, early on the EU placed its efforts, at least in part, within the framework of the UN approach. Although initially the EU and the UN seemed to be working in parallel in this area, there is a tendency towards more coordination and cooperation in the last few years, at least in respect of a number of specific African crises or subregions. For instance, there is the close cooperation in the DRC, where the EU not only conducted operation Artemis to assist the UN, but is also assisting in the setting up of an Integrated Police Unit in Kinshasa.[131] Furthermore, the UN and the EU have studied ways in which the international community can assist in strengthening the Economic Community of West African States (ECOWAS) capacity in the area of peace and security and have examined how to develop synergies between the two organisations in the region.[132] EU officials also participated in a UN Department of Peacekeeping Operations assessment mission to Burundi in February 2004.[133]

Finally, a number of structural cooperation measures regarding conflict prevention have been taken in the implementation of the EU-UN Joint Declaration on cooperation in crisis management of 24 September 2003.[134] For example, the

---

[126] EU Doc. 10327/04, n. 106, 5-6.

[127] See n. 114 and 115.

[128] 'EU and UNDP agree on strategic partnership for conflict zones and democratic governance', 28 June 2004, <http://europa-eu-un.org/articles/lv/article_3614_lv.htm>.

[129] Ibid. (this partnership was concluded on 28 June 2004 – ibid.).

[130] See also Chapter 3 in this volume.

[131] This project is funded by the European Development Fund and may be followed by an ESDP mission, see EU Doc. 10327/04, n. 106, 10.

[132] This has been followed up with a number of specific activities: ibid., 3-4.

[133] Ibid., 3.

[134] See n. 105.

Commission services have 'launched a "desk-to-desk" dialogue with integrated UN teams on five pilot countries and have agreed to share early warning information on these countries'.[135]

4. CONCLUDING REMARKS

In the light of the developments outlined above, it can be concluded that, after some initial hesitations in the area of peace operations,[136] the EC/EU-UN relationship, both generally and in the field of conflict prevention, is good and is becoming even better. Nevertheless, more progress is needed. First of all, both organisations are still developing their own conflict prevention policies and instruments; more cooperation is needed in order to fully exploit their respective expertise, comparative advantages and complementarity. Second, systematic cooperation has only been initiated in recent years and many of the original agreements on such cooperation have yet to be (fully) implemented. Third, while cooperation is increasingly structured rather than *ad hoc*, the general legal framework for cooperation is still underdeveloped, relying mostly on soft instruments such as the Joint Declaration on cooperation in crisis management. Finally, it is regrettable that, even under the EU Constitution, the UN will not have one single EU contact point and the EU will still speak through several voices in the UN. In short, EU-UN cooperation, both in general and in the field of conflict prevention, is on the right track but there is still much work ahead. For the sake of 'a secure Europe in a better world', it is vital that this work be done sooner rather than later.

---

[135] Doc. 10327/04, n. 106, 3.

[136] See T. Tardy, 'Limits and opportunities of UN-EU relations in peace operations: implications for DPKO', September 2003, available at <http://www.gcsp.ch/e/about/News/Faculty-articles/Tardy_UN_EU_Peac_Ops.pdf, 3-4>.

Chapter 18
A CULTURE OF CONFLICT PREVENTION:
OSCE EXPERIENCES AND COOPERATION WITH THE EU

by Edwin Bakker[1]

1. INTRODUCTION

The term conflict prevention is widely used. However, sometimes peacekeeping and crisis management are referred to as conflict prevention. These activities may indeed reduce the spread of violence, but they are usually applied once the threat is clear and present. The key to *preventive* action is to respond to the warning signs *before* they ignite. This is easier said than done, however, as there is no perfect system for identifying the factors that may trigger conflict. What is required is reliable information, contacts with the parties involved, a mandate to intervene, political support, and a timely response.

As a security organisation with a strong focus on conflict prevention, the Organisation for Security and Co-operation in Europe (OSCE) has developed many different tools to identify situations and developments that have the potential to escalate into violent conflicts and to react rapidly. This chapter investigates these tools and discusses lessons that can be learned from OSCE experiences in conflict prevention. Next, it investigates cooperation between the OSCE and the European Union in this field. Finally, the chapter deals with the question of what the EU could learn from the distinctive role and experience of the OSCE and discusses the benefits of increased cooperation.

2. THE OSCE

With its 55 participating States the Organisation for Security and Co-operation in Europe is the world's largest regional security organisation. All the European states take part in the Organisation, although – otherwise than the name suggests – non-European states also participate in the OSCE. The United States of

---

[1] Dr. E. Bakker is a researcher at the Netherlands Institute of International Relations 'Clingendael', The Hague, and the secretary of the executive committee of the Netherlands Helsinki Committee.

V. Kronenberger and J. Wouters, eds., The European Union and Conflict Prevention
© 2004, T·M·C·ASSER PRESS, The Hague, The Netherlands

America and Canada, both of which have for many decades played an important role in European security issues given their membership of NATO, are active participants in the OSCE. The Central Asian states that gained independence after the break-up of the Soviet Union have also become full participants of this 'European' organisation. In addition, the Organisation maintains special relations with a number of countries on the periphery of the OSCE region.[2]

Consequently, the geographical scope of the OSCE is not restricted to the European continent, but encompasses the region of the Northern Hemisphere from Vancouver to Vladivostok. Within this region the OSCE sees important duties for itself in the avoidance of conflicts (early warning and conflict prevention), the control of conflicts that could result in violence (conflict management), and the reconstruction of societies that have been torn apart by violence (post-conflict rehabilitation). In addition to these activities with respect to (potential) conflicts, the OSCE is also engaged in many other fields such as arms control and the associated Confidence and Security-Building Measures (CSBMs),[3] cooperation in the economic and environmental fields, supervision of compliance with human rights, and the observation and (where necessary) organisation of elections. These activities can be understood as long-term conflict prevention.

The OSCE's attention to a broad range of activities is based on the definition of security that the OSCE – and its predecessor, the Conference on Security and Co-operation in Europe (CSCE) – adopted from the very beginning, which can be described as comprehensive security. The concept of comprehensive security is based on the principle that politico-military issues are not solely or primarily of importance in the maintenance of security and stability, but that the protection and promotion of human rights and the fundamental freedoms (for both individuals or sections of the population) as well as economic and environmental issues should all be integral elements of security policy. Moreover, emphasis is placed on their mutual coherence, i.e., the interdependence between the various security dimensions; stagnation in one dimension has a negative effect on the other security dimensions. The essence of the principle is the following: security is indivisible.[4]

This principle of the indivisibility of security is not interpreted solely in terms of the various security dimensions; it also gives cause to the perception that the

---

[2] The OSCE has collaborated with the countries around the Mediterranean Sea which do not participate in the OSCE. And during the past decade the OSCE has entered into special relations with three Asian partners, i.e., Japan (since 1992), South Korea (1994), and Thailand (2000).

[3] Confidence- and Security-Building Measures are provisions for the exchange and verification of information regarding the participating States' armed forces and military activities, as well as certain mechanisms promoting cooperation among participating States with regard to military matters. The aim of these measures is to promote mutual trust and to dispel concern about military activities by encouraging openness and transparency.

[4] E. Bakker and B. Bomert, *The OSCE and the Netherlands as Chairman-in-Office* (The Hague, Netherlands Helsinki Committee 2003), p. 1.

security of one state cannot and may not be considered separately from another state. Threats to the security of one state or group of states can threaten the security in all states. Consequently, the maxim is: security can be achieved solely by cooperation with others, and never at the cost of or in competition with others. As a result, alongside the term comprehensive security also the term cooperative security is used. All states that participate in the OSCE have an (equal) interest in cooperation.

This principle is also reflected in the decision-making structure of the Organisation. On the basis of shared security based on mutual cooperation all participants have the same status and (must) have the same voice in the decision-making process; an essential component emphasising a persuasion-based rather than a coercion-based approach to conflict prevention. The shadow-side of this principle of consensus on political decisions (not on operational ones) is that mini-states such as Liechtenstein, Monaco, San Marino or the Holy See could block OSCE decision-making. In other words, a decision is taken only when none of the 55 participants have expressed their disapproval. It should be stressed that the principle of consensus has more than once been an obstacle to the Organisation's decision-making process. According to the Dutch *Advisory Council on International Affairs* (AIV),

> 'the states are entitled to have a say in all decisions, down to any level of detail they wish. And that is indeed what happens, although obviously not all states simultaneously take the same amount of interest in every single topic of debate. The level of interest tends to vary from topic to topic. When preparing decisions, the Chairmanship needs to consult a wide range of States in order to gauge the level of their interest and must also remain constantly alert to the danger of giving other States the impression that their own views are not being taken sufficiently seriously. As a result of this need to involve so many parties, the OSCE's decision-making process is not transparent to outsiders, is slow-moving, and is characterised by a constant search for compromise'.[5]

The Chairman-in-Office (C-i-O)[6] plays a pivotal role at the OSCE, acting primarily as an honest broker in the process of building consensus. This Chairmanship rotates among the participating states, with a new country taking over the task each year.

A second characteristic of decision-making in the OSCE is the status of its decisions. Once taken, they cannot be legally enforced, since the OSCE does not

---

[5] AIV, The Netherlands and the Organisation for Security and Cooperation in Europe in 2003: Role and Direction (AIV 2002), p. 22.

[6] The C-i-O is vested with overall responsibility for executive action and the coordination of current OSCE activities. This includes: coordination of the work of OSCE Institutions, representing the Organisation, and supervising activities related to conflict prevention, crisis management and post-conflict rehabilitation. The Chairmanship rotates annually and is held by the Foreign Minister of a participating State. The origin of the institution lies with the Charter of Paris for a New Europe (1990). The Helsinki Document 1992 formally institutionalized this function.

have a legal status according to international law – despite the fact that the Conference for Security and Cooperation in Europe was rechristened as the Organisation for Security and Cooperation in Europe in 1994, in order to reflect its character as a permanent organisation with its own responsibilities. In the mid-1990s, the OSCE did, however, acquire the status of a UN regional arrangement under the terms of Chapter VIII of the UN Charter.[7] Nonetheless, its decisions only have political status.

In the following section the primary institutions and mechanisms in the OSCE's conflict prevention regime will be examined. The main focus of attention will be on instruments that contribute most directly to conflict prevention.

3.   CONFLICT PREVENTION BY THE OSCE

As described above, the avoidance of conflict through early warning and early action is one of the main assignments of the OSCE – as laid down in, among others, the CSCE Helsinki Document.[8] Moreover, the above characteristics of the organisation – in particular its comprehensive approach to security, cooperation as a mode of interaction, decision-making based on consensus and the procedural rather than institutional character – predisposes the OSCE to an active conflict prevention role. To play this role, the Organisation possesses a number of instruments. In fact most of the political decision-making structures and operational structures – directly or indirectly – deal with conflict prevention. The instruments that are most directly aimed at responding rapidly to situations and developments that have the potential to escalate into conflicts are the following operational structures (in alphabetic order):

- *Fact-finding and rapporteur missions*
  These are usually comprised of short-term visits by experts and/or leading politicians or diplomats; the objective is to become acquainted with the facts during an on-the-spot visit. These missions report to the OSCE bodies. They are also employed to assess whether – and, if so, the extent to which – the OSCE should initiate missions and field operations.[9]

---

[7] In 1992, the then CSCE entered a new phase in its relationship with the United Nations. In the Helsinki Document it was stated that the CSCE is a regional arrangement in the sense of Chapter VIII of the Charter of the United Nations. CSCE Helsinki Document: the Challenges of Change (Helsinki 1992), Section IV 'Relations with International Organizations, Non-Participating States, Role of Non-Governmental Organizations (NGOs)', para. 2.

[8] CSCE Helsinki Document: the Challenge of Change (Helsinki 1992), Section III 'Early Warning, Conflict Prevention and Crisis Management (including Fact-finding and Rapporteur Missions and CSCE Peacekeeping, Peaceful Settlement of Disputes)'.

[9] CSCE Helsinki Document: the Challenge of Change (Helsinki 1992), Section III 'Early Warning, Conflict Prevention and Crisis Management (including Fact-finding and Rapporteur Missions and CSCE Peacekeeping)', paras. 12-16.

- *High Commissioner on National Minorities*
  The Office of the High Commissioner on National Minorities was established to identify and to seek the early resolution of ethnic tensions that might endanger peace, stability or friendly relations between OSCE participating States.[10]

- *(Long-term) Missions and other field operations*
  Although the scope and the tasks assigned to the various missions (including election monitoring missions) and other field operations can exhibit a wide variation,[11] one can state that by virtue of the missions' presence on the spot they usually constitute the OSCE's 'eyes and ears' in the field.

- *Personal representatives of the Chairman-in-Office*
  Leading diplomats or (former) politicians may be requested by the Chairman-in-Office to carry out a specific short-term task in connection with the prevention of conflicts, or crisis management. For example, in 1997 the former Austrian Chancellor Mr Vranitzky played an important role in the restoration of stability and the prevention of the re-escalation of the conflict in Albania.[12]

In addition to the operational structures that are active in the field, the OSCE possesses political decision-making structures that complete the array of OSCE means to gather reliable information, to establish contacts with the parties, to gather political support, and to formulate timely responses and structures that have a mandate to intervene politically. These structures are (in alphabetic order):

- *Ad hoc steering groups*
  Steering groups comprised of a limited number of members assist the Chairman-in-Office (C-i-O) as the need arises. The three members of the Troika – the past, the current and the future C-i-O – are always members of these steering groups, supplemented with representatives from states whom the Chairman-in-Office believes may be able to make a contribution to the resolution of the specific problem.[13]

---

[10] Mandate of the HCNM, CSCE Helsinki Document: the Challenge of Change (Helsinki 1992), Section II 'CSCE High Commissioner on National Minorities'.

[11] Missions and other field activities are usually established by a decision of the Permanent Council, with the agreement of the host country. No two mandates are the same, underlining the flexibility of this instrument.

[12] CSCE Helsinki Document: the Challenge of Change (Helsinki 1992), Section I 'Strenghtening CSCE Institutions and Structures', para. 22.

[13] CSCE Helsinki Document: the Challenge of Change (Helsinki 1992), Section I 'Strenghtening CSCE Institutions and Structures', paras. 16-21.

- *The Conflict Prevention Centre (CPC)*
  Under the guidance of the Secretary General, the CPC provides support for the Chairman-in-Office and other OSCE negotiating and decision-making bodies in the fields of early warning, conflict prevention, crisis management, and post-conflict rehabilitation. To assist in this, it maintains an Operations Centre to identify potential crisis areas and to plan for future missions and operations. The Forum for Security and Cooperation Support Unit in the Conflict Prevention Centre covers politico-military aspects of security in the OSCE area. In 2003 the, until recently rather small, CPC intends to diversify its role, with significant additional responsibilities in the fields of analytical capacity and border-related issues. It has taken on additional staff to meet its increased workload.[14]

- *The Forum for Security Cooperation*
  This Forum meets on a weekly basis in Vienna and deals with military aspects of security in the OSCE area. It aims to create an atmosphere of openness and transparency regarding military issues, and to develop measures to reduce the risk of armed conflict. The Forum's work focuses on the implementation of OSCE confidence- and security-building measures. The Forum has also begun to address emerging security issues, such as the use of force in internal conflicts and the spread of small arms and light weapons.[15]

- *The Permanent Council*
  In addition to being responsible for the day-to-day business and decision-making of the Organisation, the Permanent Council also holds informal and committee meetings, enabling representatives to exchange views on various issues pertaining to the OSCE, and to raise concerns regarding developments in the OSCE area.[16] As a permanent forum for multilateral dialogue and political consultations, the Permanent Council can be regarded as 'the king-spider in the OSCE's web of conflict prevention'[17] or 'an ongoing security council without privilege'.[18]

---

[14] The origin of the CPC lies with the CSCE Charter of Paris for a New Europe (1990), 'Supplementary document to give effect to certain provisions contained in the Charter of Paris for a New Europe', Section I 'Institutional Arrangements', para. F.

[15] CSCE Helsinki Document: the Challenge of Change (Helsinki 1992), Section V 'CSCE Forum for Security Co-operation'.

[16] The predecessor of the Permanent Council, the Permanent Committee, was created at the Rome Meeting of the Ministerial Council, CSCE Ministerial Council: CSCE and the New Europe – Our Security is Indivisible (Rome 1993), Section VII 'CSCE Structures and Operations'.

[17] A. Bloed, 'The OSCE main political bodies and their role in conflict prevention and crisis management', in M. Bothe, et al. (eds.), *The OSCE in the maintenance of peace and security: conflict prevention, crisis management and peaceful settlement of disputes* (The Hague, Kluwer 1997), p. 35.

[18] J. Cohen, *Conflict prevention in the OSCE. An assessment of capacities* (The Hague, Netherlands Institute of International Relations 'Clingendael' 1999), p. 19.

- *Procedures for the peaceful settlement of disputes*
  Over the course of the years the OSCE has developed a number of measures
  for use in times of crisis or increasing tension that are intended to promote
  direct contacts between the parties to a dispute, as well as the other parties
  involved. For example, the Moscow Mechanism provides for the participation of a minimum of six OSCE states (consequently in this instance a consensus is not required) in an expert mission to a country when these states
  perceive the threat of a crisis in a specific country.[19] In addition to issues of
  relevance to the human dimension, similar mechanisms and procedures have
  also been developed for 'unusual military activities'. Pursuant to the Vienna
  Mechanism states are under the obligation to furnish information when so requested by another state.[20]

Of the above-mentioned conflict prevention instruments, the Missions and other
field operations and the High Commissioner on National Minorities contribute
most directly to conflict prevention. For a better understanding of their capacities
to prevent conflict, a closer look at these operational structures is required.

3.1 OSCE Missions and other field operations

The decision to establish, extend and conclude field operations is usually taken
by the Permanent Council;[21] this body decides on the mandate, the number of
staff, and the budget. Initially it is usually decided to carry out a field operation
for a shorter period of time (from several months to one or two years). Supplementary decisions may subsequently result in the extension of the period and/or
the modification of the mandate, the scope and the budget so as to accommodate
changed circumstances.

In the past decade, the decision to establish a Mission or other field operations
has been taken quite often. As a result, the number of OSCE Missions and other
field operations has expanded considerably. The Organisation began its first Mission in September 1992, i.e., the long-term mission (since concluded) in Kosovo,
Sandjak and Vojvodina (former Yugoslavia). Ten years later, the OSCE has Missions or offices at almost twenty locations in Europe and Central Asia (see figure

---

[19] The Moscow Mechanism has been activated on six occasions. For instance, it was activated in
1992 by the, then, twelve states of the European Community and the United States on the issue of
reports of atrocities and attacks on unarmed civilians in Croatia and Bosnia-Herzegovina. More recently, in December 2002, ten participating States invoked the Mechanism with regard to
Turkmenistan.

[20] This consultation mechanism was activated extensively during the first phase of the Yugoslav
crisis (1989-1990).

[21] The Permanent Council is the body for regular political consultation and decision-making on
all issues pertinent to the OSCE and is responsible for the day-to-day business of the Organization.
Its members, permanent representatives of the 55 OSCE participating States, meet weekly in Vienna.

1). In many ways this field presence constitutes the Organisation's core business to which no less than 80 per cent of its total budget is allocated.[22]

Although the mandate, the number of staff and the available budget vary between Missions and field operations, they are usually assigned two duties. The first of these duties is to provide support to and to promote local political processes designed to prevent conflicts and to foster conflict management; the second is to provide information and submit reports to the OSCE concerning political and other developments in the host state. In this light, the Missions and field operations are frequently referred to as the 'eyes and ears of the Organisation'.[23] In one form or another, all mandates for the field operations encompass duties to monitor compliance with the OSCE's principles and obligations – in particular with respect to human rights; the support of democratisation processes; the promotion of the rule of law; and the encouragement of political dialogue both between the national authorities and their subjects and between governmental and non-governmental organisations.

Both short-term and long-term Missions contribute to conflict prevention. The short-term missions – fact-finding and expert or election observation missions – investigate specific situations of a human dimension or military nature. They produce the reliable information and establish contacts in (potential) conflict regions, which are required to respond quickly and adequately to potential threats to stability and security. The long-term Missions fill the gap between the short-term Missions and traditional peacekeeping, and as such have carved out a new preventive mode of operation.[24] They provide not only reliable information and contacts, but also have a mandate to intervene and – due to their presence in the area – are able to respond quickly to situations and developments that may lead to conflict. Moreover, the ongoing presence of the long-term Missions or 'Presences' and 'Assistance Groups' enable them to perform an early warning role by understanding tensions and analysing the potential that these might have for destabilising a situation and then acting in specific ways to address them. In the case of the former Yugoslav Republic of Macedonia, the OSCE Spill-over Mission to Skopje was actively involved in defusing tensions that arose in connection with attempts to establish a private Albanian university, which was regarded as illegal by the authorities of FYROM.[25]

Not all Missions are, however, primarily focused on the prevention of conflicts. It should be stressed that a number of missions mainly focus on the reconstruction of a society and a state in the phase subsequent to the resolution of a conflict. This is, for instance, the case for the OSCE's largest Mission: the one in Kosovo. Other Missions and field operations are primarily aimed at conflict man-

---

[22] PC.DEC/527, 30 December 2002.
[23] Bakker and Bomert, op. cit. n. 4, at 22.
[24] Cohen, op. cit. n. 18, at 86.
[25] Cohen, op. cit. n. 18, at p. 109.

Figure 1. OSCE missions and field operations (as of March 2003)

Date begun	host country	head of mission	budget 2003 (x EUR1,000)
14-08-1992	Macedonia	C. Jenness (Canada)	16,804
13-12-1992	Georgia	J.-M. Lacombe (France)	20,970
04-02-1993	Moldova	W.H. Hill (USA)	1,026
01-12-1993	Tajikistan	M. Gilbert (France)	3,009
06-12-1994	Minsk Group	three co-chairs	2,212
11-04-1995	Chechnya (Russia)[a]	J. Inki (Finland)	1,847
08-12-1995	Bosnia-Herzegovina	R.M. Beecroft (USA)	20,742
18-04-1996	Croatia	P. Semneby (Sweden)	10,767
27-03-1997	Albania	O. Lipponen (Finland)	4,288
18-09-1997	Belarus[b]		899
23-07-1998	Kazakhstan	I. Venczel (Hungary)	1,252
23-07-1998	Kyrgyzstan	A. Idil (Turkey)	1,668
23-07-1998	Turkmenistan	P. Badescu (Romania)	1,078
01-06-1998	Ukraine[c]		1,146
01-07-1999	Kosovo[d]	P. Fieschi (France)	48,469
22-07-1999	Armenia	R. Reeve (UK)	1,133
16-11-1999	Azerbaijan	P. Burkhard (Switzerland)	1,366
14-12-2000	Uzbekistan	A.K. Erozan (Turkey)	1,273
11-01-2001	Yugoslavia	M. Massari (Italy)	9,085

[a]   As of 1 January 2003, no agreement has been reached between the OSCE and the Russian Federation on the extension of the mandate of the OSCE Assistance Group to Chechnya. As a result, the mission has ceased its activities and must be closed by 21 March 2003.

[b]   The Permanent Council decided to create a new OSCE office in Minsk, from 1 January 2003, replacing the OSCE Advisory and Monitoring Group.

[c]   Ambassador P. Burkhard (Switzerland) was Project Coordinator until February 2002. No successor has been as yet appointed.

[d]   The Federal Republic of Serbia & Montengro

Source: E. Bakker and B. Bomert, *The OSCE and the Netherlands as Chairman-in-Office* (The Hague, Netherlands Helsinki Committee 2003), pp. 42-43.

agement, such as in the case of the Mission to Georgia. According to its original Modalities and Financial Implications approved in December 1992, the objective of this Mission was to promote negotiations between the conflicting parties in Georgia which are aimed at reaching a peaceful political settlement.

In Georgia, Kosovo and elsewhere, the Missions work closely with other organisations that are active in the field, such as the United Nations and NATO peacekeeping forces, the Council of Europe, the European Union, refugee organisations, and international and local non-governmental organisations. In Serbia and Montenegro, for instance, the OSCE cooperates with the Office of the United Nations High Commissioner for Refugees, to provide advice and support in order to facilitate the return of refugees to and from neighbouring countries and from other countries of residence as well as of internally displaced persons to their homes within the territory of the Federal Republic of Yugoslavia. In Bosnia-Herzegovina, the OSCE and its Mission have closely cooperated with the European Community Monitoring Mission in order to ensure the efficient, timely and cost-effective operation of the OSCE Mission. The Mission has also established a very close cooperation with the Office of the High Representative, SFOR, UNHCR, the Council of Europe and local NGOs among others.

3.2   The High Commissioner on National Minorities (HCNM)

At the beginning of the 1990s it became clear that the world had allowed itself to be totally surprised by the re-emergence of the 'old' ethnic tensions in Central and Eastern Europe subsequent to the collapse of Communism. These tensions were often accompanied by political instability, riots and violent actions. Internal crises in Yugoslavia and the former Soviet Union acquired both a regional and an international dimension. In view of these developments, in 1992 the CSCE adopted the proposal submitted by the Netherlands to appoint a High Commissioner on National Minorities. The High Commissioner would provide an instrument for the prevention of conflicts and for crisis management.[26] The Dutch politician and diplomat Max Van der Stoel was appointed the first High Commissioner on National Minorities, with his office in The Hague. His term of office was extended on several occasions; in 2001 he was succeeded by the present incumbent, the Swedish diplomat Rolf Ekéus.[27]

The HCNM's mandate describes the High Commissioner as an instrument for the prevention of conflicts by means of early warning and early action at the very beginning of a (potential) conflict. This mandate is based on the perception that action on minorities issues should be taken as quickly as possible, before the outbreak of violence. This pertains to issues whereby the HCNM is of the opinion that they could escalate into a conflict, creating a hazard to peace, stability, and peaceful relations between OSCE participating States. The mandate bestows two main duties on the High Commissioner. Firstly, he must try to gain control of or reduce tension involving minorities. Secondly, he must detect threats of a conflict. He is required to warn the OSCE in the event that he cannot control a specific situation with the resources at his disposal. The OSCE bodies can then exercise their discretion in deciding whether to take any action that may be re-

---

[26] According to his mandate, 'The High Commissioner will provide "early warning" and, as appropriate, "early action" at the earliest possible stage ....' CSCE Helsinki Document 1992, ch. II, Art. 3.
[27] Bakker and Bomert, op. cit. n. 4, at 30-34.

quired.[28] In addition, the HCNM has occasionally reported to non-OSCE bodies. The High Commissioner has sometimes been asked by the European Commission for Democracy through Law (Venice Commission) to give his assessment of countries with which he is engaged. The HCNM has also cooperated with the EC. During the drafting of progress reports on potential accession members, notes were compared on the general situation of minorities in a particular country, the approximation of laws and the extent to which they adhered to international standards. Moreover, Van der Stoel was able to use the Commission for carrots as well as sticks. In a few instances he urged the Commission to support specific minority-related projects.[29]

The HCNM has a number of tools available for the performance of his mandate. The most important of these are the collection of information, on-site consultations, the provision of advice from experts, the formulation of reports and the issuing of recommendations to governments, and calling in and collaborating with the Permanent Council and other OSCE bodies.

The collection of information is an extremely important element of the High Commissioner's work. The availability of the appropriate information at the appropriate time is indispensable to his ability to offer his services at as early a stage as possible in times of increasing tension. His staff in The Hague forms the closest source of information; however, a great deal of information is obtained in the field, in particular from non-governmental organisations representing specific minorities. Local partners, both governments and the minorities, also constitute an important source of information. In conclusion, the High Commissioner can also call on OSCE Missions for information about and insights into the local situation.

The on-site consultations are a second important instrument for the High Commissioner, for which purposes he does not require special permission to visit the relevant country. In the period between 1993 and 2001 Van der Stoel held more than one hundred on-site consultations in almost twenty OSCE participating States. His most frequent visits were to the former Yugoslav Republic of Macedonia, Slovakia, Croatia, Estonia, Latvia, and Romania. The current High Commissioner has also visited a number of countries.

The issue of recommendations to governments, often as a result of a visit, constituted perhaps the most important instrument of the first HCNM. His recommendations did not pillory the relevant government; instead they tried to

---

[28] The High Commissioner's mandate is subject to a number of restrictions. Among other things, he or she may not become involved in issues connected to national minorities when terrorism plays a role. Moreover, the High Commissioner is not intended to serve as an ombudsman or complaints department for national minorities. In addition, action in regions with acute and violent ethnic conflicts also fall outside the scope of his mandate.

[29] W. Kemp (ed.), *Quiet diplomacy in action: the OSCE High Commissioner on National Minorities* (The Hague, Kluwer Law International 2001), pp. 99-100.

convince the government that the country's stability would benefit most by granting specific rights or freedoms to members of the national minorities. In addition
to the issue of recommendations to governments, the HCNM also regularly pub-
lishes general reports and recommendations.[30] These reports and recommendations have contributed to the necessary amendment of national legislation, as well
as the implementation of consultation mechanisms – or at least dialogue – between governments and the representatives of minorities.

The above-mentioned concrete achievements in the field of legislation, the
contribution to the creation of consultation mechanisms and other results may be
considered a success. But have these achievements also contributed to the prevention of the use of force and violence? The next section focuses on the question
of success or failure of the activities of the HCNM as well as the OSCE Missions
and other field activities with regard to conflict prevention.

4. EXPERIENCE AND LESSONS LEARNED

What holds true for any remarks regarding the success (or failure) and the effectiveness of policy-making is also relevant to similar remarks regarding conflict
prevention: it is difficult to determine whether or not and to what extent these efforts and approaches have indeed led to positive results. Nonetheless, a number
of activities and approaches may be ascribed a positive influence on developments that have the potential to escalate into violent conflicts. The OSCE, in particular through its Missions and HCNM, has gained a great deal of experience
and expertise in the field of conflict prevention. Based on its successes and failures, the following ten lessons learned can be distinguished.

- *Long-term approach*
  The potential positive influence of OSCE Missions on developments that
  may escalate into violent conflicts is (partly) ascribed to the long-term presence in conflict areas. This enables the OSCE to establish extensive and useful networks and long-lasting contacts with the parties. These networks and
  contacts have proved to be essential requirements to be able to respond to the
  warning signs before they ignite and, thus, to allow the prevention of conflicts.

- *Presence on the spot*
  Another characteristic of the OSCE, which may have led to positive results,
  is its general structure in which a presence on the spot is linked to and sus-

---

[30] Examples include general reports on the position of the Roma in a number of OSCE participating States and recommendations pertaining to the rights of minorities with respect to the use of their
language and their rights in connection with education.

tained by high-level political consultation mechanisms in Vienna or at special (Ministerial) meetings or councils. With 'eyes and ears' in the field and with direct access to the governments of participating States, the OSCE as a whole has been capable to react quickly to developments that may lead to conflict.

- *Barriers to early action*
  The capacity of the OSCE instruments to quickly respond to situations and developments that may lead to conflict are sometimes partly undone by, among other things, the time-consuming (consensus) decision-making procedure.[31] Moreover, although from a political and diplomatic perspective the Organisation is often able to send officers rapidly to the relevant location, its conflict teams – observers, policy-makers, experts, police units, let alone military personnel – are often only deployed after a longer period of time. Thanks to his mandate, the High Commissioner on National Minorities is far less confronted with barriers to react quickly to potentially dangerous developments. The first High Commissioner was in fact often praised for his quick presence on the spot.

- *Silent diplomacy*
  Compared to other conflict prevention efforts, the HCNM represents one of the most highly developed instruments for early warning and preventive measures. Not only the quick reaction of the first High Commissioner to increasing tensions, but his activities in general have been given uniformly high ratings by political figures[32] and in the scholarly literature.[33] The factor that is often distinguished as a very important part of the effectiveness of the HCNM is his silent diplomacy. Behind the scenes, the High Commissioner offers options for consideration to disputing parties, and engages parties in informal discussions on sensitive issues that require discretion if not secrecy.

- *(Political) Flexibility*
  The (political) flexibility of the OSCE is also related to the political decision-making structures that provide for continuous dialogue and a review of situations and developments within the OSCE area. In addition, its mandate is

---

[31] Bakker and Bomert, op. cit. n. 4, at 44.

[32] According to UN Secretary General, Koffi Annan, 'In the High Commissioner on National Minorities, the OSCE has found a valuable mechanism for the identification of situations of ethnic tension, allowing them to be managed without recourse to violent conflict', in *OSCE Annual Report 2002*, p. 66.

[33] W. Zellner, *On the Effectiveness of the OSCE Minority Regime. Comparative Case Studies on Implementation of the Recommendations of the High Commissioner on National Minorities of the OSCE. A Research Project of IFSH* (Hamburg, CORE 1999) p. 4. See also E. Bakker, 'Van der Stoel acht jaar HCNM' (1993-2001), in B. Bomert, et al. (eds.), *Jaarboek vrede en veiligheid 2001* (Nijmegen, CICAM 2002), pp. 171-186.

flexible and is not limited by any rigid agenda, enabling the Organisation to react quickly to any challenge, especially new ones.[34]

- *Qualified personnel*
  The quality of the personnel of Missions and other OSCE field activities does not always meet the standards that are needed to address potential conflicts. Finding the right people at the right time is another problem confronting the OSCE. The Organisation has learned that more attention needs to be devoted to the quantity and quality of the teams. The search for the number of appropriate experts can – notwithstanding the formation of the Rapid Expert Assistance and Co-operation Teams (REACT)[35]– still be characterised as a process of scraping together the necessary manpower and expertise.[36]

- *Political will*
  Despite the OSCE instruments in the field and despite its mechanisms, in a number of cases the OSCE has not been able to gather the political will to prevent conflict. Political will – the key commodity in promoting effective multilateral conflict prevention – was lacking in cases such as Chechnya and Kosovo. These cases show that the OSCE is as strong and effective as the participating States (or the host state) want it to be.[37] Other conflict areas in which the OSCE was not able to prevent the (re-)escalation of tensions are the Caucasus region and Tadzhikistan.

- *Comprehensive approach*
  The OSCE's comprehensive approach towards security may be considered a positive contribution to conflict prevention. The Missions and other field operations have gained much experience with the concept of comprehensive security; integrating politico-military issues with the protection and promotion of human rights and the fundamental freedoms as well as economic and environmental issues into a broad security policy. This approach has enabled the OSCE to address problems in the economic and human dimension early before they grow into acute crises with effects on political security: essential for

---

[34] A. Zagorski, 'The OSCE in the context of the forthcoming NATO and EU extensions', 13 *Helsinki Monitor* (2002), p. 221 at 229.

[35] This rapidly deployable capability will cover a wide range of civilian expertise to provide assistance, in compliance with OSCE norms, in conflict prevention, crisis management and post-conflict rehabilitation. REACT was created (at the 1999 Istanbul Summit) to improve the OSCE's ability to address problems before they become crises and to deploy quickly the civilian component of a peacekeeping operation when needed.

[36] Bakker and Bomert, op. cit. n. 4, at 45.

[37] See also J. de Hoop Scheffer, Address to the OSCE Permanent Council, Vienna, 13 January 2003, Netherlands Ministry of Foreign Affairs AVT02/BZ69240.

a truly preventive stability policy.[38] Moreover, by addressing not only direct causes in their larger context, the comprehensive approach also deals with deeper causes of conflict.

* *Fragmentation and duplication*
  However, the OSCE's comprehensive approach to security also gives rise to the risk of a fragmentation of its attention to issues and its priorities. This could result in a situation in which the Organisation is involved in extensive discussions about a range of issues for which it possesses neither the manpower nor the financial resources required for an appropriate in-depth approach. Moreover, a continued expansion of the Organisation's duties is accompanied by a risk of the duplication of activities which are already being (more efficiently) addressed by other (inter)national government bodies and organisations.[39]

* *Cooperation with NGOs*
  The OSCE in general and its Missions in particular have attained substantial experience with conflict prevention through cooperation with non-governmental organisations. The long-term Missions often approach conflict prevention as a form of community-based development; an attempt to achieve stability and social justice through the creation of a critical civil society and by way of democratisation of political practices.[40] The High Commissioner on National Minorities has also established extensive networks and valuable contacts with non-governmental organisations.

5.   COOPERATION BETWEEN THE OSCE AND THE EU

Cooperation between the OSCE and the EU with regard to conflict prevention or the prevention of re-escalation of conflicts is not new.[41] Teamwork in this area dates back to the early 1990s, in connection with the Union's efforts during the Yugoslav conflict. The OSCE was involved in the implementation of the Brioni Accords of 7 July 1991 (which put an end to armed hostilities in Slovenia) and the subsequent activities of the European Community Monitoring Mission

---

[38] W. Ischinger, 'The OSCE in the European Concert', in Institute for Peace Research and Security Policy at the University of Hamburg, (ed.), *OSCE Yearbook 2000: Yearbook on the Organization for Security and Co-operation in Europe* (Baden-Baden, Nomos 2001), p. 39.

[39] Bakker and Bomert, op. cit. n. 4, at 43.

[40] J. de Wilde, 'Conflictpreventie op hellend vlak?', 31 *Vrede & Veiligheid* (2002) p. 447 at 452.

[41] It is very difficult to determine whether OSCE activities are primarily aimed at conflict prevention and the prevention of re-escalation or that they are primarily aimed at conflict management and post-conflict reconstruction. Therefore, I have also discussed examples of cooperation between the OSCE and the EU that are only indirectly aimed at preventing future conflict.

(ECMM). The OSCE and the European Union also worked closely together in assisting the implementation of the sanctions imposed by the United Nations Security Council on the Former Republic of Yugoslavia and *Republika Srpska*. The OSCE established Sanctions Assistance Missions (SAMs), which were coordinated by a Brussels-based Sanctions Committee (SAMCOMM). This committee was financed and partly staffed by the European Union.

In Albania, the OSCE and the European Union have been able to go a step further. The OSCE and the EU initiated a Friends of Albania Group (FOA), which held its inaugural meeting in Brussels in September 1998. The OSCE provides the overall framework for the Group, and co-chairs, together with the European Union, the plenary sessions. The Group is open to countries and international institutions that wish to actively support Albania in its development efforts. The Group provides, *inter alia*, a forum for mutual information, consultation and coordination on political, financial, economic and security-related matters with respect to Albania. In April 2002, under the auspices of the Chairman-in-Office and the Spanish European Union Presidency, it held its Sixth International Conference.

Another example of the coordination of political and economic approaches to post-conflict rehabilitation is the case of Moldova, where the OSCE Mission collaborated with the European Union TACIS programme. This project aims to obtain the agreement of both sides to the conflict, the Government of Moldova and the Trans-Dniestrian authorities. Projects under this programme include a shared reconstruction project to repair wartime damage and to reopen a bridge that is part of a major highway between Chisinau and Odessa. This reopening was of symbolic importance; as a sign of hope and as a restored link between Moldova, the Trans-Dniestrian region and Ukraine. Moreover, the prospects of mutual economic benefits from the project were a key in persuading the sides to take this step in restoring contacts and comments between the right and left bank of the River Dniester.

In the field of election observation and technical assistance, the OSCE, together with the European Commission, participated in a joint needs-assessment mission to the former Yugoslav Republic of Macedonia to assess the election environment prior to the 2000 municipal elections and to identify possibilities for technical assistance projects. The International Election Observation Mission set up for the Russian presidential elections in that same year closely cooperated with the EU Technical Assistance for the Commonwealth of Independent States (TACIS) project on capacity building in the field of election monitoring.[42] Similar examples of cooperation in the field of election observation include cases such as the Belarus presidential elections in 2001.

Cooperation between the OSCE and the EU in Belarus run by the authoritairan president Lukashenka, goes beyond election observations, however. The EU also

---

[42] OSCE Annual Report 2000 on OSCE Activities, 2001, ch. III, para. 1.2.2.

supports OSCE activities politically.[43] The EU backed the OSCE as relations between the OSCE Assistance and Monitoring Group and the Belarusian authorities came under pressure in the course of 2002. Tensions between Minsk and the Organisation culminated when the last remaining international mission member left Belarus at the end of October after the Mission had been denied any extension to its accreditation. The EU issued a number of statements expressing support for a continued OSCE field presence in Belarus. Eventually, the Belarusian authorities and the OSCE agreed on a new OSCE Office in Minsk that will 'assist the Belarusian Government in further promoting institution-building, in further consolidating the Rule of Law and in developing relations with civil society, in accordance with OSCE principles and commitments'.[44]

In Central Asia, the EU finances many OSCE projects. In fact, almost half of the projects of ODIHR in Central Asia during 2002 were EU-funded.[45] ODIHR and the EC also run a joint programme for advancing human rights and democratisation in the region. This project covers two main themes: strengthening the rule of law by providing assistance for the reform of the region's penitentiary system, human rights bodies and relevant legislation; and building capacity within civil society through human rights monitoring training and other assistance projects. Other major programmes aimed at advancing democracy and human rights that were jointly implemented were located in the Caucasus, Belarus, and South-Eastern Europe.[46]

5.1 Increasing and improving cooperation and coordination

In the last few years, cooperation with the European Union (EU) has continued to expand. As the EU is developing a new policy on conflict prevention and civil conflict management along lines similar to the OSCE's policy, consultations in Brussels focused on conflict management capabilities and REACT, and cooperative interaction between the two organisations.[47] Increased cooperation has led to the appointment of a Liaison Officer and informal high-level meetings between the Council of the EU and the OSCE. In August 2002, for instance, senior officials of both organisations met in Helsingborg at the Regional EU Conference on Conflict Prevention to discuss common values, common action, and common commitment.[48] The panel on common action addressed lessons learned from

---

[43] E. Bakker, 'Spionerende monitoren: De OVSE in Wit-Rusland', 167 *Oost-Europa Verkenningen* (2002), pp. 52-61. See also M. Wohlfeld, 'EU enlargement and the future of the OSCE: the role of field missions', 14 *Helsinki Monitor* (2003), pp. 52-64.

[44] PC.DEC/526, Vienna, 30 December 2002.

[45] OSCE Annual Report 2002 on OSCE Activities, 2003, p. 100.

[46] OSCE 2003, op. cit. n. 45, at 69.

[47] OSCE 2001, op. cit. n. 42, ch. III, para. 4.1.1.1.

[48] Pannellists included the former and present HCNM, the Secretary General of the OSCE, EU Commissioners and Ministers for Foreign Affairs of EU Member States.

practical cooperation in the field, policy development and division of labour in cases such as FYROM, Kosovo and Central Asia.

Common action and common commitment are not only discussed. Today, the EU and the OSCE also cooperate closely in fields such as the planning of new Missions and the development of shared selection criteria and training programmes for new staff. Policing issues is another area of increased coordination and cooperation. In fact, policing issues were one of the priorities in 2002. The OSCE Senior Police Adviser consulted with police representatives from the European Community (EC) on planned cooperation in the former Yugoslav Republic of Macedonia. These discussions resulted in a Memorandum of Understanding between the OSCE and the EC on police-related issues in that country.[49]

In general, cooperation is being increased. During the Spanish Presidency of the European Union, for instance, the C-i-O, accompanied by the Secretary General, participated in Brussels on 29 January 2002 in the first ever meeting with the EU's Ministerial Troika, thus inaugurating this new type of dialogue anticipated in the document adopted by the EU in 2001 on the reinforcement of cooperation between the EU and the OSCE. In addition to high-level contacts and to the regular updates on OSCE issues by the C-i-O to the General Affairs and External Relations Council and by Portugal within the framework of the Political and Security Committee and in the Common Foreign and Security Policy (CFSP) working groups in Brussels, which helped to enhance coordination and cooperation between the OSCE and the EU at headquarters level, the Portuguese Chairmanship endeavoured to increase collaboration between the two Organisations in the field. To this end, Portugal put forward two working documents in Brussels which were approved by the EU partners: one on EU/OSCE cooperation on Central Asia and another on enhancing cooperation and articulation between international organisations and institutions working in South-Eastern Europe, with particular focus on EU/OSCE collaboration in view of the Stabilization and Association Process.[50]

5.2 Terrorism

One particular security issue on which the OSCE and the EU cooperate that deserves special attention is terrorism. Traditionally, the OSCE deals with terrorism within the context of conflict prevention. Until 11 September, however, the Organisation did not give high priority to the problem of terrorism, except for the situation in the Central Asian states and Russia.[51] This changed after '9-11', which served as a catalyst for reviewing the existing cooperative instruments and

---

[49] OSCE 2003, op. cit. n. 45, at 100.
[50] MC(10).DOC/1/02, Porto, 7 December 2002.
[51] R. Zaagman, 'Terrorism and the OSCE. An overview', 13 *Helsinki Monitor* (2002), p. 204 at 206.

looking into ways of improving interaction among various organisations and initiatives. Cooperation with, among others, the EU developed against the background of an ensuing need for increased coordination of international efforts. It was driven in particular by decisions of the 2001 Ministerial Council meeting in Bucharest and the 2002 Ministerial Council meeting in Porto. In Bucharest, the OSCE participating States pledged to 'reinforce and develop bilateral and multilateral cooperation within the OSCE, with the United Nations and with other international and regional organizations, in order to combat terrorism in all its forms and manifestations'.[52]

OSCE cooperation with other international organisations with regard to terrorism culminated in a high-level meeting on preventing and combating terrorism, which was organised and hosted by the Portuguese OSCE Chairmanship in June 2002 in Lisbon. The participants – among them representatives of the European Union, the Council of Europe, NATO, the UN, the Commonwealth of Independent States (CIS), Interpol and many others – agreed on the need to reinforce the sharing of information and expertise. They confirmed their focus on strengthening cooperation in order to tackle effectively the problems which terrorism feeds upon, in particular: trafficking in arms, drugs and human beings; organized crime; money laundering; and persistent regional conflicts and sources of instability. In other words, they confirmed their focus on preventing terrorism instead of 'fighting' terrorist organisations and dealing with terrorist acts as such.

With terrorism firmly on the agenda, the Porto Ministerial adopted the OSCE Charter on Preventing and Combating Terrorism, which recalled the OSCE's role as a regional arrangement under Chapter VIII of the United Nations Charter and reiterated the OSCE's commitment undertaken in the framework of the Charter for European Security 'to co-operate more actively and closely with each other to meet these challenges'.[53] For the first time, regional and sub-regional organisations and initiatives within the OSCE area, as well as partners outside the OSCE, were invited to participate in an OSCE Ministerial Council meeting. At these and other occasions, inter-institutional consultation on terrorism was further developed. At the Tripartite Meeting of the OSCE, the UN and the Council of Europe – also attended by the EC – in Strasbourg, the discussion focused on the fight against terrorism, intercultural and inter-religious dialogue and on the practicalities of cooperation on the ground, including research and training.[54] One specific geographical area in which these discussions and consultations may lead to concrete joint programmes is Central Asia. In this region, the OSCE and the EU could link issues related to the fight against terrorism to existing programmes

---

[52] Bucharest Ministerial Declaration (3-4 December 2001), II. Decision on Combating Terrorism and the Bucharest plan of action for combating terrorism, MC(9).DEC/1.

[53] OSCE Charter for European Security, Istanbul, 19 November 1999, para. I, Art. 4, SUM.DOC/1/99.

[54] OSCE 2003, op. cit. n. 45, at 98.

and initiatives in the field of trafficking, democratization, the rule of law, and human rights. These programs and its offices in this region as well as those in the Kaukasus region are in fact the most important assets of the OSCE with which the Organisation can make a contribution to the 'fight' against terrorism.

5.3 Future

Given the evolving security situation in the OSCE area and with an increasing number of OSCE participating States becoming members of the EU and NATO, cooperation and coordination with the EU will become even more important in the future.[55] Both organisations have expressed the wish to further enhance cooperation in the field of conflict prevention. In May 2001, the OSCE Secretary General and the EU Ambassador Bjurner at the OSCE discussed the work of the EU on conflict prevention and possible areas for OSCE-EU cooperation. In addition to the contacts between the OSCE Chairmanship and Secretariat and future EU Presidencies, the EU Ambassador encouraged Secretariat-to-Secretariat contacts between the two organisations. Bjurner also spoke in favour of visits by OSCE heads of missions to the EU Political and Security Committee, which would give the EU Member States a better understanding of the various situations in the field.[56] Addressing the OSCE Permanent Council last year, the High Representative for the Common Foreign and Security Policy (CFSP), Javier Solana, confirmed that the OSCE and the EC are natural partners. He also stated that cooperation between the EU and OSCE, especially in view of EU enlargement, will strengthen and deepen throughout the coming years.[57] Already this year (2003), cooperation at the working level will be enhanced by the introduction of regular meetings at senior official level. These will complement day-to-day cooperation by means of regular informal contacts at expert level between the Commission, the Council Secretariat and the Secretariat of the OSCE.[58] It should, however, be noted that the implementation of the Commission's proposals regarding cooperation with the OSCE in the area of conflict prevention, notably by developing common modules and programmes for staff training for field operations (cf., the OSCE's REACT system) is still at an early phase.

---

[55] Cooperation between the EU and the OSCE may not only be institutionalised on a more practical level, but may also have a legal basis in the Constitution for Europe. In the Convention's Draft Treaty of 18 July 2003 it is stated in Chapter VII 'The Union's Relations with International Organisations and Third Countries and Union Delegations', Article III-229, para. 1, 'The Union shall establish all appropriate forms of cooperation with ... the Organisation for Security and Cooperation in Europe ...'.

[56] OSCE Secretary General, OSCE Annual Report 2001 on Interaction Between Organisations and Institutions in the OSCE Area, 26 November 2001 SEC.DOC/2/01.

[57] OSCE 2003, op. cit. n. 45, at 100.

[58] OSCE 2003, op. cit. n. 45, at 100.

6.   Concluding Remarks

In the coming years, it is hoped that the evolving European Security and Defence Policy will enable the EU to gradually dominate the responsibility for security management in Europe. Moreover, the EU will increasingly expand its 'out of area' operations; geographically and with regard to new areas of activity, including conflict prevention. In the 1990s, this area had been largely seen as the domain of the OSCE. This development is regarded by some as threatening the OSCE's very right to exist. Surely, the ambition of the EU to assert a common foreign, security and defence policy can hardly remain without any effect on the Organisation. Wherever it thinks it is appropriate, the EU is likely to be increasingly willing to apply its conflict prevention and crisis management tools directly and no longer through the OSCE. Eventually, it can block any action by the OSCE simply because of a desire to prove its relevance.[59] And if the EU and the OSCE are rivals in a deadly fight, there can be only one outcome: the death of the OSCE. However, it is too early to tell what the effect of the EU's enlargement and its evolving Security and Defence Policy will be. Many relevant questions remain unanswered. What will be the consequences of the fact that many Participating States will not join the EU in the foreseeable future and what role can the OSCE play in an OSCE area that will continue to be divided? Will the OSCE be able to maintain or create its own niche in the field of conflict prevention, conflict management and post-conflict rehabilitation? Will it develop other aspects of its work, for example its role as a negotiation framework, or the activities of the OSCE Institutions such as the HCNM? And will the OSCE be able to develop a better geographic balance and a better balance between the dimensions of its work and to improve modalities of cooperation with other organisations, especially the EU and NATO?[60]

Nonetheless, it can be argued that in the medium term the EU and the OSCE are likely to share conflict prevention efforts. The EU has economic and political resources at its disposal that are incomparable with those of the OSCE. The OSCE, on the other side, has much experience, networks and infrastructure in working 'in the field'. Both organisations realise that they have a lot to gain from combining efforts and from sharing their experiences. The EU can learn from the OSCE approach and make use of the many OSCE conflict prevention instruments to prevent the (re-)escalation of the many potential conflicts that still exist in Europe. In the long run perhaps the most positive outcome of a transfer of OSCE experience and lessons learned to the EU could be the transition of culture: a transition of a culture of reacting to crises that have already escalated – which currently characterises the EU approach to security – to a deep-rooted culture of conflict prevention that responds to warning signs before conflicts actually ignite.

---

[59] Zagorski, loc. cit. n. 34, at 225.
[60] Wohlfeld, loc. cit. n. 43, at 55.

Chapter 19
NATO CRISIS MANAGEMENT AND CONFLICT PREVENTION

by John Kriendler[1]

1. INTRODUCTION

This chapter considers the basis for the Alliance's role in crisis management and conflict prevention and how that role and the tools that the Alliance can bring to bear have evolved, particularly in the post-Cold War period. It also considers NATO's[2] cooperation with Euro-Atlantic Partnership Council (EAPC) and Partnership for Peace (PfP) partners and with other key international organisations, that contribute to international peace and security, in crisis management and conflict prevention, and, in particular, recent developments in NATO-EU relations.[3]

Crisis management and conflict prevention, including non-Article 5 crisis response operations, have been major themes in the continuing adaptation of the Alliance to the post-Cold War security environment. The new Strategic Concept adopted in Rome on 8 November 1991 emphasized the importance of crisis management, stating: 'The success of Alliance policy will require a coherent approach determined by the Alliance's political authorities choosing and coordinating appropriate crisis management measures as required from a range of political

---

[1] Professor of NATO and European Security Issues at the George C. Marshall European Center for Security Studies. The views expressed in this article are those of the author and do not reflect the official policy or position of the George C. Marshall European Center for Security Studies, the US European Command, the Department of Defense or the US Government. I am grateful to the suggestions received from Diego Ruiz Palmer, Head, Planning Section, Operations Division, NATO, and Professors Michael Mihalka, Graeme Herd and Tuomas Forsberg of the George C. Marshall European Center for Security Studies. Any errors of fact or judgement are my responsibility.

[2] Although not strictly accurate, I use NATO synonymously for the Atlantic Alliance.

[3] The NATO allies are: Belgium, Canada, the Czech Republic, Denmark, France, Germany, Greece, Hungary, Iceland, Italy, Luxembourg, the Netherlands, Norway, Poland, Portugal, Spain, Turkey, the United Kingdom and the United States. The EAPC/PfP partners are: Albania, Armenia, Austria, Azerbaijan, Belarus, Bulgaria, Croatia, Estonia, Finland, Georgia, Ireland, Kazakhstan, the Kyrgyz Republic, Latvia, Lithuania, Moldova, Romania, Russia, Slovakia, Slovenia, Sweden, Switzerland, Tajikistan, the former Yugoslav Republic of Macedonia, Turkmenistan, Ukraine and Uzbekistan. Bulgaria, Estonia, Latvia, Lithuania, Romania, Slovakia and Slovenia joined NATO on 29 March 2004.

V. Kronenberger and J. Wouters, eds., The European Union and Conflict Prevention
© 2004, T·M·C·ASSER PRESS, *The Hague, The Netherlands*

and other measures, including those in the military field'.[4] It also highlighted the importance of conflict prevention: 'In the new political and strategic environment in Europe, the success of the Alliance's policy of preserving peace and preventing war depends even more than in the past on the effectiveness of preventive diplomacy and successful management of crises affecting the security of its members.... In these new circumstances there are increased opportunities for the successful resolution of crises at an early stage'.[5] It also called for dialogue and cooperation with the CSCE and other institutions 'to prevent conflict since the Allies' security is inseparably linked to that of all other states in Europe'.[6]

The Strategic Concept adopted in Washington on 24 April 1999 went even further, listing crisis management and conflict prevention under the rubric 'fundamental security tasks' of the Alliance. It stated: '[...] in order to enhance the security and stability of the Euro-Atlantic area: Crisis Management: To stand ready, case-by-case and by consensus, in conformity with Article 7 of the Washington Treaty, to contribute to effective conflict prevention and to engage actively in crisis management, including crisis response operations'.[7] The Strategic Concept also recognized the need for 'military capabilities effective under the full range of foreseeable circumstances' as 'the basis of the Alliance's ability to contribute to conflict prevention and crisis management through non-Article 5 crisis response operations'.[8] The allies noted that NATO's preparedness to carry out such operations supports the broader objective of reinforcing and extending stability and often involves the participation of NATO's Partners and that it will make full use of partnership, cooperation and dialogue and NATO's links to other organisations to contribute to preventing crises and, should they arise, defusing them at an early stage.[9]

2.   CRISIS, CRISIS MANAGEMENT AND CONFLICT

Although it would be helpful to be able to begin with an agreed definition of crisis, there is no NATO or other internationally-agreed definition. However, a NATO subcommittee working in the field of operations research developed – but did not agree – a definition that, although general, is useful. It suggested that a crisis could be understood as 'a national or international situation where there is a

---

[4] NATO, 'The Alliance's New Strategic Concept', adopted by Heads of State and Government in Rome on 9 November 1991, para. 32.

[5] Ibid., paras. 31and 32.

[6] Ibid., para. 33.

[7] NATO, 'The Alliance's Strategic Concept', Press Release NAC-S (99) 65, 24 April 1999, para. 10.

[8] Ibid., para. 29.

[9] Ibid.

threat to priority values, interests or goals'.[10] This definition is sufficiently comprehensive to cover all the different categories of crises to which NATO might have to respond: collective defense, collective security, for which a crisis response operation might be required, or a natural, technological or humanitarian crisis. One problem that this definition highlights is that crisis, like beauty, is in the eye of the beholder, and one of the complexities of NATO crisis management is that what may be a crisis for one ally or partner may not be for others. This is one reason why the process of consultations among allies is so important. Concerning 'conflict', the focus is on preventing or resolving armed conflict, understood as one part of the broad crisis spectrum, which ranges, along a scale of escalation and then de-escalation, from peace to disagreement to confrontation to armed conflict to build down to new stability.

As for 'crisis management', it is most usefully understood as the 'organisation, procedures and arrangements to control crisis and shape its future course'. Key elements of this definition are: (1) bringing the crisis under the *control* of the crisis managers and (2) permitting them to *shape the future course* of the crisis. Crisis management activities range from information acquisition and assessment, analysis of the situation, establishment of goals, development of options for action and comparison, implementation of a selected option, including, where necessary, military action, and analysis of reaction/feedback.

Although the Alliance also has no agreed definition of conflict or conflict prevention, the former can generally be understood as a 'fight, battle or war'.[11] A sociological definition is 'a relationship between two or more parties (individuals or groups) who have, or think they have, incompatible goals'.[12] And violent conflict would be conflict where the parties resort to violent means. A useful definition of conflict prevention is: 'any structural or intercessory means to keep intrastate or interstate tensions and disputes from escalating into significant violence and use of armed force, to strengthen capabilities of potential parties to violent conflict for resolving such disputes peacefully and to progressively reduce the underlying problems that produces these issues and disputes'.[13]

---

[10] This definition was developed by the Ad Hoc Working Group within Panel VII of the Defence Research Group (AC/243), but was not agreed, as noted.

[11] Merriam-Webster's Collegiate Dictionary, available on line at <www.m-w.com/cgi-bin/dictionary>, accessed on 25 March 2002.

[12] Simon Fisher, Jawed Ludin, Sue Williams, Steve Williams, Dekha Ibrahim Abdi and Richard Smith, *Working with Conflict: Skills and Strategy for Action* (Birmingham, Zed Books 2000), p. 4.

[13] Michael Lund, 'Preventing Violent Intrastate Conflicts: Learning Lessons from Experience' in Paul van Tongeren, Hans van de Veen and Juliette Verhoven, *Searching for Peace in Europe and Eurasia: An Overview of Conflict Prevention and Peace-building Activities* (Boulder, Lynne Rienner 2002), pp. 19-91.

3. BASIS FOR CRISIS MANAGEMENT AND CONFLICT PREVENTION

Based on the Washington Treaty, NATO has been in the crisis management and conflict prevention business since its inception. Although the terminology was not used at the time, the commitment in Article 4 to consult when any ally perceives a threat to its security, sovereignty or territorial integrity and in Article 5 to regard an attack on one or more allies as an attack on all and to respond were later referred to as the basis for 'NATO crisis management'.

Allied Heads of State and Government highlighted the importance of consultations pursuant to Article 4 in the 1999 Strategic Concept, which identified 'consultations' as the second of the Alliance's 'fundamental security tasks'. The language of Article 4 is mirrored in the Partnership for Peace (PfP) invitation, which states: 'NATO will consult with any active participant in the Partnership if that Partner perceives a direct threat to its territorial integrity, political independence, or security'.[14] A number of PfP members have perceived such threats and have requested consultations, during which allies have agreed to take action to address the problems raised.[15]

Article 5, the second essential element of NATO crisis management, contains two parts: (1) the commitment to view an attack against one as an attack against all, and (2) the commitment to assist in concert by such action each member deems necessary, including the use of armed force. Article 5 can best be understood as fundamentally a statement of deterrence to would-be attackers, a statement made credible, despite its less than categorical nature, by the existence of the necessary capabilities (reflected in the integrated military structure, force commitments and readiness levels) and the evident political will to respond to any attack.

4. EVOLUTION OF NATO CRISIS MANAGEMENT

With the radical evolution of the security environment, the kinds of crises which allies have agreed the Alliance should manage and the kinds of conflicts which it sought to prevent changed dramatically as did the tools that the Alliance could bring to bear. The nature and modalities of NATO's cooperation with other international organisations, which contribute to international peace and security, in particular the UN, the EU and the OSCE, have also evolved significantly. During

---

[14] NATO, Partnership for Peace: Framework Document, adopted by the Ministerial Meeting of the North Atlantic Council/ North Atlantic Cooperation Council, NATO Headquarters, Brussels, 10-11 January 1994.

[15] As just one example, in response to Albania's request following the 1997 collapse, allies agreed to a variety of measures, including assistance in developing Albania's national crisis management organisation and procedures.

the Cold War, the kinds of crises that the Alliance faced where largely, but not exclusively, military, and the kinds of crisis management and conflict prevention tools where also therefore largely, but again not exclusively, military. What is meant by NATO crisis management has therefore evolved. In the post Cold War era, the focus is on crises resulting from tensions and antagonisms generated by ethnic conflicts, extreme nationalism, intrastate political strife, failed or inadequate political change and severe economic problems, and, since 11 September 2001, terrorism and the threat posed by weapons of mass destruction.[16]

The new approach was set out in 1991 in Rome as part of the alliance's New Strategic Concept, referred to above. The new approach encompassed a broader approach to security and greater opportunities to achieve long-standing objectives through political means. Key aspects of the new approach included: (a) more active use of political and diplomatic means, (b) close interaction and cooperation with other international organisations,[17] and (c) significant changes in NATO's command and force structures.

Further significant changes in the field of crisis management and conflict prevention took place at the Washington Summit in April 1999, already referred to above. In general terms, the Strategic Concept and Washington Summit Declaration delineated a broad approach to security, encompassing complementary political and military means and emphasizing cooperation with other states that share the Alliance's objectives and with other international organisations. Special emphasis was given to developing the European Security and Defence Identity within NATO. Allies noted that 'a coherent approach to crisis management, as in any use of force by the Alliance, will require the Alliance's political authorities to choose and coordinate appropriate responses from a range of both political and military measures and to exercise close political control at all stages'.[18]

The allies also stated that, in light of the demanding nature of conflict prevention and crisis management operations and the requirement for the same qualities of cohesion, multinational training, and extensive prior planning needed for Article 5 situations, such operations would be handled through the same Alliance structures and procedures used for Article 5 operations.[19] Allies agreed to a number of measures to ensure the NATO would have the necessary military capabilities for all NATO missions including contributing to conflict prevention and crisis management.

Measures agreed upon at the Prague summit, including enlargement, the Prague Capabilities Commitment, the NATO Response Force and the new com-

---

[16] The 1999 Strategic Concept appeared to treat terrorism as something to be dealt with under Article 4, but the North Atlantic Council took a different approach in its 12 September 2001 decision.

[17] In 1992 NATO agreed to support, on a case-by-case basis, according to its procedures, peacekeeping operations under a UN mandate or the authority of the OSCE.

[18] NATO, 1999 Strategic Concept, para. 32.

[19] Ibid., para. 29.

mand arrangements all contribute to the Alliance's conflict prevention and crisis management capabilities. Allies also gave additional impetus to cooperation with the EU in crisis management, as well as in other areas, stating that: 'Events on and since 11 September 2001 have underlined further the importance of greater transparency and cooperation between our two organisations on questions of common interest relating to security, defence, and crisis management, so that crises can be met with the most appropriate military response and effective crisis management ensured'.[20]

5.   CRISIS MANAGEMENT OBJECTIVES

Despite the lack of an agreed definition of crisis, there are agreed objectives of NATO crisis management. In general terms, these objectives are along the following lines: (1) contribute to reducing tensions to prevent them becoming crises; (2) manage crises which have arisen effectively to prevent them from becoming conflicts; (3) ensure timely civil and military preparedness for all degrees of crisis; (4) if hostilities break out, control the response, prevent further escalation and persuade any aggressor to cease his attack and withdraw from Allied territory; and (5) finally, when further escalation or hostilities have been stopped or are under control or when other kinds of crises have been successfully managed, de-escalate. An additional objective, which is less formally enshrined in Alliance documents, but is adhered to in practice, is to look at each crisis (and each crisis management exercise) from the perspective of lessons that can be drawn to maintain and enhance NATO's crisis management capabilities.[21]

6.   KEY CRISIS MANAGEMENT PRINCIPLES

There are also agreed principles for NATO crisis management, which also apply in other areas of Alliance decision-making. First, the North Atlantic Council (NAC) (or in some cases the Defence Planning Committee (DPC), on which France is not represented), at whatever level it meets (Heads of State and Government, ministers, ambassadors or their representatives) is the highest authority of the Alliance and can take decisions for common action. The second principle is that all decisions taken in the Council or the DPC (and all other NATO bodies)

---

[20] NATO, Prague Summit Declaration, 21 November 2002, para. 11.
[21] The fourth objective is obviously not applicable to technological, natural and humanitarian crises.

are expressions of national sovereignty, and are therefore taken by consensus.[22] Third, nations have delegated to their representatives in Council (or the DPC) the responsibility of representing all elements of their governments, including political, economic, defence and civil emergency planning, among others. Finally, at every step in the process there is political control of the military: no decision regarding formal planning, deployment or the use of military forces can be taken without the necessary political authorization by the Council or DPC.

7. NATO CRISIS MANAGEMENT ORGANISATION

In understanding how NATO crisis management works, it is useful to look at the role of key committees and staffs. The North Atlantic Council, or in certain cases involving the integrated military structure the Defence Planning Committee, plays, as noted, the paramount role. To undertake effective, timely crisis management, the North Atlantic Council and/or the Defence Planning Committee (DPC) have four distinct but related functions. The first function is to provide the focal point in the Alliance for the exchange of intelligence and information. Within the Alliance, the process of sharing intelligence and information is continuous, but frequently the most sensitive and latest information is exchanged in the Council or the DPC, sometimes in restricted sessions with very limited participation from delegations, the international staff and the international military staff. A second function is to act as a forum for consultation where allies can express and compare their views on key developments. Even if all allies had the same intelligence and information, which is never the case, their different geostrategic situations and interests would be likely to lead them to different conclusions about what is happening in a particular crisis, how it is likely to evolve, the implications of the crisis, and how it could and should be addressed. By comparing views, a collective view should emerge which will be, hopefully, better informed, more nuanced and more likely to succeed. A third function is that, short of decisions for collective action, Council or DPC meetings also provide a forum which allies can use, when they chose to, to align their individual policies to be mutually supporting. Finally, the Council (or the DPC) serves as a forum to harmonise views in the form of collective decisions on measures to be taken where there is the political will to do so.

In fulfilling these crisis management functions, the Council/DPC is supported by other principal committees, of which the following are the most important. The Policy Coordination Group (PCG) is a senior political/military body that provides advice on politico-military issues. The Political Committee (PC), which is

---

[22] The only exception to consensus are decisions taken in the Defence Review Committee (DRC), where by custom, an ally cannot oppose agreement of other allies concerning that country's force plans.

comprised, in almost all cases, of the political advisors of each allied delegation, provides advice on political developments and options, including a public affairs strategy for any crisis. The Military Committee (MC), which is composed of senior military officers representing the Chiefs of Defense and on major occasions, the Chiefs of Defense themselves, is the primary source of military advice and military policy recommendations and is responsible to the Council/DPC for the overall conduct of military affairs of the alliance. NATO Headquarters in Brussels is not a military headquarters and the Military Committee is not a military command. The actual conduct of military operations is the responsibility of the recently established Allied Command Operations, which is strictly bound by guidance from the political authorities, which the Military Committee translates into more detailed direction. Finally, the Senior Civil Emergency Planning Committee (SCEPC) is responsible to the Council/DPC for civil emergency planning aspects of crisis management. It ensures civil preparedness and deals with civil support for military operations and all other Civil Emergency Planning issues.[23]

7.1   The crisis spectrum

A key requirement of a crisis management system, which NATO crisis management organisation and procedures are designed to ensure, is the ability to deal with crises throughout the entire crisis spectrum. This includes the pre-crisis period of stability and peace as well as all stages of crisis. Taking the most complex case, a crisis potentially involving military operations aimed at helping to gain control of the crisis and to influence its course, the following distinct stages can be identified: (1) peace, (2) escalation (including disagreement, confrontation and armed conflict) and (3) de-escalation (including build-down and new stability). A similar, but less complicated set of categories could be applied to technological, natural or humanitarian disasters.

7.2   Consultation process

The end of the Cold War and the need to face very different kinds of risks in a radically transformed security environment brought about significant changes in the intensity and duration of consultations and decision-making. During the Cold War, the threat was clear and well understood, and it was possible to rely, for the most part, on off-the-shelf and well-rehearsed plans to determine how to respond. This usually made for rapid decision-making on clearly framed issues in NATO's large-scale exercises, where these issues arose. Moreover, as the threats were, as noted above, largely – but not exclusively – military in nature, as were the responses, once the decision was taken to engage, it was largely up to the alliance

---

[23] More detailed information on the roles of each of these committees is available at the NATO website at <http://www.nato.int/>.

armed forces to undertake the tasks that allies had agreed. In the post-Cold War security environment, the risks are more complex and unpredictable, and, if no longer existential, no less sensitive and are subject to intensive press and public scrutiny. In light of the kinds of issues which have characterized crisis response operations such as those in Bosnia-Herzegovina, Kosovo, the former Yugoslav Republic of Macedonia and Afghanistan, allies have been insisting on much more intensive involvement in planning and approval of planning and much more detailed and protracted political oversight than was the case with most Cold War scenarios. This is reflected in frequent and long Council meetings, sometimes daily and sometimes more than once each day.

8. SUPPORTING ELEMENTS FOR NATO CRISIS MANAGEMENT AND CONFLICT PREVENTION

In addition to the crisis management organisation described above, NATO has developed a variety of key elements to support crisis management and conflict prevention, including: (1) staffs and physical facilities; (2) commonly agreed arrangements and procedures; and (3) measures which can be taken to prevent or respond to crisis.

8.1 Staff and physical facilities

The recently reorganized NATO international staff (IS) and the international military staff (IMS) provide necessary support for crisis management and conflict prevention as they do for all Alliance matters. Without going into detail about information that is available elsewhere, it is useful to emphasize aspects of the IS restructuring, instituted in August 2003, specifically designed or likely to enhance NATO's crisis management and conflict prevention capabilities. Of particular importance, a division for operations was established (these functions had previously been performed by the Defense Plans and Operations Division) to 'provide the operational capability required to meet NATO's deterrence, defense and crisis management tasks. Responsibilities include NATO's crisis management and peacekeeping activities and civil emergency planning and exercises'.[24] The overall objective of the restructuring was to adapt NATO Headquarters in Brussels to better reflect the Alliance's new missions and priorities and to enable the international staff to function more effectively under very different conditions than those which obtained during the Cold War. Many aspects of the restructuring are likely, therefore, to have an impact on crisis management and conflict prevention.

---

[24] NATO, 'Restructuring NATO HQ', *NATO Issues,* available at <http://www.nato.int/issues/restructuring/index.htm>.

In addition to the overall support for crisis management and conflict prevention provided by the IS and IMS, there is a joint task force which makes particularly important contributions. The Crisis Management Task Force (CMTF)[25] coordinates advice to the Secretary General and the drafting of proposals and recommendations, including for operational planning, through the key committees and, subsequently, to the NAC. It helps to avoid presenting the NAC with individual sets of recommendations from NATO committees dealing with different disciplines. The requirement to coordinate advice to the SG and Council was identified in 1995 as IFOR deployed into Bosnia, and resulted in the establishment of a multi-disciplinary Crisis Management Task Force, designated at that time as the Bosnia Task Force (BTF). This multi-disciplinary task force is an integral part of the NATO crisis management organisation. It meets frequently to address ongoing operations and cooperation with other international organisations.

Physical facilities are also required for effective crisis management and conflict prevention. Rapid, reliable, secure, redundant communications are essential. NATO communications systems, which have been updated and modernized, provide for classified message traffic, integrated data networks and secure and nonsecure voice communications. These systems are supported by two major communications bearer systems: a space-based system using NATO-owned satellites and the NATO terrestrial transmission system, covering the European land mass.

A second key supporting facility is the NATO Situation Center (SITCEN). It was established by the North Atlantic Council in 1968: (1) to assist the North Atlantic Council, the Defense Planning Committee and the Military Committee in fulfilling their respective functions in the field of consultation; (2) to serve as a focal point within the Alliance for the receipt, exchange, and dissemination of political, military and economic intelligence and information; and (3) to act as a link with similar facilities of member nations and the major NATO Commands.

The NATO Situation Center serves as a central NATO focus for crisis management and conflict prevention by, among other things, ensuring a continuous flow and exchange of information and intelligence between NATO Headquarters, the Strategic Commands and NATO capitals, monitoring political, military and economic matters of interest to NATO and capitals and maintaining and updating background information for the crisis management staffs. The NATO Situation Center is also designed so that it can house the crisis management organisation in crisis, but this function has only been used in exercises since the end of the Cold War, due to the lesser magnitudes of the crises dealt with (compared to Cold War scenarios) and greatly increased interconnectivity within NATO Headquarters in Brussels.

---

[25] This was previously known at the Bosnia Task Force (BTF) and subsequently as the Balkans Task Force (BTF). It also meets as the Afghanistan Task Force.

8.2 Arrangements and procedures

In addition to staff elements and physical facilities, NATO has developed and refined comprehensive, detailed arrangements and procedures for: (1) the identification and monitoring of crisis situations, (2) exchange of intelligence and information, (3) production and circulation of assessments to support consultation and collective decision-making, (4) press and public relations, (5) civil emergency arrangements, and (6) communications, among many others. In essence, arrangements and procedures have been developed, promulgated, tested, practiced, updated and refined for the crisis management organisation. Both the experience of actual crises and crisis response operations and NATO-wide crisis management exercises, in some cases involving PfP partners and other international organisations, provide lessons which enable revision of arrangements and procedures.

8.3 Crisis management measures

For timely action in response to a potential or developing crisis, NATO has also learned that it is essential to have a variety of different measures or possible responses in place so that they do not have to be developed on an *ad hoc* basis for each new crisis. In deciding what to do about a given situation, the Council/DPC has a wide range of measures, which allies have agreed upon, from which to choose. These measures have been agreed and compiled in various documents, but their application in a particular situation requires consideration on a case-by-case basis. These measures have been substantially revised since the end of the Cold War to seek to ensure that they are relevant for the contemporary crisis environment, but with only partial success.

Measures include: (1) diplomatic, economic and military preventive measures, (2) a large variety of military response options, and (3) a spectrum of precautionary measures. Two of these compilations, the Inventory of Preventive Measures (IPM) and the Catalog of Military Response Options (MRO) have a number of similarities. They are both designed largely for reference and use by the political authorities, usually in the early stages of crisis and both are lists or menus, rather than systems, and can be drawn from and amended as the situation warrants. In addition, in the case of the MRO the visibility of the measures is explicitly considered as the degree to which the measures can be perceived can affect how the crisis develops. To take obvious examples, one would hope that increasing intelligence gathering would not be 'visible' and would not therefore influence how protagonist(s) react. On the other hand, increasing the readiness of forces would certainly be visible and would be likely to have an impact. Examples of the preventive measures could include: messages, trade restrictions, expressions of support for threatened states, closure of ports and airports and special programs in favor of threatened states. Examples of military response options could include:

cancellation of military cooperation, confidential military consultations, request inspections and evaluation visits, surveillance, increased readiness and activation of forces. There are also a variety of contingency operation plans, which can be drawn on for detailed operational planning if required.

In addition to these lists or menus of measures, NATO also has a system for assuring preparedness and timely response in crisis for civil and military commands, agencies and headquarters, and national military units and agencies. The NATO Precautionary System (NPS) provides a mechanism to initiate actions for the overall preparedness of the alliance to support military action and comprises a wide range of civil and military measures to ensure that actions and reactions are timely, coordinated and appropriate. The NPS assures comprehensive political control and eliminates preplanned sequences and powers delegated in advance which had characterized the Alerts System, which was used and better suited for the Cold War. Some measures request nations and direct major subordinate commanders to take certain actions. Others include action for NATO agencies. Measures cover the entire spectrum of Alliance operations including general operations, force readiness, intelligence, logistics and civil preparedness among others. Once the decision has been taken to implement a measure, national authorities and major subordinate commanders have a detailed list of steps to take in the NATO precautionary system manual. The NATO Precautionary System is directly linked to national precautionary systems in each allied country. It has been updated, usually annually, on the basis of lessons learned from NATO and NATO-led operations and also the more or less annual NATO-wide crisis management exercises.[26]

9. NATO CRISIS RESPONSE SYSTEM (NCRS)

Although the measures and precautionary system described above are still in effect, they were used only sporadically and selectively during NATO and NATO-led operations in the Balkans, and a small number of precautionary measures was implemented following the 9/11 attacks. In consequence, Allies decided that a new comprehensive, integrated, full spectrum, user-friendly crisis response system was needed.

The North Atlantic Council issued guidelines for the development of a NATO Crisis Response System (NCRS) in August 2001, and the system has now been developed and used in exercises but not yet agreed by the allies. It is designed to provide for required preparedness and support for crisis and conflict prevention, crisis management and Article 5 and non-Article 5 operations. Once implemented it is designed to increase the ability of the Alliance and, where appropriate, non-

---

[26] These are intended to take place annually but have been sometimes cancelled in the light of the demands of ongoing operations.

NATO nations to prepare for, and respond to, the full range of crises that the Alliance might be required to face. The NCRS comprises a full range of measures and is intended to enable the Alliance and, where appropriate, non-NATO nations to react in a timely, coordinated and discriminate manner.

The NCRS has a number of components, including, among others, preventive options and crisis response measures. Preventive options are designed to foster crisis management and conflict prevention by assisting the Council in its consideration of possible responses to emerging or actual crises. Crisis response measures are intended to ensure Alliance preparedness for responding to the full range of potential crises. The NCRS is designed to be complementary to and act interactively with the NATO Intelligence and Warning System (NIWS), described below, NATO's Operational Planning System (MC 133) as well as Civil Emergency Planning (CEP) crisis management arrangements.

Once the NCRS is agreed, it will be necessary to adjust national crisis management systems, which are patterned on the NATO system and must be able to interact with it. The draft NATO NCRS was used for the crisis management exercise in 2004. Once it is agreed, the Inventory of Preventive Measures, the Catalogue of Military Response Options and the NATO Precautionary System will be cancelled. The NCRS is a far-reaching adaptation of NATO's crisis management system which brings the different elements together in a comprehensive, interconnected system designed to be easier to use. It will require a substantial testing and shakedown period, but should make an important contribution to better, faster, better-informed crisis management consultations and decision-making and implementation. Its comprehensive, integrated approach is a major improvement over the fragmented measures, which are currently in effect.

10. NATO INTELLIGENCE WARNING SYSTEM (NIWS)

One of the many lessons that NATO relearned in NATO and NATO-led operations in the Balkans was the importance of early warning for effective conflict prevention and crisis management. Early warning provides more time to analyze, plan and prepare a response and, in the event of intervention, enhances its likelihood of success. Early warning can also contribute to virtually all elements of the crisis-management decision cycle, including the establishment of goals to be achieved, development of courses of action and their comparison, eventual implementation of a chosen option, and finally analysis of the reaction of the protagonists and necessary readjustment. Because of the importance of early warning, in the early stages crisis management and conflict prevention procedures focus on information acquisition, assessment and analysis.

As in so many other areas, the evolving post-Cold War security environment necessitated dramatic changes in the focus of early warning and in early warning methodologies. First there was a need to look at a much broader range of poten-

tial crises and then to adopt the methodologies to this broader range and the generally changed circumstances. Cold War warning systems, which were based on
essential steps an adversary would have to take for military action, were no
longer relevant or applicable. Instead new systems have been developed which
focus on political, economic, social developments, as well as on military ones.
Another change was a need to take into account the increased interaction among
different international organisations in the field of international peace and security.

In keeping with this need to develop new warning methodologies, NATO developed a new intelligence warning system (NIWS) that is designed to be much
more inclusive than its predecessor and to take account of the risks identified in
the Alliance's 1999 Strategic Concept. It is based on the informed judgment of
analysts and relies on qualitative analytical processes, not the more mechanical
measurement of multiple, precisely defined and specific events, as was the case
during the Cold War. The new system covers not only threats to NATO, but also
a wide variety of military and non-military risk indicators, including uncertainty
and instability in and around the Euro-Atlantic area, and the possibility of regional crises on the periphery of the Alliance. Moreover, it both provides warning
of any developing instability, crisis, threats, risks, or concerns that could impact
on the security interests of the Alliance and it monitors de-escalation of a crisis.

'Warning' is not an event, but a cyclical process in which an identifiable crisis, risk or threat is assessed, a warning problem is defined and a critical indicator
list is developed. Clearly, this is more difficult in today's more complex and less
predictable security environment. Next, the critical indicators are continuously
monitored and the assessment matrix is updated as required, warning is issued,
and the cycle resumes. The crucial sub-text to this process is recognition that the
effectiveness of warning is dependent upon the extent to which it is integrated
into the crisis management and response measures available to decision-makers.[27]

11.   PUBLIC INFORMATION STRATEGY

Another area of substantial change as a result of lessons learned from operations
in the Balkans has been NATO's approach to public information and the media.
During the Kosovo air campaign, NATO was overwhelmed with press and media
queries, which it was not in a position to respond to effectively. The need to have
a fully developed and coordinated public information strategy for crisis management was clear. It was recognized that the way NATO's message is communi-
cated to the media can have a critical impact on the potential protagonists and on

---

[27] For more detail see John Kriendler, 'Anticipating Crisis', 4 *NATO Review* (2002), available on
line at <http://www.nato.int/docu/review/2002/issue4/english/main.htm>.

public opinion in the potential or actual protagonist country and allied as well as other countries.

In response to the initial problems experienced during the air campaign, including Milošević's active media efforts, NATO established a Media Operations Center (MOC) to bring high-level media expertise to bear and to anticipate media issues, develop responses and coordinate media efforts in Allied capitals. The Media Operations Center was an important improvement and has now been incorporated into NATO's crisis management organisation and procedures. A NATO conference room has been equipped with the necessary computer and other communications terminals, and the internal procedures have been developed so that a MOC can be activated at short notice.

NATO also recognized that a crisis management public information strategy needed to achieve the following objectives: sustain public support from the outset of military operations and present and communicate the missions positively, effectively and consistently, both within allied countries and in the broader international environment. The following were seen as necessary to accomplish this, among many other requirements: (1) a pro-active strategy, developed as part of the operational planning process, identifying key issues and messages and seeking to anticipate problems before they arose; (2) precise coordination between the NATO and national spokespersons, (3) a NATO headquarters crisis management public information organisation that can be surged in times of crisis, (4) standard operating procedures for the organisation, (5) identification of a single Alliance spokesperson or close coordination between spokespersons, and (6) effective military as well as civilian spokespersons, able to respond quickly, but accurately, to media queries.

12. PARTNERSHIP ACTIVITIES

As already noted, the allies emphasized the importance of NATO partnership cooperation activities, including the Euro-Atlantic Partnership Council (EAPC), Partnership for Peace (PfP), The NATO Russia Council (NRC), the NATO/Ukraine Commission (NUC) and the Mediterranean Dialogue, in crisis management and conflict prevention.

These activities and the countries that participate in them have contributed to and can contribute to crisis management and conflict prevention in a number of ways. One important contribution is structural reduction of tension through adoption of democratic norms and practices, settlement of outstanding disputes and defense reform by countries that aspire to membership in the Alliance or in PfP. This can be seen dramatically in the reforms adopted by the seven countries invited to join the Alliance at the Prague summit in 2002. NATO's cooperation activities also contribute to crisis management and conflict prevention through the active discussions of potential or ongoing crises. These consultations focus attention on sensitive issues and allow for ventilating views in ways that my help to reduce tensions. A third aspect of support for crisis management is the political weight that partnership countries (those that participate in the bodies listed above) as well as others that contribute to NATO-led crisis response operations lend to NATO-led efforts to address crises. This is reflected in statements adopted by these bodies, such as those adopted by the Euro-Atlantic Cooperation Council regarding the September 11 attacks, as well as positions they adopt in other international organisations dealing with these same issues. Finally and certainly not least important, partners have also made substantial contributions to NATO-led crisis response operations in the form of armed forces and essential host nation support such as air, land, and maritime transit and basing and other facilities.[28]

These developments all post-date the Cold War, of course, and continue to evolve. There have been significant changes in all of the areas of partnership, in particular the continued development of an enhanced and more operational partnership. *Inter alia*, NATO has been seeking to (1) further develop partners' potential role in crisis prevention and crisis management, (2) consider means to transition from non-crisis PfP relations to crisis use of PfP assets, and (3) look at issues related to releasing additional classified information to partners and other international organisations during crisis. One of many areas of significant change is the degree to which partners can participate in decisions related to crisis management operations. Although allies make the final decision on the planning and execution of a crisis response operation, there has been significant improvements in the timeliness and quantity of information provided to Partners, the amount of time they have to react and the degree to which their views are taken into account before decisions are taken by allies.

Reflecting the importance of partner contributions to NATO-led crisis response operations, the Washington Summit agreed the Political Military Framework for NATO-led PfP Operations (PMF) which provides essential building blocks for partner integration into command and political structures, including partner participation in: (1) operational planning, (2) command arrangements and (3) political consultations and decision-making. Allies and partners agreed that the process of information and consultation with contributing partner nations significantly facilitated deployment of NATO-led operations with significant partner participation. Periodic reviews of the PMF provide opportunities for allies and partners to refine it. While partners are unlikely to ever have as much information as early as they would like or as much influence on the decisions taken, they are considerably better off in all these areas than was the case with IFOR or SFOR and have recognized the progress that has been made.

---

[28] As just one example, SFOR is presently comprised of contingents from: 16 allies, eight PfP partners and three others.

13.   Cooperation with Other International Organisations

Cooperation with other international organisations that contribute to international peace and security is another important facet of NATO's role in crisis management and conflict prevention. Although the Washington Treaty contains explicit references to NATO's commitment to the principles of the UN Charter and the United Nations, there was little contact between NATO and the UN or other international organisations during the Cold War. One of the many important changes in the 1991 Strategic Concept was a recognition of the need to address the broader approach to security though cooperation between NATO and other international organisations. With respect to the Alliance's role in promoting international peace and security, the 1991 Strategic Concept explicitly recognized 'the valuable contribution being made by other organisations such as the European Community and the CSCE, and that the roles of these institutions and of the Alliance are complementary [...]'[29] In the section dealing with crisis management and conflict prevention the 1991 Strategic Concept stated that: 'The potential of dialogue and co-operation within all of Europe must be fully developed in order to help to defuse crises and to prevent conflicts since the Allies' security is inseparably linked to that of all other states in Europe. To this end, the Allies will support the role of the CSCE process and its institutions. Other bodies including the European Community, Western European Union and United Nations may also have an important role to play'.[30] This same point was made in the Rome Declaration on Peace and Cooperation adopted at the same time, which noted that 'a framework of interlocking institutions' was needed and that NATO was working 'toward a new European security architecture in which NATO, the CSCE, the European Community, the WEU and the Council of Europe complement each other [...]. This interaction will be of the greatest significance in preventing instability and divisions that could result from various causes, such as economic disparities and violent nationalism'.[31]

Efforts to initiate such a cooperative approach got off to a difficult start. The UN had responded unenthusiastically to NATO's initial efforts at contacts to consider developments in Yugoslavia as UN officials did not consider contacts between the UN and NATO concerning Yugoslavia to be appropriate. However, despite the well-known difficulties over UNPROFOR, NATO-UN contacts proved essential and developed substantially to mutual benefit at virtually all levels, that of the Secretaries General, NATO and UN Headquarters and, once NATO-led forces were deployed in the Balkans, in the field. The utility of continuous liaison was eventually reflected in the assignment of International Military Staff officers to UN Headquarters in New York and, for a period, the

---

[29] NATO, 1991 Strategic Concept, para. 27.
[30] Ibid., para. 33.
[31] NATO, Rome Declaration on Peace and Cooperation, 8 November 1991, para. 3.

assignment of a UN liaison team to NATO Headquarters in Brussels. These liaison arrangements made a major contribution to more effective interaction between the organisations.

Close liaison arrangements were also established with the OSCE. This included periodic, reciprocal staff visits, led by the Director of Crisis Management and Operations from NATO and the Head of the OSCE Conflict Prevention Center, to exchange detailed views on developments of current or potential interest and to consider ways to enhance cooperation between the two organisations and contacts between action officers in both institutions. Close liaison was also established between the UN Organisation for the Coordination of Humanitarian Assistance (UN OCHA) and NATO Civil Emergency Planning Officials as well as with other international organisations concerning the Kosovo air campaign and then KFOR.

Although these contacts with the UN and OSCE did not achieve the goal of enhancing more simultaneous military and civilian planning for crisis response operations, they did contribute to enhancing cooperation between the organisations which facilitated both strategic and tactical responses as the organisations worked together in Bosnia Herzegovina, Kosovo and eventually Macedonia. The North Atlantic Council report on lessons learned from NATO and NATO-led operations in the Balkans noted the importance of liaison with the UN and OSCE, as well as other organisations, and recommended working out arrangements to be able to quickly undertake similar arrangements for future crisis response operations. The continuing importance of cooperation with the OSCE in the fields under discussion is reflected in the Prague Summit Declaration, which states that: 'To further promote peace and stability in the Euro-Atlantic Area, NATO will continue to develop its fruitful and close cooperation with the OSCE, namely in the complementary areas of conflict prevention, crisis management and post-conflict rehabilitation'.[32]

14.   NATO – EU RELATIONS

Another important but complicated aspect of NATO's contribution to conflict prevention and crisis management is the progress made in developing a strategic partnership with the European Union 'so that they can bring their combined assets to bear in enhancing peace and security'.[33] I will consider the background only briefly but focus on some of the lessons learned from recent cooperation and some ongoing issues.

---

[32] NATO, Prague Summit Declaration, para. 12.
[33] NATO, 'NATO After Prague: New Members, New Capabilities and News Relations', NATO Office of Press and Information NATO.

In considering NATO-EU relations, it is useful to keep in mind two leitmotivs of such relations, as Jolyon Howorth and John T.S. Keeler have pointed out: (1) an effort to 'rebalance' or strengthen NATO by developing a 'European pillar within NATO' and (2) a number of institutional innovations reflecting the increasing drive for European autonomy.[34] In addition to EU capability improvements being seen as enhancing NATO's overall effectiveness, NATO support for the EU was also seen as providing an alternative to NATO action. Another rationale for NATO support was that the EU would require NATO assets – such as deployable headquarters, strategic lift, and satellite intelligence – for larger operations. Finally, such support was seen as reinforcing the transatlantic partnership. Experience in UN, NATO and NATO-led operations in the Balkans, which demonstrated European dependence on the US, gave increased impetus to European efforts to develop a European Security and Defence Policy (ESDP) with the necessary capabilities for both civilian and military crisis management.

Following the 1999 EU Cologne decisions to give the EU the means to implement a European Security and Defence Policy including its commitment to its Headline Goal for Petersberg missions,[35] NATO agreed that that it was willing to support operations led by the EU, when NATO as a whole was not involved, building on the mechanisms which had been developed between NATO and the WEU.[36]

After a long delay, due to a lack of agreement on participation by non-EU Allies in EU defense matters, on 16 December 2002, a joint declaration was adopted by the European Union and NATO opened the way by providing a formal basis and framework for cooperation between the two organisations in crisis management and conflict prevention.[37] The agreement outlines the political principles for EU-NATO cooperation. There was also agreement on a substantial agenda of common work, including a definition of the modalities for effective mutual consultation, cooperation and transparency. NATO reiterated its commitment to achieve a close, transparent and coherent NATO – EU relationship. Eventual agreement in the spring of 2003 on the detailed modalities to implement 'Berlin plus'[38] included arrangements and procedures for (1) assured EU access to NATO planning capabilities, (2) presumption of availability of pre-identified NATO capabilities and common assets, (3) identification of European command

---

[34] J. Howorth and J.T.S. Keeler (eds.), *Defending Europe: The EU, NATO and the Quest for European Autonomy* (Palgrave, Macmillan 2003), p. 4.

[35] Humanitarian and rescue, peacekeeping and combat forces in crisis management, including peacemaking.

[36] NATO, Washington Summit Communiqué: An Alliance for the 21st Century, 24 April 1999, paras. 10 and 11.

[37] NATO, 'EU and NATO adopt framework for co-operation', *NATO Update,* available on line at <http://www.nato.int/docu/update/2002/12-december/e1216a.htm>; accessed 12/8/03.

[38] Referring to the decisions taken at the Berlin meeting of NATO foreign ministers in 1996.

structure options including further developing the role of Deputy Supreme Allied Commander Europe (DSACEUR) to assume his European responsibilities, and (4) further adaptation of NATO's defence planning to address requirements for EU-led operations.[39] In addition, agreement had been reached on provisions for the exchange and protection of classified information and documents between the two organisations, essential for effective cooperation in conflict prevention and crisis management.[40]

The Prague summit gave additional impetus to NATO-EU relations in the area of crisis management. It was agreed that: 'Events on and since 11 September 2001 have underlined further the importance of greater transparency and coopera-tion between our two organisations on questions of common interest relating to security, defence, and crisis management, so that crises can be met with the most appropriate military response and effective crisis management ensured'.[41]

14.1 Cooperation in Southern Serbia and FYROM

In early 2001, in a good example of things working in practice before the detailed arrangements had been fully worked out and agreed, NATO and the EU, with OSCE participation, engaged in successful joint efforts to defuse conflict in Southern Serbia and to prevent civil war in the former Yugoslav Republic of Macedonia. Although procedures had not yet been agreed for NATO-EU consul-tations and NATO support for the EU, NATO and the EU worked together effec-tively to establish the necessary conditions for a return to peace and stability in two situations where full-blown conflict would have been very likely without these efforts.[42] In the case of Southern Serbia, these efforts included joint state-ments and visits by the EU High Representative for Common Foreign and Secu-rity Policy Affairs Javier Solana and NATO Secretary General Lord Robertson, the dispatch of missions of NATO and EU officials, who engaged in shuttle di-plomacy and complex negotiations, which resulted in the adoption by Belgrade of confidence building measures and guarantees for the Albanian population of Southern Serbia, including amnesty and a demilitarization agreement for the eth-nic Albanian militants and phased reduction of the Ground Safety Zone.

In the case of the violence in the former Yugoslav Republic of Macedonia, the NATO Liaison mission in Skopje and the Secretary General's special representa-tive Mark Laity, played a key role in orchestrating NATO's contribution to secur-

---

[39] NATO, Washington Summit Communiqué, para. 11.

[40] European Union Council Decision 2002/211/CFSP of 24 February 2003 concerning the con-clusion of the Agreement between the European Union and the North Atlantic Treaty Organisation on the Security of Information.

[41] NATO, Prague Summit Declaration Issued by the Heads of State and Government participat-ing in the meeting of the North Atlantic Council in Prague on 21 November 2002, para. 11.

[42] For a succinct description of the NATO role, see Mihai Carp, 'Back from the Brink', 4 *NATO Review* (2002), available on line at <www.nato.int/docu/review/2002/issue4/art2/_pr.html>.

ing an end to the fighting and creating conditions to disengage the FYROM Army and security forces and the so-called National Liberation Army (NLA). Following the adoption of a framework agreement brokered by the EU and US at Ohrid on 13 August, NATO dispatched Operation Essential Harvest to collect NLA weapons. The hallmarks of both these efforts were protracted, close, mutually supporting cooperation between NATO and the EU. These two cases are successful examples of highly pragmatic cooperation, drawing on the respective strengths of the international organisations that contributed, which achieved significant results, and can serve as models for future cooperation.

14.2 Operation Concordia

In a concrete test of the agreed arrangements, the EU took over NATO's Task Force Fox mission in Macedonia on 31 March 2003, which it renamed Operation Concordia. Operation Concordia ended on 15 December 2003, and it is still too early to make definitive judgments, but some preliminary lessons can be drawn. Operation Concordia was seen as a test case for ESDP. NATO military authorities considered that NATO Task Force Fox objectives had been achieved and that there was no military rationale for continuing the operation, but political imperatives prevailed.[43] In considering lessons from Operation Concordia, it should be remembered that it was small, relatively risk free, with a force structure in place, with NATO advice available from a NATO military liaison office in Skopje and with NATO assets available in the vicinity in the event that assistance was needed. In other words, Operation Concordia was an almost perfect ESDP demonstration project. That being said, the operation went smoothly, demonstrating the efficacy of NATO-EU cooperation and ESDP capabilities in this limited operation. However, some EU officials expressed concern at the insertion of an additional and unexpected level of NATO command, NATO's Regional Headquarters Allied Forces Southern Europe (AFSOUTH), in Naples, Italy, which they considered diluted EU control of the operation. AFSOUTH served as the operational command under DSACEUR acting as EU strategic commander from EU Headquarters established at SHAPE.

14.3 EU follow on force for SFOR

A much more substantial test of NATO-EU relations, arrangements for NATO-EU cooperation and ESDP is now expected in the second half of 2004, when the EU will take on the tasks presently being accomplished by SFOR in Bosnia-Herzegovina. By way of background, on 24 February 2003, the UK and France called for the EU to take-over the NATO mission in Bosnia in early 2004 with a

---

[43] Views expressed by a senior SHAPE officer on 14 October 2003.

credible force. However, at the Madrid ministerial in June, according to press reports, the US was unenthusiastic about a take over by mid-2004, saying that it was too early even to start discussions. A senior US official reportedly said 'that there was still much for the Western defense alliance to do in Bosnia, including rounding up of indicted war crimes suspects, stamping out the threat of terrorism and uniting the country's ethnically divided society'.[44] On 4 September, the German Defense Minister Peter Struck and the French Defense Minister Michèle Alliot-Marie, pushed for the EU to take over the NATO mission, and at their meeting on 7 October 2003, EU defense ministers said they hope to take on the mission in the second half of 2004.[45] At the informal meeting of NATO Colorado Springs on 9 October, NATO defense ministers expressed broad support for such a take-over.[46] It is likely that the evolution in the US position is related to US commitments in Iraq and Afghanistan.

Although the security situation in Bosnia-Herzegovina has improved, and NATO is planning to further reduce the size of SFOR, from 13,000 in 2003 to from 6,000 to 8,000 in 2004, in the context, *inter alia*, of a more regional approach to its Balkans operations, taking on this task will be much more challenging for the EU. It is a big, complex operation, with a considerably higher risk than Operation Concordia. The High Representative for Bosnia-Herzegovina Lord Ashdown recognized this when he emphasized this would have to be a 'serious' operation. 'It cannot come in on the cheap. It has to come in as an effective force capable of securing the peace. It has to do it with bayonets fixed and flags flying.'[47]

15. CONCLUSIONS

Since the end of the Cold War, NATO has increased its focus on crisis management and conflict prevention and has improved its crisis management and conflict prevention organisation, procedures and tools. It has also demonstrated, in Bosnia-Herzegovina, in Kosovo, in Macedonia, in Afghanistan and in supporting the Polish deployment in Iraq (with force generation, communications and logistics), the political will to use these tools and their efficacy.

This chapter has focused largely on the civilian aspects of NATO crisis management and conflict prevention; however, I wish to emphasize, as Allied Heads of State and Government and the Secretary General have repeatedly, that the necessary military capabilities are essential for NATO to be a credible and effective

---

[44] *Reuters*, 3 June 2003.

[45] Ian Black, 'Ashdown backs creation of EU Bosnia force', *The Guardian*, 8 October 2003.

[46] Peter Spiegel, 'EU Closer to taking Bosnia peace role from NATO', *Financial Times*, 10 October 2003.

[47] Quoted in Ian Black, op. cit. n. 45.

actor in the future in these areas. The Prague Summit decisions reflect this emphasis clearly in their multifaceted approach to enhancing NATO's military capabilities. The NATO Response Force, the Prague Capabilities Commitment and the new command arrangements are all intended to address the serious capability shortfalls that allies have identified, increase the speed of the process of transformation of allied forces and ensure that the command structure is capable of responding to the challenges of rapid deployment for high-intensity operations wherever and whenever required. While there had been some disappointing progress towards addressing the capabilities' shortfalls pursuant to the Defense Capabilities Initiative (DCI) agreed at the Washington Summit and some progress since Prague, the reluctance by allies to increase defense expenditures will inhibit making the necessary changes. Continuing capability shortfalls will be a serious impediment to effective crisis management and, to a lesser degree, conflict prevention.

A related essential ingredient for successful NATO crisis management and conflict prevention is political will. Even the greatly improved instruments and procedures that NATO has developed will be of little avail if allies cannot agree in a timely manner, or at all, to use them. As reflected in the much more rapid engagement in Macedonia than in Kosovo, which was still much more rapid than in Bosnia-Herzegovina, allies appear to have learned that early engagement is more likely to be effective. These were sensitive and complex issues, but allies were able to agree and to persevere even in the case of significant pressure. Unfortunately the kinds of engagement for which the NATO Response Force is being prepared make it unlikely that the necessary consensus to use it will be easily achieved. The presumption of participation, explicit in the way the NATO Response Force is being stood up, may make such agreement more difficult, since it will be more difficult for allies, whose forces are participating in an NRF rotation, to opt out of an operation during that rotation (something they have been able to do easily until now for non-Article 5 crisis response operations).[48] National constitutional requirements on the part of some allies for parliamentary approval of such deployments are an additional complicating factor, likely to slow down decision-making. In addition, the way in which NATO decision-making works with 26 allies will have an impact on reaching agreement for crisis response operations, but I do not share the view that consensus decision-making at 26 will be substantially more difficult than at 19. That does not mean that it will be easy, but the number of different views is unlikely to increase, and the class of 2004 is likely to wish to avoid making decision-making more difficult.

---

[48] SIPRI Director Alyson J.K. Bailes considers that can be found, 'but only if a political initiative is taken outside NATO by countries/organisations to request use of Alliance capabilities', in Alyson J.K. Bailes, 'The Future of European Security: NATO, the EU and Transatlantic Relations after Iraq', Speaking notes for address at Reykjavik on 25 June 2003.

Concerning NATO-EU relations, despite significant progress in successfully preventing conflict in Southern Serbia and Macedonia and agreeing the complex procedures for consultations in peacetime and crisis and to provide NATO support for EU-led operations, suspicions and political impediments continue to complicate relations. The tensions that arose in the fall of 2003 regarding the establishment of an independent EU operational planning capability and a change in UK views on the inclusion of defense in what is known as 'structured cooperation', were reflected in US Ambassador Nicholas Burns calling for a special meeting of the North Atlantic Council to address these matters and his statement that EU plans represented 'one of the greatest dangers to the transatlantic relationship'.[49] European reassurances and efforts to dampen the tensions notwithstanding, Washington's concerns do not appear to have been fully assuaged. The degree to which these differences impede cooperation in crisis management and conflict prevention remains to be seen.

---

[49] Judy Dempsey, 'US to confront Brussels over defence policy', *Financial Times*, 17 October 2003.

Chapter 20
NO PEACE WITHOUT HUMAN RIGHTS: THE COUNCIL OF EUROPE AND CONFLICT PREVENTION

by Jan Kleijssen[1]

1. INTRODUCTION

'There should come into being a Council of Europe [...] to [...] prevent renewed aggression and the preparation of future wars .... Anyone can see that this Council when created must eventually embrace the whole of Europe and that all the main branches of the European family must some day be partners in it'.

Winston Churchill spoke these prophetic words in a radio broadcast on 21 March 1943. His vision conceived in the darkest days of World War Two led to, some six years later, the signing of the Statute[2] of the Council of Europe. This Statute was signed in London on 5 May 1949 by 10 European democracies.[3]

Although Churchill had envisaged an Organisation to prevent conflicts, the Council of Europe's statute did not explicitly refer to this. In view of the relationship between its founding states, it was perhaps not surprising that they did not consider conflict prevention between them to be a priority. Instead, it was given a mission to promote and defend pluralist democracy, human rights and the rule of

---

[1] Jan P.A. Kleijssen, LL.M, M.A. is Director of the Private Office of the Secretary General of the Council of Europe. This contribution has been written in a personal capacity only.

[2] Cf., Statute of the Council of Europe, Article 1:

(a) The aim of the Council of Europe is to achieve a greater unity between its members for the purpose of safeguarding and realising the ideals and principles which are their common heritage and facilitating their economic and social progress.

(b) This aim shall be pursued through the organs of the Council by discussion of questions of common concern and by agreements and common action in economic, social, cultural, scientific, legal and administrative matters and in the maintenance and further realisation of human rights and fundamental freedoms.

(c) Participation in the Council of Europe shall not affect the collaboration of its members in the work of the United Nations and of other international organisations or unions to which they are parties.

(d) Matters relating to national defence do not fall within the scope of the Council of Europe.

[3] By Belgium, Denmark, France, Ireland, Italy, Luxembourg, the Netherlands, Norway, Sweden, and the United Kingdom

V. Kronenberger and J. Wouters, eds., The European Union and Conflict Prevention
© 2004, T·M·C·ASSER PRESS, The Hague, The Netherlands

law. Political commitment to these values and principles became a precondition for membership of the Organisation. The ultimate aim of achieving greater unity between its members was to be promoted by common action on behalf of its Member States in a wide range of fields of intergovernmental cooperation.

The only area specifically excluded from the Council of Europe's mandate are matters related to national defence. This, however, has not prevented the Organisation from intensively dealing with matters relating to international security. Indeed, much of its work has had a direct impact on security and stability in Europe, as will be set out below.

Churchill had foreseen a truly pan-European Council of Europe. However, for many years, as a result of the Iron Curtain, the Council's membership remained limited to the western half of Europe. During this period however, it had already demonstrated its capacity to integrate countries that had freed themselves from totalitarian regimes. Thus, in 1977 Greece was readmitted (under the Colonels' regime, it had withdrawn when it was about to be excluded) and Portugal and Spain were admitted in 1976 and 1977 respectively, following the restoration of democracy.

The fall of the Berlin wall finally enabled the Council of Europe to achieve what it had been set up to do from the beginning: to unite the whole of Europe on the basis of common values, enshrined in its major legal instruments.

Today, the geographical part of Churchill's vision has nearly been fulfilled. With the accession of Monaco in October 2004, the Council of Europe will have 45 Member States, stretching from Reykjavik to the Baring Straits and representing over 800 million Europeans. Only Belarus, which still suffers under a repressive regime, is absent from the European democratic family.

This contribution will examine how, in the over 50 years of its existence, the Council has responded to Churchill's call of 'preventing aggression and the preparation of future wars'. Within this contribution, 'wars' is understood as any form of armed conflict, be it within a state, between states, or against the international community, in the form of international terrorism.

2. CAPABILITIES IN CONFLICT PREVENTION

The Council of Europe's capability to promote political dialogue and to ensure practical cooperation on the basis of fundamental values at the intergovernmental and interparliamentary level, is the key to its role in conflict prevention.

Political dialogue is particularly intense within the Parliamentary Assembly, one of the two organs of the Organisation.

Made up of delegations from national parliaments, which must always include representatives of government and opposition parties, the Assembly (composed of 313 Representatives and an equal number of substitutes) can justifiably claim to represent all European citizens. Apart from expressing the whole gamut of European political opinions, it has consistently acted as the engine-room of the Organisation by raising issues, often in a pioneering way. It has been effective in putting pressure on governments and in proposing innovative solutions. It has initiated a large number of Council of Europe legal instruments.

Political dialogue also takes place within the other organ, the Committee of Ministers. The Deputies, a Committee of permanent representatives (Ambassadors) meet in Strasbourg every week in plenary session, as well as regularly in subordinate working groups.

Unfortunately, the potential of this organ remains very much under-exploited. The Permanent Representatives too rarely receive instructions to tackle sensitive political issues which many governments apparently prefer to deal with in other institutions, or on a purely bilateral basis. Sometimes intense parliamentary pressure or an initiative by the Secretary General is required to put controversial issues, such as Chechnya, on the agenda. Progress has been made in recent years with the EU States meeting as a group and attempting to present a common position.

Efforts are further being made to coordinate the EU's policy also through the so-called COSCE forum in Brussels.[4]

An interesting new and very recent development was the making public of a critical report on Armenia and Azerbaijan in September 2003. It is to be hoped that this will constitute a precedent for more active involvement by the Committee of Ministers in dealing with problems in Member States.

The Secretary General plays an important role. Being elected by the Parliamentary Assembly, he clearly enjoys a political mandate, enabling him to take action and to intervene directly with governments as the guardian of the Organisation's values. He further acts as the spokesperson for the entire Organisation.

The current Secretary General, Mr Walter Schwimmer, elected in 1999 for a five-year period, frequently uses this political mandate to take initiatives in crisis situations. These include, for example, the question of political prisoners in Azerbaijan, political stability in Moldova, the human rights situation in the Chechen Republic of the Russian Federation, and the problems of Roma in several Member States. While this 'quiet diplomacy' mostly goes unnoticed by the media, it is often very effective. Where the support of Member States is only lukewarm or token, however, the Secretary General's possibilities are limited.

---

[4] COSCE is the Working Party on the Organisation for Security and Cooperation in Europe and the Council of Europe. It was set up by a decision of the Permanent Representatives Committee of the Council of the European Union (COREPER).

3. CONFLICT PREVENTION THROUGH LEGAL INSTRUMENTS

The Council of Europe does distinguish itself from other organisations by the large number of binding obligations that Member States have entered into and by the sophisticated mechanisms ensuring the compliance of Member States with these obligations. The high degree of objectivity guaranteed by these mechanisms contributes significantly to instilling confidence between Member States.

Several of the most sophisticated legal instruments concern human rights. There can be no doubt that violations of human rights are an important cause of armed conflict. By ensuring the observance of these rights the Council is therefore addressing an important root cause.

The unique feature of the European Convention on Human Rights (ECHR) of 1950 is its control mechanism. The protection of fundamental rights is entrusted to a permanent European Court of Human Rights. It can be seized both by States and by individuals. Its judgements are legally binding upon the Council of Europe Member States. Even in politically highly sensitive cases, its judgements are implemented – even if not always immediately.

Protecting national minorities has become one of the most serious and pressing issues in Europe today. Ethnic and racial tensions, simmering over the years, have resurfaced often in acute form and even as armed conflict, as the recent tragedies in South East Europe have shown.

The Framework Convention for the Protection of National Minorities was adopted by the Committee of Ministers in November 1994 and it entered into force in February 1998. It is the first ever legally binding multilateral instrument devoted to the protection of national minorities.

As a counterpart to the Framework Convention, the European Charter for Regional or Minority Languages came into force in March 1998. It recognises that the right to use a regional or minority language in private and public is an inalienable right.

The European Commission against Racism and Intolerance (ECRI) is an independent body which makes recommendations to governments, both generally and individually, on combating racism and xenophobia, anti-racism and intolerance. Its general policy recommendations deal, *inter alia*, with combating intolerance of Islam, violence against Roma, and the abuse of the internet for racist propaganda.

Torture is said to be the best recruiting agent for armed insurgents or terrorist movements. The Convention for the Prevention of Torture and Inhuman or Degrading Treatment or Punishment complements the protection available under the European Convention on Human Rights by establishing a European Committee for the Prevention of Torture (known as the CPT) composed of independent and impartial experts from a variety of backgrounds, including the law, medicine, prison affairs and politics.

The Council of Europe's European Commission for Democracy through Law, better known as the Venice Commission, has provided constitutional advice in a number of conflict areas, notably in South-Eastern Europe. The Commission is composed of independent experts. In addition to the representatives of the 45 Council of Europe Member States, it has many observers, including from Canada, Mexico, Japan and the United States.

The European Cultural Convention, also open to non-Member States, provides the framework for a large variety of activities to promote intercultural dialogue and respect for diversity. Such dialogue and respect are vital elements of a democratic society. On the other hand, the absence of such dialogue and a lack of respect have often fuelled violence.

These major legal instruments and mechanisms are clearly making a contribution to conflict prevention. They could, however, be even more effective, if, like the ECHR, they would all have to be, obligatorily, ratified by all Member States.

4. Conflict Prevention Through Long-Term Institutional Cooperation

In addition to the above legal instruments, the long-term institutional cooperation activities of the Council of Europe are important tools.

Following the collapse of the communist regimes in Central and Eastern Europe in 1989, the Council of Europe embarked on a programme of cooperation and assistance with these countries, aimed at helping them to carry out democratic reforms and at integrating them into European structures.

These programmes focus on democratic institution building, constitutional reform, harmonisation of legislation with European standards, in particular the European Convention on Human Rights, reform of the judiciary, electoral reform, media legislation, reform of education curricula, minority rights and protection, training for law officers, development of local democracy and the promotion of civil society.

These programmes are being adapted to help prevent the (re-)emergence of particular conflict situations, on a case-by-case basis. A concrete example: educational reform in Bosnia and Herzegovina.

5. Monitoring Obligations and Commitments

Direct negotiation and the use of political leverage in the context of obligations linked with the accession to membership are also amongst the Council of Europe's specific capabilities.

Besides emphasising the general membership obligations under the Statute of the Council of Europe, the Parliamentary Assembly has established over recent years a comprehensive list of political commitments which had to be accepted by the authorities of the countries applying for membership. The Committee of Ministers has taken these commitments as the basis of its decision to admit a State to the Organisation.

These commitments concern, *inter alia*, endeavours to prevent or overcome conflictual situations with political means, in line with democratic principles and respect for human rights.

The Assembly has created a special monitoring procedure to verify compliance with these commitments. The reporting and debates in the Parliamentary Assembly are public and are organised on a country-by-country basis.

A monitoring procedure also exists in the Committee of Ministers which follows a thematic approach (freedom of information, local democracy, independence of the judiciary, etc.) across all Member States.

Sanctions are possible when the political will to cooperate is found to be lacking. For example, the Parliamentary Assembly suspended the voting rights of the Russian delegation in April 2000 (and restored them in January 2001) because of the human rights situation there.

Persistent failure to comply with the Organisation's principles could result in expulsion from the Organisation.[5]

In the accession procedure of Armenia and Azerbaijan, the governments of these countries, in addition to other obligations, committed themselves to intensifying joint efforts with a view to achieving a peaceful settlement of the Nagorno-Karabakh conflict. The Council of Europe has offered constitutional advice on the future legal status of the area.

The conflict in the Chechen Republic of the Russian Federation is a matter of constant concern for the Organisation. The Secretary General reports to the Committee of Ministers on a monthly basis. A series of initiatives have been taken to improve the human rights situation.

For its part, the Parliamentary Assembly has set up, together with the Russian State Duma, a Joint Working Group on a political solution to the conflict in Chechnya, including consultations with Chechen Representatives prepared to commit themselves to finding a peaceful solution to the conflict and to the renunciation of violence.

The recent internal conflict in Moldova, with its possible regional repercussions, has given rise to initiatives by the Parliamentary Assembly, the Committee of Ministers and the Secretary General, aimed at restoring political dialogue be-

---

[5] Article 8 of the Council of Europe Statute states: 'Any member of the Council of Europe which has seriously violated Article 3 may be suspended from its rights of representation and requested by the Committee of Ministers to withdraw under Article 7. If such member state does not comply with this request, the Committee may decide that it has ceased to be a member of the Council as from such date as the Committee may determine.'

The full text of the Statute of the Council of Europe can be consulted at the following website <http://conventions.coe.int/Treaty/EN/CadreListeTraites.htm>.

tween government and opposition. These have resulted in a de-escalation of the crisis and a resumption of political dialogue within the country.

In the above cases, the Council of Europe has demonstrated its capability of contributing to preventing the outbreak, resumption or aggravation of conflicts in its Member States, as well as to post-conflict rehabilitation. Its degree of success, however, depends to a large extent on the political will of its Member States.

6. FIELD PRESENCE

The Council of Europe's presence in the field, which only started to develop in recent years, has probably become the most visible part of the Organisation's conflict prevention efforts.

In the *Chechen Republic* of the Russian Federation, the Council of Europe experts were for several years the only internationals present. They assist the Special Representative of the President of the Russian Federation for ensuring human and civil rights and freedoms in the Chechen Republic. In June 2002 the new mandate for a Council of Europe presence was confirmed and the tasks of the experts were enlarged to include support for the development of public authorities, self-government, judiciary and education. Following a targeted bomb attack on the experts, and a general deterioration of the security situation, this activity was temporarily suspended in May 2003.

In *Pristina* the mandate of the office is to assist UNMIK in the implementation of UN Security Council Resolution 1244, in particular in the area of legal standards, the judiciary and more recently in the field of decentralisation and reform of local self-government.

Also, in *Skopje,* the Council of Europe's representative assists the EU Special Representative in the implementation of the 'Ohrid Agreement' and the local authorities in the decentralisation reform and in a number of other areas within the Organisation's competence.

In *Belgrade,* the Special Representative of the Secretary General has an overall coordination role to ensure that the post-accession programme with Serbia and Montenegro is implemented and that full dialogue with other international institutions in the field takes place. Progress in the implementation of the post-accession programme is being monitored by the Committee of Ministers.

In *Sarajevo* the Organisation has been present since the end of the conflict, initially with the specific task of assisting in the implementation of the Dayton Peace Agreement and of preparing the country for membership in the Organisation. Bosnia and Herzegovina also has a vast post-accession programme designed to help it fulfil all the commitments linked to membership. Monitoring its implementation has already begun.

In *Tirana*, a major contribution was made to enabling political dialogue between the Socialist and Democratic Parties, ending a dangerous stand-off. Assistance has been provided in democratic reforms, in particular in the field of the judiciary and electoral legislation. The interplay with other international organisations has been a key to ensuring coherence of action.

In *Chisinau*, major efforts were successfully made to resolve the internal conflict (which may well have had regional repercussions) through restoring political dialogue between the government and the opposition. Legal expertise has been offered so as to contribute to efforts to end the Transdnistria conflict.

In *Yerevan, Baku* and *Tbilisi*, advice on electoral and judicial reform are key activities, together with monitoring the human rights situation and political development.

These field missions, a new feature in the Council of Europe's operations, have proved to be an invaluable complement to the more traditional activities carried out in Strasbourg.

7. CONFLICT PREVENTION THROUGH SPECIFIC TOOLS

The Parliamentary Assembly and the Congress of Local and Regional Authorities of Europe (CLRAE) regularly observe elections at national and regional levels. Their action, often in cooperation with other international organisations, has a fraud-deterrent effect and their findings enjoy wide respect.

The Assembly's parliamentary diplomacy is involved in confidence building and conflict prevention through activities by its President, *ad hoc* Committees, by special missions mandated by its Bureau (Chechnya Joint Working Group, Belarus Group), by targeted actions of its Political Groups (the Albania crisis in 1997), and by regular reports on specific situations (such as Chechnya, Nagorno-Karabakh, Cyprus).

The CLRAE follows, through special missions and reports, the relations between central, regional and local authorities (Moldova/Gagausia, 'the former Yugoslav Republic of Macedonia'). The Congress has, furthermore, set up Local Democracy Agencies (LDA) which aim at confidence building between different ethnic, religious or linguistic communities, as well as at building partnerships between towns and regions, improving local democracy and fostering dialogue and transfrontier cooperation in areas with different minorities (e.g., in South-East Europe).

Under the aegis of the Committee of Ministers, several intergovernmental activities have a direct bearing on conflict prevention. These include:

- *the promotion of civil society*. By making use of the Participatory Status granted to over 400 international non-governmental organisations and through special programmes of training and regional networking among

NGOs, the Organisation aims to strengthen the role and political responsibility of sub-regional and local actors from civil society;

- the Confidence-Building Measures Programme (CBM) provides support for pilot projects, the primary objective of which is to increase the knowledge of European values and principles and to promote tolerance and understanding between people, as well as to improve inter-community relations within a specific region or between specific countries (South-East Europe, the Caucasus, Cyprus);

- the Democratic Leadership Programme (DLP) brings together young political leaders from different countries, helping them to acquire basic knowledge of European standards and good governance, as well as skills in democratic problem-solving and decision-making. Particular support is given to regional initiatives promoting such democratic leadership (Moscow School of Political Studies, Tbilisi School of Political Studies, emerging Network of Schools for South-East Europe).

8. COOPERATION WITH THE EUROPEAN UNION

The pioneering role of the Council of Europe in preparing candidate states for membership of the European Union has been widely acknowledged by the states concerned, as well as by the EU institutions. Although this is nowhere formally stated, the Copenhagen political criteria for EU membership are, in fact, largely modelled on the accession criteria of the Council of Europe.[6]

In the coming years, the Council of Europe's assistance will be essential in enabling South-East European states to submit their candidature.

Relations between the Council of Europe and the EU are based on Article 303 TEC which stipulates that: 'The Community shall establish all appropriate forms of cooperation with the Council of Europe'.

This takes place in a number of ways. There are annual High-Level 'Quadripartite' meetings (CiOs, Secretary General of the Council of Europe and the Commissioner). The EU Commission participates in the sessions of the Council of Europe's Committee of Ministers, in the meetings of the Ministers' Deputies and their political subordinated bodies (GR-EDS, GR-OSCE, GR-EU). There are annual Senior officials meetings with the European Commission, complemented by regular targeted meetings linked to the respective enlargement processes. Joint Council of Europe – European Commission assistance programmes for demo-

---

[6] See further on this question, M. Rantala, 'The Council of Europe' in A. Ott and K. Inglis (eds.), *Handbook on European Enlargement – A Commentary on the Enlargement Process* (The Hague, TMC Asser Press 2002), pp. 67-74.

cratic and legal reforms, good governance for a number of transition countries and regions (South Caucasus, North Caucasus, including Chechnya, Ukraine, Moldova, Albania) have been gradually developed.

A joint declaration on cooperation and partnership signed in April 2001 by the Council of Europe's Secretary General Walter Schwimmer, and Commissioner Chris Patten underlined the political significance of this common action which should include all areas of common concern and cover such crucial matters as human rights, democratic institution building, the judiciary, local government and the protection of national minorities. There have been invitations to the Council of Europe's Secretary General and High Officials to attend meetings of the PSC, COSCE and subsidiary bodies.

The Parliamentary Assembly and the European Parliament have recently increased their contacts and joint sessions are now organised on a regular basis.

It is encouraging that the European Convention proposed a direct reference to cooperation with the Council of Europe for the Constitution of the European Union. Moreover, it agreed to propose that the European Union shall seek accession to the European Convention on Human Rights. Such an accession would considerably reinforce human rights protection in Europe,[7] which, as argued above, is a cornerstone of conflict prevention.

In 2004 the European Union enlarged to 25 members. Others will follow. However, several European states will, in the coming years, either not be able, or not be willing to join. The Council of Europe is the ideal forum for political dialogue between the enlarged EU and the European non-EU states. A Third Council of Europe Summit, to take place on 16 and 17 May 2005 in Warsaw, is being prepared to determine the Organisation's future role alongside an enlarged European Union. An associated membership of the European Union in the Council of Europe is among the proposals to be discussed.

9. CONCLUSION

Conflict prevention is without doubt less visible than conflict resolution. Whereas ending an existing conflict is certain to attract much media attention, it is much less rewarding to prevent conflicts. Indeed, if a conflict does not actually emerge, it is difficult to prove that this was thanks to successful prevention. Equally, it is difficult to prove that the money invested in such prevention was well spent. Fireproof doors and carpets are much less fascinating than a roaring fire engine.

---

[7] On this issue see, e.g., J. Polakiewicz, 'The Relationship between the European Convention on Human Rights and the EU Charter of Fundamental Rights – Some proposals for a coherent system of human rights protection in Europe' in V. Kronenberger (ed.), *The European Union and the International Legal Order: Discord or Harmony?* (The Hague, TMC Asser Press 2001), pp. 69-92.

Thus, paradoxically, whereas the cost of conflict prevention is infinitesimal compared to that of conflict resolution, governments seem much less inclined to make this investment. Political capital may be won through highly visible conflict mediation. It is less likely to be obtained on the basis of hardly visible long-term action.

The Council of Europe is best known for its protection of human rights, rule of law and pluralist democracy throughout the entire European continent. It is through these activities it is also making a major contribution to conflict prevention.

Churchill's vision of the Council of Europe is today a reality. Together with an enlarged European Union it is ideally placed to ensure that on the old continent indeed 'all will be well'.

Chapter 21
COOPERATION BETWEEN THE EU AND THE G8 IN CONFLICT PREVENTION

by John Kirton[1]

1. INTRODUCTION

Along with the United Nations (UN), the Group of Eight (G8) and the European Union (EU) are the international institutions that stand on the front lines of the growing global effort to prevent the visible proliferation of deadly conflict in the post-cold war world.[2] The G8 first took up conflict prevention in the modern sense as a self-contained, general subject in its own right at its 1993 G7 Tokyo Summit, devoted increasing attention to it in each subsequent year, and chose it as a major focus from 1999 to 2003. The EU, starting in 1999, had by 2001 approved a formal Commission communication for mainstreaming conflict prevention in its development assistance policies, and for supportive regional integration, trade and cooperation links, unveiled the Council's programme for the Prevention of Violent Conflicts, and started to explore the instruments of cooperation it could use. As the twenty-first century got underway, it was thus clear that both the G8 and EU had chosen conflict prevention as part of their central contribution to global governance in a still violent world.

In each case, there is a vibrant debate about why each institution has chosen the conflict prevention cause, what each has accomplished in its early efforts, and

---

[1] Associate Professor of Political Science, Fellow of Trinity College, Research Associate of the Munk Centre for International Studies, and Director of the G8 Research Group, at the University of Toronto in Canada.

[2] The emphasis here is on the visibility rather than the actual record of the proliferation, as there is solid evidence to suggest that the incidence of interstate and even intrastate deadly conflict was greater during the cold war period than in the years since; see David Malone, 'The G8 and Conflict Prevention: From Promise to Practice?' in John Kirton and Radoslava Stefanova (eds.), *The G8, the United Nations and Conflict Prevention* (Aldershot, Ashgate 2004), pp. 43-58. Nonetheless, the toll of the post-cold war legacy of deadly conflict not prevented is formidable indeed; see J. Kirton and R. Stefanova, 'Introduction: The G8's Role in Global Conflict Prevention', in J. Kirton and R. Stefanova (eds.), *The G8, the United Nations and Conflict Prevention* (Aldershot, Ashgate 2004), pp. 1-20.

V. Kronenberger and J. Wouters, eds., The European Union and Conflict Prevention
© 2004, T·M·C·ASSER PRESS, *The Hague, The Netherlands*

what role each will, can and should play in the years ahead.[3] Yet few have seriously reflected on how their respective contributions have been, and might be, enhanced and rendered more effective by improved cooperation between the two.[4]

Such a reflection begins by taking full account of the distinctive international institutional characteristics of the G8, as a group of democratic major powers devoted to the preservation and global promotion of open democracy, individual liberty and social advancement. Today's G8 was born in November 1975 when the leaders of France, the United States, Britain, Germany, Japan and Italy assembled at the Château de Rambouillet on the outskirts of Paris for what was billed as a one-time gathering devoted to economic affairs. But led by US Secretary of State Henry Kissinger, the group quickly developed as a modern, democratic version of the 19th-century Concert of Europe, centred on an annual Summit in late spring or summer, hosted in turn by each member, and adding Canada in 1976, the European Community (for issues within its competence) in 1977, and a newly democratic Russia in 1998. As a concert form of global governance, the G8 has deliberately avoided those attributes so beloved by contemporary American liberal-institutionalist scholars of 'legalization' – notably, a formal, internationally negotiated and domestically ratified and entrenched charter, and a separate and thus quasi-autonomous international secretariat or bureaucracy all its own.[5] Rather, the leaders of the world's powerful democracies have cherished the G8 as a form that they can and do directly dominate, where they are fully free to set new directions and take hard decisions on the toughest issues to guide global order, and where they can rely on their authoritative control over their own highly capable national governments, and most of the world's consequential regional and multilateral intergovernmental organizations, as well as their moral suasion as popularly elected leaders, to put their decisions into effect. Over the years the leaders have been supported by an ever more elaborate network of G8 officials who prepare their annual Summit, by stand-alone forums of

---

[3] In the case of the G8, see John Kirton, et al., 'The G8 and Conflict Prevention: Commitment, Compliance, and Systemic Contributions', in J. Kirton and R. Stefanova (eds.), op. cit. n. 2, at 59-85; Malone, op. cit. n. 2; Michael Schmunk, 'Ein neuer Global Player? Moeglichkeiten und Grenzen der G-8 Aussenminister', 8 *International Politik* (2000), pp. 59-65; Christoph Schwegmann, 'Modern Concert Diplomacy: The Contact Group and the G7/G8 in Crisis Management', in J. Kirton, et al. (eds.), *Guiding Global Order: G8 Governance in the Twenty-First Century* (Aldershot, Ashgate 2001), pp. 93-122; and Gina Stephens and Kristiana Powell, 'From Good Intentions to Good Practice: The G8 and Conflict Prevention', in J. Kirton and R. Stefanova (eds.), op. cit n. 2, at 193-211.

[4] For a tentative start, see Reinhardt Rummel, 'Advancing the European Union's Conflict Prevention Policy', in J. Kirton and R. Stefanova (eds.), op. cit. n. 2, at 113-141; Klemens Fischer, 'The G7/G8 and the European Union', in J. Kirton, et al. (eds.), op. cit. n. 3, at 123-142; and Heidi Ullrich and Alan Donnelly, 'The Group of Eight and the European Union', 5 *G8 Governance* (1998), <www.g7.utoronto.ca/governance/gov5> (August 2003).

[5] Kenneth Abbott, Robert Keohane, Andrew Moravcsik, Anne-Marie Slaughter and Duncan Snidal, 'The Concept of Legalization', 54 *International Organization* (2000), pp. 401-420.

G8 ministers now covering many portfolios in their national governments, and by a plethora of official-level bodies, including one for conflict prevention. With a clear mission and mandate, with a defined membership, with a core agenda, with a highly patterned and well-recognized set of procedures and decision-making rules, with a formidable capacity to raise and reallocate budgetary resources to provide public goods, and with a 'constitutional' capacity to reinforce, reform and replace the multilateral, 'hard law' intergovernmental organizations of old, the G8 Summit and larger system indeed form an intergovernmental institution, and one that does much, for good or ill, to authoritatively allocate values, and determine who gets what, in the global community as a whole.

At first glance, the G8, along with the EU, might appear as an unlikely global conflict preventer. For both were born as bodies with a geographically restricted membership and preoccupation, and with a formal agenda focused on classic economic matters, rather than global-transnational or political-security affairs. The basis for their conflict-preventing effectiveness, and for their synergistic cooperation, flows in part from the many parallels between the two institutions. Both began life with an agenda – on trade, development and, nascently, the environment – that is now known to be integrally linked to the conflict prevention task. Both bodies also began with a clear political vision and global vista that have propelled their institutional development and work to this day. Both contain an array of major powers balanced between, on the one hand, the old traditional military security 1945 United Nations Security Council (UNSC) Permanent Five (P5) veto powers of Britain, France, the United States and Russia, and, on the other, the new more 'civilian' security powers of Germany, Italy, Japan and Canada that have been frozen out in perpetuity from a place in the inner core of the UN security management system fixed in 1945. Both the G8 and EU had front-line seats on the neighbouring Balkans, where the upsurge in genocidal violence from 1990 to 1999 provided the animating shared shock that propelled both the G8 and the EU into a major conflict prevention effort. And both bring to this broader task an impressive record in having prevented conflict for many decades among their once-warring members, despite the ongoing challenges in Northern Ireland, along the Franco-Spanish border and in Chechnya to the east.

Equally importantly, both the G8 and EU emerged, in the 1970s, as institutionalized summit-directed systems, controlled by democratically elected leaders who had a comprehensive agenda, who could link old issues in new ways and create new issue areas, who could introduce innovative principles and norms, and who could make collective commitments that their national governments would faithfully comply with and implement back home.[6] To this foundation, the G8 added the unique advantage of including and engaging the powerful, globally residing

---

[6] Susan Hainsworth, 'Coming of Age: The European Community and the Economic Summit', Country Study No. 7 (Toronto, University of Toronto, Centre for International Studies 1990), <www.g7.utoronto.ca/scholar/hainsworth1990/bispre.htm> (August 2003).

and relevant United States and Japan, along with Canada and now Russia. The EU uniquely added a partly supranational, 'hard law'-governed, strong and steadily strengthening international bureaucracy of its own to help ensure that its deliberations, directions and decisions were put into effect.[7]

This chapter explores, primarily from the perspective of the G8, how these two largely similar, but also consequentially different, international institutions of the G8 and EU have come, and could come, together in the global conflict prevention task. It argues that their existing individual efforts and cooperation in conflict prevention have been respectable, but that much more could and should be done together in the years ahead. Propelling this past, present and prospective cooperative effort and effectiveness is, first, the surging global demand for conflict prevention in the post-cold war, globalizing, post-September 11th world.[8] The second driver is the inadequacy of the required supply of effective conflict prevention action from a United Nations system still largely trapped in a 1945 design that privileges non-interference in the internal affairs of sovereign states as the ultimate value, and that assigns the responsibility and privileges for security, including preventing conflict, to a UNSC P5 that excludes the now formidable capability and distinctive approaches of Germany, Italy, Japan, Canada and the ever more powerful and supranational EU itself.[9] The third driver also explains why it is the G8 and the EU, rather than other regional or plurilateral bodies such as the Organisation for Economic Co-operation and Development (OECD),[10] that have stepped into the lead to cope with this growing supply-demand gap. This driver is the powerful configuration of international institutional characteristics shared uniquely by the G8 and EU: a global predominance and internal equality of capability among members, a still-constricted participation, common democratic and human rights values, and direct political control by democratically and popularly elected leaders, exercised through institutionalized summitry where a full comprehensiveness of vision and flexibility of action prevail. It is this par-

---

[7] John Ruggie, 'Territoriality and Beyond: Problematizing Modernity in International Relations', 47 *International Organization* (1993), pp. 139-174.

[8] J. Kirton and R. Stefanova (eds.), *The G8, the United Nations and Conflict Prevention* (Aldershot, Ashgate 2004).

[9] John Kirton, 'The G8, the United Nations, and Global Security Governance', in John Kirton and Junichi Takase (eds.), *New Directions in Global Political Governance: The G8 and International Order in the Twenty-First Century* (Aldershot, Ashgate 2002), pp. 191-208.

[10] The OECD did begin work with its Development Assistance Committee's (DAC) concern since 1995 with development cooperation in conflict situations, and with the DAC's 1995 creation of the Task Force on Conflict, Peace and Development Co-operation. In May 1997, the DAC's High Level Meeting approved a policy document on 'Conflict, Peace and Development Co-operation on the Threshold of the 21st Century'. In April 2001, the DAC High Level meeting approved a new policy document, 'Helping Prevent Violent Conflict: Orientations for External Partners', and converted the Task Force into a network to encourage members to mainstream conflict prevention into their policies. This OECD activity can be viewed as a common resource for, and the connector of, the G8 and EU in their conflict prevention work.

ticular configuration of characteristics that makes the G8 and EU, whatever their defects in deadly conflict crisis management and response, exceptionally well tailored to meet the global conflict prevention challenge in the post-cold war era and particularly in the difficult years that lie ahead.

2. THE G8'S ROLE AND INITIATIVES IN CONFLICT PREVENTION

Conflict prevention in the broadest sense has been a concern of the G7 since its inaugural 1975 Summit at Rambouillet, France.[11] Here the leaders publicly declared in their concluding communiqué that the new institution's central mission was to promote globally the values of open democracy, individual liberty and social advancement. They further noted that the Group was vigilantly seeking to manage tensions across the long frozen, East-West, cold war divide. But it was only amidst the proliferating disasters of the post-cold war, rapidly globalising world of the 1990s that the G7 and soon G8 (with Russia increasingly involved from 1992 to 2002) began to focus directly on conflict prevention in its modern sense of short- and long-term engagement to stop, before it starts, the outbreak or spread of any collective violence and the activities that precipitate and propel such violence.

The G8's identification of conflict prevention as a self-contained, general subject in its own right, requiring new instruments and interventions, began at the 1993 Tokyo Summit. Inspired in part by UN Secretary General Boutros Boutros-Ghali's 1992 *Agenda for Peace*, the G7 leaders first referred directly to conflict prevention and highlighted the importance of strengthening the UN's capacity for 'preventive diplomacy'. Naples 1994 repeated this call. At Halifax in 1995, the G7 leaders assumed the responsibility for conflict prevention themselves, asking not only the UN to act more quickly, but also the G7 countries to coordinate more closely, 'in the prevention, management and resolution of conflicts'.[12] They specifically affirmed the need for the early warning of crises and field entry of international personnel, the role of regional organisations, improved analysis of conflict-related early warning information with respect to human rights and refugees, and focusing development assistance on those with 'a demonstrated capacity and commitment to use them effectively', while taking into account trends in 'military and other unproductive spending'.

During its subsequent seven-year Summit hosting cycle, from 1996 to 2002, the G7 and (after 1997) the G8 moved ever more expansively to create the concept, and commit itself to the cause, of conflict prevention on a global scale. At French-hosted Lyon in 1996, G7 leaders included conflict prevention as part of

[11] This section draws on J. Kirton and R. Stefanova, op. cit. n. 2.
[12] G7, 'Halifax Summit Communiqué', Halifax 16 June 1993, <www.g7.utoronto.ca/summit/1995halifax/communique/index.html> (August 2003).

their new globalization *problèmatique*, highlighting the importance of democracy, human rights and good governance, limits on unproductive and excessive military expenditure, the need for a comprehensive approach that included police training, the importance of action against landmines and conventional weapons harming children, and the use of flexible instruments, including the role of regional organisations. Yet also underscored, at this French-hosted Summit, were the primary role of the United Nations, the ultimate right of self-defence, action in the post-conflict phase, and instruments such as mediation by the UN. At US-hosted Denver in 1997, conflict prevention became a priority, acquired an African emphasis, and added sustainable development, a broad array of societal actors, the 1997 policy guidelines of the OECD's Development Assistance Committee (DAC), and African leadership and local capacities as key elements in the conflict prevention task. Yet the G8 continued to emphasize the central role of the UN. British-hosted Birmingham in 1998 was much the same.

The big breakthrough into concentrated, comprehensive, coherent work on conflict prevention came when the G8 hosting prerogative moved beyond those who were privileged members of the UNSC P5. In the lead-up to the German-hosted 1999 Cologne Summit, the G8 Foreign Ministers, inspired by their efforts in helping to bring a successful end to the conflict in Kosovo, called for innovation in conflict prevention, especially in regard to long-range democratic institution-building.[13] Their leaders at Cologne endorsed the call. The G8 Foreign Ministers held their first ever theme-specific meeting in Berlin in December 1999, devoted to conflict prevention. They asked their political directors to work, in the new Conflict Prevention Officials Meeting (CPOM), to translate the general Cologne consensus into specific initiatives for approval and action by leaders at the Japanese-hosted G8 Okinawa Summit the following year.[14]

At Okinawa the leaders delivered, authorizing action on the five specific items of conflict diamonds, conflict and development, small arms and light weapons, children in conflict and international civilian police. The Italian-hosted Genoa G8 Summit in 2001 again expanded the field of vision and action, adding the role of the private sector, water and women to the list. It also had the G8 Foreign Ministers issue a self-assessment of how G8 members had complied with their conflict prevention commitments made the year before. The Canadian-hosted 2002 G8 Summit in Kananaskis, the first held after the terrorist attacks on North America on September 11th, 2001, was preoccupied with the need to respond to the new crisis of terrorism. Its mainstream, Foreign Ministers-driven conflict prevention process concentrated heavily on Afghanistan. But the G8 Foreign Ministers' meeting at Whistler, British Columbia, did much to codify and extend the broader

---

[13] Risto Penttilä, 'The Role of the G8 in International Peace and Security', Adelphi Paper 355 (Oxford, Oxford University Press 2003), pp. 70-74.
[14] J. Kirton, et al. (eds.), *Guiding Global Order: G8 Governance in the Twenty-First Century* (Aldershot, Ashgate 2001).

work. And the leaders at Kananaskis mainstreamed – indeed gave priority to – conflict prevention in their ambitious, central G8 Africa Action Plan.[15]

The current, now eight-year cycle of Summitry (with Russia added as a host for 2006) began under French hosting at Evian in June 2003. The G8 Foreign Ministers' meeting, held in Paris immediately before the Summit, saw its conflict prevention work focus again on Afghanistan, both at that meeting and through a special conference held immediately before. The Summit itself again moved to mainstream conflict prevention operationally on the Kananaskis model, through the leaders' follow-up work on the G8 Africa Action Plan. More broadly, building on the earlier G8 successes with conflict diamonds in 2000 and the role of the private sector in 2001, the French highlighted the need for a 'responsible market economy'. It was a theme within which the American passion to combat corruption, and the British proposal on the Extractive Industries Transparency Initiative (EITI) successfully, if not easily, found a place. Evian thus showed that at a French-hosted Summit, which launched the current cycle, the three traditional G7 members that proudly protected their position on the UNSC P5 could come together to continue and expand the G8's conflict prevention work.

3. THE DEVELOPMENT OF G7/8-EU COOPERATION IN CONFLICT PREVENTION

As the G8 has forged ahead with this ever more ambitious conflict prevention program in recent years, it would appear, at first glance, that the EU has been irrelevant as a cooperative partner in this cause. Indeed, most existing analyses of the EU's record in, and potential relevance to, the G7/8 omit any serious reference to the political-security field in general and the conflict prevention component in particular.[16] Yet a closer examination reveals that the EU has been an essential partner in the G7/8's successes in conflict prevention. It has played this part in large measure by allowing an otherwise historically constrained Germany to assume a leadership role, by bringing the voice of a broader European Community that includes the smaller, non-G8 members to offset that of P5-focused France and Britain, and by balancing the increased weight and traditional orienta-

---

[15] Michele Fratianni, et al., *Sustaining Global Growth and Development: G7 and IMF Governance* (Aldershot, Ashgate 2003).

[16] See, for example, Sylvia Ostry, 'Canada, Europe and the Economic Summits', paper presented at the All-European Canadian Studies Conference, The Hague, 24-27 October 1990, <www.library. utoronto.ca/g7/scholar/ostry1990/index.html> (August 2003); Susan Hainsworth, op. cit. n. 6, <www.g7.utoronto.ca/scholar/hainsworth1990/bispre.htm> (August 2003); Pascal Lamy, 'The Economic Summit and the European Community', Bissell Paper No. 4 (Toronto, University of Toronto, Centre for International Studies 1988), <www.g7.utoronto.ca/scholar/lamy1988/index.html> (August 2003).

tion of P5-member Russia as it has become an increasingly influential member of the G8.

Despite French reluctance, what was then the EEC first came to the Summit, in the person of Roy Jenkins, President of the Commission, in 1977 to deal with the largely economic issues in which the EU had competence. By 1982 the EU found itself involved in the G7's growing political-security agenda as well. But it was the end of the cold war that allowed the EU to carve out a conflict prevention niche for itself, when the 1990 G7 Summit, hosted by President George Bush in Houston, Texas, asked the EU, at German urging, to take the lead role in designing and delivering an assistance program to the newly liberated states of Central and Eastern Europe. This role was expanded through EU contributions to the major assistance programs mounted by the G7 for the ever more democratic Russia, starting with the German-hosted Munich Summit of 1992. This included the important EU part in the G8's work on nuclear safety in the former Soviet Union, and the EU's participation in the G7's inter-sessional Moscow 'Nuclear Safety and Security Summit' co-hosted by France and Russia in 1996. This summit focused on preventing illicit trafficking of nuclear material. In its 'Programme for Preventing and Combatting Illicit Trafficking in Nuclear Material', the Summit emphasized that the 'criminal diversion of nuclear material could assist states or terrorist groups to bypass the carefully crafted controls of the international nuclear non-proliferation regime and permit them to construct or otherwise acquire a nuclear or radiological weapon'.[17]

EU-G8 cooperation on conflict prevention moved in 1999 beyond this broader tableau of terrorism, crime, nuclear safety and assistance to post-communist governments. The catalyst was the failure of the prevailing EU and G8 approach in the Balkans, where the European Council meeting in the spring of 1992 and the subsequent German-hosted G7 Summit at Munich in 1992, had proclaimed the readiness of both bodies to use all necessary means to ensure that their humanitarian relief would get through to the innocent victims it was intended to help.[18] On 24 March 1999, the G7 members, through the North Atlantic Treaty Organization (NATO), initiated an air war against Yugoslavia to prevent the growing genocide in Kosovo. In the lead-up to the Cologne G8 Summit, the G8 leaders made it clear to both Slobodan Milošević and Russia's Boris Yeltsin that they were prepared to inject ground combat forces under non-permissive conditions to complete the task. This historic, highly successful move of the G7/8 into a com-

---

[17] G7 plus Russia, 'Programme for Preventing and Combatting Illegal Trafficking in Nuclear Material', 20 April 1996, <www.g8.utoronto.ca/summit/1996moscow/program.html> (August 2003).

[18] More broadly, the creation of the Bosnian Contact Group, which included the EU and all G8 members save Canada, came from the 'initiative of EU negotiator David Owen, who had gained positive first hand experience with the Contact Group in Namibia' (R. Penttilä, op. cit. n. 13, at 27). The Namibian Contact Group was formed in the late 1970s by the Western members of the UNSC P5, who had found it necessary to include Canada and Germany, from the start to the end.

bined conduct of conflict and prevention of genocide depended critically on Germany's position as host of the G8 for 1999 and simultaneously as president of the EU and the Western European Union (WEU) for the first half of 1999. Germany developed the 'Fischer Plan,' with five principles for lasting peace; it took them to the EU and NATO, and chose the G8 as the appropriate forum for implementation due to Russia's inclusion. Germany delivered the program through an April 1999 meeting of G8 Political Directors in Dresden, a follow-up meeting in Petersburg, a G8 Foreign Ministers' meeting in June and a decision by G8 leaders, for the first time with Yeltsin in agreement, at the Cologne Summit itself. Vital to the success was the appointment as mediators by Russia of Viktor Chernomyrdin and by the G8 of Finland's President Martti Ahtisaari, who had the backing of the EU and who held the EU Presidency for the second half of 1999.[19]

This success over Kosovo, after the failures of traditional approaches in the Balkans and Africa during the previous decade, led directly to the German-hosted G8 Foreign Ministers' meeting on conflict prevention, held on 16-17 December 1999 in Berlin. Its origins dated back to a December 1998 paper on how the G8 could deal with conflict prevention, a paper that the initially unenthusiastic German Foreign Minister, spurred by the conflict in Kosovo, accepted in January 1999. The proposal, along with the G8's response to Kosovo, was leveraged by the Germans through, *inter alia*, the EU's Directors of Common Foreign and Security Policy (CFSP), the EU and its four individual G8 members, as well as the WEU, NATO and the Organization for Security and Co-operation in Europe (OSCE). By the G8 Foreign Ministers' meeting held just before Cologne, there was an agreement that the Berlin meeting would take place as Germany's 'Millennium' event to mark the end of its year as host.

As part of the major breakthroughs it made in launching the G8's conflict prevention program, the Berlin meeting affirmed the need for an integrated, comprehensive approach that included the 'economic, financial, environmental, social and development policies'[20] where the EU held competence and capacity. It also affirmed the role of regional organizations such as the EU and, particularly, the OSCE. Vital to the success and even existence of the meeting was the formula found by the German Presidency to address the issue of Chechnya, at a gathering that all G8 members, including Russia's Igor Ivanov, decided finally to attend. The separate 'Chairman's Statement' on Chechnya declared that the need for a culture of prevention that applied to 'all of us' existed alongside Russia's territo-

---

[19] Gunther Pleuger, 'The G8: Heading for a Major Role in International Peace and Security?', in Winrich Kuhne and Jochen Prantl (eds.), *The Security Council and the G8 in the New Millennium: Who Is in Charge of International Peace and Security?* (Ebenhausen, Stiftung Wissenschaft und Politik 2000), pp. 83-84; R. Penttilä, op. cit. n. 13, at 44-45.

[20] G8 Foreign Ministers, 'Conclusions of the Meeting of the G8 Foreign Ministers' Meeting', 13 July 2000, <www.g7.utoronto.ca/foreign/fm000713.htm> (August 2003).

rial integrity and right to fight terrorism, that a political solution in Chechnya would be 'a valid contribution to future conflict prevention for the conflict-torn Caucasus', and that there was a need for 'an urgent stepping up of international aid'.[21] While the appeal to Russia was made in the name of its membership in the OSCE and Council of Europe, the incentive of a stronger relationship between Russia and the EU was significant in its success. The importance of the prospect of enhanced partnership with a weighty EU, voiced in the name of a G8 in which the EU was a virtually full member, also displayed its conflict prevention influence in the G8's Cologne Summit appeal to Greece and Turkey to resume talks over Cyprus.[22]

At a meeting of G8 Political Directors in Kyoto in February 2000, the Japanese followed the Germans in adopting conflict prevention as their Foreign Ministers' theme for their year as host, having failed to find an adequate substitute featuring an all-Asian theme. At Kyoto a group was established to prepare an action plan on conflict prevention for the G8 Miyazaki Foreign Ministers' meeting that spring. Although the French resisted, the Germans found it easy to form alliances with the other G8 EU powers, such as Britain, in the freewheeling, informal atmosphere of the G8, to make further, faster progress than they could in the more formal confines of the EU itself. Thus Miyazaki succeeded in producing the action program that the Berlin meeting, beset by intra-G8 and intra-Russian divisions, had not.

For Genoa in 2001, the Italians under Prime Minister Giuliano Amato identified conflict prevention as a major theme and made considerable advances at the Foreign Minister level. Yet at the Summit level itself, several factors worked against them, including the advent of Silvio Berlusconi as Italian Prime Minister on the Summit's eve, the unprecedented violence at Genoa during the Summit, the arrival of George Bush as US President and major divisions between him and French-led Europe over the Kyoto Protocol on Climate Change in particular and America's apparent unilateral approach to the world in general. At Genoa, the EU was represented not just by the Commission but also by an 'outside' or non-G8 member as President of the Council, in the person of Belgian Prime Minister Guy Verhofstadt. He spoke more than any other leader at the Summit table, joining with France's Jacques Chirac to criticize the US for Kyoto and its unilateralism, but also complaining that he had not been involved in the preparatory process for the Summit. As a result, there was little real exchange among leaders at the Summit, leaving the Summit-level advances on conflict prevention to come from the visiting African leaders seeking G8 help for their new approach to African development.

---

[21] G8 Foreign Ministers, 'G8 Chairman's Statement', 16-17 December 1999, <www.g7.utoronto. ca/foreign/fm991216chair.htm> (August 2003).

[22] J. Kirton, 'The G8: Heading for a Major Role in International Peace and Security?', in W. Kuhne and J. Prantl (eds.), op. cit n. 19, at 73-82.

This African legacy from Genoa, the unifying force of the September 11th, 2001, terrorist attacks, and the presence of Spain's Jose Maria Aznar (known as a shrewd, stable businessman) as the European Council representative made the 2002 Kananaskis Summit a much more productive affair. At the lead-up G8 Foreign Ministers' meeting in Whistler, British Columbia, one of the most delicate conflict prevention issues was the Middle East, where both the US as well as the EU and European members (thanks in part to large official development assistance programs) had a major role. The Canadians, led by their Foreign Minister, Bill Graham, as Chair, succeeded in getting the US and the Europeans together on a common statement that largely endorsed the plan President Bush had released in Washington a few days before. A last-minute all-European caucus acquiesced in the statement that came from the Canadian Chair, rather than demand a negotiated consensus of the full G8. A similar dynamic and result emerged among the leaders at Kananaskis when the Middle East was discussed. The quick consensus here helped the Summit move to unveil, as its centrepiece achievement, the ambitious G8 Africa Action Plan. The plan put conflict prevention in first place and highlighted the instruments where EU competence and capacity loomed large.

At Evian in 2003, a similar story unfolded, as the leaders' conflict prevention-related agenda focused heavily on Africa and the Middle East, where the EU role stood out. Although Greek Prime Minister Konstantinos Simitis attended as President-in-Office of the European Council, the EU case was largely carried by Romano Prodi, the veteran President of the European Commission. As an individual who had also had G8 Summit experience as a popularly elected leader of a G8 country, he was exceptionally well positioned to make the EU voice effectively heard.

4. CREATING CLOSER COOPERATION FOR TWENTY-FIRST CENTURY
    CONFLICT PREVENTION

In the coming years, the major challenge for the G8 will be how to keep its newly launched conflict prevention program alive, expanding, relevant to the new problems the international system produces and, above all, moving from agenda setting, norm-developing and collective decision-making into effective implementation in the field. This challenge is heightened by the potentially diversionary, new preoccupation with the post-September 11th campaign against terrorism and the rebuilding of Afghanistan, and by the divisions and diversions caused by the spring 2003 war in Iraq. Institutionally, within the G8, the challenge is compounded by the fact that the hosting cycle has passed to the UNSC P5 members of France in 2003, the United States in 2004, Britain in 2005 and now Russia in 2006. Hosting only returns to the G8 conflict prevention enthusiasts of Germany in 2007, Japan in 2008, Italy in 2009, and Canada in 2010.

In contemplating the desirable evolution of G8-EU cooperation on conflict prevention during the current G8 hosting cycle, several advantages of a closer relationship stand out from the perspective of the G8. First, as the G8 moves toward implementation, the EU offers the organizational capacity, institutional memory and a permanent representational presence in countries abroad that the G8, as an informal institution devoid of its own secretariat, lacks – as it will continue to lack, and as it should. Here, the EU brings a sensitive experience with G8 affairs through the presence of individuals, such as Romano Prodi and, before him, Jacques Delors and Pascal Lamy, who have served as leading G7 heads or sherpas and gone on to assume prominent leadership positions within the EU. Second, the EU, as a multinational organization, has developed internally the habits of international accommodation and consensus building that G8 national governments, alone or even all together, have honed to a lesser degree, but that are vital in conflict prevention implementation. The EU is thus particularly well equipped for a conflict prevention program that requires both long-term continuity and multiperspectival restraint and care. Third, as the EU expands to include more members, it will increase the already formidable expertise, multiperspectival sensitivity and international legitimacy it now brings to the conflict prevention task. Fourth, the 'outer' or non-G8 EU members, such as the Netherlands, Belgium, Spain and Portugal, as well as the EU through its Africa, Caribbean and Pacific states (ACP) arrangements, have an impressive global array of special relationships with those countries within which conflict prevention is most needed. Regionally, these range from the African epicentre through the Americas, as well as to Asia. The EU and its ACP relationships also offer an abundance of critical resources, from official development assistance through trade to other assets, which are required for conflict prevention. Taken together, a G8 that wants to move in its conflict prevention activity from innovative agenda-setting into effective action needs a closer relationship with the EU.

How might the closer relationship that the G8 needs with the EU on conflict prevention be constructed in the coming years? Here, one might be tempted to start with a relatively safe, EU-centred strategy of concentrating on the accepted areas related to conflict prevention where the EU already has long had supranational competence – notably the 'soft flanks' of trade, development and environment – and take the relatively easy steps of harvesting the low hanging fruit that lies in these fields. A second, more ambitious strategy, is to focus in the first instance on the hardcore power centres and strengths of the G8 as an institution, and on the particular issues where the most leverage on the challenge of conflict prevention itself might reside. Building largely on this latter foundation, it is appropriate to envisage an incrementally implemented program of three somewhat overlapping phases. This strategy would start with modest steps in the 2003-2006 period when the UNSC P5 members host the G8, become much more ambitious from 2007 to 2010 when the non-UNSC P5 G8 members assume the Presidency of the G8, and potentially take a great leap forward in 2011 when the next, now potentially nine-year cycle of Summitry begins.

For the first phase, from 2003 to 2006, the immediate challenge is the skepticism of the Bush administration in the United States, expressed in 2001 and 2003, about whether the world really needs the G8 for Foreign Ministers' meetings and more broadly as well.[23] Thus the initial task is to maintain the recently institutionalized G8 momentum and mobilize the EU's capacity for conflict prevention delivery, particularly given the reluctance of the US to take up this latter task.[24] Here the G8 and EU should work with, rather than be deterred by, the avowed and apparent aversion to the institutionalization of the G8 on the part of France, the US and Britain, for the actual record of these rhetorical skeptics demonstrates their revealed preference for G8 institution-building of some strength. Institutionally, the first step is to create a more permanent and powerful CPOM, with a work program more integrated into that of the leaders themselves. The second step is to keep alive the new G8 Development Ministers' forum, born in 2002 and institutionalized in 2003, by inspiring a 2004 installment with an agenda that extends to the development dimensions of conflict prevention.

Substantively, these two institutional advances could be made attractive to all G8 members and to its 2004 American host, by having these forums, and the now closely linked leaders' Summits themselves, focus on two issues. The first issue is the American's favourite of terrorism, with an emphasis on the root causes of lack of development and democracy that could lead to the domestic (as well as international) terrorism that could constitute a trigger event or take-off process for violent conflict to draw nigh. The second is to build on the Evian 2003 Summit's success with the theme of 'responsible market economy', and fuse the favourite American and British components of corruption and EITI respectively with the earlier G8's accomplishments on conflict diamonds and the role of the private sector in conflict prevention. In both cases, the permanent CPOM and the stronger G8 Development Ministers' forum could charge the EU with the lead role in implementation and delivery, just as the G7 Summit hosted by President George Bush in Houston, Texas, in 1990 did in assigning the EU the lead on the then highly political issue of assistance to the newly liberated Central and East European states.

---

[23] This skepticism flows not just from a 2003 Iraq war-bred rational calculation of the US advantage in relying on *ad hoc*, task-specific coalitions of the willing, rather than the permanent G8 concert where diffuse reciprocity and mutual adjustment are the order of the day (see R. Penttilä, op. cit. n. 13). It flows also from Bush's preference, following his father as President, for one-on-one encounters that are more private and informal than collective affairs. The Bush style is in sharp contrast to that of Presidents Bill Clinton and Jimmy Carter before him, who relished the collective analytically based exchange in a G8-sized seminar.

[24] Frank Loy, 'US Approaches to International Conflict Prevention and the Role of Allies and International Institutions', in J. Kirton and R. Stefanova (eds.), op. cit. n. 2, at 103-112.

As part of this first phase, two desirable procedural reforms could be usefully introduced. The first is to have the G8 host schedule its Summit so that the EU Council President, if from a non-G8 member, would attend at the very end of his or her six-month term, rather than at the very start. This would ensure that the 'outside' President is part of the full G8 preparatory process, and has a much stronger knowledge and politically based claim to speak on behalf of the full EU. For its part, the EU could improve the integration of both the current and forthcoming Council Presidency into the G8 preparatory process, in the spirit that the Germans followed with the Finns in the great conflict prevention breakthrough year of 1999.

The second phase would run from 2007 to 2010, but could begin earlier by taking advantage of British enthusiasm in 2005 and the centrality that the G8 has for the new and rapidly evolving Russia that will host in 2006. Institutionally, this stage would see the development of the G8 Foreign Ministers' forum to the point where it becomes as robust as its fellow G8 Finance Ministers' body. It would do so both in the intensity and year-round coverage of its meetings 'at eight' and in its 'outreach' to involve additional participants, as the now G8 Finance Ministers' forum has done with the Group of Twenty (G20) and the Financial Stability Forum. It would further involve the more modest step of having the existing G8 Finance Ministers' institutions (including their Deputies forum) and their broader extensions, take up the finance-related aspects of conflict prevention, building on Britain's EITI. It would finally have the more fluid forum for G8 Ministers of the Interior and Justice move beyond their current preoccupation with terrorism to take up the tasks of conflict prevention that involve, or could involve, civilian police. Should the Foreign or Interior Ministers prove slow in moving in this direction, the Development Ministers' forum could set the pace. Once again, the EU, especially when Germany in 2007 and Italy in 2009 assume the chair, could be assigned G8 mandates for delivery and further policy development.

Substantively, the attractive agenda for this phase of G8 institutional development, would again map the issue preoccupations of the host. It would thus, with Britain 2005 in mind, focus first on the finance aspects of conflict prevention, with Africa serving as the privileged region in this regard. The focus on civilian police, and the broader governance issues associated with it (starting with the judiciary and court system, but extending to civilian control of security forces and the place of para-military forces), could come as a subsequent step.

The third phase, starting in 2011, takes advantage of the G8's launch of a full new cycle of summitry that year, with G8 founder and the great architect of global governance France serving as the host. This propensity for an ambitious great leap forward on the part of the G8 could be matched by a much more robust EU. By then, enlargement, a meaningful Common Foreign and Security Policy and capable, deployable military rapid reaction forces as well as a more democratic polity would be accomplished EU facts. As a result two major steps could be contemplated.

The first step would be to create a G8 ministerial-level institution, with the EU as a full and mandate-seeking member, for the civilian heads of intelligence and defence ministries. Its mission would be to foster G8 and broader cooperation on the specific critical conflict prevention tasks of intelligence sharing for early warning systems, and planning for preventive deployments, as well as dealing with extensions of the traditional military-related tasks of small arms and light weapons (SALW) and of children in conflict. In both cases, it would be the civilian rather than uniformed leadership that would be involved in the first instance, in recognition of the core need to prevent rather than conduct conflict.

The second step would be to insert into the next hosting cycle starting in 2011 the new, steadily more supranational EU itself, by allowing it finally to host a Summit of its own, sometime between 2011 and 2020. It would do so at a location of its own choice, perhaps where one of its major institutions (such as the Commission or the European Parliament) is housed. Such a step would be appropriate if the EU had by then largely overcome its democratic deficit, and moved much closer to having a head who was a popularly and democratically elected leader, as are all the other G8 Summit participants. At that point, a full, hosting membership for an enlarged EU would do much to increase the internal equality and global predominance of the G8's capabilities – the structural factors that are critical to the effectiveness of the G8 as a centre of global governance. The EU-as-Summit host would further restore to the G8 the historic balance between UNSC P5 and non-UNSC P5 members, and the slight numerical bias toward the latter, that has prevailed since 1976 but that will be tilted toward the former when Russia hosts in 2006. With the EU inserted into the hosting cycle, it would be appropriate to anticipate, and appeal for, EU leadership on the G8's conflict prevention agenda, both on an ongoing annual basis and as a centrepiece theme for the first Summit the EU hosts.

Even as part of this third or a potential fourth step, one of the often recommended G8 reform proposals should be firmly set aside. This is the suggestion that the EU itself should eventually replace the four individual European members at the leaders' table, in the G8 Foreign Ministers meeting, and elsewhere, as it has from the start at the Trade Ministers' Quadrilateral. This idea is thought to be a useful way of lowering transaction costs by further constricting participation, and increasing American buy-in and binding to a forum Americans sometimes feel is dominated by European countries that loomed large in the world of 1945 but that no longer do so today. Yet eliminating the Germans and Italians who have led the G8's conflict prevention program, and the British and even the French who have come along in valuable ways, would be a major loss. It would be especially costly at a time in the G8's conflict prevention program when individual national capacities, as well as those of the EU collectively, are needed to implement the G8's conflict prevention programs, in Africa above all. Without the presence of those individual nations, the single EU voice could well become unduly dominated by the 'big four' behind the scenes, rather than remaining relatively free to express the views of the EU's ever increasing smaller members, which are not there at the G8 table in their own right. And as shown by the sharp difference between Genoa 2001 and the Summits before and after it, a single European voice criticizing George Bush's America does much less to induce G8 conflict-preventing cooperation than does a diversity of European voices in which Britain's Tony Blair, Italy's Silvio Berlusconi, Spain's Jose Maria Aznar and the EU Commission's Romano Prodi are free to take the American side, to serve as transatlantic bridge builders or to use their individual special relationship with the United States to bind America to the G8 conflict prevention initiatives that Europe has done so much to pioneer and produce.

Chapter 22
CONFLICT AND DEVELOPMENT: THE ROLE OF THE WORLD BANK

by Ian Bannon[1]

1. AN EVOLVING APPROACH OVERVIEW

Although the World Bank was created to help rebuild European countries devastated by World War II, putting the 'R' back in the International Bank for Reconstruction and Development, the full title of the World Bank, has been a case study in institutional change for the multilateral agency. This article examines the evolution of the Bank's approach to conflict and development, the way it has gone about implementing this agenda and some of the challenges it faces.

At the time of the creation of the UN Department of Humanitarian Affairs (UNDHA), now the Office for Coordination of Humanitarian Affairs (OCHA), no one working in the relief and rehabilitation programs of Liberia, Kurdistan or the former Yugoslavia could be heard to question 'where is the Bank?' As the premier, wholesaler of development assistance, better known for the controversy over structural adjustment, its absence was taken for granted. Yet, by the time that East Timor's struggle for independence burst on to the world scene, a Bank team was in the vanguard of the rehabilitation and reconstruction wave. Today, the Bank is active in a wide range of conflict-affected countries and is looking to re-engage in a number of very poor performers, who are often beset by conflict or have never recovered from its after-effects.

At the time when the international community worried about the relief to the development gap and the need to ensure a continuum – did it exist or could it be achieved? – certain visionaries at senior UN and World Bank levels saw that the institution could well fill a gap between emergency aid and the onset of reconstruction and development assistance. At the same time certain Bank staff were prepared to demonstrate that Bank projects could start to operate to good effect on the heels of humanitarian aid without waiting for the peace to be a matter of recorded history.

---

[1] Ian Bannon is Manager of the World Bank's Conflict Prevention and Reconstruction Unit, Washington.

V. Kronenberger and J. Wouters, eds., The European Union and Conflict Prevention
© 2004, T·M·C·Asser press, *The Hague, The Netherlands*

A critical turning point, early in the World Bank presidency of James Wolfensohn, was the reconstruction program in Bosnia, where in 1995 a trust fund was established upstream of Bank lending, followed by emergency lending mobilized more rapidly and across a wider range of activities than previously. The Bosnia experience had come in the heels of the Bank's new role in the West Bank and Gaza, where in 1994 it was asked to administer the multi-donor Holst Fund. The Bosnia program, however, broke the mould, and formed the basis for a new post-conflict framework which was to become within three years an operational policy. Following Bosnia were a series of programs in Rwanda, Kosovo, Sierra Leone, other Balkan states, East Timor, the Democratic Republic of Congo (DRC) and the Greater Great Lakes Region, and most recently Afghanistan. No one doubts that the next post-conflict reconstruction challenge would bring similar major contributions from the Bank.

In 1998, mindful that this new direction was not without its problems or detractors, the Bank's evaluation arm, the Operations Evaluation Department (OED), took a long hard look at the institution's post-conflict performance.[2] Though it found many unanswered questions in the transition from conflict to development, and judged the Bank's performance uneven, it concluded that the institution had a definite comparative advantage in supporting peace, at least where certain prerequisites and other actors were in place. The links between sustainable peace and development – economic stability, good governance, employment generation, access to social services and so on – were compelling. In addition, the Bank was in a prime position to support donor coordination and to mobilize substantial reconstruction funds.

Few in the humanitarian and donor community disagreed in principle or argued for the Bank to withdraw. The Brahimi report was equally positive about the Bank's contribution. But was the Bank equipped to do the job, and what about preventing conflict rather than helping with the clean up? Looking back over a decade, the OED review noted that 16% of Bank lending was already tied up in post-conflict settings so the institution was in too deep to withdraw – now it had to get it right.

While a small, post-conflict unit located in the center and comprised mainly of ex UN and NGO staff advanced the agenda as far as it could, the real changes became apparent in the Bank's Regions, where operations and country relations are managed. Funding, analysis and expertise started flowing toward demobilization and reintegration programs, land-mine clearance, people- and community-centered rehabilitation rather than a narrow focus on infrastructure, the special needs of child soldiers, and a broader approach to good governance. As one NGO commentator dryly put it, 'so the Bank has discovered peace'. But what the Bank

---

[2] World Bank, *The World Bank's Experience with Post-Conflict Reconstruction* (Operations Evaluation Department. Washington, D.C. 1998).

had really discovered was that in practice post-conflict was where we all wanted to get to, but it was not always the starting point.

Five years on from the OED study it is neither rhetoric nor an exaggeration to say that post-conflict reconstruction has been mainstreamed in Bank operations. The Bank still has much to learn about post-conflict reconstruction and it could always do with greater speed and nimbleness in environments that cry out for a quick response, but the processes and mind-sets to learn from post-conflict experience and to try to respond quicker are in place and well established within the institution.

As the Bank's post-conflict reconstruction agenda took hold, and with the costs, complexity, risks and visibility of recovery operations running so high, attention then turned to prevention. Here, research and events had an unexpected convergence. The operational policy of 2001, *Development Cooperation and Conflict*, defined the Bank's approach to conflict-affected countries, not just post-conflict. The new policy recognized that the Bank's role might extend beyond post-conflict reconstruction to a more proactive role in conflict-affected and vulnerable countries. It called for Bank assistance to 'minimize potential causes and be sensitive to conflict', while acknowledging there was much to learn in this area.

Then, findings from the Bank's research arm (DECRG), under Paul Collier, opened up the global debate on the economic causes and consequences of conflict. For an institution well stocked with economists, there had been surprisingly scant economic analysis or explanations of conflict in the Bank. Bank economists were inclined to think of conflict as an exogenous shock, akin to a natural disaster or an adverse swing in the terms of trade – something bad and unfortunate that happened from time to time and which was either 'not our problem' or in any case 'there was not much we could do about it'.

Collier's research reaffirmed the links between conflict and poverty, confirming the everyday observations of other agencies and NGOs, but also added new insights, new at least to some – for example, that the temptation from having lootable natural resources (alluvial diamonds for example) and swelling numbers of unemployed youth, greatly heightens the risks of conflict. Other findings were more controversial and sparked a lively debate which came to be known as the 'greed versus grievance' debate. The main point of contention centered around whether this was too focused on economic explanations of conflict and thus ignored genuine grievances and the broader discourse on causation, a discourse that tended to be dominated by political scientists. Irrespective of the outcome of the debate, it is clear that Collier's work changed the nature of the discussion on conflict and forced most to at least question or cast a wary eye on the prevailing discourse on grievance as the driver for civil wars.

The events of September 11, 2001 also prompted the Bank to look anew at its mission and mandate. The proximity of the attacks had a palpable personal effect on Bank staff and led to a genuine soul-searching and re-examination of the core

Bank mission. President Wolfensohn was quick to articulate what most staff felt – that the poverty mission was more important than ever. It was not that poverty led to terrorism – the poor are not the enemy – but a sense that 'failed states' offered fertile soil on which terrorism could thrive. Although small-scale terrorists can lurk in the shadows of any society, September 11 showed that large scale terrorism needs territory outside the control of a recognized and reputable government. Staff in the Bank wondered aloud, 'should we have been absent from Afghanistan for so long, was there anything we could have done differently?'.

September 11 also roughly coincided with another important round of research and ensuing policy discussion, which came to be known as the 'aid effectiveness' debate. In a nutshell, it argued, based on careful research, that aid was effective in spurring development but only when recipient countries adopted sound policies and nurtured effective institutions. When they did not, aid was a waste of taxpayers' money. This debate carried important policy implications for the donor community. It implied that donors should be more selective in allocating aid, rewarding the good performers and, in the extreme, totally cutting off the bad performers – a 'tough love' approach. While the case for stricter allocations of aid based on performance was persuasive and becoming accepted, there was also a sense of unease about setting the bad performers completely adrift. A large number of poor people live in these countries and, through no fault of their own, suffer the consequences of incompetent and cleptocratic governments. September 11 added a new dimension by painfully showing that the problems of poor performing countries would not be contained within their own borders.

The Bank's considered response to the convergence of September 11 and the outcome of the 'aid effectiveness' debate was to set up a task force to take a fresh look at its approach to countries across a broad spectrum of poor performance and vulnerability, now known as the 'low-income countries under stress' (LICUS) initiative. In a relatively short time, and without creating new instruments or bureaucratic responses, the work of the task force brought a more nuanced approach to the focus on good governance, policy reform and service provision in circumstances of chronic instability, or 'zero-generation' reforms. In essence, it articulated the need for some form of engagement, even if at a very low and modest level, that could offer some, even dim, possibility of policy reforms and change. This, some humanitarian workers and analysts had been seeking for years as a complement to their work.

Taking its cue from the operational policy, research findings – notably that post-conflict countries had over a 40% chance of recurring conflict during the first five years after the onset of peace – and evolving international practice, the Post-Conflict Unit was renamed the Conflict Prevention and Reconstruction (CPR) Unit. Now piloting conflict analysis in vulnerable countries, the Unit continues to be the focal point for the Bank's conflict agenda and administers the Post-Conflict Fund. This fund kick-starts the Bank's re-engagement with conflict-affected countries through grants to governments and a wide spectrum of

UN and NGO relief and rehabilitation agencies. While post-September 11 concerns muted critics who previously detected 'mission creep' in the Bank's conflict agenda, so the Bank's CPR Unit in collaboration with the Bank's Regions and Networks, set about the task of translating the reality of 'no development without peace' into operational possibilities for Bank assistance and partnerships.

As the complexities of conflict prevention and its causes unfold, new issues emerge for the Bank to ponder. What should be the type and level of assistance in poor performing or conflict-vulnerable countries? How to deal with moral hazard questions in these cases? What should be the Bank's level of engagement when the conflict is taking place? Is the 'do no harm' approach enough, or should the Bank be far more proactive in conflict prevention? And what do we mean by conflict prevention anyway? How should the Bank align its operations and performance-based lending to human rights considerations and what definition of human rights should it use? How do we distinguish bad performers from those that are merely suffering from the aftershocks of the conflict and will likely make a full recovery? Since aid is a zero-sum game, how do we provide extra assistance to those recovering from conflict without punishing those that through a combination of good policies, institutions and good luck, managed to steer clear of conflict? Who takes over financing when emergency funds run out? How does the Bank work with donors, or partner with smaller humanitarian and development agencies, without crowding out the market or impeding their speed and flexibility? Like Tolstoy's unhappy families, does the uniqueness of each conflict and its attendant emergency, preclude a preplanned division of labor or does it boil down to committed implementation on a case-by-case approach?

The remainder of this paper explores the Bank's rules of engagement in conflict-affected countries and some of the challenges and themes it is seeking to address. The paper first sketches the operational implications of the Bank's evolving approach to conflict and development leading in light of its new policy (Section II). It then reviews recent experience with a number of key Bank policies, instruments and approaches commonly used in work with conflict-affected countries, including engagement modalities, poverty strategies, LICUS and the Comprehensive Development Framework (Section III). The fourth section looks at new approaches and tools that are being developed to better address the development challenges posed by violent conflict, including a better understanding of the economics of conflict, knowledge gaps and new insights in areas such as gender, HIV/AIDS, community-driven development, and governance and the rule of law. The paper then briefly describes recent developments with respect to Bank financing of post-conflict recovery efforts. Section VI reviews the growing importance of knowledge management and key partnerships. A concluding section underlies remaining challenges.

2. CONFRONTING MORE COMPLEX CHALLENGES

The World Bank's role in addressing the ravages of violent conflict is historical. Some of the first Bank loans helped rebuild European countries devastated by World War II and over the ensuing decades it has sought to respond to the challenges of post-conflict reconstruction. The Bank initially concentrated on providing financial capital and rebuilding physical infrastructure, but in a post-Cold War era marked by an increase in the number and severity of civil conflicts, it had to adapt to different and more complex challenges. As discussed earlier, two cases in the mid-1990s in particular highlighted this growing complexity. In 1994 the Bank became the administrator for the multi-donor Holst Fund for the West Bank and Gaza, and in 1995 it was asked to take the lead with the European Commission in planning and coordinating international assistance for post-conflict recovery in Bosnia-Herzegovina. Realizing that it faced a far more difficult post-conflict environment and growing expectations on the part of the international community, the Bank decided to create a locus of expertise in post-conflict reconstruction and to examine the framework under which it operated. To this end, in 1997 the Bank created the Post-Conflict Unit in the Social Development Department, and in February 1997 the Executive Directors endorsed the paper entitled *Framework for World Bank Involvement in Post-Conflict Reconstruction*.[3] The new framework provided a rationale and guidelines for Bank involvement in countries in transition from conflict.

With poverty both a cause and a consequence of conflict, and in line with evolving international initiatives to explore the potential role of development assistance in preventing conflict, the Bank sought to redefine its reconstruction role more broadly in the context of a comprehensive development framework – from an approach focused on rebuilding infrastructure to one that seeks to understand the root causes of conflict, to integrate a sensitivity to conflict in Bank activities and to promote assistance that minimizes the potential causes of conflict. In line with this shift in focus, in January 2001 the Executive Directors approved Operational Policy/Bank Procedures 2.30 (OP/BP 2.30), *Development Cooperation and Conflict*, which provides a strategic framework and sets the parameters for Bank engagement in countries affected by conflict.

OP/BP 2.30 goes beyond the 1997 framework by requiring the active consideration of conflict issues in all Bank activities – in countries that are vulnerable to conflict, in countries affected by conflict, and in countries in transition from conflict (post-conflict). The adoption of OP/BP 2.30 has enhanced the Bank's capacity to respond rapidly and flexibly, defining rules of involvement, Bank objectives in relation to the conflict phases countries which typically go through, and reasserting guiding principles for Bank engagement. The main features of OP

---

[3] World Bank, *A Framework for World Bank Involvement in Post-Conflict Reconstruction* (Washington, D.C. 1997).

2.30 include: (i) definition of the different levels of Bank engagement in different conflict settings; (ii) integration of sensitivity to conflict in Bank assistance through conflict analysis; (iii) the importance of working in partnership; and (iv) demarcation of Bank activities in conflict situations in line with its mandate and Articles of Agreement. BP 2.30 determines: (i) the procedures that apply in deciding the type and level of Bank engagement in a country affected by conflict; (ii) the guidance that staff may receive; and (iii) how conflicts and Bank operational responses are reported to the Board.

In line with this broader focus on incorporating a sensitivity to conflict in all Bank activities, the Post-Conflict Unit was renamed the Conflict Prevention and Reconstruction (CPR) Unit, in the Social Development Department, within the Environmentally and Socially Sustainable Development (ESSD) Network. While overall responsibility for Bank work in conflict-affected countries lies with the Bank's Regions and country teams, the CPR Unit provides a Bank focal point for policy advice, operational support, knowledge management, training and external partnerships. In addition, the CPR Unit manages the Post Conflict Fund. With respect to financial issues, the Resource Mobilization Department (FRM) is responsible for policy related to the allocation and use of IDA resources in post-conflict countries, and Credit Risk (FINCR) in cases involving IBRD countries, general financial policy and arrears.

While OP/BP 2.30 sets the overall context and provides a flexible framework for Bank engagement with countries affected by conflict, it also makes it clear that, in line with the mandate specified in its Articles of Agreement, the Bank does not engage in peace-making or peacekeeping, does not provide direct support for disarming combatants, and does not provide humanitarian relief, all of which are functions assumed by the United Nations and other agencies or donors.

3. POLICIES AND INSTRUMENTS

This section briefly reviews experience with a number of key Bank policies, instruments and approaches used in conflict-affected countries. These include the different levels of engagement linked to the different phases of conflict, conflict analysis as an input to strategies and programs, the special circumstances of Poverty Reduction Strategy Papers in conflict-affected countries, new approaches under the LICUS initiative and the links with conflict, and the Comprehensive Development Framework in conflict settings.

3.1 Levels of bank engagement

OP/BP 2.30 sets out three stages of Bank engagement in conflict-affected countries depending on the stage of the conflict and the Bank's ability to deploy its normal array of assistance instruments:

- *Watching Brief*

  The Bank may initiate a Watching Brief where normal Bank assistance is no longer possible due to conflict or its aftermath (e.g., Somalia, Sudan). The Watching Brief allows the Bank to maintain a minimum level of engagement, monitoring evolving socio-economic conditions and prospects for change, and to thus be in a better position to re-engage when conditions permit. As part of the Watching Brief, the Bank may support additional activities at the country's request.

- *Transitional Support Strategy (TSS)*

  The TSS is a short- to medium-term Bank assistance strategy for a country in transition from conflict that does not have a Country Assistance Strategy (CAS) or where conditions are not yet appropriate to prepare a full-fledged CAS (e.g., Afghanistan, Sierra Leone, Timor-Leste). The TSS may be in place for up to 24 months and may be renewed for additional periods with the endorsement of the Executive Directors.[4] A TSS is typically closely aligned with the objectives and sequencing of priorities in peace accords and recovery plans; its assistance priorities will most likely differ from those under a CAS.[5]

- *Country Assistance Strategy (CAS)*

  As a post-conflict country successfully transitions out of conflict, the Bank can revert to a normal CAS. In some instances of overt conflict, continued assistance may still be possible under a full-fledged CAS, without recourse to the Watching Brief and TSS stages, if the Bank determines it can still assist the country to meet its development objectives (e.g., Colombia, Sri Lanka).

The latest Quarterly Monitoring Report on Conflict-Affected Countries covers 41 countries and areas that are considered to be conflict-affected.[6] Of these, 6 are in non-accrual status, 3 have Watching Briefs, 13 have a TSS, and 20 are under a CAS. Over three quarters (32 countries) of the 41 conflict-affected countries are low income, of which 28 are IDA and 4 are blend countries.

The three levels of engagement set out in OP/BP 2.30 are appropriate and provide considerable flexibility to tailor Bank involvement and assistance depending

---

[4] The final TSS is made available to the public in the same manner, and subject to the same conditions, as a CAS.

[5] Priorities may include the reintegration of refugees or internally displaced populations, demining operations, demobilization and reintegration of ex-combatants, psycho-social support for traumatized populations, and targeted programs for the demobilization of child soldiers and women combatants.

[6] Countries/areas are included in the report at the discretion of the Bank's Regional Offices, using a broad definition of conflict-affected, including spillover effects from neighboring countries in active conflict.

on the stage of the conflict. The small number of Watching Briefs likely reflects the difficulties the Bank has faced in maintaining even a limited or passive monitoring effort in countries where there are little prospects for a turnaround, either in the conflict or in improved policies and governance, that would justify moving to a TSS. Implementation of the Low-Income Countries Under Stress (LICUS) Task Force recommendations aims to address these difficulties – including lack of management attention, administrative budgets and staff incentives – by proposing different modes of engagement for this group of countries (see section 3.5 below for a discussion of the relationship between LICUS and conflict-affected countries). As strategic approaches to LICUS are developed and tested, we would expect to see a greater use of the Watching Brief mode as well as a more proactive and strategic design of Watching Briefs, in line with the approach proposed for LICUS. For countries where the Bank is re-engaging under a LICUS mode, a note describing the re-engagement approach will be brought for discussion to the Board.

3.2 Conflict analysis and sensitivity to conflict

OP 2.30 calls for the integration of sensitivity to conflict in Bank assistance through analytical work, including conflict analysis. The CPR Unit has developed a Conflict Analysis Framework (CAF) to help Bank teams analyze more systematically the links between poverty and conflict when preparing strategies, policies and programs.[7] Conflict-sensitive approaches that take into account factors that can trigger or affect vulnerability to conflict may help to prevent the onset, exacerbation, or resurgence of violent conflict. The CAF has been informed by the Development Economics Research Group's (DECRG) program on the economic causes of conflict, as well as the CPR Unit's work and international best practice and experience in conflict analysis and early-warning systems methodologies.[8]

Conflict analysis frameworks can be a useful tool when applied carefully and sensitively. They can play a valuable role in assisting country teams to gain a better and more systematic understanding of the root causes of conflict and how development interventions may mitigate or worsen conflict risks – or as a minimum, ensure that Bank activities do no harm. A number of steps are being taken to encourage the use of conflict analysis tools, including: (i) development of the CAF tool as part of the Bank's social analysis methodology,[9] which allows

---

[7] World Bank, 'The Conflict Analysis Framework (CAF): Identifying Conflict-related Obstacles to Development', 4 *CPR Dissemination Notes* (2002).

[8] For a recent application of a conflict assessment framework carried out in partnership with DFID, USAID, and UNDP, see: World Bank, 'Nigeria Strategic Conflict Assessment: Methodology, Key Findings and Lessons Learnt', 11 *Social Development Notes: Conflict Prevention & Reconstruction* (2003) and Institute for Peace and Conflict Resolution. *Strategic Conflict Assessment: Consolidated and Zonal Reports.* (Abudja, Nigerian Presidency 2003).

[9] See the World Bank Social Analysis Sourcebook (August 2002) available at <www.worldbank. org/socialanalysissourcebook>.

its use as stand-alone analysis or as part of an upstream macro-social analysis; (ii) the CPR Unit in partnership with country teams will test the approach in a number of pilot countries in order to further refine the framework and demonstrate its usefulness; (iii) CAF techniques and approaches will be incorporated in the annual staff training offered by CPR in collaboration with DECRG and WBI; (iv) where there is receptivity by country teams and client governments, we will look for opportunities to incorporate conflict analysis into PRSP processes and LICUS pilot countries; and (v) the CPR Unit is developing a Peace and Conflict Impact Assessment tool, which will complement the CAF with a micro approach which can better target individual projects and programs.

3.3 A Comprehensive Development Framework (CDF) in conflict-affected countries

The CDF principles – introduced by the Bank in 1999 and adopted in 2001 – provide a sound framework for the development and implementation of OP 2.30, by introducing a holistic approach to conflict, development and poverty reduction. They reinforce the centrality of country owned development strategies implemented in partnership with all stakeholders and development partners. In 1999, the CDF Secretariat introduced a system for tracking experience with implementing the CDF principles at country level and a growing number of conflict-affected countries are covered by these assessments. A key focus has been drawing lessons across countries in different stages of transition from conflict to peace. The assessments suggest that the CDF principles have provided a basis for addressing the challenges faced by conflict-affected countries. In the short run, the CDF calls for and encourages the use of mechanisms for national dialogue and building consensus on long-term national priorities, establishing more immediate road-maps for needed reforms and the development or strengthening of systems of governance. In the long run, the CDF helps to improve development effectiveness by focusing the efforts of stakeholders and development partners on consolidating peace and achieving lasting development results.

3.4 Poverty Reduction Strategies in conflict-affected countries

The Poverty Reduction Strategy Paper (PRSP) process had not been fully developed at the time that OP/BP 2.30 was discussed with the Board. Reducing poverty is clearly a more complex and difficult task in countries affected by conflict than in peaceful ones. As noted in the Bank's most recent Quarterly Monitoring Report on Conflict-Affected Countries, 12 of the 41 conflict-affected countries had formulated an Interim-PRSP but only one had completed a PRSP. Thus, over the coming year there will be a considerable number of countries that will have to wrestle with the design and implementation of poverty reduction strategies in environments made substantially more complicated by the presence of conflict, either overt or as a high risk factor.

Countries affected by conflict face a two-way relationship between conflict and poverty – pervasive poverty makes societies more vulnerable to violent conflict, while conflict itself creates more poverty. At the same time, conflict has a negative effect on the ability of countries to formulate poverty reduction strategies. Countries emerging from violent conflict are markedly different from peaceful countries, where the challenge is to promote higher sustained growth and design effective poverty reduction policies. First and foremost, post-conflict countries face a high risk of reverting to conflict, especially during the first five years. In addition, post-conflict countries often confront massive human, physical, economic, social and institutional dislocation, and the choices they must make are correspondingly more difficult. Countries facing a high risk of conflict must also look at the development challenge through a different lens, paying particular attention to their vulnerability to conflict and the impact that strategies and policies may have in mitigating or aggravating the risk of conflict.

Although there is recognition that PRSPs for conflict-affected countries should differ from those of more peaceful ones, there is no consensus, let alone best practices, on how to integrate the conflict nexus or the key elements of conflict-affected PRSP processes. The recent report *Review of the Poverty Reduction Strategy Paper (PRSP) Approach – Main Findings*, concluded that the PRSP framework should be sufficiently flexible for the special needs of conflict-affected countries. While this is indeed the case, the report recognizes that special guidance and the development of best practices are required, for staff, governments and stakeholders, on how to support and adapt the PRSP processes in countries where conflict is an important development issue. The main objective over the short to medium term must be to consolidate peace – poverty strategies and policies cannot succeed without it. PRSPs in conflict-affected countries therefore should look and feel very different from other countries. For example, it will be important to focus on the factors that affect the risk of conflict. The quality and reliability of poverty data are likely to be lower, and so too will be the poverty diagnosis. Outcome indicators may specifically address targets and agreements in peace accords. Participatory processes and the role of civil society are likely to be very different in cases where territorial security may not be fully restored, where there are deep social, political, ethnic or religious cleavages in society, and where there is little experience with participatory processes after years of violence and mistrust. Poverty strategies will need to pay special attention to issues generated by the conflict itself, such as the removal of land-mines, the special needs of refugees, male, female and child ex-combatants, war-wounded and widows. Economic policies also need to be more flexible, taking into account the specific constraints resulting from the conflict and the primary objective of ensuring peace and political stability. Although the formulation of the full PRSP can take several years, it is nevertheless important that the process provides input at an early stage into the reconstruction program for which the broad objectives typically need to be laid out soon after the end of the conflict.

To address these issues, the CPR Unit in collaboration with the Poverty Reduction Group in PREM (PRMPR), the LICUS Unit in OPCS and the IMF, is initiating a medium-term work program to better evaluate PRSP processes in conflict-affected countries, develop specific guidance and best practices, disseminate lessons learned and provide targeted support to countries and Bank country teams that request assistance in addressing conflict and development issues in the PRSP process. This effort will be supported by DFID and will include collaboration with other PRSP partners, including UNDP and other interested bilateral donor agencies.

3.5 Low-Income Countries Under Stress (LICUS) and conflict

There is a substantial overlap between countries classified as Low-Income Countries Under Stress (LICUS) and conflict-affected countries. LICUS are significantly more prone to large-scale and violent conflict than other low-income countries. Hence policies and strategies that can mitigate the effects and reduce the risk of conflict are a greater priority in LICUS than elsewhere.[10] Poor economic performance, manifested in low growth and pervasive poverty, is itself a strong risk factor. In general terms, all LICUS are conflict-prone, although not all conflict-affected countries are LICUS.

Given the considerable overlap between LICUS and conflict-affected countries, the LICUS Unit in OPCS and the CPR Unit are developing a joint work program to support the implementation of the LICUS Task Force recommendations and to assist and guide the preparation of LICUS pilot strategies (e.g., Angola, Central African Republic, Haiti and Sudan). Since poor policies and governance failures are the defining characteristics of LICUS, bringing together conflict and governance issues has added value to our approach in conflict-affected countries. While each post-conflict situation is different, countries emerging from conflict tend to confront many of the same underlying problems of governance that affect LICUS, including: lack of confidence by economic actors; weak state capacity, especially in judicial, financial, fiscal, administrative and regulatory functions; large informal economy and parallel markets; poor economic policies; widespread unemployment, especially among the young; lack of skilled labor and low secondary school enrolment; and damaged or obsolete physical capital. These governance and institutional weaknesses markedly increase the risk that violent conflict will reignite. Given these risk factors, we expect that the combined LICUS and CPR perspectives will enrich the Bank's approach to conflict prevention and sustainable post-conflict reconstruction.

---

[10] World Bank, *World Bank Group Work in Low-Income Countries Under Stress: A Task force Report* (Washington, D.C. 2002).

4. ANALYSIS, TOOLS AND INTERVENTIONS

To complement its new policy on conflict, the Bank has been developing a set of analytical tools and interventions to better address the challenges of conflict prevention and reconstruction. Key among these has been the path-breaking research on the economics of conflict, as well as capacity and experience in a number of areas relevant for conflict-affected settings.

4.1 Understanding the causes of conflict

The Economics of Conflict. In 1999, the Bank's Development Economics Research Group (DECRG) began a major research effort to study the economics of conflict and violence.[11] As a result of its findings and the debate it has sparked, policymakers have gained considerable insight into the factors that affect the risk of violent internal conflict and its duration, including: poverty and low economic growth; the importance of primary commodities, such as diamonds and oil, in fueling conflict; the role of diasporas and ethnic dominance; and low levels of secondary school enrolments, especially for young males. In a second phase of this research, now nearing completion and in partnership with Yale University, the Bank is undertaking individual country case studies to assess the general applicability of the economics of conflict model, complementing the framework with a political economy analysis of conflict and its triggers. The results and major implications of this work have been published in a World Bank Policy Research Report.[12]

The Global Governance of Natural Resources and Conflict. Recent research undertaken by the Bank and others suggests a strong linkage between rents from natural resource extraction and violent conflict. Such revenues have fueled and financed devastating conflicts in a large number of countries and regions.[13] With support from the Norwegian Trust Fund for Environmentally and Socially Sustainable Development, the Bank has launched a Project on the Governance of Natural Resources. Its aim is to build a solid body of theoretical and applied research on the links between natural resource extraction and violent conflict, to review interventions that can be effective in enhancing the global governance of trade in these resources, to suggest practical approaches to improve the transparency of resource revenues (e.g., oil and gas) and to reduce rents from the illegal

---

[11] Information on DECRG research on conflict and the PPR can be found at <http://www.worldbank.org/research/conflict/>.

[12] *Breaking the Conflict Trap: Civil War and Development Policy* (Washington, D.C, World Bank 2002).

[13] The G8 Africa Action Plan issued during the G8 Kananaskis Summit in June 2002 states the commitment to work with African governments, civil society and others to address the linkages between armed conflict and the exploitation of natural resources.

trade in commodities with strong links to conflict (e.g., conflict rough diamonds, tropical timber, coltan and other precious metals).

Within the Bank, the Project is a combined effort involving DECRG, the CPR Unit and the joint Bank/IFC Oil and Gas Policy Division (COCPO). The Project is also mobilizing a broad coalition of international stakeholders, including the UN system, the IMF, NGOs (such as Global Witness, the Open Society Institute, Fauna and Flora International), private companies in extractive industries, and multilateral organizations including the European Commission and OECD/DAC. Following a workshop in December 2002 hosted by *Agence Française de Développement*, bringing together this wide group of stakeholders to review the results of the first round of research, the Project produced a set of policy recommendations and suggestions for global action.[14]

4.2   Conflict and development: filling gaps and new insights

As the Bank gains experience and carries out additional research on conflict and development issues, it is identifying gaps that need to be filled and developing new insights that can help to improve development effectiveness. Some recent examples include: the gender dimensions of conflict, a better understanding of the links between education and conflict, patterns of post-conflict aid and absorptive capacity, and policy reform priorities in post-conflict countries.

Gender. Women and men experience violent conflict in very different ways. As the Bank broadened its approach to conflict and in line with its continuing efforts to mainstream gender, it became clear that the gender dimensions of conflict require special attention. The challenge is not only to respond to the special but often neglected needs of women resulting from the conflict, but also to build on the positive, often temporary, changes in social structures and norms brought about by the conflict, to support more equal gender relations in reconstruction and longer-term development processes.

Experience in post-conflict reconstruction suggests that the demobilization and reintegration phase poses particular difficulties for women and girl soldiers. Demobilization programs almost exclusively focus on male ex-combatants, overlooking female combatants. When a conflict ends, female ex-combatants may suddenly become invisible – even in Angola where 30% of the armed forces were female or in Sierra Leone where females accounted for up to 30% of the RUF.[15] In addition to the female ex-combatants, there are other affected groups also neglected when peace and demobilization come. These include abducted girls, excombatants' families, war widows and women in the host community. As the Bank has built up greater experience in demobilization and reintegration pro-

[14] Ian Bannon and Paul Collier (eds.), *Natural Resources and Violent Conflict: Options and Actions* (Washington, D.C, World Bank 2003).
[15] Jennifer Michelle. n.d. 'Women and Girls in the Military'. *Unprocessed draft.*

grams, it is increasingly focusing on the special needs of female ex-combatants and other affected groups. A recent study distills key lessons.[16]

Social structures and norms are severely disrupted during conflicts. Traditionally defined roles and responsibilities are transformed as people develop survival strategies to cope with the new realities that emerge from conflict. Gender relations, in particular, are affected by conflict as women and men assume new roles and responsibilities during and after the conflict. However, once the conflict ends women and girls are generally expected to quietly revert back to their pre-conflict roles, giving up freedoms, social capital, labor market participation, political influence or networking capabilities they may have gained as a result of the conflict. Their leadership skills and experience are often downplayed. The design of post-conflict reconstruction programs needs to adopt an explicit gender focus, especially to understand these dynamics and respond to them. A recent good example is the approach adopted in Afghanistan, which emphasizes the use of local institutions and the need to provide Afghan women with the tools to develop their own gender agenda and leadership skills, as a way to effectively and less controversially engender Afghanistan's reconstruction.

Women are not solely victims of conflict, but can also make tremendous contributions to conflict resolution, management and peace building processes. Introducing a gender sensitive lens to conflict analysis frameworks and post-conflict reconstruction strategies can help in understanding both women's and men's roles as actors, not just victims. In many post-conflict situations, women are cast purely as overburdened victims of physical and mental abuse. A more careful gender analysis can bring out how women respond to difficult situations – their coping and survival strategies, their marshalling of scarce resources and the means by which they generate social capital to cope with the effects of the conflict – and how to tap these potentials during the reconstruction phase and beyond.

The Post Conflict Fund has played an important role in supporting innovative approaches to gender in conflict-affected countries. Activities funded by the PCF include:

- The UNDP-executed 'Community Action for the Reintegration and Recovery of Youth and Women' in the Democratic Republic of the Congo, to address the particular challenges women face when attempting to reintegrate into their communities and gain sustainable livelihoods;

- The 'Knitting Together Nations' project in Bosnia, to create sustainable employment opportunities for Bosnian women in inter-ethnic activities such as the production, marketing and sale of traditional knitwear;

---

[16] Nathalie de Watteville, 'Addressing Gender Issues in Demobilization and Reintegration Programs' *Africa Region Working Paper Series* (Washington, D.C, World Bank 2002).

- The 'Women Reconstructing Southern Africa' program, implemented by the African Women's Alliance for Mobilizing Action, to finance capacity-building activities for emerging women leaders in rural villages;

- The 'War Widows and Welfare project in Indonesia' with the National Commission on Violence Against Women, to help poor widows recover their economic capacities in areas of Indonesia and Timor-Leste affected by violence; and

- In Afghanistan prior to the fall of the Taliban regime, short-term job-related training for Afghan women's NGOs, and the 'Afghan Female Teachers In-Service Training' project in Peshawar (Pakistan), implemented by Save the Children USA and the Swedish Committee for Afghanistan, designed to train female Afghan teachers to educate girls in the camps but also to provide the trained female teachers that Afghanistan would need during the reconstruction phase.

Education and Conflict. The impact of conflict on education systems is profound and lasting, resulting in a shortage of resources, a reduction in access and coverage, lower teaching and learning quality, the collapse of management structures and capacity, and the undermining of core values. The recent Bank commitment to accelerate progress toward Education for All (EFA) prompted an analysis by the Education Team in the Human Development Network, of which countries were not on track to achieve EFA. The results indicated that 89 countries were not on track to achieve universal primary education by 2015, of which 29 were seriously off track. One quarter of the 60 countries not on track are conflict affected, as are over one-third of the 29 countries that are seriously off track. Clearly, conflict is a significant obstacle to achieving EFA targets.

   Although the impact of conflict on education systems, and the role that schools and education systems can play in fostering the attitudes, values and social relations that underlie much civil strife are relatively well understood, less attention has been paid to the opportunities for transformation of education systems after conflict, and of the potentially positive contribution of education to the reconstruction of post-conflict society. At the same time, although there has been considerable progress in thinking through the Bank's role in post-conflict reconstruction generally, this has not been matched by much analysis that focuses specifically on education.[17] To fill this vacuum, the Education Team, in collaboration with the CPR Unit, has launched a comprehensive study on Education and Post-Conflict Reconstruction. The main objective of the study is to review expe-

---

[17] A recent initiative can be found in Marc Sommers, 'Children, Education and War: Reaching Education for All (EFA) Objectives in Countries Affected by Conflict', 1 *Conflict Prevention and Reconstruction Unit Working Paper Series* (2002).

rience of education system reconstruction in post-conflict countries and to identify lessons that can assist in the achievement of EFA goals. The study, based on
an overview of all conflict-affected countries, and a number of desk reviews and
in-depth country case studies, will cover three broad themes: (i) the impact of
conflict on education systems; (ii) strategies for system reconstruction; and (iii)
the contribution of education to rebuilding social cohesion and social capital. The
study is expected to be completed in the second half of 2003.

   Conflict and the Spread of HIV/AIDS. War and disease have been grim
partners since the advent of war, but HIV/AIDS and its lethal nexus with conflict
now poses a new and more daunting threat. Conflict is an important vector of
HIV/AIDS, a virus responsible for killing more than ten times as many people in
Africa as the conflicts themselves.[18] Although there are a number of factors affecting the interplay of HIV/AIDS and conflict, there is also an important gender
dimension. A striking aspect of recent conflicts is the deliberate targeting of civilians and the widespread use of rape as a systematic tool of warfare. Although not
a new phenomenon, the systematic use of sexual violence against women is an
important manifestation of how recent conflicts have been waged and how indirect effects can rapidly spread to civilians. The likelihood of contracting HIV during rape is very high due to the violent nature of the act, often resulting in
wounds which facilitate infection, and the fact that in conflict settings victims are
often raped repeatedly, substantially increasing the risk of transmission. At times
of conflict, civilians, particularly women and girls, are often left in conditions of
extreme poverty as economic and social structures fray. As a result they may be
forced to rely on commercial sex to survive.

   In many low-income countries, the prevalence rates of sexually transmitted
diseases among military personnel usually exceed those of the civilian population
by a factor of two to five, and this is also true with regard to HIV. Prevalence
rates tend to be higher in conflict countries due to the more risky sexual behavior
of combatants, coupled with their living conditions, mobility, age and removal
from families and communities for long periods. As a result of large and often
massive population movements induced by armed conflict, civilians are at greater
risk of becoming infected. Displacement by conflict is often associated with undermining of social cohesion and relationships, promiscuity, inadequate shelter
and commercial sex.[19] In addition, conflicts lead to the virtual collapse of health
systems, often where peacetime access was already low to begin with. In conflict-
affected countries there is also an increased need for transfusions and blood is
less likely to be screened, increasing the risk of HIV transmission. Civilians who
manage to survive an armed conflict may still face the prospect of slow, painful
deaths years after peace has been secured. Of the 17 countries which each have

---

   [18] Stefan Elbe, 'HIV/AIDS and the Changing Landscape of War in Africa', 27 *International Security* (2002), pp. 159-177.
   [19] UNAIDS, 'HIV/AIDS and Conflict' (*UNAIDS Fact Sheet*, No. 2, July 2002).

over 100,000 children orphaned by AIDS, 13 are in conflict or highly vulnerable.[20]

As the Bank and the international community set about addressing the HIV/ AIDS pandemic, there is a need to explicitly confront the devastating interplay with conflict. In addition to presenting an additional and powerful reason to invest more heavily in preventing conflicts from erupting in the first place, there are some emerging lessons on additional steps that can be taken. These include the allocation of funds to fight the spread of HIV/AIDS in refugee camps and the provision of testing and counseling services in demobilization camps for ex-combatants. Another important emerging lesson is the need to engage directly with the armed forces and police leaderships, Ministries of Defense and other relevant line ministries, since uniformed services represent both a high-risk group and a major HIV/AIDS vector. This is, of course, an extremely difficult and delicate task and may not necessarily be a Bank comparative advantage, but international experience suggests it can be done, as in the cases of Thailand and Uganda, where substantial decreases were achieved in HIV prevalence rates in the armed forces.

Absorptive Capacity in Post-Conflict Reconstruction. As pointed out in a recent IMF paper, aid to post-conflict countries is typically abundant and can reach extraordinarily high levels – both in per capita terms and relative to the size of the economy – when the country is at the center of international attention, but tends to decline very rapidly as attention fades.[21] Ongoing and preliminary research by DECRG[22] on the role of aid in stimulating growth in post-conflict countries, suggests that: (i) increased aid is indeed effective in augmenting post-conflict growth; (ii) it needs to approximately double; and (iii) the pattern of aid disbursements should probably rise gradually during the first four years[23] and then taper back to normal levels by the end of the first post-conflict decade. Capacity to absorb aid productively is limited in the first three or four years after a conflict, but then improves – in fact, there is a transitional phase during which absorptive capacity itself is recovering.

Although further analysis is required to confirm these results, they do call attention to the need to match disbursement patterns with the absorptive capacity in post-conflict countries, the need for all donors to pay increased attention to the timing, not just the level, of financial support in post-conflict countries and the design of such support. There is a strong *a priori* case to focus most initial post-conflict assistance on building absorptive capacity, which by its very nature will

[20] Idem.

[21] Dimitri G. Demekas, Jimmy McHugh and Theodora Kosma, 'The Economics of Post Conflict Aid', *IMF Working Paper*, WP/02/198. (International Monetary Fund, Washington, D.C. 2002).

[22] World Bank, 'Aid, Policy and Growth in Post-Conflict Countries', 2 *Conflict Prevention and Reconstruction Dissemination Notes* (2002).

[23] Given the five- to eight-year disbursement profiles of most IDA grants and credits to countries recovering from conflict, IDA disbursements typically show such a gradual rise.

not involve large disbursements, and budget support especially to meet the recurrent costs of new administrations while they build up their revenue generating capacity, rather than more complex and ambitious projects that will burden absorptive capacity.

Reform Priorities. Recent research in DECRG is also looking at whether policy priorities for growth, as measured by Country Policy and Institutional Analysis (CPIA) ratings, should be distinctive in post-conflict settings. Using the broad policy categories of macro, sectoral and social in the CPIA ratings, tentative findings suggest that among policies the key priorities for improvement, relative to an otherwise similar society without a recent history of conflict, should show an earlier and stronger emphasis on social relative to macro policy priorities. The results do not imply that macro policies are not important, only that where small tradeoffs may be involved between social and macro policies, social policies, especially those that foster inclusion, should be assigned somewhat higher priority in post-conflict countries. The positive effects on growth are likely the result of a strong signaling effect for the private sector on the government's commitment to peace and reconciliation.[24]

4.3   Approaches and interventions

A number of approaches and Bank interventions in conflict settings have proven effective over the years. These include increasing emphasis on community-driven development and social capital, demobilization and reintegration programs, support for the removal of land-mines, and the role of governance and the rule of law in conflict prevention.

Social Capital, Community-Driven Development and Conflict. In addition to physical destruction, societies emerging from conflict face an erosion of bridging social capital (between different groups) and linking social capital (relations between government and communities), high levels of mistrust, deep social cleavages, and often increased ethnic or religious polarization. These conditions undermine the basis for joint community actions and the social cohesion that needs to underpin a country-owned development effort.[25] At the same time, intrastate conflicts are fought within the borders of one country, so that when peace breaks out citizens often return to their communities to live side by side with former adversaries. In recent years, the Bank has increasingly focused on the need to rebuild communities and their social capital from the bottom up, by adopting a community-driven development (CDD) approach to post-conflict re-

---

[24] *Breaking the Conflict Trap: Civil War and Development Policy.* (Washington, D.C, World Bank 2002).

[25] Nat J. Colletta and Michelle L. Cullen. *Violent Conflict and the Transformation of Social Capital: Lessons from Cambodia, Rwanda, Guatemala, and Somalia* (Washington, D.C., World Bank 2000).

construction and to development efforts in conflict-affected communities.[26] The Bank's Community Reintegration and Development Project in Rwanda relies on a CDD approach to support the reintegration of returning refugees, social rehabilitation and increased decentralization. In Colombia, the Program for Development and Peace in Magdalena Medio, supported by a Bank project, promotes a community-based participatory approach to development and peace in one of the country's most conflictive regions.[27] Indonesia's Kecamatan Development Project, launched in 1998, is based on CDD principles and operates throughout the country including areas with overt conflict or which are conflict vulnerable.

Rebuilding bridging and linking social capital is essential for sustainable reconstruction and development. The Bank's growing emphasis on, and emerging lessons from, the application of a CDD approach in conflict settings suggests that it has enormous potential to rebuild the social fabric of communities and perhaps to make communities more resilient to conflict. What has been lacking so far is a systematic evaluation of CDD approaches in conflict, an organizing conceptual framework to evaluate lessons and adaptations to different types of conflicts and country settings, quantification of its impact on social capital, interaction with different governance levels, and whether CDD approaches in conflict settings are ultimately more developmentally efficient and cost-effective. In order to begin addressing these questions, the CDD and Social Capital Group in the Social Development Department, in collaboration with the CPR Unit and WBI, are designing a 2-year research effort on CDD and conflict, supported by the Norwegian Trust Fund for Environmentally and Socially Sustainable Development. A research program with DECRG will examine ways of measuring the impact of a CDD approach on social capital in conflict-affected areas of Indonesia, relying on a control group approach to contrast the effects with communities not adopting CDD approaches.

Demobilization and Reintegration Programs. The Bank has provided assistance to 16 countries (27 projects) in the design and financing of demobilization and reintegration programs aimed at the reinsertion of former combatants into productive civilian life. Working in close partnership with the United Nations and national development agencies, who typically handle the security side during the post-conflict phase (i.e., disarmament, weapons destruction and reform of the armed forces and police), the Bank supports assistance to ex-combatants as they transition out of conflict and into productive civilian life, including, where appropriate, the financing of transitional safety nets. This includes facilitating access to productive assets, credit and training. In societies that have been torn by conflict,

[26] For a recent review of Bank experience in community-driven reconstruction programs, see Sarah Cliffe, Scott Guggenheim and Markus Kostner, *Social Development Papers: Conflict Prevention & Reconstruction*, CPR Working Paper No. 7 (Washington, D.C., World Bank 2003).

[27] World Bank, 'Colombia: Development and Peace in the Magdalena Medio Region', 6 *Conflict Prevention and Reconstruction Dissemination Notes* (2001).

reintegration is not only an economic problem, but must also involve rebuilding social capital and the ability of societies and communities to manage and become more resilient to conflict. In addition to working with ex-combatants to heal the psychological wounds of war through counseling and group support, the Bank also works with communities to rebuild the social relations and trust necessary for successful social reintegration. The special needs of child soldiers[28] and women affected by conflict[29] also receive special attention.

Demining. Bank Operational Guidelines for Financing Land Mine Clearance were issued in February 1997, although mine clearance operations were already underway in Bosnia and Croatia, and under preparation in Angola, Azerbaijan and Cambodia. The Guidelines broke new ground, not only in establishing criteria for Bank financing of demining activities but also in emphasizing the need for a commitment by recipient governments not to lay new land-mines anywhere in the country that would in any way undermine the execution or development objectives of the project. The World Bank was represented at a senior level at the 1997 Ottawa Conference to Ban Landmines and since issuing its Operational Guidelines has pursued partnerships with key actors involved in demining, including the International Committee of the Red Cross and the United Nations Mine Action Service. The CPR Unit has prepared a staff guide for the preparation and design of land-mine projects.[30]

Governance and the Rule of Law. Weak and collapsed states have also been a central part of the story of spiraling conflict. In many war-torn countries, as the state weakens the struggle for power and control over resources leads to predation and an unending cycle of violent conflict and suffering. In many cases, the illicit control and trade of natural resources allows easy access to arms and the financing of conflict. Combine this situation with a post-Cold War world of cheap and accessible weapons and there is a ready formula for civil war. With the weakening of the state's ability to provide security and the incipient privatization of violence, the rule of law often crumbles, with the greatest impact on poor and vulnerable populations, especially on their physical security, livelihoods, property and human rights.

The Bank's effort in recent years to strengthen its support for good governance, anti-corruption and the rule of law is an additional and important element in mitigating conflict risks. Fighting corruption, improving the rule of law and increasing transparency and accountability, can substantially reduce the sources of conflict. The rule of law, coupled with a functional, accessible and independent

---

[28] Beth Verthey, 'Child Soldiers: Preventing, Demobilizing and Reintegrating', *Africa Region Working Paper Series*. (Washington, D.C., World Bank 2001).

[29] Nathalie de Watteville, 'Addressing Gender Issues in Demobilization and Reintegration Programs', *Africa Region Working Paper Series* (Washington, D.C., World Bank 2002).

[30] Jacques Bure and Pierre Pont, 'Land-Mine Clearance Projects: Task Manager's Guide', *Social Development Papers: Conflict Prevention & Reconstruction*, CPR Working Paper (forthcoming).

judicial system, not only serves as a disincentive to criminality and the resolution of conflict through violent means, but is also an essential element of the enabling environment to attract foreign and domestic investment. But it is also important to address legal gender disparities that may impose severe restrictions on rights and access to economic empowerment. For example, inequities in laws and regulations can be important obstacles to the successful reintegration of female ex-combatants into civilian life. Women and girls may be legally deprived of the right to own land, women and widows may not be allowed to rent, and a combination of legal restrictions and social custom may impede women's and girls' access to the formal credit system. The law can be an important tool for empowerment and inclusion, can play a major role in making societies less vulnerable to violent conflict, and can contribute to effective reconstruction and development programs in post-conflict countries. Continued analytical work on the role of legal systems in conflict-affected countries can add considerable value to the Bank's work.

5.   FINANCING SOCIAL AND ECONOMIC RECOVERY: RECENT DEVELOPMENTS

As a critical part of its broadened approach to conflict and development, the Bank has created new financing tools and revised existing instruments in order to provide more effective and timely financial support during the post-conflict reconstruction phase. This section reviews key financing sources and modalities applied in conflict-affected countries.

5.1   Dealing with debt and arrears in post-conflict countries

Countries emerging from conflict have sizeable needs for financial assistance, and the Bank has worked with the International Monetary Fund (IMF) to help ensure that these countries have early access to financial resources once conditions warrant. Many countries emerging from conflict also have high external debt levels that can be a serious, and frequently unsustainable, drain on their resources. The Bank has worked with the IMF to help these countries access debt relief, especially under the Heavily Indebted Poor Countries (HIPC) Initiative, as soon as the necessary conditions are in place to assure that the freed resources will be appropriately used. A joint Bank-Fund paper on this issue (*Assistance to Post-conflict Countries and the HIPC Initiative*) was considered by the Boards in April 2001. That paper also described the two institutions' efforts to help resolve the difficulties of post-conflict countries with large protracted arrears.

The Bank has also worked to improve its ability to provide early support for reconstruction in countries that are showing a strong commitment to re-establishing peace. As authorized in the IDA12 agreement, FRM developed a framework for the provision of pre-arrears clearance grants to post-conflict countries with large and protracted arrears. This framework was approved by the Board on 31 July 2001. Previously, IDA resources could not be used to support the early recovery efforts of countries in arrears, thus delaying at a critical time IDA's support for peace processes and immediate post-conflict recovery efforts. The Democratic Republic of Congo and Afghanistan have so far benefited from pre-arrears clearance grants. IDA has also helped the recovery efforts in Timor-Leste and Kosovo, which were not members of IDA.

5.2   Increasing financial flows: IDA modifications

In response to the challenges posed by the special circumstances of post-conflict countries, the IDA13[31] agreement endorses a new methodology to enable the Bank to more systematically calibrate IDA's response to the different post-conflict phases. While this methodology sharpens the focus on performance – in line with the stronger emphasis on performance in all IDA countries – it also emphasizes the need for judgment in taking account of the complexities and heterogeneity of post-conflict settings. Performance is measured by a set of Post-Conflict Progress Indicators (PCPI) and allows for the provision of exceptional levels of IDA resources to eligible countries for a limited period (three years, which can be extended for up to two more years). Following this exceptional period a country will normally be expected to return to IDA's regular allocation process. The precise level of resources is determined on the basis of a set of performance indicators designed specifically for post-conflict countries. PCPI indicators include performance on governance, human security, and progress toward peace, all of which are critical factors for assessing the stability and readiness of a country to use additional resources effectively.

Another key change in IDA13 is the authorization of an expanded use of IDA grants during the IDA13 period, in the range of 18 to 21% of overall IDA13 resources. Post-conflict countries, eligible for exceptional IDA allocations based on PCPI ratings, may receive up to 40% of their IDA allocation as grants for a limited period, once their arrears have been cleared.[32] Furthermore, in special cases, grants could be made available to territories within member countries that are under UN administration on an interim basis. Within this allocation and grants envelope, post-conflict countries with large and protracted arrears will continue to be also eligible for limited grant financing prior to arrears clearance under the same provisions as in IDA12. Countries currently classified as post-conflict un-

---

[31] IDA13 refers to the 13th replenishment of IDA, the World Bank's concessional lending facility.

[32] The precise percentage varies annually depending on the number of eligible post-conflict countries, and on other claims on the overall amount of IDA13 grant resources. For FY03 the percentage is set at 29%.

der IDA guidelines are: Afghanistan, Angola, Burundi, Democratic Republic of Congo, Republic of Congo, Eritrea, Guinea-Bissau, and Sierra Leone, in addition to the UN Managed Territory of Kosovo.

5.3   Responding to crises and supporting innovations: the Post-Conflict Fund

The Post-Conflict Fund (PCF), part of the Bank's Development Grant Facility (DGF), was set up in August 1997 to support countries in transition from conflict to sustainable peace and economic development. The aim of the PCF is to position the Bank through constructive engagement in countries where normal instruments cannot be used or may not be appropriate. PCF grants place a premium on: (i) innovative approaches to conflict and development; (ii) partnerships with donors, the UN system and NGOs; (iii) appropriate exit strategies, especially in terms of potential for replicability and scaling up; and (iv) scope for using grants to leverage additional funding and thus enhance impact. The PCF Secretariat in the CPR Unit coordinates, reviews and screens proposals, and monitors existing grants. Proposals are approved by the PCF Committee, a Director-level committee including representatives from the Social Development Department, the CPR Unit, Regional Vice-Presidencies, DGF and the Legal Department. Grants can range from $25,000 to $1million, which can be exceeded for multi-year programs.

As with the Bank's evolving approach to conflict, the PCF has also evolved and adapted to new demands. In June 1999, the Executive Directors endorsed trust fund status for the PCF to enable donor contributions and more efficient management of funds in the 'stop-start' environment of operations in conflict-affected countries.[33] The range of grant proposals that could be considered was also broadened, in line with the broadened mandate provided by OP/BP 2.30, including, for example, conflict analysis, capacity building, community development, youth-at-risk, psycho-social and mental health in post-conflict populations, and focused research on the causes of conflict. With the demand for support exceeding the availability of funds, PCF is currently exploring collaboration with the LICUS Unit to harmonize work programs and help enhance the PCF funding base.

The PCF was subject to an independent external evaluation completed in February 2002,[34] which found that the Fund had broken new ground and generated new partnerships. In spite of the high risk context, the evaluation noted the high

---

[33] To date, the PCF has received contributions from the Netherlands, Belgium, Switzerland, UNDP and UNHCR accounting for 9.5% of total committed funds, with the remainder ($48.9 million) coming from the Bank's net income through DGF.

[34] Robert Muscat and Michael Morfit, *Breaking New Ground: An Independent Evaluation of the World Bank Post-Conflict Fund* (Maryland, Development Alternatives, Inc. Bethesda 2002).

performance ranking of grants. It concluded that the PCF now needed to enhance its knowledge management role by feeding the experience back into mainstream Bank operations. The PCF Secretariat has developed a strategy to implement the evaluation's recommendations over the next three years.

Grant approvals over the first five years of the PCF total $53.5 million for 110 projects across 30 countries, with commitments running at 84% and disbursements at a healthy 73%. The Africa and ECA regions have received the highest share of approved grants (37% and 32%, respectively). Partners have included governments, transitional authorities, UN agencies and a variety of NGOs.[35] Examples of PCF grants include:

- In Afghanistan, prior to the fall of the Taliban regime, a watching brief to support economic and sectoral analyses, and a teacher training program for Afghan refugees in Pakistan, targeting women and girls;

- In Somalia, a grant to support delivery of health services through the International Federation of Red Cross and Red Crescent Societies, and a watching brief focusing on macroeconomic and socioeconomic data collection and analysis;

- In Tajikistan, a project to empower women through socioeconomic development;

- A grant for capacity building and development in Timor-Leste;

- The Travnik mental health program in Bosnia addressing the psycho-social legacies of conflict;

- An institutional capacity-building program for demobilization and reintegration in Eritrea;

- A program for the reintegration of vulnerable street children in urban areas of the Democratic Republic of Congo;

- A grant to support local capacity building in demining in Sri Lanka; and

- In Yugoslavia, the Southern Serbia Municipal Improvement and Recovery Program to reinforce inclusive local development efforts in the Presevo Valley.

---

[35] Information on all approved PCF grants can be found at <www.worldbank.org/pcf>.

5.4   Leveraging resources: Multi-Donor Trust Funds

Multi-Donor Trust Funds are often used to mobilize resources and provide flexible financing mechanisms in conflict environments, especially to fund activities considered essential or urgent by the recipient government and donor community, and which are not easily covered through normal Bank or donor funding mechanisms.[36] In some instances and on a case-by-case basis, the Bank has utilized its net income to make grants to post-conflict countries before a normal lending relationship can resume and has leveraged these resources by establishing multi-donor trust funds. The Holst Fund in West Bank Gaza was a pioneering example of this financing formula for conflict countries. Examples of such funding arrangements include:

- West Bank Gaza: the $269 million Holst Fund (with 27 donors) coupled with a $380 million trust fund from Bank net income;

- Bosnia: $150 million trust fund for emergency projects ($25 million in grants, $125 million in concessional loans);

- Kosovo: a $60 million two-year trust fund financed from Bank net income, following initial PCF funding for priority community driven projects and recurrent education and health expenditures;

- Timor-Leste: a $80 million multi-donor trust fund started with $10 million of Bank net income, and initial PCF funding following a joint assessment mission;

- Sierra Leone: administration of a $12 million multi-donor trust fund for disarmament, demobilization and reintegration, in tandem with a $25 million IDA credit for the reintegration of war-affected populations; and

- Greater Great Lakes Region: $350 million trust fund for demobilization and reintegration.

6.   KNOWLEDGE MANAGEMENT AND PARTNERSHIPS

The CPR Unit, in collaboration with internal and external partners, plays a key role in the development and diffusion of innovative research on the root causes of

---

[36] A review of the World Bank's experience with Multi-Donor Trust Funds in post-conflict reconstruction can be found in Salvatore Schiavo-Campo, 'Financing and Aid Management Arrangements in Post-Conflict Situations' *Social Development Papers: Conflict Prevention & Reconstruction*, CPR Working Paper No. 6 (Washington D.C., World Bank 2003).

conflict, the aggregation and synthesis of good practices and lessons learned, provision of training for Bank staff and management of a number of important external partnerships related to conflict and development.

6.1   Best practices and lessons learned

Over recent years, the Bank has gained considerable knowledge based on its operational experience and analytical work on conflict-affected countries. The challenge is to process, distill and make this knowledge available to staff who have to address the special developmental challenges posed by violent conflict. This process of accumulating knowledge and good practices is being strengthened in the Bank. In some areas, such as the demobilization and reintegration of ex-combatants, the design of post-conflict reconstruction programs, or the removal of landmines, the Bank already has considerable experience and its best practice lessons are helping in the design and implementation of assistance strategies in a number of countries. A CPR good practice guide is being compiled and developed by the CPR Unit to further strengthen Bank knowledge and capacity in responding to the needs of conflict-affected countries.[37]

6.2   Staff development and capacity building

Continuous staff training and development is an important part of building Bank capacity to assist conflict-affected countries. To ensure that Bank staff are better equipped to respond to the more complex development challenges posed by countries emerging from conflict, the Bank first developed its own training module on war to peace transition. More recently and in line with the broadened mandate on conflict provided by OP/BP 2.30, the CPR Unit in collaboration with DECRG and the World Bank Institute (WBI), developed a consolidated three-day training course, *Development and Conflict: Operational Agenda*, last offered in March 2003 in Washington, D.C. Although mainly directed at Bank staff, the course reserved a few places for interested external partners. This training course will be offered annually and will be periodically updated as the Bank builds its store of knowledge and operational experience on conflict and development. In addition, the CPR Unit in collaboration with internal and external partners regularly sponsors workshops, seminars and publications on conflict-related issues, aimed at keeping staff updated on evolving issues and practices.

6.3   External partnerships

Probably more than in other settings, cooperation and partnerships with other stakeholders is critical in conflict settings. The increasingly complex political, so-

---

[37] The CPR Good Practice Database, which is still under development, can be accessed at: http://lnweb18.worldbank.org/ESSD/essd.nsf/CPR/GPHomePage

cial, economic and international dimensions of conflict require that the Bank works in close partnership with other key actors and stakeholders. This includes the UN system, regional banks and organizations, as well as NGOs and civil society organizations.

Working with the UN at the Institutional and Country Level. UN Secretary General Kofi Annan has made the challenges of the prevention of armed conflict one of the top priorities of his second term. In 2000, the Secretary General released his *Report on the Prevention of Armed Conflict,* calling for a paradigm shift from a culture of reaction to a culture of prevention and setting out his vision to develop the conflict prevention capacity of the UN. The prevention of armed conflict was a prominent theme during the Millennium Summit, when leaders of the world supported the Secretary General's call to move from a culture of reaction to a culture of prevention. Building on the Secretary General's *Report on the Prevention of Armed Conflict* and his report on the follow-up to the Millennium Declaration, the Heads of all UN Agencies (UN System Chief Executives Board) last year agreed that the conflict prevention and the development agendas should be mutually reinforcing, stressing the drain in resources brought about by conflict-resources that could otherwise be devoted to development.

The Bank, while fully respecting its apolitical approach, has joined several UN standing bodies with observer status: the Executive Committee on Peace and Security, a high-level advisory and coordinating body; the Framework Team for Coordination, a mechanism for early warning and preventive action among 14 UN participating departments, program and agencies; and the UN Development Group. While the Bank does not provide humanitarian relief, it participates in the Inter-Agency Standing Committee and seeks to strengthen coordination with UNHCR and UNDP during conflict emergencies and the humanitarian and relief phases of post-conflict reconstruction. The Bank also takes part selectively in the Mine Action Advisory Group.

From an operational perspective, the Bank has either co-led or joined assessment missions to post-conflict countries, such as Timor-Leste, Eritrea, the Republic of Congo and Afghanistan. Together with the UN Secretariat and agencies, we are exploring possible collaboration on strategies for conflict-affected regions, in Central Asia and West Africa.

Three important collaborative efforts have been recently agreed with the UN. The first is the partnership with UNHCR and UNDP to promote a more integrated approach to address the repatriation, reintegration, rehabilitation and reconstruction needs (the '4Rs' approach) of refugees and internally displaced persons in countries emerging from conflict. The joint effort is designed to be a country-owned, bottom-up approach, taking specific country cases to determine how country teams in the field can best work together to smooth the transition from relief to post-conflict reconstruction and development, and to build a body of best practices on successful transitions. Following consultations with respective country teams, Eritrea, Sierra Leone and Sri Lanka have been identified as pilot countries. The second axis of collaboration is around the LICUS partnership with UNDP, where four pilots are also under way (Angola, Central African Republic, Somalia and Sudan) to develop and implement LICUS country strategies in line with the recommendations of the LICUS Task Force. The third is the joint review with UNDP of recent experiences in the preparation of Needs Assessments in Post-Conflict Reconstruction. The study, funded jointly by the CPR Unit and UNDP's Bureau of Crisis Prevention and Recovery, is being carried out by GTZ.

Working with the IMF. The IMF provides assistance to countries emerging from conflict in three ways: technical assistance with a focus on rebuilding capacity to formulate and implement economic policies; economic policy advice; and financial assistance, including through the IMF's emergency post-conflict assistance facility which can be accessed at a relatively early post-conflict stage. Emergency post-conflict assistance can be provided in those situations where: (i) there is an urgent balance of payments need to help rebuild reserves; (ii) the country's institutional and administrative capacity is disrupted as a result of the conflict so that the member country is not yet able to develop and implement a comprehensive economic program that could be supported by a Fund arrangement; (iii) there is nonetheless sufficient capacity for policy planning and implementation, and demonstrated commitment on the part of the authorities (to provide adequate safeguards for the use of Fund resources); and (iv) Fund support would be part of a concerted international effort to address the aftermath of the conflict in a comprehensive way. IMF staff are in the process of reviewing the Fund's experience in assisting post-conflict countries, with a focus on its economic policy advice, to see if there are lessons to be learned and ways to make the assistance more effective.

As discussed throughout this paper, the Bank will continue to work closely with the Fund in a number of key areas in support of conflict-affected countries. These include the need to apply the PRSP framework flexibly in conflict-affected countries, the clearance of arrears and early access to HIPC in post-conflict countries, and close collaboration among country teams in the design of post-conflict reconstruction programs and capacity building in economic policy and public administration.

Partnering with Conflict Networks. The Bank has played an active role in contributing to policy formulation, and in disseminating and facilitating the exchange of knowledge among key players working on conflict-related issues. This is a critical two-way street, as the Bank also gains tremendously from the knowledge and experience of external partners. The Bank is an active member of two key international conflict networks designed to exchange knowledge and experiences in the conflict field. The first is the OECD/DAC Network on Conflict, Peace and Development Cooperation (CPDC). The Bank participated actively in CPDC's extensive work to develop guidance on conflict prevention for OECD members, issued in 2001 (OECD, 2001). The second is the Conflict Prevention and Post-Conflict Reconstruction Network (CPRN), which the Bank helped to establish and is a more informal network of agencies, governments, NGOs and think-tanks involved in conflict-related work. CPRN has a rotating chair and a focus on implementation issues relative to OECD/DAC's focus on policy development.

Regional Banks and Organisations. Over the past decade, regional banks have become important actors in international efforts to assist conflict-affected countries and they have been strengthening their capacities in conflict mitigation and post-conflict reconstruction. For example, in post-conflict countries or regions, such as Cambodia, Timor-Leste and Mindanao in the Philippines, the Bank and the Asian Development Bank (ADB) are closely coordinating their activities. Collaboration with ADB, as well as with the Islamic Development Bank is also being strengthened in the reconstruction of Afghanistan. A Memorandum of Understanding between the African Development Bank (AfDB) and the World Bank, including post-conflict collaboration, is being operationalized. As part of this agreement, the Bank is discussing extending Bank training in conflict and development to staff from AfDB. In Latin America, the Bank has worked closely with the Inter-American Development Bank supporting donor coordination and reconstruction programs in Central America, and more recently in formulating an approach to Haiti, also in collaboration with the Organization of American States and the Pan-American Health Organization.

Further efforts are required to strengthen collaboration with the EU/EC and the European Bank for Reconstruction and Development. While Bank country teams work closely with counterpart teams in the Commission and EBRD in a number of conflict-affected countries, there is a need to improve collaboration and working arrangements at the central, policy level – as is the case with other multilateral bodies such as the IMF and UN system, and key bilaterals.

Working with NGOs. NGOs and other civil society organizations participate actively in many Bank programs in conflict-affected countries. At a broader level, the Bank held consultations and discussions with key international NGOs in preparing OP/BP 2.30 and has since maintained an active dialogue with interested NGOs on its implementation. In addition, NGOs are major recipients of PCF grants. Over 30 non-governmental entities have received PCF grants, including: Save the Children, Catholic Relief Services, CARE, the International Federation of Red Cross and Red Crescent Societies, International Committee of the Red Cross and ACTIONAID, as well as a number of local NGOs.

7.   CONCLUSIONS

Although the World Bank has come a long way in recent years in addressing the nexus between conflict and development, it cannot yet claim to be smoothly operating as a vital cog in the much-sought humanitarian-development continuum. But, the process of institutional adaptation inside the organization, the Bank's willingness to learn from its own experience and the convergence of external factors, has greatly contributed to a narrowing of the gap. At the same time, as the World Bank continuously adapts and evolves, the process is generating new questions and issues, which will pose additional challenges in the years to come.

Adoption of OP/BP 2.30 has made a major contribution to the Bank's ability to address issues of conflict and development. It provides a comprehensive and flexible framework within which to frame Bank assistance to countries affected by conflict. Since the adoption of the new policy, the Bank has made considerable progress, building on strong internal and external partnerships, in developing the tools and the analytical and operational underpinnings needed to implement its new policy. As a result of the impetus provided by OP/BP 2.30, concerted effort across Bank networks and the dedication and commitment of country teams working in difficult conflict environments, the Bank has been able to build considerable knowledge and expertise in a very challenging area, and as a result is now seen as making a major and leading contribution to the efforts by the international community to build a safer world and thus to contribute more effectively to a world free of poverty.

Looking ahead, we expect to continue to focus on drawing lessons from the Bank's involvement in a wide range of conflict-affected countries. The fact that every conflict is different requires us to constantly evaluate and assess our various approaches and interventions, and, with our partners in the international community, to continue to develop and fine-tune our tools and instruments. In parallel, we need to deepen the Bank's path-breaking work on understanding the root causes of conflict and extract from it policy prescriptions and actionable recommendations.

Looking inside the Bank, we face an important but complex challenge in more fully integrating a sensitivity to conflict in Bank assistance, including more targeted and tailor-made advice on PRSP processes in conflict-prone settings. In addition, there are a number of areas that intersect with conflict and where we need to deepen our understanding of complex interactions or fill important knowledge gaps. These include the links between HIV/AIDS and conflict, the role of education systems in creating greater resilience to or exacerbating the risks of conflict, more integrated consideration of gender and conflict, and the role that CDD approaches can play in reweaving the social fabric of war-torn societies. An important area requiring greater attention is the rule of law, and how to ensure that it contributes to empowerment and inclusion, and ultimately to making societies less prone to violent conflict. Discussions are underway across networks to better define the issues and develop work programs across Bank units that can deepen our knowledge and improve our operational practices.

PART THREE

EXPERIENCE OF OTHER ACTORS

PART THREE B

OTHER ACTORS

Chapter 23
PREVENTING CONFLICT: A EU-INTERNATIONAL
COMMITTEE OF THE RED CROSS COMMON INTEREST

by Stéphane Kolanowski[1]

1. INTRODUCTION

The International Committee of the Red Cross (ICRC) has worked around the world since 1863 to protect and assist those affected by an armed conflict or internal violence. It is a humanitarian organisation with its headquarters in Geneva, mandated by the international community[2] to act as the guardian of international humanitarian law, and is the founding body of the International Red Cross and Red Crescent Movement.

It is interesting to note – and this is important to better understand the ICRC's role and position in conflict situations – that the ICRC has a unique status in international law, placing it outside the traditional dichotomy of International Organisations *versus* NGOs. Indeed, the ICRC is not composed of Member States; it is not an intergovernmental organisation. On the other hand, it is not an NGO in the traditional sense of the term for many reasons. Among the most important of these reasons, one can identify the mandate which the ICRC has received from the international community and its special relationship with States. This relationship allows the ICRC to have a constant and close dialogue with States and, at the same time, to remain independent. Only if it is free to act independently of any government or other authority can the ICRC serve the interests of victims of conflicts (the need for dialogue with all the parties to a conflict, and access to the victims), which lies at the heart of its humanitarian mission. A rather extensive State and international organisation practice has emerged to reinforce this *sui generis* status, such as the granting of observer status at the UN General Assembly, the numerous seat agreements which the ICRC has signed,

---

[1] Stéphane Kolanowski (LL.M.) is a Legal Advisor to the ICRC Delegation to the European Union, Brussels. The views and opinions expressed in this contribution are the author's alone and do not necessarily reflect the views and opinions of the ICRC.

[2] The ICRC's mandate is to be found in the four Geneva Conventions of 12th August 1949 and their Additional Protocols of 8th June 1977. As of 1st October 2003, 191 States are party to the 1949 Conventions.

V. Kronenberger and J. Wouters, eds., The European Union and Conflict Prevention
© 2004, T·M·C·ASSER PRESS, *The Hague, The Netherlands*

and the granting of some privileges before national and international jurisdictions.[3]

The role of the ICRC is described in its mission statement as follows:

'The International Committee of the Red Cross is an impartial, neutral and independent organization whose exclusively humanitarian mission is to protect the lives and dignity of *victims of war and internal violence* and to provide them with assistance. It directs and coordinates the international relief activities conducted by the [International Red Cross and Red Crescent] Movement in *situations of conflict*. It also endeavours to prevent suffering by promoting and strengthening *international humanitarian law* and universal humanitarian principles'.

This extract from the ICRC mission statement is rather clear: the ICRC is working *in* situations of armed conflict and internal violence. One may then ask why the ICRC considers conflict prevention to be part of its activities while this should really be outside the scope of its operations.

In fulfilling its mandate, the ICRC is driven by the principles of humanity, which means that everything has to be done to protect the lives and dignity of human beings, including doing the utmost possible to prevent suffering. In an ideal world, the ICRC would be useless, but one has to acknowledge that we are far from living in an ideal world. Indeed the concept of conflict prevention has to be understood in a broad sense, which includes not only preventing a conflict from occurring, but also, in a tense or conflict situation, preventing the worsening of a situation, preventing atrocities from occurring, preventing the spread of a conflict, and preventing the resumption of a conflict. We believe that activities which help to achieve a long-lasting peace are also, in a sense, conflict prevention activities.

In this brief contribution, we will try to show how the ICRC can contribute to conflict prevention, and how the European Union (EU) and the ICRC can work in a complementary fashion (while fully respecting of the ICRC's independence!) towards a common goal.

2. THE INTERNATIONAL COMMITTEE OF THE RED CROSS AND CONFLICT PREVENTION

The ICRC's contribution to preventing conflict is rather modest, but not non-existent and certainly not insignificant.[4] Gustave Moynier[5] already stressed this in

---

[3] For more details, see A. Lorite Escorihuela, 'Le Comité international de la Croix-Rouge comme organisation *sui generis*, remarques sur la personnalité juridique internationale du CICR', 3 *Revue Générale de Droit International Public* (2001), pp. 581-616.

[4] This part is based on J.-L. Blondel, 'Rôle du CICR en matière de prévention des conflits armés: possibilités d'action et limites', 844 *RICR* (2001), pp. 923-946; as well as on the Guidelines on con-

the very first days of the ICRC while shaping what would later become the International Red Cross and Red Crescent Movement (hereafter, the 'Movement').

While speaking of the Movement and conflict prevention, it is worth keeping in mind the definition of peace given by the Movement in 1986 and included in the Preamble of its Statute:[6] 'by its humanitarian work and the dissemination of its ideals, the Movement promotes a lasting peace, which is not simply the absence of war, but is a dynamic process of cooperation among all States and peoples, cooperation founded on respect for freedom, independence, national sovereignty, equality, human rights, as well as on a fair and equitable distribution of resources to meet the needs of peoples'. Peace is indeed a dynamic process and requires constant attention and a long-term commitment. The ICRC motto *per humanitatem ad pacem* also shows the ICRC's position regarding conflict prevention.

In a way, the prevention dimension is present in most ICRC activities. Indeed, preventive action includes different elements that are always present, but in varying degrees depending on the situation. Such elements signal the imminence or the probability of an event or a crisis (alerting, informing, giving early warning), thereby providing the possibility to prepare oneself by anticipating possible events and undergoing specific training, finally preventing violations of international humanitarian law. This, however, does not comprise a pre-established range of activities.

With regard to the prevention of armed conflict, the main role of the ICRC is to urge States to adopt the necessary measures and, when appropriate, to supply them with information and analysis to help them assume their responsibilities in a more pertinent way. The ICRC is bound by its principle of neutrality, which has as its consequence that the ICRC cannot play a role in political negotiations aimed at averting an imminent armed conflict, but it can, on occasion, make a significant contribution through preventive diplomacy, its good offices and the creative use of its role as a neutral intermediary. The ICRC will not, however, take any initiative that could result in a party to a conflict restricting access to the victims of that conflict, or that might endanger its delegates or employees. In the missile crisis in Cuba (1962) for instance, the ICRC was asked by both parties to set up a system of ship inspections in order to ease the tensions between the protagonists. The ICRC accepted the request, even though inspecting ships, especially within the framework of an embargo, is not really what the ICRC is supposed to do. In that particularly tense context, the ICRC believed that this was

---

flict prevention adopted by the ICRC Assembly Council on 28 January 2002 as a chapter of its doctrine (the public version of the text can be found in 846 *Revue internationale de la Croix-Rouge (RICR)* (2002), pp. 463-466).

[5] A. Durand, 'Gustave Moynier and the peace societies', 314 *RICR* (1996), pp. 532-550.

[6] 'Adoption of the Statues and the Rules of Procedure of the International Red Cross and Red Crescent Movement', in *Report of the 25th International Conference of the Red Cross, Geneva 23 to 31 October 1986*, 256 *RICR* (1986), pp. 340-388.

an important task in order to prevent the outbreak of a conflict that could have been on a huge scale, and the fact that the parties trusted the ICRC to carry out such a sensitive task meant that this was probably the only organisation which was able to carry out such work. The way in which events turned out made the inspections irrelevant, and the ICRC never in fact embarked on such inspections. Nevertheless, the debate and the thinking behind these events were quite instructive in many aspects, including the role of the ICRC in easing tension on the eve of a potential conflict.

When peace initiatives fail and conflict breaks out, the preventive effort does not cease entirely but is transformed into a drive to promote respect for international humanitarian law. This body of law is a core element of the protection of victims of armed conflict. Its development, dissemination and implementation form an integral part of the protection of individuals in such troubled times. By spreading knowledge of humanitarian law and monitoring its application, it is possible to avert, or at least limit, abuses and to prevent their recurrence. The rules protect the victims, and the purpose of all ICRC activities in this area is precisely to ensure that the rules laid down by humanitarian law are respected, and thus to forestall violations. Experience has taught us that compliance with the law enhances security, and respect for humanitarian law facilitates the resumption of dialogue between the parties, the conduct of the necessary negotiations and the restoration of peace.

During conflict situations, the ICRC can also act as a facilitator and lend its good offices to assist warring parties to resume contact with each other, either to address humanitarian problems caused by the conflict or to seek a political solution thereto, it being understood that the ICRC itself will not take part in political discussions on the settlement of the conflict.

The end of active hostilities never means that peace is fully restored, and many enormous challenges remain. The capacity of the ICRC to prevent the initial outbreak of an armed conflict is limited, although it can do much to create a climate of respect for the individual through its educational work and its efforts to promote human dignity. It can, on the other hand, play an important part in the prevention of renewed conflict, by helping to establish conditions which are conducive to reconciliation and social reconstruction and thereby to consolidate peace. For the same purpose, the Movement as a whole, thanks to the complementary nature of its components' mandates and expertise, can carry out vital work on a long-term basis.

The three approaches (before, during and after a conflict) are present in all ICRC activities and are also reflected in its structure and organisation. For instance, the ICRC has assigned an active role to regional delegations[7] in analysing

---

[7] The ICRC has regional delegations in Abidjan, Dakar, Harare, Lagos, Nairobi, Pretoria, Yaounde, Bangkok, Kuala Lumpur, New Delhi, Suva, Tachkent, Buenos Aires, Caracas, Mexico City, Budapest, Kyev, Moscow, Washington, Kuwait and Tunis.

situations, anticipating crises, providing extensive training in and the formation of international humanitarian law, as well as increasing cooperation with the National Red Cross and Red Crescent Societies to improve their emergency preparedness. Such activities are of particular importance in terms of conflict prevention.

It must be underlined that a major effort is being undertaken to develop international humanitarian law and to promote its implementation. The ICRC's active participation in international legal work aimed at providing more effective protection for the individual, at preventing excessive violence and the use of excessively cruel weapons or weapons that cause unnecessary suffering is also part of a consistent approach to preventive actions.

The work of the ICRC's Protection Division is a crucial one, not only concerning the immediate consequences for the individual entitled to legal protection, but also in the mid to long term when trying to achieve a long-lasting peace. Indeed, by preventing torture, by promoting decent conditions of detention, by tracing people and bringing family members together, the ICRC is working towards preparing a favourable environment for reconciliation and peace.

One must not forget the teaching of international humanitarian law and the spreading of its principles. Armed forces, police and security forces, universities, but also schools form an audience of particular interest to the ICRC. It is worth mentioning a programme called 'Exploring humanitarian law' that the ICRC has developed for young people. Exploring humanitarian law is an educational programme aiming to introduce adolescents to the basic rules of international humanitarian law and to help them embrace principles of humanity in their daily lives and the way they assess events at home and abroad.

This programme was first implemented in Northern Ireland and it immediately had a rather positive impact on young people in that country. Today, this programme is carried out in many countries throughout the world, including in the Russian Federation, Israel and the Occupied and Autonomous Territories, Serbia and Montenegro, as well as many other countries in Europe, the Middle East, Africa, Asia and the Americas. Although this body of law applies to conflict situations, it conveys a powerful message concerning the value of human dignity, which can encourage individuals and groups to desist from violence and thereby to peacefully settle disputes.

During the last International Red Cross and Red Crescent Conference (the 28th International Conference, 2-6 December 2003), the 15 EU Member States and the 10 acceding countries commonly pledged to promote awareness of International Humanitarian Law and its principles, including to young people, for instance on the basis of that specific programme.[8]

---

[8] The pledges can be found on the ICRC web site. See, as an example, the Italian pledge at <http://www.icrc.org/APPLIC/P128e.nsf/va_PBA/4EB5E3A220719B57C1256DF3004BFE3F? openDocument&section=PBP>.

A series of other activities also have a role to play in terms of conflict prevention, but these cannot be developed in such a brief contribution. These activities are, for instance, ones which are linked to the demobilisation of combatants, including child soldiers, or a sensitive approach to post-conflict rehabilitation.

It must be underlined that the particular status of the ICRC, not being an intergovernmental organisation but having a particular relationship with States (as party to the Geneva Conventions of 1949), as well as the structure of the Movement, allow the Red Cross and the Red Crescent to be present and active at each and every level of society, and in virtually each and every country. Such a wide presence, and the confidence that the Movement is able to gain with different actors are key elements to an effective conflict prevention policy.

3. THE EU AND INTERNATIONAL COMMITTEE OF THE RED CROSS: A COMMON INTEREST IN PREVENTING CONFLICTS

Before presenting some aspects of the relationship between the EU and the ICRC, it must be stressed that the ICRC maintains and develops relations not only with the EU, but also with most of the international and regional organisations.[9] The ICRC being neutral, impartial, and independent – and willing to be perceived as such – it is essential to maintain dialogue with different relevant organisations in different parts of the world. The level of dialogue will of course depend on the structures and competences of the organisations.

Already in 1968 the ICRC had contact with the European Communities, which were financially supporting the ICRC relief activities in Nigeria (Biafra). Since then the relationship has increased, especially with the development of the EU's Common Foreign and Security Policy (CFSP) and the opening of the ICRC Delegation to the EU in June 1999. It may be recalled that the EU itself is a successful example of conflict prevention. Preventing new conflict from occurring in Europe was both at the origin and the driving force of the construction of Europe and, today, of its enlargement, which in a way is a project designed to promote reconciliation, stability and peace.

Most EU-ICRC cooperation in terms of conflict prevention takes place in the form of constant dialogue, at different levels, in Brussels as well as in the field. This dialogue is reinforced by important financial support and substantial political support to the ICRC which the EU expresses both officially and publicly.

It is important for the ICRC to maintain constant dialogue with international actors such as the EU. At the field level there is regular dialogue between the

---

[9] The ICRC not only has a close relationship with the United Nations system, but also – among others – with the Council of Europe, the OSCE, NATO, the Movement of Non-Aligned Countries, ASEAN, the League of Arab States, the Organisation of Islamic Conference, the Organisation of American States, the African Union, the East African Community, the Economic Community of Western African States, the Southern African Development Community, etc.

ICRC Delegations and the Representations of the European Commission as well as with the Member States. Such dialogue is essential as it allows discussions and an exchange of views and analysis between people living in the same tense situation. Discussions on specific situations are also carried out in Brussels with ICRC personnel from the field or from the headquarters (Geneva) placing the dialogue in a broader context.

The ICRC maintains regular dialogue in Brussels with the European Parliament, the European Commission, and the Council of the EU, including the General Secretariat.

With the European Parliament this dialogue takes the form of hearings, mainly before the Development and the Foreign Affairs Committees. Bilateral discussions with some Members of the European Parliament or some administrators can also occur when there is a specific interest. Exchanges of views and opinions are more substantive with the Commission and the Council due to their respective roles and responsibilities. On a regular basis, the ICRC Head of Delegations (field) or Head of operations for a specific area (Headquarters) visit interlocutors from the Commission (DG Development, including ECHO – the European Community Humanitarian Office, and DG External Relations), as well as from the General Secretariat of the Council of the EU. Senior ICRC officials are also invited, when necessary, to brief some Council Working Groups on topics or situations and to present them with the ICRC perspective and opinion. Such discussions are very useful for both the ICRC and the EU institutions in operational terms, including in terms of conflict prevention, within the meaning explained above.

During the last few years, the ICRC has entered into a structured dialogue with the EU that is not limited to discussions on specific situations, but also includes strategic dialogue with the Commission and the Council at the level of the ICRC Director of Operations and the ICRC President. Such dialogue permits problems to be addressed in their global context and it also permits going beyond a specific country or region in situation analysis, including regional or international efforts towards preventing conflicts. For instance, the ICRC Director of Operations meets annually with the Director General for External Relations from the Council of the EU's General Secretariat; he maintains regular dialogue with the Policy Unit advising the CFSP High Representative, Mr Javier Solana; and he conducts a yearly strategic dialogue with the ECHO's senior officials. The ICRC President is invited every six months (under each Presidency) to brief the Political and Security Committee (PSC) within the Council on issues of concern to the ICRC. These issues can of course involve questions related to conflict prevention. He also meets, when necessary, with the CSFSP High Representative, as well as the Commissioner for Development and the Commissioner for External Relations.

The EU institutions issued several documents on conflict prevention. We will not go into their substance and indeed, that is not the purpose of this contribution, but it is worth mentioning that most of them refer to international humanitarian law and/or to the ICRC. For instance, the Report presented to the Nice European Council by the Secretary General/High Representative and the Commission in December 2000[10] mention, as key recommendations, to intensify the dialogue with the ICRC and to systematically support the right of access to potential conflict zones by the ICRC. The EU Programme for the prevention of violent conflicts,[11] endorsed in June 2001 at the Göteborg Summit, underlines the importance of an 'effective partnership', and it mentions the need to foster the exchange of information, dialogue and cooperation with humanitarian actors such as the ICRC.

The dialogue and exchanges of views and opinions were indeed intensified. Within the line of this Programme, the ICRC Vice-President was invited to participate at two EU Regional Conferences, one that was held in Helsingborg in August 2002 and another in Athens in May 2003. At those two Conferences the ICRC Vice-President placed emphasis on the importance of disseminating international humanitarian law as well as humanitarian values not only to the military, but also to the civilian population, including to the young people.[12]

Finally, it worth having a look at the EU priorities for the 58th United Nations General Assembly,[13] and more specifically at points 29 to 31, stating that:

'29. The European Union stresses the importance of the activities of the International Committee of the Red Cross (ICRC) as a neutral and impartial organisation.

30. The EU and the ICRC have a shared interest in disseminating the main provisions and fundamental principles of international humanitarian law as widely as possible. These principles contribute fundamentally to the goal of conflict prevention.

31. The EU and ICRC should consolidate and deepen the political dialogue taking the ICRC's unique mandate into account'.

To sum up, one can say that the EU and the ICRC have different mandates, different status and different means, but there is indeed a clear common interest in doing the utmost possible to prevent new conflict from occurring, preventing a deterioration in a violent situation, preventing spread of armed conflict, and preventing resurgence of a conflict.

---

[10] Improving the Coherence and Effectiveness of the European Union Action in the field of Conflict Prevention, Nice, 7, 8 and 9 December 2000. Text can be found at <http://register.consilium.eu.int/pdf/en/00/st14/14088en0.pdf>.

[11] The text can be found at <http://register.consilium.eu.int/pdf/en/01/st09/09537-r1en1.pdf>.

[12] The text of the ICRC's contribution to the Helsingborg meeting can be found at <http://www.icrc.org/Web/Eng/siteeng0.nsf/iwpList74/9DAF0CDB12CFDFFEC1256C24005808FA>.

[13] Adopted by the 21st July General Affairs Council. The text can be found at: <http://europa-eu-un.org/article.asp?id=2624>

Nevertheless, the ICRC can only focus on humanitarian and international humanitarian law aspects of conflict prevention. It cannot be involved in the important political component of conflict prevention. It must be stressed once gain that humanitarian operations can never be a palliative to political problems. But taking into account the ICRC's mandate and status, as well as its means of intervention, the ICRC and the EU can work in an effective complementary manner towards preventing conflicts around the world.

Chapter 24
NON-GOVERNMENTAL ORGANISATIONS–EU RELATIONS IN CONFLICT PREVENTION: TWO UNEQUAL BUT COMPLEMENTARY PARTNERS

by Heike Schneider[1]

1. INTRODUCTION

Neither the Non-Governmental Organisations (hereinafter NGOs) nor the EU would like to be seen as blind or lame. But the picture of the lame leading the blind comes to my mind when thinking about the relationship between NGOs and the EU in the area of conflict prevention. Conflict prevention requires a huge variety of capacities and activities and neither the NGOs nor the EU disposes of all of them. The lame and the blind will find their way only when they cooperate.

Conflict prevention is an area where many actors are active. States through their development or foreign affairs ministries, the UN, the European Commission, NGOs and many others are all engaged in this area. Conflict prevention NGOs relate in many ways to the other actors, including the European Union. The nature of this relationship between NGOs and the European Union is the subject of this chapter.

The EU regards cooperation with NGOs in the area of conflict prevention as useful and aims to promote it. The Gothenburg Programme on the prevention of violent conflicts, which was endorsed by the European Council in June 2001, sets out as one of the four priority areas the building of effective partnerships for prevention. In order to do so, 'exchange of information, dialogue and practical cooperation with humanitarian actors such as the ICRC, relevant non-governmental actors and academic organisations should also be strengthened'.[2] In its communication on conflict prevention adopted in April 2001, the Commission stated that it 'intends to stress conflict prevention in its contacts with NGOs (both human rights-based and others) to try and identify those which might play a significant role in conflict prevention. The Commission will give higher priority, through the

---

[1] Head of the European Peacebuilding Liaison Office (EPLO), Brussels. EPLO brings together 19 conflict prevention NGOs based in Europe.
[2] EU Programme for the Prevention of Violent Conflicts, 15-16 June 2001, p. 5.

V. Kronenberger and J. Wouters, eds., The European Union and Conflict Prevention
© 2004, T·M·C·ASSER PRESS, *The Hague, The Netherlands*

European Initiative for Democracy and Human Rights, to activities that contribute to the prevention of conflicts and help to deal with the consequences of conflicts'.[3]

Going beyond this statement of a general willingness to cooperate with NGOs many questions arise. How does this cooperation look in practice? And why should the EU cooperate with NGOs? What is the specific contribution of NGOs to conflict prevention?

It is equally interesting to ask why NGOs should engage with the EU. The simple answer is that the EU has an enormous potential to prevent violent conflicts, a subject which will be dealt with in further detail by most of the other chapters of this book. Also, NGOs can obtain support, both political and financial, from the EU for their activities.

This chapter will discuss four main questions:

1. How do NGOs prevent conflicts? What types of activities do they carry out and how do they relate to the EU?
2. Why should the EU cooperate with NGOs? What is the potential of NGOs to prevent conflicts, and what is their added value?
3. How is this potential used by the EU? What is the reality of the cooperation?
4. What are the challenges for the future? How can the cooperation in conflict prevention between NGOs and the EU be improved?

2. NGOs' CONFLICT PREVENTION ACTIVITIES

2.1 Conflict prevention as an approach to external affairs and as a specific kind of activity: clarification of terms

'NGOs'are part of civil society. More precisely, NGOs belong to the kind of civil society organisations which do not pursue profit as an objective. Instead the NGOs which are the topic of this chapter aim to prevent violent conflicts.

It is important to stress that the objective of conflict prevention NGOs is not to prevent conflicts but rather to prevent VIOLENT conflicts. The term *conflict prevention* is used throughout this text to mean activities which aim to reduce structural tensions or prevent the outbreak, escalation or recurrence of violence. The distinction between conflict prevention and other areas of politics, such as development cooperation, and human rights is not a clear-cut one. In every society there are different interests and therefore conflicts arise. Conflict prevention NGOs, contrary to development or human rights NGOs, become active only once

---

[3] European Commission, *Communication from the Commission on Conflict Prevention* (Brussels, 11 April 2001, COM (2001) 211 final), p. 28.

there is a risk that these conflicts become violent. As it is not always easy to tell when a society will be able to manage a conflict peacefully and when it will not, the boundary between other activities and conflict prevention is blurred and there is an overlapping area of activities.

But conflict prevention can be distinguished from similar activities through two main elements. First, there is an awareness of a risk that a violent conflict will break out which is founded on an analysis of the conflict. The second element is the intention to prevent the outbreak of violence through the activities carried out. So, while it is possible that development cooperation has by accident a conflict prevention effect, it is also possible that it exacerbates tensions.[4] It would therefore make little sense to refer to development cooperation as a conflict prevention activity *per se*. Similarly, I consider trade, human rights or development cooperation as conflict prevention activities only if they are based on an analysis of the conflict situation and are consciously targeted to prevent the outbreak of violence.

In so far as any activity, be it development cooperation, the negotiation of trade agreements, or the building of roads as well as more 'pure' conflict prevention activities such as reconciliation or mediation, can have these two elements, conflict prevention is as much a specific approach to external affairs as it relates to a specific kind of activity.

2.2   The many aspects of NGOs' conflict prevention activities: operational, policy and capacity building

NGOs perform a huge variety of activities to prevent conflicts.[5] To understand these activities and the relationships NGOs have with the EU institutions it is important to categorise them.

NGOs can contribute to the prevention of conflicts through two kinds of activity, through changing policies or through operational activities. When NGOs become active at the policy level they aim at decision-makers who have an influence on the conflict but are not themselves a party to the conflict. When they become operational they aim to influence the actors in the conflict, their behaviour, and attitude and the underlying structures of the conflict. Through their operational activities NGOs address local policymakers and other relevant

---

[4] See Mary B. Anderson, *Do no Harm: How Aid Supports Peace – or War* (Boulder and London, Lynne Rienner Publishers 1999).

[5] For an overview of NGO conflict prevention activities see: *'People Building Peace. 15 Inspiring Stories from Around the World'*, (Utrecht, European Centre for Conflict Prevention, in cooperation with the International Fellowship of Reconciliation (IFOR) and the Coexistence Initiative of State of the World Forum 1999). One can also access the websites of NGOs. The websites of 19 conflict prevention NGOs who work on or with the EU can be accessed from the website of EPLO, the European Peacebuilding Liaison Office <www.eplo.org>. EPLO functions as a liaison office between its NGO members and the EU.

local actors. At the policy level NGOs address the EU or other (local) actors who are not themselves part of the conflict but can have an influence thereon, e.g., the African Union. In the case of the EU becoming a party to the conflict NGOs might extend their operational activities to the EU.

A third category of activities is training or capacity building. NGOs train staff of other NGOs and staff working for governments, including Commission officials, and engage in capacity building of their southern partners.

The role of NGOs and the degree of importance NGOs attribute to the various activities has been changing. Many NGOs limit themselves more and more to fund raising and capacity building and leave the implementation of projects to local partners. When northern NGOs discuss policies with EU staff, they try to involve their local partners more and bring them to Brussels to meet decision-makers there. At the same time they now give more priority to strengthening the capacity of their southern colleagues to carry out lobbying activities themselves.

Policy dialogue, operational activities and training all give rise to different kinds of relationships between NGOs and the EU. When performing operational tasks European NGOs conclude contracts with the European Commission. Sometimes European NGOs implement contracts themselves, sometimes their southern partners. Increasingly southern NGOs receive funding from EU delegations in their country directly and are themselves responsible for the implementation of projects. With regard to their advocacy role, European NGOs engage themselves in a policy dialogue with EU institutions, often jointly with their southern colleagues. At the same time they try to enhance the capacity of their southern colleagues to lobby EU delegations in their country and to link directly to the EU. Through training EU officials NGOs simultaneously have some influence on EU policy.

3.   THE POTENTIAL FOR EU-NGOs COOPERATION IN CONFLICT PREVENTION

Why should NGOs play a role in conflict prevention? And for what reasons should the EU cooperate with them? What exactly is their potential? I propose to discuss these questions with regard to the different kinds of activities which NGOs perform. What is their added value in policy dialogue, in activities on the ground and in training?

3.1   The contribution NGOs can make through policy dialogue

3.1.1   *Policy dialogue and campaigning*

At the policy level, two forms of activities can be distinguished, namely lobbying or policy dialogue and campaigning. When NGOs' representatives advise decision-makers on what can be done in a certain country to avoid the recurrence of violence this is called lobbying. A good example is the paper that International Alert and Saferworld usually in cooperation with the European Platform and EPLO, draft for the EU presidencies and in which they make recommendations for the rotating EU presidencies on how to promote conflict prevention during their term. The objective of lobbying or policy dialogue is to provide expertise and to give advice to decision-makers.

Policy dialogue usually takes place on the basis of substantial research, which has been carried out over months if not years. I will therefore include in the category of policy dialogue also conflict prevention research in all its aspects, be it conflict impact assessment or early warning or research into the proliferation of small arms. Some NGOs such as the Conflict Prevention Unit of the Clingendael Institute, the Berghof Center or Swisspeace mainly carry out research and some other NGOs such as International Alert, Saferworld or Oxfam carry out research on a regular basis. The specificity of this kind of research is that NGOs try to be action-oriented, to develop and improve practical methods and instruments for conflict prevention and to elaborate policy options for decision-makers.

Policy dialogue takes place in Brussels between the EU and EU-based NGOs, but it also takes place between the EU, partner countries and NGOs based in these countries. The Cotonou Agreement,[6] which is the most advanced of all regional instruments in this respect, foresees the involvement of local civil society in the political dialogue between the ACP country and the EU. Also, according to the Cotonou Agreement, NGOs should be involved in the drawing up of the Country Strategy Papers, which outline the EU support for the development strategy of the ACP countries.

Campaigning is done to create political will. When NGOs launch a campaign they first of all want to mobilise the population. The more the better. The objective is to draw the attention of the wider public to a particular problem through demonstrations, media and signatories' campaigns. The idea behind this is that politicians are sensitive to the concerns of the general public and might change policies due to campaigns because they want to be re-elected. A good example of a successful campaign is the anti-landmine campaign. Similar to lobbying, the objective is to influence policies but campaigning addresses decision-makers only indirectly. As campaigning only aims indirectly at decision-makers, it will not be discussed any further in this chapter.

---

[6] The Cotonou Agreement is a trade, development and political cooperation agreement concluded between the EU, its Member States and 77 States from Africa, the Caribbean and the Pacific. It has a financial envelope of EUR 15.2 billion plus 10 billion from the financial envelopes of previous years' euros to be spent over six years.

3.1.2   *The role of policy dialogue in conflict prevention*

Lobbying or policy dialogue is important in many policy areas, but in conflict prevention lobbying is essential. Without a strong development cooperation lobby, aid to poor countries is probably going to decrease, but it will continue. The picture for conflict prevention is different. In this field lobbying is almost a condition *sine qua non*. The reason for this is simple. Conflict prevention is an activity for which it is almost impossible to obtain credit. If it is successful, nobody will hear about the activities. But even if people do hear about the activities they will wonder whether they were really necessary, because there is no conflict in this region. If conflict prevention is not successful, one does not get the credit either, even though one might have made serious efforts.

Conflict prevention is caught in an incentive trap. Staff working on foreign affairs is constantly busy managing crises which have already made headlines in the newspapers. And it is very difficult to get conflicts which are not yet in the headlines on the agenda, and which in the case of effective action will never be in the headlines. This is true even when there is in principle an openness and a readiness to work on conflict prevention. It does not make things any easier that conflict prevention is normally not an issue in elections. NGOs therefore have an important role to play in reminding decision-makers of their commitment to conflict prevention.

Besides insisting on the need for and encouraging decision-makers to engage in conflict prevention, NGOS also have a capacity to influence positively the quality of conflict prevention policies and to strengthen their democratic legitimacy.

NGOs, especially those that function more as think-tanks, can bring additional expertise. Many NGOs have developed a special expertise after having worked in a certain area over a number of years. They have become experts on a specific region such as the Great Lakes or the Horn of Africa or in a specific topic like conflict rough diamonds or small arms. Through their direct contact, interaction and dialogue with people who are affected by EU policy, NGOs have often developed alternative expertise. They can add certain aspects to the discussion, that would otherwise have been overlooked and they can draw attention to the concerns of the people on the ground. NGOs thereby further a more inclusive, a deeper and a more comprehensive discussion, that is able to take the interests and concerns of the different people better into account and lead to more rational solutions.

Governments or the EU cannot obtain feedback as regards their conflict prevention policy from the public through elections. Possibilities for criticism and appraisal, therefore, have to be organised in other ways. A structured dialogue between the Commission and the NGOs can fulfil this function.

NGOs, with a capacity to reach out, have a potential to further public discussion and to draw the attention of a wider public to conflict prevention issues and to organise a structured dialogue. They inform people, they critically assess policies and challenge governments with alternative proposals.

In addition to their outreach capacity some NGOs can claim to be representative. Certain NGOs, namely those linked to mass organisations such as the churches and the unions, have a huge and democratically organised membership, which allows them to speak out on behalf of huge parts of society and to make the voice of those people heard.

Certainly NGOs are a very heterogeneous group of actors. Some are linked to mass organisations, some function as think-thanks and others focus very much on one area and have become real experts in that particular field. But it is due to this diversity that NGOs can bring the wide range of views existing on a certain topic to the attention of the EU so that the institutions can take better informed policy decisions, reach more rational and at the same time more democratic solutions.

The EU needs to recognise this democratising potential of NGOs even more urgently than its Member States, because it is only insufficiently democratically legitimised through the European Parliament and the Council. The Members of the European Parliament are directly elected but they have little influence in foreign policy. The members of the Council are only indirectly legitimised, in so far as they are members of democratically elected governments in their countries and yet it is them who take the decisions in foreign policy. A European public opinion has only started to develop. Very few newspapers systematically discuss EU politics. EU politics are neither an issue in national elections, which essentially legitimise the Council, nor in the elections for the European Parliament. MEPs are normally elected according to the performance of their party in their home country. People do not discuss EU politics in the same way as they discuss national politics, because they know so little about the EU and because information is not always readily available.

NGOs can contribute to bridging the gap between Brussels and the Member States and can function as a crystallising point for a European Public. NGOs, especially when they are organised in European networks, can inform people in the EU member countries, they can critically assess EU policies and can launch a Europe-wide discussion. By contributing to the development of a European public, NGOs reinforce the existing legitimising mechanisms of EU politics.

3.1.3 *Conditions for a fruitful policy dialogue*

NGOs can contribute to making conflict prevention policies more rational and, at the same time, more legitimate. This potential can be realised if the EU and NGOs fulfil certain requirements.

A fruitful policy dialogue is possible if the NGOs are independently, autonomously and transparently organised. A policy dialogue also requires from NGOs that they have a potential to reach people through broad membership or a capacity to launch discussions and to distribute information. Obviously NGOs also need to have enough expertise and resources to carry out their activities.

The need for resources and the importance of remaining independent are issues. Some NGOs, Quaker NGOs being one example, accept government funding only in exceptional cases when they can be sure that this funding does not affect their work. Other NGOs have set themselves a limit and accept only up to, for example, 10 or 15% government funding. They regard government funding as multiplying the funding they receive from civil society. Still other NGOs try to delink the sources of funding from potential sources of influence by diversifying their income and working with different donors. The issue is very complex. One can also argue that an NGO which receives 100% or a huge part of its income from one government and does not need to apply for funding for every project, is more independent than an NGO that needs to obtain funding which is approved for every single project. It is clear that other factors such as the formal structure of the NGO, how rooted it is in and the political support it receives from civil society also play a role.

On the part of the Commission a fruitful dialogue implies a transparent structure, an active information distribution policy and a readiness to engage in dialogue with NGOs on all major issues. The Commission should also support NGOs' policy work. It is not enough to consult NGOs, if the NGOs do not have enough staff to follow it up, to distribute the information, and to assess it. Launching a public discussion should be seen as a public good which benefits all and should therefore be government funded. The Commission needs to support public discussion financially as it does with many other public goods and as some Member States do with political parties or foundations. Finally, the Commission should give more priority to dialogue with NGOs so that EU officials have sufficient time for dialogue with civil society.

3.2   The contribution NGOs can make through their operational activities

The principal 'operational' activities of NGOs consist at providing resources, guidance and technological support to local peace processes. The term 'operational' is slightly ambiguous. Many northern NGOs would tend to reject the idea that they are operational and describe their role as fund-raisers, capacity builders and, more generally, as trying to find the support of politicians and the wider public for the work of their partners in the 'south'. The actual degree of involvement of expatriates differs from one organisation to another and also depends on the context. While some European organisations have an office with an expatriate as country director, other NGOs simply visit their partner as and when they consider it to be useful. But the division of labour between 'northern' and 'southern' NGOs is not the issue of this chapter. I will therefore still employ the term 'operational' and refer to the joint work of both partners.

The Commission, in its communication on conflict prevention, distinguishes several ways by which NGOs can contribute to conflict prevention, all of them operational: 'By virtue of their support for the development of civil society and democracy, NGOs are key actors in long-term conflict prevention. They are often present on the ground in situations where official state structures are absent. They can also function as grass roots mediators as well as reliable and neutral observers in situations where there is no international presence. Mediation activities of specialist NGOs have sometimes proved decisive in a crisis'.[7]

With this paragraph the Commission refers to the same two kinds of NGO activities which the UN Secretary General in his Report to the Security Council on the Prevention of Armed Conflict also distinguishes: 'NGOs can contribute to the maintenance of peace and security by offering non-violent avenues for addressing the root causes of conflict at an early stage. Moreover, NGOs can be an important means of conducting Track Two diplomacy when governments and international organizations are unable to do so'.[8]

It is indeed useful to distinguish between these two kinds of activities. Whereas the one kind of activities focuses on the actors in the conflict, the other focuses on the (root) causes of the conflict, the underlying structures. Johan Galtung, one of the pioneers of peace and conflict research, in addition distinguishes between attitudes and behaviour of the actors in the conflict.[9] In his conflict triangle, Galtung sets out three aspects of a conflict: causes, attitudes and behaviour. The additional distinction in attitudes and behaviour is helpful as in some conflicts it might be useful to first focus on the behaviour and to ensure that violent behaviour discontinues. At the same time, the conflict triangle reminds us that event though there is no violent behaviour there might still be a need to work on the attitudes, the perceptions of the conflicting parties, but also the objective reality of the conflict, its actual cause.

The conflict triangle sets out the three main elements of a conflict. Only if all three elements are tackled, is conflict prevention work done. The conflict triangle sets out the agenda for conflict prevention, and allows for a comprehensive description and classification of conflict prevention activities. It is therefore a helpful instrument to assess the contributions which NGOs can make to preventing violent conflicts.

How do NGOs address the three elements of a conflict – behaviour, attitudes and root causes?[10] What do they do differently from, e.g., government actors? What can NGOs contribute to what others cannot?

---

[7] European Commission, *Communication from the Commission on Conflict Prevention* (Brussels, 11 April 2001, COM (2001) 211 final), p. 28.

[8] Report of the Secretary General, *Prevention of armed conflict* (United Nations, General Assembly, Security Council, fifty-fifth session, Fifty-sixth year, June 2001), p. 32.

[9] Johan Galtung, 'Violence, Peace and Peace Research', 3 *Journal of Peace Research* (1969), pp. 167-192.

[10] For a much more comprehensive description of NGO activities using Galtung's conflict triangle, see Tim Wallis and Mareike Junge, *Enhancing UK Capacity for a UK Capacity for Handling Conflict: The Rationale for a UK Civilian Peace Service* (London, Peaceworkers UK 2002), chapter 2.

3.2.1 *Working on behaviour*

Working on the behaviour of the parties to a conflict is traditionally seen as a pre-rogative of the state and more precisely either the police or the military. It is be-lieved that acts of violence can only be stopped by the military or the police. Yet, there are powerful civilian tools which allow violence to be contained, at least in some circumstances. Peace-brigades International, for example, accompanies po-tential victims of violence 24 hours a day in order to dissuade acts of violence against them. Other civilian tools are a large presence of people from outside the conflict situation, or monitoring, which includes the recording, reporting and the dissemination of information.

The strengthening of what Marie Anderson refers to as local capacities for peace also falls into this category. Local capacities for peace are 'the things that connect people to each other'. They could be markets, infrastructure, shared val-ues, language, etc. These connections are active and important even in situations of open violence and allow people to connect with each other and to (re)build re-lationships.[11]

3.2.2 *Working on attitudes*

NGOs work on the attitudes of the conflicting parties, the second element of the conflict triangle, through a variety of activities. They bring together groups and individuals from different communities through sports events, job programmes or integrated schooling projects. Through these activities they try to challenge preju-dices and stereotypes, and to encourage dialogue and relationships. Work on atti-tudes includes track two initiatives. 'Track Two Diplomacy encompasses peace efforts embarked upon by unofficial, non-governmental organisations and indi-viduals who specialise in conflict management. Private peacemakers try to gener-ate non-governmental citizen interactions between parties in a conflict. Their aim is to help resolve conflicts by surpassing the logic of power politics and to en-courage communication, understanding and collaboration between antagonistic communities'.[12] Whereas it is the objective of the official Track One Diplomacy to reach peace agreements between governments, Track Two wants to promote the mutual understanding between larger groups of people and get them to en-gage, to support and at times even to carry the peace process forward. Activities include problem-solving workshops, acting as messengers and go-betweens to help set up dialogue between antagonistic communities offering mediation

---

[11] Mary B. Anderson and Angelika Spelten, *Conflict Transformation. How International Assis-tance Can Contribute?* (SEF (Stiftung Entwicklung und Frieden) Policy Papers No. 15, 2000), p. 3.

[12] Jos Havermans, 'Private Professionals for Peace', in European Centre for Conflict Prevention, *People Building Peace. 35 Inspiring Stories from Around the World* (Amsterdam, Bureau M&O 1999), p. 166.

courses to local leaders, organising seminars and conferences and private one-on-one diplomacy behind the scenes.

Both the Commission and the Secretary General agree that NGOs can carry out mediation activities when international organisations or governments cannot. But Track Two negotiations should not just be seen as a fall-back option if Track One negotiations fail. In fact, Track Two can be complementary to Track One. If it is possible to create synergies between the two processes, this can bring the peace process forward. The relationship between the two tracks is an issue on its own.[13] Both approaches have their advantages and limitations through the different stages of a conflict. And progress at the other level might still be possible when there is a deadlock at one level. This progress can then lead to a breakthrough at the other level, especially if there is a good relationship between level one and level two. John Lederach makes this point. 'The most significant gap of interdependence we face is rooted in the lack of responsive and coordinated relationships up and down the levels of leadership in a society affected by protracted violent conflict. High, middle-range and grassroots levels of leadership rarely see themselves as interdependent with the other levels in reference to peace-building until they discover they need them, usually when the process is under enormous stress and time constraints. If pursued the resulting relationship suffers manipulation or instrumentalist superficiality'.[14]

3.2.3   *Working on the root causes of conflict*

In addition to working on the attitudes and the behaviour of conflicting parties, NGOs also try to address the root causes of conflict. There are different categories of root causes. The EU very usefully distinguishes between four different kinds of root causes:

1. Imbalances of political socio-economic or culture opportunities;
2. Lack of democratic legitimacy and effectiveness of governance;
3. Absence of opportunities for the peaceful conciliation of group interests;
4. Lack of an active and organised civil society.

Many examples can be found of the way in which NGOs can play a part in addressing root causes. Those with a development background work on unequal distribution of wealth through poverty alleviation projects and they try to em-

---

[13] For a brief discussion, see Cordula Reinmann, 'Assessing the State of the Art in Conflict Transformation', in Berghof Research Center for Constructive Conflict Management, The Berghof Handbook for Conflict Transformation <http://www.berghof-center.org/handbook/articles/articles_mf.htm>, 2003), p. 4.

[14] John Paul Lederach, 'Justpeace – The Challenge of the 21st Century', in European Centre for Conflict Prevention, *People Building Peace. 35 Inspiring Stories from Around the World* (Amsterdam, Bureau M&O 1999), p. 30.

power poor parts of society and to strengthen their participation in politics. Other NGOs work to strengthen the democratic legitimacy of governments through, for example, human rights work. They monitor the human rights situation and promote public awareness of human rights and human rights education. They organise human rights training for police officers or advise on security sector reform, with the objective of making security forces more accountable. NGOs also strengthen the capacity of a society to deal with conflicts in a peaceful manner. They strengthen civil society and support, for example, independent and pluralist media. Other examples are peace education and non-violence training for ex-combatants or criminal gangs and others who might tend to react violently in everyday situations. Another important area is support for peace constituencies. Peace constituencies are groups of society which are in favour of peace. They can be women's groups, religious communities or (parts of) the business sectors. The NGO Common Ground supports a Women's Peace Centre in Burundi, which brings together Hutu and Tutsi women. The success of this project is due to the fact that women in Burundi are traditionally seen as connectors between the two ethnic groups and they promote understanding between the two groups.

3.2.4   *What NGOs can contribute to prevent violence, what governmental actors cannot*

There are many arguments for the involvement of civil society in the peace process. One of the most important ones is the often insufficient capacity of a government to secure peace. 'There is more and more evidence from the world's war zones for example, that many so-called sovereign states and governments lack a monopoly of coercive capacity and are incapable of bringing order to territory under their control. Far from governing on behalf of and for the people (their citizens), they are either unable to extend legitimate authority and security to citizens or are intensely predatory and exploitative'.[15]

An obvious example of such a situation is the North Eastern part of the Congo, over which the Central government does not have any control. Other examples of what is sometimes quite drastically called 'failed states', are the anarchic situations in Sierra Leone or Somalia, where the rule of law does not really exist, or to a lesser extent the Caucasus and parts of the Balkans where the government is either corrupt or where its power is undermined by organised crime. In these countries governments no longer undertake their tasks of providing security and peace and consequently one needs to consider other ways to do so and to work with civil society to ensure the rule of law, and to fight against corruption

---

[15] Kevin Clements, 'The Interdependence of track 1, 2 and 3, and the Fields of Human Rights, Humanitarian Assistance, Development Cooperation', in Berghof Research Center for Constructive Conflict Management, The Berghof Handbook for Conflict Transformation <http://www.berghof-center.org/handbook/articles/articles_mf.htm>, 2003), p. 3

and organised crime. At the same time, it is crucial not to undermine the capacity of the state even further, but rather to try to strengthen it.

Even worse, there are cases where the governments are more part of the problem than of its actual solution. They might have the means to provide security and to make peace, but they do not use them, because they have an interest in continued violence. This is not to say that the state should not be involved in the peace process and it does not mean that all parts of civil society are in favour of the process. We know that in some conflicts parts of the business sector or religious communities have actively supported violence or have even been directly involved. It is merely a warning that sometimes it might be difficult to involve the state in the peace process and that it might be important to involve those parts of civil society who want peace and thereby hopefully also convince the state and its government of the peace process.

A similar argument, while not necessarily questioning the capacity of a government for coercive powers, questions its legitimacy. 'Conflict resolvers, therefore, have always been somewhat ambivalent towards State and Political systems. On the one hand, there is a willingness to acknowledge the importance of the state while on the other, there is a critique of the state's monopoly of power and a rejection of threat and coercion as the primary means for generating order and stability'.[16] NGOs would rather try and modify behaviour by working with and through civil society groups.

In Nigeria, for example, the government tries to prevent the outbreak of violence between different ethnic groups by sending in soldiers. It is very doubtful whether this can be the solution. People are afraid of the military because they have experienced them plundering their villages. While the government certainly has its part to play in the peace process, e.g., through a just distribution of the oil revenues, it is equally important to work with the different populations to bring them together and to try to increase mutual recognition of their legitimate needs, to increase their mutual understanding and to work on prejudices and hatred.

In addition, NGOs often enjoy more trust on the part of the local population, especially if they are local or work with local staff. This, in turn, gives them unique access to people and places. Through this unique access and their cooperation with locals they have a first hand understanding of the conflict. And, finally, NGOs are more likely than International Organisations to remain in a conflict area for a longer period of time and support the, at times, very long peace processes.

3.2.5 The framework for successful operation cooperation

This contribution has tried to show how NGOs, through various operational activities, contribute to the prevention of violent conflicts. Whether they are suc-

---

[16] Idem, p. 4.

cessful or not depends (amongst other things) on a number of conditions that need to be fulfilled on the side of the NGOs and the Commission.

The first condition is obviously a high degree of professionalism, including a thorough understanding of the conflict. But professionalism is not limited to intellectual capacities. It includes political and psychosocial skills. Private peacemakers must try to achieve and maintain balance and even-handedness and avoid acting as advocates for one of the parties in a conflict. It is also difficult to deal with the emotions of people directly engaged in a conflict.[17]

The organisational structure matters. NGOs must have a capacity to manage funds, enough expertise and resources to carry out their activities and they should be organised in a transparent structure. To support local peace processes it is usually best to have a long-standing partnership with NGOs in the relevant country. In conflict prevention, however, more than in 'ordinary' development cooperation or humanitarian assistance, a good case can be made to send expatriates as outsiders, as they are normally perceived to be more neutral.

On the side of the Commission a high degree of professionalism is required, too. Commission staff needs to have a very good understanding of the conflict and they need to have experience in working with civil society. It is a common problem that in conflict affected countries, civil society has been suppressed and is not effective. In some cases NGOs are even part of the conflict. The Commission can only use the potential NGOs' offer if it knows them well and has experience with working with them. As the Commission 'deconcentrates' increasingly decision-making power to delegations, this is not only true for staff in Brussels but also for staff in delegations. To secure the involvement of all the NGOs that are relevant for the peace process and not only those that are based in the capital or those that already have experience with working with the EU delegations, a proactive approach should be taken in informing and contacting local NGOs.

In so far as the organisational relationship between the Commission and NGOs is concerned it is important that the Commission distributes EU funds according to clear and transparent criteria and also supports the capacity building of NGOs. Finally, the EU should make cooperation with NGOs more of a priority so that Commission staff has time to deal also with the effective, but time-consuming, small NGO projects.

3.3   The contribution NGOs can make through training and capacity building

NGOs offer training courses on a huge variety of issues including conflict analysis, conflict-sensitive planning management and implementation of development

---

[17] Jos Havermans, 'Private Professionals for Peace', in European Centre for Conflict Prevention, *People Building Peace. 35 Inspiring Stories from Around the World* (Amsterdam, Bureau M&O 1999), p. 167.

cooperation, 'Do no Harm', early warning and preventive action, mediation and facilitation training, alternative dispute resolution, use of media for peacebuilding, human rights and election monitoring.

Training and capacity building are becoming more and more important. As has been mentioned above, northern NGOs are gradually changing their role from 'implementators' of projects to supporters of their local partners, which usually involves capacity building and advising them on their organisational development. They train their partners in conflict management and provide them with education resources. Saferworld, for example, together with its local partners, has produced a manual on the Cotonou Agreement and conflict prevention in the Horn of Africa.

While training their partners NGOs build up what is frequently referred to as a 'healthy' civil society and they thereby strengthen the capacity of a society to deal with conflicts. Northern NGOs assist marginalised parts of civil society to be empowered and to make their voice heard.

In addition to training NGO staff, NGOs also train government officials including Commission staff.

The added value of NGOs in this area mainly lies in their hands-on experience in conflict prevention and their first-hand understanding of conflicts. Training obviously requires a high degree of professionalism, and experience. The best training comes from NGOs who have tested and themselves used the methods they teach.

4. THE REALITY OF EU-NGOs COOPERATION

Section three of this chapter has tried to show what NGOs can bring to conflict prevention which other actors cannot, how NGOs engage in policy dialogue, how they work on the three aspects constituting conflict through their operational activities and how they carry out this training. It should go without saying that this does not mean that NGOs are the sole important actors in conflict prevention. But I have tried to show that NGOs play a specific and important role, which often cannot be taken aboard by other actors such as the UN and/or the EU. To what extent does the EU make use of this potential?

4.1 Policy dialogue

NGOs have an informal policy dialogue with the Commission, especially with its Crisis management and conflict prevention unit, but also with the geographic desk officers of the Commission and with the Council. This dialogue, however, is not structured and organised in a very *ad hoc* way. In 2001 17 European conflict prevention NGOs set up the European Peacebuilding Liaison Office to facilitate dialogue with the EU. Since then EPLO has been informing its members about

EU conflict prevention policies and has organised many meetings with EU representatives and NGOs to exchange information and discuss conflict prevention issues.

The Commission, the Council and NGOs have been discussing the organisation of regional meetings, where experts from the institutions and from the NGOs would discuss conflict prevention strategies for certain countries or regions. So far, however, only a few meetings have taken place and there is no systematic approach to this.

Some of the regional instruments of the EU foresee a dialogue with local civil society. The most advanced of these agreements both with regard to conflict prevention and the involvement of civil society is certainly the Cotonou Agreement.

Article 11 of the Cotonou Agreement foresees that 'The Parties shall pursue an active, comprehensive and integrated policy of peace-building, and conflict prevention and resolution within the framework of the Partnership (...)'. Cotonou at the same time stipulates that NGOs should be informed and consulted on cooperation strategies and that they should be involved in the political dialogue, which plays a central role in conflict prevention. Article 8 deals with political dialogue between the partners, which is meant to cover all the aims and objectives of the Agreement. Much of the article deals with the inclusion of conflict issues in the dialogue, thereby using dialogue itself as a conflict prevention tool: 'Through dialogue, the Parties shall contribute to peace, security and stability and promote a stable and democratic political environment'. (Paragraph 3) 'Broadly based policies to promote peace and to prevent, manage and resolve violent conflict shall play a prominent role in this dialogue, as shall the need to take full account of the objective of peace and democratic stability in the definition of priority areas of cooperation'. (Paragraph 5).

Dialogue is not only meant between ACP and EU partners, but also amongst the ACP countries at whatever appropriate level: regional, sub-regional and national. Civil society organisations are to be included in this dialogue.

Article 8, therefore, as well as putting conflict issues on the agenda of the EU-ACP dialogue, actively encourages dialogue at the local and regional level.

It is difficult to check to what extent the EU engages via its delegations with civil society in all 77 ACP countries. There are some notable exceptions, but generally it appears that this does not happen in a systematic way. Three years after the signing of the Cotonou Agreement, the Commission is still in the process of developing guidelines for its delegations for cooperating with local civil society. What is true for Brussels is also true for the delegations. The extent to which dialogue occurs depends very much on the individuals in question.

This impression was confirmed through some research carried out by EPLO on the mainstreaming of conflict prevention. When we asked southern NGOs about the involvement of civil society into the programming of the country strategy papers, we heard quite divergent opinions about civil society participation. One stated that a section of civil society organisations had been consulted during the preparation of the Country Strategy Paper. The other, however, did not believe that there was proper consultation in general at the inception of the papers and that the consultation process, being both insufficient and inadequate, was organised after the key document had already been produced. On top of this, the same contact complained that they had facilitated consultation, as opposed to the Commission delegation or the National Authorising Officer. Whilst one contact believed that awareness had been raised concerning participatory rights in the Cotonou Agreement, the other stated that almost none of the civil society groups knew about this initiative, attributing this to the EU's and the government's fear of giving civil society organisations participatory rights in case they backfire.

Some NGOs have undertaken considerable efforts to inform their local colleagues about the possibilities which Cotonou offers. One of the most important initiatives is the civil society guide 'Understanding the EU – a civil society guide to development and conflict prevention policies' produced by Saferworld and its partners, the Inter-Africa Group and the Africa Peace Forum, and in collaboration with the Conflict Prevention Network.

Generally speaking, it seems that Policy dialogue on conflict prevention issues between EU institutions and European NGOs, on the one hand, and local NGOs, on the other, is not ideal. But it needs to be acknowledged that there has been considerable progress.

The situation looks different as far as research is concerned. EC Funding for research into conflict prevention is limited. The Commission, the European Parliament and the Council used to finance a network of conflict prevention experts, CPN (Conflict Prevention Network), but the call for proposals was cancelled at the end of 2002, and it appears that the Commission is not going to replace this very valuable instrument. As the Commission itself does not have a policy or research unit for conflict prevention it is important for it to keep in touch with the research carried out and the policy options developed by others. It is not yet clear how the Commission is going to do this. DG Research has a huge research budget from which it also funds some University research on conflict prevention. There are also budget lines for training, studies and meetings with experts. Still desk officers frequently complain that they do not receive enough training and if they attend meetings, they feel they are not relevant to their work. Maybe the challenge is to fund more action-oriented research and to develop, jointly with desk officers, more practical tools for conflict prevention.

4.2 Operational cooperation

The Commission has two financial instruments to finance cooperation in external affairs, the Community budget and the European Development Fund (EDF). Under the Community budget there are between 70 and 80 budget lines for external relations, most of them for development cooperation. The EDF is the financial instrument of the Cotonou Agreement, concluded between 77 countries from Africa, the Caribbean and the Pacific, the EU and its Member States.

Conflict prevention is supposed to be mainstreamed into development cooperation and the other external policies. So the Commission should fund conflict prevention programmes, or at least projects which are conflict sensitive, under all of its budget lines for external affairs and under the EDF wherever there is a need for it.

The Commission does not have figures either on the amount spent on conflict prevention nor on the amount spent on NGOs' conflict prevention activities. But the Commission has figures on how much funding is channelled through NGOs. In its communication on the participation of non-state actors in EC development policy[18] the Commission gives precise figures on how much of the funding available under the different external aid Budget lines is channelled through non-state actors, of which NGOs are an important part.

In addition, it is possible to see how seriously conflict prevention is taken by looking at the different programmes and policies which govern the budget lines. The two points taken together – non-state actor involvement and the importance attributed to conflict prevention – gives us an idea of how the EU cooperates with NGOs in the area of conflict prevention with regard to specific projects on the ground.

The external budget lines can be divided into two groups: geographic and thematic. With regard to the amount of funding the most important thematic ones are the following:

- Co-financing budget line;
- European Initiative for Democracy and Human Rights (EIDHR);
- Humanitarian Assistance;
- Food Aid and Food Security.

The co-financing budget line was specifically created to co-finance development activities proposed by NGOs. The focus of this budget line is human and social development. If projects aim towards these objectives and include a conflict prevention dimension, the Commission might fund them. When one looks at the call for proposals launched in December 2002 it becomes evident that there is an awareness of conflict prevention issues. The call for proposals sets out the following criteria for the priority that is given to projects:

- 'support and facilitate the linking of rehabilitation and development operations in countries emerging from a crisis following natural or man-made disasters;

---

[18] European Commission, *Participation of non-state actors in EC development policy* (Brussels, 7 November 2002, COM (2002) 598 final).

- undertaken in countries affected by conflict and/or where official EC cooperation is suspended, unavailable or reduced'.

EIDHR is the only budget line that – at least until 2003 – explicitly allocated certain parts of the funding to conflict prevention. In the 2002 call for proposals under this budget line and in its Update adopted in January 2003 conflict prevention is a subpriority under one of the four main priorities. It has been identified as an area of intervention for the EIDHR in many countries. Conflict prevention activities to be promoted by the Commission include:

- Early warning, mediation, reconciliation and confidence-building measures from grass roots and international NGOs;
- Common training modules for civilian staff to be deployed in international missions.[19]

An allocation of 4 million Euros for the year 2002 and 12 million Euros for 2003-4 has been made. Cooperation with international, regional and local organisations involved with peace initiatives is to be supported. The inclusion of local actors in mediation activities is especially encouraged.

The Commission also sees conflict prevention as an important area under the EIDHR at the regional level. At this level, however, the Commission usually cooperates with actors such as the UN, the OSCE, the African Union, SADC and not with NGOs. Overall, around 80% of the funding of the EIDHR goes to NGOs.

With its 2004 EIDHR programming update the Commission now wants to move away from indicative sub-thematic allocations towards an approach that addresses issues in amore mainstreamed or cross-cutting manner. It is planned that all funding from the EIDHR shall take into account the objectives of conflict prevention and conflict resolution by favouring project proposals that include these aspects in their specific project objectives.

ECHO, the Office administering the Humanitarian Aid of the European Commission, takes a rather purist approach to humanitarian assistance. ECHO's stated policy is 'to keep humanitarian assistance at arm's length of politics'. While there are good arguments for doing this, it is not an easy task, given the fact that 80% of ECHO's aid is delivered in conflict zones. ECHO states that it is committed to 'do no harm' principles, but ECHO has not yet explained how it is going to implement this principle and how it is going to avoid the fact that its humanitarian assistance will have negative effects on conflict dynamics.

There seems to be room for more reflection on the relationship between humanitarian assistance and conflict and a need for increasing the conflict sensitiveness of ECHO staff. This is true even if ECHO sticks to its purist approach and

---

[19] EIDHR Programming Document 2002-2004, p. 8.

just wants to make sure – to the extent possible – that aid reaches the beneficiaries and is effective.

ECHO has taken the first steps to increase the conflict awareness of its staff. A fair number of desk officers participated in training courses on 'Local capacities for peace approach-Do no harm' in October 2001, a course which was given by NGOs. But due to the high staff turnover and the small training budget, which does not allow for a sufficient number of courses, the impact of this training is limited.

ECHO channels more than half of its funds through NGOs. It is however worrying that ECHO states quite frankly that its cooperation with NGOs does not extend to conflict prevention. At the same time, it is also clear that a number of ECHO's partners, be it ActionAid, Oxfam, World Vision and others are highly conflict sensitive and will make sure that aid is delivered as effectively as possible and does not fuel conflicts.

The Food Aid and Food Security departments of the European Commission have not yet developed a concept for dealing with conflicts, although this is certainly an important issue as well. So the Commission does not yet ensure that food aid and food security is promoted in a conflict-sensitive way.

Another horizontal budget line of interest is the Rapid Reaction Mechanism (RRM). The RRM is a small but very important budget line with about 25 Million euro per year. It was created to allow the EC to respond quickly to countries experiencing a violent crisis and to support short-term measures. The idea is that after a short time – usually six months – the EC can follow up with the more traditional funding instruments. NGOs are eligible partners under the RRM regulation but the Commission channels most of the funds through governments and International Organisations. One example for Commission support to NGOs was the RRM funding for NGO media work in DRC on issues pertaining to the Inter-Congolese Dialogue.

Besides the thematic budget lines, the EC budget also foresees funding for cooperation certain regions. Before looking at them it is useful to look at the cooperation with ACP countries which is governed by the Cotonou Agreement and funded from a second financial instrument: the European Development Fund (EDF).

Amongst the regional cooperation instruments, the Cotonou Agreement is certainly the most interesting, both in terms of conflict prevention and in terms of cooperation with NGOs. The Cotonou Agreement recognises the important role which NGOs can play in the cooperation process.[20] Article 4 stipulates that non-state actors will be provided with financial resources. The programming guidelines foresee that up to 15% of the funding foreseen for a specific country can be

---

[20] For more information on this, see ECDPM, *Cotonou Infokit: Obtaining Resources* (Maastricht, ECDPM 2001).

allocated to NGOs. Also the agreement stipulates that NGOs are informed, consulted and involved in the cooperation strategies.

In principle NGOs can access funds from the EDF through three different channels. NGOs can join forces with the government and design and implement programmes together under the National Indicative Programme. Under the framework of decentralised cooperation non-state actors can propose their own projects. This form of cooperation might be accessible to some NGOs. Thirdly, if the National Indicative programme foresees micro projects, then NGOs can apply for funding for such projects.

However, will NGOs be able to seize these possibilities? And how realistic is the 15% or even 10%? Many NGOs have criticised the fact that the National Authorising Officer has to agree on all projects, including those submitted by NGOs. In many conflict-prone countries, governments might not so readily share what they consider to be their funds with civil society organisations.

Also, the EU still spends most of its development funds on roads. Some 32.5% of the resources available under Cotonou will be spent on transport followed by 31% on social infrastructure and services. This would not be a problem, if conflict prevention was fully mainstreamed into these areas. But as the latter is not the case, it appears that neither the EU nor the ACP countries take conflict prevention as seriously as the Cotonou Agreement suggests.

A good example is the Civil Society Fund set up by the delegation in Ethiopia to support projects of local non-state actors in the areas of human rights, governance, and conflict prevention. A total of 10 million Euros has been allocated to this fund.

On the whole, however, it appears that conflict prevention and cooperation with NGOs in this field, will in many ACP countries only become a priority if the Commission actively – and much more than it used to do – pushes for this objective.

Cooperation with NGOs under the other regional agreements differs quite substantially from one instrument to the other. According to the Commission communication on cooperation with non-state actors the amounts allocated to non-state actors vary between around 4% and 25%.

Whereas under the Commission's programme for the Mediterranean, MEDA, only 3.9% of the funds go to NSA, 25.8% of the whole funding available under the geographic instruments for Latin America and 23.5% of the funding available under the geographic instruments for Asia goes to NSA. It is however not clear how much of this funding for non-state actors goes to NGOs' conflict prevention activities.

The regional instrument for the Balkans is the CARDS programme. 'One of the priorities for CARDS regional funds is to support democratic stabilisation and civil society, including minority rights, media and good governance. As a complement to the CARDS national programmes and the EIDHR, non-governmental activities in the fields of human rights, fundamental freedoms and sustainable development will be promoted'.[21] These are all areas with a strong conflict prevention potential, but no figures are available on how much of the CARDS funds are allocated to these areas. With regard to NGO participation CARDS seems to be somewhere in between the Asia and Latin America programmes and the Middle East, with 12.7% of the funding going to NSAs.

From the Eastern Europe and Central Asia programme 12.1% of the funding goes to NSA. Partnership and Cooperation Agreements are the basis for cooperation with the 13 countries of Eastern Europe and Central Asia which benefit from the TACIS programme. There is no specific provision for involving NSA in the preparation of the indicative and action programmes. 'Support for civil society' has been selected as a priority in the majority of the CSPs.[22]

So the picture of EU-NGO operational cooperation is very nuanced. There is one budget line with which the Commission explicitly supports NGO conflict prevention activities. Under the other budget lines the involvement of NGOs and the importance attached to conflict prevention varies.

4.3   Training and capacity building

There is very little support from the Commission for the capacity building projects of EU NGOs for southern NGOs. Only under the EIDHR can the building capacity of international, regional or local organisations involved in conflict prevention be supported.

Under the Cotonou Agreement local NGOs have direct access to EDF funding for capacity building. In marked contrast to the three other ways of funding, the National Authorising Officer only has to agree on the global amount of resources allocated to this type of activity and not on the individual projects.

EU NGOs have trained Commission officials. Due to limited funds for training and due to the difficulties in accessing them, this has only occasionally occurred. One example was when World Vision trained ECHO staff on 'Local capacities for peace approach-Do no harm' in October 2001.

The Commission has set up a network of training institutions based in the Member States that train civilians for EU crisis management missions in the areas of the rule of law and civilian administration. Some Member States have asked NGOs to carry out this training. In the UK, for example, Peaceworkers UK are responsible. The courses include training in human rights, democracy and conflict prevention issues. This is a very important initiative which merits further development.

---

[21] European Commission, *Participation of non-state actors in EC development policy* (Brussels, 7 November 2002, COM (2002) 598 final), p. 13.

[22] Idem.

5. Conclusion: The Vision for EU-NGOs Cooperation

There are two main arguments for cooperation with NGOs. The first one concerns the policy dialogue. If EU institutions engage with NGOs more rational and more democratically legitimised solutions can be found. With regard to EU support for operational NGO activities and training, the main argument is the effectiveness of the peace process and the need to involve civil society within it. In the broad majority of cases there are many factors which lead to the outbreak of violence. These factors are economic and political, some of them can be controlled by the government, others are beyond its control. This means that peace building can only be effective, when all actors cooperate. Those working on economic development, those advising on security sector reforms, those working with the government and those working with civil society. Only where there is a regular and intensive exchange of ideas and experiences, programmes and strategies and when all the actors discuss how they can cooperate and create synergies, can peace be achieved.

The EU has made progress in cooperating with NGOs in the area of conflict prevention. During the last few years, the EU has created a good policy framework for conflict prevention and the Commission has undertaken efforts to mainstream conflict prevention into development cooperation. With its communication on the participation of non-state actors in EC development cooperation the Commission has taken a first step in ensuring that cooperation with NGOs is more fruitful. The most concrete progress has been achieved by the Cotonou Agreement and its provision on the participation of civil society and on conflict prevention. The next huge but very important step could be to include similar provisions to those in the Cotonou Agreement within other frameworks for regional cooperation.

What is missing is a coherent policy on dialogue with NGOs. Yes, there is the Cotonou, but under the other regional instruments it depends very much on the goodwill and interest of individual delegation staff or staff in Brussels, whether dialogue with NGOs is taking place. The same is true for dialogue on sectoral issues. A more systematic and in-depth policy dialogue is therefore needed, if the EU wants to benefit from the contribution which NGOs can make to finding more rational and democratic solutions.

Also the EU has never developed a consistent policy for cooperating with the NGOs. The share of funding that is channelled through non-states actors differs hugely from one regional instrument to the other. This might be due to the different situations in the different regions, but it is a fact, that the EU has never really discussed this aspect. In its communication on cooperation with non-state actors, it only describes the status quo, how the Commission currently engages with NGOs and the different mechanisms involved. It does not discuss the question of how this relationship should look like nor does it look at the different models practised in the Member States.

In some cases operational cooperation with conflict prevention NGOs is limited because insufficient attention is being paid to conflict prevention issues. This has been the case in humanitarian assistance, where more than half of the funding goes to NGO projects, but where conflict prevention is not seen as a relevant issue. In other cases conflict prevention is taken seriously, but the potential of cooperation with NGOs is underestimated and is not fully exploited. This is the case with the RRM.

And while the Cotonou Agreement includes excellent provisions both for cooperating with civil society as well as for conflict prevention, the challenge for the EU now lies in its implementation. The EU has a tradition of focusing on the economic aspects of development cooperation. It is still in a process of moving from measuring effectiveness by the amounts of allocated funding to measuring actual results, the change achieved on the ground. The coming years will show whether the EU will manage to shift towards a more comprehensive political engagement.

To achieve this, the EU will need to provide concrete guidance on how to implement the Cotonou provisions on conflict prevention and on civil society participation for its staff in Brussels and for the delegations.

Engaging with local NGOs is not always easy. In situations with a risk of violent conflicts, NGOs are often weak, suppressed, and divided. It might be difficult to judge the background of NGOs. It is therefore crucial that delegations have adequate staff with good local knowledge. At the same time it is also important that the EU cooperates with a broad range of NGOs, not simply those based in the capital, but also those from across the whole variety of political, religious or ethnic spectrum.

It also seems that there is potential with regard to increasing the conflict sensitivity of Commission staff. Due to the huge amounts of aid administered by the Commission, but also due to its responsibility in agriculture and trade, the EU has a huge impact on conflicts in developing countries. There is a clear need for the EU to ensure that the impact of community policies on conflicts does not exacerbate tensions but contributes to the prevention of violence.

The Commission has tried to mainstream conflict prevention into its development cooperation, through the distribution of 'conflict indicators' and through the facilitation of workshop seminars on conflict issues. Such workshops were the responsibility of the Conflict Prevention Network (CPN), created in 1997 and disbanded in 2001. Now, the Conflict Prevention Unit has taken over this role. Although keen to enhance the expertise and training of Commission staff *vis-à-vis* conflict prevention, there exist no formal structures committing the CPU to this, so it occurs on an *ad hoc* basis. The consequence of this has been that some officials have not really been made very sensitive to conflict issues. Some desk officers have failed to receive the 'conflict indicators' prepared by the CPU, and others have felt that the organised seminars were not relevant to their country or region. In relation to its huge staff and the high staff turnover, the training budget of the Commission is insufficient.

Finally, political will is crucial. The EU needs to make both conflict prevention and cooperation with civil society more of a priority, so that dialogue with civil society is no longer considered a luxury and desk officers will find time to work on conflict prevention.

The EU is now developing a security concept. This is a litmus test that will show how seriously the EU takes conflict prevention. Will it base itself on a more traditional understanding of security in which arms and the threat of violence play a crucial role, or will it try to respond to the new security challenges such as terrorism and violence from non-state actors and develop a more comprehensive security concept, which also addresses the root causes of conflicts and is aware of the importance of involving civil society in peace-building processes? Security cannot be built against the background of huge parts of the population living in outright poverty and feeling excluded from important political processes. Security requires poverty elimination, the promotion of human rights, and democratisation at the national, regional and global levels. If we do not want anarchy we need rules to govern international and global relations. Rules must be enforced, but they must first and foremost be respected and agreed upon. The EU has a reputation as a 'soft power' using political and economic means. When in the past it has used these means in a coordinated way the EU has been successful. A good example of this is the Balkans. With the EU being the most important trading partner of most countries in the world, the biggest donor of development aid and potentially an important political actor, the EU is in a better position than any other actor to respond adequately to the new security threats and to prevent the outbreak of violence.

Chapter 25
THE EUROPEAN UNION'S ROLE IN PROMOTING THE PREVENTION OF VIOLENT CONFLICTS WITHIN THE BUSINESS SECTOR

by Vincent Kronenberger[1]

1. INTRODUCTION

In 2000, a well-known and important report, *The Business of Peace*, underlined the challenges which companies face when operating in conflict-prone countries: dealing with repressive or corrupt regimes; benefiting from 'war economies'; facilitating illegal or illicit activities; exploiting strategic resources; managing security arrangements; creating a 'honey-pot' effect through large-scale investments; promoting responsible distribution of public revenues generated by business operations, deciding on withdrawal versus 'constructive engagement'; engaging in the role of a diplomat or political player; undertaking collective corporate action versus individual activities; measuring and accounting for responsible wealth creation; managing company reputation; and establishing the limits of effective business engagement in social investments and conflict prevention.[2] While the role of a few, large transnational companies in fuelling or exacerbating violent conflicts is generally acknowledged,[3] little attention has been paid to the contribution of

---

[1] Doctor of Law, legal secretary at the Court of First Instance of the European Communities, Luxembourg. I would like to thank Jan Wouters, Kim Eling, Meri Rantala and Javier Niño-Pérez for their invaluable comments on the draft of this article. Naturally, all views expressed remain entirely personal and do not reflect those of my institution.

[2] Jane Nelson, et al., *The Business of Peace: The Private Sector as a Partner in Conflict Prevention and Resolution* (London, International Alert, Council on Economic Priorities and the Prince of Wales International Business Leaders Forum 2000), executive summary, p. 4, available at <http://www.international-alert.org/publications.htm#business>.

[3] See OECD Working Paper on International Investment, *Multinational Enterprises in Situations of Violent Conflict and Widespread Human Rights Abuses* (Paris, OECD May 2002), notably at p. 24: 'Some serious concerns have been raised. Companies' activities have placed them in close proximity to human rights abuses (some well documented, others only allegations). Companies have provided billions of US dollars in revenues to corrupt regimes, and, by signing confidentiality agreements with them, have at times appeared to be "silent partners" in wrongdoing. In addition to the human suffering that companies may indirectly be party to, this causes problems for the international policy and business communities as they try to build the case for the benefits of foreign direct investment'. Cf., also, the report by B. Manby, *The price of oil: Corporate Responsibility and Human Rights violations in Nigeria's oil producing communities* (New-York, Human Rights Watch 1999) and the recent discussion by the UN Security Council on the role of business in conflict prevention, peacekeeping and post conflict peace-building, Press Release SC/8058, 15 April 2004.

V. Kronenberger and J. Wouters, eds., The European Union and Conflict Prevention
© 2004, T·M·C·ASSER PRESS, *The Hague, The Netherlands*

companies to the prevention of violent conflict,[4] as well as to the initiatives of international organisations in developing and enhancing such a contribution. This chapter aims to scrutinise the role of the European Union (hereinafter the 'EU'), the territory on which numerous transnational corporations are located,[5] concerning the promotion of conflict prevention in the business sector. After examining the EU's achievements (section 2.), this article will discuss the EU's role in the promotion of conflict prevention initiatives by the business sector (section 3.), as well as the instruments it has at its disposal which might achieve these objectives (section 4.). However, before embarking upon this study, a few preliminary remarks need to be made. These relate to the definition of the expressions 'conflict prevention' and 'business sector' used in this contribution (section 1.1) as well as some explanations regarding the reasons for involving companies in the prevention of violent conflicts (section 1.2).

1.1 What is meant by 'conflict prevention' and the 'business sector'?

Conflict prevention has both operational and structural dimensions.[6] Operational conflict prevention comprises short-term measures which aim to avoid imminent violence. Structural conflict prevention refers to medium and long-term measures meant to tackle the root-causes of violent conflicts or the factors which may lead to such conflicts. Such measures also pursue the objective of avoiding any re-eruption of conflict. Although tackling the deep causes of conflicts is probably the most efficient means to prevent any eruption or reignition of conflicts, these causes are multiple. In its 2001 Communication on conflict prevention,[7] the European Commission listed the following non-exhaustive causes: poverty, economic stagnation, uneven distribution of resources, weak social structures, undemocratic governance, systematic discrimination, oppression of the rights of minorities, destabilising effects of refugee flows, ethnic antagonisms, religious

---

[4] See, however, the studies of J. Nelson, et al., op. cit. n. 2; A. Gerson, 'Peace-Building: private sector's role', 95 *American Journal of International Law* (2001), at 102-119; P. Champain, 'Assessing the Corporate Sector in Mainstreaming Conflict Prevention', in L. van de Goor and M. Huber (eds.), *Mainstreaming Conflict Prevention. Concept and Practice* (Baden-Baden, SWP Conflict Prevention Network, Nomos Verlagsgesellschaft 2002), pp. 145-172 and A. Wenger and D. Möckli, *Conflict Prevention. The Untapped Potential of the Business Sector* (Boulder-London, Lynne Rienner Publishers 2003).

[5] Among the 100 largest firms ranked by foreign assets (by UN ECOSOC) in 1999, 46 were located in the Member States of the EU and their main business sectors were natural resources exploitation (in particular, petroleum, gas and electricity), chemicals and pharmaceuticals, motor vehicles, beverages and food, telecommunications and electronics.

[6] See, e.g., Chapters 3 and 4 of the Final Report of the Carnegie Commission on Preventing Deadly Conflict (1997), available at <http://www.wilsoncenter.org/subsites/ccpdc/pubs/rept97/finfr.htm> and A. Wenger and D. Möckli, op. cit. n. 4, p. 35; see also, Michael S. Lund, 'Preventing Violent Conflicts: Progress and Shortfall' in P. Cross (ed.) *Contributing to Preventive Action* (Baden-Baden, SWP, Conflict Prevention Network Yearbook 1997-1998, Nomos 1998), p. 21, at 27-28.

[7] COM (2001) 211 final, 11 April 2001.

and cultural intolerance, social injustice and the proliferation of weapons of mass destruction and small arms.[8]

While the business sector has, in general, little to do with operational conflict prevention, it has important potential for cooperating in the efforts to combat, at an early stage, the root-causes and factors of conflicts, in particular by enabling local populations to profit from the benefits of peace.[9] Consequently, this contribution will focus on structural conflict prevention, including post-conflict reconstruction as a means to minimise the reignition of conflicts, rather than operational conflict prevention.

Moreover, the present author has deliberately chosen the expression 'business sector' for its general and wide characteristics. While transnational corporations[10] – also often called multinational enterprises[11] – are large legal entities that are facing most of the challenges of operating in violent or conflict-prone States, it is nevertheless important not to forget the role of small and medium-sized enter-prises (hereinafter 'SMEs') in this context. SMEs represent a large part of the business economy, accounting for approximately two-thirds of employment and 60% of value-added in the European Community (EC).[12] The 'internationalisa-tion' of SMEs[13] implies that their operations in third States may occur in violent or potentially violent contexts. In third States where businesses are essentially lo-cal, SMEs are often the sole providers of employment and may therefore be con-sidered as guarantees for socio-economic stability.

From another perspective, a recent study by the NGO International Alert has classified businesses into three simple categories.[14] The first category refers to

---

[8] Communication, p. 5.

[9] See section 1.2 below.

[10] According to the UN Draft Norms on the Responsibilities of Transnational Corporations and Other Business Enterprises with Regard to Human Rights, a 'transnational corporation' is defined as 'an economic entity operating in more than one country or a cluster of economic entities operating in two or more countries, whatever their legal form, whether in their home country or country of activ-ity, and whether taken individually or collectively': see the version of August 2003 adopted by Resolution 2003/16 of the UN Sub-Commission on the Promotion and the Protection of Human Rights (UN. Doc E/CN.4/Sub.2/2003/L.11 at 52 (2003)). On 20 April 2004, the Commission on Hu-man Rights decided, without a vote, to recommend that the UN ECOSOC Council confirm the im-portance and priority it accords to the question of responsibilities of transnational corporations and related business enterprises with regard to human rights. The Commission also requested the Office of the High Commissioner for Human Rights to compile a report setting out the scope and legal sta-tus of existing initiatives and standards in this area. However, the Commission indicated that the draft norms had not been requested and had no legal standing (cf., Decision 2004/116 in Doc. E/CN.4/2004/L.11/Add.7, 22 April 2004, p. 81). The draft norms are available at <http://www.unm.edu/humanrts/links/norms-Aug2003.html>.

[11] Cf., OECD Guidelines for Multinational Enterprises, available at <www.oecd.org/daf/invest-ment/guidelines/> which, however, do not provide any definition of the concept. See further on these guidelines, section 2.1 below.

[12] Commission staff working paper: Creating an entrepreneurial Europe: the activities of the Eu-ropean Union for small and medium-sized enterprises (SMEs), SEC (2003) 58, 21 January 2003, p. 16.

[13] Idem, p. 103.

[14] International Alert, 'Supporting and Enhancing the Business Sector's role in Peacebuilding', 3 Global Policy Notes (2002), at 1, available at <http://www.international-alert.org/publications.htm#business>.

rogue companies and industries which directly profit from a conflict environment. According to International Alert, as far as these actors are concerned, States may have little choice other than to criminalise them or their activities. In the second category fall investing companies which inadvertently heighten instability in host societies. Actions in relation to such undertakings relate to the suppression of the negative impact which their operations have. Finally, the third category encompasses local business communities as a peace-building constituency. Although useful, this categorisation appears to be over-simplified. It indeed opposes somewhat too abruptly, large foreign companies, the operations of which would either profit from conflict or have negative impacts, to local businesses the actions of which would, apparently systematically, offer peace-building potential. This classification also seems to imply that, if companies are making profits in a conflict environment, their presence in that State would be illegitimate. If such an interpretation is correct, it appears to disregard the fact that the companies' presence may also have, to a certain extent, positive intended or unintended effects on local communities, such as, e.g., the creation of employment or the continuation of socio-economic programmes launched in host countries. In those cases the foreign companies involved will often face the dilemma between whether it is wiser to leave the country abandoning at the same time autochthonous people to their fate or to remain in the country but to subject their employees to possible physical danger and themselves to material damage, criticism and/or boycotts by stakeholders, including consumers.

1.2   Why involve companies in the prevention of violent conflicts?

It is undisputed that the main responsibility for the prevention of violent conflicts lies on States and international organisations, among which is the EU. One may wonder, however, whether, beyond moral values, there are rational reasons for involving companies in such initiatives. In fact, the participation of companies in conflict prevention will be all the more active and efficient once they understand the economic interest in doing so.[15] From a general point of view, it has rightly been pointed out that the idea of involving companies in the prevention of conflicts finds its origin in the changing nature of both conflicts and international relations.[16] While conflicts have shifted from inter-state to intrastate, which often implies the direct involvement of civil society, in particular the business community, international relations have experienced the growing participation of eco-

---

[15] P. Champain, op. cit. n. 4, at 148, calls this 'understanding the business case' of 'the economic benefits of peace'.

[16] A. Gerson, op. cit. n. 4, p. 102 and Wengler and Mökli, op. cit. n. 4, at 21-25. The latter authors indicate that, between 1989 and 2000, there were more than 100 intrastate violent conflicts but only seven inter-state armed conflicts around the world.

nomic operators through a mixture of trade liberalisation and privatisation,[17] in what is usually now called globalisation. More precisely, in their search for new markets, often located in unstable countries, companies are increasingly facing conflicts, which may turn into violence. Such violent conflicts create costs for the operations of companies.[18] Six main kinds of costs can be identified: material damage, security and risk management costs, personnel costs, costs related to the business environment, in particular, the disruption of basic infrastructures and networks, as well as reputation costs if the companies are considered by public opinion and investors, justified or not, to be too much involved in or to be the cause of violence.

A rational solution is therefore to avoid or to lower such costs by trying to pre-vent the eruption of the causes of conflicts, in particular their root-causes. How-ever, the problem is that such costs may be considered as an acceptable burden if the companies think that their operations are or will be more lucrative. For in-stance, fierce competition over natural resources may lead certain companies to deliberately disregard respect for human rights or to ignore the negative impact of their activities on local communities, in order to retain their market. In other words, if they do not capture the market, another company will get it. Under pres-sure from NGOs, 'ethical' pension funds, consumers, as well as, in some cases, companies themselves, the companies' responsibility towards autochthonous populations has been admitted as a correlation to the growing role which they play in the international economic sphere. Hence, the involvement of companies in the prevention of violent conflicts may also be seen as part and parcel of the external dimension of Corporate Social Responsibility (hereinafter 'CSR'). How-ever, the concept of CSR, 'whereby companies integrate social and environmen-tal concerns in their business operations in their interaction with their stakeholders on a voluntary basis',[19] does not yet fully correlate with the multifaceted dimension of conflict prevention. According to empirical studies, companies do not generally see conflict prevention as part of CSR,[20] whereas

---

[17] Including, e.g., the privatisation of security: see on this subject, D. Lilly and M. von Tangen Page (eds.), *Security Sector Reform: The Challenges and Opportunities of the Privatisation of Secu-rity* (London, International Alert 2002).

[18] A 2001 research programme undertaken in Sri Lanka estimated that this country, without the war, would have created approximately 103,000 more jobs in the tourist industry alone and foreign direct investment (FDI) would have been five times higher than the level at that time. It is also esti-mated that the rate of economic growth between 1982 and 1988 would have been 5.4% rather than 4.6%: see: *Cost of the war*, National Peace Council of Sri Lanka (London, Marga Institute and Inter-national Alert 2001) quoted by P. Champain, op. cit. n. 4, at 148.

[19] Communication from the Commission concerning Corporate Social Responsibility: A business contribution to Sustainable Development, COM (2002) 347 final, 2 July 2002, at 5.

[20] Cf., Collaborative for Development Action, *The Role of Business in Conflict Resolution and Peace Building*, Corporate Engagement Project Issue Paper, February 2003, available at <http://www.cdainc.com/cda/cda-publications.php#cep>.

NGOs call for an explicit link between CSR and conflict prevention.[21]

Anyhow, as with CSR, companies face problems in mainstreaming or integrating conflict prevention into their business operations. According to one study,[22] this operation comprises five main components:

- understanding the business case;
- using frameworks to analyse the conflict (mainly the dynamics of the conflict, the actors and the role of the company);
- familiarity with conflict prevention processes (namely a six-stage process comprising research and analysis, stakeholder consultation, problem solving, implementing practical projects, institutionalising business engagement and documenting the lessons learned);
- availability of relevant skills and tools (e.g., technical expertise but also risk assessment tools);
- adherence to guidelines and regulations.

While the last point has received some attention, the others are more difficult to appraise. In any event, at each of these stages, the support of third parties may be needed. In this respect, the EU may have a role to play. As indicated above, the following sections will examine the shift from rhetoric to action which the EU has embarked upon (section 2.), the EU's role in the promotion of conflict prevention initiatives by the business sector (section 3.), and whether the instruments the EU possesses which are targeted at companies can achieve these objectives (section 4.).

2.   FROM RHETORIC TO ACTION

The EU's actions towards the promotion of conflict prevention among the business sector have, so far, been limited in scope. They often remain at the stage of rhetoric and good intentions (section 2.1). However, noticeable concrete actions have been undertaken, especially as regards companies which are active in the natural resources sector (section 2.2).

2.1 **Rhetoric and good intentions**

In its 2001 Communication on conflict prevention, the Commission expressed its

---

[21] International Alert and Saferworld, *Ensuring Progress in the Prevention of Violent Conflict: Priorities for the Greek and Italian EU Presidencies 2003*, April 2003, p. 6, available at <http://www.international-alert.org/>. This idea was also supported by numerous interventions in the discussion held by the UN Security Council on 15 April 2004, op. cit. n. 3.

[22] P. Champain, op. cit. n. 4, at 148-154.

commitment to 'promoting actively the OECD guidelines for multinational enterprises which aim at encouraging businesses to behave responsibly when operating abroad, in particular in developing countries'.[23] While, at the time, the communication also announced that the Commission's Green Paper on CSR would 'address the issue of conflict prevention and the role which business can play in this field',[24] the 2001 Green Paper fell short of this promise. Although the Green Paper identified an external dimension of CSR, extending to the respect of human rights by companies operating in third countries,[25] it did not dedicate any space to the role that the EU and companies could play together in preventing conflicts. The EU Programme for the prevention of violent conflicts endorsed at the June 2001 European Council meeting in Göteborg, while echoing the Commission's communication, asked that 'methods for EU co-operation with the private sector in the field of conflict prevention be developed, drawing, *inter alia*, on progress made by the UN Global Partnership, the OECD guidelines for multinational enterprises and the G8'.[26] To date, however, no such methods are in place.[27] These statements give some indications as to how the Commission and the Member States perceive the role of the European Union in this field. Basically, two points can be made: on the one hand, the EU appears to be satisfied by making references to benchmarks developed by other international forums (section 2.1.1). On the other hand, the EU appears to set goals for itself which are too ambitious (section 2.1.2).

2.1.1 *Benchmarks developed in other international forums*

International organisations have developed a number of initiatives in order to encourage or strengthen the respect of human rights and internationally agreed social and environmental standards by companies. Such initiatives comprise the OECD guidelines for multinational companies,[28] the International Labour Organisation (ILO) Tripartite Declaration on principles concerning multinational enterprises and social policy and the Declaration on fundamental principles and

---

[23] Communication, op. cit. n. 7, p. 20.

[24] Idem.

[25] See the Green Paper entitled 'Promoting a European framework for corporate social responsibility', July 2001, pp. 14-16. See on this subject, the comprehensive study by A.J.C. Gatto, *The European Union and Corporate Social Responsibility: Can the EU contribute to the Accountability of Multinational Enterprises for Human Rights?* (Leuven, Working Paper No. 32 Institute for International Law, September 2002), available at <http://www.law.kuleuven.ac.be/iir/eng/index.html>.

[26] EU Programme for the Prevention of Violent Conflicts (9537/1/01 REV 1), Göteborg, June 2001, available at <http://ue.eu.int/en/Info/eurocouncil/index.htm>.

[27] Note that the Implementation of the EU Programme for the Prevention of Violent Conflicts (9991/02) presented by the Presidency to the European Council in Seville on 21-22 June 2002 did not even mention the role of the business sector in this area. This report is available at <http://ue.eu.int/en/Info/eurocouncil/index.htm>.

[28] Available at <www.oecd.org/daf/investment/guidelines/>.

rights at work,[29] the UN Global Compact initiative,[30] as well as the recently proposed UN Norms on the responsibilities of transnational corporations and other
business enterprises with regard to human rights.[31] As their names suggest, all
these initiatives are not specifically targeted towards conflict prevention. However, they do participate in the fight against the root-causes of conflicts.

As noted above, the EU refers to benchmarks developed in other international
forums for companies to behave responsibly. So far, the Commission and the
Member States do not seem to share the ambitions of the European Parliament to
develop a *sui generis* European code of conduct for Community companies operating abroad, in particular in developing countries,[32] and a legally binding framework with sanctions for companies which contribute to conflicts.[33] It is therefore
worth dedicating some lines to the above-mentioned international efforts which
the EU supports.

The first and most quoted instrument by EU institutions is the OECD guidelines for multinational enterprises.[34] These guidelines were originally adopted as
part of the OECD Council Declaration on International Investment and Multinational Enterprises in 1976. The guidelines have undergone several amendments,
the last and most important one being the revision of 2000. They provide for voluntary non-binding principles and standards for responsible business conduct, addressed by adhering States[35] to their multinational enterprises. The guidelines are
divided into nine chapters. They contain, besides general recommendations, principles on information disclosure, principles of good behaviour in employment
and industrial relations, including the contribution to the abolition of child labour
and the elimination of all forms of compulsory labour, recommendations on the
protection of the environment, public health and safety, on the fight against brib-

---

[29] The first Declaration was adopted in Geneva in November 1977, the second was adopted in
Geneva in June 1998. The aim of the Tripartite Declaration of Principles 'is to encourage the positive contribution which multinational enterprises can make to economic and social progress and to
minimize and resolve the difficulties to which their various operations may give rise, taking into account the United Nations resolutions advocating the Establishment of a New International Economic
Order'. The Tripartite Declaration refers to a vast number of ILO Conventions and Recommendations. An addendum to the Tripartite Declaration was adopted in Geneva in November 1995 and it
added a list of relevant ILO instruments adopted since 1977. The texts of both Declarations are
available at <http://www.ilo.org/public/english/standards/norm/sources/>.

[30] See <http://www.unglobalcompact.org/Portal/Default.asp>.

[31] Draft Norms approved by the UN Sub-Commission on the Promotion and the Protection of
Human Rights on 13 August 2003, op. cit. n. 10.

[32] European Parliament resolution on EU standards for European enterprises operating in developing countries: towards a European Code of Conduct, *OJEC* [1999] C 104/180.

[33] Cf., European Parliament Resolution on the Commission Communication on Conflict Prevention, *OJEC* [2002] C 177E/291, at 294.

[34] Note that, within the framework of Article 304 TEC, the European Community has established
a close cooperation with the OECD (cf., Protocol No. 1 to the OECD Convention of 14 December
1960). Although the Community is not *de jure* a Contracting Party to the OECD, it benefits from a
de facto membership status. Moreover, all its Member States are also members the OECD.

[35] Currently the Member States of the OECD, plus Argentina, Brazil and Chile.

ery, on the protection of consumer interests, on science and technology, as well as on competition and taxation. The guidelines are not a substitute for and cannot override national law and regulations. They should not place a multinational enterprise in a situation where it faces conflicting requirements.[36] The promotion of, and a consultation mechanism on, the guidelines is established in each adhering country, through National Contact Points which report annually to a central body, the OECD Committee on International Investment and Multinational Enterprises (CIME), overseeing the functioning of the guidelines.

Although the guidelines represent, as the OECD puts it, 'the only comprehensive, multilaterally endorsed code of conduct for multinational enterprises',[37] and are even considered as the 'European Union's standard of reference in the field of CSR',[38] they suffer from two main and related shortcomings. On the one hand, the guidelines are, in conformity with traditional international law, only addressed to governments, not to the enterprises themselves. Hence, it will often depend on the dynamism of each National Contact Point to promote the guidelines on its territory. Moreover, given the often highly complex and hybrid structure of multinational companies, which are, by the way, not defined in the guidelines, implementation issues may often arise as to the exact material scope of the recommendations. Even though it stems from the 2000 review of the guidelines that they should apply to companies in the adhering States, including for operations by their subsidiaries or affiliated companies abroad, it is likely that overseeing the actual implementation of the guidelines by companies for such operations will be an extremely difficult task. This issue relates to the second shortcoming: the geographical scope of the guidelines is limited to OECD members, Argentina, Brazil and Chile, therefore excluding the most important bulk of countries where conflict potentials exist and where the recommendations could, if promoted and applied there, possibly prevent their eruption.[39]

As far as these problems are concerned, the European Commission has recently put forward the proposal that, in each of the European Community's external agreements a new phrase be inserted according to which the Parties (or the Community and its Member States) would 'remind their multinational enterprises of their recommendations to observe the OECD guidelines for multinational en-

---

[36] See OECD guidelines, text, commentary and clarifications, 31 October 2001, p. 12, available at <www.oecd.org/daf/investment/guidelines/>.

[37] See Policy Brief, The OECD Guidelines for Multinational Enterprises (Paris, OECD June 2001), p. 7, available <www.oecd.org/daf/investment/guidelines/>.

[38] J. Niño-Peréz, 'The European Debate on Corporate Social Responsibility and Conflict Prevention', speech delivered at a conference organised by the German Federal Ministry of Economic Cooperation and Development and the Development Policy Forum in Bonn on 26 November 2003, p. 2.

[39] One could argue that the non-binding character of the guidelines could be a third deficiency. However, as will be developed below, the complexity of the area may not be adapted to imposing a general binding framework on companies.

terprises, wherever they operate'.[40] This should naturally not mean that the Contracting Party to the agreement with the Community and its Member States would, even indirectly, be adhering to the OECD guidelines. However, it would give a clear message to the authorities of that State together with the Community companies operating there that the recommendations, in particular as far as human rights, labour rights and combating bribery are concerned, should be adhered to. As far as the present author is aware, such a phrase has, so far, only been inserted in a 'Joint Declaration concerning guidelines to investors' to the Association Agreement between the European Community and its Member States, on the one part, and Chile, on the other, signed on 18 November 2002.[41] It seems that the Commission's services are also intending to insert such a reference in the ACP Economic Partnership Agreements (EPAs).[42] The negotiations on these agreements were launched on 27th September 2002 within the framework of the 2000 Cotonou Partnership Agreement and are intended to be concluded in 2007.[43] Contrary to the case of the Association Agreement with Chile, a State that is already a signatory to the OECD guidelines, the insertion of such a declaration in the EPAs would raise the awareness of non-adhering countries to the guidelines.

Another often quoted instrument is the UN Global Compact.[44] This initiative, directly addressed to business leaders, was proposed by the UN Secretary General Kofi Annan at the World Economic Forum in Davos in January 1999. The UN Global Compact, concretely launched in July 2000, is aimed at bringing companies (and business and industrial associations) together with UN agencies,[45] labour and civil society to support 10 principles derived from the Universal Declaration of Human Rights, the ILO Declaration on Fundamental Principles and Rights at Work and the Rio Declaration on Environment and Development. These 10 principles are:

---

[40] Communication from the Commission of 2 July 2002 concerning Corporate Social Responsibility: A Business Contribution to Sustainable Development, COM (2002) 347 final, p. 24.

[41] Cf., the agreement published in *OJEC* [2002] L 352/1. In conformity with a Council Decision of 18 November 2002, the agreement is being temporarily and partially (trade chapter) applied until the national parliaments of the Member States ratify it. The first Association Council of the Agreement held on 27 March 2003 called upon national parliaments to speed up their ratification process.

[42] Cf., J. Niño-Peréz, op. cit. n. 38, p. 3.

[43] See *Economic Partnership Agreements. A new approach in the relations between the European Union and the ACP countries* (Brussels, European Commission 2002), p. 3, available at <http://www.europa.eu.int/comm/development/body/publications/descript/publ_10_en.cfm>.

[44] Quoted, e.g., in the Council Resolution on the CSR Green Paper, *OJEC* [2002] C 86/3, point 16. The EU Programme for the Prevention of Violent Conflicts, adopted by the European Council in Göteborg (June 2001) refers to the UN Global Partnership which is an indirect reference to the UN Global Compact.

[45] The five core UN agencies participating in the UN Global Compact are the United Nations Environment Programme (UNEP), the United Nations Development Programme (UNDP), the ILO, the Office of the High Commissioner for Human Rights (OHCHR) and the United Nations Industrial Development Organisation (UNIDO).

- businesses should support and respect the protection of internationally proclaimed human rights within their sphere of influence;
- they should make sure that they are not complicit in human rights abuses;
- businesses should uphold the freedom of association and the effective recognition of the right to collective bargaining;
- they should uphold the elimination of all forms of forced and compulsory labour;
- they should uphold the effective abolition of child labour;
- they should eliminate discrimination in respect of employment and occupation;
- businesses should support a precautionary approach to environmental challenges;
- they should undertake initiatives to promote greater environmental responsibility; and
- they should encourage the development and diffusion of environmentally friendly technologies;
- they should work against all forms of corruption, including extorsion and bribery. [46]

The UN Global Compact is a voluntary corporate responsibility initiative.[47] In 2003, this network encompassed more than 1,000 companies, over half of them being from developing countries.[48] In terms of transparency and image, these companies can certainly benefit from being quoted among the participants in the UN Global Compact. However, participation does not give any guarantee that the principles are complied with in the field. Not surprisingly, one of the critical issues faced by the UN Global Compact Office is controlling the implementation of the principles to which companies commit themselves. The UN Global Compact Office acknowledges that it has neither the capacity nor is it designed as a static verification instrument.[49] Nevertheless, in January 2003 it adopted a new strategic approach according to which participating companies are asked to communicate the ways in which they are implementing the 10 principles quoted above using their annual reports and/or other prominent public reports. Such an approach is to be welcomed. In the same vein, the UN Global Compact has decided to establish a 'task force to develop a process to address companies

---

[46] The inclusion of this 10th principle on transparency and corruption was discussed during the Global Compact Leaders Summit convened on 24-25 June 2004.

[47] The network is managed by an office located at the UN headquarters in New York, chaired by Mr. George Kell.

[48] UN Global Compact Annual Report 2002-2003, available at <http://www.unglobalcompact.org/irj/servlet/prt/portal/prtroot/com.sapportals.km.xmlformpreview?XMLFormID=KMNews&show/test=dc95dd24-f600-0010-0080-de24db575b11>, p. 7.

[49] See, Global Compact Database of Companies, available at <http://www.unglobalcompact.org/Portal/>.

engaged in "egregious violations" of the 10 principles'.[50] The fact that the UN Global Compact directly addresses companies is certainly one of the reasons for its rapid success. For participating companies, the public image benefits are immediate. From the point of view of the organisation, the close contact with companies is of assistance in better understanding the problems they may face, in the field, as regards conflicting requirements between international standards to which they commit themselves and legislation, regulations and/or practices of their host State.

Whereas the EC/EU explicitly intends to promote the OECD guidelines, both by its participation in the OECD and, more recently, by specific references to those guidelines in external agreements, its interest has been less explicit towards the UN Global Compact. Naturally, one reason may well be that the Community does not participate directly in initiatives developed under that body. However, it does have an observer status at the ILO, one of the core agencies of the UN Global Compact. A possible way to develop relations with the UN Global Compact would be to initiate cooperation in the field between delegations of the Commission in third States and the Global Compact local networks so far launched in over twenty States.

By its references to instruments developed by other international organisations, the EU obviously wishes to avoid any overlapping. However, as mentioned above, none of these instruments are specifically targeted at the prevention of conflicts, although, in the long-term, they may be beneficial to that aim. This very cautious approach by the EU institutions is paradoxically accompanied by over-ambitious aims.

2.1.2   Setting ambitious aims?

In Göteborg, the European Council called for a *method for cooperation* to be developed with the business sector. The European Council did not, however, provide any indications as to which method the Heads of State and Government possibly had in mind, which kind of cooperation could be proposed and with whom such cooperation should be developed. What appeared to be clearer was that the Commission would have to develop such a method. Interestingly, in its publicly available documents, the Commission does not even mention any cooperation with the business sector. Hence, its documents relating to CSR, in so far as they are relevant for businesses in preventing conflicts, solely encourage the development of guiding principles ensuring the effectiveness and credibility of private codes of conduct.[51] These documents illustrate that the Commission has not yet foreseen, at least officially, a particular type of cooperation with compa-

---

[50] Report on Advisory Council Meeting, 16 July 2003.

[51] Cf., Communication from the Commission of 2 July 2002 concerning Corporate Social Responsibility: A Business Contribution to Sustainable Development, COM (2002) 347 final, p. 18.

nies concerning their role in the prevention of conflicts. A particular method is therefore even further away from the agenda. The reasons for discrepancies between the ambitious aims of the European Council and the lack of action on the part of the Commission in this respect may be numerous. Generally speaking, Member States are often keen to set ambitious political aims, without fully considering of the human, financial and technical means by which to achieve them. A more technical reason may be that the rapid concern over conflict prevention issues within the Commission has focused more on what the EU/EC could do as an international organisation on its own or in cooperation with other organisations rather than scrutinizing how to better involve the business sector (or civil society in general) in preventing the emergence of conflicts. Basically, working with the private sector has not been a high priority on the agenda of the EU's conflict prevention goals. This is unfortunate given the potential that the EU/EC as an 'economic giant' may have in being involved in cooperation with companies in what is called 'economic peace-building'.[52] This may also be related to the lack of any clear institutional responsibility within the Commission and, in fact, no real overlapping between competent Directorates General (DG). Hence, DG External Relations is in charge of conflict prevention but it does not primarily focus on involving the business sector, whereas CSR falls under the responsibility of DG Employment and Social Affairs, but does not, in principle, encompass conflict prevention, despite its multifaceted feature.[53] The conjunction of these circumstances probably lies at the origin of the lack of an official method to cooperate with the private sector in the prevention of conflicts.

It is worth noting that, so far, the European Council has not called for coercive actions to be adopted and imposed on European companies, unlike what has been proposed on several occasions by the European Parliament[54] and echoed by some NGOs.[55] As will be discussed below, although the binding character of texts could seem attractive to lawyers, the most important issue that one faces is to monitor the enforcement of principles to which companies are, or would be, subject when they operate in third States with violent conflict potential. Whether or not a text is legally binding in the EU does not dramatically change this problem, while possibly raising more legal issues in this already complex area.

More realistically, one could reflect on the kind of methods for cooperation which the EU/EC could initiate with the business sector. Traditional means such

---

[52] Cf., Wenger and Möckli, op. cit. n. 4, especially at 153.

[53] It has already been noted that, according to empirical studies, companies do not generally see conflict prevention as part of CSR: cf., Collaborative for Development Action, 'The Role of Business in Conflict Resolution and Peace Building', Corporate Engagement Project Issue Paper, February 2003, available at <http://www.cdainc.com/cda/cda-publications.php#cep>.

[54] See, European Parliament Report of 9 November 2001, point 13.

[55] International Alert, Safer World, Intermón Oxfam, in cooperation with EPLO and European Platform for Conflict Prevention, 'Putting conflict prevention into practice: Priorities for the Spanish and Danish EU Presidencies 2002', January 2002, p. 20 available at <http://www.international-alert.org/publications.htm#eu>.

as meetings and discussions with the industry and the Member States could be developed and coordinated by the Commission. NGOs and representatives of other international organisations (e.g., UN, ILO, OECD and the World Bank) could and probably should be associated with these meetings, in what could be called a Multistakeholders European Forum on Conflict Prevention.[56] Indeed, it is only with such public-private partnerships in the field of conflict prevention that a real comprehensive strategy can be established. It is time to acknowledge that cooperation with companies and sharing know-how in this field can support efforts undertaken by international organisations, States and NGOs.

In assisting the Commission in the coordination of such meetings, the parties could exchange information relating to the experiences of European companies in third States faced with potential or actual conflict situations. The information would include the negative and positive impact of their businesses in the State of operations, e.g., on local communities, an analysis of the common features of these experiences and defining any possible actions to be undertaken by the Commission and the Member States in promoting, in particular, good behaviour in specific geographic regions or business sectors with the full cooperation of companies. An extensive share of the know-how is particularly important in order to avoid generalising practices which might be efficient in one conflict-related zone but irrelevant in another. A striking example relates to the hiring policy of local staff by companies. Many companies announce – and are often encouraged to adopt[57] – neutral policies with regard to, for example, the ethnic origins of local staff, opting for recruitment policies only based on merit. However, as emphasised by a recent study,[58] within many conflict areas, one issue underlying conflict is the historical disadvantage of some groups as compared to others. Hence the historically privileged group(s) will have traditionally better access to advanced education, often required by a merit-based corporate recruitment policy. In such a situation, the results of a neutral hiring policy can therefore unintentionally favour one group over the others which exactly overlap with and match the divisions which lie at the very heart of the conflict.[59] Such an example illustrates the difficulties of promoting a standard conflict prevention roadmap for companies in their business operations. In the author's opinion, this is precisely why the compilation and cautious analysis of extensive empirical information is a

---

[56] Such a forum could be associated with or incorporated into the Community CSR Multi-Stakeholders forum launched in October 2002.

[57] Cf., e.g., Wenkler and Möckli, op. cit. n. 4, p. 152 who refer to the Multi-Cultural Transformation programme of Deloitte Touche Tohmatsu in South Africa which encompasses a targeted workplace diversity initiative.

[58] Mary B. Anderson, 'Developing Best Practice for Corporate Engagement in Conflict Zones: Lessons Learned from Experience', paper presented in Bonn on 26 November 2002 and available at <http://www.cdainc.com/cda/cda-publications.php#cep>.

[59] Ibid., p. 3.

precondition to launching initiatives such as a Community standard code of conduct for companies operating in conflict-potential countries.

In the field, the Community could develop the role of the Commission's delegations in third States in cooperating with local NGOs and companies. This cooperation could materialise by gathering information to be processed later on the impact which local (in particular SMEs) and/or European companies' activities and investments have within the host State, as well as the development of concrete projects to be defined, enhancing tri-sector partnerships (involving public sector, NGOs and companies), in line with the European Union's strategy on the prevention of conflicts.[60] The development of such partnerships would probably benefit the credibility of companies in the prevention of violent conflicts,[61] while the involvement of the Community could lessen any adverse risks inherent in the projects.

2.2 Concrete actions

So far, the most prominent action concerns the engagement of the EC 'in breaking the link between rough diamonds and violent conflicts and supporting the Kimberley Process'.[62] During the past decade, the trade in rough diamonds[63] has fuelled violent conflicts in particular in Angola, Sierra Leone, Liberia and the Democratic Republic of the Congo. One of the most well-known and documented examples was the funding of UNITA's war efforts in Angola through the control of large productive areas in order to, *inter alia*, buy arms.[64] Whilst the UN Security Council imposed sanctions on Angola, Sierra Leone and Liberia as well as the parties in the conflicts, including, under certain conditions, prohibiting the

---

[60] On tri-sector partnerships, see Tri-sector partnerships – Preventing and Resolving Disputes with Communities and NGOs' Business and Partners for Development, Briefing Note 6, available at <http://www.bpd-naturalresources.org/html/pub_working.html>. Tri-sector partnerships provide examples of cooperation between public organisations, companies and NGOs which improve the impact of concrete business and investment projects within the local communities of the host State by integrating social concerns, better understanding between the parties involved and/or providing a forum for discussion and the prevention of disputes.

[61] Cf., Wengler and Möckli, op. cit. n. 4, p. 170.

[62] Göteborg European Council, June 2001 and recital 2 of Council Regulation (EC) No. 2368/2002 of 20 December 2002 implementing the Kimberley Process certification scheme for the international trade in rough diamonds, *OJEC* [2002] L 358/28.

[63] The diamond industry pipeline is divided into eight stages: 1) exploration and prospecting; 2) mining and recovery of rough diamonds; 3) sorting, valuation and supply of rough diamonds; 4) dealing; 5) manufacturing (i.e., cutting and polishing, leading to polished diamonds); 6) jewellery manufacturing; 7) jewellery wholesaling; 8) jewellery retailing.

[64] For a comprehensive study on the trade in diamonds during the civil war in Angola, see the Report by Global Witness, 'A rough trade. The role of companies and governments in the Angolan Conflict', December 1998, available at <http://www.globalwitness.org/reports/show.php/en.00013.html>.

import of rough diamonds from those countries,[65] a number of loopholes remained which enabled traders, sometimes with the tacit acceptance of importing
States, to circumvent such measures. The industry considers that, at its peak in
1999, the trade in conflict diamonds accounted for less than 4% of the world's
annual rough diamond production.[66] However, the diamond industry rapidly understood that its commercial interests should exclude any potential linkage with
the funding of rebel movements and the suffering and death of civilians in countries devastated by civil wars.[67] In May 2000, the South African government convened a meeting in Kimberley for all interested parties (governments, NGOs and
industry) to meet and discuss a way forward. A series of meetings followed
which came to be known as the Kimberley process. In December 2000, the UN
General Assembly voted unanimously to support the process.[68] The discussions
focused on the introduction of an agreement establishing an international certification scheme ensuring the proper tracing of legitimate rough diamonds. On 29
October 2001, the Council authorised the Commission to negotiate the agreement
on behalf of the Community on the basis of Article 133 TEC (former Article 113
TEC). The agreement, which was signed on 5 November 2002,[69] falls within the
Community's Common Commercial Policy. For the purposes of the agreement,
the Community, as a Participant, is therefore considered as a single territory.
Consequently, the Community is also responsible for the proper implementation
of the agreement. To this end, the Community has adopted Regulation (EC) No.
2368/2002 which 'sets up a Community system of certification and import and
export controls for rough diamonds'[70] and which is directly applicable in the

---

[65] Cf., in particular, Security Council Resolutions 1173 of 12 June 1998 and 1176 of 24 June
1998 concerning Angola, 1306 of 5 July 2000 concerning Sierra Leone, and 1343 of 7 March 2001
concerning Liberia. Although the Security Council expressed concern over the illegal exploitation of
natural resources in the Democratic Republic of the Congo (cf., e.g., its Resolution 1457 of 24 January 2003 calling upon the Panel of Experts on this topic to inform the OECD of companies which
are in contravention of the OECD guidelines for multinationals enterprises and lately Resolution
1499 of 13 August 2003), the Security Council has not yet adopted a Resolution banning the export
of conflict rough diamonds from that country.

[66] World Diamond Council, 'The essential guide to implementing the Kimberley Process', February 2003, p. 11 available at <http://www.worlddiamondcouncil.com>.

[67] In this respect, it is interesting to note that the First World rough diamond company, De Beers,
has recently developed a brand marketing strategy through its wholly-owned subsidiary DTC (Diamond Trading Company) to sell diamonds under the so-called Forevermark which is a proprietary
device identifying selected diamonds originating from DTC in a way which indicates their conflict-
free origins. Forevermark diamonds are intended to be natural, untreated, not from areas of conflict,
consistent with the best environmental practices and social behaviour and should be ethically sound:
see on this, Commission Decision 2003/79/EC of 25 July 2001 declaring a concentration to be compatible with the common market and the EEA Agreement, De Beers/LVMH, *OJEC* [2003] L 29/40,
points 42 and 107.

[68] UN General Assembly Resolution 55/56 of 1 December 2000.

[69] The agreement is annexed to Council Regulation (EC) No. 2368/2002. In the summer of 2003,
there were 58 Participants in the scheme: for the list of participants, see <http://www.kimberley
process.com/news/info1.asp?Id=26>.

[70] Art. 1 of Council Regulation (EC) No. 2368/2002, op. cit. n. 62.

Member States. Basically, only rough diamonds exported from a Participant to the Kimberley Process and certified by a Participant's competent authority as being in compliance with the Kimberley Process scheme will be allowed within the Community.[71] The Regulation entered into force on 31 December 2002. However, the entry into force of a number of core provisions, including those on import and export certificates, were suspended until the application of those provisions could be ensured within the Participants' territories. This materialised on 13 February 2003 by the publication of two amendments to Regulation 2368/2002.[72]

Moreover, since the fundamental idea of the scheme, as implemented by the Regulation, is to limit the free international trade of rough diamonds between Participants to the Kimberley Process and non-Participants, WTO Members participating in the scheme considered it necessary to request the WTO General Council to grant a waiver from Articles I, paragraph 1, XIII, paragraph 1 and XI, paragraph 1 of the GATT 1994.[73] 'Recognising the extraordinary humanitarian nature of this issue and the devastating impact of conflicts fuelled by the trade in conflict diamonds on the peace, safety and security of people in the affected countries',[74] the WTO General Council granted a waiver to the notifying Members from 1 January 2003 until 31 December 2006.

Under the agreement, each Participant is required to adopt an internal control system in order to ensure the elimination of the presence of conflict diamonds from shipments of rough diamonds imported into and exported from its territory.[75] The efficiency of the process will therefore rely heavily on the administrative capacities of each Participant. Discrepancies in the quality of internal controls between the Participants may be the most important weaknesses of the whole system.[76] The system is nevertheless based on mutual confidence in con-

---

[71] See Art. 3 of the Regulation.

[72] Regulation (EC) 254/2003 *OJEC* [2003] L 36/7 and Regulation (EC) 257/2003, *OJEC* [2003] L 36/11.

[73] GATT 1994 refers to GATT 1947; Article I, para. 1, GATT 1947 concerns the Most-Favoured Nation Treatment; Article XI, para. 1 prohibits quantitative restrictions on imports and exports; Article XIII, para. 1 prohibits any discriminatory administration of quantitative restrictions.

[74] Recital 6 of the WTO General Council decision of 15 May 2003, WT/L/518, 27 May 2003 available at <http://www.wto.org/>.

[75] Sect. IV (a) of the agreement.

[76] The Final Communiqué of the First Kimberley Process Plenary Meeting, which took place in Johannesburg on 28-30 April 2003, recognised the difficulties experienced by various Participants in implementing the scheme and referred a series of issues to specialised working groups (communiqué available at <http://www.kimberleyprocess.com/news/documents.asp?Id=51>). The creation of a Participation Committee was decided at that meeting. Its purpose was to vet Participants as to whether they had legislation implementing the Kimberley Certification Scheme. The result was that a large number of countries were dropped from the list of Participants issued in July 2003. Another unfortunate weakness is that, according to Annex I of the agreement which relates to general recommendations formulated for the Participants, Participants that produce diamonds and that have rebel groups suspected of mining diamonds within their territories are merely 'encouraged' to identify the areas of rebel diamond activity.

trols,[77] a well-known notion in the trade in goods within the Community. In order to support the administrative control capacities of each Participant, the diamond industry, through a body specially created to coordinate the industry's position, the World Diamond Council (WDC), proposed to create a system of warranties of conflict-free rough diamonds. Basically, the rough diamond industry has committed itself to ensuring that after the importation of certified rough diamonds subsequent sales transactions must include a notice on the invoice that the diamonds purchased are conflict-free.[78]

While Section IV of the Kimberley Process certification scheme takes note of this undertaking,[79] Regulation 2368/2002 lays down stringent criteria in order to be listed as an organisation representing traders in rough diamonds for the purposes of the Regulation. The Regulation chiefly requires the organisations to trace rough diamonds and to prohibit the purchase of rough diamonds from suspect or unknown sources of supply, to create and maintain records of invoices received, to undertake the independent auditing of invoices and transactions, to supervise their membership and to apply sanctions against those traders which have committed serious violations of the undertakings. They must also inform the Commission and the relevant Community authority (of a Member State) of their membership and any change of members, and to allow access to the relevant Community authority to any information needed in order to assess the proper functioning of the system and the industry self-regulation. It is of course too early to say whether the system proposed by the industry will be efficient. However, it is in the industry's own interests to make the system work in order to avoid any loss of credibility and the introduction of legally-binding unilateral measures im-

---

[77] Note, in this respect, Recital 13 of the Agreement: 'Recognising that an international certification scheme for rough diamonds will only be credible if all Participants have established internal systems of control designed to eliminate the presence of conflict diamonds in the chain of producing, exporting and importing rough diamonds within their own territories, while taking into account that differences in production methods and trading practices as well as differences in institutional controls thereof may require different approaches to meet minimum standards'.

[78] Since 1 January 2003, each invoice for every transaction in rough diamonds must bear the following text: 'The diamonds herein invoiced have been purchased from legitimate sources not involved in funding conflict and in compliance with United Nations resolutions. The seller hereby guarantees that these diamonds are conflict-free, based on personal knowledge and/or written guarantees provided by the supplier of these diamonds'; text quoted from World Diamond Council, 'The essential guide to implementing the Kimberley Process', February 2003, p. 5 available at <http://www.worlddiamondcouncil.com/>. See also the industry's system of self regulation adopted on 29 October 2002 available at <http://www.diamonds.net/news/newsitem.asp?num=7578&type=all&topic=Kimberely%20Process>.

[79] Sect. IV relating to the 'Principles of Industry Self-Regulation' reads as follows: 'Participants understand that a voluntary system of industry self-regulation, as referred to in the Preamble of this Document, will provide for a system of warranties underpinned through verification by independent auditors of individual companies and supported by internal penalties set by industry, which will help to facilitate the full traceability of rough diamond transactions by government authorities'.

posed on them by the Participants.[80] Actually, the diamond industry is actively participating in the review mechanism set up under point 20 of the Kimberley agreement and has played a key role in introducing an effective monitoring mechanism. However, one important loophole in the system is that it does not provide for the traceability of diamonds through the whole chain of production, trading and selling. Indeed, only rough diamonds fall within the system. Of course, this corresponds to the exact scope of the Kimberley certifying scheme. However, an industry-wide system of warranties, covering polished diamond dealers and retailers as well as diamond jewellery retailers, would have demonstrated the total commitment of the industry to combating the trade in conflict diamonds.

Nevertheless, the Kimberley Process illustrates that cooperation between the industry, States and international organisations, including the Community which hosts the world's leading rough diamond producer and seller accounting for 60% of the trade in rough diamonds, is possible.[81] The opponents to the involvement of the business sector may argue that such an agreement – or even a more far-reaching one – could have been adopted without the industry's participation. That might be true. It is, however, important to remember that international agreements only exist if they are put into effect and applied. It is arguable that without support from the diamond industry the agreement would never have been applicable. The industry's undertakings at least ensure that it will do its utmost to support compliance with the agreement. In this respect, it is probable that the industry's commitment will be all the more effective that the market for the exploitation and sale of rough diamonds is concentrated among a few multinational companies. In other words, the industry's commitments can be easily enforced. It is debatable, however, whether comparable commitments by the private sector could be made within a highly competitive market with few or no entry barriers. Indeed, in a very competitive market where numerous economic operators are active, organisations may face difficulties in bringing all the actors around the negotiating table and ensuring that the undertakings agreed upon are in fact respected. This may be one of the reasons for the lack of participation on the part of the diamond jewellery operators in the Kimberley certification scheme. With this reservation in mind, the active involvement of the private sector (upstream market players in rough diamonds) in the Kimberley certification scheme may possibly serve as an example for future Community actions in relation to the exploitation of other natural resources which may exacerbate tensions in conflict-

---

[80] It should be noted that Article 17, para. 7(b) of the Regulation imposes on the Commission the obligation to take 'necessary measures', in accordance with the comitology procedure referred to in Article 22, paragraph 2 of the Regulation, if, on the basis of reports, assessments or other pertinent information, the Commission comes to the conclusion that the system does not function properly and the issue has not been adequately addressed.

[81] The Community actually accounts for at least 80% of the global trade in rough diamonds.

prone third States or fuel such conflicts. In this respect, concrete actions have recently been announced in the fight against illegal logging.

Illegal logging takes place when timber is felled in violation of domestic laws.
A number of empirical studies have emphasised the linkage between illegal logging and the fuelling of violent conflicts, their exacerbation[82] or the undermining
of democratic principles and human rights.[83] This linkage lies explicitly at the
origin of a recent Commission proposal for an EU Action Plan on Forest Law Enforcement, Governance and Trade (FLEGT).[84] The proposed Action Plan notes
that illegal logging may cause human and environmental damage, but also represents a loss of revenue for the timber-producing countries of 10-15 billion euros
per year.[85] Strong evidence suggests that a significant share of the trade in timber
is likely to be based on illegally harvested timber.[86] As far as the involvement of
the private sector is concerned, the Commission Communication is particularly
interesting in two respects.

Firstly, the Communication makes an explicit reference to the Kimberley Process and relies on this example to launch the idea of the introduction of a system
of EC import control for illegally harvested timber. Such a system would be
based on draft bilateral or regional 'Forest Partnership Agreements' with producing and exporting third States on the certification of legally harvested timber.[87]

---

[82] See, for example, the study undertaken by Global Witness in Liberia, *Logging Off* (London,
September 2002) which urges the UN Security Council to adopt an export ban on timber originating
in Liberia until it is demonstrated that trade does not finance any armed groups, including the former
Revolutionary United Front (RUF). This study is available at <http://www.globalwitness.org/reports/
show.php/en.00006.html>.

[83] Cf., e.g., the study carried out by D. Reyes and L. Zandvliet, *A look at the operational activities of logging companies in Cameroon*, (Cambridge (US), Collaborative for Development Action,
Corporate Engagement Projects June 2002) available at <http://www.cdainc.com/cda/cda-
publications.php#cep> who, after having observed that 'enabled by the prevalence of corruption, illegal logging is pervasive, eliminating incentives for good behaviour' (p. 20), also note (p. 26) that
'the relationship between logging companies and local communities is currently not characterised by
large-scale violent conflict. However, there are indications that when resources disappear and livelihoods have been destroyed, tensions in the country could rise, a circumstance that some people
within Cameroon predict could result in violence. Company policies are currently based on the assumption that the forest will disappear in the next five to ten years. Hence, they see little benefit in
establishing good relations with local communities but, instead, focus their energy on logging as
much as they can in the shortest possible time'. See also in an even more dramatic tone concerning
logging in Mozambique, D. Reyes, 'An evaluation of Commercial Logging in Mozambique' (Cambridge (US), Collaborative for Development Action, Corporate Options March 2003) available at
<http://www.cdainc.com/cda/cda-publications.php#cep>.

[84] Communication from the Commission to the Council and the European Parliament, 21 May
2003, COM (2003) 251 final, in particular pp. 4-5.

[85] Idem, p. 4.

[86] Ibid., p. 9.

[87] The EC Treaty legal basis for concluding such agreements is not discussed by the Action Plan.
In this respect, one could argue that, like the Kimberley Process certification scheme, such agreements, because of their trade character, could be concluded on the basis of Art. 133 TEC (Common

Logically, exports which do not carry such a certificate would be prohibited from entering into the Community customs territory.[88] Those bilateral or regional agreements would initially cover a limited range of solid wood products (round-wood and rough sawnwood), possibly extending to other product categories if feasible. This system is considered to be an alternative to a multilateral frame-work, like the Kimberley agreement, which is too complex to establish in the short-term.

Secondly, the proposed Action Plan dedicates a whole section to 'private sec-tor initiatives based on principles of CSR'.[89] According to the Communication, 'the private sector has a key role to play in combating illegal logging, and can exert a direct and positive influence through the network of business relationships extending from the forest to the market place'. The Commission does not appear to favour legislative measures being imposed on companies. On the contrary, it prefers to 'encourage the private sector in the EU to work with the private sector in timber-producing countries according to voluntary codes of practice for timber harvesting and procurement, supplemented by rigorous voluntary independent au-dit of the supply chain.'[90] In this respect, the Commission quotes the initiatives developed by the Tropical Forest Trust (TFT), an organisation established to as-sist the purchasers of tropical timber to source from sustainably-managed forests and to build capacity for certification.[91]

Commercial policy). However, their aims will most probably also support sustainable forest manage-ment principles. Consequently, one could also defend the view that these agreements could be based on Art. 175(1) TEC (Environmental policy). In accordance with the case law of the Court of Justice of the EC, the selection of the appropriate legal basis must be made objectively when examining the purpose of the Community measure. When such measures pursue twofold aims, the legal basis will be the one required by the main or predominant purpose or component. By way of an exception, if the objectives pursued are inseparable with no hierarchy between them, the Community measure must be founded on the corresponding legal bases: see Case C-281/01, *Commission* v. *Council* [2002] ECR, I-12049, at paras. 33-35.

[88] Communication, op. cit. n. 84, pp. 11-14.

[89] Idem, p. 16.

[90] Ibid., p. 16. Note that the idea of voluntary codes of conduct in this sector is not new. In its 4th Environment Action Plan adopted by the Council on 19 October 1987, the Community already an-nounced that companies established in the Community should adopt such codes as far as the import of tropical hardwood was concerned. This idea was reiterated in the Commission Communication on conservation of tropical forests, adopted on 16 October 1989 (*OJEC* [1989] C 264/1, at 18).

[91] Ibid., p. 17. The TFT was established in March 1999 to assist companies trading in tropical hardwood garden furniture to secure reliable supplies of certified hardwood, according to the Forest Stewardship Council (FSC) certification scheme. The TFT, which is no longer limited to garden fur-niture, has three membership categories: producing members, supplying members who manufacture and/or trade in wood products and buying members who sell to end-users. TFT currently has 26 member companies established in South-East Asia (Vietnam, Indonesia), Africa (South Africa), Eu-rope and the USA. TFT members, especially buyers, are not required to buy only from TFT suppli-ers but they must instruct the non-TFT suppliers to ensure that, within a given period, they will phase out tropical hardwood products of unknown origin. TFT undertakes different projects to pro-mote the use of the FSC certification scheme in South-East Asia (Vietnam, Malaysia and Indonesia). For more information on the TFT's aims, requirements and projects, see <http://www.tropical foresttrust.com/>.

As noted above in relation to conflict diamonds, a policy of certification and the involvement of the private sector may achieve the best and most efficient results when few economic operators are active on the market. Whereas this point is acknowledged by the FLEGT Communication from the Commission,[92] the market structure of trade in timber, as well as the diversity of interests among the industry might considerably slow down the efforts to build an efficient system with the aim of phasing out the trade in illegally harvested timber. Enhanced controls and actively combating corruption within the producing States as well as a certain approximation of laws governing the trade in timber should be essential elements for such a system to function properly. The industry must also understand that, in the long-term, due, in particular, to the financial impact of consumer awareness in importing countries, it is economically sound to exclude illegally harvested timber from entering international trade. If a great deal still needs to be done, by adopting its Action Plan, the Commission has already announced its intention to act swiftly. The Member States and the European Parliament will need to demonstrate their commitment to follow this path, whereas the Community organisations of timber importers should already prepare themselves for drafting a common code of conduct in close cooperation with the Commission.

In spite of these positive initiatives, the EU needs to define its role in the promotion of conflict prevention within the business sector. This question is developed in the following section.

3. WHICH ROLE FOR THE EU?

By adopting, in 2001, what can be called a conflict prevention strategy, the European Union has set conflict prevention high on its agenda. However, as the developments in the previous section indicate, the EU's role towards the business sector is rather unclear and, at least, lacks a systematic outlook. If official willingness to cooperate with companies in this area has been expressed, the results are still rather limited. This may be due to the complexity of the issue and the lack of interest on the part of a number of companies in investing their time, energy and money in such initiatives. Another reason may also be that the EU has not yet decided on the role it wishes to play with regard to the business sector. However, one of the difficulties is that the EU may be faced with different roles to play, without necessarily setting priorities. Indeed, the EU may opt to facilitate the companies' analysis of countries with violent conflict potential (risk analysis) and/or promote companies' compliance with international standards adopted by other organisations and/or develop its own standards, including legislative measures, for Community undertakings investing in third States and/or provide for specific answers and incentives in selected sectors, such as in the extractive industries. Setting priorities is naturally a political choice. However, such a choice

---

[92] Cf., Communication, op. cit. n. 84, p. 17.

should be based on an objective assessment of what the EU does best. As we have discussed above, the EU has, so far, been working in two directions:

- promoting compliance by Community-based undertakings with voluntary international standards adopted in other international organisations, in particular the OECD; and

- participating in and reflecting upon the trade control of commodities fuelling conflicts, with the cooperation of the business sector.

These two elements have a common denominator: pragmatism. With relatively few human and financial resources, the EU institutions have obviously decided not to duplicate what already exists and have opted to work in an area which they know well, i.e., trade. However, at least with respect to Community-based companies, it is difficult to imagine the EU's role being limited to these tasks. Indeed, if the aim is to compel companies to integrate conflict prevention into their business operations, the EU needs to support companies in the five stages described in section 1.2 above. The Commission has a crucial role to play in this respect since, given its missions, it is in daily contact with companies and has a unique 'power of attraction' (e.g., the capacity to bring companies around the table) and a 'power of conviction' enabling it to be heard by the business community as a whole. Concerning stages 1 and 2, namely understanding the 'business case' and using frameworks to analyse the conflicts, the EU institutions, and especially the Commission, could undertake and/or coordinate empirical studies which are much needed, in particular, in order better to assess the 'economic benefits of peace'. These studies could be carried out within the framework of the Commission's Country Strategy Papers (CSPs)[93] but also the EC Conflict Prevention Assessment Mission Reports.[94] Whereas these reports already provide important and useful information for the business community,[95] it is, however, regrettable that, as far as the EC Conflict Prevention Assessment Missions are concerned, their reports pay very little attention to an evaluation of the country's

---

[93] In its Communication on conflict prevention, the Commission identified the CSPs (assessment papers focusing on development cooperation) as key tools to integrate conflict prevention in the programming of development cooperation. The risk factors are now systematically checked when drafting each CSP.

[94] These pilot missions are financed under the Rapid Reaction Mechanism and may also contribute more conflict prevention oriented CSPs. Missions have been sent to Nepal (Report published in January 2002), Indonesia (Report in March 2002), Afghanistan (Report in April 2002), Tajikistan (Report on rehabilitation in June 2002), Pakistan (Report on education in June 2002), the South Pacific (Report on Papua New Guinea, Solomon Islands and Fiji Islands in June 2002), Sri Lanka (Report in August 2002). All reports are available at <http://europa.eu.int/comm/external_relations/cpcm/mission/ and http://europa.eu.int/comm/external_relations/cfsp/news/ip_01_255.htm>.

[95] Especially when it comes to risk factors identified in each of the countries, possibly leading to the eruption of violent conflicts.

situation by local and foreign businesses, as well as to their contribution to the prevention of conflicts.[96] More focused research on the subject could be carried out, in particular, by Community delegations in third States, together with international and local NGOs as well as businesses already active in the countries concerned. Such information could also be very helpful to ensure familiarity by companies with conflict prevention processes, helping them to mainstream conflict prevention in their business operations (stage 3). Within this stage, it has been mentioned that consultation with stakeholders is an essential element. Although this should obviously take place at the local level (e.g., discussions and cooperation with representatives of local communities, women's organisations, local trade associations), the EU could contribute to developing a more coordinated dialogue between NGOs and Community companies operating in conflict-prone States. If a number of Community companies have already established partnerships with NGOs, in particular in the assessment of their CSR or human rights commitments, these initiatives are isolated and uncoordinated at the Community level. Regular dialogue and the sharing of know-how could therefore be coordinated by the Commission across different sectors of activity. This could also include the possible creation of a Community-wide conflict risk assessment network for businesses and NGOs (stage 4). As far as stage 5 is concerned, the question is whether a specific EU conflict prevention code of conduct for the business sector operating in third States is necessary and whether it is sufficient.

As noted above, in 1999 the European Parliament called for the adoption of a model Code of conduct for European businesses operating in developing countries.[97] While welcoming and encouraging voluntary codes of conduct, the European Parliament called for the adoption of a model code of conduct for European businesses which would, at least, incorporate applicable international standards[98]

---

[96] The report of the EC Conflict Prevention Assessment Mission on Nepal, dedicates two short paragraphs to the (passive) attitude of local businesses towards the conflict (cf., point 3.8.5). The report on Indonesia identifies economic welfare as an element for peace-building but does not consider it as a priority of the Community's conflict prevention strategy to be developed for Indonesia. The report also does not discuss the (positive or negative) role of businesses in the eruption of local violent conflicts in that country. The report on the South Pacific region identified SMEs as 'allies for peace' (p. 48) that the EU should support. The report on Sri Lanka identifies the business community as being both positive and negative towards the settlement of the conflict (cf., point 5.2.2 of the report). All reports are, however, silent on the role which Community companies play in these countries.

[97] Resolution of the European Parliament on EU standards for European enterprises operating in developing countries: towards a European Code of Conduct, *OJEC* [1999] C 104/10.

[98] The Resolution referred to the following instruments: the ILO Tripartite Declaration of Principles concerning Multinational Enterprises and Social Policy, the OECD guidelines for Multinational Enterprises; in the field of labour rights: the ILO core Conventions; in the field of human rights: the UN Declaration and different Covenants on Human Rights; in the field of minority and indigenous peoples' rights: ILO Convention No. 169, Chapter 26 of Agenda 21, 1994 Draft UN Declaration on the Rights of Indigenous Peoples, UN Declaration on the Elimination of All Forms of Racial Discrimination; in the field of environmental standards: UN Convention on Biological Diver-

and include the consideration of new standards being currently developed. This model would contribute to the standardisation of voluntary codes of conduct adopted by companies.[99] Aware of the importance of monitoring the proper functioning of voluntary codes of conduct based on the model proposed, the European Parliament called on the Commission to study the possibility of setting up a European Monitoring Platform (EMP) in close collaboration with the social partners, NGOs from North and South and representatives of indigenous and local communities.

Although this Resolution was solely targeted at companies' operations in developing countries and did not specifically mention the prevention of violent conflicts nor was it aimed at businesses' operations in conflict situations,[100] its content clearly revealed the aim of proposing to European companies that they should integrate structural conflict prevention policies into their operations. However, the Resolution was not followed by any action.[101] Two years later, in reaction to the Commission Communication on conflict prevention, the European Parliament adopted a Resolution whereby it proposed, *inter alia*, 'that the harmful influence which certain private and public undertakings have in unstable regions should be acknowledged by creating a legally binding framework with sanctions for companies which contribute to conflicts'.[102] Such a legally binding framework with sanctions raises several issues.

First, its legal basis is unclear. The Explanatory statements of the Resolution are silent on this question.[103] Currently, Community law which is applicable to undertakings does not apply extraterritorially. Hence, provisions governing com-

---

sity, the Rio Declaration and the European Commission proposal for the development of a code of conduct for European logging companies (COM (89) 410) and the relevant UN Conventions in the fields of protection of the environment, animal welfare and public health; in the field of security services: Common Article 3 of the Geneva Conventions and Protocol II, and the UN Code of Conduct for Law Enforcement Officials; in the field of corruption: the OECD anti-bribery convention and the European Commission communication on legislative measures against corruption (COM (97) 192).

[99] Cf., the Explanatory statements by the Committee on Development and Cooperation, MEP Richard Howitt (Rapporteur), in its Report on EU standards for European Enterprises operating in developing countries, Doc. A4 0508/98, 17 December 1998.

[100] Note, however, that the European Parliament (point 5 of the Resolution) 'believe[d] that a code should recognise the responsibilities of companies operating in conflict situations by incorporating the Amnesty International Human Rights Principles for Companies, Human Rights Watch Recommendations to companies and the UN Code of Conduct for Law Enforcement Officials'.

[101] As noted above, neither the Commission Communication of 2001 nor the Göteborg European Council have explicitly called for the introduction of such a code of conduct. So far, the Commission has a marked preference for sector-specific voluntary codes of conduct adopted by companies themselves.

[102] Point 14 of European Parliament Resolution of 13 December 2001 on the Commission communication on Conflict Prevention, *OJEC* [2002] C 177 E/291, at 294.

[103] Cf., Report on the Commission communication on Conflict Prevention, Committee on Foreign Affairs, Human Rights, Common Security and Defense Policy, Joost Lagendijk (Rapporteur), Doc. A5-0394/2001, 9 November 2001.

pany legislation (Article 44, paragraph 2(g) TEC) only concern companies established within the Community. On the other hand, it is well-known that agreements and concerted practices by companies located abroad or abuses of dominant positions by such companies that have an effect on trade between the Member States of the Community may infringe Community competition law rules (Articles 81 and 82 TEC).[104] However, such an extension of Community competition law cannot be considered as extraterritorial application since the criterion for application relates to the place of the effects of the anti-competitive behaviour at issue, namely the Community. According to the Resolution's proposed rationale, the situation with regard to applicability and jurisdiction would be the reverse of what occurs under Community competition law. The sanctions would be imposed on companies – whether they would be established within the Community or elsewhere is not clear from the text of the Resolution – for breaches of the legally binding framework committed in third States. This would mean that such a Community measure would have extraterritorial application. Such a measure would resemble the Helms-Burton Act, adopted in the United States, to impose trade sanctions against companies operating in Cuba.[105] As far as companies established outside the Community are concerned, there is currently no legal basis within the Treaty which would enable the Community to adopt such sanctions. Article 301 TEC, which enables the Community to cease or reduce, either partially or totally, economic relations with third States is, in the present author's opinion, unlikely to be extended to undertakings which cannot be considered as a constitutive part of the official authorities of those States.[106] As far as Community-based companies are concerned, as indicated above, Com-

---

[104] In its Case 114/85, *A. Ahlström Oy* v. *Commission* ('*Wood Pulp*') [1988] ECR p. 5193, the Court of Justice considered that an agreement concluded outside the Community was covered by Community competition law rules because it was *implemented* within the Community. In a subsequent case (T-102/96, *Gencor Ltd* v. *Commission* [1999] ECR II-753), the Court of First Instance of the European Communities found that a proposed merger between South African platinum group metal production undertakings could be prohibited under the Community Merger Regulation (4064/89) because of sales within the Community since it was foreseeable that the proposed concentration w[ould] have an immediate and substantial effect in the Community. On this subject, see, e.g., I. Nitsche, 'Extraterritoriality and International Cooperation: The State of Play in EC-USA Relations in Competition Matters', in V. Kronenberger (ed.), *The European Union and the International Legal Order: Discord or Harmony?* (The Hague, TMC Asser Press 2001), pp. 273-295.

[105] On this, see, e.g., J. van den Brink, 'Helms-Burton: extending the limits of jurisdiction', 44 *Netherlands International Law Review* (1997), pp. 131-148 and J. Huber, 'La réaction de l'Union européenne face aux lois Helms-Burton et d'Amato', 408 *Revue du Marché commun et de l'Union européenne* (1997), pp. 301-308.

[106] Note that Art. 301 TEC has been used by the Community together with Arts. 60 (movement of capital) to combat the financing of terrorist groups and persons linked to the Afghan Taliban regime, including after the collapse of that regime (cf., Council Regulations 467/2001/EC, *OJEC* [2001] L 67/1 and 881/2002/EC, *OJEC* [2002] L 139/9, also based on Art. 308 TEC). These regulations are subject to annulment proceedings which are, at the time of writing, pending before the Court of First Instance of the European Communities (Case T-306/01).

munity law only imposes certain sanctions or fines for infringements of competition law rules that take place within the Community. Consequently, it appears that, at the current stage of Community law, no legal basis exists for introducing such a system. However, it is interesting to note that Article III-224 of the draft Constitution for Europe proposes to entrust the Council with the possibility to adopt restrictive measures against natural or legal persons, as well as non-State groups or entities, similar to those currently adopted under Article 301 TEC against third States.[107] Since that provision does not mention whether those non-State actors should be located within or outside the territory of the Union, one could assume that such measures could be targeted towards all companies, irrespective of their place of establishment. However, it is uncertain whether such restrictive measures could be adopted independently of sanctions against third States.

Second, if, for the time being, one excludes the idea of extraterritorial application of Community law for companies not located within its territory, a system whereby only Community-based companies would be sanctioned for having contributed to the fuelling or the exacerbation of conflicts would be politically questionable and might not attain the goal of reducing violence. Indeed, it is possible that, faced with the risk of being sanctioned, companies established within the Community would, instead of introducing conflict prevention policies, establish themselves in other parts of the world, with more 'understanding' for companies. The proposed framework would obviously not support the overall objective of preventing the eruption of conflicts, while deterring the Community from continuing to positively influence the policy of companies relocated abroad.

Finally, as far as concrete implementation is concerned, one may wonder about the efficiency of such a legally binding framework as compared to voluntary codes of conduct. Indeed, notwithstanding the difficulties in adducing evidence of a direct or indirect contribution by a company in a given conflict,[108] positive results may be better achieved by adherence to fully accepted self-imposed measures. This is not to say that the Community could not influence the drafting of certain codes of conduct, so that there is an accepted (negotiated) commitment to adhere to certain standards which would otherwise be ignored, or to create positive incentives for companies to behave in accordance with such codes. However, given the complexity of the issues that companies are facing in the field, legally binding measures adopted at Community level may simply be ignored and be inapplicable because of their general and unspecified character. In the present author's opinion, the real question concerns less the legal nature of

---

[107] See the Draft Treaty establishing a Constitution for Europe, *OJEC* [2003] C 169/1 at 72.

[108] A related question would also concern identifying the judicial bodies responsible for establishing a breach of the framework. Since sanctions normally fall within the competence of Member States, it would be natural that national courts are competent to decide on breaches of the framework. It is likely that, if the Commission or the Council would be allowed to impose sanctions, a judicial review (a challenge by the company) would fall within the competence of the Court of First Instance of the European Communities.

the texts than their concrete implementation, as well as their independent and transparent monitoring by audit bodies. It is probably at those stages that most work will have to be done and could be carried out by the Community institutions without excluding, at the monitoring stage, the adoption of binding measures.

4.   WHICH INSTRUMENTS ARE OR COULD BE AVAILABLE?

The EU is an economic giant. It possesses a wide range of policies and instruments which are targeted towards companies established or providing activities within its territory. Those policies and instruments remain, so far, unused in order to promote the integration of conflict prevention within the business sector. A general explanation lies in the lack of extraterritorial application of Community instruments and/or an appropriate legal basis. For instance, Community Company law acts, based on Article 44, paragraph 2(g) TEC, are aimed at facilitating the establishment of companies within the Community, and are not instruments to prevent conflicts. This section intends to briefly discuss some of these policies where the integration of conflict prevention within the business sector, if advisable for policy objectives, may nevertheless lead to several problems.

4.1   EC company law

Within the Community, the approximation of company law is based on Article 44, paragraph 2(g) TEC with the aim being to coordinate 'to the necessary extent the safeguards which, for the protection of the interests of members and others, are required by Member States of companies or firms (...) with a view to making such safeguards equivalent throughout the Community'.[109] Legislative measures can basically be divided between 'basic' company law Directives, and Regulations[110] on the one hand, and Directives relating to accounting obligations, on the

---

[109] In general on this topic, see, e.g., V. Edwards, *EC Company Law* (Oxford, Oxford University Press 2000).

[110] See First Council (Company Law) Directive 68/151/EEC, *OJEC* [1968] L 65/8, amended by Directive 2003/58/EC as regards disclosure requirements in respect of certain types of companies, *OJEC* [2003] L 221/13; Second Company Law Directive 77/91/EEC (formation of public limited liability companies and the maintenance and alteration of their capital), *OJEC* [1977] L 26/1; Third Company Law Directive 78/855/EEC concerning mergers of public limited liability companies, *OJEC* [1978] L 295/36; Sixth Company Law Directive 82/891/EEC concerning the division of public limited liability companies, *OJEC* [1982] L 378/47; Eleventh Company Law Directive 89/666/EEC concerning disclosure requirements in respect of branches opened in a Member State by certain types of company governed by the law of another State, *OJEC* [1989] L 395/36; Twelfth Company Law Directive 89/667/EEC on single-member private limited-liability companies, *OJEC* [1989] L 395/40; Council Regulation (EEC) No. 2137/85 on the European Economic Interest Grouping (EEIG), *OJEC* [1985] L 199/1; Council Regulation (EC) No. 2157/2001 of 8 October 2001 on the Statute for a European company (SE), *OJEC* [2001] L 294/1 (entry into force on 8 October 2004);

other.[111] So far, EC Company legislation does not take into consideration either CSR or, *a fortiori,* conflict prevention measures adopted by companies, because of a lack of an appropriate legal basis.

Together with a number of NGOs, the European Parliament has called on the Commission (and more generally the Community) to ensure that consideration would be given, with an appropriate legal basis, to incorporating core labour, environmental and human rights international standards in EC Company law.[112] The idea is essentially to oblige companies to report systematically to stakeholders, whether governmental or non-governmental, on the impact of their activities, while ensuring, at the same time, a proper independent auditing thereof.[113] It is clear that this call was primarily aimed at activities of European companies abroad (including those of their subsidiaries) and may, therefore, also relate to the consequences of their activities in conflict affected or conflict-prone States. In particular, several NGOs and stakeholders support the view that companies should be obliged to report on the funding of foreign governments, which may support the exacerbation of conflicts.[114]

Council Regulation (EC) No. 1435/2003 of 22 July 2003 on the Statute for a European Cooperative Society (SCE), *OJEC* [2003] L 207/1 (applicable from 18 August 2006). Proposals for a Directive on takeover bids and a Directive on cross-border mergers of companies with share capital are still being discussed.

[111] Fourth Company Law Directive 78/660/EEC on the annual accounts of certain types of companies, *OJEC* [1978] L 222/11, as amended by Directive 2003/38/EC on the annual accounts of certain types of companies as regards amounts expressed in euro, *OJEC* [2003] L 120/22; Seventh Company Law Directive 83/349/EEC on consolidated accounts, *OJEC* [1983] L 193/1; these two directives have been amended by Directive 2003/51/EC which modernises and updates accounting rules, *OJEC* [2003] L 178/16; Eighth Company Law Directive 84/253/EEC on the approval of persons responsible for carrying out the statutory audits of accounting documents, *OJEC* [1984] L 126/20; Regulation (EC) No. 1606/2002 of the European Parliament and of the Council of 19 July 2002 on the application of international accounting standards, *OJEC* [2002] L 243/1 and Commission Regulation (EC) No. 1725/2003 of 29 September 2003 adopting certain international accounting standards in accordance with Regulation (EC) No. 1606/2002 of the European Parliament and of the Council, *OJEC* [2003] L 261/1.

[112] See its 1999 Resolution cited above at n. 97, point 27.

[113] Several companies have already implemented, on a voluntary basis, independent auditing by NGOs in the field of labour law or human rights. A recent example is given by Carrefour, one of the world leaders in the distribution of commodities, that has signed an agreement with the International Federation of Human Rights whereby the latter, together with local NGOs, audits the firm's clothing suppliers (based in Asia) as to whether they respect ILO Conventions. It has been reported that, in cases where the audit revealed abuses or wrongdoings, the supplier complied with the audit's results within three months, whereas in only 3% of the cases was the supplier agreement terminated. Adopting such schemes probably also encourages companies to 'compete' for best solutions within their sector.

[114] As illustrated by a survey carried out by the OECD, many companies in the extractive sector acknowledge that they fund foreign governments and consider this as part of their support to civil society, although very few question the use that these revenues are being put to: see, *Multinational Enterprises in Situations of Violent Conflict and Widespread Human Rights Abuses* (Paris, OECD Working Paper on International Investment 2002), p. 27.

The European Parliament's invitation has not been followed up. The current draft Constitution for Europe (cf., draft Article III-23) does not propose to take its concerns into account, Article III-23 being a pure transcript of the current Article 44, paragraph 2(g) TEC. Although the draft Constitution includes the Union's Charter for Fundamental Rights, it is difficult to foresee how such reference could enlarge the scope of application of EC company law rules.

One may, wonder, however, whether a flexible interpretation of Article 44, paragraph 2(g) TEC could not be defended. This interpretation would lie in a number of assumptions. The first would be that a large number of Member States would have imposed on their companies reporting obligations concerning their conflict prevention initiatives.[115] Such obligations could be considered as affording guarantees to stakeholders and other interested parties, in the sense of Article 44, paragraph 2(g) TEC, that companies respect certain fundamental principles when doing business. As was mentioned above, one of the problems with conflict prevention measures adopted by companies concerns their monitoring. Monitoring starts from the assumption that a transparent reporting system exists in order to carry out such a task properly. If a large number of Member States would impose conflict prevention reporting obligations on their companies, including for their consolidated activities (namely their subsidiaries abroad), would coordination at the Community level be necessary to render those guarantees equivalent, since those companies might be subject to different sets of rules in the Member States?

Such a view can easily be considered as an abuse of current EC Company law rules, as they would be used for purposes that they do not, and are not supposed to, govern. Moreover, it also overlooks the problem of the extraterritorial application of Community company law. Indeed, subsidiaries (operating in third States) of companies established within the Community are governed by the law of their host State. Consequently, they remain subject to that State's company legislation. In addition to the interference with the legal system of a third State that this represents,[116] the proper enforcement of these reporting obligations would probably be excessively difficult. These problems probably render the European Parliament's proposal unviable, unless the EC Treaty is substantially revised.

---

[115] A source of inspiration may come from France where Article 116 of the provisions of the Act on New Economic Regulations (*Loi n° 2001-420 sur les nouvelles régulations économiques*, JORF 16 May 2001, p. 7776) requires, since 1 January 2002, that all publicly traded companies have to annually report 'on the way in which the company takes into consideration the social and environmental consequences of its activities'. The relevant provisions of this article read as follows: 'Le rapport (annuel) [...] comprend également des informations, dont la liste est fixée par décret en Conseil d'État, sur la manière dont la société prend en compte les conséquences sociales et environnementales de son activité. Le présent alinéa ne s'applique pas aux sociétés dont les titres ne sont pas admis aux négociations sur un marché réglementé. [...] Les dispositions [...] prennent effet à compter de la publication du rapport annuel portant sur l'exercice ouvert à compter du 1er janvier 2002'.

[116] With all political and economic challenges that this may incur.

4.2 Competition law and policy

Introducing conflict prevention measures into business policies may be seen by some companies as a factor which lowers their competitiveness. In effect, being demanding as to the way in which one's company operates in third countries so as to ensure a balance, e.g., between the welfare of indigenous peoples and minorities and business operations, can be seen as an economic and competitive burden, particularly when competitors are less, or not at all, attentive to the matter. However, as explained above, operating in States afflicted by conflicts creates costs, including reputation costs. Hence, companies operating in conflict-prone third States may, in the long run, have a competitiveness advantage if they introduce appropriate business policies into their daily operations. Setting aside, as mentioned in section 3. above, the extraterritorial application of EC competition law, the issue here is whether current EC competition rules, which only apply in so far as the anti-competitive behaviour concerned (anti-competitive agreements between undertakings, abuse of a dominant position or a merger reinforcing a dominant position) has an effect on the territory of the Community (or the European Economic Area), could affect conflict prevention measures adopted by Community-based companies. Such a situation may occur, for example, if on a given market, two or more companies, having an important market share, would agree to limit their suppliers of certain goods or services to those whose products and services participate in the concerned companies' certification scheme with the aim of ensuring the distribution of guaranteed conflict-free and sustainable products or services. This situation could resemble the Kimberley process mechanism but would be introduced on the initiative of private companies. Such a system would have a tie-in effect which would be particularly effective if the parties to the agreement have very important market shares, e.g., in the distribution of commodities in one or several Member States. Suppliers abroad would have no other choice than to participate in the scheme or choose not to export to the Community. The agreement could then well be considered as particularly efficient in preventing conflicts, but also at the same time lowering competition within the Community. Indeed, the agreement could be caught by the prohibition of Article 81(1) TEC, since it could very well lower the range of products/services supplied within the Community and ensure the parties to the agreement the possibility to maintain price levels and differentials. Assuming that the agreement would fall within Article 81(1) TEC, the next question would then be whether such an agreement could be considered justified on the grounds listed in Article 81(3) TEC. Would such an agreement be considered to promote technical and economic progress ensuring a possible share of the profits to the end-users, as laid down in Article 81(3) TEC? Could consumers within the Community be considered to benefit from an agreement that is primarily intended to benefit peoples located in third States? Whilst the reply is naturally uncertain, one may wonder whether current Community competition law rules could appropriately resolve the problem.

Another question which arises is whether the Community could promote a conflict prevention dimension in a wider competition policy context. Indeed, if efforts are made to ensure that Community-based companies are behaving in their operations abroad in accordance with a set of international standards for the welfare of local populations, such efforts should not prejudice companies established in the Community as compared to their foreign competitors. Consequently, if conflict prevention is to be seriously taken into consideration and mainstreamed within the operations of the business sector, the task of the Community would be to ensure that it is part of multilateral economic discussions. Hence, in the present author's opinion, should a worldwide agreement on competition be adopted,[117] certain fundamental principles relating to the responsibility of companies in violent conflicts and their participation in 'socio-economic peace-building' should be part of the deal.

4.3   Enterprise and trade policies

In the context of the internal market, the Community has developed the free movement of goods and services both through mutual recognition of technical requirements, conformity assessments and certification imposed by Member States on products and services, and, when this does not function properly, through the approximation of laws and harmonisation. The idea behind such a policy is to reduce the impact of technical requirements imposed by Member States on producers, enabling a balance to be achieved between free trade together with a high degree of protection of public interests.

As technical barriers to trade also exist between the Community and third States, the Community has entered into the WTO Agreement on Technical Barriers to Trade (TBT) and has also concluded a number of bilateral agreements which are aimed at the mutual acceptance of test reports, certificates and marking made by competent authorities of the Contracting Party, having a comparable level of technical development and having a compatible approach concerning conformity assessment.[118] These agreements are based on mutual confidence concerning the quality of tests and the competence of competent conformity assessment bodies.

---

[117] The December 1996 WTO Ministerial Conference in Singapore decided to set up four new working groups, one dedicated to the interaction between trade and competition policy. This subject is now part of the Doha Development Agenda adopted at the Fourth WTO Ministerial Conference in Doha, Qatar, in November 2001. Negotiations should have started at the Fifth Conference in Cancún, Mexico, in September 2003, but the delegations remained entrenched, particularly on the issues launched in Singapore, among which is a multilateral framework for competition policy.

[118] 1 November 1998 with Canada, 1 December 1998 with the United States, 1 January 1999 with Australia and New Zealand, 1 May 2000 with Israel in the sector of chemicals good laboratory practices (GLP), 1 January 2002 with Japan and 1 June 2002 with Switzerland.

As mentioned above, the Kimberly Process certification scheme is also based on the same principle, although not all the Contracting Parties to this agreement have comparable standards for certification. This is one of the reasons why the rough diamond industry needed to be closely involved in the process. However, despite certain lacunae, the Kimberly certification scheme has the necessary merit to remain in existence.

The question is whether the Community could not develop sector-specific standards according to which goods and services manufactured in third States would be conflict-free or would respond to sustainable development conditions, such as respecting ILO Conventions. The participation of companies in this process would be essential, since a number of them have already developed private sector-based schemes ensuring that their suppliers comply with set standards which, as indicated above, might not always necessarily comply with EC competition law, but which could constitute a proper basis for further work to be developed by Community institutions.

4.4   Cooperation and development policies

Whereas the Community's cooperation and development policies[119] are not essentially targeted towards companies, they may, however, be powerful tools to integrate conflict prevention considerations into the business sector. This can be seen from two angles: on the one hand, in respect of Community-based companies participating in Community programmes and, on the other, concerning the business sector in recipient countries.

As far as the first category is concerned, it must be clear that companies working in third States under Community funding should be irreproachable in terms of proper management of funds, neutrality in respect of ethnic or local community tensions, as well as compliance with basic international standards that the Community advocates for the international sphere. In this respect, it is interesting to note that in a Resolution adopted in 1999, the European Parliament

'call[ed] on the Commission to enforce the requirement that all private companies carrying out operations in third countries on behalf of the Union, and financed out of the Commission's budget or the European Development Fund, act in accordance with the Treaty on European Union in respect of fundamental rights, failing companies would not be entitled to continue to receive European Union funding, in particular its instruments for assistance with investment in third countries, [and] call[ed] on the Commission to prepare a report on the extent to which private companies to which it awards contracts have been made aware of these obligations'.[120]

---

[119] On these policies in relation to conflict prevention, see Chapter 9 in this volume.
[120] Resolution of the European Parliament, quoted above n. 97, point 23.

The present author is not aware of any follow up to this suggestion. A publicly available systematic study on this question would be welcomed, together with a study on how these obligations have been complied with. Particular focus could be given to the problems faced when conflicts erupt, as well as the reactions of those companies to the situation.

As far as the development of the business sector in third States is concerned, more extensive and intensive support from the Community would be requested, in particular in post-conflict reconstruction programmes. Indeed, for local populations having experienced several years of violent conflict, peace needs to bring socio-economic development. As some authors have rightly pointed out, 'while poverty and despair are a breeding ground for violence and extremism, the prospect of prosperity and a better future are a powerful incentive to convince people of the benefits of peace.'[121] It is rather striking to note that, in 2001, the Community provided € 14 million (out of total payments of € 168 million) to the revitalisation and development of the private sector in Bosnia and Herzegovina,[122] whereas economic growth in the country is slowing down together with a decrease in financial aid, the creation of viable business is neglected and unemployment remains at 40% of the population.[123]

Although macro-economic cooperation aid is important, the Community's financial commitments towards developing a stable business sector in third States, in particular local business initiatives, should be strengthened. In this respect, an overall assessment of the quantitative and qualitative achievements would be welcomed. So far, the development of the private sector is considered as a cross-cutting issue and is often combined with the funding of infrastructure projects, i.e., the strengthening of the business environment. Whereas in ACP countries the European Community has set itself a strategy for private sector development,[124] in particular supporting the idea of business cooperation agreements between Community and ACP companies, there is currently, to the present author's knowledge, no systematic evaluation of the results of this strategy. Such an assessment would be particularly useful in order to assess whether the strategy has put into practice 'the conviction' on which it is based to the effect that 'sustainable private sector development is both facilitated by and contributes to the strengthening of democracy, the rule of law and human rights (including property rights) as recognised in the Universal Declaration of Human Rights, the Africa, American and European Conventions on Human Rights'.[125]

---

[121] Wenger and Möckli, op. cit. n. 4, p. 135.

[122] The figures are extracted from the Annual Report 2001 on the EC Development Policy and the Implementation of the external assistance (Brussels, European Commission 2002) available at <http://www.europa.eu.int/comm/development/body/publications/descript/pub7_2_en.cfm>.

[123] See The Economist, 27 September 2003, p. 32.

[124] Communication from the Commission to the Council and the European Parliament, A European Community Strategy for private sector development in ACP countries, COM (98) 667 final, 20 November 1998.

[125] Idem, p. 9.

5. CONCLUSION

The business sector has an important role to play in the prevention of violent conflicts. Companies can contribute to preventing the eruption of conflicts and, by their participation in socio-economic peace-building, can avoid the reignition of violent conflicts. Although in 2001 the EU announced its intention to initiate co-operation with the business sector in the prevention of violent conflicts in third States, two years later concrete actions are still rather limited. Moreover, some of the instruments which the EU possesses are, in their current form, either unsuitable for promoting the integration of conflict prevention policies with the operations of companies or may raise delicate legal and political issues, such as the rather extensive extraterritorial application of Community law. Keeping this in mind, and given the complexity of violent conflicts, their origins and the problems which companies face in the field, this contribution has argued that, for the time being, the EU should not impose a general legally binding framework on Community undertakings. Conversely, time is ripe for the EU institutions to launch and coordinate a multi-stakeholders' forum on conflict prevention and to encourage sector-based codes of conduct. For their proper implementation, it would be essential to have efficient monitoring mechanisms. Consequently, discussions on how to impose appropriate reporting and monitoring systems on companies that have accepted such codes should also be part of the agenda.

CONCLUSION: TOWARDS A COMPREHENSIVE EU POLICY ON CONFLICT PREVENTION

J. Solana recently remarkably summarised:

'[o]f all policy objectives, the prevention of violent conflict is the most ambitious, the most demanding and the most thankless. It requires the imagination to see ahead to the consequences of our inaction. And it demands the political will and courage to take preventive action where this is costly, dangerous or unpopular and where the benefits may never be seen. Address a crisis and you will be praised. Prevention is often unseen. It requires a different level of political courage'.[1]

As the contributions to this book have shown, since the previous four to five years, the European Union has set conflict prevention as a major objective of its external policy, both in a short-term perspective, i.e., by recourse to either political or, more recently, military instruments in crisis situations, and in terms of structural conflict prevention, namely with the aim to address the root causes of conflict. Conflict prevention as one of the EU's key policy objectives will even be given a constitutional ranking when the Treaty establishing a Constitution for Europe (hereafter 'the Draft Constitution') will enter into force. Indeed, pursuant to Article III-193(2)(c) of the Draft Constitution,[2]

'[t]he Union shall define and pursue common policies and actions, and shall work for a high degree of cooperation in all fields of international relations, in order to [...] preserve peace, prevent conflicts and strengthen international security, in conformity with the purposes and principles of the United Nations Charter, with the principles of the Helsinki Final Act and with the aims of the Charter of Paris, including those relating to external borders'.[3]

---

[1] Summary of the speech delivered at the Conference on Conflict Prevention, Dublin, 31 March 2004, p. 2, available at <http://ue.eu.int/cms3_applications/applications/solana/list.asp?BID=107& lang=EN&cmsid=335>

[2] For the purpose of this conclusion, we will use the text of the Draft Constitution as laid down in IGC Doc. No. 86/04 of 25 June 2004, i.e., the provisional consolidated version of the Draft Treaty establishing a Constitution for Europe, available at <http://ue.eu.int/showPage.ASP?id=251&lang =en>.

[3] Furthermore, conflict prevention is mentioned twice as part of the Draft Constitution's provisions on the European Union's common security and defence policy: see Articles I-40(1) and III-210(1).

V. Kronenberger and J. Wouters, eds., The European Union and Conflict Prevention
© *2004, T·M·C·Asser press, The Hague, The Netherlands*

This provision gives support to the idea that the EU wishes to consolidate its efforts in this area in a more systematic and coherent way. From a pure policy perspective, however, it remains to be seen whether the focus on conflict prevention will remain as high after the enlargement to 25 Member States. Notwithstanding this uncertainty, the ambition of a consistent and mainstreamed conflict prevention objective has, so far, provided few results. Naturally, it should be borne in mind that the systematic insertion of conflict prevention in EU policies may only achieve tangible results in the medium and long-term. More time and appropriate analytical tools, in particular as regards the impact assessment of the EU's actions, are needed in order to evaluate whether the ambitions are turned into reality and whether those actions have tangibly achieved their aim. However, the difficulty of assessing the efficiency of conflict prevention initiatives or policies is exacerbated by the fact that their benefits are usually unnoticed. Moreover, a debate on the potentially negative impact of (internal and external) EU policies should probably be added to the scrutiny.[4] The mere fact of inserting a conflict prevention dimension into the existing policies or external instruments of the EU may not be sufficient, if these policies or instruments remain chiefly the same. Although it is very unlikely that, as such, EU/EC policies directly contribute to the eruption of conflicts in third States, one should not underestimate their potential for contributing to the root causes of conflicts abroad and even for exacerbating existing conflicts. A deeper and more comprehensive multidisciplinary reflection may be needed on that topic.

To a varying degree, the chapters of this book have pointed out different challenges that the EU's conflict prevention strategy faces, which may turn into shortcomings if no appropriate answers are found in the short and medium term. In brief, three main challenges can be identified: a) intra-EU institutional and coordination challenges; b) financial and human capacity issues; and c) the question of establishing an appropriately structured division of labour with other international organisations. These points will be developed hereunder.

Intra-EU institutional and coordination challenges. Under the current institutional framework, a certain division of tasks has emerged between the two main EU institutions active in conflict prevention, along the lines of their respective competences: the Commission is essentially responsible for actions in the long-term, structural conflict prevention falling within the so-called 1st pillar, whereas the Council – in addition to its role in conflict management – mainly bears responsibility for short-term conflict prevention, which essentially falls within the scope of the CFSP. From a conflict prevention perspective, such a division intrinsically causes problems of coordination and coherence. For instance, in terms of conflict indicator resources, the Commission relies on its network of delegations present in over 120 third States, whereas early warning bodies (the Policy Unit,

---

[4] Cf., Chapter 13 above.

the EU Military Staff and the Joint Situation Centre) within the General Secretariat of the Council mainly retrieve information from outside resources, including diplomatic reporting from Member States.[5] To a certain extent, the use of a constellation of conflict indicator and early warning resources should be welcomed. It certainly ensures the possibility for the cross-checking of information and ultimately better policy assessments. However, it also has shortcomings in terms of duplication of work and proper exchange of information between all concerned parties, namely the Commission, the Council bodies and the Member States. Moreover, the Council's dependence on external intelligence resources, with the exception, to a certain extent, of the role of the EU Satellite Centre, the mission of which is to support the decision-making of the Union in the context of CFSP/ESDP[6] essentially by providing data originating in earth observation satellites, remains worrying. Although the EU Satellite Centre's missions currently include the provision of data within the scope of the Petersberg tasks and early warning,[7] it is regrettable that the Draft Constitution does not lay the grounds for the creation of a European intelligence agency, based on the existing EU Satellite Centre, enabling the EU to rely on more independent resources of its own. Of course, the association of the Commission within the Council's Political and Security Committee (PSC) and its participation (through it own officials) within the Policy Unit attached to the Secretary General/High Representative for CFSP (SG/HR) were aimed at preventing information flow and coordination deficiencies inherent in the institutional framework. Good personal relations between External Affairs Commissioner C. Patten and SG/HR J. Solana have certainly decreased possible tensions and conflicts between the two institutions. However, the system depends too heavily on such circumstantial factors.[8] As admitted by the SG/HR himself in the context of his proposal for a European Security Strategy, the cre-

---

[5] See Chapters 1 and 2 above.

[6] Article 2 of the Council Joint Action of 20 July 2001 on the establishment of a European Union Satellite Centre, *OJEC* [2001] L 200/5. The Satellite Centre is formally an agency of the European Union, under the political supervision of the Political and Security Committee (PSC) within the Council, and under the operational direction of the SG/High Representative for CSFP.

[7] As indicated above, according to the Draft Constitution, conflict prevention missions in EDSP will find a legal basis in the Constitution. This implies that the EU Satellite Centre will also be legally in charge of supporting those missions.

[8] See the cogent diagnosis of the current institutional imbroglio made by Mr. Gunter Pleuger, an alternate member of the Convention on the Future of Europe, in his Working Document No. 17 of 5 November 2002 which bears the telling title 'Double hat': 'Greater demands will be placed on an enlarged Union, especially in the field of external relations. The Union must enhance its capability to act in this area in order to meet these increased demands. For this it is vital that the Union speaks with one voice to the outside world on external relations issues. Moreover, the Union must strive for greater coherence in the formulation and implementation of foreign policy decisions. The relationship between the External Relations Commissioner and the High Representative for the CFSP is a key issue here. The current good cooperation due to the personal qualities of the present office holders should not blind us to the rivalry inherent in the current system. We must overcome these structural weaknesses.'

ation, in the recent years, of different instruments and capabilities, each of which having its own structure and rationale, now requires them to be brought together with the objective being to create synergy through a more coherent and comprehensive approach.[9] In this respect, the Draft Constitution entails two important institutional changes[10] that may positively boost institutional coordination and coherence in conflict prevention actions: the creation of a Union Minister for Foreign Affairs[11] and the correlative establishment of a European External Action Service.[12] Under the Draft Constitution, the functions currently exercised by the SG/HR and External Affairs Commissioner are to be merged and reinforced under the responsibility of one single person, the Union Minister for Foreign Affairs. However, the Union Minister for Foreign Affairs should exercise those functions under two hats. On the one hand, for questions belonging to the CSFP/ESDP, he/she contributes to those policies and carries them out 'as mandated by the Council'.[13] On the other hand, 'for responsibilities falling to it in external relations and for coordinating other aspects of the Union's external action', the Union Minister for Foreign Affairs is one of the Vice-Presidents of the European Commission. The consequence is that in exercising those responsibilities, and, as the Draft Constitution emphasizes, 'only for these responsibilities', the Union Minister for Foreign Affairs is bound by the Commission's procedures 'to the extent that this is consistent with' his or her conducting the Union's CFSP and ESDP and presiding over the Foreign Affairs Council.[14] Although the text only refers to 'procedures' and not rules, this indication certainly should mean that the Union Minister for Foreign Affairs, when acting as the Vice-President of the Commission in charge of external affairs (and exercising his or her voting rights within the Commission), should be bound by Article I-25(7) of the Draft Constitution, which provides that, in carrying out its responsibilities, the Commission shall be completely independent and that European Commissioners shall neither seek nor take instructions from any government or other institution, body, office or agency. Although the exercise of these two functions by one single person entails a certain dose of schizophrenia, it may at the same time enable the Union to have a more consistent external policy, in particular by bridging short-term and

---

[9] European Security Strategy, 12 December 2003, p. 13, available at <http://ue.eu.int/cms3_applications/applications/solana/index.asp?lang=EN&cmsid=246>.

[10] It should be borne in mind that the Draft Constitution also foresees the merging of the current three pillars under a single framework. Such a merger might also entail some structural changes capable of having positive coordination effects between the current pillars. However, the differences in the decision-making processes of the current CFSP and EC pillars will chiefly remain.

[11] See in particular Articles I-27 and III-197 of the Draft Constitution. For a first analysis, see J. Wouters, 'The Union Minister for Foreign Affairs: Europe's Single Voice or Trojan Horse?', forthcoming in *Liber Amicorum Fred Kellermann* (The Hague, T.M.C. Asser Press 2004).

[12] Declaration on the creation of a European external action service, *OJEU* [2003] C 169/1, at 99.

[13] Article I-27(2) of the Draft Constitution, op. cit. n 2.

[14] Article I-27(4) of the Draft Constitution.

structural conflict prevention together under the same direction. To paraphrase J. Solana, 'in a crisis there is no substitute for unity of command'.[15] As far as the European External Action Service is concerned, Article III-197(3) of the Draft Constitution indicates that this service should assist the Union Minister for Foreign Affairs in fulfilling his or her mandate. Given the dualistic role assumed by the Minister, the European External Action Service shall comprise officials from relevant departments of the General Secretariat of the Council and of the Commission as well as staff seconded from national diplomatic services of the Member States. As the former Commission delegations are renamed 'Union delegations' and are to operate under the authority of the Union Minister for Foreign Affairs,[16] the delegations' policy role will be broadened as their mandates will include CFSP/EDSP aspects. This will also enable them to have more expertise in and dedicate more attention to the latter areas, in particular, when providing information on early warning/conflict indicators to the Brussels headquarters. However, this ambition must be followed by an appropriate allocation of financial and human resources. That remark leads us to the second main challenge which faces the European Union's conflict prevention strategy.

Financial and human capacity challenges. Several chapters in this book[17] have pointed out the difficulties in correctly evaluating the EU's budget allocation for conflict prevention projects. These difficulties stem from the multifaceted dimension of conflict prevention and the EU's pillar structure. Whereas the 2003 EU budget allocation for external actions amounted to 8,335 billion euros, a large amount of this budget did not directly support conflict prevention actions. Conversely, within the total amount indicated above, the CFSP budget title B8 included merely 7.5 million euros of budget appropriations for conflict prevention and crisis management, excluding, by definition, all missions financed under the Community budget, among which are those financed under the Rapid Reaction Mechanism (RRM) and the European Initiative for Democracy and Human Rights (EIDHR). The difficulty in correctly assessing the amount which the EU spends annually on conflict prevention would not be that problematic if it was not combined with two more fundamental issues: a) the inconsistencies in decision-taking mechanisms and b) burdensome implementing procedures.

The first aspect lies in the different procedures that exist between financing operations under the Community budget and the CFSP budget. On the one hand, when an action falls within the competence of the Community the measure is financed by the Community budget, the Commission being responsible for the

---

[15] European Security Strategy, op. cit. n. 9, p. 13.

[16] See Article III-230 of the Draft Constitution, pursuant to which Union delegations in third countries and to international organisations shall represent the Union and shall operate under the authority of the Union Minister for Foreign Affairs and in close cooperation with the Member States' diplomatic and consular missions.

[17] Cf., especially Chapters 4, 6 and 9.

adoption of those measures. On the other hand, when an action falls within the ambit of CFSP, that measure will be financed under a separate title of the EU budget or by the Member States,[18] the Council being responsible for adopting those measures, which, in principle, require unanimity.[19] Although the Commission has widened it competence over the years,[20] in particular concerning civilian aspects of conflict prevention and management, there are still areas where identical measures, such as the operations concerning the collection of small arms, depending on the regions where those operations are undertaken, fall either under the competence of the Commission (for ACP countries) or under the competence of the Council, and are consequently financed differently. Such problems should be avoided by limiting the competence of the Council under the CFSP solely to operations having military or defence implications, all other field operation measures, including those aimed at the prevention of conflicts, being financed under the Community budget. This would certainly ensure some consistency, accelerate decision-taking and also, in principle, speed up budgetary appropriations. Unfortunately, such a possibility seems unlikely when one reads Article III-215 of the Draft Constitution. That provision chiefly reiterates the current Article 28 TEU, abandoning, however, the requirement that the Council decides unanimously on allocating operating expenses to the Member States as an exception to the principle that those expenses should fall within the scope of the EU budget, unless they have military or defence implications. Article III-215(3) of the Draft Constitution also introduces an innovation particularly relevant for conflict prevention. Indeed, it obliges the Council to – unanimously[21] – adopt a 'European decision establishing the specific procedures for guaranteeing rapid access to appropriations in the Union budget for urgent financing of initiatives in the framework of the common foreign and security policy, in particular for preparatory activities for tasks as referred to in Articles I-40(1) and III-210'. The latter provisions refer, *inter alia*, to conflict prevention and peace-keeping tasks outside the Union. If Article III-215(3) implies that the use of the CFSP budget under the current system has not always been as efficient as it should have been, it also allows the Council to remain the decision-taking institution as far as conflict prevention initiatives falling within the scope of CFSP, including their preparatory phase, are concerned.

In relation to the implementing procedures, it is unfortunate that a number of geographic or thematic instruments do not take into account the urgency of situations. The implementing procedures of these instruments are not properly adapted to a good preventive mechanism which, by definition, needs to be efficient and

---

[18] Cf., Article 28 TEU.

[19] Article 23 TEU.

[20] On the basis of Article 47 TEU which provides that nothing in the TEU shall affect the EC Treaty.

[21] This follows from Article III-201(1) of the Draft Constitution.

rapid. The creation of the RRM has largely facilitated a speedier response in a number of crisis situations, including in 'situations threatening to escalate into armed conflict or to destabilise the [beneficiary] country (...)', in particular by enabling the Commission to act without the consultation of Member States' committees. However, the yearly budget of the RRM, which falls under the Community budget title B.7, will remain at only 25 million euros until 2006. If, at first sight, the RRM achievements look positive, a systematic evaluation of the RRM should be undertaken by the Commission so that this instrument would eventually receive more funds. Another problem relating to implementing procedures is the involvement, to various degrees, of the beneficiary countries in the programming and/or identification stages of projects. As far as conflict prevention projects are concerned, the involvement of the beneficiary country may considerably slow down projects aiming to address the root causes of conflicts, such as the promotion of certain segments of society. Such projects should, in reality, be decided without the participation of the beneficiary country, as is done under thematic instruments such as the human rights regulations. These shortcomings lead one to ask whether it would not be appropriate for the Community to create a specific conflict prevention instrument, having its own budget line within the Community budget title B7, which would solely be dedicated to financing conflict prevention projects, in particular those aiming at structural conflict prevention, as a complement to the RRM. Such an instrument would have a number of advantages. It would clearly give conflict prevention more visibility and would take into consideration the specific nature of conflict prevention projects. However, it may slow down the progress in mainstreaming conflict prevention in other EU policy areas. Another option could be to add a conflict prevention dimension in current geographic aid instruments, freeing, for instance, the Commission from the involvement of beneficiary countries. The insertion of this new dimension in external aid instruments would possibly enable more projects managed by non-State actors – and NGOs in particular – to receive more financial support.[22]

In terms of human capacity, beyond the importance of enabling the EU institutions to have sufficient human resources, in particular in the Commission's Conflict Prevention Unit, the increasing role played by delegations also requires more and better training of their staff in the whole spectrum of issues relating to conflict prevention. Since delegations will bear increasing responsibility in the allocation of aid and will have an increasing role both in relation to the identification of crises and the formulation of efficient responses, the training of their staff will need to be upgraded. NGOs can play an important role in this respect, as well as training missions of international organisations, such as those of the OSCE.[23]

---

[22] For current data on the funding of NGOs' projects, see Chapter 24 above.
[23] See Chapter 18 above.

Evidently, the training of staff at headquarters should not be underestimated either, in order to increase the skills of officers in conflict prevention issues. In addition to the exchange of staff with other international organisations, joint pilot training courses should be further developed, along the lines of the course organised for Human Rights officers by the OSCE, the UN High Commissioner for Human Rights, the EU institutions and the Council of Europe in 1999.

Seeking an appropriately structured division of labour with international organisations. According to the TEC, the Community enjoys privileged relations with two international organisations, namely the Council of Europe and the OECD,[24] which both play a role in the prevention of conflicts, the first one essentially by the promotion of human rights and the rule of law on the territory of its Member States,[25] the second one particularly by supporting development and co-operation programmes and promoting the respect of fundamental principles by multinationals.[26] The United Nations, the OSCE and NATO are only mentioned cursively in the TEU, the first two by reference to their constitutive texts,[27] the third one with reference to its position as a defence organisation within the framework of the ESDP.[28] The chapters of this book[29] have pointed out that, whether the EU enjoys special relations with international organisations or not, its cooperation with those organisations in the area of conflict prevention has remained *ad hoc* rather than properly structured. So far, in relation to conflict management and prevention, only EU-NATO relations rely on agreements concerning EU access to NATO planning and other capabilities for engaging in its own military operations (Berlin-plus agreements).[30] The lack of an appropriately structured relationship often lies at the heart of duplication of work, loss of resources and ultimately the loss of credibility as far as all actors are concerned.[31] This fact has been admitted by the Commission in its recent Communication on the European Union and the United Nations.[32] Although the Communication provides evidence of positive initiatives to better synchronise EU-UN activities for conflict prevention, both on the ground and between headquarters, systematic steps are called for through a more frequent, more operational and more carefully organised dialogue

---

[24] See respectively Article 303 and Article 304 TEC.

[25] Cf., Chapter 20 above.

[26] Cf., Chapter 25 above.

[27] Cf., Article 11 TEU.

[28] Cf., Article 17 TEU. Note that the World Bank and the G 8 are not mentioned at all in the TEU.

[29] Cf., Chapters 16 to 22 above.

[30] Cf., Chapter 19 above.

[31] Cf., Chapter 16 above.

[32] Communication from the Commission to the Council and the European Parliament, COM (2003) 526 final, 10 September 2003.

between the two organisations.[33] Such bilateral systematic cooperation should indeed be welcomed.[34] Coordinated actions at headquarters and in the field are certainly essential for efficient responses to nascent crises and conflicts. Efforts to facilitate the exchange of staff may also prove positive in the long run. However, one may ask whether it would not be advisable for the EU to enter into more formalised arrangements with the UN, in particular as far as civilian aspects of conflict prevention are concerned. The same is true for relations with regional organisations such as the OSCE and the Council of Europe. Once again the Draft Constitution may lay the necessary grounds for introducing a more structured cooperation between the EU and other organisations. First, according to Article I-6 of the Draft Constitution, the EU will enjoy legal personality, which implies that it should be able to join, as a *sui generis* Contracting Party, organisations having non-economic aims, provided that those organisations allow non-State organisations to join them. The EU, in particular through its delegations acting under the authority of its Minister for Foreign Affairs, may therefore use that possibility to coordinate its position with the organisations concerned and influence the decisions adopted there. Second, it is worth noting that, as far as the UN and the OSCE are concerned, Article III-229 of the Draft Constitution provides that the Union shall establish all appropriate forms of cooperation with (the organs of) those organisations. It is suggested here that such a provision should be put into effect in the area of conflict prevention by entering into cooperation agreements with those organisations and, in the case of the UN, its specialised agencies and subsidiary organs. When it comes to the OSCE, such a cooperation agreement could include mutual exchange of information on early warning and conflict prevention assessment, access to OSCE training missions in the field, and modalities for the EU to mandate more systematically – as the EC has done on some occasions – the High Commissioner for National Minorities for early action. The agreement could also include provisions governing when, where and how one of the two organisations could take the lead in specific field missions. For instance, for OSCE States having no prospect of EU membership, the former could assume the core responsibility for coordinating diplomatic *démarches* and the wide range of short-term conflict prevention instruments; since the OSCE is also clearly considered to be a regional arrangement in the sense of Chapter VIII of the UN Charter[35] and since it is generally admitted that such regional arrangements can, on their own initiative, only adopt non-coercive actions on the territory of their Con-

---

[33] Idem, p. 15. Note that, as far as cooperation in crisis management is concerned, the EU and the UN have adopted a Joint Declaration on 24 September 2003 (cf., Press 266 Doc. No. 12510/03), the implementation of the military component of which was discussed by the EU Political and Security Committee and endorsed on 9 June 2004 (cf., Doc. No. 9638/1/04 Rev. 1). See also Chapter 17 in this volume.

[34] Cf., Chapter 17 above.

[35] Cf., UN General Assembly Resolution 52/22 (16 January 1998).

tracting Parties,[36] the deployment of conflict prevention missions (of a military or civilian dimension) by the EU could, legally speaking, be safely implemented under the auspices of the OSCE.[37] For other conflict prevention missions outside the territory of the EU, those actions would need to be authorised by the UN Security Council, if they have a coercive nature or be agreed by the State authorities (or parties in dispute) of the country(ies) concerned if they are only civilian missions. When it comes to structural conflict prevention, given the limited resources of the OSCE, it would be quite understandable that the EU would take responsibility for the actions falling within that scope, in particular on the basis of its policy instruments relating to trade, environment, development and cooperation. Such a cooperation agreement, whatever its modalities, would give a strong impetus to a comprehensive approach towards conflict prevention in Europe and in its close neighbourhood. It would also clearly demonstrate the EU's commitment to avoiding entering into competition with other international organisations, while it would admit that its resources, capacities and priorities should not duplicate what already exists. On some occasions, the EU could also conceive its role as an 'implementing organisation' putting into effect decisions agreed upon in other international forums such as the UN and the G8. In this latter respect, Chapter 21 above made concrete proposals for coordinating, in a three-phase approach from 2003 to 2011, G8 summits and ministerial meetings with EU presidencies, enabling the EU to adopt the role of a mandate-seeker and delivery organisation of the G8, in which it would ultimately acquire the status of a full member.[38] The dichotomy described above – on the one hand, a leader role for the EU in its close neighbourhood and, on the other, a role of mandate-seeker and delivery organisation under the lead of other organisations in other parts of the world – appears to be the leitmotiv of the European Security Strategy proposed by J. Solana at the Thessaloniki European Council in June 2003, and endorsed at the Brussels European Council of 12-13 December 2003.[39] On a global scale, the text stresses the central role that the UN should play in maintaining peace and security, with support from the EU, while, on a European scale, the document puts emphasis on the EU's leading role in its neighbourhood. However, the exact relationship between regional organisations in Europe, such as the OSCE and the Council of Europe, is not addressed.[40]

---

[36] See, e.g., E. Kodjo, 'Article 52' in J.P. Cot and A. Pellet (sous la dir. de), *La Charte des Nations Unies, commentaire article par article* (Paris, Economica 1985), p. 796. Coercive actions by regional arrangements outside their territory might be considered illegal if these actions do not benefit from a mandate by the UN Security Council.

[37] For earlier support for such a position, see V. Kronenberger, 'La dimension institutionnelle de la Politique européenne commune de sécurité et de défense', 10 *Europe* (2000), p. 3, at 7.

[38] Cf., Chapter 21, section 4.

[39] 'A Secure Europe in a Better World', op. cit. n. 9.

[40] The document indicates that 'Regional organisations also strengthen global governance. For the European Union, the strength and effectiveness of the OSCE and the Council of Europe has a particular significance', at p. 9.

Overall, the three main challenges described above converge around the same issue: setting priorities proportionate to the EU capacities. Too often, priorities or targets are set at a disproportionate level in relation to the human, financial and institutional capacities of the EU. This often leads to disillusion and discouragement both within and outside the EU. This is not to say that ambitions should only stick to available capacities. Capacities should be adapted to priorities and it is realistic to acknowledge that priorities which are too ambitious can only lead to failure. The EU should therefore select carefully its priorities concerning: a) what it can do better than other actors (Member States alone, other international organisations) (priority actions and policies) and b) where it could implement those actions better than other actors (geographical priorities). This is undoubtedly the idea behind the European Security Strategy cited above. Although the document does not consider conflict prevention alone, it does contribute to the EU objective of preventing the eruption and reignition of conflicts and to setting priorities in this respect. Hence, geographically, it is envisaged that the EU should extend the zone of security to its close neighbourhood, i.e., Europe at large, including the Southern Caucasus, and the Mediterranean countries, including the resolution of the Arab-Israeli conflict. These geographical priorities are understandable for a European organisation. They also make sense after the diplomatic and military successes which the EU has had in preventing the escalation of violence in Macedonia, although recent events show that stability and peace remain fragile and point out that further efforts from the EU are needed, in particular in terms of socio-economic peace-building. However, one may wonder whether the African continent (and not merely Mediterranean countries), given the endemic conflicts and crises it is confronted with and the particular responsibility which EU Member States have towards their African counterparts, should not be placed higher on the security agenda of the EU. The fact that, within the three strategic security objectives identified in the European Security Strategy,[41] Africa is only mentioned cursively and not, as such, within the strategic priority of building security in Europe's neighbourhood, is a rather preoccupying factor. Even if one admits that Africa as a whole is not in the vicinity of the EU, forgetting that continent is all the more surprising when one considers that the European Security Strategy extends the definition of its neighbourhood to the Arab world.[42]

---

[41] Those are: a) addressing the threats; b) building security in our neighbourhood; c) an international order based on effective multilateralism. Note that, in the first draft of the European Security Strategy, threats (terrorism, weapons of mass destruction...) came last, whereas building security (extending security) came first. It has been suggested that this change can be seen as a political message to emphasise that the EU shares US concerns: see S. Biscop, 'The European Security Strategy. Implementing a Distinctive Approach to Security', 82 *Sécurité et Stratégie* (2004), p. 18, available at <www.irri-kiib.be/papers/Artikel%20V&S%20ESS.pdf>.

[42] European Security Strategy, op. cit. n. 9, p. 8.

In general, to the devastating intra and inter-State wars spreading in Africa, the EU's responses have remained rather limited. From a mainly reactive attitude, in particular concerning the possibility of diversion of Community (European Development Fund) financial resources to military purposes in the African, Caribbean and Pacific (ACP) States involved in armed conflicts,[43] efforts to concentrate on conflict prevention in a more systematic way have only taken off with the conclusion of the Cotonou Agreement – the partnership (framework association) agreement between the EU and 77 ACP States –, signed in 2000 and which entered into force in April 2003. From an institutional and legal perspective, one should welcome the importance of inserting provisions in that agreement whereby the prevention of violent conflicts is an integral part of the political dialogue between the Parties (Article 8, paragraph 3) and according to which the Parties pursue an 'active, comprehensive and integrated policy of peace-building and conflict prevention and resolution within the framework of the Partnership' (Article 11, paragraph 1). These provisions lay the ground for institutionalised dialogue and mutual action. However, as pointed out in Chapter 9 above, the fact that projects to be financed remain subject to the agreement of the ACP country concerned both at the programming and identification stage is problematic, since its involvement may exclude, or at least considerably slow down, projects aiming to address the root causes of conflicts, such as the promotion of certain segments of society. In concrete terms, conflict prevention projects under the Cotonou Agreement would certainly benefit if the Commission would enjoy more flexibility as far as programming and project identification are concerned.[44] The Commission should also issue clear guidance on the implementation of the conflict prevention provisions of the Cotonou Agreement. In the short-term, the fact that, even before the entry into force of Article 96 of the Cotonou Agreement,[45] the EU initiated early consultations with individual ACP States (namely Haiti,

---

[43] Commission Communication to the Council and the European Parliament on cooperation with ACP States involved in armed conflict, COM (1999) 204 final, 19 May 1999. See also the Resolution of the European Parliament on the communication, *OJEC* [2001] C 197/390.

[44] Although the flexibility afforded to the Commission by the Rapid Reaction Mechanism (Regulation 381/2001, *OJEC* [2001] L 57/5) has partially circumvented this problem since some ACP States have benefited from interventions under the RRM, it should, however, be noted that this instrument is aimed at responding to a 'situation of crisis or emerging crisis' which, by definition, does not encompass projects having long-term conflict prevention purposes.

[45] Article 96 of the Agreement allows a Party (the Community, a Member State or an ACP State) to ask for consultations with another Party should it be considered to have failed to fulfil an obligation stemming from respect for human rights, democratic principles and the rule of law in order to remedy the situation, except in cases of special urgency (i.e., cases of particularly serious and flagrant violations of one of the essential elements, that require immediate action). If consultations do not lead to a solution acceptable to both Parties, are refused or in case of special urgency, appropriate measures may be taken. Appropriate measures are taken in accordance with international law and they must be proportional to the violation. It is understood that suspension would be a measure of last resort.

Liberia, Fiji, Ivory Coast and Zimbabwe)[46] where human rights, democracy and/ or the rule of law were considered to be violated, may give some indications as to how the EU may put pressure on the State concerned, in particular by threatening to suspend or freeze European Development Fund resources, with the aim being to preventing the escalation of violence and, eventually, the eruption of conflicts. However, apart from the non-African islands of Fiji, where financial aid resumed in part in November 2003, the examples mentioned above also show the limits of such threats when they are not coupled with stronger involvement. In this respect, the principle of ownership, as one of the leading principles governing EU-African relations in conflict prevention,[47] whereby African capacity in identifying problems and resolving them should be encouraged and strengthened, in particular through the African Union and African sub-regional organisations,[48] ought not to be interpreted by EU institutions and Member States in such an extreme way that, in reality, it would leave Africans struggling on their own. As indicated above, not mentioning Africa as one of the strategic objectives of Europe's security leaves the bitter impression that the EU does not link its own security to that of the African continent. The EU should therefore incorporate into its security strategy the objective of conflict prevention in Africa and allocate necessary funding and resources in that respect. In the light of the existing instruments that the EU possesses, putting emphasis on Africa as a geographic strategic objective of the EU security strategy cannot be considered to be disproportionate.

The two other strategic objectives emphasised in the European Security Strategy, i.e., a) addressing the threats and b) supporting effective multilateralism should be welcomed. Among the first category falls regional conflicts and state failure. The examples given in those sections (problems in Kashmir, the Great Lakes Region, the Korean Peninsula, the Balkans, the Middle East, in the first group and Somalia, Liberia and Afghanistan in the second group) do not appear totally consistent with the second strategic objective whereby the EU should, as a priority, assume leading responsibility in its neighbourhood. However, this is compensated by the emphasis, in the third security strategy objective, on the EU's supporting role to ensure effective multilateralism, in particular by being committed to upholding and developing international law and by admitting the primary responsibility of the UN Security Council for the maintenance of international peace and security.[49] From a conflict prevention perspective, it can be regretted that the EU has not seized the opportunity to clearly establish that it would not undertake any preventive military action without the mandate of the

---

[46] On these consultations, see O. Babarinde and G. Faber, 'From Lomé to Cotonou: Business as Usual?', 9 *EFARev.* (2004) p. 27, at 44-45.

[47] See Chapter 15 above.

[48] See the Presidency conclusions of the Brussels European Council of 12/13 December 2003 (Doc. 5381/04, 5 February 2004), point 78. In the European Security Strategy (op. cit. n. 9), the African Union is mentioned as making 'an important contribution to a more orderly world' (p. 9).

[49] European Security Strategy, op. cit. n. 9, p. 9.

UN Security Council, and, where it is possible, the consent of the State authorities concerned. On the contrary, the text, as far as policy implications for the EU are concerned, appears somehow ambiguous since it stresses that 'we need to be able to act before countries around us deteriorate, when signs of proliferation are detected, before humanitarian emergencies arise. Preventive engagement can avoid more serious problems in the future. A European Union which takes greater responsibility and which is more active will be one which carries more political weight'.[50] This conclusion is true provided that the EU fully respects international law. As emphasised above, if conflict prevention missions or actions do not generally interfere with international law, then it is still the case that, coercive military actions by a regional organisation – possibly considered as a regional arrangement according to Chapter VIII of the UN Charter – with the aim of preventing conflicts from emerging or reigniting, cannot be undertaken without the mandate of the UN Security Council. The EU will not gain political weight if it acts contrary to that principle. This issue, although politically and legally sensitive, could have been stressed in the European Security Strategy.[51]

Within a few years, the EU has built a genuine conflict prevention strategy. In the long-term, the endorsement of the European Security Strategy in 2003 and the adoption of the Draft Constitution, to be signed in Rome on 29 October 2004 and hopefully ratified by all Member States soon thereafter, have provided a firm basis for major initiatives by the EU in the coming years, provided that there is sufficient political will to pursue these efforts. In the short-term, a practical and important test for EU credibility will be the transfer of responsibility at the end of 2004 from the NATO-led mission SFOR in Bosnia-Herzegovina for the maintenance of peace in that country. It will take a few years again to assess whether the EU's conflict prevention strategy has overcome the challenges it currently faces.

Vincent KRONENBERGER
Jan WOUTERS

---

[50] Idem, p. 11. Note that the words 'pre-emptive engagement', which appeared in the June 2003 draft European Security Strategy was wisely replaced in the final text by 'preventive engagement', such terminology being further adrift from to the word 'pre-emption' which has been used in the context of the US invasion of Iraq.

[51] See also S. Biscop, op. cit. n. 41, p. 23.

DETAILED TABLE OF CONTENTS

PART TWO B
Towards a structural conflict prevention

PART THREE
Experience of other actors

PART THREE A
International organisations

INDEX